THE VISUAL FIELDS

A textbook and atlas of clinical perimetry

THE VISUAL FIELDS

A textbook and atlas of clinical perimetry

David O. Harrington, A.B., M.D., F.A.C.S.

Clinical Professor Emeritus of Ophthalmology, University of California School of Medicine, San Francisco, California; Consultant in Ophthalmology, Veterans Administration Hospital, Fort Miley, San Francisco, California

FIFTH EDITION

with **460** *illustrations*
and **9** *plates, with* **5** *in color*

The C. V. Mosby Company

ST. LOUIS • TORONTO • LONDON 1981

A TRADITION OF PUBLISHING EXCELLENCE

Editor: Eugenia A. Klein
Manuscript editor: Emilie F. Fall
Designer: Susan Trail
Production: Linda Stalnaker

FIFTH EDITION

Printed in the United States of America

The C. V. Mosby Company
11830 Westline Industrial Drive, St. Louis, Missouri 63141

Library of Congress Cataloging in Publication Data

Harrington, David O., 1904-
The visual fields.

Bibliography: p.
Includes index.
1. Perimetry. 2. Visual fields. I. Title.
[DNLM: 1. Perimetry. 2. Visual fields. WW
145 H299v]
RE79.P4H3 1981 617.7′5 81-2558
ISBN 0-8016-2059-7 AACR2

GW/CB/B 9 8 7 6 5 4 3 01/B/021

Affectionately dedicated to my family

MARY LOUISE

ERIN

KEVIN

Foreword

This comprehensive text by Dr. Harrington is the excellent contribution to the literature one would expect from the author. Knowledge of the subject, thoroughness in examination, and meticulous attention to detail are combined with originality. While other publications cover limited parts of the field of perimetry, this text fills out the scotomatous patches.

When Dr. Harrington was a staff member of the Department of Neurological Surgery, his interest in neuro-ophthalmology developed and led to detailed training in this field. Later, when he became the ophthalmological consultant for the Departments of Neurology and Neurological Surgery, he included among his students not only the ophthalmologists but also the undergraduates and resident staff of these related departments.

For his expert advice as a consultant, those specialties in the University of California have profited greatly and they acknowledge their debt.

This presentation is that of a thoroughly grounded, broadly prepared, and experienced teacher of his subject. Just as quantitative methods increased the diagnostic value of perimetry, the original methods here presented offer additional help. The correlation of visual field interpretation with anatomy is of particular value. These various closely related specialties are greatly enriched by this contribution, and its practitioners cannot fail to profit greatly from it.

†Howard C. Naffziger

B.S., M.S., M.D., F.A.C.S., F.R.C.S.
(Honorary) England

Late Professor Emeritus, Neurological
Surgery, University of California School
of Medicine, San Francisco, Calif.

†Deceased, March 21, 1961.

Preface to fifth edition

The continued popularity of this book and the need for the fifth edition are evidenced by its increased readership among ophthalmologists and its continued use in training programs not only in ophthalmology but also in neurology, neurosurgery, and internal medicine. Both domestic and foreign sales of the book have increased. In the past two years a Spanish translation has been published, which should further expand interest in perimetry and visual field analysis.

In recent years there has been a continuing search for perimetric instruments and techniques that would simplify and speed up the examination of the visual fields. With the advent of increasingly sophisticated minicomputers it has become possible to program a variety of visual field tests; with some techniques it is claimed that the patient can examine his own field.

As might be expected, the electronics engineers have been quick to exploit this interesting and lucrative field. The result is a plethora of new automated and computer-assisted perimeters with which it is said that visual fields may be examined with great accuracy, reproducibility, and speed, with minimal attention from a technician and no supervision whatever from the ophthalmologist who is ultimately responsible for the interpretation of the data supplied by the computer. This is roughly equivalent to having the physician request a computer-assisted tomograph (CAT) or a visually evoked response (VER) without ever having performed a clinical examination of the patient.

A number of these automated perimeters are examined in this edition for comparison with each other and with more standardized instruments and time-tested methods.

When used as screening devices, these instruments are capable of detecting deficits in the visual fields that may then be investigated on the tangent screen, the Goldmann perimeter, or the Tübinger perimeter for diagnostic characteristics such as shape, size, density, position in relation to fixation, and hemianoptic borders. When so used they are a valuable and rapid examination technique, albeit still a screening method and in many cases no faster or more accurate than a well-performed examination on the tangent screen or Goldmann bowl.

As indicated in the foregoing paragraphs, major changes in this edition have to do with instrumentation and techniques of examination, but the largest part of the book continues to deal with interpretation and analysis of visual field defects as they present themselves in the examinations with the tangent screen, the Goldmann perimeter, or the Tübinger instrument. In order to become proficient in such analyses it is necessary for the perimetrist to conduct his own examination and to develop his own individual techniques. The tangent screen examination, either static or kinetic, is the most efficient method of teaching perimetry, which is one reason it is so valuable a method.

All of the new computerized perimeters automatically record the random presentation of static stimuli of variable luminance for the detection of visual field defects. Some of them have effectively shortened the examination time, while others have actually lengthened it.

It is an undeniable fact that most perimetry is now performed by technicians, and these technicians are hard to find, must be highly trained, and are hard to keep! The physician must be the trainer, which means he must first train himself. It is to be hoped that the pendulum will not swing too far in this direction, thus driving the physician completely out of the visual field examining room. Some patients are incapable of responding to an automated pattern of stimuli and must therefore be studied by other techniques. In such situations great patience and flexibility are needed, properties not to be found in computers.

In addition to the rewriting of the first three chapters of this book I have updated Chapter 12, on the toxic amblyopias. In spite of the tremendous increase in the use of drugs and chemicals that might be expected to adversely affect the eyes, relatively few of them harm the sensory pathway or the visual fields. A thorough search of the literature was required to uncover this fortunate fact.

While computerized tomography has revolutionized neurodiagnosis and is of enormous help in neuro-ophthalmology, it should not be allowed to replace careful visual field studies, history taking, and ophthalmoscopy. We should continue to discourage uncontrolled requests for CT scans in the absence of clinical indications, such as visual field defects. It then becomes an expensive abuse of the procedure. A number of the more than thirty new illustrations in this edition show the valuable and close correlation between visual field studies and the CT scan. In most instances the visual field defects were supported by the computerized tomography.

Visual-evoked response (or potential) to various pattern and light stimuli is an increasingly valuable tool in the diagnosis of lesions of the visual pathway, especially those in the optic nerves. This truly objective method of measuring visual field defects is discussed and illustrated in this edition.

Most of the new illustrations are additions to those in the fourth edition, but some are substitutes for older and less desirable charts and photographs.

The literature pertinent to visual field studies continues to be voluminous. Articles, books, symposia, and monographs published since 1976 have been culled for information that would update this fifth edition. The bibliography has been expanded, but no attempt has been made to make it all inclusive.

I am indebted to those residents in the Department of Ophthalmology of the University of California who have accepted the challenge of perimetry and have assisted in the collection of data on the many interesting new cases seen in our visual field clinic and conferences. I have, as always, personally performed the visual field examination on all new cases reported in this edition.

I am much indebted to Miss Hilda Leavy, who edited and typed the new manuscript pages; to Mrs. Joan Weddell, who executed the new illustrative visual field charts; and to Michael Narahara and Bruce Morris for their excellent photographic work in this new edition.

David O. Harrington

Preface to first edition

This book is a clinical guide to the examination and interpretation of the visual fields. It is based upon twenty years' experience in the teaching of perimetry to graduate students of ophthalmology, neurosurgery, and neurology and results from a long-held desire to crystallize this teaching experience for the student and the busy practitioner.

The examination of the visual fields is a subjective test. The interpretation of the results of such a subjective examination is dependent upon many factors, not the least of which is the personality of the patient and the examiner and the rapport between them. It is not possible to evaluate the results of a visual field study performed by a technician as well as if you had performed it yourself. No two perimetrists will conduct their study of the visual fields in exactly the same manner. No perimetrist should use exactly the same technique of examination on every patient. Responses will differ depending on age, speed of comprehension, state of health, rapport with the examiner, and many other factors. It follows, therefore, that the visual field examination must not be conducted according to a rigid routine, and that ingenuity must be exercised to obtain the most information from the test. With this in mind, the section of this book devoted to the techniques of perimetry is couched in general terms as far as the actual conduct of the visual field examination is concerned. At the same time the student is supplied with the tools required to perform the examination and an account of their construction and the general principles underlying their use.

No methods or instruments for visual field examination have been described unless I have used them with personal satisfaction. Whenever possible, techniques have been simplified. It is my sincere conviction that elaborate machinery is unnecessary for adequate perimetry, and that the simpler methods focus attention on the capabilities of the examiner rather than on the instrumentation employed. In short, the man behind the perimeter is more important than the equipment he uses.

No other diagnostic procedure available to the ophthalmologist offers a challenge or opportunity equal to that of perimetry. The examination of the visual field need not be the tedious chore that it is usually considered. There is great personal satisfaction to be derived from the careful quantitative study of a visual field defect, its interpretation and correlation with other signs and symptoms of disease, and its analysis and evaluation in terms of the localization and pathology of the lesion in the visual pathway which produced it.

I have tried, in this book, to communicate my enthusiasm for visual field study to the reader just as I have tried through the years to pass it on to my students. If the book is successful in this it will have served its purpose well.

For my own interest in the study of the visual fields I am largely indebted to three men:

To Dr. Frederick Cordes, who saw the need for a perimetrist and student of neuro-ophthalmology in his Department of Ophthalmology at the University of California School of Medicine, and who encouraged me in every way to pursue the study which would lead to a teaching position on his staff.

To Dr. Howard C. Naffziger, in whose Department of Neurosurgery at the University of California I served for a period, and who has given me continuing help and encouragement through the years by affording me unusual opportunities to examine many of the patients on his service, both clinic and private. He taught me to follow the patient from the perimeter to the operating table and to correlate my visual field studies with the pathological lesions which produced them.

To Dr. H. M. Traquair, on whose service in the Royal Infirmary in Edinburgh I spent most of a year, who taught me the techniques of visual field examination and interpretation which are so obviously reflected in this book. All persons interested in the visual fields will be forever indebted to Dr. Traquair for his work in advancing and popularizing the concept of quantitative perimetry and the importance of the visual field examination in the diagnosis of lesions of the visual pathway.

It has also been my good fortune to have had the highest degree of cooperation and understanding from such other outstanding clinicians in the Departments of Neurosurgery and Neurology as Dr. O. W. Jones, Jr., Dr. Howard A. Brown, Dr. Edwin Boldrey, Dr. John Adams, and Dr. Robert Aird, not to mention the long list of young men on the Resident Staff whose loyalty and cooperation are so essential to a long-term study such as this.

All of the material in this book is drawn from personal experience in the study of the visual fields. It is a compilation of my own clinical experience and, as such, it emphasizes the clinical viewpoint. I have, of course, drawn freely from the literature for the chapters on the anatomy of the visual pathway and its vascular supply. I have long been convinced that the clinical perimetrist must have such a background for the proper understanding of his subject.

Because of my experience with Dr. Traquair I have naturally tended to reflect his teachings and adhere to his broad concept of the quantitative examination of extrafoveal visual acuity, but only in so far as I was able to apply them in my own experience.

The old cliché that "one picture is worth ten thousand words" is nowhere more applicable than in a book of this type. Illustrative material is essential to the understanding of visual field interpretation. This book was originally conceived as an atlas, and this concept is underscored by the retention of the word "Atlas" in the title.

I am proud of the illustrations in this book, which are almost entirely original and have been drawn largely from my own case records. The anatomical drawings are from sketches which are a composite of my own dissections and a study of the classic literature on the subject. I am indebted to Dr. William Hoyt for assistance in the preparation of the sketches for Figs. 36, 37, 38, 40, 45, 49, 50, and 51. Where I have borrowed directly from the literature it has been with the author's permission, as noted in the legends.

I have been most fortunate in securing the services of a notable group of artists whose patience and unusual skill are reflected in their work.

Miss Sylvia Ford, formerly of the University of California Medical Illustration Department, Division of Ophthalmology, is responsible for Plates I to IX. Miss Kay Hyde, Medical Illustrator for the U.S. Veterans Administration Hospital at Fort Miley, San Francisco, has drawn most of the black and white illustrations, both anatomical and visual fields, and has given me the utmost in cooperation and assistance. Mrs. Laura Gilleland, of the University of California Medical Illustration Department, has supplemented Miss Hyde's work on visual field charts and black and white anatomical drawings. Mr. Ralph Sweet, Chairman of the Department of Medical Illustration at the University of California, drew the central panel of Plate VIII and has given much valuable advice and assistance in reviewing many of the drawings as they were completed. A number of the photographs are the expert work of Mr. Henry Rafael at the U.S. Veterans Administration Hospital in San Francisco.

No acknowledgment would be complete without paying tribute to the tedious work and infinite patience of Miss Myrtle Gable and Mrs. Elizabeth Valentine, who read, corrected, and typed the manuscript from its original longhand script.

David O. Harrington

San Francisco, 1956

Contents

Plates

THE VISUAL FIELDS

A textbook and atlas of clinical perimetry

Introduction

The visual field is that portion of space in which objects are simultaneously visible to the steadily fixating eye. It is somewhat more than one half of a hollow sphere, situated before and around each eye of the observer, within which objects are perceived while the eye is fixating a stationary point on its inner surface. Objects that are visible on the inner surface of this sphere act to stimulate the various portions of the retina and, through the conducting nerve fiber bundles of the visual pathway, the visual cortex in the calcarine areas of the occipital lobes. The varying degrees of intensity of these stimuli depend on (1) the proximity of the stimuli to the visual axis, (2) the size of the stimuli (the number of retinal elements covered by their image), (3) the brightness of the stimuli (the lumens of light emitted from their surface), and (4) the integrity of the receptors of the stimulus.

Traquair's apt comparison of the visual field to "an island hill of vision surrounded by a sea of blindness" has firmly established in clinical practice the quantitative method of perimetry as advocated by Bjerrum, Rönne, Sinclair, and Walker. It has focused our attention on the measurement of the field of vision in terms of visual acuity and is the basis for the profile charting of visual field defects in static perimetry.

When one considers that retinal sensitivity is greatest in the foveal area and decreases in direct proportion to the distance of the rods and cones from the fovea, it will be apparent that visual acuity within the visual field does likewise. It follows, then, that small objects are seen with distinctness within the visual field only when they are near the visual axis and that larger and brighter stimuli are required if they are to be perceived in the peripheral field.

Visual acuity as measured with the Snellen letters also varies with the proximity of the test letter from fixation. In the normal eye with 20/20 vision at fixation, acuity decreases rapidly in the peripheral field so that at 2 degrees from fixation it is reduced to 20/30. At 3 degrees, visual acuity is approximately 20/40; at 5 degrees, it is 20/70; at 10 degrees, vision measures 20/100; at 20 degrees, vision is 20/200; and at 40 degrees, it is about 20/400.

In terms of visual acuity, the hollow sphere of the visual field becomes the "island hill of vision surrounded by the sea of blindness." Objects nearest the visual axis are seen with greatest clarity, as though they were situated on a peak directly below the observer's eye. As the contour of the hill slopes downward and outward from the peak toward the shoreline, smaller objects become invisible and only stimuli of gradually increasing size or intensity are seen. Because of the relative constancy of visual acuity in different portions of the visual field in normal eyes, the island of vision has a remarkably constant shape and size.

The island is oval in shape with a regular coastline rising abruptly from the sea in precipitous cliffs. These cliffs are surmounted by a sloping plateau that rises toward an eccentrically placed summit, which in turn slopes steeply upward to a needlelike peak. Beside the summit is a pit or well that extends downward to the level of the sea. This is the blind spot.

To the normal eye, viewing this island as from a helicopter poised directly over the peak, the entire panorama of its surface is in view but, as in any panoramic view, the objects nearest the observer are the most distinct. Thus, minute objects on or near the summit of the peak are seen with greatest clarity, whereas those situated on the plateau must be larger to be visible. On the coastline at the bottom of the cliffs, only large patches of white are visible.

The limits within which a certain sized object can be seen by the normal observer can be surveyed on the hill as a contour line and plotted on a map or chart. These are the *isopters* of the normal field. The normal isopters or contour lines are relatively constant in size and shape, but they show certain characteristic variations and abnormalities as a result of disease affecting the visual pathway. The correct interpretation of these variations in visual acuity within the visual field, and hence of the isopters, may make it possible anatomically to localize within the visual pathway the site of the lesion that has produced the variation.

If we know the normal visual acuity for any portion of the visual field, i.e., if we know the isopter or contour line within which a stimulus subtending a given visual angle is visible to the normal eye, we can then correctly interpret variations from this normal in terms of damage to the visual pathway.

The surface of the retina receives an image of objects in the visual field in much the same manner as a photographic film records a landscape. The nerve fiber bundles of the retina are arranged in a pattern that is repeated in the visual pathway from the optic nerve through the chiasmal decussation and on into the cortical visual center in the occipital lobes. The visual field corresponds to an inverse cross section of the visual pathway at any point from the receptor organ in the retina to the terminal center in the occipital cortex. Thus any defect or abnormality of the visual field may, through correct interpretation, reflect disease or damage to a specific portion of the visual pathway.

It is the purpose of perimetry to detect these revealing defects in the visual field, to measure them quantitatively in terms of visual acuity, and to chart them as normal or abnormal contour lines or isopters.

Perimetry, then, is a special type of psychophysical examination. It requires a trained examiner with a knowledge of the available techniques and instruments and their special physical and optical properties.

The clinical applications of perimetry also demand knowledge of the anatomy and physiology of the visual pathway and its contiguous structures and the psychologic factors that may influence the responses of the individual subjected to the test.

THE ART AND SCIENCE OF PERIMETRY

The aim of perimetry is to quantitatively examine visual acuity in all portions of the visual field. This implies careful survey of the island hill of vision and its subsequent contour mapping, or, in the case of static perimetry, its profile in any given meridian.

All manner of variations in the surface and coastline of the hill should be detectable and later subjected to analysis and interpretation. Because of the complexity of the terrain, no single instrument or method of examination will suffice to survey the entire hill adequately, and the perimetrist must be aware of the limitations of a given method and the point in the examination when one instrument or method should supplant another.

There is an art to the proper examination of the visual field that is being more and more neglected in recent years.

With the increased complexity and sophistication of the instruments of perimetry, there is a tendency to view the visual field examination as a wholly scientific procedure, the end result of which is an objective measurement of visual function that is immutable, exact and repeatable. The fallacy of this view is readily seen when one realizes that the visual field examination is a psychophysical evaluation of an individual's visual and mental status at a given time. No matter how elaborate the instruments, the test is subjective, cannot be considered truly scientific, and, in many ways, is more of an art than a science.

The only truly scientific method of visual field examination is the objective measurement of visual-evoked response of the optic cortex. Variations of the technique have received increasing attention in the past decade.

With more demand on the ophthalmologist's time to include an increasing number of complicated procedures in a routine eye examination, less time is allowed for visual field testing. Faced with the need to do tonometric, tonographic, gonioscopic, fluorescein angiographic, ophthalmoscopic, photographic, biomicroscopic examinations, and all objective tests, the harassed clinician understandably delegates such subjective examinations as history taking, vision testing, refraction, and perimetry to paramedical personnel.

These subjective examinations require a degree of psychic evaluation that will often determine the validity of the findings. The visual field examination cannot be isolated from the total evaluation of the patient. The physician must assess these values and the more important the visual field studies are to the establishment of a diagnosis the greater the need for the personal attention of the clinician. Only the physician can practice the art of perimetry.

There are numerous case reports in this book that illustrate the need for great flexibility in the visual field examination. In some instances only minimal threshold stimuli will suffice to detect early, subtle deficits that may be all-important in establishing a diagnosis. In other cases the grossest stimulus, such as a waving white towel, is needed to demonstrate a field defect characteristic of a specific disease process in the visual pathway. In many instances the visual field loss is the only diagnostic finding and may be missed or misinterpreted because of the limits imposed by a rigid examination technique.

Carefully examined and analyzed visual field defects are often the only guide available to the neurologist or neurosurgeon in his search for the location and nature of intracerebral pathology. The computerized tomography (CT) scan is of great value but may not be any more reliable than the visual field and adds greatly to the expense of the neurologic examination.

The time-consuming routine visual field examination will lose its drudgery when the perimetrist faces the challenge of each individual patient as a psychobiological problem from whom all possible information is to be extracted. It is rare indeed that some information cannot be obtained from a patient concerning his peripheral visual acuity. Fields of a sort and much information as to brain damage can be obtained from semicomatose patients, from psychotic patients, from small children, and even from animals. Obviously, other than standard techniques must be used in these instances.

PART ONE

Examination of the visual field

The examination of the visual field should be geared to the patient's responses. One should not expect the same subjective responses to visual stimuli from a senile old man as from an alert and intelligent young woman. The aged or ill must be given more time, and a single answer cannot be relied on; the defect must be checked and rechecked until the examiner is certain of the analysis of it. If the perimetrist will show an obvious interest and enthusiasm for the test, the patient will often enter into the spirit of the "game" and thereby increase its diagnostic value.

Before the examiner actually settles down to the task of "taking the field," there are many useful hints or clues that may indicate the presence of a visual field defect:

1. When questioned directly, the patient may give a history of a positive scotoma and some patients can actually draw out the limits of their defect.
2. Observation of a patient's manner of avoiding obstacles as he walks into a room will sometimes indicate the presence of a homonymous hemianopsia or an inferior field defect.
3. A statement by the patient that he spills his food at the table will, if elaborated, indicate the area of the field defect responsible for the errors.
4. The manner in which the Snellen test letters are read may reveal the nature of a visual field loss. The patient may volunteer the information that he sees the first letter better if he looks at the second one. Patients with chiasmal lesions and bitemporal hemianopsia will frequently start reading the test line backward. If, after correction of refractive error, a patient leaves out parts of letters, reading F for E, C for O, or P for R, it may indicate a tiny scotoma.
5. A history of deficient color vision of recent origin may indicate a relative color scotoma.
6. The description by the migrainous patient of his scintillating scotoma may vary according to his experiences. Thus he may give the classic picture of the expanding circle of jagged light and color or he may compare it with a pool full of leaping fish. His transient hemianopsia may be described as a mist or a fog, or a heat haze rising from a pavement, or water running down a window-

pane. The same variations may be found in descriptions of hallucinations. In all instances careful attention should be paid to the patient's own wording in describing his symptoms.

All of these and many other subjective visual complaints when analyzed and correctly interpreted may point the way to a specific field defect and save much time when the visual field is tested.

The instruments of perimetry are legion and the methods of eliciting a visual field loss may vary from the use of a waving flashlight to the presentation of a 0.25-mm fused silver wire test object on the card of a stereocampimeter. Almost all serious students of perimetry have at one time or another devised their own special instruments. It is to be noted that the instruments that have survived and have been widely adopted are simple in design and construction. It remains to be seen if our modern, complicated and computerized instruments will stand the test of time.

Elaborate self-recording pantographs have numerous objectionable qualities, whether they use mechanical test object carriers or light projection of the stimulus onto the perimeter arc or tangent screen. The simplicity of the pantograph of the Goldmann perimeter, however, has much to commend it. The pantographs of the Auto-Plot screen and the Tübinger perimeter are simple and accurate in design. The instruments use light-projected stimuli that can be turned on or off at will during movement of the stimulus from one part of the field to another as is done when the field is examined statically with the Tübinger, modified Goldmann, and some of the newer automated perimeters. The need for elasticity in performing the examination of the visual field has already been stressed, and the introduction of a mechanically actuated test object, whether it be a paper or plastic disc, a steel ball moved by a magnet, or a projected spot of light, reduces the opportunity of quickly varying the size, position, and intensity of the stimulus. Although mechanical and self-recording perimeters and tangent screens may make it possible to perform more routine visual field examinations in a given time, it does not follow that these examinations are more carefully or exhaustively carried out. It is easy to understand why the perimetric technician who does a large number of examinations by rote would prefer one of the various forms of mechanical perimeters, but it is rare that such a technician understands the nature of the disease in the visual pathway being examined. Because of its slow and tedious nature, profile or static perimetry must usually be delegated to a technician. These technicians must have other tasks to perform from time to time to vary the monotony of continuous visual field examination.

In almost every instance the students who have contributed most to the examination and interpretation of the visual field have used equipment and techniques of great simplicity. The methods and instruments of Bjerrum, Rönne, Peter, Ferree and Rand, Sloan, Walker, Lloyd, Evans, Traquair, Goldmann, Harms, and Aulhorn have stood the test of time and use. They have been elaborated upon, but they have not been greatly improved.

A summary of Goldmann's requirements and fundamentals of exact perimetry follows:

1. To perform exact relative perimetry with white targets, adaptation equilib-

rium must be established, contrast between target and perimeter background must remain constant, and basic illumination must not show appreciable change.

2. Under such conditions, quantitative relationship may be found between targets of varying size. A quantitative comparison of the sensitivity of individual retinal points thus becomes possible on the basis of perimetric data gained with different sized targets.
3. The function of any retinal point is characterized not only by its different sensitivity but also by its power of summation for different sized targets. The summation power of the normal retina is constant over wide areas of the visual field. Distinct perception decreases summation, whereas dark adaptation seems to increase it.
4. The visual field as tested with white stimuli is influenced by the sharpness of the target border. Refractive errors and cloudy media diminish the relative field considerably. The inner isopters in particular should be examined only with corrective lenses, and visual fields in patients with opacities of the media must be evaluated with caution.

Examination of central or foveal visual function and peripheral vision must always go together. One cannot say that visual acuity is reduced to 20/50 and the visual field is normal. In such circumstances there must be a general depression of all isopters, such as might occur with opacities of the media, or there must be a central scotoma detectable with proper perimetric techniques.

Visual field examination is a threshold measurement. It is, of course, impossible to examine every point in the entire field of vision, so in practice a limited number of areas are selected for testing. The selection of these sites may be random or purposeful. In testing these selected points, the minimum light stimulus is measured that is required to produce a response by the patient. Threshold stimulation can take place in total darkness or against a background of measured luminance. In the latter case one is measuring the minimum contrast between stimulus and background. This difference threshold is the smallest measurable difference in luminance between a stimulus and its background. The Goldmann and Tübinger perimeters, and recent modifications of these instruments, measure visual function in the visual field by determining differential light sensitivity of a number of positions by means of difference threshold measurements.

There are a number of factors that determine this difference threshold measurement:

1. Physical characteristics of the stimulus
2. Preretinal factors such as pupil size, media opacities, and refractive error
3. Receptive and neural factors
4. Psychologic factors that have been mentioned before
5. General health of the patient

All of these will be considered in the examination and analysis of specific visual field deficits.

CHAPTER 1

Perimetry without special instruments

It is not always possible to perform a visual field examination under ideal conditions. In examinations in the home, of bedridden patients, or in hospitals where perimetric instruments are not available, considerable ingenuity may be required in utilizing existing facilities as effective substitutes for the usually employed methods of testing. The lack of standard perimetric equipment is no excuse for failure to examine the visual field. The diagnostic value of the test in certain cases makes its attempt mandatory, and it is surprising how often perimetry with improved methods and equipment will yield information that is of clinical importance.

CONFRONTATION TEST

Of all the methods of perimetry, the confrontation test is probably the most widely used. It has become a part of the routine physical examination performed by many physicians and certainly by the majority of neurologists and neurosurgeons. It is frequently used by the optometrist and the ophthalmologist as a rapid, qualitative screening test of the visual field. The confrontation test is generally considered to be a crude and purely qualitative method, suitable only for elicting very gross defects in the peripheral field and quite useless for finer testing or any form of scotometry.

It is my opinion that all the possibilities of the confrontation test have never been fully exploited and that, when properly performed, the test may be of great value. In many situations it is the only practical form of clinical perimetry available: for instance, in the examinations of small children, mentally disturbed patients, or very ill or semiconscious persons.

As a rule the confrontation test is performed with examiner and patient facing each other about a half-meter apart, the examiner wiggling an index finger in each of the four quadrants of the field and asking the patient whether he can see it. When used in this manner, the method is capable of detecting only the most gross defects, and a negative result is too often recorded as a normal field when, in fact, there may be defects of considerable size and density. In performing a confrontation examination, the examiner should pay attention to the light source and its position, the nature of the background, the test object used, and the patient's responses, both subjective and objective (shift of fixation). The method should never be considered as a substitute for more precise methods of perimetry but only as an adjunct. However, because there are times when it is the only available method, it should be practiced diligently, utilizing all possible refinements so that experience may be gained in the examination and the interpretation of the results.

R. C. Welsh has described a useful variation of the confrontation field that roughly quantitates peripheral visual acuity and that may be used as a gross screening test. Instead of the usual stimulus of a wiggling finger, he asks the patient to count one or two fingers in the peripheral field while maintaining central fixation. By increasing the distance from 500 mm to 3 or 4 meters, he makes the test more sensitive and can test the field out to 40 to 60 degrees from fixation. I have used this finger-counting field examination as a quick preliminary test to obtain information as to which areas of the field require more careful exploration and analysis. It is also adaptable to simultaneous double stimulation.

A proper confrontation examination is performed with the patient, his back to the light, facing the examiner at a distance of about one-half meter from the examiner. If possible a uniform and dark background should be behind the examiner and the intensity of the light should be capable of variation. The patient uses the examiner's eye as a fixation point for the eye being tested while he covers his other eye with the palm of his hand or an occluder patch. With a suitable test object it is often possible to outline the blind spot, thus demonstrating what is meant by disappearance of the stimulus. Test objects may vary in size and type, but in general the 2-, 5-, or 10-mm disc or plastic sphere is most suitable when attached to the end of a dull black (felt-covered) wand about 2 feet in length. With the patient fixating on the examiner's eye, the test object is moved from the periphery of the patient's field in an arc simulating the curve of an imaginary perimeter. Little practice is required to estimate with considerable accuracy the number of degrees from fixation at which the object appears in the field, and the object is then moved slowly in toward fixation to uncover any gross scotomas that may be present. Paracentral and central scotomas, hemianopsias, and quadrant defects can often be surveyed with considerable accuracy. When the patient demonstrates good central visual acuity, a 5-mm test object is probably the stimulus of choice; however, there is no limit to the size of the object that may be profitably used, from a 2-mm white bead to a large sheet of paper or a naked ophthalmoscope light.

Another stimulus of considerable versatility that is useful in confrontation testing is the electroluminescent self-luminous target (Lumiwand), which will be described later. The short arm of the wand used in a dimly lighted room provides an easily controlled target that can be moved about rapidly in the peripheral field and can be turned on and off so that the patient never knows in which sector it will appear. Its size can be varied and its use, preliminary to more elaborate perimetry, may often point out the areas of the field requiring more careful study. It is an especially useful stimulus for evaluating the visual fields in young children.

Fig. 1-1. Confrontation test using simultaneous double stimulation.

A valuable elaboration of the confrontation test is one that makes use of the extinction phenomenon. In this examination both sides of the visual field are tested simultaneously. This method of double stimulation, which may be used both monocularly and binocularly, will be considered separately as a special technique (Fig. 1-1).

Lars Frisén has described a simple qualitative confrontation test for the central visual field that does not change its character with varying illumination. The test is based on the association of defects with disturbed color perception involving an apparent desaturation and a predictable change in hue of a colored test object. (See also notes on color perimetry.) Red and blue frosted light bulbs were used as test objects and the examinations were run in parallel with quantitative kinetic perimetry with good correlation between the two methods.

BEDSIDE PERIMETRY

Bedside perimetry applies to the methods of testing the visual field at the bedside in the hospital or at home or under any circumstances when the usual techniques or instruments of perimetry are not available.

There have been many attempts to design a practical perimeter or tangent screen sufficiently light and portable to use in examining the visual field of a patient too ill to be moved from bed or unable to assume a sitting position. Most of these instruments have been too heavy for the patient to hold for any length of time, and others have been so bulky and complicated as to be, in fact, no more portable than the standard equipment. The two most widely used instruments are probably the Schweigger hand perimeter and a 2-foot square of black or gray cardboard. Both of these instruments are light in weight, but they have the major disadvantage of a very short distance between eye and fixation point and a consequent reduction in the sensitivity of the test. Of the two, the tangent screen is probably the more useful.

Another useful device is an adaptation of the umbrella perimeter in which an ordinary black umbrella is covered on its inner side with black felt or velvet so as to hide the steel ribs. The handle is cut off at whatever length is desired, depending on the size and radius of curvature of the umbrella. The end of the handle is rested against the cheek under the eye being tested.

Ordinary spherical or disc test objects mounted on felt-covered wands are used. The umbrella is so light that it may be held over a reclining patient, and it offers a wide field and a long enough radius to be of value in scotometry. When not in use, it may be cased with its test objects and wands in a cardboard or metal mailing tube.

Actually there is very little difference between bedside perimetry and office perimetry except that the former requires somewhat more ingenuity in the utilization of existing materials and less dependence on the usual standard equipment. For example, an adequate tangent screen field can be taken on a reclining patient by using a room wall with a piece of adhesive material stuck to it at a suitable height for fixation. The patient is turned on his side and moved so that his face is at the edge of the mattress, and the field is plotted as though the temporal field were at the ceiling and the nasal field near the floor. If the wall is white or light colored, a black-headed pin mounted on a wooden applicator stick may be used as a contrasting test object.

The self-luminous wand (Lumiwand), which uses its own electroluminescent source of light, is especially useful at the bedside. It is portable and, because it is used in a dim or even dark room, requires no special background; it can be used as a quantitative test by varying the stimulus size from 1 to 10 mm and the luminance from 9 to 1 footlamberts.

Whichever method is used, it is the duty of the examiner to make the most of the equipment at hand and to improvise as required with this equipment, using ingenuity and imagination in the conduct of the test.

CHAPTER 2

Instruments of perimetry and their use

Perimetric instruments have been devised in almost infinite variety, and yet the basic specifications for a good perimeter or tangent screen have remained essentially unchanged in spite of all attempts to improve them. While basic principles of perimetry remain constant, the instrumentation becomes more and more sophisticated. The long search for more rapid and less tedious methods of visual field testing has largely removed this very important subjective sensory examination from the hands of the ophthalmologist and made it the responsibility of highly trained paramedical technicians or, in the case of automated perimetry, the patient himself.

This has resulted in the development of a plethora of new instruments, from the Goldmann perimeter and its several copies, used primarily for kinetic perimetry, to the Tübinger instrument, capable of kinetic examination of the field but mainly used for static perimetry.

Along the way a number of screening devices for rapid visual field examination have been developed, beginning with the multiple pattern method of Harrington-Flocks (see Fig. 3-2) and followed by the Globuck screen, the Friedmann field analyzer, and a series of automated and computerized perimeters, some of which are used as screeners and some for definitive field examination. All of these instruments use randomized presentation of multiple stimuli in automated patterns, recorded automatically with the patient, in effect, performing his own visual field examination. The ultimate in sophisticated instrumentation is that used by the Octopus perimetery, which performs automated computer-assisted perimetry but which still requires the presence of a technician and is still a subjective examination. Beyond this we must go to the increasing improvements and use of visual-evoked response (VER) for a truly objective analysis of visual deficits (see Fig. 3-8).

PERIMETERS

The theoretically ideal perimeter would be one half of a hollow sphere, with a radius of curvature of at least a meter, with the patient's eye at the center of the sphere and the examiner outside the sphere but still able to observe the patient for attentiveness, fixation, and reactions. The larger the sphere the more accurate would be its detection of visual field defects of all types, including scotomas. If such an instrument included (1) complete freedom of movement of the test stimuli in all directions, (2) rapid interchangeability of test object size, brightness, and color, (3) a pantograph for automatic recording of the position of the stimulus at any given moment, and (4) computer-assisted randomized stimulus presentation and recording, it is likely that most other methods of visual field examination could largely be eliminated.

There have been a number of short-radius sphere and projection perimeters, but none have embodied as many desirable features as that of Hans Goldmann, which has become the standard instrument throughout the rest of the Western world (Fig. 2-1). An example of an excellent set of specifications for a perimeter is found in the descriptive brochure written by Goldmann and supplied with the instrument by the manufacturer:

> It is a spherical projection perimeter with a recording device. A Nitra lamp illuminates a circumscribed peripheral area above and inside the bowl which is of 300 mm. radius and painted matte white. The lamp is shaded from the rest of the hemisphere by a hood. A por-

A B

Fig. 2-1. Goldmann perimeter. **A,** Front view showing projection system. **B,** Rear view showing pantograph. (Courtesy Haag-Streit Co., Berne, Switzerland.)

tion of the light is sent by a condenser through a hollow lever arm containing the projection system for the perimeter target. By this means slight variations in the brightness of the lamp affect background and target luminosity equally. The movement of the projection arm is produced by a pantograph controlled by a handle which slides on a vertical plate of opal glass illuminated from behind on the back of the perimeter. This plate carries the recording chart. Each position of the handle corresponds exactly with the position of the spot of light on the hemisphere. By slow movement of the handle across the surface of the chart the visual fields may be examined for 95° on each side of fixation. A telescope through the back of the hemisphere allows for constant observation and control of the patient's eye and in it is a light, variable sized, fixation point. A slide allows the target to vanish and reappear noiselessly. The projected targets are ellipses of varying sizes from 1/16 mm.^{2} to 64 mm.^{2} and are easily changed by stops. A series of neutral filters permits geometric reduction in the luminosity of the targets from 100 millilamberts to 3.16 millilamberts. The basic luminosity of the target has been fixed at thirty-three times that of the background and a photometric device is incorporated in the instrument to ensure the constancy of this ratio. If a perimeter does not automatically keep this contrast between background and target luminosity a constant, it is unusable for exact relative perimetry, and previous projection perimeters have not done so. Hitherto such a constancy has only been found with perimeters using paper targets.

Because of the importance of this constant ratio of background to target luminosity, the photometric adjustment of the perimeter should be effected before each examination, but after the patient is seated before the instrument since lighter or darker faces and clothes can alter the background luminosity by several percent.

The perimeter may also be equipped with color filter for red, green and blue.

It will be seen from the preceding description that this instrument is admirable from a theoretical point of view. If Goldmann's standards are adhered to, the photometric adjustment of the instrument before each examination is a requirement of accuracy; and if not made, the projection system as an accurate method is nullified. Other valid objections to the instrument are (1) its small radius, (2) its considerable bulk, which generally requires a special room for its use, and (3) its initial cost.

Whereas the method of static perimetry (also called lightsense perimetry or profile perimetry) has been known for over three decades and has been under continuous investigation for most of that time, it is only now gaining the recognition it deserves. Until recently the method was considered a research tool, unsuited for widespread clinical use. However, the development of a practical instrument by Professor H. Harms and Professor E. Aulhorn of the University of Tübingen in Germany (Fig. 2-2) has popularized the method, and static perimetry is now being used and studied in clinics around the world. It constitutes the basis for all of the newer automated perimeters that present static suprathreshold stimuli in randomized and computer-controlled patterns.

The method consists of presenting stationary (or static) stimuli in a series of exposures, usually along a series of meridians in the bowl of the perimeter. The stimuli are projected light spots, similar to those of the Goldmann perimeter, but they remain static while their luminance is increased by measured increments of light until the patient signals that the stimulus is visible. The stimulus is then moved to a new location on the meridian and again the luminance is increased from zero to visibility. This is repeated usually at 1-degree intervals within the central 15 degrees of the

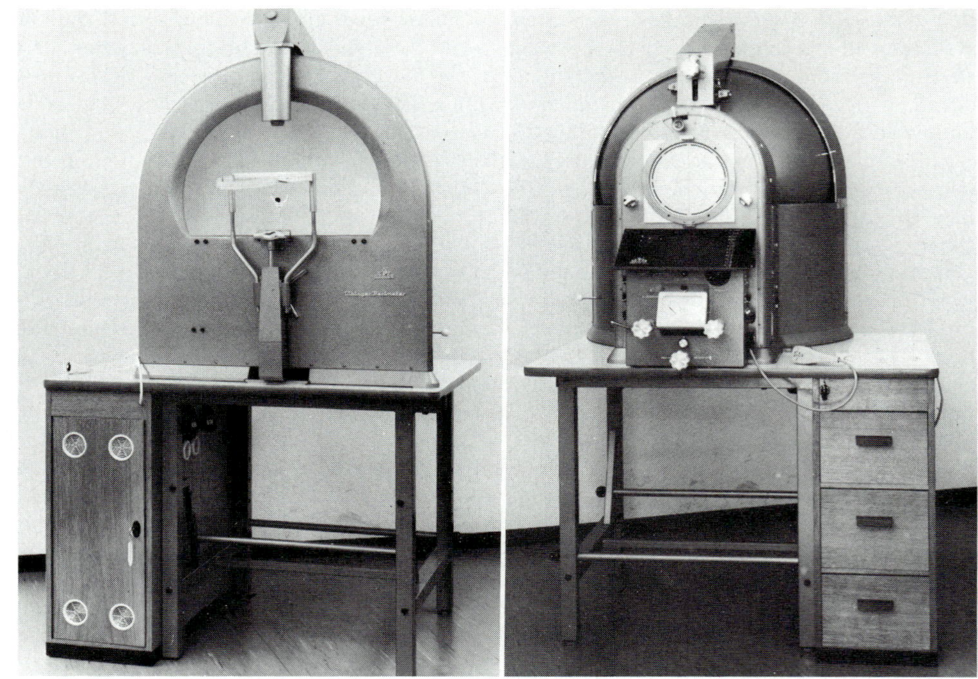

Fig. 2-2. Tübinger perimeter. **A,** Front view showing projection system. **B,** Rear view showing controls, pantograph, and charts for both static and kinetic perimetry. (Courtesy Oculus Optikgerate, Dutenhofen, Germany.)

field and at 5-degree intervals in the peripheral field. Thus, approximately fifty stimulus exposures must be made along a single meridian, with each exposure started at zero luminance and increased by increments of light until the patient sees the projected spot. Stimulus size may be varied in the same manner as with the Goldmann perimeter.

Usually the examination is made along four meridians (90, 180, 135, and 45 degrees), which would be adequate coverage of the field. If depressions are discovered, they may be explored along new meridians or in a circular fashion. Kinetic perimetry may be performed on the same instrument.

Theoretically, it is possible to examine the entire visual field at 1-degree intervals, but this, of course, would require approximately 15,000 exposures and a year of time.

As each meridian of the field is examined, it is charted by pantographic means on special charts supplied with the instrument (see Figs. 2-20 and 2-21). The plot of the exposures is a cross section through the hill of vision or a profile study of this cross section showing its peak, slope, blind spot, and any abnormal depression on its surface. In this it differs from kinetic or isopter perimetry, which charts the contour lines of the hill of vision. What is measured and charted in static perimetry is the light threshold in the different areas of the visual field.

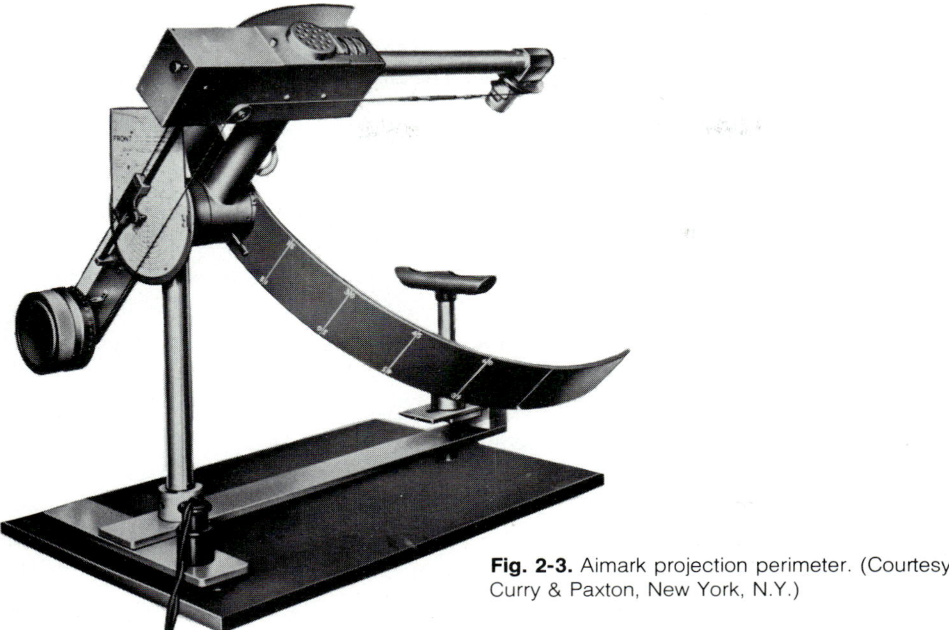

Fig. 2-3. Aimark projection perimeter. (Courtesy Curry & Paxton, New York, N.Y.)

The measurement of the difference threshold by static perimetry is accurate and is one of the most fundamental functions of the visual system. The only variable is the luminance; all other factors that might influence the level of difference threshold are kept constant.

Kinetic perimetry also measures light sensitivity. As in static perimetry, the difference threshold is measured at multiple points in the visual field. The method of measurement, however, is different and an extra variable, the movement of the stimulus, is introduced. Stimulus luminance remains constant, but position varies. Static perimetry produces a vertical section or profile of the "island of vision." Kinetic perimetry produces a horizontal section through the island.

Static perimetry is more accurate than the kinetic method but is less flexible in its application. Kinetic perimetry is more dependent on the knowledge and skill of the examiner and the cooperation of the patient.

The Tübinger perimeter has its greatest usefulness in the detection and assessment of the earliest visual field defects in glaucoma. It should be used in combination with kinetic perimetry on the tangent screen to obtain maximum information from these defects. Because of its relative simplicity, inexpensiveness, and portability, the arc perimeter is still an instrument in fairly common use. It is a segment of a hollow sphere in the form of an arc that rotates through 360 degrees about a central axis. Thus by rotation of the arc, all areas within the hollow sphere of the visual field may be tested in sequence.

The general specifications of an acceptable arc perimeter are largely satisfied by the British-made Airmark projection perimeter (Fig. 2-3).

EXAMINATION WITH THE PERIMETER

During examination of the visual field with the perimeter, it is essential that the patient be comfortably seated and relaxed. The nature of the test should be briefly explained to him.

A system of signals should be agreed on, such as a tap on the table when the test object appears. The patient should be instructed to signal when he becomes conscious of the test object, as distinct from the carrier, and also to indicate its disappearance immediately. Hand signals are better than verbal responses.

The light in the examining room should be diminished but of sufficient intensity that the examiner may constantly observe the patient's eye and its fixation.

The size of the test object chosen for the first examination will depend on a number of factors: (1) the patient's central visual acuity, (2) the state of the media of the eye, and (3) the patient's mental status, speed of cerebration, reaction time, and ability to concentrate on the examination as judged by responses to previous portions of the eye examination. When in doubt, a 3-mm object is a good average starting stimulus.

It is generally not necessary to chart each meridian as it is taken, unless the visual field defect is complicated by several appearances and disappearances of the object along the arc. In most instances and with a little practice, three or four meridians can be memorized as they are examined before stopping to chart them.

The movement of the test object along the arc of the perimeter will vary somewhat in speed with the size of the object and the patient's reaction time. A movement rate of 3 degrees per second is recommended. It is generally best to start temporally in the far periphery of the field, moving the object slowly and smoothly in toward fixation. Except for certain special tests, the object should not be wiggled or oscillated. A rapidly moving object actually subtends a larger visual angle than its size and therefore tests a different isopter from what was intended. This is one reason why very thin wire test object carriers are unsatisfactory, since they tend to vibrate with movement or the slightest hand tremor.

One should be able at any time in the course of the examination to cause the test object to appear or disappear at will or to bring it into view from obscurity while maintaining it in a stationary position. This is accomplished by mounting the stimulus on the *side* of the carrying wand rather than at its tip or by having one side of the test object black and the other side white. In this way the test object can be flipped over and made to disappear. It can then be brought back into view by slowly or quickly rotating the carrying stick.

Patients must be frequently subjected to this disappearance of the test object in order to evaluate the alertness of their responses and the accuracy of their fixation.

Provision is made for this need to periodically hide the stimulus in the various projection perimeters. It is also accomplished with great facility with the electroluminescent stimuli, to be described later.

When the patient signals that he has seen the stimulus, a mental note is made of its position and the movement of the object is slowly continued inward while the patient is cautioned to signal when it disappears. If the movement is too fast, the object may "pass through" a scotoma so rapidly that the patient is unaware of its disappearance before it appears again. By locating and outlining the normal blind spot, the examiner has an excellent idea of how fast or how slow to proceed with any given individual and at the same time can instruct the patient in what is meant by the disappearance and appearance of the test object.

Each of eight or more half-meridians is generally examined in the same way. When a visual field defect is encountered, its size, shape, and density should be exhaustively studied using as many meridians and changes of arc position as are required and quantitatively surveying its outline and depth with multiple test objects of graduated size. Too much time should not be spent in a routine examination of the intact portions of the visual field, in order that more time may be spent on a careful analysis of such defects as are detected.

When readily interchangeable test objects on hand-held wands or carriers are used with the perimeter, a considerable degree of latitude is obtainable in the examination of the central field. Somewhat more care is needed in the examination of small scotomas because of the short radius of the instrument.

In the past two decades there have been much interest and debate in the literature on the relative merits of static and kinetic perimetry. Conventional perimetry with moving test objects has been variously designated as topographic, isopter, or kinetic perimetry, whereas the methods of perimetry that measure light thresholds directly at a series of fixed locations within the visual field by varying the luminance of the test objects are variously known as lightsense, quantitative, profile, or static perimetry.

The Goldmann spherical projection perimeter makes possible precise and reproducible gradations in the visibility of the test object by varying either the object's area or its contrast with the background, or both.

Goldmann used conventional or kinetic perimetry with moving test objects to find the changes in area and luminance of the projected test object that would produce the same alteration in the limits of the visual field. Some of his studies were conducted with test objects moved automatically at a constant rate of speed, a method designated as skiascotometry. The Goldmann perimeter can also be equipped for static perimetry as well as for automated perimetry.

Both Harms and Weekers and La Vergne strongly advocated the method of static perimetry and have stated that it is more accurate and will also detect early defects not revealed by the conventional kinetic method.

In conventional kinetic perimetry, the visual field is explored with a moving test object of fixed luminance to locate points at which this luminance becomes visible for a given stimulus area. Static perimetry uses test objects of varying area located at fixed positions in the visual field with a gradual increasing of luminance to the threshold of visibility.

Threshold measurements made by kinetic perimetry cannot be as precise and reproducible as those made by static perimetry, because the rate of movement of the test object and the promptness of response by the patient when the stimulus appears and disappears introduce unavoidable variations in the plot of the field. The principal reason for using location of the test object (as in conventional kinetic perimetry) rather than luminance (as in static perimetry) as the variable is that exploration of the entire visual field in a number of meridians is much less time consuming by kinetic perimetry.

In clinical studies static perimetry is a valuable supplement to conventional methods as a means of precisely exploring the density of a field deficit already located by kinetic methods. In glaucoma it is particularly useful as a means of detecting depressed acuity in the Bjerrum area in the form of a small, often isolated, scotoma, which may later be explored on the tangent screen with moving targets.

Eric Greve has combined single and multiple stimulus static perimetry in the study of glaucomatous visual field defects using the Friedmann field analyzer and the Tübinger perimeter.

Jayle has further explored the matter of variable luminance with a modified Goldmann perimeter, with which he can vary both test object and background luminance using both static and kinetic perimetry. He is thus able to examine the visual field under photopic or light-adapted conditions, under which the greatest stimulation is to the cones; scotopic or dark-adapted conditions, under which rod stimulation is greatest; and mesopic or mid-dark–adapted conditions, under which rods and cones are equally stimulated.

Widespread acceptance of the Goldmann perimeter and the more recent enthusiasm for the Tübinger perimeter and the method of static perimetry advocated by Harms and Aulhorn have stimulated comparative studies and encouraged new methods and refinements in perimetric techniques that are still in a state of evolution.

As mentioned earlier, a number of automated perimeters have been developed, tested, and sold in the past ten or more years. Theoretically, these devices enable the patient to conduct his own visual field examination in a fairly comprehensive manner, with any defects being automatically charted. All of these instruments, in fact, require a technician to initiate and monitor the examination. Some demand more attention than others. The speed of the examination (one of the chief advantages cited over conventional perimetry) is largely determined by the subjective responses of the individual patient and the assistance required of the technician. The examination remains a subjective one in spite of a complex system of computerization and automation.

It is said that highly skilled perimetrists are not needed to conduct these examinations, but most proponents are careful to emphasize that the instruments are screening devices and were not designed to replace the skilled perimetrist, who must analyze the field deficits detected by the perimeter and, in many cases, gather more detailed data by conventional kinetic or static perimetry on the Goldmann instrument or the tangent screen.

Four of these automated and computer-assisted perimeters will be briefly examined in more detail. They are the Baylor Visual Field Programmer (House of Vision Instrument Co., Chicago), the Fieldmaster Automated Perimeter (Synemed Inc., Berkeley), the Perimetron (Coherent, Medical Division, Palo Alto), and the Octopus system (Interzeag Ag Schlieren, Switzerland).

The Baylor Visual Field Programmer was designed to provide an exactly repeatable test procedure year to year, patient to patient, and examiner to examiner and uses a preprogrammed microprocessor to present stimuli and record responses (Fig. 2-4). It consists of a small computer, a control panel, and a display board that attaches to a Goldmann-type perimeter, replacing the translucent surface on which the recording paper is placed. The display board contains an array of light-emitting diodes that are illuminated sequentially by a computer through a selection of pre-

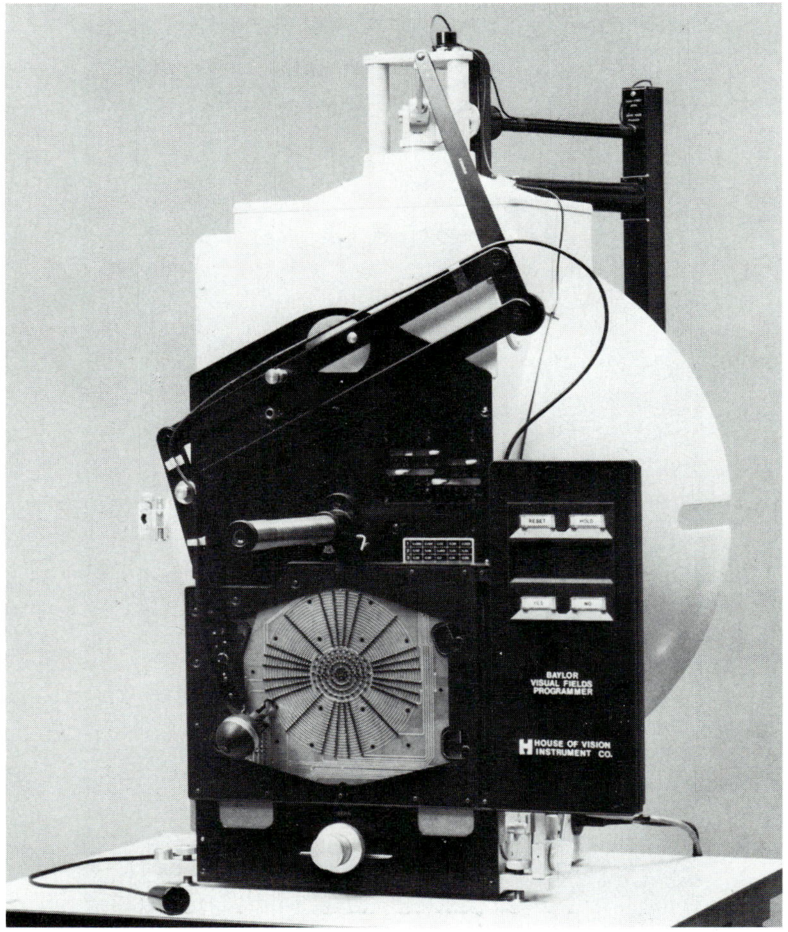

Fig. 2-4. Baylor Visual Field Programmer. (Courtesy House of Vision Instrument Co., Chicago, Ill.)

programmed visual field testing procedures. Three programs are available depending on the number of test locations desired; from 116 in the basic program to 439 for the glaucoma program, utilizing a modification and extension of the Armaly-Drance screen, to 516 test points for the extended program of special value for testing neurologic deficits. Stimuli are presented statically or kinetically depending on their location. Attachment of the module to a Goldmann-type perimeter does not interfere with the use of the instrument as a regular kinetic perimeter. A Goldmann-type visual field examination can therefore be performed concentrating on the defective areas detected by the programmer. Because of the relative simplicity of the module and the fact that it can be used on an existing Goldmann instrument, its initial cost and maintenance expense are appreciably less than for some of the other automated perimeters.

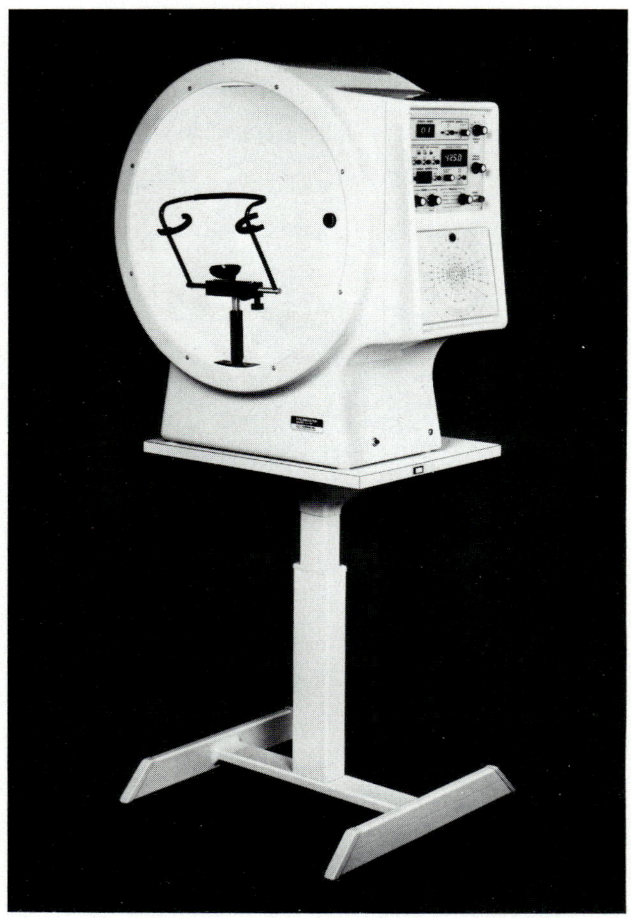

Fig. 2-5. Fieldmaster Automated Visual Field Plotter. (Courtesy Synemed, Inc., Berkeley, Calif.)

The Fieldmaster Automated Perimeter utilizes a quick randomized test procedure referred to as "suprathreshold static perimetry." It has been thoroughly tested and the results compared with the findings of expertly examined Goldmann perimeter fields by Keltner and associates. They found a very close correlation between the deficits detected by the Fieldmaster and those found by kinetic perimetry on the Goldmann instrument. Their efforts were directed toward a rapid, quantitative screening technique. Target luminance is initially adjusted to a level assumed to be above normal threshold sensitivity, and the targets are then presented at locations throughout the visual field in random sequence.

The Fieldmaster instrument (Fig. 2-5) consists of a hemispherical cupola of 300-mm radius with 99 holes placed at strategic locations in the visual field. Fiberoptic elements positioned behind each hole provide the target illumination from a single central light source. During the examination, each spot lights up in a random sequence and the patient depresses a button for each target seen. The location of each response is recorded on a heat-sensitive paper. Dark spots on the chart indicate locations where the target is seen, whereas unfilled spots denote locations where the stimulus is not seen (see Fig. 2-23). Accurate fixation is monitored continuously so that changes in fixation will elicit a warning tone and stop the program until proper fixation is resumed.

Luminance of the background and the stimuli can be varied by independent controls. The background luminance may be varied between 1 and 45 apostilbs (asb), whereas the test spot luminance may be varied from 5 to 1,000 asb. Exposure duration of the test spot and time interval between exposures may also be controlled. Manual selection and presentation of individual test spots can be performed, and there is provision for an automatic recheck of all missed test spots on an individual run. Programs may be selected for testing the full visual field, the central 30 degrees only, or the periphery only. For the most commonly used time intervals, each test run of 99 spots takes less than two and one-half minutes to complete.

In spite of the high degree of standardization and the close correlation between the Fieldmaster and Goldmann fields, Keltner and associates emphasize that the Fieldmaster is not intended as a replacement for the Goldmann perimeter and the tangent screen and should not be regarded as such. It is an automated screening device requiring subjective responses that must be monitored and interpreted by a trained technician. Its proper use may stimulate renewed interest in visual field testing.

The Perimetron computerized projection perimeter system is designed to be operated by an unskilled technician and offers a high degree of standardization, repeatability, and versatility to the visual field examination (Fig. 2-6). It is more than a limited purpose screening device.

The heart of the system is a computer that stores multiple test protocols and that controls the stimulus brightness, position, speed of motion, and exposure time. Repeatability in testing is assured, with no variation from one examiner or examination to the next.

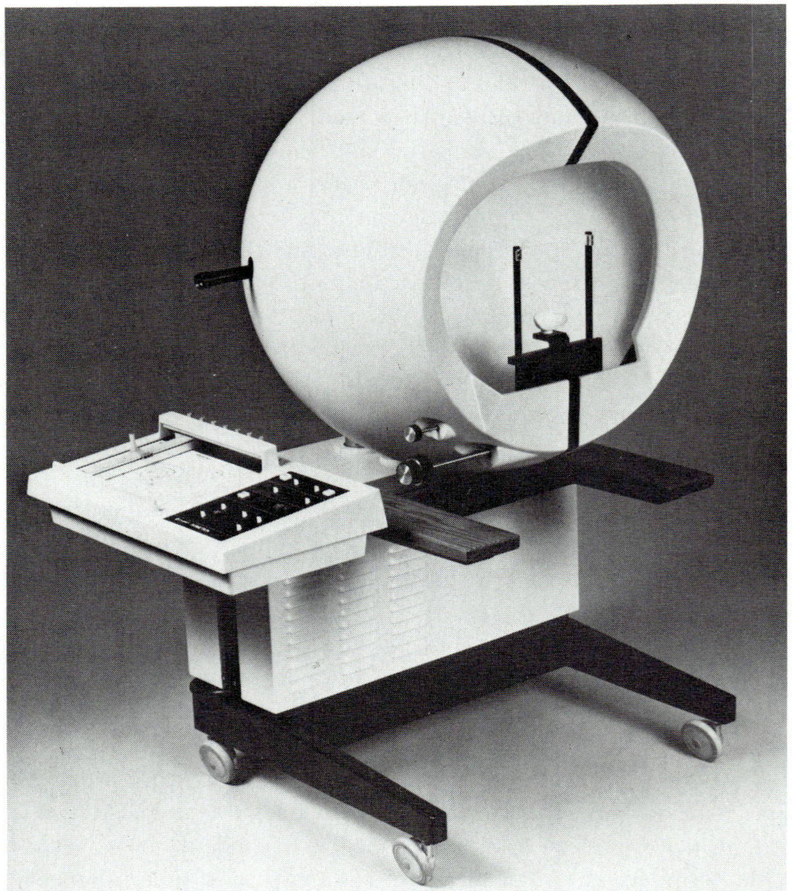

Fig. 2-6. Perimetron automated perimeter. (Courtesy Coherent, Medical Division, Palo Alto, Calif.)

The computer protocols are patterned after the most effective manual perimetric techniques. Stimuli are automatically moved from nonseeing to seeing areas or randomly presented to spot-check any point within the visual field.

Multiple-isopter protocols are available to check both central and peripheral fields, including one for glaucoma screening after the Armaly-Drance technique. This program combines suprathreshold stimuli to kinetically check the horizontal meridians along with a large number of spot checks within the 30-degree central field. A static perimetry test is available for mapping cross-section profiles through existing field defects.

At the end of the examination the field is automatically plotted with conventionally labeled isopters. Interpretation of the visual field defects is the same as on the charts of the Goldmann perimeter, since the design incorporates the Goldmann standards of bowl size, illumination, and stimulus size and intensity.

In the likely event that new and better perimetric techniques evolve in the

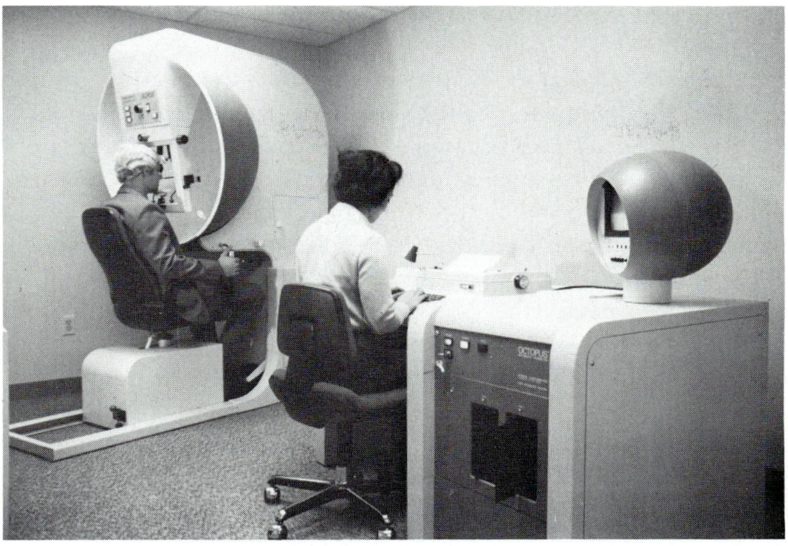

Fig. 2-7. Octopus perimeter system. Fixation monitored on video screen. (Courtesy Hitron Corp., East Providence, R.I.)

future, the Perimetron can be reprogrammed and no other change in the instrument would be required.

The Octopus system of automated and computer-assisted perimetry is a most sophisticated instrument developed over the past ten years by Fankhauser at Bern, Switzerland. It has been studied and tested intensively by a large number of investigators and has been declared superior to Goldmann kinetic perimetry and Tübinger static perimetry in the early detection and analysis of visual field defects, especially those associated with glaucoma (Fig. 2-7).

The Octopus perimeter system is a measuring instrument combined with a computer. The computer controls and supervises the instrument, which in turn supplies the computer with information. Further information is added in the patient's history. The computer processes this information and provides printouts of various forms. Fixation is monitored by the operator through a video system that is highly accurate and sensitive to eye movement or lid closure.

Printouts of the results of a visual field examination may be recorded on a Diskette in the form of a numerical table or a profile graph, or in half-tone density steps. These Diskettes may store a large number of individual visual field examinations, which can be retrieved for comparison at a later date.

Experiences with the Octopus system of perimetry indicate that it is more sensitive in detecting visual field loss than manual perimetry, either kinetic or static, in about 80% of the glaucomatous eyes that were examined. Relative scotomas were the field defects most frequently missed by manual perimetry. Octopus automated perimetry had few false negative examinations.

Even with the standardization of perimeters, both kinetic and static, the visual fields plotted by different examiners may vary widely and the limits of error may be considerable.

Goldmann has stated that every point in the visual field has its own threshold, its relation to its surroundings, and its error function. Therefore neither contour nor profile perimetry can give a complete description of a visual field; this can only be done by point-for-point testing. The examiner arbitrarily determines the number and distribution of the points to be investigated. Too few points give inadequate information; too many points tire the patient and render his responses unrealiable. The stimuli should be presented at random in the field, and the number, distribution, and density can be determined accurately only by a computerized automated perimeter with variable and flexible programs.

Such complex and elaborate instrumentation is necessarily very expensive, requires expert monitoring by trained technicians, and needs maintenance and repair services. It takes a minimum of 17 minutes to examine each eye and is very little faster than a well-done Goldmann field examination. It is unlikely that it will soon be available as an office procedure to the general clinical ophthalmologist. In its proper setting, however, it will inevitably teach us much about the true nature of the visual field in both health and disease.

For the moment we will need to be content with the information obtainable with expertly performed examinations with the Goldmann perimeter, the Tübinger perimeter, various screening devices, and definitive exploration of small relative defects in the visual field as detected by careful quantitative perimetry on the tangent screen.

A thorough knowledge of the principles of visual field examination and interpretation of defects is necessary before we can delegate perimetry entirely to an automated and computerized instrument. Not all patients can be successfully examined by automated perimetry; the interpretation of visual field defects is still the responsibility of the ophthalmologist whether the defects are discovered by manual or automatic methods.

The continuing search for more rapid and reliable visual field examination is understandable. Manual perimetry is tedious and time consuming and requires a skilled technician for its proper performance. Such technicians are expensive, hard to find, and harder to keep. The result is that the visual field examination is often entirely neglected or inadequately performed.

Despite the advantages of automated perimetry, it is still a technique of limited capability in the detailed and definitive assessment and analysis of visual field deficits once they have been found.

TANGENT SCREENS

Of all the techniques of perimetry, the examination of the visual field with the tangent screen is the most flexible. It is subject to certain limitations, however, and therefore should not be considered as supplanting the perimeter examination but as supplementing it. When properly performed, so that all of its possibilities are exploited, the tangent screen technique is capable of eliciting 90% of visual field defects either wholly or in part.

Whereas the perimeter is used most effectively to record perception in the peripheral field, the tangent screen finds its area of greatest usefulness within 30 degrees of fixation. All of the automatic computer-assisted perimeters described above concentrate on the 30-degree field as the most frequently used programmed visual field but are capable of examining the field out to 90 degrees from fixation. It should be remembered, however, that the effective area of tangent screen use can be doubled to 60 degrees temporally and nasally by simply moving the fixation target from the center to the periphery of the screen and utilizing its entire width to plot one-half the visual field. When tangent screen examination is conducted at one-half meter, the width of the field increases to 50 degrees (Fig. 2-8). Inasmuch as a high percentage of visual field defects detected on the perimeter in the peripheral field extend inward to within the 30-degree radius, they are also detectable, at least in part, with the tangent screen. It is for this reason that I have reversed the

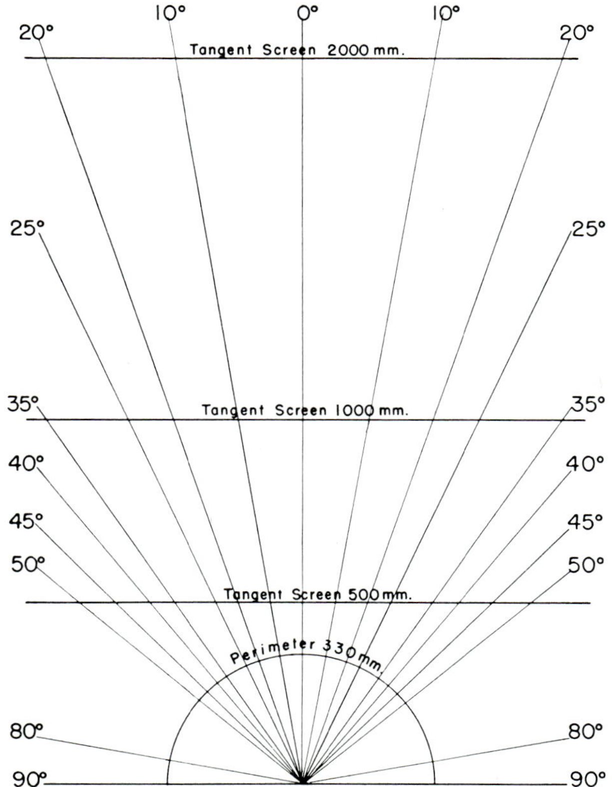

Fig. 2-8. Effect on size of visual field produced by varying distance between observer and tangent screen.

usual routine of visual field testing and prefer to perform the tangent screen examination first and follow it with the perimeter examination if indicated.

Practice with the tangent screen will increase the elasticity of the method and will make it possible to perform comprehensive surveys of the visual field in a minimum of time and with a maximum of efficiency.

Most of the advocates of tangent screen perimetry have designed their own instruments and, as is the case with perimeters of various designs, the simplest equipment has stood the test of time. Bjerrum, whose name is frequently given to the tangent screen, pioneered the method by using the back of his consulting room door. Rönne, Sinclair, Traquair, and Walker studied and used the method exhaustively and established with it the present concept of quantitative perimetry.

Because of the unlimited number of distances at which the screen may be used, the visual angles subtended by test objects of varying size upon its surface are almost infinite in number. Used at close range with test objects up to 75 cm in diameter, the tangent screen is capable of testing the depth and density of the almost absolute defect, whereas with the 0.5-mm test object at a distance of 2 or even 4 meters, it provides the most accurate measure of visual acuity within the central area of the field. For the same reason, a defect in the field that is 1 cm in diameter when examined at 300 mm, will at 2 meters be magnified in all detail to 6 cm and will be of more diagnostic value because its shape, size, uniformity, and density can be studied more accurately.

The tangent screen also lends itself to perimetry with electroluminescent stimuli and acts as an efficient background for flicker fusion frequency fields.

It is my opinion that tangent screens should be individually designed and constructed according to the needs, office space, and desires of the perimetrist. Variations that have been proposed are minor and have been dictated largely by individual problems encountered by the designer. With this in mind, the following list gives the general specifications of a good tangent screen, some of the permissible variations, and some details of my own preference in screens:

1. If space permits, the screen should be 2 meters square.
2. It may be fixed on a wall, either stretched on a wooden frame or hung from a curtain roller, so that it can be rolled up out of the way when not in use. If the roller type is used, it should be weighted at the bottom and, in addition, fastened to the floor when opened up ready for use so that it does not sway back and forth while being marked with pins or chalk.
3. The best material is a soft-finished cloth, such as black felt.
4. If the screen is marked by stitching to indicate the meridians and degrees from fixation, such stitching should be done in dull black thread. The meridians should be marked at 30-degree intervals and the circles at 5, 10, 15, and 20 degrees for the 2-meter distance, which is 10, 20, 30, and 40 degrees at 1 meter (Fig. 2-9). Two blind spots should be indicated on each side of fixation, one for the 2-meter distance and one for the 1-meter.
5. If the screen is entirely unmarked, it may be used at any distance from the

Table 1. Natural tangents useful in perimetry

Degrees	Tangent value	Degrees	Tangent value
1	.01746	19	.34433
2	.03492	20	.36397
3	.05241	21	.38386
4	.06993	22	.40403
5	.08749	23	.42447
5.5	.09629	24	.44523
6	.10510	25	.46631
7	.12278	26	.48773
7.5	.13065	27	.50953
8	.14054	28	.53171
9	.15838	29	.55431
10	.17633	30	.57735
11	.19438	35	.70021
12	.21256	40	.83910
13	.23087	45	1.00000
14	.24933	50	1.19175
15	.26795	55	1.42815
15.5	.27732	60	1.73025
16	.28675		
17	.30573		
18	.32492		

Minutes	Tangent value
1	.000291
5	.001454
10	.002909
15	.004363
20	.005818
30	.008727
40	.011636
50	.014545

To obtain measurement of degrees in millimeters, multiply the tangent value by the distance in millimeters of the observer from the tangent screen. For example: 5 degrees on the tangent screen at 1 meter equals 0.8749 × 1000 equals 87.49 mm radius; 2 degrees on the tangent screen at 500 mm equals .03492 × 500 equals 17.46 mm radius.

Any intermediate distances can be calculated from the tangent scale; therefore, if the perimetrist finds it more convenient to work at 500 mm and 1 meter or at 1.5 and 3 meters, the screen may be marked accordingly.

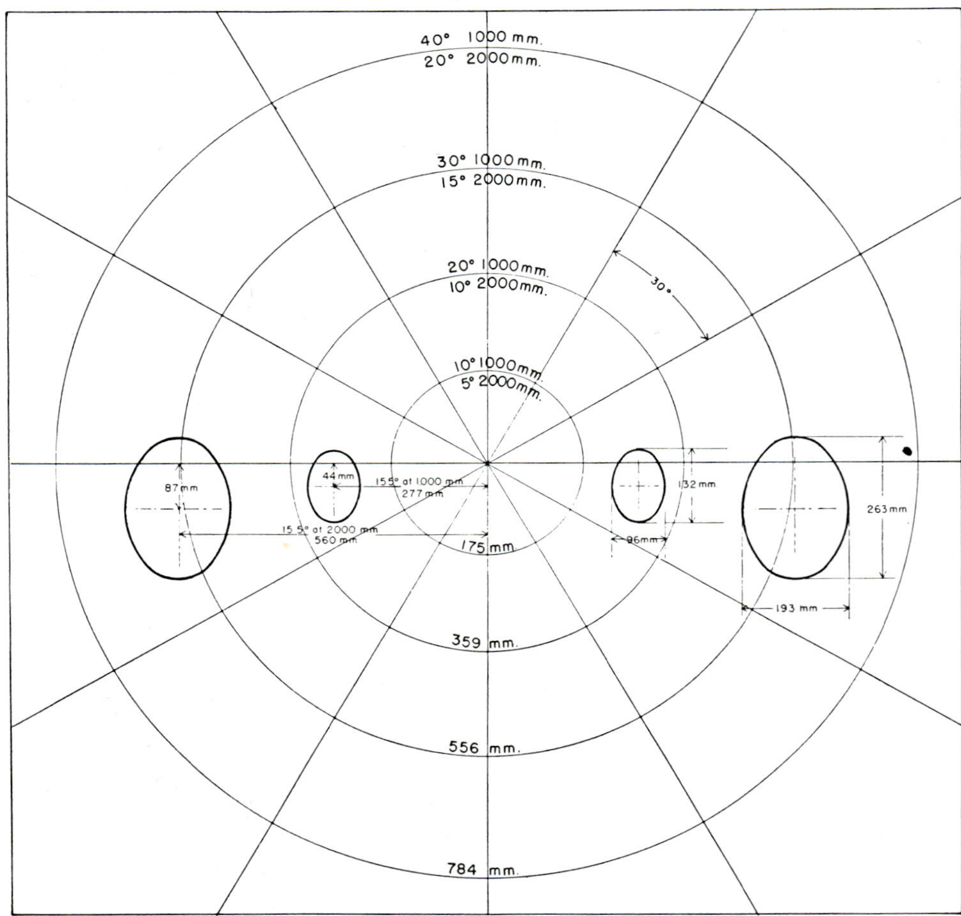

Fig. 2-9. Dimensions of markings on tangent screen. For screen to be used at both 1 and 2 meters, radial distances in millimeters from fixation are averaged. For example, tangent 15 degrees at 2 meters = 0.26795 × 2000 = 535.9 mm; tangent 30 degrees at 1 meter = 577.3 mm. Average of these two figures = 556.6. To obtain exact dimensions for construction of 1-meter or 2-meter tangent rule, consult Table 1.

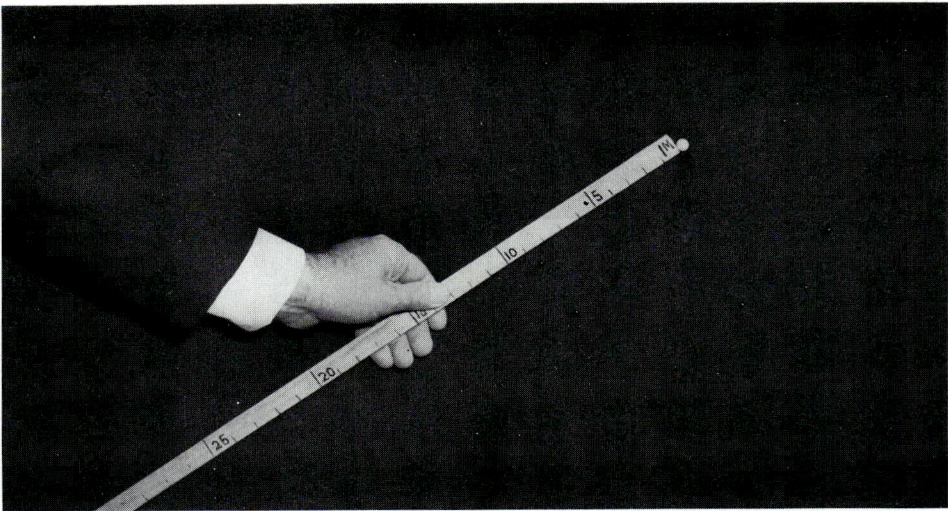

Fig. 2-10. Tangent rule in use for charting visual field from unmarked tangent screen. Black pins, placed in screen at time of examination, form circle of approximately 10 degrees radius as measured on 1-meter tangent rule.

patient and fixation may be shifted in any direction from its center. The outlines of the field on the unmarked screen are pinned or chalked out and then transferred to the chart by means of a tangent rule (Fig. 2-10). A tangent rule may be easily calculated and constructed for any given distance by means of the tangent scale and the following simple formula:

Tangent value × Distance in millimeters = Radius of circle in millimeters

6. It should always be possible to examine the field on the tangent screen at varying distances, two of which are multiples of 2 (i.e., 500 mm and 1 meter, 1 and 2 meters, 1.5 and 3 meters, and 2 and 4 meters). Whether the screen should be fixed and the patient movable or vice versa will largely depend on the availability of space or the arrangement of the consultation or perimeter room. When the screen is generally used at one distance (e.g., 1 meter) a convenient substitute for the tangent rule is a thin black cord fastened at one end to the fixation point and knotted at intervals of 2 degrees in the central position and 5 degrees in the periphery.
7. Fixation targets should be capable of variation from 1 to 100 mm. Circles of varying size are used for fixation when testing for small central scotomas. White tapes may be attached to the two upper corners of the screen so that they can be crossed in the center when testing for large, dense, central scotomas. The patient fixates where he thinks the tapes will cross even though he cannot see the actual crossing point. All fixation targets should be readily available and easily fastened to or removed from the screen.

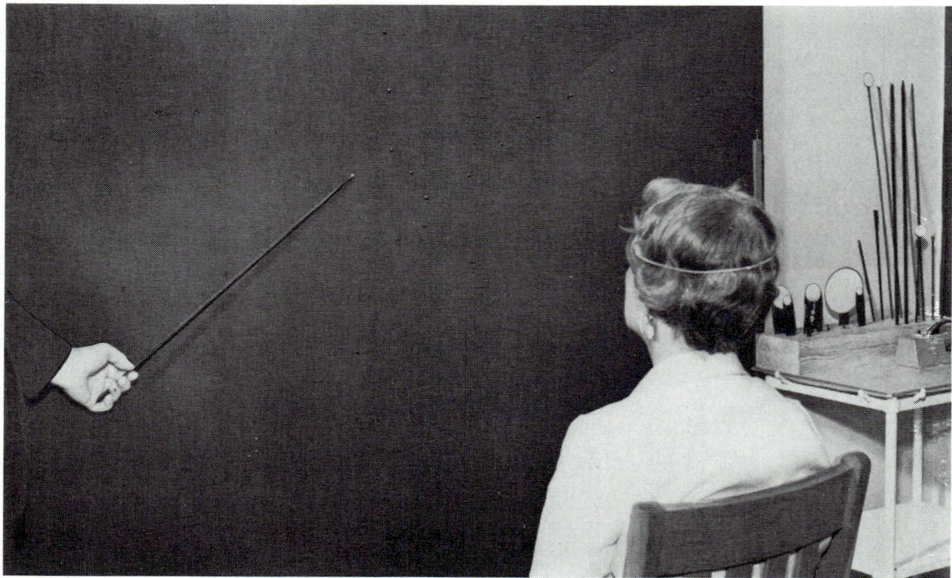

Fig. 2-11. Wall-mounted tangent screen in use at distance of 1 meter. Standard illumination and reflecting test object on hand-held carrier are used.

Fixation by proprioceptive sense may be made on the patient's index finger held against the center of the tangent screen when central visual acuity is markedly reduced by the presence of a dense central scotoma. This, of course, shortens the distance to the screen and thereby reduces the size of the field defect, but it assures accurate fixation, which may not otherwise be possible.

8. Adequate and even illumination of the tangent screen has always been a problem. Theoretically, equal light should come from all four sides, of such intensity as to give 7 footcandles of light on the center and all other areas of the screen. This requires a cumbersome and usually fixed and expensive installation. Practically, it is possible to obtain adequate and quite even illumination by means of simple spotlights directed from above and placed slightly to one side. Occasionally it is necessary to use two spotlights, depending on the distance from light to screen. The ordinary outdoor advertising reflector lamp, which gives a spot of about 6 feet in diameter at about 6 feet distance, is generally adequate. If the light is found by photometric examination to be too bright, it can be brought to the proper intensity by filtering through paper or plastic discs of various sizes pasted on the center of the lamp. Lighting requirements will be somewhat different in almost every installation and must of necessity be dealt with individually. It should be possible to vary the intensity of illumination so as to decrease stimulus intensity. This may be done with a simple and inexpensive rheostat in the light circuit.

Fig. 2-12. Auto-Plot tangent screen. (Courtesy Bausch & Lomb, Inc.)

A simple and relatively inexpensive tangent screen with pantographically controlled projected light stimuli is manufactured by Bausch & Lomb, Inc. (Fig. 2-12). This instrument is compact and easy to operate. The movement of the projected stimulus is controlled by the handle of the pantograph, which charts the field synchronously. The 1-meter tangent screen is unmarked neutral gray vinyl plastic. The patient has an unobstructed view of the screen, and the examiner may observe the patient's fixation at all times. The size of the test object may be quickly changed, and the stimulus may be extinguished at will.

A number of recent modifications of this instrument have increased its flexibility and value. It is now possible to use the screen at both 1 and 2 meters. Since projected stimulus and background screen are independently illuminated, a wide variety of luminances and contrasts can be accomplished.

I prefer to use a 2-meter-square black felt screen on a light wooden frame mounted on the consultation room wall. A chin rest is not necessary. Experience has shown that a patient is usually more comfortable and relaxed when seated naturally in a straight-backed chair. Fixation is adjusted for height either by moving the fixation target up or down on an unmarked screen or by raising or lowering the patient's chair or stool. Fixation targets are printed on dull black cardboard in matte white and may be fastened anywhere on the screen. Another very satisfactory fixation target is a dull white plastic disc with a small central hole through which it may be fastened to the screen with a black-headed pin.

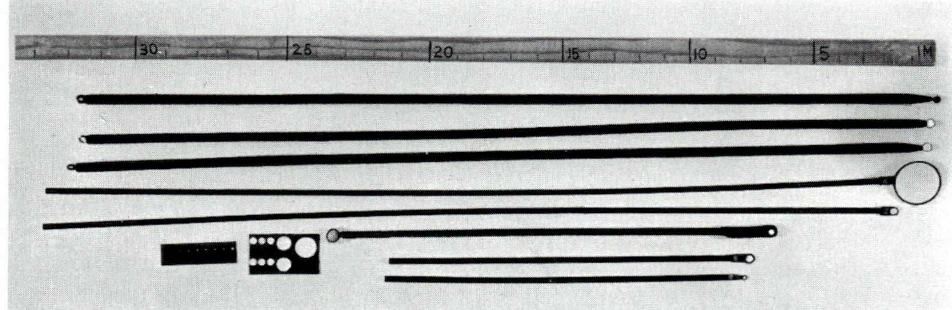

Fig. 2-13. Types of test objects and test object carriers. These include spherical, plastic disc and printed stimuli, and also homemade tangent rule.

An electroluminescent panel lamp* may be mounted on the wall behind a hole cut in the tangent screen. To vary the size of the fixation spot, a rotatable diaphragm containing openings of 2, 5, and 10 mm may be affixed to the edge of the panel lamp. Such a self-luminous target may be used with standard reflecting test objects or with electroluminescent stimuli in a dark or semidark room. Very large fixation targets may, of course, but cut from white drawing paper in the shape of circular discs. After the field has been marked out on the screen with dull black-headed pins, it is transferred to the chart by means of the tangent rule (see Fig. 2-10). The rule may be marked on one side for the 1-meter distance and on the other for the 2-meter distance. Other rules can be calculated for any distance desired and marked in ink on a strip of wood or scratched on a metal strip (Fig. 2-13).

EXAMINATION WITH THE TANGENT SCREEN

Examination of the field on the tangent screen is essentially the same as on the perimeter except that the method allows for more flexibility in exploring defects. The field defect is marked out with pins as it develops and later is transferred to a graphic chart by measurement with the tangent rule or by reference to the stitched markings on the screen.

It is generally advisable to start the routine examination at the 1-meter distance (see Fig. 2-11). The 1-meter distance provides sufficient magnification of scotomas to enable their detection with relative ease and at the same time encompasses approximately 30 to 35 degrees of the field, which is enough to include all but the most peripheral defects. If it becomes necessary to explore small central scotomas or to outline a defect in greater detail, the 2-meter or even the 4-meter distance may be used (see Fig. 15-50).

The size of the fixation target used will depend on the central visual acuity as tested with the Snellen test letters, the state of the refractive media, etc.

The use of corrective lenses during the test will also depend on the refractive

*Manufactured by Sylvania Electric Co. and obtainable at most hardware stores.

error and the area of field being explored. It is obvious that a patient with very high myopia should wear corrective lenses if a scotoma within the 10-degree circle is being explored. Bifocal lenses may depress the lower field. When in doubt, give the patient a trial lens with the spherical equivalent of his distance correction, which he may then hold close to his eye while having his field examined. This will eliminate interference from spectacle frames and at the same time give maximum visual field with a minimum of spherical aberration. By moving the lens slightly before the eye, the examiner may explore even the more peripheral portions of the tangent screen field without distortion.

After carefully instructing the patient in what is expected of him and arranging a system of verbal or hand signals, one may begin the examination of the visual field on the tangent screen.

It is advisable first to outline the blind spot by way of instructing the patient in perimetric technique and also for diagnostic purposes. A 20-mm test object will immediately be seen in the peripheral field and will completely disappear in the blind spot. With a test object of this size, its disappearance into the blind spot will be a dramatic demonstration to the patient of what is meant by the loss or absence of the stimulus.

After the blind spot has been located, it should be outlined carefully for any extensions. For this purpose a change to a 1-, 2-, or 3-mm test object is in order, depending on central visual acuity, mental alertness, etc. With small stimuli it is possible to detect early nerve fiber bundle scotomas. As in the examination with the perimeter, the object must be moved slowly, steadily, and without vibration toward the fixation target.

At regular intervals the stimulus should be made to disappear by flipping the wand. If small spherical targets are being used, they should be mounted on the side of the wand near its tip. A sudden rotation of the wand causes the target to disappear, and if the patient is alert, he will detect this loss of stimulus immediately and will so report. If he does not report this, his attention must be called to the fact that, although he still sees the wand, the stimulus on its end is no longer visible. If large targets are being used, one side should be black so that it can be turned over and made to disappear against the black screen.

When the examination is resumed, the test object may be slowly brought into view while remaining in the same area of the tangent screen, and the patient should again detect its presence. This maneuver is particularly important in critically analyzing an already discovered defect for size, shape, and density (e.g., in quantitative exploration of a glaucomatous nerve fiber bundle defect). With the electroluminescent stimuli of the Lumiwand (see Fig. 2-16), the stimulus may be turned on and off at will by pressing the button on the handle. An infinite number of stimuli may be randomly presented and areas of deficit may be studied in detail.

Any points of disappearance and reappearance are marked with a black pin so that the field defect can be seen to grow as the test progresses. It is convenient to start by exploring the oblique meridians and, if they are normal, then to examine the vertical and horizontal meridians.

If at any point in the test an area of defect appears, it should be immediately explored for size, shape, and density. This is done by moving the test object from the blind to the seeing areas, at right angles to the border of the defect. Having established the size and shape of the area of visual loss for a given test object, one then establishes its density, uniformity, the sharpness of its borders, and other characteristics by examining it with larger and larger stimuli. If, on the other hand, the defect was first detected with farily large stimuli, its size and shape should be established for smaller objects and sometimes for color. A defect that at first appears to be an isolated scotoma in the upper nasal quadrant, when tested with the 6-mm test object at a distance of 1 meter, may be only the denser area of a fully developed nerve fiber bundle defect as tested with a 1- or 2-mm object.

When answers are conflicting and confusing, when the test object seems to "come and go," when the patient is obviously uncertain as to whether he sees the test object or its carrier, probably too small a stimulus has been chosen to begin testing. If the patient fatigues quickly, it is best to let him rest for a while or even to finish the examination at another time. If the patient is mentally sluggish, senile, or too ill to respond to an average examination, the tempo must be slowed down to match his reaction time. Finally, there are some patients on whom it is quite impossible to conduct a tangent screen examination in the ordinary sense, and it is useless to go through the motions of a routine test when the results are not amenable to interpretation. For these individuals special techniques must be used.

The examiner's approach to the patient must be varied according to the needs of the situation. Some patients must be constantly exhorted to maintain position, fixation, and attention, whereas others become nervous or even distraught and hysterical when badgered into compliance with the requirements of the examination. With the tangent screen, even more than with the perimeter, too much reliance must not be placed on the accuracy of the first examination. Almost every patient will give a more reliable response to a second test if time will permit it.

Because the tangent screen examination is so flexible, certain and invariable rules for its conduct are difficult to establish and, in fact, none should be set. Only common sense backed by experience in the taking of many fields will supply the knowledge necessary to conduct a reliable and efficient examination in every instance. This is the "art" of perimetry and it cannot be replaced by automated and computerized techniques no matter how elaborate or ingenious.

In all instances the tangent screen examination should be conducted by the ophthalmologist or under his close supervision. The interpretation of the field loss can be made correctly only when the examiner has the opportunity of evaluating the patient's attitude and responses and the reproducibility of the findings. The character of visual field defects (i.e., their size, shape, and density) should be analyzed by the examiner *during* the examination rather than from the completed chart, which graphically illustrates the defect. Although it is possible for a technician to *detect* a field deficit, only the ophthalmologist is qualified to analyze and properly interpret its characteristics so as to obtain the most possible information.

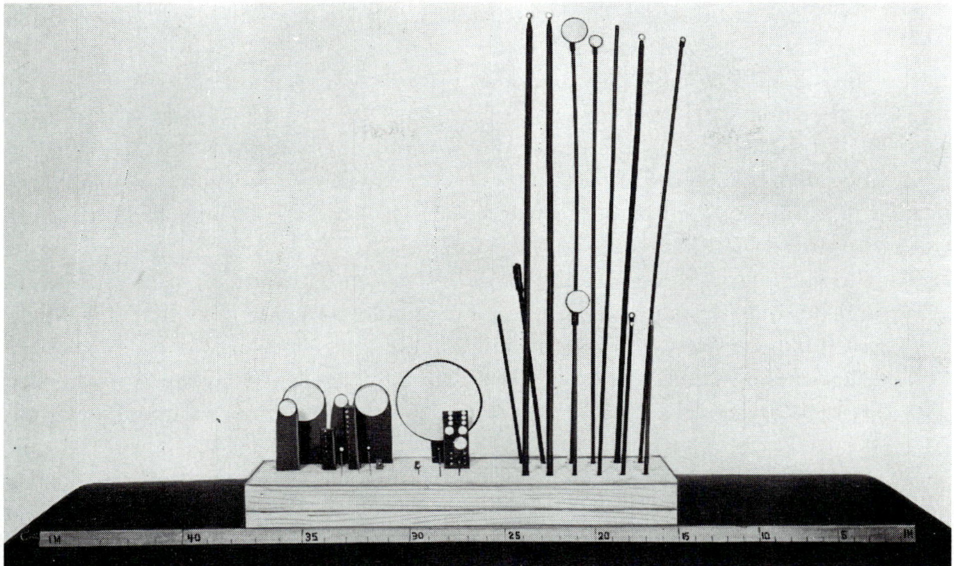

Fig. 2-14. Test objects and carriers in convenient table rack, which may also be wall mounted.

TEST OBJECTS AND TEST OBJECT CARRIERS

There are certain fundamental requirements for good test objects (Figs. 2-13 and 2-14). Minor variations are quite permissible, and there is no ideal test object suitable for all conditions. Certain general specifications should be met as follows:

1. They should be capable of being quickly and easily varied in size in both white and color.
2. They should not be allowed to become soiled or faded; in other words, they should be replaceable or cleanable.
3. It is desirable to be able to use the same test objects on both the arc perimeter and tangent screen.
4. It should be possible to insert the test object easily into the carrier in such a way that no bright pin or metal rim is visible.
5. It should be possible to flip or reverse the test object easily during the examination so as to cause it to disappear or reappear at will in order to test the patient's responses.
6. Colors should be as nearly saturated as possible and are probably best when homemade from carefully selected papers that have been kept away from light until ready to use.

Test object carriers should also adhere to certain basic specifications but may vary in details of construction.

1. They should be rigid enough so that there is a minimum of vibration when moved along the arc of a perimeter or across the face of a tangent screen.

2. They should be about 1 foot long for the perimeter and about 2½ or 3 feet long for the tangent screen.
3. They should be inexpensive and simple in construction so as to be readily replaceable.
4. The tip that receives the removable test object should be so constructed that the pin on which the object is mounted or the paper on which it is printed will slip easily and completely into the carrier. In this way only the object and the carrier will be visible to the patient.
5. The carrier should be painted a dull black with paint that will remain dull and nonreflecting after long use, or it should be made of dull, matte finish, plastic, or covered with felt, or flocced with a sprayed-on material to simulate felt. A felt-covered wooden or plastic ⅛-inch dowel or rod is the most practical type of carrier. These are easily made by hand stitching a strip of felt around the rod.

Few, if any, of the commercially made test objects or carriers adhere to all of the preceding specifications, although each has certain advantages. The spherical test objects in common use today have the advantage that they are easily cleaned and kept bright and new looking. They do not become shiny with use, they are well made and durable, and their colors are relatively fast. They have the disadvantage that they cannot be reversed and made to appear and disappear at the will of the examiner when they are mounted on the end of the carrier. This disadvantage is overcome by mounting them on one side of the tip of a felt-covered rod with a diameter of more than 5 mm. Large spherical test objects cannot be hidden this way, which is one reason why I prefer flat or disc-shaped stimuli in sizes larger than 5 mm.

Spherical test objects also reflect the light from only a portion of their surface when a single source of illumination is used and therefore present a smaller stimulus than would be indicated by the actual diameter of the sphere. This may be readily demonstrated when a spherical test object is coated with luminescent paint and exposed to a source of ultraviolet light. The carrier that is usually supplied with these spherical test objects is unsatisfactory. It is a brass rod with an opening at each end and is painted dull black or gray. In a very short time, the openings become enlarged so that they will not hold the fine pins on which the 1-mm and 0.5-mm objects are mounted. The paint quickly becomes shiny with handling and chips off where it is brought into contact with the metal arc of the perimeter.

The test objects mounted on fine wire that are supplied with certain perimeters are too fragile to stand long use. They vibrate with the slightest movement or tremor of the hand and are too short to be used on the tangent screen.

A very satisfactory type of test object can be made of flat discs of matte finish black and white plastic fused together over a pin that has had its head clipped off with a wire cutter and the cut end flattened with a hammer blow. The discs may be fused together over the pin with heat or bonded with glue. They may be cut to any size from sheets of the plastic material. They remain dull in finish and may be cleaned with a damp cloth. Since one side of the disc is white and the other black, they can be quickly reversed during the test to check the patient's responses and fixation. They are difficult to make in sizes less than 3 mm.

Another acceptable type of test object is that made by printing a spot of the proper size of thin matte finish black cardboard sheet. A great number of spots varying in size from 0.25 to 50 mm may be printed on a single sheet and cut from the sheet with scissors as needed (Fig. 2-15). Thus, hundreds of test objects can be made for a few cents. At the first sign of soiling, the object may be discarded for a new one. Very large objects are cut according to need from cheets of black cardboard that have been painted solid white on the other side so that they may be reversed at will. The test objects may be printed in white or in blue, red, or green. The carrier for these test objects is a ⅛-inch wand made of dull black plastic beveled and slotted at one end to receive the small piece of cardboard on which the test object is printed. These plastic wands retain their dull finish, there is no paint to chip off or become shiny, and they are very inexpensive. They may be made in any desired length for use with perimeter or screen.

As already mentioned, constant luminance of test objects used in tangent screen perimetry is difficult to attain. The problem has been to design a test object for tangent screen examination that would maintain a constant, measurable, standardized level of brightness at all times under all conditions of background illumination. This standard is possible only with stimuli that are self-illuminating (i.e., contain their own light source).

The use of fluorescent phosphors activated by ultraviolet light, which thus becomes their own light source, was a partial solution of this problem.

I have designed a self-luminous stimulus* that utilizes the phenomenon of

*Lumiwand, manufactured by Jenkel-Davidson Optical Co., San Francisco, Calif.

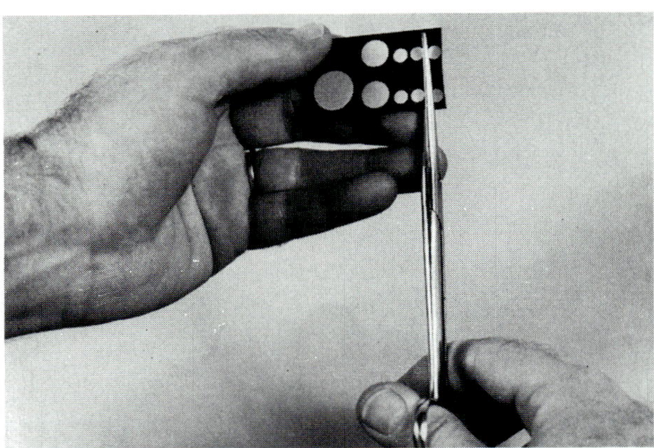

Fig. 2-15. Printed test objects being cut from sheet for mounting in slot of test object carrier.

electroluminescence to produce an area type of light source. The light remains constant over its area but may be varied in intensity by measured amounts and may be turned on or off at will.

The light-producing elements (phosphors) are zinc sulfide crystals together with a suitable activator such as copper. An activated crystal in the presence of a pulsating electrical field converts electric energy into light. The quantity and quality of the light depend on the nature of the crystal and the activator and on the characteristics of the exciting electric field. The brightness and color of the light change with both voltage and frequency.

The light of the special Panalescent lamp* is emitted uniformly over its entire face, which has a diameter of 10 mm. The lamp is connected through a meter-long black hollow tube to its power source in the battery handle. It is turned on by pushing one of the three buttons on the front of the handle. The button is kept depressed as long as one wishes to expose the stimulus. Thus the light may be flashed momentarily, or it may be turned on continuously while moving from one part of the screen to another; or it may be turned off, moved, and turned on again. The three buttons vary the voltage delivered to the lamp so that the luminance varies from 9 footlamberts when the top button is pressed to 3 footlamberts when the middle button is pressed to 1 footlambert when the bottom button is used.

The wand should be covered with a sheath of black felt to minimize its visibility.

The size of the stimuli is varied from 1 to 10 mm by sliding small perforated pliable black opaque polyethylene caps over the 10-mm disc on the end of the wand. The caps have openings of 1, 2, 3, and 5 mm (Fig. 2-16, *A*). Thus there are fifteen different stimuli available with five variables as to size and three as to luminance. The 10-mm disc with 9 footlamberts of luminance is a farily gross test, whereas the 1-mm stimulus with 1 footlambert of luminance is a very sensitive stimulus suitable for detecting early minimal defects in the visual field.

A short wand that may be attached to the battery handle is available for use with nonprojection perimeters and for confrontation testing.

In clinical use the stimulus is best exposed against a black felt screen that is shielded from any direct light so that the wand of the Lumiwand is invisible to the patient and only the light stimulus can be seen when the button is pressed. The room light should be sufficient, however, to allow the examiner to observe the patient's fixation and also to prevent dark adaptation. This can be accomplished by having light come from the side so that the patient can be seen but the surface of the screen is protected by a light baffle. It can also be accomplished by having a very small night-light fixed to the wall above the screen and directed down toward the patient (Fig. 2-16, *B*).

The stimulus is thus presented, under mesoptic background illumination, with a minimum of distraction from the wand, either as a moving (kinetic) or stationary (static) target. It is my practice first to outline the blind spot with the 5-mm stimulus. If responses are good, the examiner can be sure that there is good fixa-

*Supplied by Sylvania Electric Products, Inc.

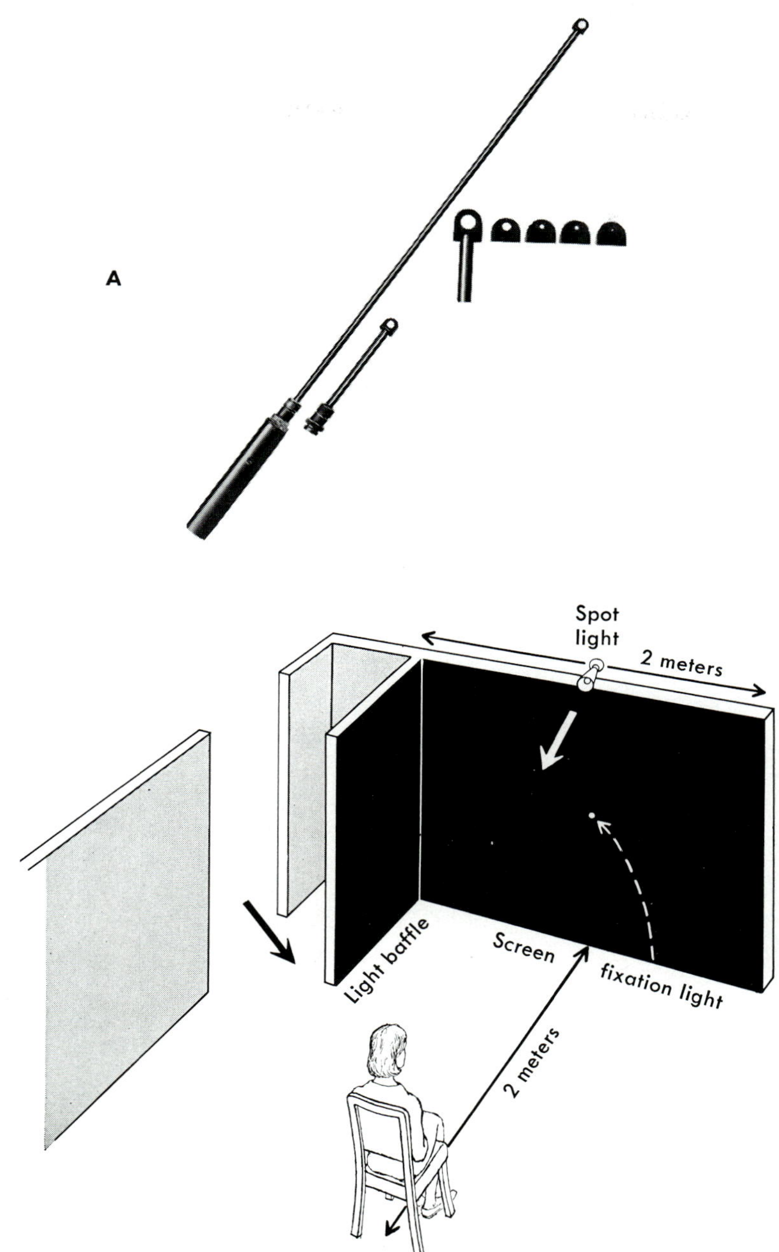

Fig. 2-16. A, Lumiwand showing long wand and battery handle for tangent screen, short wand for confrontation and arc perimeter use, and polyethylene caps to vary stimulus size. **B,** Arrangement of tangent screen room for use with electroluminescent stimuli (Lumiwand) showing electroluminescent fixation spot and methods of allowing light to fall on patient while keeping surface of screen darkened.

tion by the patient. The 1-mm cap is then slipped onto the lamp and the target is presented in the peripheral field, extinguished, moved to a new area, lighted by pressing the button, extinguished, moved to a new area until the entire field has been explored. The patient cannot see the wand if outside illumination of the screen is correct. He does not know in which area of the field the stimulus will appear next. The duration of exposure of the stimulus may vary from a momentary flash to continuous exposure of the moving target as in conventional (kinetic) perimetry. Momentary exposure of a static target has increased the sensitivity of the test. By using three measured increments of stimulus luminance in a stationary target of variable size, static perimetry is accomplished with the Lumiwand on the tangent screen. By varying voltage, and thus brightness, with a rheostat, threshold sensitivity may be measured with some accuracy with a static stimulus in any area of the visual field.

CHARTS

Charts for recording the visual field are a method of indicating a flat projection of a hemispherical surface and of recording the survery of the hill of vision in terms of contour or isopter lines. Thus the field will be graphed as a series of irregular circles with areas where the contour lines are close together, indicating a steep slope to the hill, and other areas where they are widely separated. There will

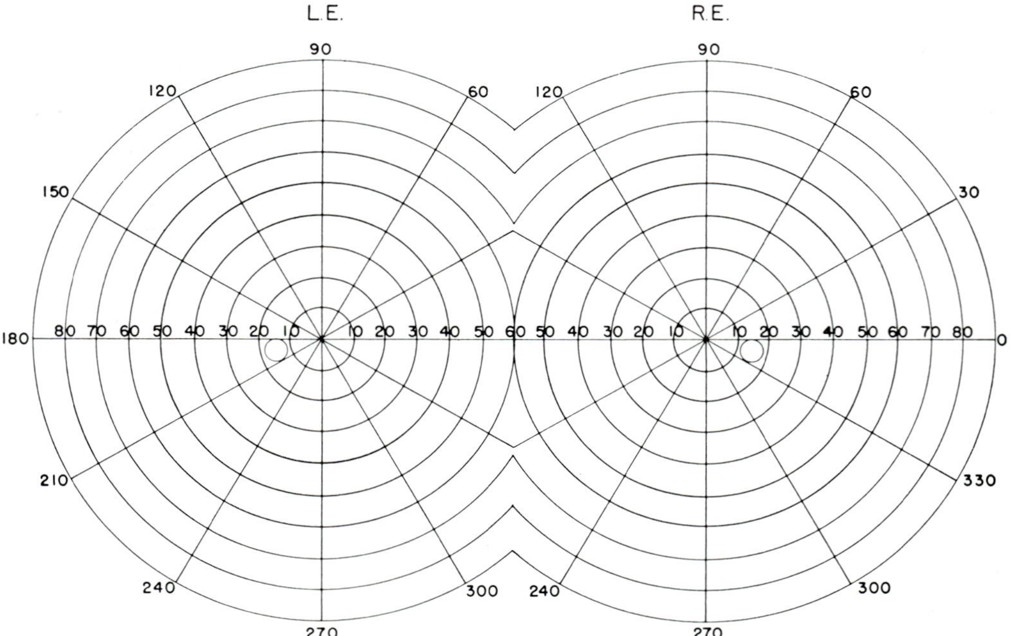

Fig. 2-17. Simple chart for recording visual field from examination with arc perimeter.

be depressions and large segments in which the map shows the hill of vision to be eroded away. These may be indicated as erosions of the shoreline, sector defects, or ravinelike depressions extending from the center outward, or central or eccentric depressions or pits, which are charted as scotomas.

All of these variations in the visual field must be recorded in graph form, and for this purpose standard printed charts have been developed that show the meridians tested, the distances from fixation in degrees, and the relative position and size of the normal blind spot (Figs. 2-17 and 2-18).

Perimetrists tend to vary their charts in minor ways for their own purposes, and manufacturers of perimetric instruments print charts suitable for their particular instrument (Fig. 2-19). Self-recording perimeters, of course, must have their own charts scaled to the specific pantograph of that instrument, and they are usually monocular charts.

Static perimetry measures the profile or section of sensitivity of the hill of vision, and the results of the examination with static stimuli are charted both as the profile of the hill and in terms of its contour lines or isopters. The Tübinger perimeter uses several special monocular charts that fit its pantographic device (Figs. 2-20 and 2-21).

There are numerous types of perimetric charts, one for use on the perimeter with outside circles indicating a field of 90 or 95 degrees, one for use with static perimetry, and one for the tangent screen with more widely spaced circles and an outside limit of 30 to 35 degrees. Within certain limits there is the possibility of almost endless variety:

1. The charts should be simple with a minimum number of meridians, degree circles, and numbers printed on them.
2. Charts should be binocular. Right and left eye should be indicated and the chart should be printed as the patient sees the visual field and not accord-

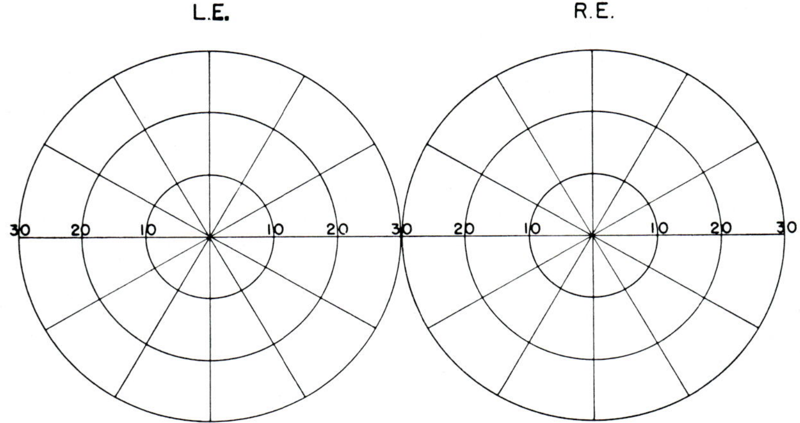

Fig. 2-18. Chart for recording visual field from tangent screen examination.

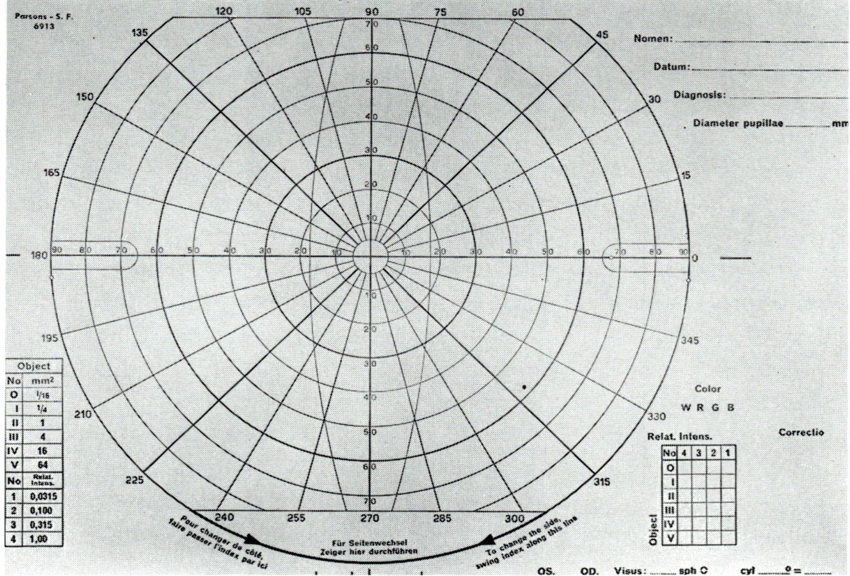

Fig. 2-19. Chart for Goldmann perimeter.

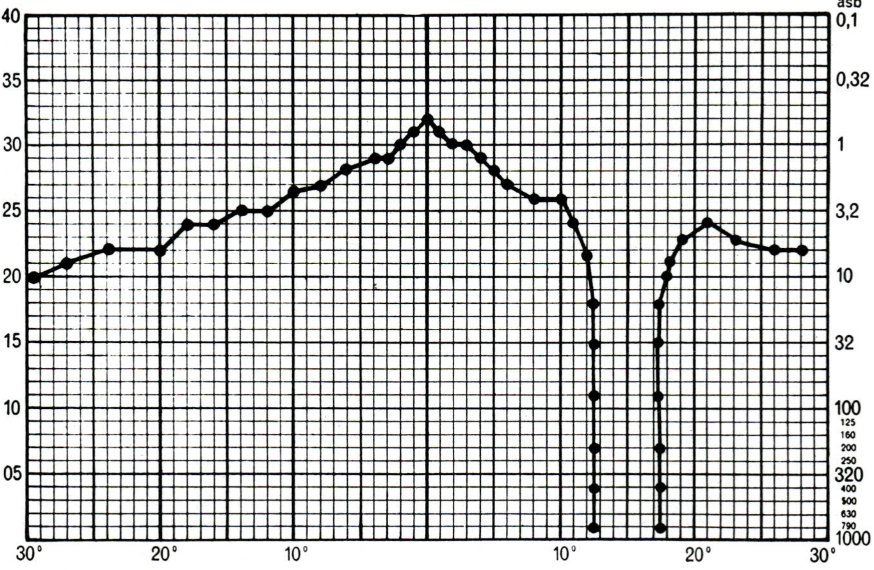

Fig. 2-20. Recording chart for static or profile perimetry with Tübinger perimeter showing normal section of sensitivity profile for central portion of field.

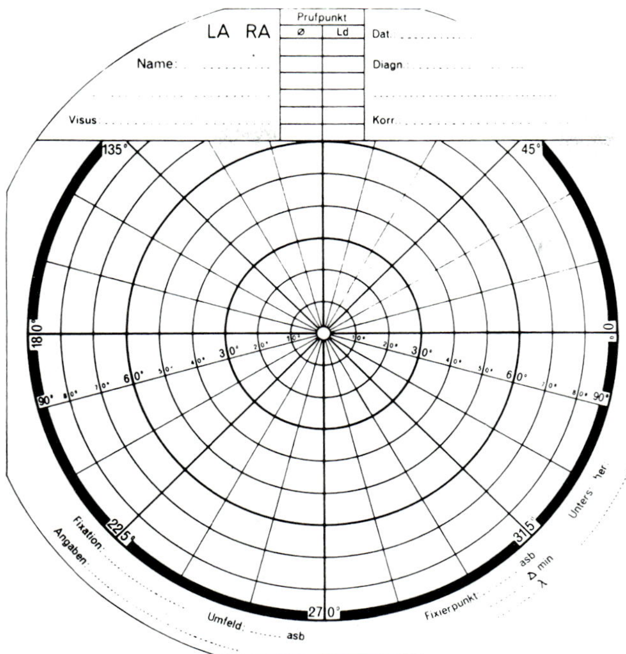

Fig. 2-21. Recording chart for kinetic perimetry on Tübinger perimeter.

ing to the anatomy of the visual pathway. Space should be available for indicating the patient's name, the date, the examiner's name, the isopters tested, and the corrected visual acuity. Where letter size folders are used for keeping records, as in institutions and clinics, it is advantageous to print three or four perimeter charts on one side of a sheet and a like number of tangent screen field charts on the reverse. The paper may be colored for easy identification in the folder. In this way several visual field examinations may be seen at a glance and progress or regression followed clearly and easily. I prefer to have perimeter and tangent screen charts printed in pads on gummed paper, which may then be glued to the record opposite the date and notations of the rest of the eye examination, thus giving the whole picture for that day at a glance. These may be printed in any desired size from 2 by 3½ inches on up.

3. The charts should be well printed by the use of zinc cuts or by silk-screen method on good tough paper that will take ink well.
4. Notation of the isopters tested may be made directly on the chart or to one side with arrows indicating the isopter line. Isopters should be indicated as a fraction, the numerator indicating the size of the test object in millimeters and the denominator the distance of the patient from fixation in millimeters. Thus the fraction 3/2000 indicates quite clearly what test object was used

and at what distance. Notation of isopters in degrees of visual angle subtended by the test objects gives only a part of the information desired.

5. Special charts are used for each of the previously described automated perimeters and are different for each instrument (Fig. 2-22). The Fieldmaster chart is a prototype and shows the overall number of stimuli, their locations, and the stimuli "missed" in the examination of an eye with advanced open-angle glaucoma (Fig. 2-23, *A*). The chart for the Baylor programmer is similar to but not identical with that for the Fieldmaster. The Perimetron chart is very similar to the Goldmann, and its isopters are interpreted in much the same way (Fig. 2-24). The Octopus system uses three types of notation of visual field deficits (Fig. 2-25); a numerical chart that indicates depressed areas of the field by decreased number values; a profile chart for static perimetry similar to that used for the Tübinger instrument; and a "density step" chart that prints out the visual field, automatically indicating depressed areas (relative to absolute) by increasing density of the printout (see Fig. 2-23).

Dr. Ben Esterman has devised a pair of useful grids that evaluate the perimeter and tangent screen field on the basis of the field's functional value to the patient.*

*Grids may be purchased from Manhattan Eye, Ear & Throat Hospital, 210 East 64th St., New York, N.Y.

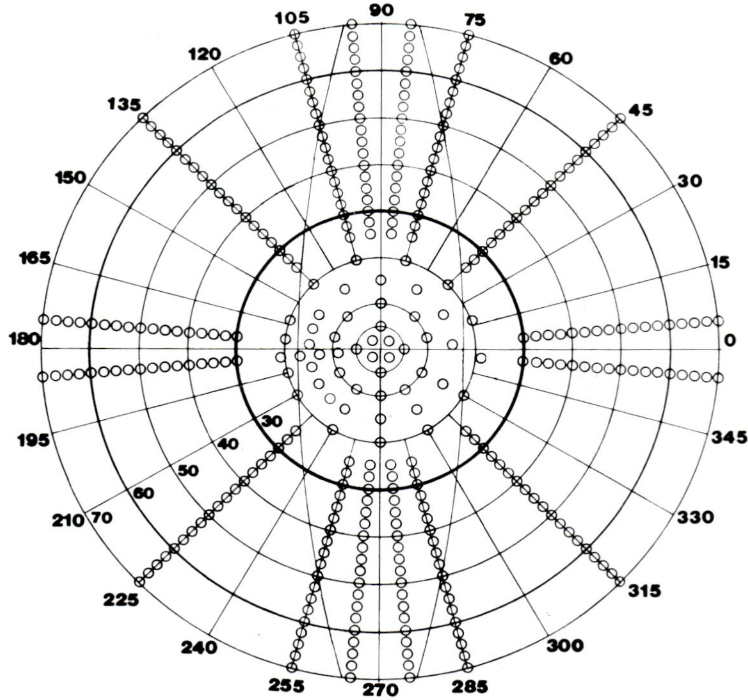

Fig. 2-22. Recording chart for Baylor Visual Field Programmer, extended program left eye.

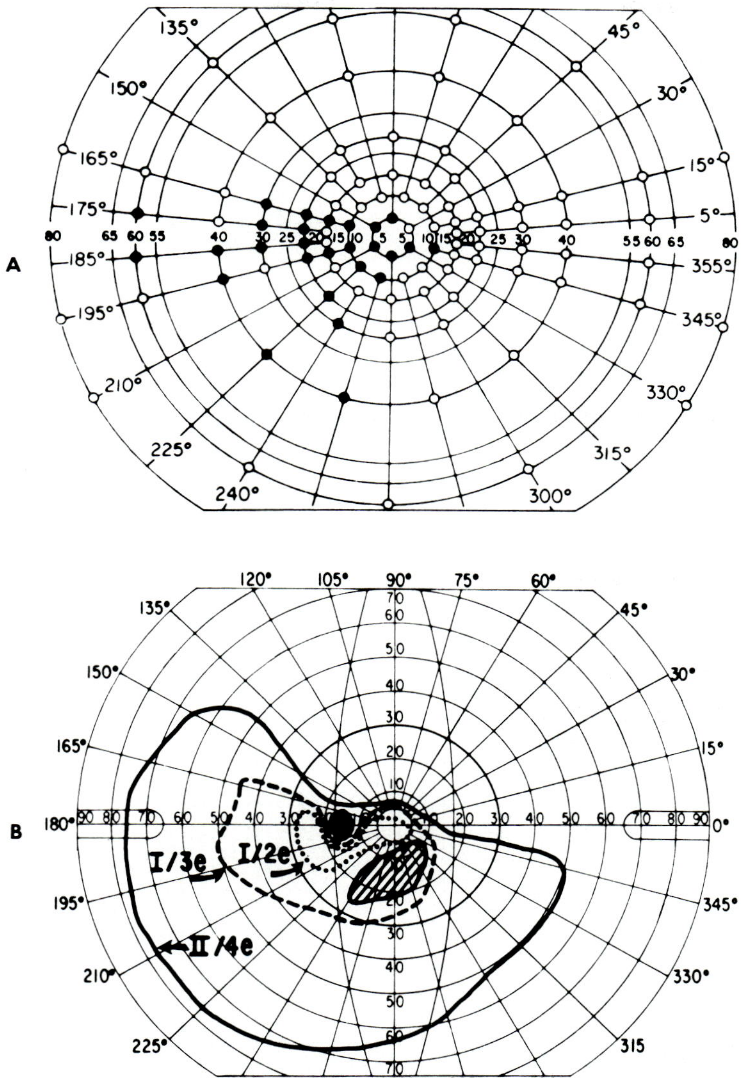

Fig. 2-23. A, Recording chart for Fieldmaster automated perimeter showing area of field deficits (black dots) in a case of glaucoma. Stimulus I/3e with 135 asb luminance. **B,** Goldmann perimeter recording of visual field defects shown in **A.**

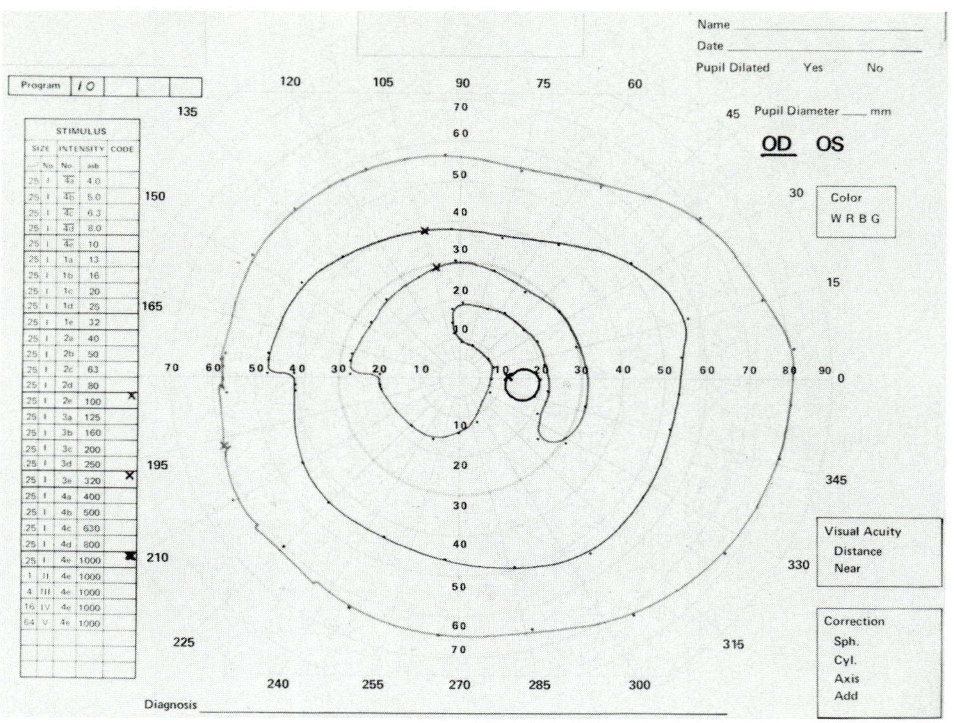

Fig. 2-24. Circular recording chart for Perimetron automated perimeter showing nerve fiber bundle defect. (Courtesy Coherent, Medical Division, Palo Alto, Calif.)

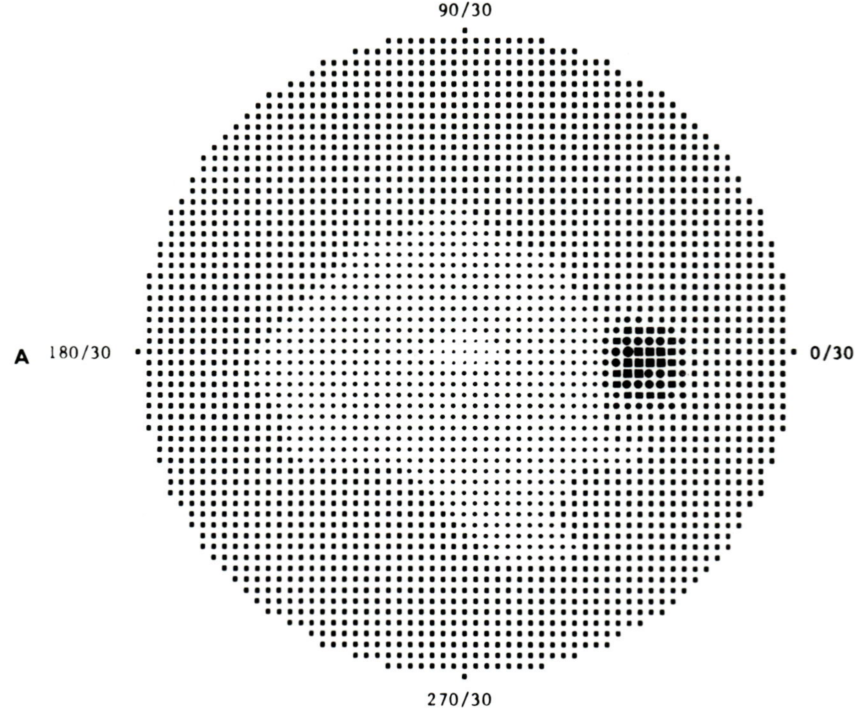

Fig. 2-25. For legend see opposite page.

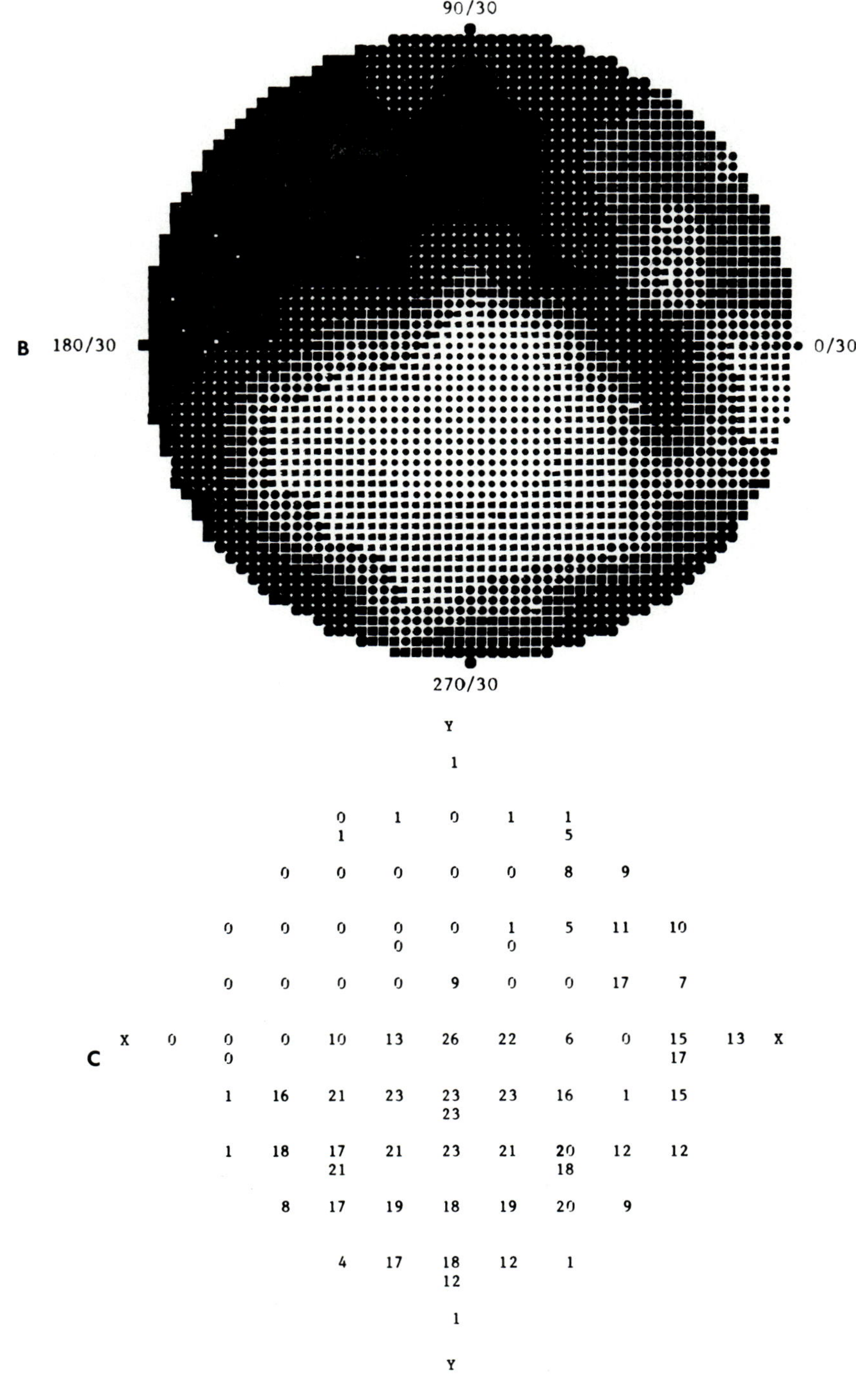

Fig. 2-25. A, Recording gray scale chart of normal Octopus visual field. Average sensitivities for age group 18 to 39 years. (Courtesy Hitron Corp., East Providence, R.I.) **B,** Gray scale chart of Octopus visual field defects in a case of advanced glaucoma with nerve fiber bundle defect. **C,** Numerical chart of Octopus visual field defect seen in **B.** Note lack of stimulus response in area of scotoma and upper nasal field.

This scale is in contrast to the present AMA scale, which scores percentage of field loss based on area alone. The Esterman method assumes that not all areas of the visual field have equal value to the patient, since (1) the paracentral area is more important than the periphery, and (2) the lower half of the field is more useful than the upper half in reading, walking, and working. The inequality of the various areas makes the grid a relative value scale that should be especially valuable in evaluating functional loss in industrial, military, and medicolegal cases.

CHAPTER 3

Special perimetric techniques

In the constant search for a quicker, more objective, less tedious, and less complicated method of visual field examination, many special methods have been advocated.

Perimetry in diminished light has become so much a part of standard procedure that filters for decreasing the test object brightness are included as standard equipment in the projection perimeters previously described.

It is common knowledge that clouding of the media of the eye (or interposing a filter before the eye) will materially alter the visual field, usually in the direction of exaggerating the defect. Variations in test object luminosity and background luminosity have all added their bit to our increasing knowledge and have succeeded at times in uncovering field defects much earlier in their development than with standard illumination.

EXTINCTION PHENOMENON

One of the important developments in the field of perimetry has been Bender's application to visual field study of the method of simultaneous double stimulation for the purpose of eliciting the extinction phenomenon.

"Clinically speaking, extinction of sensation is defined as a process in which a sensation disappears or a stimulus becomes imperceptible when another sensation is evoked by simultaneous stimulation elsewhere in the sensory field. But the definition needs modification because there are so many variations in the manifestation and in the conditions under which the phenomenon occurs."

Bender selected the term *extinction* because the first patient in which he studied the phenomenon in detail had a wound of the left parieto-occipital region of the brain and described the phenomenon "as if the 'light' in the right field was extinguished by the stimulus introduced in the left field." As soon as the stimulus was removed from the left field, he again saw the stimulus on the right.

Extinction does not occur in every patient with homonymous hemianopsia. It does not always occur on each examination of the same patient but may be elicited in seven or eight out of ten tests. It does not always imply a complete loss of sensation but may show only a decrease or obscuration of the sensation, whether visual or painful.

When used as part of the confrontation test (see Fig. 1-1), it adds value and refinement to the examination; and, in fact, I have had numerous experiences in which a rough confrontation examination using double simultaneous stimulation revealed a homonymous hemianopsia that had remained undetected by careful perimetric examination by standard methods with a single stimulus.

In using the method of double stimulation on the perimeter, the examiner exposes two equal-sized test objects on their carriers simultaneously in opposite halves of the visual fields and advances them from the periphery toward fixation at equal speeds. As the perimeter arc is rotated through the various meridians, the two stimuli are exposed in opposite quandrants, 180 degrees from each other. The patient is asked to indicate whether he sees one object or two, and also where they are located, while he is steadily fixating the central target. The examiner may present a single object in the right field and then in the left field and then in both right and left fields simultaneously. In each case the patient is asked to say whether he sees one or two objects and to indicate their location. This alternate single and double stimulation should be quickly repeated eight or ten times. In cases of true extinction, the patient will fail to perceive one of the two stimultaneously exposed objects seven or eight out of ten times and the extinguished test object will always be in the same hemianoptic half or quadrant of the field.

It will be evident from the foregoing discussion that there is an inherent flexibility in the method of simultaneous double stimulation and that this flexibility may be applied in a variety of ways, depending on the ingenuity of the examiner.

There is, as yet, no satisfactory explanation as to why extinction occurs. It is a fact of clinical value, however, that the extinction pattern is most often seen in the patient with parietal lobe disease.

AMSLER GRID

The Amsler grid has long been used for the detection of very small central scotomas and metamorphopsia in early diseases of the macula. It is a subjective test in which the patient fixes attention on the center dot of a white grid on a black background and describes the appearance of the grid lines at or close to fixation. Distortion of the grid lines around fixation indicates the presence of metamorphopsia such as might occur with macular edema. Absence of portions of the central grid indicates a scotoma. The test is very useful in explaining impaired visual acuity due to minute lesions of the maculae.

The Amsler grid patterns have been used for dynamic visual field testing in the examining chair or at the patient's bedside. By rotating the grids and using 1-mm or 2-mm spherical test objects at 35.6 cm, one is able to plot visual field defects out to approximately 45 degrees in all meridians.

As with tangent screen examination, preliminary outlining of the blind spot is necessary to assure that fixation is steady.

The test is economical and time saving and detects visual field loss in neurologic disease and in eyes with glaucoma with a high degree of accuracy.

ANGIOSCOTOMETRY

Measurement of the retinal vessel shadows at the upper and lower poles of the blind spot (angioscotometry) has been studied intensively, and it is believed that widening of the angioscotomas corresponds closely with fiuctuations in intraocular pressure in early cases of glaucoma (see Chapter 11). The examination of angioscotomas is tedious and time consuming and has not been widely adopted.

FLICKER FUSION FREQUENCY FIELDS

Much of the credit for the practical application of the method of visual field examination commonly known as flicker fusion frequency fields (FFF fields) belongs to Miles, Weekers, and Roussel.

The critical point at which a flickering light of decreasing frequency is first perceived to flicker is a phenomenon that lends itself well to clinical use in testing the perception of small areas of the retina. Unlike other tests of the visual field, the flicker fusion frequency depends on the length of the latent period between the light stimulus and the response and on the ability of cones or groups of light-adapted elements, including cones and their pathways, to recover from the inhibitory period following one stimulus and to become receptive to another.

Flicker fusion frequency is a number. Gradations of perception are measured without the use of various-sized test objects or targets.

The development of electronic instruments for the production of accurately measured rates of flicker has made it practical to apply this method of perimetry to the clinical examination of defects in the visual field. A commerically made stroboscope is adapted for the examination by attaching the strobe light to the end of a wand and enclosing it in an opaque hood so that only a 5-cm area of the light will be seen. This 5-cm opening is covered with ordinary white translucent paper to diffuse the light. The wand carrying the stroboscopic light is connected to the electronic instrument or stroboscope, which measures the rate of flicker on a dial. The wand with its flickering strobe light may be used against the background of an ordinary tangent screen at 1-meter distance, and the field can be examined to a distance of 30 degrees from fixation.

A portable commercial stroboscope that can be easily adapted for FFF field examination is the Stobotac.* Adaptation of the stroboscope is accomplished by removing the flash tube and the reflector and soldering the ends of a 6-foot, four-wire cable to the lugs on the flash tube socket. The four prongs of the flash tube itself are then soldered to the appropriate wires of the cable. The last 2 or 3 feet of the cable are passed through a rigid steel or aluminum tube to form a wand by means of which the light can be controlled in its movement in front of the tangent screen. The tube itself is covered with thin typing paper and this in turn in covered with an opaque hood with an opening 5 cm square over a portion of the bulb. Numbers are applied with India ink on the dial of the instrument to read in flashes per

*Manufactured by the General Radio Corporation, Cambridge, Mass.

second instead of hundreds per minute. Each number on the dial is multiplied by 100 and that number is divided by 60. For example, the number 30 multiplied by 100 equals 300, divided by 60 equals 50.

The patient is placed before the tangent screen and one eye is covered. He is directed to look at the light and the dial is turned so that first the light is steady and then gradually it begins to flicker at a slower and slower rate. This acquaints the patient with the nature of the test. The rate of flicker is then increased until the light appears to be steady and then gradually is reduced from a fused level of flicker until the patient says "now" as soon as the flicker becomes apparent. The normal rate of flicker fusion frequency at fixation is about forty-two flashes per second. In the periphery of the field, the detectable flicker rate if fifty or more, out to the 20-degree tangent. When an area appears depressed, the test should be repeated in that area. In visual fields where hemianopsia is suspected, readings should straddle the vertical dividing line. Comparative studies of flicker rate on the two eyes are particularly useful in diseases that may be unilateral, such as glaucoma. The fields are plotted on regular tangent screen charts as a series of numbers scattered throughout the various areas of the field so that areas of depressed

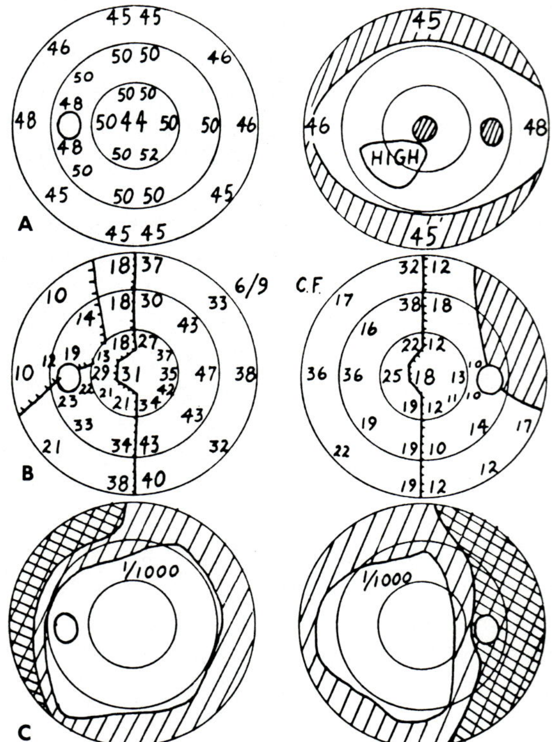

Fig. 3-1. Flicker fusion frequency fields. **A,** Normal field. **B,** Field of patient with pituitary adenoma. **C,** Same visual field examined on tangent screen. (From Miles.)

flicker rate perception are seen at a glance. These areas may be shaded to show the visual field defect more clearly (Fig. 3-1).

The flash rate should be reduced fairly rapidly to avoid fatigue but not so rapidly that the patient cannot find the end point at which he first detects a flicker. Some practice is required in determining this speed of change. Flicker fusion perimetry has been used with excellent results in the study of various neuro-ophthalmologic lesions, such as pituitary tumors and tumors involving the suprachiasmal visual pathway.

MULTIPLE PATTERN METHOD OF VISUAL FIELD EXAMINATION

Because the methods of visual field examination are complex and time consuming, they are not as widely or routinely used as they should be. It is difficult for the average busy ophthalmologist to perform a visual field examination on every patient. There has been a need for a rapid, reasonably accurate, screening method that would detect visual field defects in a high percentage of the unknown number of persons with these defects.

All screening methods of examination designed for rapid evaluation of disease states are imperfect, but without them many persons are denied the chance of any examination whatever and disease that might have been detected is neglected. This is true of the visual field examination, since the majority of persons never have the benefit of this examination.

To meet the needs of an accurate screening method of visual field examination, I have developed, with Dr. Milton Flocks, the multiple pattern method of visual field examination (Fig. 3-2). The method utilizes the principle of tachistoscopic,

Fig. 3-2. Instrument for examination of visual field by multiple pattern method. Front view showing pattern card in position and examiner's finger on switch button. Pattern is shown at instant of flash.

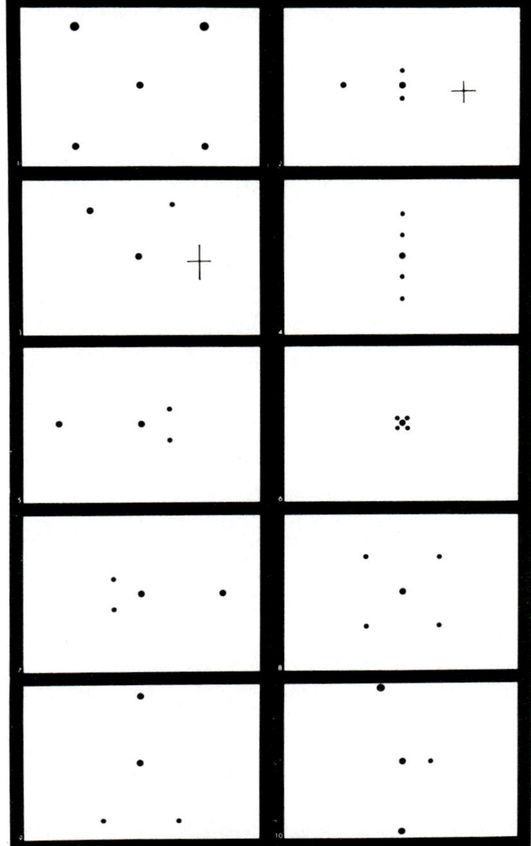

Fig. 3-3. Patterns of multiple pattern method of visual field examination.

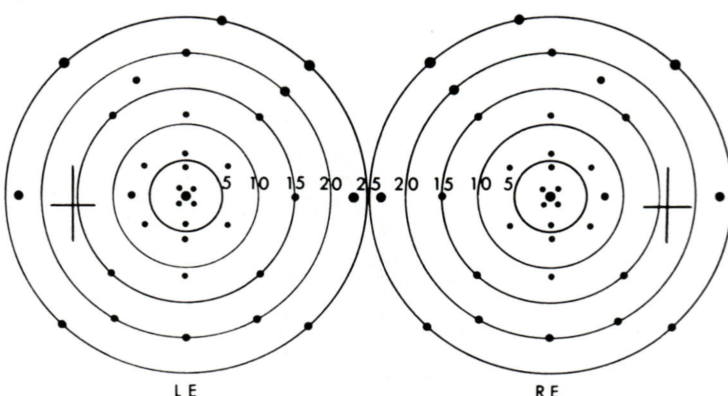

Fig. 3-4. Composite of ten patterns for each eye of multiple pattern method of visual field examination, demonstrating location of stimuli in central area of visual field. This may be used as recording chart to check off erroneous responses during examination.

or flash, presentation of simple, abstract patterns of dots and crosses to the fixing eye (Fig. 3-3). These dots act as visual stimuli in the various parts of the visual field. The patterns are printed in white fluorescent sulfide ink on white cards, so that with ordinary room light only a black central fixation dot is visible. When the card is illuminated by a flash of ultraviolet radiation (black light) of ¼-second duration, the pattern stands out clearly against the background of the card and acts as a stimulus to extrafoveal vision in that area. The duration of the flash of black light that activates the pattern is sufficient to allow the subject to see the pattern but is too short to allow a shift of fixation. If a poı tion of the visual field is defective, the stimulus of the pattern in that area will not be seen and the patient will describe the pattern erroneously. A composite of thirty-three stimuli covers most of the visual field within the 25-degree radius. Errors in describing the patterns may be checked off on a chart of the pattern composite as a means of recording the examination (Fig. 3-4).

The pattern cards are bound in a book of twenty cards with an Amsler grid on the back cover for the testing of macular function. The patterns are exposed one at a time in a box containing the black-light tube covered by a tubular Corning No. 5874 filter and equipped with a chin rest so that the patient's eye is at a fixed distance of 330 mm from the card. The instrument will plug into any convenient 110-volt light socket.

The back of the easel is dull black. In the center is a luminescent fixation spot so that the back may be used as a standard tangent screen of 330-mm distance, utilizing fluorescent sulfide test objects.

In the center of each card is a 5-mm black dot for fixation. In a moderately well-lighted room of uniform brightness, the pattern is completely invisible until activated by the ultraviolet light. The brighter the room, the less contrast there will be between the pattern stimuli and the background and the greater will be the sensitivity of the test. If a light meter is available, the measure of room light on the card should be approximately 5 footcandles.

The first ten cards of the series are exposed to the right eye. The second ten cards present the same stimuli in different sequence to the left eye.

All patterns exhibit three or more stimuli in the visual field, some on each side of the vertical meridian.

The ten patterns for each eye are made up of round dots that vary from 1 to 8 mm in diameter, the larger dots being at the peripheral limits of the field and the 1-mm dots close to fixation.

In comparative visual field studies with the multiple pattern method of examination, patients with abnormal visual fields of all types were encountered. In most instances, the response to the patterns indicated the location and the general type of visual field loss and was consistent with the subsequent tangent screen examination (Fig. 3-5).

The limitations of the test must be recognized. It is a screening device, *not* a substitute for, but is a supplement to, our standard perimetric techniques.

Since the introduction of the Harrington-Flocks multiple pattern visual field

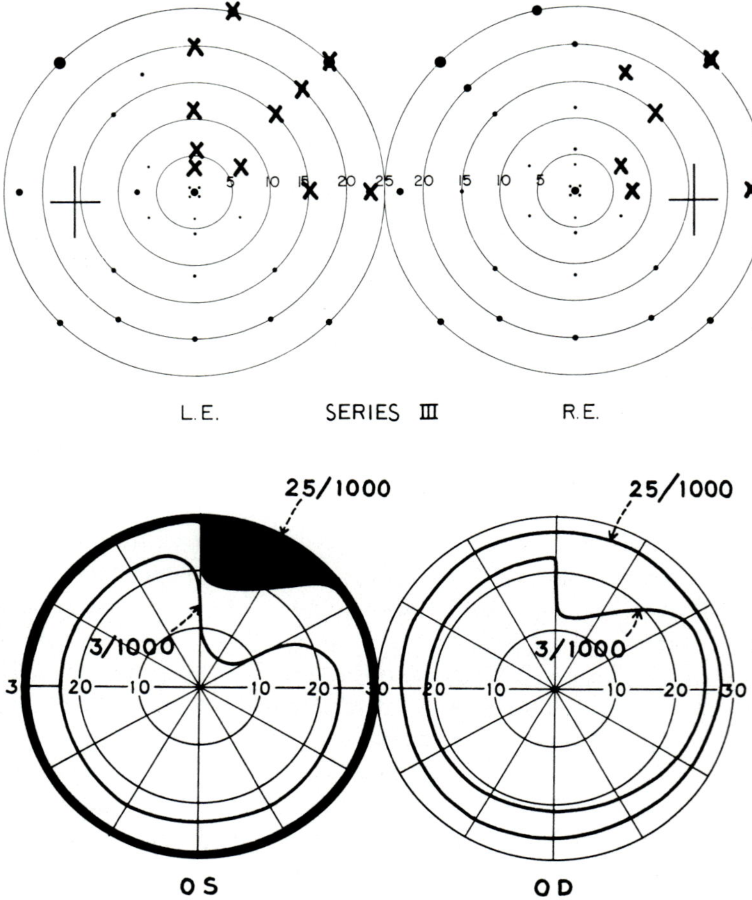

Fig. 3-5. Responses to multiple pattern method of visual field examination and comparative tangent screen field study of incongruous homonymous hemianopsia resulting from cerebral vascular disease of left temporal lobe.

screener in 1954, many modifications have been developed, most of them more sophisticated, complicated, and expensive than the original device. These include the Globuck screen, the Friedmann visual field analyzer, the Fieldmaster automated perimeter, and the Octopus system of automated computer-assisted perimetry.

Recently, Flocks and associates have designed a system of mass visual screening by means of television that presents on the ordinary home television set videotaped programs that can be used for screening of visual acuity and visual fields by means of broadcast television. Test patterns are largely based on those used in the Harrington-Flocks field screening apparatus. Results were compared with Goldmann visual field studies with excellent correlation. Ninety percent of those patients with defects of visual acuity or visual field were detected by the television test. Again it is emphasized that this test is a screening device and not a definitive visual field examination.

The multiple pattern method of visual field screening, using static, suprathreshold, tachistoscopic presentation of multiple stimuli is the precursor of all of the modern automated computer-assisted perimeters described above. There are still many Harrington-Flocks instruments in use today.

Armaly has developed a method of selective perimetry as a screening device in glaucoma, in which a large number of positions in the central visual field are examined both kinetically and with static stimuli. Seventy-two positions are examined by static perimetry on the 5-, 10-, and 15-degree parallels, and a selected number of nine positions in the nasal periphery and two in the temporal periphery are examined kinetically.

Drance has modified the Armaly technique and devised a method of his own for defects in the temporal field. He feels that these methods are highly accurate but still feels that any defect found by the screening method should have a more accurate visual field analysis.

COLOR PERIMETRY

The use of colored test objects in perimetry has been advocated by some authors and condemned by others. It is my opinion that our present method of color perimetry (as compared with careful quantitative perimetric methods using white stimuli) is definitely not worth the effort involved except in special circumstances to be described. Even the strongest advocates of color perimetry are careful to emphasize the complexities of the method and the difficulty of interpreting the results. Traquair cautiously advocated the use of colored test objects in certain types of visual field defects, notably in tobacco amblyopia, but he warned repeatedly that the usefulness of color perimetry was limited.

Walsh and Hoyt advocate the use of colored stimuli and believe, with Bender and Kanzer, that defects for colored objects appear before disturbances for form and for black and white stimuli. Inability to recognize colors in visual half-fields may be partial or total. When the visual field is defective for colors, it is also altered for white; but demonstrating the color deficit may be much easier.

When color vision, as tested with the HRR and Ishihara color plates, is defective in one eye, there will be a deficit in the visual field of that eye for colored stimuli. This is seen most often in lesions affecting the optic nerve. When both eyes show defective color vision, the field defect is likely to be bitemporal, implicating the chiasm. It should be noted that acquired cerebral color blindness associated with homonymous hemianopsia may result from massive lesions, either vascular or tumor, of the occipital cortex.

The most useful color for examination of the peripheral field is red, and it is not uncommon to find a paracentral scotoma or a bitemporal hemianopsia in the $^{5}/_{1000}$ or $^{10}/_{1000}$ isopter for red stimuli. When testing the foveal area of the visual field, it is sometimes possible to exaggerate a central scotoma with blue stimuli.

These visual field defects, which may be detected with farily large colored stimuli, can also always be found with small white stimuli and also with reduced illumination and with static perimetry. It may be that substituting colored for white test objects is simply a way of reducing the strength of the stimulus without reducing its area. From a practical point of view, the presentation of large colored stimuli, such as the Lars Frisén color confrontation test, is a quick supplement to more definitive perimetric studies. In certain conditions such as tobacco amblyopia, minute foveal lesions, optic nerve disease, and suprachiasmal and infrachiasmal lesions, the use of colored stimuli may give valuable information.

PEDIATRIC PERIMETRY

Visual field studies are uncommonly performed on children, especially under the age of 10 years. This is because it is usually assumed in advance that such examinations are unreliable or even impossible to perform, and this assumption in turn seems to be predicated on the belief that such examinations must be conducted in the same manner and with the same techniques as those employed with adult patients. Such assumptions are invalid.

When variations in technique are applied with some flexibility and imagination, significant motor responses may be obtained from patients with various field defects that make verbal communications between patient and examiner unnecessary and thus make perimetric evaluation possible in totally deaf patients, in patients with an insurmountable language barrier, in psychotic patients, including psychotic children, in semicomatose patients, and even in dogs in which homonymous hemianopsias have been induced by intracranial surgery.

Such motor responses to visual stimuli are variously seen as (1) the shift in ocular fixation that occurs suddenly and repeatedly when the stimulus is brought from a blind to a seeing area in the visual field, (2) movement of the head toward the stimulus, (3) pointing motions, sometimes almost involuntary, and (4) changes in facial expression elicited by stimuli in the seeing area as contrasted to the anopic portion of the field.

For example, a left homonymous hemianopsia in an infant 1 year of age was detected by watching his facial expression respond happily to a pleasurable visual stimulus presented on his right side as contrasted with total inattention to the same stimulus presented on the left. In this case moving hands or lights elicited a variable and inconsistent response of head movement that was inconclusive on repeated testing, and the infant has been declared congenitally blind. It was then noted that the baby reacted with bright smiles to a game of peekaboo with his older brother. The brother was then used as the visual stimulus, playing the game, without sound, first on the left and then on the right side, with invariable pleasurable response by the baby on the right and inattention on the left. The field defect and the presence of right congenital cerebral aplasia were confirmed several years later with both the multiple pattern method and standard tangent screen perimetry.

The most useful form of visual examination for infants and young children under the age of 6 years is the confrontation technique. The short attention span of children in this age group makes a quick, simple test mandatory, and the child's central fixation can be maintained best by a constant patter of talk on the part of the examiner or one of the parents. It is usually wise to have the small child seated on the mother's lap where she may, if necessary, also control head movements. Sometimes the father or a familiar friend or sibling makes a good fixation point over the examiner's head or shoulder.

The peripheral field in four quadrants may be checked in a matter of seconds using a small toy as a stimulus. If the child has brought a favorite doll to the examination, I use this as the initial test object, switching quickly to my own collection of toys in decreasing size depending on the response.

Such toys can be purchased in almost infinite variety in metal, plastic, or rubber at most department stores. The larger ones such as dolls, animals, toy autos, or a monkey that moves up and down on a stick are simply hand held and are brought into view from the peripheral field until the child turns eyes or head to look or reach for the object.

This confrontation test may be quantitated by decreasing the size of the stimulus. Miniature toys such as plastic dolls, soldiers, cowboys, Indians, animals, and autos can be glued to the end of a pencil or black plastic knitting needle (Fig. 3-6).

Deficient responses in one area of the field may be explored with these miniature stimuli and, if cooperation is good, with small bright beads stuck on the point of the knitting needle.

Another effective method of quantitation is to reduce the room illumination during the test until just enough light remains to observe the child' responses.

Fig. 3-6. Miniature figures mounted on pencils for use as test objects.

If the child is old enough to walk, or even to crawl about, another useful variant is to toss three or four miniature toys or bright beads on the floor on each side of the room and to observe the manner and speed with which he retrieves these objects.

In testing the confrontation field of small children, the short wand of the electroluminescent Lumiwand is especially effective. The test is done in a room that is just light enough to allow the examiner to observe the child's responses, head movements, and shifts of ocular fixation. The wand is held in the peripheral field where, in the dim light, it is completely invisible. The button activating the light is pushed and the child involuntarily turns his eyes or head toward the light if visual acuity is normal in that area of the field. Grossly delayed or absent response is the rule in anopic portions of the field.

Older children (6 to 10 years of age) will respond quite accurately and often verbally to the standard method of presenting the targets on the tangent screen.

By making a game of "catching the fireflies" in which 2-mm electroluminescent stimuli are made to wink on and off in different areas of the darkened tangent screen, one can get consistent and accurate responses from small children. By this method I have detected a bitemporal hemianopsia in a 4-year-old girl who was later operated on for craniopharyngioma.

It must also be remembered that the responses of children vary as widely as their intelligence. The examiner of very young patients will sometimes find himself using sophisticated methods of perimetry with excellent results, and accurate quantitative visual field studies are often accomplished with a little patience and friendliness.

Another extraordinarily successful type of pediatric visual field examination is that afforded by the Harrington-Flocks multiple pattern method. I have found the method quite accurate, and, on occasion, it has revealed diagnostic visual field loss that was unsuspected or had been missed by examination with standard perimetric methods.

In theory, a child should be able to count the dots as they appear on the pattern cards. It is therefore of most value with children 6 years of age and over. I have, however, used it successfully with children under 4 years of age, who pointed to the targets they had seen even though the could not count them.

Fig. 3-7, *A*, shows the multiple pattern visual field composite chart of a 6-year-old sexually precocious boy with a suprasellar chorion epithelioma with chiasmal pressure from above. The subsequent tangent screen field study, which was conducted without difficulty, revealed an inferior temporal quadrant defect with a sharp vertical border indicating chiasmal involvement. The perimetrically localized lesion was confirmed at an autopsy.

If a child is over 6 years of age, it is quite possible to undertake definitive and quantitative perimetric studies on both tangent screen and perimeter. I have succeeded, with less time and trouble than with the average adult, in demonstrating a 0.5-degree central scotoma in a 7-year-old boy with an eclipse burn of the fovea.

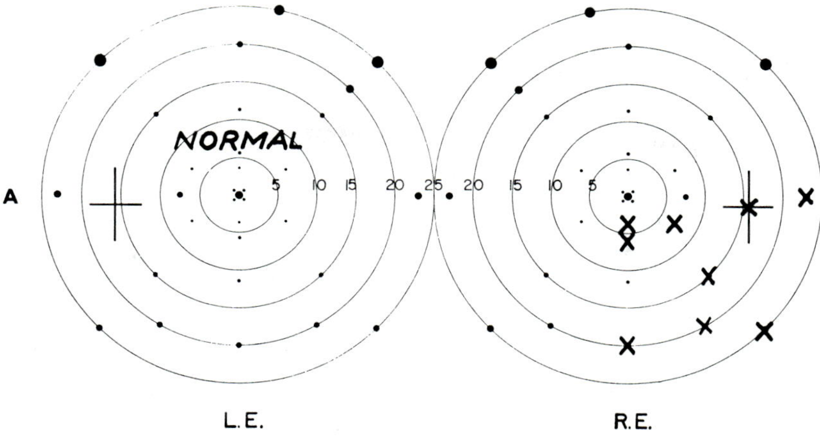

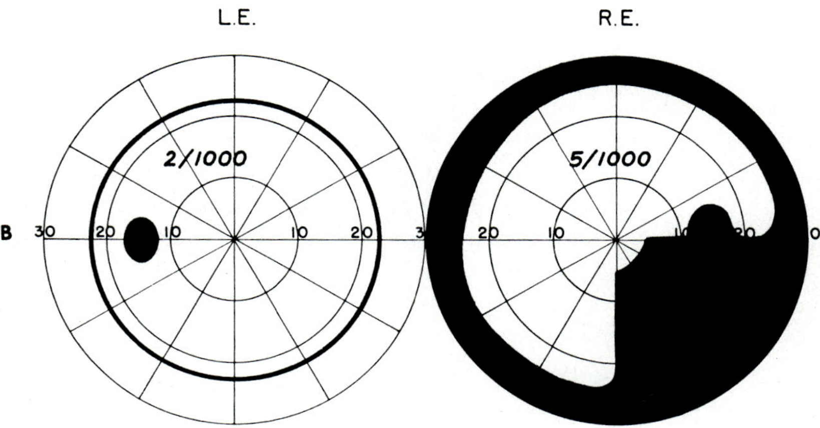

Fig. 3-7. A, Composite of multiple pattern cards showing right inferior temporal quadrant defect in 6-year-old sexually precocious child with suprasellar chorion epithelioma. **B,** Tangent screen field study of same child.

On another occasion an 8-year-old child, who had been diagnosed as hysterical, was able to outline with great accuracy a typical arcuate nerve fiber bundle defect resulting from a healed and very small area of juxtapapillary choroiditis. The fundus lesion was diagnosed retrospectively after the field defect indicated its presence and position.

The incidence of hysterical amblyopia of varying degree and severity is very high in the group 10 to 15 years of age. In the majority of these patients, the visual deficit is reversible, and frequently these children are so amenable to suggestion that the elaborate routine of a complete ophthalmologic examination is sufficient to "cure" their amblyopia. No other part of the examination is as important to the diagnosis as the tangent screen study of the visual field.

In the typical case there will be a gross concentric contraction, sometimes to within 6 or 8 inches from fixation with 2-, 5-, or 10-mm or even larger stimuli. If the field is examined at 1 meter and again at 2 meters (or, alternatively, at 500 mm and 1 meter), the contraction will be the same size in inches on the screen for both distances. This is a true *tubular* field and cannot be the result of organic pathology, which would produce a cone of vision with the contracted field twice as large at 2 meters as it is at 1 meter. A true tubular contraction is spurious and must be functional or hysterical in origin.

In the process of repeated examination, it is often possible, through suggestion, to expand the field gradually so that at the end of the procedure the previously contracted field has become quite normal. It is well to perform this examination without witnesses. If done in the presence of parents, it causes the child to lose face and reversal of the defect may become much more difficult. Such therapeutic examination may be a source of great satisfaction to the examiner and patient alike (see Chapter 16).

In summary, the rewards or perimetric examination of children are considerable. The techniques call from some ingenuity, flexibility, and patience and are a challenge to the examiner. The detection of diagnostic defects in the visual fields of infants is quite possible. The native intelligence, alertness, and natural curiosity of small children often make it a joy to work with them.

Much diagnostic material is available if an effort is made to uncover it. The techniques of pediatric perimetry vary from the crudest forms of confrontation to the most sophisticated and quantitative analysis of complicated deficits,

VISUAL-EVOKED RESPONSE

Visual-evoked response (VER) testing has become a valuable clinical tool and is providing us with an objective method of detecting abnormalities of the afferent visual pathways. It has been known for years that regularly repeated flashes of light before the eyes produce evoked responses in the electroencephalogram recorded over the occipital cortex. Improved techniques and the development of computers permitted the averaging of an evoked response that is time locked to the stimulus. Variation of the stimulus presentation is still under study, but, whether straight multiple light flashes or rapid reversal of black and white checkerboard pattern shift is used, an abnormally prolonged latency or an abnormal wave form will often be found in patients with multiple sclerosis who have no other clinical signs or symptoms of visual system involvement. Often the abnormal VER will confirm the diagnosis of multiple sclerosis (Fig. 3-8).

VER has been clinically useful in detecting malingering and in monitoring optic nerve function during removal of a tumor compressing the chiasm.

VER can be used to measure macular function. Wave form in VER is being studied and promises to markedly increase the already great clinical potential of this method of objectively examining visual function and visual field deficits.

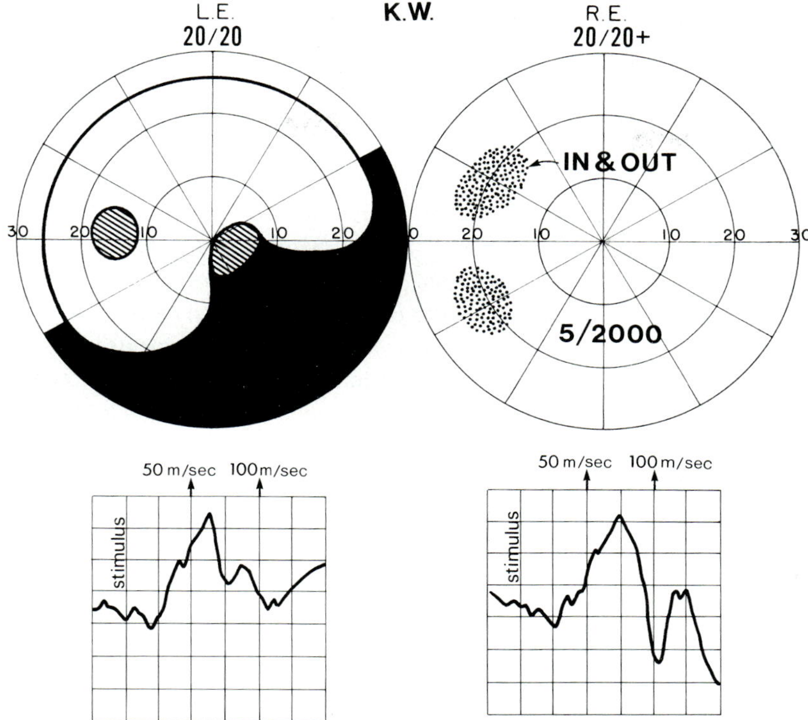

Fig. 3-8. Thirty-two-year-old white female with acute demyelinating optic neuropathy, left eye, with abnormal visual-evoked responses (VER), both eyes. Pain on rotation of eyes, vision initially depressed left eye to 20/60, improving over one-month period. Marcus-Gunn pupil and absent color perception, left eye. Visual field shows inferior nasal depression encroaching on fixation, left eye, with multiple scotomas, right eye. VER shows abnormal initial negative wave and markedly prolonged latency in initial peaks of both eyes. Diagnosis, probable multiple sclerosis.

Pattern shift VER is very useful because it can demonstrate in a quantitative fashion an abnormality of central nervous sytem function that is either subclinical on historical grounds or clinically unsuspected by ordinary neurologic or ophthalmologic examinations.

There is good evidence that the VER will make it possible to objectively measure visual acuity in infants and very small children and even to detect deficits in various areas of the visual field.

The VER in ischemic optic neuropathy is markedly different from that seen in multiple sclerosis. In the latter condition, the latency period is much prolonged, often in both eyes, while the amplitude of the wave pattern is relatively normal. In ischemic optic neuropathy, the latency period remains normal, while there is marked reduction in the amplitude.

Recent studies of VER in normal and glaucoma patients indicate that elevation of intraocular pressure reduces the amplitude of the wave pattern, especially in patients with glaucoma, where the optic nerve head appears vulnerable.

Pattern-evoked visual responses show an increase in latency in most cases of glaucoma, sometimes before visual field changes are detected. The increased latency of the VER indicates a decrease in optic nerve conduction, not unlike that found in multiple sclerosis, which may be due to interruption of axoplasmic flow at the lamina cribrosa due to localized ischemia.

Patients with definite multiple sclerosis but who do not have obvious clinical involvement of the visual system may still have an abnormal VER. An increase in latency is found in a high percentage of these patients.

Evoked cerebral potentials recorded by new computer techniques have recently become a widely used means of documenting, discovering, and defining lesions in the central nervous system. Tests are now available for examining visual, auditory, and somatosensory pathways. Lesions frequently are demonstrated on evoked potential tests but not on any other examinations. Some "silent" lesions are found despite normal physical findings.

CHAPTER 4

Anatomy of the visual pathway

Although an exhaustive discussion of the gross and microscopic anatomy of the visual pathway has no place in a book of this type, the student of perimetry should be well aware that some practical knowledge of the anatomy of the visual pathway is essential. A brief and rather general statement is certainly indicated. The bibliography devoted to the anatomy of the visual pathway is extensive, but the outstanding names are those of Brouwer and Zeeman, Polyak, Putnam and Putnam, Holmes, Clark and Hoyt. A major part of these authors' work is summarized in the second volume of *System of Ophthalmology*, by Duke-Elder and Wybar, and in *Clinical Neuro-ophthalmology*, third edition, by Walsh and Hoyt.

Much of our knowledge of the visual pathway, from the ganglion cell layer of the retina to the external geniculate body, is the result of the degeneration studies of Brouwer and Zeeman and more recently of Hoyt. These authors produced minute lesions of the retina and then studied the degeneration in the nerve fiber layer of the retina, the optic nerve, the chiasmal decussation, and the optic tract, up to and including the external geniculate body. In 1932, Stephen Polyak conducted similar experiments in which he injured minute portions of the area striata of the occipital lobe of monkeys and traced the resulting degeneration in the nerve fibers of the optic radiations. His monumental lifework was published posthumously in 1957. Numerous studies have been made on the cerebral cortex of both humans and animals, and we now have a fairly complete picture of the visual pathway from the rod and cone layer of the retina to its termination in the calcarine fissure and the operculum of the occipital lobe.

The phylogenetic development of the visual pathway has been succinctly outlined by Duke-Elder (Fig. 4-1).

In primitive animal forms, nervous activities were expressed in simple and immediate reflexes so that afferent sensory impulses were simply transformed into ready responses. With the vertebrates the sense of smell began to govern behavior, and the cerebrum became largely an olfactory center. A salient factor in the evolution of humanity was the replacement of smell by vision as the dominant sense. To accomplish this, the entire central nervous system was reorganized. The midbrain became only a relay station between the eye and the new and more efficient end station. Oculomotor function became more exact. These changes were de-

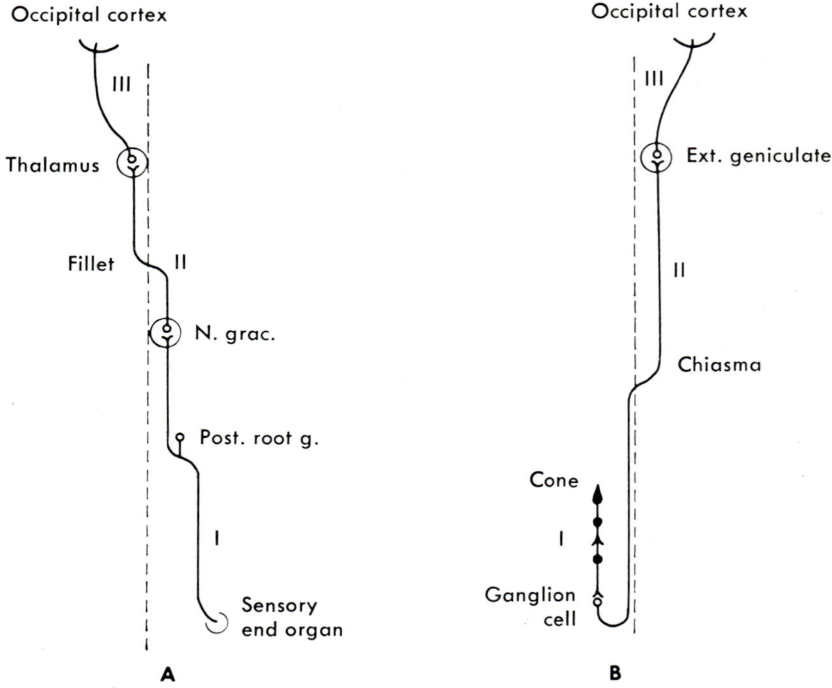

Fig. 4-1. Comparison of neurons of visual pathway with those of somesthetic sensory tract. (After Duke-Elder.)

pendent on (1) the development of a macula, which made exact vision possible, (2) the decussation of the fibers in the chiasm, which allowed physiologically corresponding areas in the two retinas to be associated for the purposes of binocular vision, and (3) profound changes in the nervous control of eye movements, which made possible conjugate movements and convergence so as to bring the two images precisely upon corresponding retinal points.

The visual pathway is a sensory tract and corresponds to the general type of afferent tract that carries impulses to the brain (Fig. 4-1). The bipolar cell of the retina is the peripheral visual nerve and corresponds to the long first-order neuron of the sensory nerve.

The layer of ganglion cells in the retina is a spread-out nucleus, comparable to the nucleus gracilis and cuneatus, and is the beginning of the second-order neuron. The retinal nerve fiber layer, the optic nerve, the nerve fiber decussation of the chiasm, and its continuation in the tract to the external geniculate body constitute the neuron of the second order and correspond to the mesial fillet of the medulla and pons, which end nearby in thalamus.

The neuron of the third order is the optic radiation that is analogous to the corona radiata of the cerebrum and, like it, ends in the cerebral cortex.

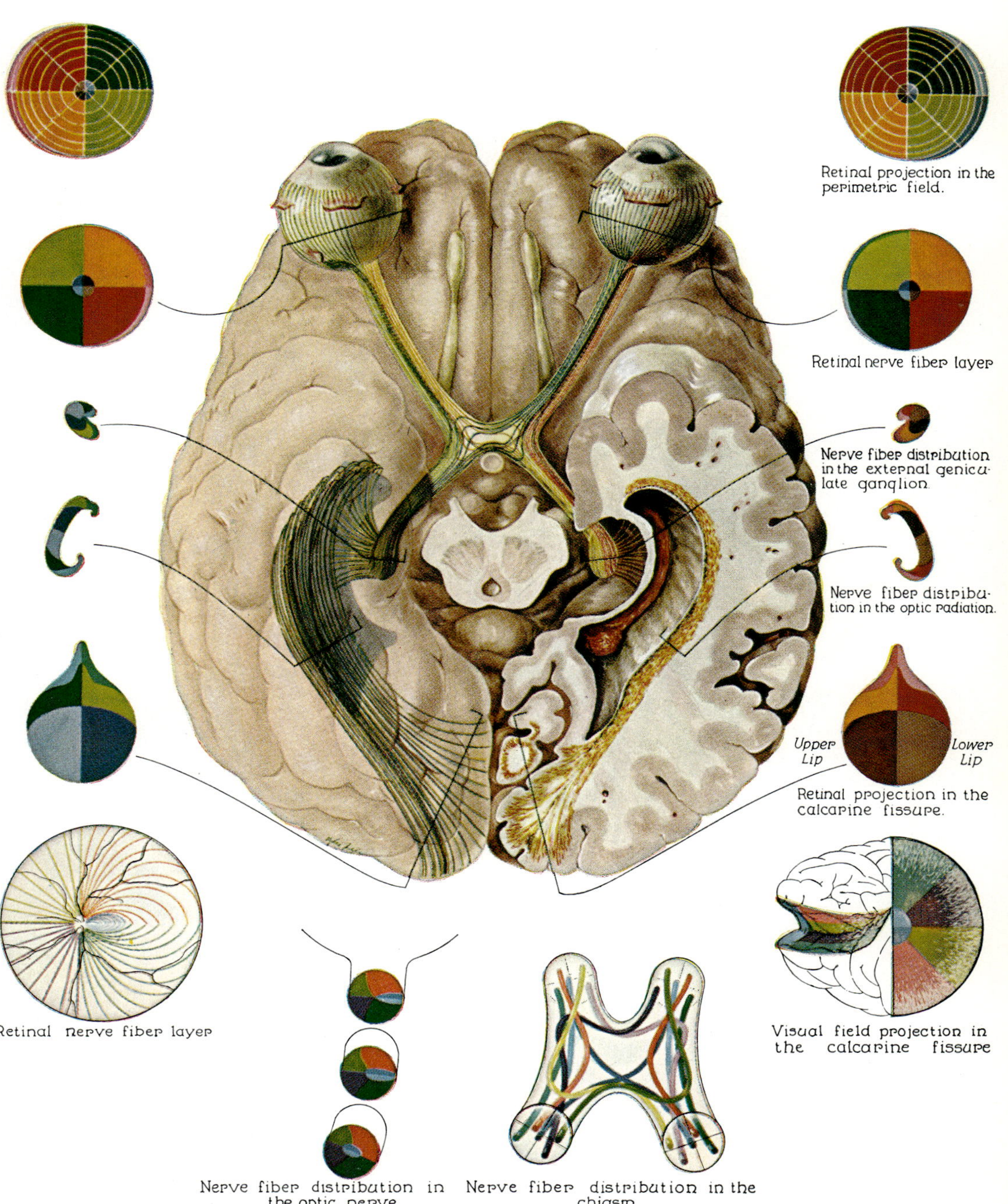

Plate 1. Anatomy of visual pathway.

The neuron of the first order is only as long as the retina is thick (0.1 to 0.5 mm). It is made up of two parts: (1) the end organ or rod and cone layer with nuclei and fibrils and (2) the bipolar cells with filaments and nuclei. The second-order neuron also begins in the retina, in the spread-out ganglion cell layer. From the ganglion cells the individual nerve fibers cross the surface of the retina and enter the optic nerve. The pattern of the nerve fiber layer of the retina is constant and characteristic (Fig. 4-2), and it arrangement is carried on relatively unchanged through the optic nerve, the optic chiasm, and the optic tract to the external geniculate body. This fiber pattern has five major parts: (1) the papillomacular bundle, divided into a superior and an inferior portion, within which are concentrated approximately 65% of the nerve fibers from the retina, (2) the superior arcuate fibers, which arch around the papillomacular bundle from the horizontal raphe to the optic nerve, (3) the inferior arcuate bundle, which arches around the papillomacular bundle from the horizontal raphe into the optic nerve, (4) the superior radiating bundle, which passes through the nasal superior portion of the retina into the optic nerve, and (5) the inferior radiating bundle, which enters the optic nerve from the inferior nasal quadrant of the retina.

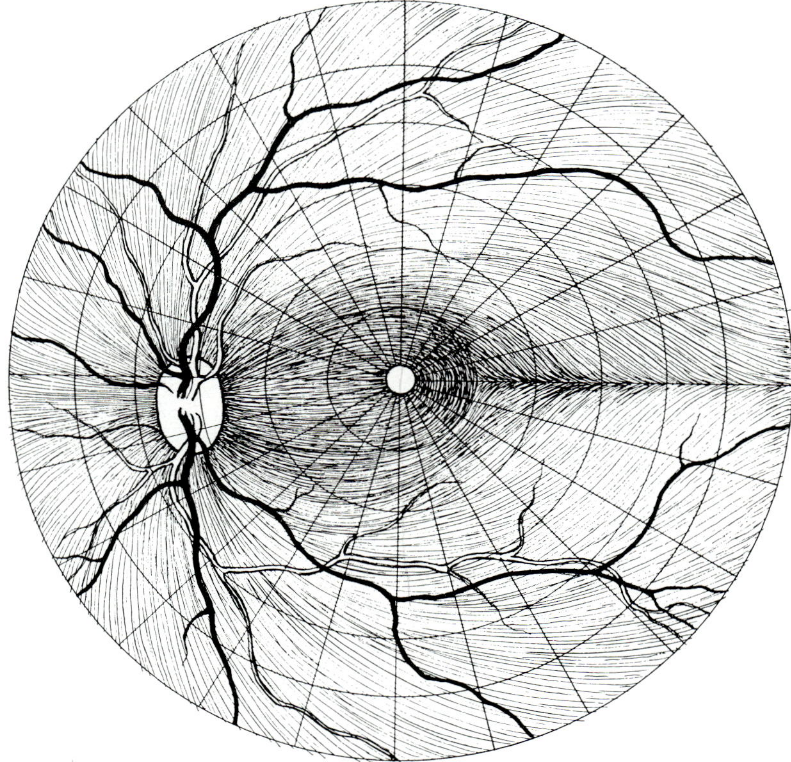

Fig. 4-2. Nerve fiber pattern of retina in its relationship to retinal vascular tree.

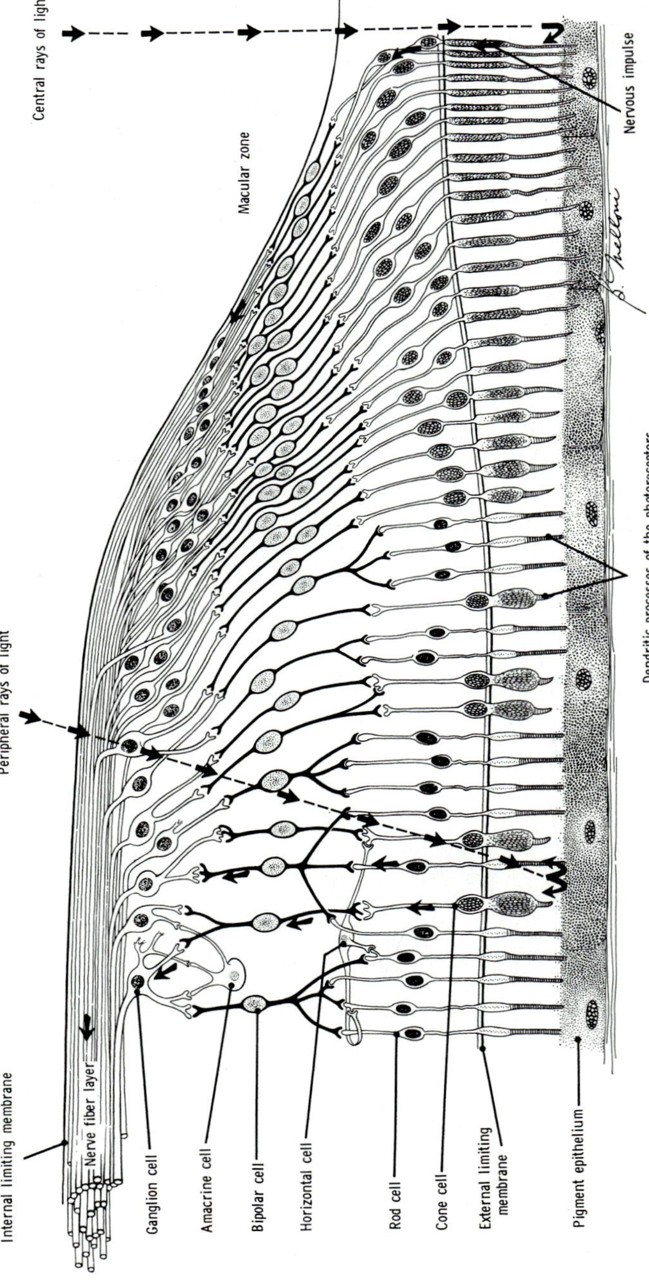

Fig. 4-3. Microscopic anatomy of retina. (From Melloni, B. J.: What's New, Abbott Laboratories.)

Recent studies by Potts and associates show that relatively tiny foveal lesions produced by photocoagulation of the retina caused the loss of from 1/6 to 1/4 of all the optic nerve fibers in the eye. The foveal lesion producing this nerve fiber destruction occupies only 0.4% of the area from which the nerve fibers originate. In addition, the majority of the destroyed nerve fibers are of the smallest size.

In optic nerve disease the first tissue to succumb may be the high fiber density, tightly packed small fibers with the greatest metabolic demand. Thus the visual loss associated with diffuse optic nerve disease takes the form of a central scotoma and loss of central visual acuity.

In entering the optic nerve, the fibers from the periphery of the retina lie in the deep or external part of the nerve fiber layer and enter the periphery of the nerve. Those from the central area of the retina lie in the internal layer of the nerve fiber layer nearest the vitreous and enter the central portion of the nerve.

Investigations by Wolter of the anatomically important optic papilla show it to be a round, sievelike structure, providing a well-protected outlet for all neurites of the nerve fiber layer of the retina that form the optic nerve. The posterior portion is formed by an intertwined structure of connective tissue fibers known as the lamina cribrosa. The anterior portion is a shallow, caplike basket of special retinal astroglia known as spider cells. All neurites of the retinal nerve fiber layer undergo in this papilla a 90-degree flexion from the retina into the optic nerve and are protected and supported at this vulnerable point by the caplike basket of spider cells, which also send many processes to the capillaries, thus acting also as a nutritive organ of the optic nerve fibers.

The glial basket of the optic papilla shows advanced atrophy in all situations that result in optic nerve fiber degeneration, and it is virtually destroyed in advanced glaucoma.

Histologically, complete atrophy of the optic nerve is practically nonexistent. Surprisingly, there are often many well-preserved nerve fiber bundles in the optic papilla even in patients who are completely blind.

In the embryologic development of the nerve fiber layer of the retina, the fovea is at first located in the temporal periphery with the temporal fibers coursing in straight radiating lines toward the optic nerve, just as they do in the adult nasal retina (Fig. 4-4). With the gradual migration of the fovea nasally toward the optic nerve, the horixontal raphe is formed, across which horizontal boundary line no retinal vessels and, presumably, no nerve fibers pass. The formation of the horizontal raphe by the indentation of the fovea forces the temporal nerve fibers to arch around the fovea in arcuate nerve fiber bundles that end abruptly at the raphe. Retinal nerve fiber axons arising in the papillomacular area between the fovea and the optic disc have been shown by Hoyt and Tudor to pass directly into the optic nerve on its temporal side adjacent to the central vessels.

Distally, in the optic nerve, the fibers are grouped in essentially the same pattern as in the retina, with the macular bundle occupying a sector-shaped area in the temporal portion of the nerve. As the chiasm is approached, the macular

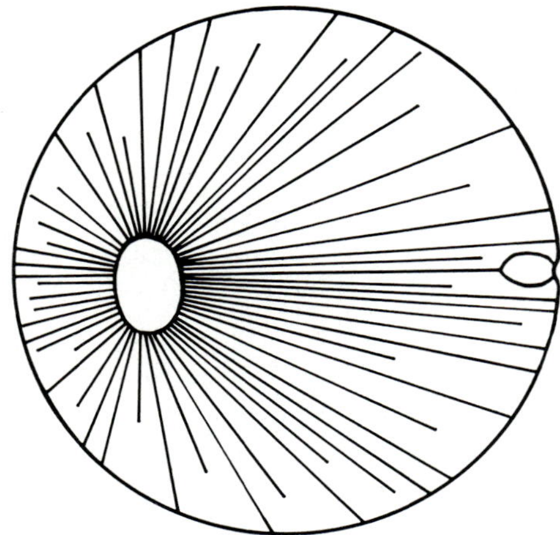

Fig. 4-4. Diagrammatic representation of embryologic position of fovea at retinal periphery before nasal migration toward optic disc and formation of raphe.

fibers move centrally into the nerve and lose their bundle arrangement to become widely and diffusely spread within the nerve.

The superior temporal fibers of the peripheral retina maintain their position in the upper outer quadrant of the optic nerve and become the superior uncrossed visual fibers of the chiasm. In similar fashion, the inferior temporal uncrossed fibers maintain their lower outer quadrant position within the nerve. There is no rotation of these fiber bundles within the optic nerve, and they enter the anterior portion of the chiasm in the same relative positions as they held within the optic nerve.

In spite of intensive study of the optic nerve pathway from the eye to the brain, the developmental mechanisms responsible for guiding incoming retinal ganglion cell axons to appropriate sites in their target nuclei, to achieve a precise topographic representation of the visual world, remain poorly understood.

Fibers in the mammalian optic nerve are generally thought to be organized retinotopically, as noted by Polyak and others.

Recent studies by Horton, Greenwood, and Hubel with electrophysiologic recording from the cat optic nerve failed to support this idea and led them to study the problem by anatomic methods more precise and reliable than those of earlier investigators. They made a localized injection of horseradish peroxidase into the lateral geniculate body of the cat, labeling a small clump of retinal ganglion cells and their axons in the optic nerve. These fibers, emanating from neighboring cells in the retina, became widely scattered through the optic nerve, indicating that retinotopic order is essentially lacking. Their technique permits a much finer resolution of the fiber arrangement in the optic nerve.

In view of these findings, it seems unlikely that the physical arrangement of fibers in the optic nerve and tract could alone account for the retinotopy present in the lateral geniculate body. Conceivably, retinotopic order is present as fibers first

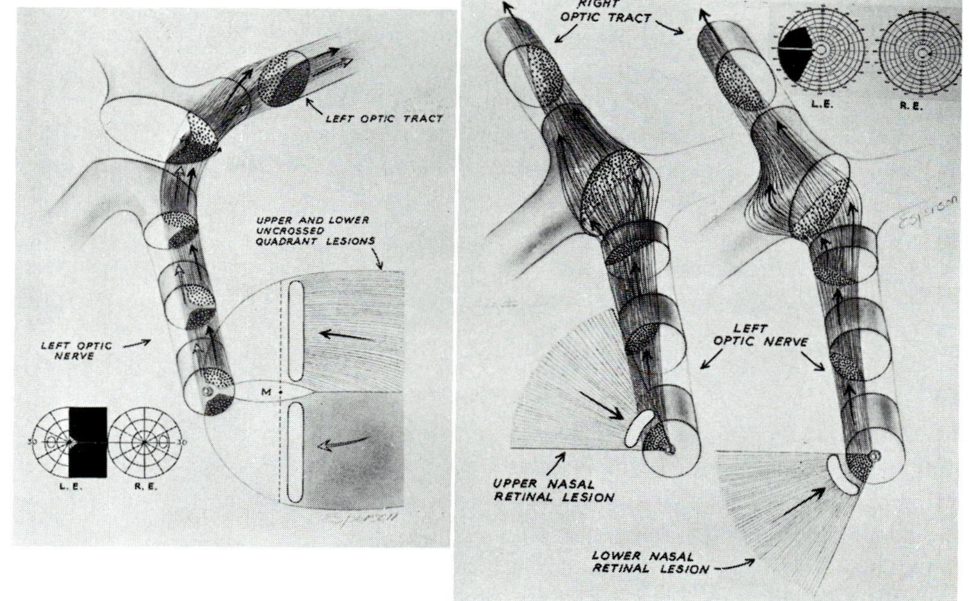

Fig. 4-5. A, Fiber projection from uncrossed retinal quadrants in the monkey. Retina is represented below on right. Vertical white bars are photocoagulator lesions. Macula, *M,* has not been destroyed. No rotation of quadrants occurs until optic tract is reached. Corresponding hypothetical visual defects are represented in lower left diagram. **B,** Visual fiber projections from upper and lower crossed retinal quadrants of the monkey. Hypothetical visual field defects caused by photocoagulation lesion are shown in upper right corner. (Courtesy W. F. Hoyt, M.D., and O. Luis, San Francisco, Calif.)

reach their targets, and their relative positions then shift during subsequent development. The authors state that critical information is lacking, namely, the temporal and spatial order of the nerve fibers on arrival at the lateral geniculate body in the embryo. They are perplexed that fibers in the mammalian optic nerve should be scattered, in view of the evidence favoring retinotopic order in the optic nerves of fish and amphibia, and they wonder if the nonretinotopic arrangement of fibers in the mammalian optic nerve may be of functional significance.

Midway through the chiasm, the upper uncrossed quadrant of fibers begins to extend more medially, whereas the lower quadrant bundle occupies the entire inferior lateral portion of the chiasm.

As these uncrossed fiber bundles pass from the chiasm into the optic tract, the inferior quadrant bundle shifts laterally to occupy the inferior lateral portion of the tract, whereas the superior quadrant fibers move from their dorsal position to a medial location in the tract (Fig. 4-5).

The crossed fiber bundles from the retina, destined to decussate in the chiasm, also follow a characteristic and constant pattern.

Inferior quadrant fibers maintain this position throughout the nerve and into the chiasm, and rotation does not occur. Superior fibers remain superior to the midportion of the chiasm. These crossed fiber bundles are tightly packed, and the axon caliber is large.

At the chiasm the inferior quadrant fibers cross immediately in the lower anterior chiasm. Some fibers loop across into the contralateral nerve at its junction with the chiasm. As the fibers approach the optic tract in the posterior portion of the chiasm, the crossed lower quadrant fiber bundle moves laterally and enters the lateral side of the optic tract.

Upper crossed quadrant fiber bundles cross in the dorsal and posterior portion of the chiasm and enter the medial and inferior half of the contralateral optic tract.

The fibers representing the temporal crescent of the visual field (i.e., the peripheral nasal retinal fibers) occupy both dorsal and ventral areas in the chiasm.

As already mentioned, the macular fibers are diffusely scattered in the optic nerve, chiasm, and optic tract, mixing freely with peripheral quadrant bundles except for a very short segment of the anterior optic nerve where they are a small and compact bundle.

Compared with the extramacular axons, macular fibers are of small caliber. They occupy a large portion of the optic nerve and chiasm and about two-thirds of the optic tracts. They mix freely with the extramacular fiber bundles.

As retinal axons pass from one optic nerve through the chiasm to the ipsilateral and contralateral optic tracts, two types of fiber segregation occur. The first type is segregation into crossed and uncrossed retinal axons. The superior axons enter the medial side of the optic tracts, whereas the inferior axons enter the lateral side. The second type of fiber segregation is rearrangement in the chiasm of retinal axons according to fiber size. Small-caliber fibers, primarily from the macular areas of the retina, rise from the central part of the optic nerve to the superior areas of the chiasm and optic tracts; large-caliber fibers, from peripheral retinal areas, descend during passage through the chiasm into the inferior portions of the optic tracts.

Looping of the extramacular (peripheral) crossed axons into the opposite optic nerve and optic tracts occurs so that at each side of the chiasm crossed fibers from both sides mingle with uncrossed fibers from the same side.

The two areas of the chiasm that contain no macular fibers are the anterior inferior chiasm and the posterior inferior chiasm. All other portions of the chiasm contain large numbers of small-caliber axons.

As each posterior limb of the chiasm enters the optic tract, it thus contains (1) uncrossed temporal fibers from the same side, (2) crossed nasal fibers from the opposite side, (3) uncrossed macular fibers from the same side, (4) crossed macular fibers from the opposite side, and (5) diffusely scattered macular fibers.

The optic chiasm, in its gross anatomy, is formed by the junction and partial decussation of the optic nerves. It is a transversely oval body averaging 15 by 8 by 4 mm in size. It lies covered by the pia mater in the cisterna basalis of the sub-

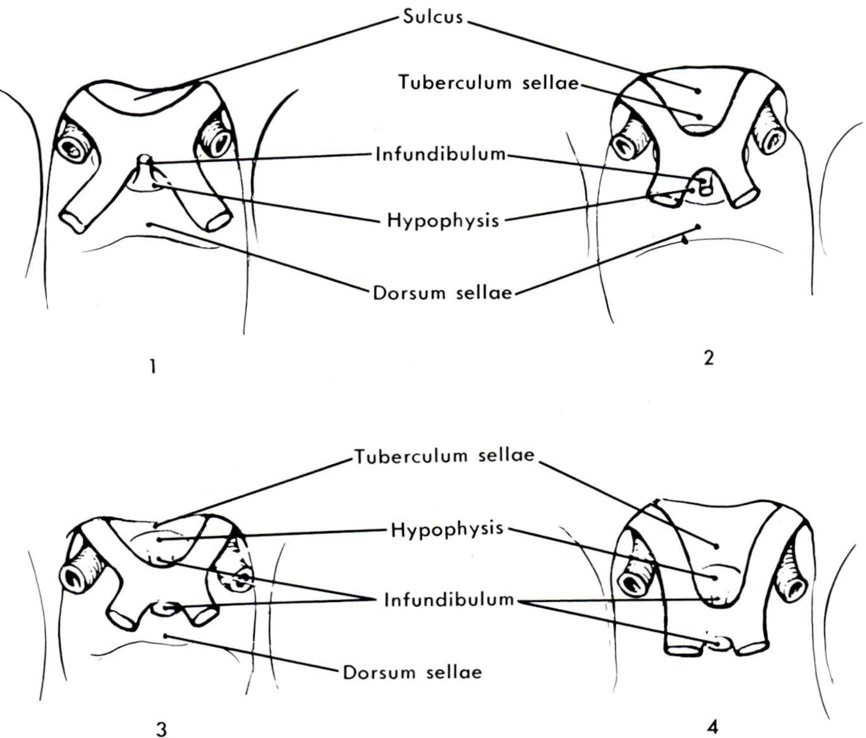

Fig. 4-6. Four positions of chiasm in relation to sella turcica: position *1* equals 4%; position *2* equals 12%; position *3* equals 80%; position *4* equals 4%.

arachnoid space, resting behind the tuberculum sellae and the sulcus chiasmaticus. It varies in its relation to the posterior part of the pituitary body; it may lie behind the dorsum sellae or, rarely, far forward of the chiasmal sulcus. In approximately 80% of cases, the center of the chiasm lies over the posterior two-thirds of the sella. Only 12% of chiasms lie directly over the center of the sella, whereas 4% are prefixed with very short optic nerves and 4% are postfixed with very long optic nerves and the center of the chiasm lying behind the sella (Fig. 4-6). The relations of the optic chiasm are as follows (Fig. 4-7): Above it lies the cavity of the third ventricle. On each side and in close contact is the internal carotid artery just before it divides into the anterior and middle cerebral arteries. In front and in very close relationship are the two anterior cerebral arteries joined by the anterior communicating artery. Posteriorly lies the interpeduncular area with the tuber cinereum and the infundibulum. Below the chiasm the pituitary body lies in the fossa of the sella turcica in the sphenoidal bone, covered by the diaphragma sellae. Occasionally a sphenoidal sinus may undermine the entire chiasm. Between the chiasm and the diaphragma sellae is the cisterna basalis.

The optic tracts begin in the posterolateral angle of the chiasm and run lat-

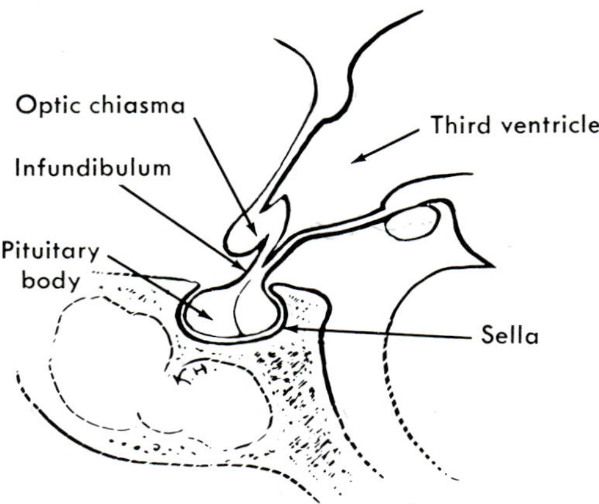

Fig. 4-7. Sagittal section through chiasm showing its relationship to third ventricle, pituitary body, pituitary stalk, sella turcica, and sphenoid sinus.

erally and backward. Each tract is a rounded band running between the tuber cinereum and the anterior perforated substance in its first portion and then continuing posteriorly as a flattened band of fibers to sweep around the cerebral peduncles in close association with the posterior cerebral artery. When the optic tract reaches the posterolateral aspect of the thalamus, it breaks into two routes: (1) a lateral and larger route that ends in the external geniculate body, the pulvinar of the thalamus, and the superior colliculus and (2) a small medial route to the medial geniculate body. The visual pathway fibers are all in the lateral route. The lateral geniculate body, which is the end station of the neuron of the second order, is in fact a part of the optic thalamus and the superior colliculus, which is a part of the midbrain.

The lateral or external geniculate body is a small oval body appearing on the posterolateral part of the pulvinar of the thalamus. It receives 80% of the fibers from the optic tract. Some of the fibers terminate in the external geniculate body, whereas others pass over or through it to the surface of the pulvinar and thence to the superior colliculus (Fig. 4-8).

The external geniculate body is the end station for the visual fibers in the optic tract. It is made up of six laminae of alternating grey and white matter. Crossed retinal projections terminate in laminae 1, 4, and 6, while uncrossed fibers terminate in laminae 2, 3, and 5. Corresponding points in both retinae are represented in the external geniculate body in vertically oriented lines or columns of cells from all six laminae. Thus the monocular organization of rods and cones is converted into a binocular arrangement of external geniculate neurons, most of which is devoted to macular vision. Irregular or partial damage to several laminae will thus give rise to asymmetrical defects in the corresponding homonymous visual fields (Fig. 4-9). The external geniculate body is the origin of the optic radiation, through which it is connected to the occipital cortex. The lateral geniculate body is highly developed in primates and has been the subject of intensive research both anatomic

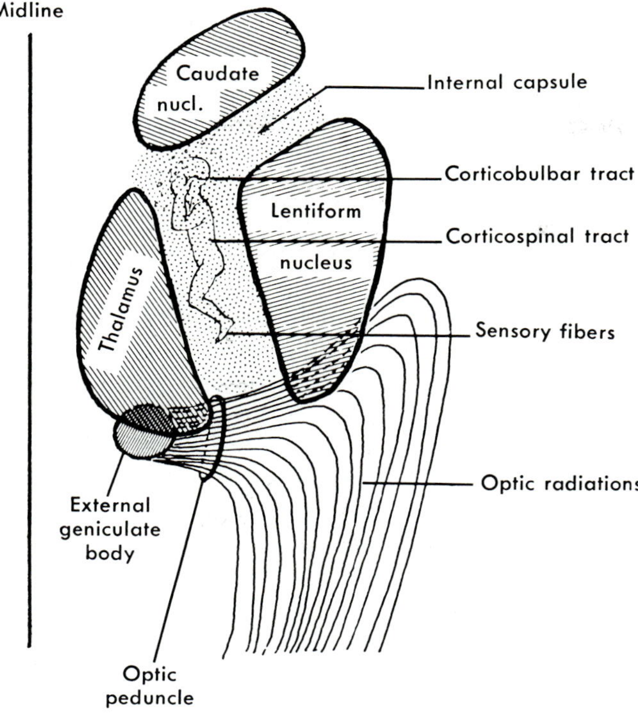

Fig. 4-8. Relationships of visual pathway in internal capsule.

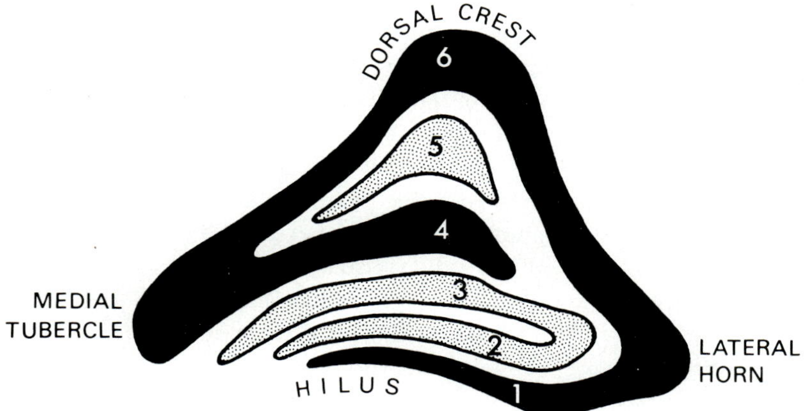

Fig. 4-9. Schematic representation of laminae in right external geniculate body. Crossed retinal projections terminate in laminae 1, 4, and 6. Uncrossed projections terminate in laminae 2, 3, and 5. Selective partial involvement of one or more of these laminae will produce asymmetrical homonymous visual field defects, depending on the extent of laminar damage.

and physiologic. The ratio of axons in the optic tract to cells in the external geniculate body is approximately 1:1. The synaptic interruption of the visual pathway within the geniculate body is further evidenced by the lack of optic atrophy in patients with extensive or complete destruction of the occipital cortex of one cerebral hemisphere, while at the same time all of the nerve cells of the ipsilateral external geniculate lamellae degenerate. Because of this absence of transsynaptic degeneration, a homonymous hemianoptic field defect unaccompanied by optic atrophy (after several weeks' time) would indicate damage to the visual pathway posterior to the external geniculate ganglion.

Hoyt has pointed out that the generalization that upper retinal fibers remain above and lower retinal fibers remain below does not hold for the external geniculate body. During the evolution of the visual pathway, the geniculate body rotated through an angle of 90 degrees. As a result the upper or dorsal retinal fibers were displaced medially and the lower or ventral fibers displaced laterally. This twist in the arrangement of the visual fibers of the retina becomes straightened out again in the optic radiations. Thus, with the exception of the area of the external geniculate body, upper retinal fibers remain upper and lower retinal fibers remain lower throughout the visual pathway.

The visual fibers are relayed on to the occipital cortex as the geniculocalcarine pathway or optic radiation, which becomes the neuron of the third order. The thalamus does not form an actual relay station in the visual pathway. The experimental work of Brouwer and Zeeman showed that lesions of the retina or of the occipital cortex do not produce degeneration in the thalamus and that extensive lesions in the thalamus do not produce hemianopsia as they do in the external geniculate body.

Just as we are indebted to Brouwer and Zeeman for much of our knowledge of the anatomy of the lower or anterior visual pathway, so too must we look to Polyak for an understanding of the main visual fiber systems of the cerebral cortex. In considering the organization and function of the visual system in general and in detail, Polyak was most precise and definite in his statements. He considered that the entire afferent visual system in primates, from its beginning in the retina to its cortical termination, is a definite anatomic and functional entity organized spatially (i.e., according to the principle of localization) (Fig. 4-10). In the peripheral portions of the visual system, from the retina to the external geniculate body, this was demonstrated experimentally by Brouwer and Zeeman and largely confirmed by Hoyt and Luis in 1962. In the central portion of the visual system, from the geniculate body to the cortex, the same principle has been demonstrated by experimental, clinical, and pathologic studies of Wilbrand, Henschen, Minkowski, Meyer, Uhthoff, Lenz, and Saenger. This work was confirmed in 1932 and 1957 by Polyak, who concluded that there is no longer reason for the continued adherence to the old view of a threefold subcortical origin of the visual radiation and no ground for support of the hypothesis of a multiple or diffuse projection of the retina, especially of the macula, on a wide region of the cerebral cortex.

The relation of the afferent visual pathway to the cortex is quite definite. One

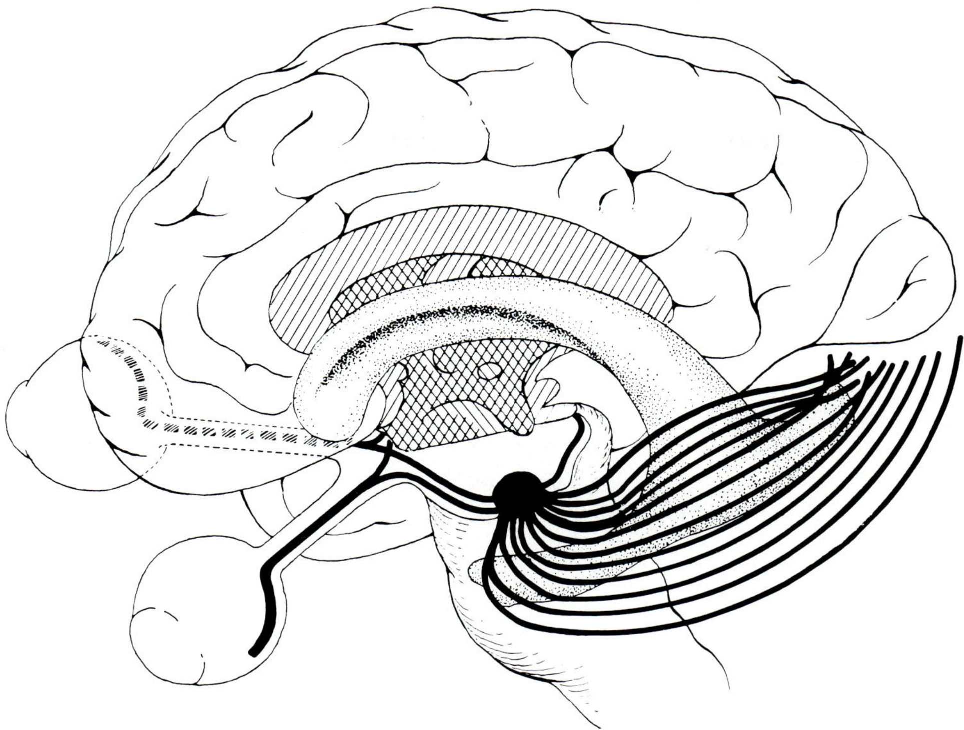

Fig. 4-10. Schematic representation of visual pathway from retina to calcarine fissure of occipital lobe. Cutaway view from gross dissections shows distribution of visual fibers in optic radiation.

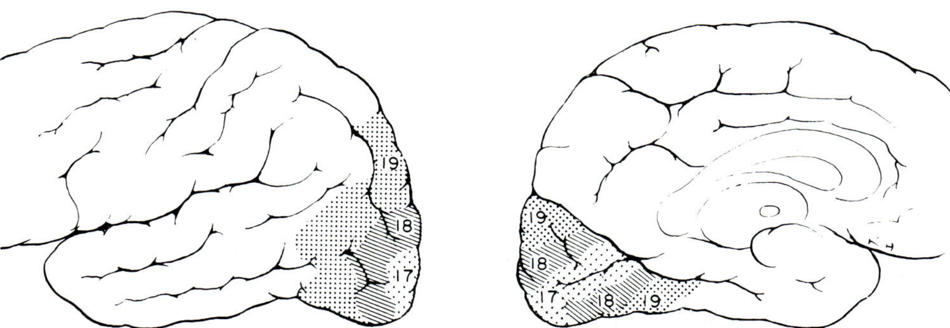

Fig. 4-11. Visual area or striate cortex in occipital lobe. Lateral and mesial views show Brodmann's area *17* (striate area), *18* (parastriate area), and *19* (peristriate area). Area *17* is sharply delineated cortical termination of visual pathway.

cortical area, the striate cortex, receives direct visual impulses from its peripheral receptor organ, the retina (Fig. 4-11). A definite small segment of the visual cortex corresponds to each minute unit of the retina. Experiments involving very small injuries in the striate cortex point toward the existence of a certain localization even in the farther spreading of the visual impulses in the hemispheres.

The strictly localistic principle demonstrates a mathematical projection of the retina on the cerebral cortex, the same principle applying also to a part of the further subcortical association connections of the visual projection cortex with the surrounding nonprojection areas of the occipitoparietal lobes. The second principle postulates the existence of short intracortical and subcortical neurons, mechanisms that are responsible for the unity of subjective psychovisual experiences.

Polyak's conclusions and discussion were largely based on experimental studies on degeneration in monkeys. The summary of his monumental work follows:

1. The external geniculate body of the betweenbrain must be recognized at present as the only and exclusive origin of the visual radiation in primates.
2. There exists only one single direct afferent visual pathway from the subcortical region to the cerebral cortex. It is the fiber system originating from the external geniculate body. The external geniculocortical radiation forms a strong fiber lamina or layer in the posterior temporal, parietal, and occipital lobes. Other fibers (afferent, callosal, and associational) mix with the afferent visual fibers.
3. The cortical termination of the visual pathway is a definite and sharply delimited area that is identical with the area striata of G. E. Smith and of Brodmann's field 17 (Fig. 4-11). It is distinguished by the strong intracortical fiber layer, the stripe of Gennari. No other areas of the cerebral cortex receive afferent visual fibers.
4. The central visual pathway above the external geniculate body is strictly unilateral. No evidence exists of a partial decussation of its fibers through the corpus callosum. The only spot, therefore, where the visual pathway undergoes a partial decussation is in the optic chiasm.
5. The fibers of the visual radiation are, on the whole, of medium size and finer than the somatic-sensory fibers.
6. The optic radiation is composed of fibers grouped into fiber bundles and arranged in parallel fashion. Each fiber bundle originates in a definite small segment of the external geniculate body and terminates in a definite small segment of the striate cortex.
7. The optic radiation or external sagittal layer of the parieto-occipital lobe can be subdivided into three anatomic-functional portions, discernible on cross section perpendicular to the long axis of the hemisphere (i.e., the dorsal horizontal branch, the ventral horizontal branch, and the vertical branch connecting both horizontal branches).
   a. The dorsal horizontal branch is composed of fibers originating from the medial or internal segment of the external geniculate body close to the thalamus, which corresponds with the upper extramacular segments of both homonymous hemiretinas including the upper monocular portion of the crossed retina. This branch supplies the striate cortex of the upper (dorsal) tip of the calcarine fissure; the most dorsomedioanterior bundle of the radiation supplies the most internal longitudinal "boundary seg-

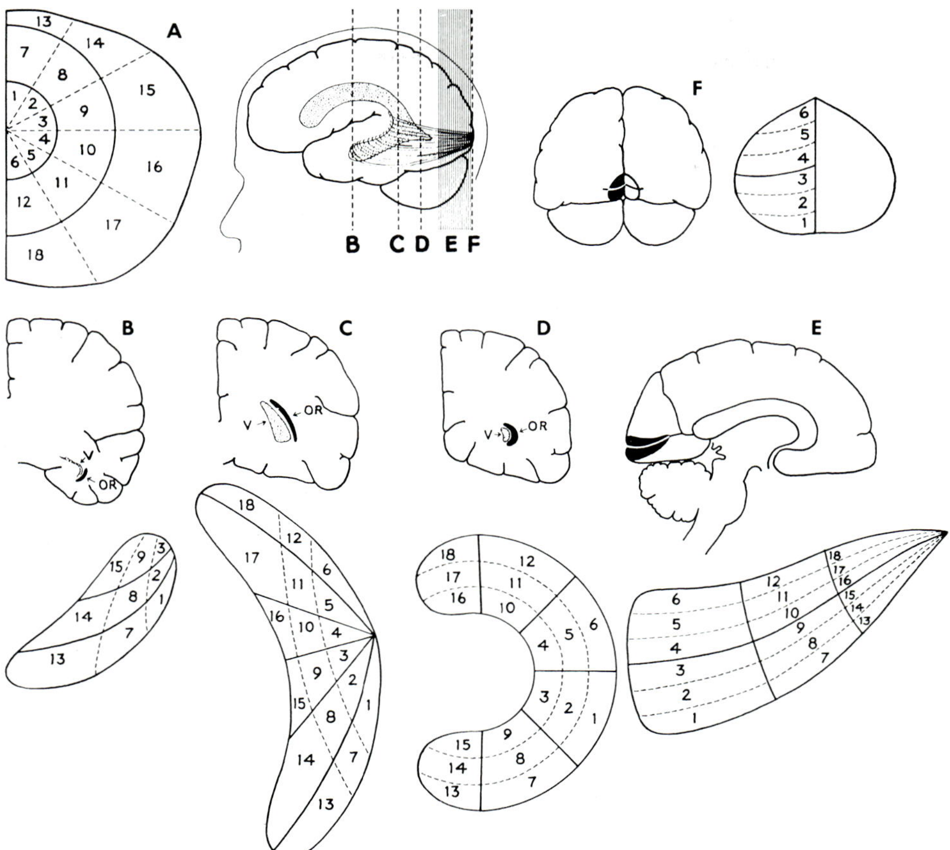

Fig. 4-12. Schematic representation of architecture of geniculocalcarine pathway with projection of striate cortex and nerve fiber bundles of optic radiation onto visual field. **A,** Right homonymous half-field divided into sectors and concentric zones representing projection of various bundles of optic radiation in temporal and parietal lobe and striate cortex calcarine fissure of occipital lobe. **B, C,** and **D,** Coronal sections, seen from in front, through temporal, parietal, and parieto-occipital lobes of left cerebral hemisphere, showing planes of section, relationship of optic radiation to lateral ventricle, and division of visual fiber bundles within the radiation into sectors and concentric zones corresponding to their projection onto visual field. Note in plane of section through temporal loop of Meyer **(B)** only the lower half of the radiation is represented and in planes **B** and **C,** which section anterior radiation, the macular fibers (*1* to *6*) are laminated on lateral surface of radiation (as postulated by Spalding, 1952); in plane **D,** which sections posterior part of radiation, the macular fibers are interposed between and completely separate the upper and lower peripheral fibers (as postulated by Polyak, 1957). **E,** Medial view of left cerebral hemisphere showing striate cortex of calcarine fissure divided according to its projection on right homonymous half-field. **F,** View from behind striate cortex at posterior tip of left occipital pole, showing projection of macular portion of right homonymous half-field.

ment" of the upper lip and successive lateral bundles supply the more lateral and somewhat caudal segments closer to the floor of the calcarine fissure and to the side of the striate area.

b. The ventral horizontal branch is composed of fibers originating from the lateral segment of the external geniculate body close to the lentiform nucleus, corresponding to the lower extramacular quadrants of both homonymous hemiretinas, including the lower monocular portion of the crossed retina. It supplies the striate cortex of the lower (ventral) lip of the calcarine fissure. The narrow zones of the striate area supplied here are probably similarly arranged longitudinally as are those in the upper lip, but in reversed order, with the most medial zones being supplied by the most ventromedioanterior bundle.

c. The perpendicular (intermediate) branch of the visual radiation is composed of fibers originating from the large intermediate segment of the external geniculate body, situated between the internal and external segments of that body. This intermediate segment corresponds to both dorsal and ventral quadrants of both homonymous hemimaculas. The vertical branch represents a considerable portion (probably more than half) of the visual radiation. It supplies the striate cortex covering the pole of the occipital lobe, the external face of the occipital lobe, or occipital operculum. The vertical branch represents in its upper half, near the dorsohorizontal branch, the upper quadrants of both homonymous hemimaculas; in its ventral half, near the ventral horizontal branch, the lower quadrants of both homonymous hemimaculas.

8. In view of the preceding statements and the results of pathologic and experimental studies of Rönne (1914) and Brouwer and Zeeman (1026), the following conclusions as to the projection of the retina upon the cortex in primates and in man may be made:

   a. The upper extramacular quadrants of both homonymous hemiretinas (the lower quadrants of the homonymous halves of the visual fields excluding the macular portion) together with the upper half of the monocular portion of the crossed retina (lower half of the crossed temporal crescent) are projected upon the anterior portion of the lower lip of the calcarine fissure.

   b. The lower extramacular quadrants of both homonymous hemiretinas (the upper quadrants of the homonymous halves of the visual fields excluding the macular portion) together with the lower half of the monocular portion of the crossed retina (upper half of the crossed temporal crescent) are projected upon the anterior portion of the lower lip of the calcarine fissure.

   c. The projection zone of the monocular temporal crescent occupies the anterior portion of the calcarine striate area, being its most peripheral zone.

d. Homonymous halves of both maculas and the fovea are projected upon the pole of the occipital lobe. The upper half of the polar striate cortex represents the upper quadrants of both homonymous halves of the maculas (the lower homonymous quadrants of the macular portion of the visual field). The lower polar half represents the lower quadrants of both homonymous halves of the maculas (upper homonymous quadrants of the macular portion of the visual fields). The fovea in particular is projected upon a middle zone stretching across the pole.
e. The horizontal meridian, dividing the upper homonymous extramacular quadrants of both hemiretinas and of the crossed monocular portion and corresponding portions of the visual fields from the lower quadrants, extends longitudinally along the bottom of the calcarine fissure. Its continuation around the occipital pole corresponds with the horizontal meridian dividing the upper and lower quadrants of both homonymous hemimaculas. The vertical line, dividing both homonymous halves of the visual fields of both eyes and passing through the pionts of fixation, is represented by the posterior boundary of the striate area. The points of fixation must therefore correspond to a central point of that boundary.

9. The bilateral or double cortical representation of each total macula, with each and all of its receptor elements connected with both hemispheres, has no anatomic foundation. The individual macular elements are represented only in one hemisphere. In other words, each macular cortex represents homonymous halves of both maculas.
10. The entire striate area receives everywhere afferent visual fibers. There are no gaps. The number of fibers per cortical square unit is larger in the occipital pole than in the calcarine fissure.
11. The small segments of the visual cortex supplied by individual bundles of the visual radiation have sharp limits and definite form. There is no overlapping of these small zones, or mingling of their respective bundles, or even a diffuse termination of individual bundles of the visual radiation in extensive portions of the visual cortex.
12. The entire efferent visual system from its beginning in the retina to its termination in the striate area of the cerebral cortex is composed of individual receptor and conductor units. These structural and functional units are strictly arranged according to the spatial principle, on the one hand, and the principle of neighborhood, on the other. Each area striata is, in some sense, a faithful copy of both homonymous halves of both retinas. There exists a full preservation of spatial relations in the visual cortex as it exists in the retina, although the absolute shape of the cortical hemiretinas is somewhat changed in consequence of the slight mutual displacement of neighboring units or segments.
13. All visual impulses, whatever their special form or quality and regardless of their ultimate destination as far as they reach the cortex of the forebrain,

first go to the striate area, from which they are distributed to other regions of the same and opposite hemispheres.

14. Since there exists a fixed arrangement of functionally different bundles or segments of the visual radiation, as well as of the peripheral portions of the visual system, which means a fixed projection of definite retinal quadrants upon definite portions of the visual cortex symmetric in both hemispheres, injuries of the visual system produce definite symptoms, depending on the location and extent of the injury. Since each of the constituent structures of the afferent visual system and of the visual cortex has its own function, its destruction is always followed by an irreparable and lasting loss of that particular function. The replacement or compensation of the lost function must be achieved by what can be called a more economical utilization of the parts remaining undamaged.

    The anatomic evidence for point-to-point representation of the retina on the occipital cortex is further supported by the physiologic experiments of Hubel and Wiesel.

    The striate cortex of the monkey was mapped by Daniel and Whitteridge with a searching stimulus in the visual field of one eye and a recording electrode implanted in various precisely localized positions in the visual cortex. They showed that each area of the retina projects to a discrete and predictable spot in the primary visual cortex.

With regard to macular representation, the anatomic facts, physiologic experiments, and clinical observations combine to compel us to conclude that the macula must be represented in the posterior portion of the area striata around the pole and not in its anterior portion.

More recently Dobelle and associates have stimulated the human visual cortex in a totally blind person and mapped the visual field position of the resulting punctate sensations of light, which are called phosphenes. Their method reverses the technique used in animals where electrical activity is elicited in the visual cortex by stimulation with punctate lights in the visual field. Their approach provides direct, localized access to human visual cortex including areas 17, 18, and 19 by means of simultaneous stimulation of multiple electrodes.

Analysis of the phosphene map indicates that successive stimulation of points further from the tip of the occipital pole produces phosphenes progressively more distant from the fixation point. These results confirm the general view of cortical organization derived from field defect studies in man and from anatomic and electrophysiologic studies in monkeys.

The macular segment of the external geniculate body, as found by Rönne and by Brouwer and Zeeman, represents a large portion of that nucleus. The fibers that originate in this segment constitute a considerable part of the radiation (nearly one half), a fact quite in accord with the greater importance of central or macular vision, and with the great number of ganglion cells in the fovea of the retina.

Since the number of macular fibers in the optic nerve, chiasm, and tract exceeds that of the extramacular fibers and since the macular segment of the external geniculate body represents more than one half of the nucleus, the macular cortex must be proportionately large, probably larger than the entire extramacular cortex, and must be located in the far more extensive region of the area striata, which covers the occipital pole.

Anatomic, physiologic, and clinical evidence for macular representation is conflicting. Anatomic evidence favors the contention that the macula is unilaterally represented, whereas the theory of bilateral representation is supported by quantitative visual field studies on patients who have had surgical resections of one occipital lobe. This view is also supported by physiologic studies on animals. Whichever theory is correct, it appears that either direct connections or callosal interhemispheric connections account for part of macular cortical function. Walsh and Hoyt predict that the controversy will be resolved experimentally by combined morphologic and neurophysiologic studies of single macular units of the retina, geniculate body, and visual cortex in monkeys.

From the preceding discussion of its anatomy, we should understand that large portions of the visual pathway are in intimate relationship with various other parts of the central nervous system and its blood supply. With rather rare exceptions, most interruptions of the visual pathway, with clinical symptoms resulting therefrom, will also present certain other neurologic disturbances in the patient. The combination of symptoms and signs from these other areas of the nervous system, with disturbances of vision, is of utmost importance in the localization of lesions within the central nervous system. The perimetrist, therefore, should be as familiar with general neuroanatomy as with the specific neuroanatomy of the visual pathway, and a knowledge of the anatomy of all of the cranial nerves and their relationship to the visual pathway is of utmost value.

CHAPTER 5

Vascular supply of the visual pathway

So many of the lesions that affect the visual pathway and produce visual field defects are vascular in nature, it is necessary to have some understanding of the blood supply of the visual pathway and of the anatomic relationships of the arteries and veins to the nerve fiber bundles.

Circulatory disturbances may affect the visual pathway either directly or indirectly. For example, a hemorrhage or ischemic infarct in the occipital lobe may produce total homonymous hemianopsia or a tiny homonymous hemianoptic scotoma, depending on its size and location. A tumor in the same area may produce extensive loss of visual field, partly by direct pressure on the nerve fiber bundles, but largely by interference with the blood supply of the occipital cortex. It is probable that the major cause of the visual field defects found in patients with a brain tumor is vascular obstruction rather than direct pressure by the tumor (Fig. 5-1).

Interference with the blood supply to the visual pathway may occur as the result of traumatic interruption of the vessels; or, on occasion, the vessels themselves may act to compress the visual fibers, as in aneurysms of the circle of Willis; or the pressure of normal or arteriosclerotic arteries on visual fibers displaced against them by a remote tumor may impede the blood flow to the visual pathway. Atherosclerotic arterial insufficiency or stenosis and occlusion may also impair the blood flow to visual centers. In general, vascular lesions can be localized with considerable accuracy by the visual field defects that they produce.

The retinal vascular supply is in two parts: (1) the choroidal circulation from the ciliary arteries, which supplies the pigment epithelium, rods and cones, and outer nuclear layers, and (2) the central artery of the retina, which supplies the remainder of the retina (Fig. 5-2).

The foveal area, the peripheral retina, and the optic nerve head have a rich network of anastomoses, and there is some anastomosis between the small branches of the central artery and those of the choroidal circulation near the optic disc.

The four main branches of the central artery follow the general pattern of the nerve fiber layer of the retina, with the superior and inferior temporal branches arching around the fovea and ending at a horizontal vascular raphe. There is anatomic and clinical evidence that the vascular demarcation at the raphe is more ex-

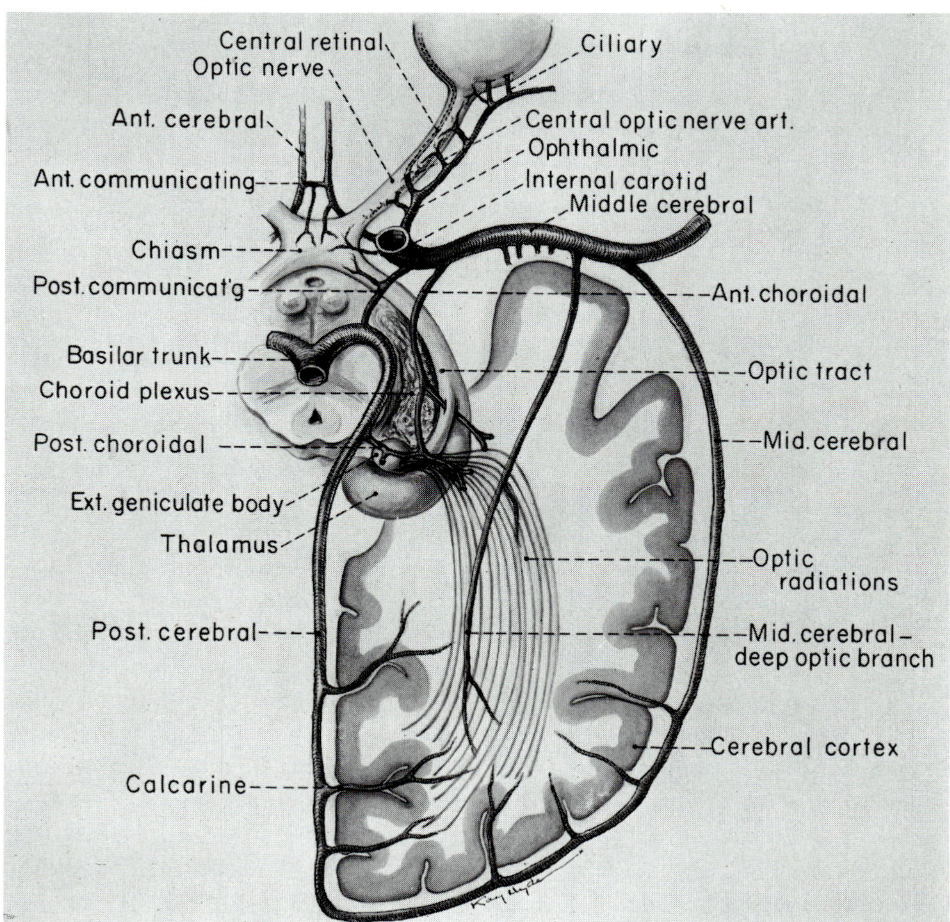

Fig. 5-1. Diagrammatic representation of vascular supply of visual pathway from retina to occipital cortex.

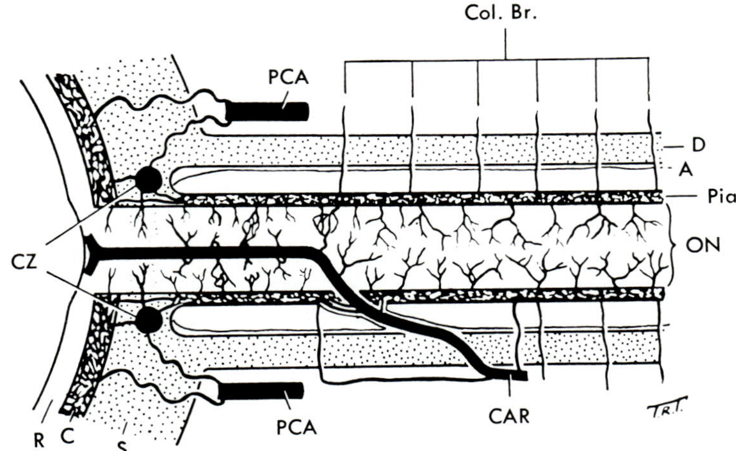

Fig. 5-2. Arterial supply of optic nerve according to Hayreh. Central retinal artery gives off branches in dural sheath. There is no central artery of optic nerve. *A,* Arachnoid; *C,* choroid; *CAR,* central artery of retina; *Col. Br.,* collateral branch; *CZ,* circle of Zinn-Haller; *D,* dura; *ON,* optic nerve; *PCA,* posterior ciliary artery; *R,* retina; *S,* sclera. (From Hayreh, S. S.: Br. J. Ophthalmol. **47:**651, 1963.)

act than in the nerve fiber bundles. The arteries lie in the nerve fiber and ganglion cell layer of the retina (see Fig. 4-2).

Increasing evidence of the importance of the vasculature of the optic nerve head in the pathogenesis of glaucomatous optic atrophy and visual field deficits has focused attention on the circumpapillary and papillary microcirculation.

Henkind and Levitzky have studied the angioarchitecture of the papilla and the lamina cribrosa. They conclude that the fine network of polygonally arranged vessels in the papilla is largely supplied from the choroid, with possible occasional retinal capillary connections. In the lamina cribrosa there is a rich capillary network supplied largely by branches of the circle of Zinn-Haller and the choroidal arterioles.

These anatomic studies are further supported by Hayreh's fluorescein angiographic studies of normal and atrophic optic nerve heads. When optic atrophy is secondary to retinal lesions, the choroidal vessels in the disc fill normally although disc fluorescence is less than normal. In all other forms of optic atrophy, there is generalized reduction in fluorescence of the disc.

Acute elevation of intraocular pressure in monkeys selectively obliterates vessels of choroidal origin in the optic disc and the peripapillary choroid. There is also reduced filling of the peripheral choroid but no obliteration of the retinal vasculature.

By means of simultaneous artificial elevation of intraocular pressure and fluorescein angiography in normal human eyes, Blumenthal and his co-workers have described controlled studies of intraocular pressure effects on the vascular bed of the eye. They have demonstrated that although the retinal and choroidal vascular systems are both derived from the ophthalmic artery these systems react quite differently to increased intraocular pressure. Blood flow ceases in the choroidal circulation at intraocular pressures significantly lower than those required to produce cessation of flow in the retinal vascular tree.

Optic disc capillaries are affected by the smallest increase in intraocular pressure, filling with dye only after the entire choroid has fluoresced. In some instances the entire peripapillary choroidal area revealed a marked decrease in fluorescence. These findings indicate that the peripapillary choroidal vessels and the optic disc vessels are the most vulnerable portion of the choroidal circulation to increases in intraocular pressure and are more readily affected than the retinal vasculature.

All this is effective support for the clinical evidence that interference with the choroidal supply to the optic nerve head in glaucoma is responsible for the cavernous atrophy and visual field defects in chronic open-angle glaucoma (see Chapter 11).

The ophthalmic artery supplies the optic nerve sheaths with a fine and rich network of vessels that anastomose with each other and with the branches of the lacrimal, middle meningeal, and short posterior ciliary arteries, in the posterior orbit. These branches from the sheath enter the nerve and supply the superior and lateral periphery of the nerve.

The ophthalmic artery shows considerable variation in its pathways in the orbit and optic nerve. The posterior ciliary arteries also vary in their origin and course. The central retinal artery originates from the ophthalmic artery in only about half the cases. In other cases it comes from a trunk common with the ciliary arteries and penetrates the inferior aspect of the nerve, ensuring vascularization of its surface areas through its pial branches and of its depth by its intraneural branches. The ciliary arteries vary in number and pattern. Vascularization of the center of the optic nerve is assured by collateral branches from the trunk of the central retinal artery in the majority of cases. The existence of an individual and separate central artery of the optic nerve is a rare variation from normal.

The central retinal artery has a major role in the blood supply of the anterior part of the optic nerve in a majority of instances, contributing to both the peripheral and the axial systems. Anastomoses are usually established by the pial branches of the central retinal artery with the recurrent pial branches of the circle of Zinn-Haller and choroidal arteries and with the pial collateral branches from the ophthalmic artery and other orbital arteries.

Anastomoses occur between branches from the vascular circle of Zinn-Haller, derived from the posterior ciliary arteries, and the anterior branch of the central optic nerve artery. Capillaries from extraorbital cerebral vessels enter the pial sheath and supply the peripheral inferior portion of the nerve.

The main branch of the central artery of the retina passes to the center of the nerve and runs forward into the optic papilla and on to the surface of the retina (see Fig. 5-2).

The rather sharp division of the three areas of optic nerve blood supply, into superior peripheral, inferior peripheral, and central, helps to explain some of the visual field defects that are so characteristic of optic nerve lesions (e.g., altitudinal field loss with sharp horizontal border). The nerve fiber bundle defects seen in patients with arteriosclerotic optic atrophy, which closely simulate the glaucoma field, are also explainable on the basis of this blood supply.

The chiasm is profusely supplied by eleven arteries and a complicated network of anastomotic arterioles. Functional defects cannot therefore be attributed to occlusion of a single artery but to an intratissue capillary disturbance caused by either degeneration or external compression.

Dawson has studied the chiasmal circulation in a most thorough fashion. Cursory inspection of the vascular networks on the optic chiasm suggests no constant pattern, but more detailed examination shows a well-defined arrangement. Two sets of arterial anastomotic systems, prechiasmal and circuminfundibular, are defined in the chiasmal region.

In a comprehensive series of autopsy observations of the arterial blood supply of the extracerebral portions of the visual pathways, Bergland and Ray studied the chiasmal circulation in great detail. They point out that the optic nerve, chiasm, and optic tracts pass through the circle of Willis (Fig. 5-3), coursing below the anterior cerebral and anterior communicating artery and above the posterior cerebral and communicating arteries and the basilar artery. This oblique course of the chiasm

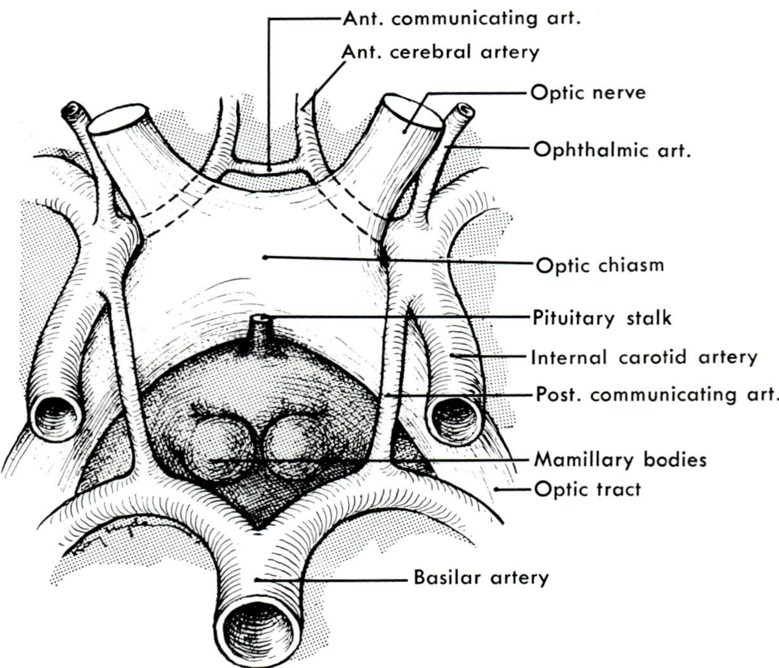

Fig. 5-3. Relationships of chiasm to basilar arterial system of brain, pituitary body and pituitary stalk, tuber cinereum, and mamillary bodies as seen from below.

through the circle of Willis permits a natural division of its blood supply into a plentiful inferior group of vessels from the carotid and posterior vessels of the circle and a sparse superior group from the anterior portion of the circle of Willis.

Most small vessels coursed toward the median eminence and infundibulum and are properly called superior hypophyseal arteries. From four to eight vessels were found on each side with many anastomoses in this complex. The superior group included one to four small vessels arising from either anterior cerebral artery. They extended to the upper surfaces of the optic nerves and tracts but only to the lateral parts of the chiasm. Vessels were seldom seen above the lamina terminalis. The many vessels entering the central part of the chiasm from below were apparent on coronal section. Silicone rubber injections of the chiasmal vasculature confirmed these observations, especially the rich arterial network of the inferior surfaces of the optic nerves, tracts, and chiasm.

In the vast majority of cases, functional disturbance in the chiasm is the result of circulatory impairment. External forces sufficient to compress, distort, or stretch the chiasm will most certainly impair the blood flow in the capillary network and result in neuronal anoxia and dysfunction.

The optic tract and external geniculate body are supplied by a whole series of vessels that enter these structures at various levels in their backward course.

In its anterior portion the tract derives its blood supply from the same arteries that supply the posterior portion of the chiasm, namely, (1) internal carotid, (2) middle cerebral, and (3) posterior communicating.

The posterior two thirds of the optic tract is supplied by the anterior choroidal artery. This artery arises from the internal carotid artery and runs backward in close association with the tract. It gives off branches to the temporal lobe and the lateral ventricle, as well as to the tract, the external geniculate body, and the beginning of the optic radiations.

The external geniculate body also receives branches from (1) the posterior choroidal artery and (2) the posterior cerebral artery.

The optic radiations are supplied by the following arteries:

1. The anterior choroidal supplies the anterior portion, chiefly the optic peduncle, after having passed through or under the optic tract and external geniculate body.
2. The posterior choroidal arteries also give a fine network of branches to the optic peduncle.
3. The middle cerebral artery, through its deep optic branch, supplies the anterior and middle portion of the radiation where it lies lateral to the ventricle.
4. The posterior cerebral artery, through its perforating branches, supplies the posterior portion of the optic radiation before it enters the area of the calcarine cortex.
5. The calcarine artery, arising from the posterior cerebral artery, supplies the posterior portion of the radiation as it passes back of the lateral ventricle and enters the occipital lobe.

Smith and Richardson have traced the course and origin of the arteries supplying the visual cortex of one hemisphere of thirty-two human brains. They found that the calcarine artery usually supplies most of the visual area but in three-fourths of the specimens it was not the only vessel supplying this area nor was its distribution restricted to this area.

Branches of the posterior temporal artery helped to supply the visual cortex in half of the specimens. These branches always supply a part of the macular area of the cortex and may be a factor in the preservation of central vision when the calcarine artery is occluded.

In some specimens there was additional supply to the visual area from the parieto-occipital artery and also a direct contribution from the middle cerebral artery. This overlapping of vascular supply with the calcarine branches of the posterior cerebral artery, the posterior cortical or deep optic branch of the middle cerebral artery (see Fig. 5-1), and the branches of the posterior temporal artery, all of which may supply a part of the macular area of the occipital cortex, is the most rational explanation for the phenomenon of macular sparing in the visual field defects resulting from severe damage to the visual cortex.

Vascular lesions of the visual pathway that produce visual field defects are common and destructive and have certain characteristics of diagnostic importance in differentiating them from other diseases affecting the visual pathway. They may affect any portion of the pathway from the retina to the occipital cortex. They are almost always sudden in onset, although they may be preceded by telltale prodromal symptoms. The resulting visual field defects are usually dense, steep-margined, and permanent.

These vascular lesions may be divided into three general categories:

1. Those that produce pressure on the nerve fiber bundles of the visual pathway, such as aneurysm and subdural hematoma.
2. Those that destroy the nerve fiber bundles by hemorrhage into them, such as retinal vascular lesions and intracerebral hemorrhage.
3. Those that give rise to infarction in the nerve fiber bundles by arterial insufficiency and occlusion, such as retinal arterial occlusion, internal carotid and ophthalmic artery stenosis and occlusion, and middle and posterior cerebral arterial occlusion with resulting cerebral infarction and extensive visual field loss.
4. Inflammatory lesions, such as giant cell optic nerve or cerebral arteritis.

Such vascular lesions are further subdivided according to their location within the visual pathway and will be considered separately under their anatomic headings.

Aneurysms that give rise to direct compression of nerve fiber bundles are most commonly located in the vessels of the circle of Willis and consequently involve the intracranial portion of the optic nerve, the chiasm, and the anterior optic tract (Fig. 5-4). They give rise to unilateral scotomas, asymmetric bitemporal visual field defects, unilateral nasal or binasal field loss, and highly incongruous homonymous hemianopsia.

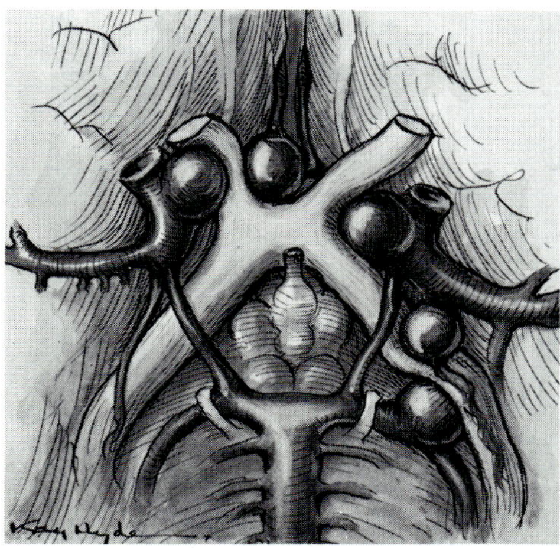

Fig. 5-4. Sites of aneurysms in basilar arterial system of brain. This is composite drawing from series of cases proved at operation, autopsy, and by angiography.

Subdural hematoma may cause direct compression of the visual pathway or, by producing herniation of the mesial (hippocampal) gyrus of the temporal lobe through the tentorial opening, compress and obstruct the posterior cerebral artery with resulting infarction in the calcarine cortex.

In direct compression of the anterior visual pathway, the resulting contralateral homonymous hemianopsia is likely to have a sloping margin and to be incongrous. When posterior cerebral artery compression from temporal lobe herniation results in visual cortex infarction, the field loss is congruous, dense, and steep-margined and is likely to be associated with ipsilateral third nerve palsy of varying degree.

Vascular lesions that damage the nerve fiber bundles of the visual pathway by hemorrhage into them may occur at any level of the pathway. Hemorrhages into the retina, either venous or arterial in origin, produce visual loss and scotomas, depending on their size and location. Hemorrhage within the optic nerve, chiasm, and optic tract is rare. The classic example of extensive visual field loss resulting from hemorrhage is that occurring from the lenticulostriate or stroke artery involving the posterior limb of the internal capsule, with contralateral homonymous hemianopsia and hemiplegia.

Intracerebral hemorrhage may occur from small arterioles in the temporal, parietal, and occipital lobe, giving rise to characteristic homonymous hemianoptic visual field loss, depending on the site of the lesion. As might be expected, the field defects are sudden in onset and usually dense. When the hemorrhage occurs in the temporal lobe, the resulting homonymous hemianopsia, if incomplete, is incongrous, whereas a very small hemorrhagic lesion of the calcarine cortex will produce exquisitely symmetric homonymous hemianoptic scotomas. Examples of such visual field defects will be illustrated in later chapters.

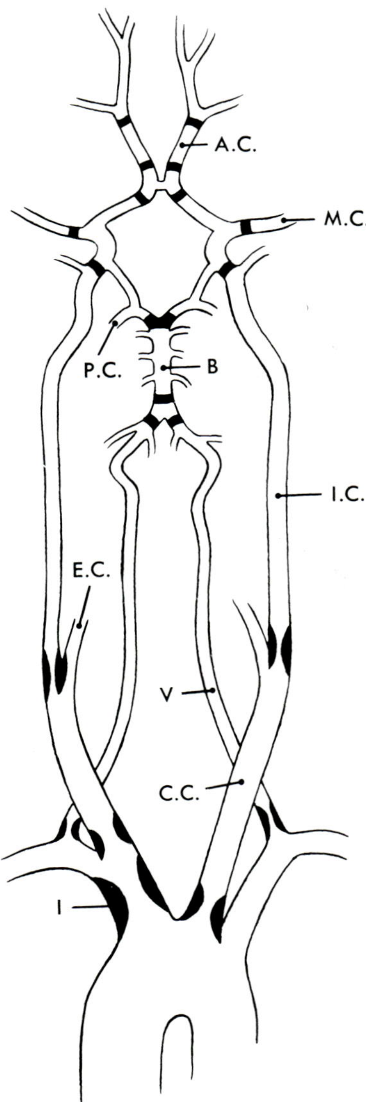

Fig. 5-5. Principal sites of atherosclerosis and plaque formation in cerebral circulation. *A.C.,* Anterior cerebral; *M.C.,* middle cerebral; *P.C.,* posterior cerebral or posterior communicating; *I.C.,* internal carotid; *E.C.,* external carotid; *C.C.,* common carotid; *V,* vertebral; *I,* innominate; *B,* basilar.

Arterial insufficiency and occlusion give rise to a wide variety of visual field defects that may be of great value in diagnosing and localizing the site of the lesion. Such occlusions are frequently preceded by periods of relative insufficiency and stenosis in the artery and its smaller branches. Attacks of arterial insufficiency give rise to transient visual loss, which may be monocular or homonymous (bilateral) and hemianoptic, and are frequently associated with transient neurologic deficits.

The transient disturbances are probably the result of the passage of small emboli through the cerebral and ocular circulation. These emboli arise from atherosclerotic plaques in the carotid, vertebral, and basilar arteries and have been photographed in the cerebral and retinal circulation (Fig. 5-5). Hollenhorst believes that the bright plaques that he described in the retinal arteries are, in fact, cholesterol crystals. Others consider them to be fat emboli.

It is probable that the cerebral and ocular emboli are of two types:

1. A fibrin-platelet microembolus that forms on an atherosclerotic plaque in the carotid artery and may reach the small vessels of the brain and retina.

   These are susceptible to lysis by plasmin and therefore do not produce permanent visual loss.
2. A lipid-debris microembolus discharged from an atherosclerotic plaque and lodging in a retinal or cerebral arteriole, producing infarction and permanent loss of function.

   These lipid-debris emboli are not lysed by fibrin and do not respond to anticoagulant therapy.

Such emboli produce transient or permanent visual field defects that are characteristic of the site of the infarct and hence are of localizing value:

1. Occlusion of the ophthalmic artery or its branches, the central artery of the optic nerve and the central retinal artery, causes sudden, permanent, and marked monocular loss of vision.
   a. If the embolus lodges in the anterior optic nerve near the lamina cribrosa, it often produces a nerve fiber bundle type of scotoma that is indistinguishable from the one caused by advanced open-angle glaucoma (see Chapter 11).
   b. When the central retinal artery is occluded, total visual loss usually results in that eye; but if the embolus obstructs only a retinal arteriole, the result is a sector-type or quadrantic visual field defect corresponding to the retinal area supplied by that vessel (see Chapter 10).
2. Stenosis or occlusion of the middle cerebral artery may result from extension of the atherosclerotic process from the internal carotid artery or from emboli. Such lesions produce cerebral infarction and typically cause contralateral homonymous hemianopsia, which is usually quadrantic and may be incongruous in character. If the ophthalmic artery is simultaneously involved, there may be a homolateral nerve fiber bundle or Bjerrum scotoma combined with contralateral homonymous hemianopsia (see Chapter 11).
3. Vertebral and basilar artery disease frequently gives rise to posterior cerebral and calcarine artery involvement, with resulting visual cortex infarction and contralateral homonymous hemianoptic field defects of sudden onset and great variety. Such defects may be total on one side, or they may take the form of small central or peripheral homonymous hemianoptic scotomas, depending on the size of the occluded vessel and the area of cortex supplied by it. They are always steep-margined and dense, frequently irregular in shape, and invariably exquisitely symmetric in the two eyes.
4. Occipital cortical infarction is an uncommon complication of cardiopulmonary bypass surgery. It manifests itself by a postoperative complaint of defective vision varying from mile transient blurring to total blindness. More frequent is the finding of homonymous hemianoptic deficits that are dense, steep-

margined, and completely congruous. These characteristics localize the lesion in the occipital cortex, and such localization has been confirmed by a computerized axial tomography (CAT) scan.

Neurologic deficits either transient or permanent are often associated with the visual distrubances just noted, their type and location being dependent on the artery involved. Localization of such lesions requires both neurologic and ophthalmologic studies.

Ophthalmodynamometry may give much information and should be routinely used when vascular insufficiency is suspected. The findings must be correlated with brachial blood pressure measurements and with all pertinent neurologic and ophthalmologic data. Final proof of arterial occlusion often rests with arteriography, but even this examination has its limitations and its risks and must be used and interpreted with some caution.

Vascular lesions are among the most frequent producers of visual field defects and as such deserve special consideration. It is often necessary to differentiate between them and neoplastic disease involving the visual pathway. Comparative examples of visual field defects of vascular origin will be shown in later chapters.

CHAPTER 6

Normal visual field

The normal monocular visual field is a slightly irregular oval measuring from fixation, approximately 60 degrees upward and 60 degrees inward, 70 to 75 degrees downward, and 100 to 110 degrees outward. The field of the two eyes together, or the binocular field, is a combination of the right and left monocular fields. The whole binocular field forms a rough oval extending to about 200 degrees laterally and 130 degrees vertically. The extreme extent of the visual field is limited by the nose and the brows, but within the anatomic restrictions imposed by these structures the normal field may be considered from a practical point of view as being made up of two portions: (1) the central field, which constitutes that portion of the visual field within the 30-degree radius of fixation, and (2) the peripheral field, which makes up the remainder of the visual field. Within these areas the normal visual field is determined by the visual acuity of the normal person in the various areas of the visual field (Fig. 6-1 and Plate 2).

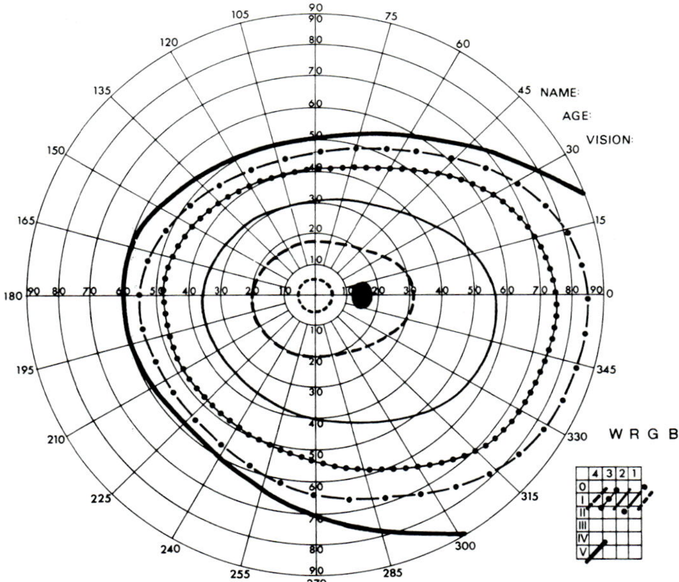

Fig. 6-1. Normal isopters of young adults measured with Goldmann perimeter.

If we refer once again to Traquair's concept of the island hill of vision, the outline of the various contours of this hill may be projected upon a map as contour lines that, in the nomenclature of perimetry, are termed isopters. The central point from which these isopters are measured corresponds to the visual axis and is known as the point of fixation. The isopters, or contour lines, are designated by the size of the stimulus and the distance at which it is viewed by the observer, expressed as a fraction. Thus the isopter for a 1-mm test object observed by the patient at a distance of 2 meters is expressed by the fraction 1/2000 and designates the specific area of the visual field within which the normal person should be able to see this stimulus.

In static or profile perimetry these stationary stimuli are presented with a luminance below threshold that is gradually increased until seen by the patient. A number of retinal spots are tested along a visual field meridian, and the graphic plot of these threshold values yields a profile section of sensitivity through the hill of vision (see Figs. 2-20 and 6-2). By this method of splitting the hill of vision and charting its profile, areas of partial loss of vision are mapped as shallow to deep depressions extending somewhat below the level of the normal profile. Absolute scotomas, mapped with the largest and brightest available stimuli, are shown as deep pits extending down to the level of the sea of blindness (e.g., the normal blind spot).

For purposes of convenience in charting, the visual field is generally divided into four quadrants. A horizontal line passing through fixation divides the field into an upper and lower half, and these in turn are divided into quadrants by a vertical

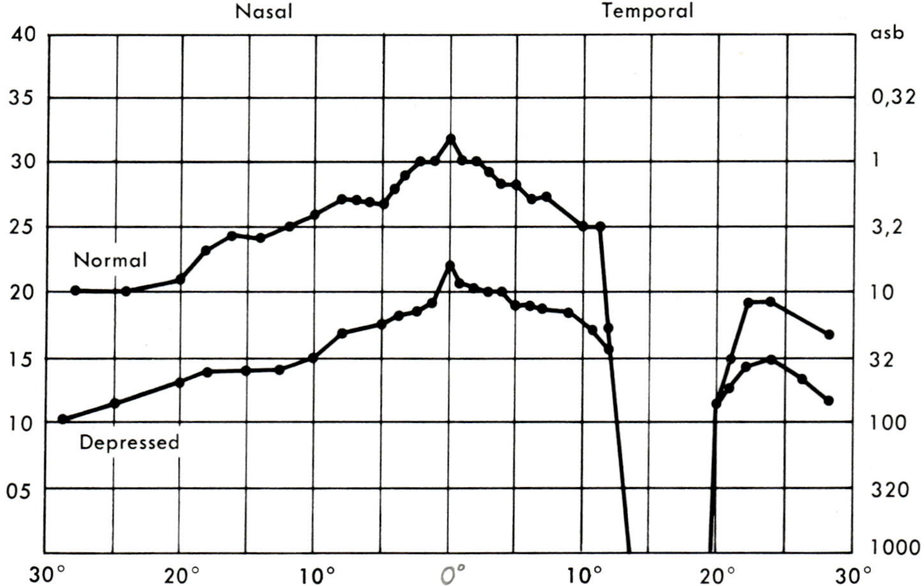

Fig. 6-2. Recording of section of sensitivity or static perimetry profile of normal and depressed visual field.

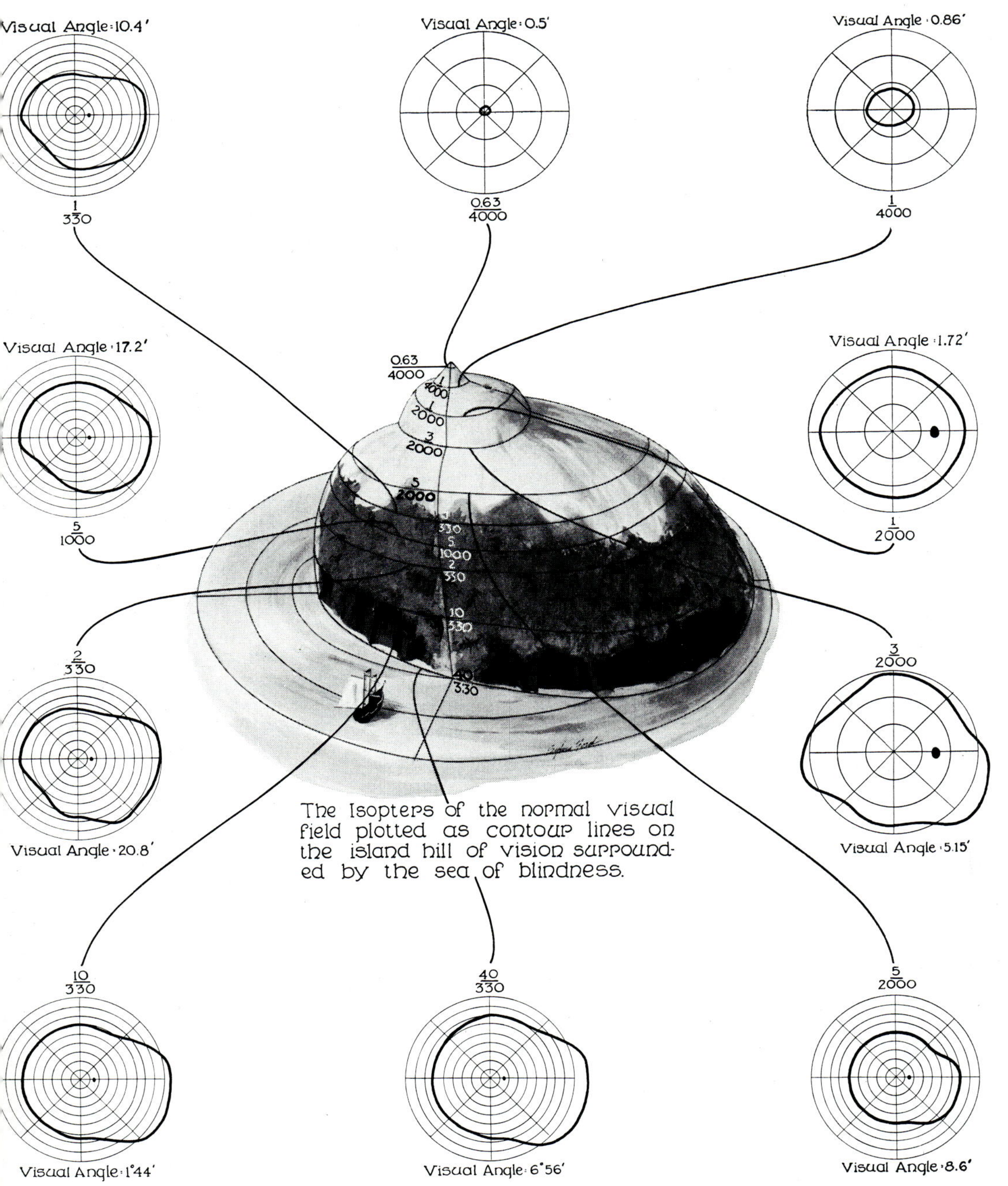

Plate 2. Normal visual field.

line also passing through fixation. The upper and lower halves of the visual field are almost equal in size, but the nasal and temporal halves of the field are quite different because of the eccentric position of the fixation point, the temporal half being considerably larger than the nasal half. This eccentricity of the field is largely caused by the configuration of the orbit and the limitation of the nasal field by the nose and brow (see Fig. 6-2).

The binocular field is made up of the overlapping uniocular fields. The central portion, which is common to both eyes, is almost circular, with an average diameter of somewhat over 120 degrees. The temporal crescent extends for approximately 30 degrees to each side of the paired portion of the binocular field. The clinical perimetrist occasionally may be concerned with the temporal crescent in the interpretation of a homonymous hemianoptic defect, but for the most part is is the uniocular field that is clinical importance.

As mentioned previously, the visual field is usually tested with varying-sized test objects at varying distances. Multiple isopters are examined with stimuli that subtend varying visual angles. It is only by this means that the relative visual acuity within the visual field can be quantitatively estimated, and it is this quantitative examination of visual acuity within all areas of the visual field that constitutes quantitative perimetry.

The isopter is designated by the fraction $\frac{\text{object}}{\text{distance}}$ or $\frac{\text{O}}{\text{D}}$ or, numerically, 1/330 or 2/2000, or whatever the notation may be that indicates the size of the stimulus and the distance at which it is used. This is readily converted to a visual angle in degrees or minutes by multiplying the fraction by the constant $\frac{180}{\pi}$, which equals 57.3. For example, to convert the fraction 2/1000, multiply it by $\frac{180}{\pi}$, which equals 0.114 degree, or 6.84 minutes, the visual angle subtended by the 2-mm test object at a distance of 1 meter.

Because there are many factors that influence the size of the normal visual field, the average isopter has varied somewhat, depending on the investigator compiling the data. Thus, the figures for the normal visual field isopters as given by Traquair vary somewhat from those of Rönne and other observers. In general, however, there is surprisingly close agreement among investigators when one considers the difficulties involved in establishing such standards for a subjective examination.

The normal blind spot is remarkably constant in position and size. It is a vertical oval with steep edges. Its center is located 15.5 degrees temporal to fixation and 1.5 degrees below the horizontal meridian. It is 5.5 degrees wide and 7.5 degrees high. Surrounding the area of absolute blindness is a narrow amblyopic zone of 1 degree in width when tested with the 1- and 2-mm test objects at a distance of 2 meters. Variations in the blind spot are of considerable clinical importance, partly because of the constancy of its normal dimensions.

It will be noted from Table 2 that the temporal limits of the 1/2000 isopter lie

Table 2. Average normal visual field isopters (visual field in degrees)

Size of test object	Distance	Isopter notation	Visual angle	Temporally	Inferiorly	Nasally	Superiorly
For white							
1 mm	330	1/300	10.32′	80	60	55	50
2 mm	330	2/330	20.70′	85	65	60	50
3 mm	330	3/330	31.08′	90	70	60	60
5 mm	330	5/330	51.60′	100	80	60	60
40 mm	330	40/330	6.56°	110	80	60	60
1 mm	1000	1/1000	3.42′	25	25	25	25
2 mm	1000	2/1000	6.84′	26	26	26	26
3 mm	1000	3/1000	10.20′	38	30	30	26
5 mm	1000	5/1000	17.10′	75	50	50	50
10 mm	1000	10/1000	34.20′	90	75	60	60
20 mm	1000	20/1000	1.14°	100	75	60	60
40 mm	1000	40/1000	2.25°	100	75	60	60
1 mm	2000	1/2000	1.70°	24	24	24	24
3 mm	2000	3/2000	5.10′	30	30	24	
5 mm	2000	5/2000	8.52′	70	50	50	50
1 mm	4000	1/4000	0.85′	10	8	10	5
3 mm	4000	3/4000	2.75′	10	12	15	10
For green							
3 mm	330	3/330	31.08′	18	12	18	10
5 mm	330	5/330	51.60′	30	24	18	18
2 mm	1000	2/1000	6.84′	3	3	4	2
5 mm	1000	5/1000	17.10′	8	5	7	5
For red							
3 mm	330	3/330	31.08′	39	15	15	15
5 mm	330	5/330	51.60′	45	29	23	26
2 mm	1000	2/1000	6.84′	5	4	6	4
5 mm	1000	5/1000	17.10′	8	5	8	6
For blue							
3 mm	330	3/330	31.08′	63	30	30	25
5 mm	330	5/330	51.60′	75	46	38	38
2 mm	1000	2/1000	6.84′	12	12	14	9
5 mm	1000	5/1000	17.10′	18	15	19	13

at 24 degrees from fixation. This is assuming that the patient is alert, rested, and in good health. It also supposes a uniformity of apparatus, illumination, and method that is almost impossible to achieve. This is not to say that perimetry is highly inaccurate but only that certain variations within the normal field are permissible. The actual size of a given isopter is of less importance than its shape, especially in relation to other isopters, and the visual acuity within its boundaries.

A depressed field in which all isopters are smaller than normal may still be a normal field for a given patient, a reduced illumination, a lessened ratio of contrast between stimulus and background, etc.

Perimetrists should have their own fields of vision examined not once but many times and under differing conditions. Only thus will they come to know the normal variations in the normal visual field.

PHYSIOLOGIC AND PSYCHOLOGIC FACTORS IN EXAMINATION OF THE VISUAL FIELD

As has been mentioned, many factors enter into the determination of the visual field in any individual. Because of this there is, in fact, no such thing as a "normal" visual field. The visual field will vary in some degree in a single individual, depending on his age, the number of times the field has been examined previously, the state of his health and general fatigue at the moment of the examination, the size of the pupils, the amount of light in the examining room, the ratio of background light to stimulus illumination, the ability of the individual to concentrate on the task at hand, and the resulting variation in his speed of response to stimuli within the visual field. In practice, these variables are of importance and must be reckoned with, especially in consecutive examinations of the visual field of a single individual over a period of time.

The steadiness of fixation of an eye will affect the size of its visual field. If fixation were completely steady, all objects in the visual field would gradually disappear, those in the peripheral field more rapidly than those in the central areas. Because complete steadiness of fixation is almost impossible, there is, during a perimetric examination, a constant slight movement of the eye. Images in the peripheral portion of the retina move slightly with these shifts in fixation, and the question of retinal fatigue is of theoretical rather than practical importance.

The degree of dark adaptation or light adaptation of the eye may be of importance in the examination of the visual field. When the eye is light-adapted, vision is said to be photopic; and when it is dark-adapted, vision is scotopic. During photopic vision the eye is adapted to illuminations commonly met in good daylight or in good artificial illumination. Light adaptation is a rapid process and is generally done within a minute or two. Complete dark adaptation is slower, requiring more nearly an hour. At levels of illumination between complete light adaptation and complete dark adaptation, the retina makes an effort to come into equilibrium with any change in illumination, so that at intermediate levels of illumination both rods and cones are active. This intermediate zone of illumination in visual field testing has been designated as mesopic, and there is good reason to believe that under such conditions the visual field examination is more accurate in uncovering pathologic defects than in the less physiologic photopic or scotopic examination. Much interesting work has been done in this area by G. E. Jayle and his co-workers, who have developed and experimented with elaborate instruments capable of producing almost unlimited variations in luminance in background and stimuli.

It should be mentioned that reduction in the illumination of the stimuli and the background has a profound effect on the visual field, whether this reduction is by means of filters or rheostats or whether it is due to the transmission of the light from the stimulus through ocular media that are not perfectly transparent. Thus one would not expect to find the same visual field defects in a glaucomatous eye with a perfectly clear lens as in that same eye with cloudy media.

Such relatively simple movements as voluntary or involuntary narrowing of the lid aperture during examination of the visual field will alter the size of the field. This may be of importance, for example, in patients with myopia or in patients with high degrees of astigmatism who narrow their lid apertures habitually. The dryness of the cornea may affect the visual field by making it very difficult for the patient to maintain steady fixation without blinking.

It has been shown that the contrast between the object and the object's background is a major factor in the measurement of visual acuity whether in the foveal area or in the peripheral portion of the visual field. The physiologic processes underlying discrimination of form depend on contrast in the image. With reduction in contrast, visual acuity apparently decreases. Within certain limits a decrease in stimulus luminosity or an increase in background luminosity in the examination of the visual field will heighten the sensitivity of the test.

Some of the variable factors influencing the size of the normal visual field are (1) age, (2) pupillary miosis, (3) clarity of the media, (4) refractive error, and (5) aphakia.

1. Age depresses the central isopters of the field so that, for example, the 1/2000 isopter falls well within the blind spot instead of just outside it and the peak of the profile of the hill of vision is lowered (see Fig. 6-2). Thus an erroneous impression may be given that there is a baring of the blind spot, which may be interpreted as a pathologic deficit. The decrease in the central isopters appears to be a continuous and gradual change progressing from youth to old age.
2. It is well known that pupillary miosis depresses both peripheral and central isopters of the normal visual field and may exaggerate the size and density of established defects. This is of particular importance in glaucoma under treatment with miotics. One should periodically examine the visual fields of such patients with their pupils dilated.
3. Decrease in the clarity of the media has a striking effect on the visual field. The presence of a cataract or vitreous opacification acts in the same way as a filter so that, in effect, the visual field is being tested under reduced illumination with consequent depression of all its isopters and exaggeration of its defects.
4. Uncorrected errors of refraction affect the visual field in several ways. A highly myopic eye should be fully corrected if the field is to be tested on the tangent screen at 2 meters; but it may require no lenses if the examination is performed at 330 mm. Presbyopia, on the other hand, requires correction for perimeter examination only.

   Areas of localized myopia (as in posterior staphyloma) or hyperopia (as in macular elevation) may show so-called refraction scotomas, which disappear when the area of depression or elevation is brought to focus with lenses. I have seen one such refraction scotoma with markedly enlarged blind spots due to extasia or posterior staphyloma of the sclera and optic nerve head. When the difference of 8 D between the macula and the nerve head was corrected with lenses, the blind spot enlargement decreased markedly while a relative depression of the central isopter shifted the scotoma to the fixation area.

5. Beasley has reported exhaustively on the effects of aphakia on the visual field. The results of his study of fifty aphakic patients showed that the multiple pattern method may be used if suitable ultraviolet filters are available. The aphakic field may be tested on the perimeter without correction if stimuli larger than 5 mm are used. Spectacle-corrected aphakic fields can be reliably tested only in the central 30 degrees. Contact lens correction of aphakia provides the best optical device for testing both peripheral and central fields. The aphakic visual field tested with contact lenses is 10 to 15 degrees smaller than the phakic field for the same-sized object. The uncorrected aphakic blind spot is slightly closer to fixation than the normal phakic blind spot and moves still closer as correction is added and vertex distance increases.

The psychologic processes of vision are of utmost importance in any consideration of the techniques of perimetry or in the interpretation of the visual fields resulting from those techniques. The subjective nature of the visual field examination has been repeatedly stressed. The examination is limited by the capacity of the patient to respond to it, and the perimetrist must be constantly on guard against making demands beyond the patient's capabilities. He must recognize that the responses of one individual to the examination may be entirely different from those of another; therefore, the time required for perimetric examination of different persons with the same disease process may vary from 10 minutes to an hour.

The experience of the perimetrist will enable the evaluation, within certain limits, of the patient's intelligence, his speed of reaction, his ability to concentrate, and his degree of suggestibility. Any or all of these factors may alter the visual field. In the perimetric examination the personal equation and the training of the clinician are of considerable importance, and no form of examination makes greater demands.

The perimetric chart, therefore, should not be regarded as conveying a mathematically accurate and precise expression of the state of the peripheral vision. It indicates only the kind and degree of defect present at that moment. It must be interpreted with a knowledge of what perimetric techniques entail and of the psychologic background of the individual whose record of peripheral vision it is.

Variations in the visual field, of physiologic and psychologic origin, are compounded and exaggerated in direct ratio to the complexity of the examining technique. Simple and flexible techniques have been stressed both in method and in apparatus. The more the perimetrist is concerned with mastery of a complicated method or instrument, the less attention can be given to the infinite vagaries of the human organism, a portion of whose nervous system is being examined.

The perimetrist must have knowledge of human anatomy, pathology, and psychology. The methods of examination must be varied according to that knowledge.

There will be numerous occasions when an examiner receives an impression of a visual field defect that is definite enough to be of considerable diagnostic value but is impossible to chart with any accuracy. In such circumstances the statement of the impression is of more value than the plotting of a chart, which is highly inaccurate and gives a false impression of precise localization.

It should be obvious from the preceding that in order to correctly interpret a visual field defect the examiner must analyze the defect in terms of its size, shape, density, and other characteristics. To be valid, this analysis must actually be accomplished during the examination itself. Therefore, in order to correctly analyze and interpret a visual field defect, the perimetric examination must be performed by the person who is to interpret the result. In short, ophthalmologists must be their own perimetrists.

Examinations of the visual field with various screening devices provide exceptions to this statement. There is only one way to conduct the field examination on the Harrington-Flocks instrument or the Friedmann analyzer; the examination is performed in the same unvarying manner. The same is true of the examination with the automated or computerized perimeters such as the Baylor Programmer, the Fieldmaster, and the Octopus system. Here the static method of randomized presentation of suprathreshold stimuli, which are programmed by computer, demands the use of complex automated instruments and a completely rigid examination technique.

PART TWO

Interpretation of defects in visual fields

CHAPTER 7

Abnormal visual fields

Three basic defects of the visual field are (1) contraction, (2) depression, and (3) scotomas.

CONTRACTION

True contraction is relatively rare. To satisfy the definition of contraction, the area of the visual field that is defective must be totally blind to all stimuli, no matter how bright or how large, presented in that area. The edge of the defect must be the same regardless of the intensity of the stimulus.

Contractions are usually peripheral defects (Fig. 7-2), but a scotoma may satisfy the definition of contraction if its boundaries are perpendicular (i.e., the same size for all stimuli) and if its area is totally blind to all stimuli, regardless of intensity, that will fit within its area. Thus the normal blind spot (in its absolute portion) can be classified as a true contraction because it is totally blind to all stimuli that can be encompassed by its area. Another example of a normal contraction in the visual field is that produced by a large nose or a very heavy brow.

A characteristic of true contraction is that if very large test objects are passed slowly across the border of the field defect from the anoptic to the seeing portion of the field the subject sees an increasingly larger portion of the stimulus as it comes into view. The stimulus is often described as though it were "a moon rising over the horizon."

Contractions may have various forms: (1) general peripheral, (2) partial peripheral, (3) sector, (4) partial hemianoptic, (5) total hemianoptic, and (6) scotomatous. The characteristics of each of these types of field loss will be discussed in detail later. They may be either monocular or binocular.

It must be understood that a true contraction of the visual field can be diagnosed only after all possible stimuli have been utilized to test it, up to and including a moving light or a waving bath towel if necessary (Fig. 7-3, *B*). One cannot state that a true contraction exists simply because of 100-mm test object is invisible in the defective portion of the field, if at the same time a test object 4 feet in diameter can be seen. It is obvious, then, that a visual field chart that shows a test for only one isopter cannot be spoken of as a contracted field. If may be a contracted field, but further isopters must be charted to prove it (Fig. 7-4, *B*).

Because true contraction with absolute defect in the visual field is rare, it is of

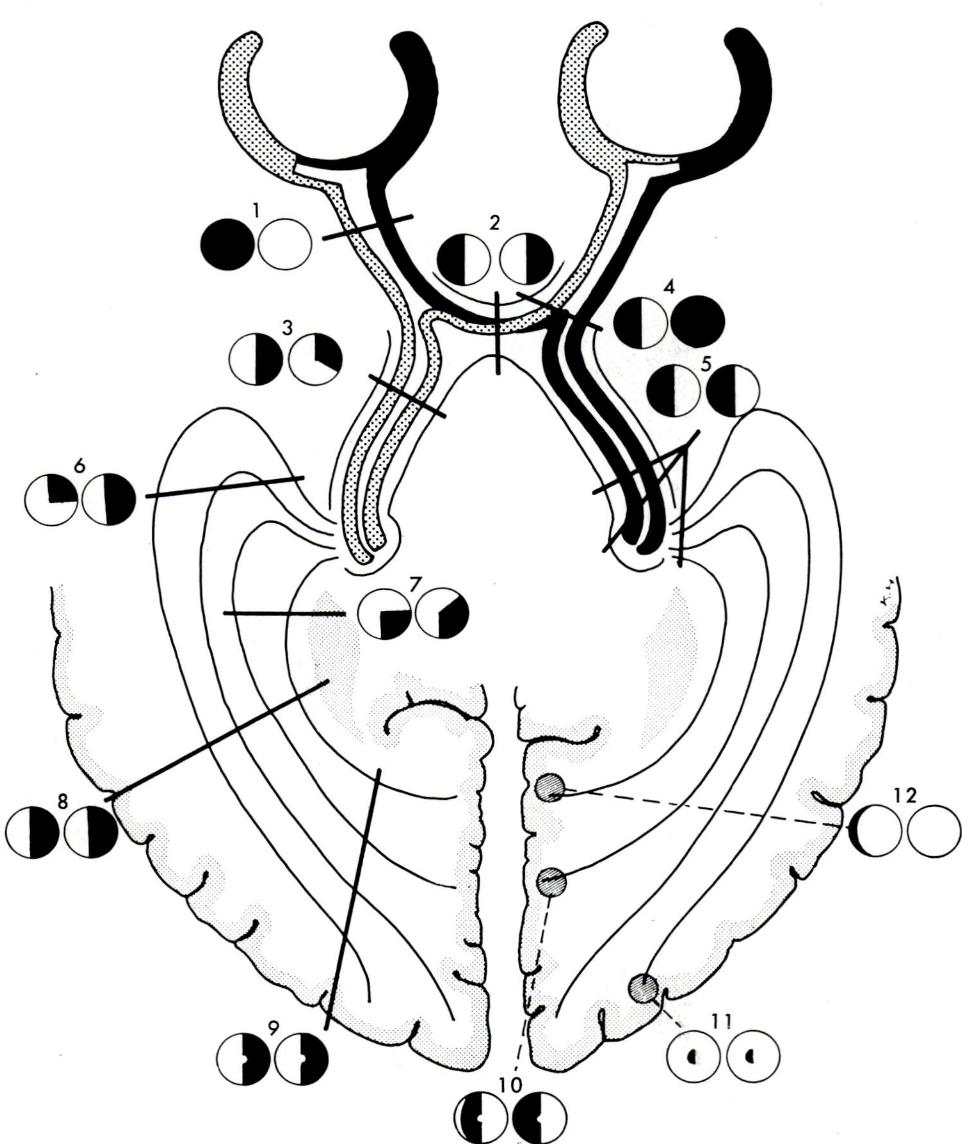

Fig. 7-1. For legend see opposite page.

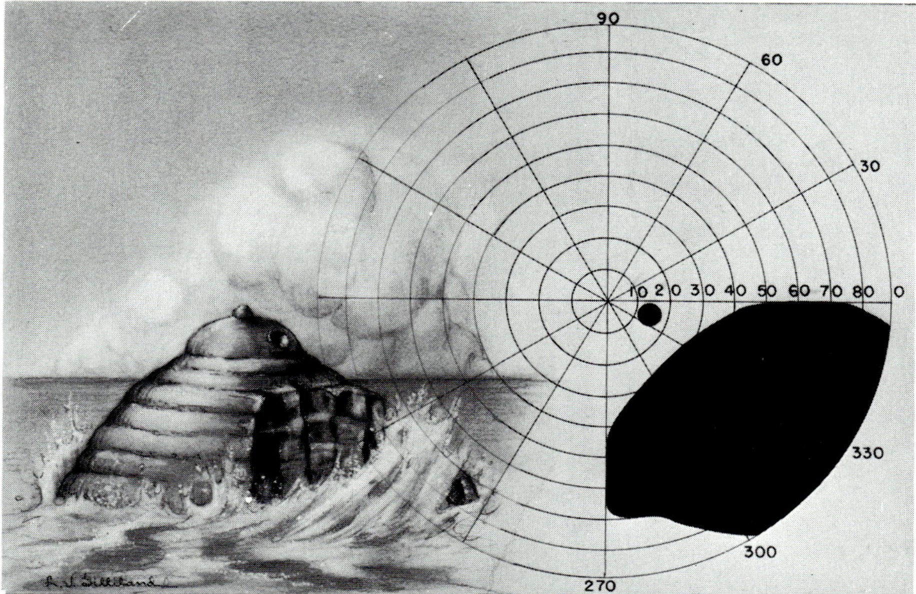

Fig. 7-2. Diagrammatic representation of erosion of coastline of hill of vision to produce contraction in peripheral visual field.

Fig. 7-1. Abnormal visual field. Schematic representation of visual pathway showing sites of total interruption of nerve fibers and various abnormal visual fields produced by such interruption.

1. Optic nerve—blindness on side of lesion, with normal contralateral field
2. Chiasm—bitemporal hemianopsia
3. Optic tract—contralateral incongruous homonymous hemianopsia
4. Optic nerve—chiasmal junction; blindness on side of lesion with contralateral temporal hemianopsia or hemianoptic scotoma
5. Posterior optic tract, external geniculate ganglion, posterior limb of internal capsule—complete contralateral homonymous hemianopsia or incomplete incongruous contralateral homonymous hemianopsia
6. Optic radiation; anterior loop in temporal lobe—incongruous contralateral homonymous hemianopsia or superior quadrantanopsia
7. Medial fibers of optic radiation—contralateral incongruous inferior homonymous quadrantanopsia
8. Optic radiation in parietal lobe—contralateral homonymous hemianopsia, sometimes slightly incongruous, with minimal macular sparing
9. Optic radiation in posterior parietal lobe and occipital lobe—contralateral congruous, homonymous hemianopsia with macular sparing
10. Midportion of calcarine cortex—contralateral congruous homonymous hemianopsia with wide macular sparing and sparing of contralateral temporal crescent
11. Tip of occipital lobe—contralateral congruous homonymous hemianoptic scotomas
12. Anterior tip of calcarine fissure—contralateral loss of temporal crescent with otherwise normal visual fields

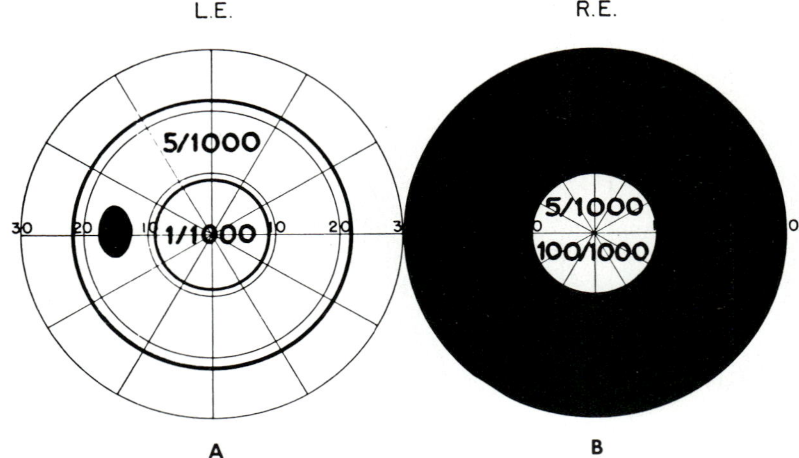

Fig. 7-3. A, Generally depressed visual field. All isopters are smaller than normal and each isopter is different is size. **B,** Contracted visual field. Field loss is absolute for all stimuli, regardless of size, and all isopters are same size.

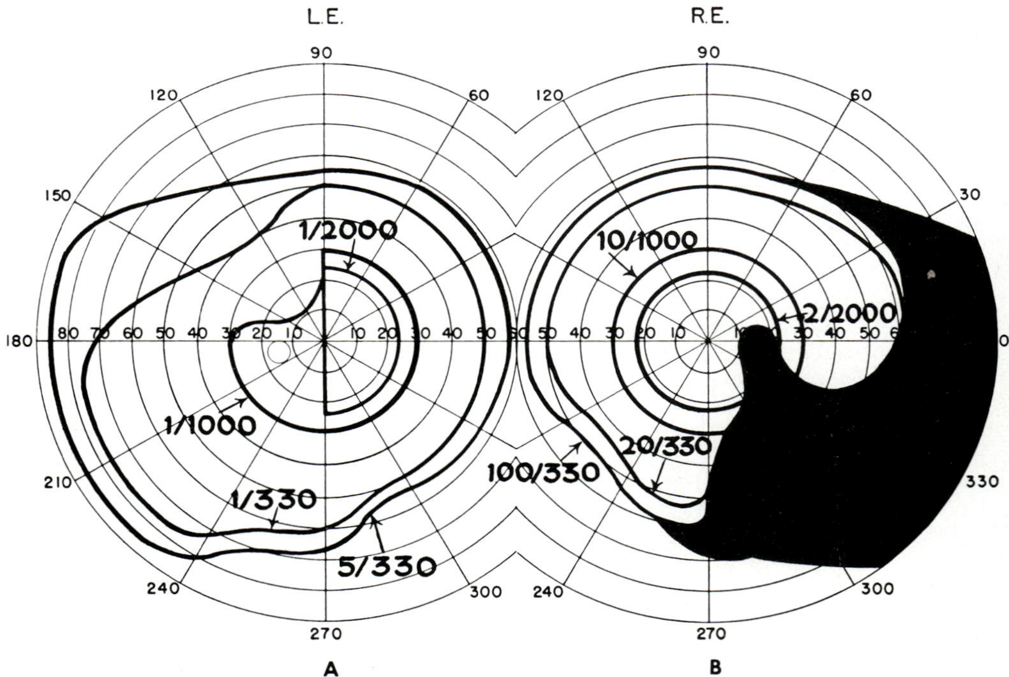

Fig. 7-4. A, Example of depression in visual field. Peripheral isopters are normal to large stimuli. Defect increases in central isopters with weak stimuli. From case of pituitary adenoma. **B,** Example of contraction in visual field. Lower sector defect is absolute and is same size for all stimuli. From case of gunshot injury to optic nerve.

considerable diagnostic importance when found and tends to narrow the differential diagnostic possibilities. It indicates a lesion that is (1) total in its effect on the visual pathway, (2) stable or nonprogressive, and (3) prognostically poor for recovery.

DEPRESSION

The great majority of visual field defects, both peripheral and central, are caused by depression of the visual acuity within a given area of the field. This visual acuity depression may be very marked (but not absolute) or very slight. It may involve only the extreme periphery or only the most minute portion of the fixation area. It may take an almost infinite variety of forms.

To determine that a visual field depression exists, at least two isopters must be studied. The more stimuli used, the more visual angles employed, and the more isopters charted, the clearer will be the nature of the visual field depression and the greater its diagnostic value. The analysis of visual field depression is the backbone and *raison d'être* of quantitative perimetry.

Scotomas and peripheral defects in the visual field are often spoken of as relative. In fact, any depression in the field is relative inasmuch as it may be present for one stimulus but not for a larger one. Thus the field may be completely normal in the 20/1000 isopter; it may show an area of dimness in the Bjerrum area for the 5/2000 stimulus; and it may develop a broad and absolute arcuate scotoma for the 1/2000 test object.

Visual field depression may be divided into (1) general depression and (2) local depression.

General depression

General depression of the visual field is one in which all the isopters are smaller than normal and some of the internal isopters are missing (see Fig. 7-3, *A*). There is a decrease in visual acuity in all areas of the visual field, including the central portion; and, in fact, the center isopters are the first and most severely affected. In general depression, the smaller and less intense the stimulus, the earlier its isopter is involved.

Using the island of vision surrounded by a sea of blindness to illustrate his point, Traquair likened visual field depression to a general sinking of the island into the sea so that all the contour lines of the island hill (isopters) became smaller or contracted. He pointed out that depression is less where the hill is steep and the contour lines are close together but becomes much more evident on areas of the hill that are gently sloping and where the contour lines or isopters are far apart. Slight depressions, then, may be most readily detected by testing the isopters that are the contour lines of the flat part of the hill of vision (i.e., those with small visual angles in the central portion of the field). This is why so many visual field defects are detectable on the tangent screen within the 20-degree circle. In this regard, then, the isopters of the central field reflect the changes that occur in the periphery (Fig. 7-4, *A*).

Static perimetry that maps the profile of the hill of vision shows even more clearly

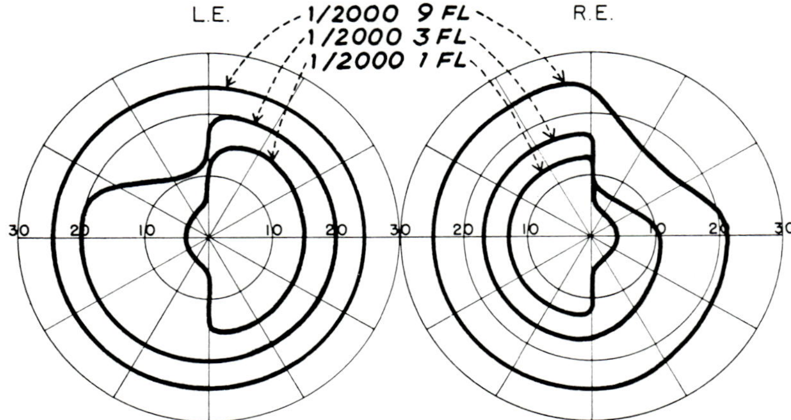

Fig. 7-5. Effect of variation in test object luminance on visual field defect produced by chromophobic adenoma of pituitary gland. Note that size of test object (visual angle) remained constant but luminance decreased from 9 footlamberts to 1 footlambert with increasing defect in visual field.

the depression of the entire field (see Fig. 6-2) or portions thereof (see Chapter 11) than does the contour map of conventional kinetic perimetry.

The generally depressed field may be produced in the normal person by decreasing the intensity of the stimulus. This may be accomplished by a decrease in illumination of the test object or by an increase in the relative background illumination; or it may be accomplished by using gray or dirty test objects or by interposing filters between the eye and the stimulus. General depression of the normal field will also result from opacities of the media of the eye, such as corneal scar, cataract, and vitreous haze; and for the same reason visual field defects due to local depression will be exaggerated.

It is possible, by varying resistance in the Lumiwand, to obtain a stimulus brightness of 1, 2, 3, or up to 10 footlamberts in the electroluminescent panel lamp, and studies have demonstrated detection of visual field defects with low luminance that had been missed under standard illumination. Known visual field defects are exaggerated in size and density when studied with decreased illumination, and in certain instances characteristics have been discovered in a field defect by analysis with variable luminance that have greatly assisted in interpretation of the defect.

In the case illustrated in Fig. 7-5, it would have been impossible to be certain that the 1/2000 isopter with standard illumination had detected a visual field loss, whereas the same isopter studied with reduced light would have revealed a characteristic bitemporal hemianopsia.

Local depression

Local depression of the visual field is the most common type of defect. It may take many forms, including scotoma, which will be discussed separately, and it has certain characteristics that should be studied in every case if the interpretation of the defect is to be of value.

Each visual field defect should be investigated and analyzed as to (1) position, (2) shape, (3) size, (4) intensity, (5) uniformity, (6) margins, and (7) onset and course.

Position

The position of the defect may vary widely. The defect may be peripheral and detectable in only the peripheral isopters with the arc or sphere perimeter; it may be central, involving only the fixation area, with normal field about it (central scotoma); or it may be a combination of both peripheral and central defect, located in any quadrant or part of a quadrant. It may be bilateral or unilateral.

Shape

The shape of the local visual field depression is of greater diagnostic value than its size or position. Besides scotomas, the most common type of local defect is the sector defect. This may be monocular or binocular. It may be wedged-shaped, regular, absolute or relative, connected to or separate from the blind spot, and limited by a vertical, horizontal, or oblique meridian.

The commonest form of monocular sector defect is that found in patients with glaucoma, in which the shape of the defect is determined by the fact that it is produced by physiologic interruption of a retinal nerve fiber bundle or bundles.

The typical binocular sector defect is hemianopsia, which may be subdivided and classified according to characteristics as follows: (1) homonymous, total, (2) homonymous, partial (congruous or incongruous), (3) homonymous quadrantanopsia, (4) bitemporal, (5) binasal, (6) crossed quadrantanopsia, (7) altitudinal, (8) double homonymous, (9) macula spared, and (10) macula split.

Total homonymous hemaniopsia (Fig. 7-6). Total homonymous hemianopsia is in reality a contraction of the visual field rather than a depression defect. It is bilateral and left-sided or right-sided, which means that there is total blindness in the temporal field of one eye and in the nasal field of the other eye. The dividing line between the seeing and nonseeing portions of the field is vertical and passes through the field directly above and below the fixation point. It may split the fixation point or it may spare the fixation point by passing a few degrees around it. Because there is no vision in any portion of the defective half of the fields, there can be no question of congruity or incongruity in the hemaniopsia, regardless of the location of the lesion or the intensity of the stimulus.

Total homonymous hemianopsia implies total destruction of the visual pathway behind the chiasm on one side. The lesion may be located at any level from the optic tract to the occipital lobe. It is probably more commonly seen in patients with vascular lesions than with tumors, and it is not an uncommon finding in patients with severe destruction of cerebral tissue from trauma.

In relation to other types of visual field defects, total homonymous hemianopsia is rather rare. Because it is usually due to widespread and severe cerebral tissue destruction, it is frequently associated with other neurologic signs and symptoms.

Partial homonymous hemianopsia. Partial homonymous hemianopsia is by far the most common visual field defect resulting from damage to the visual pathway in its

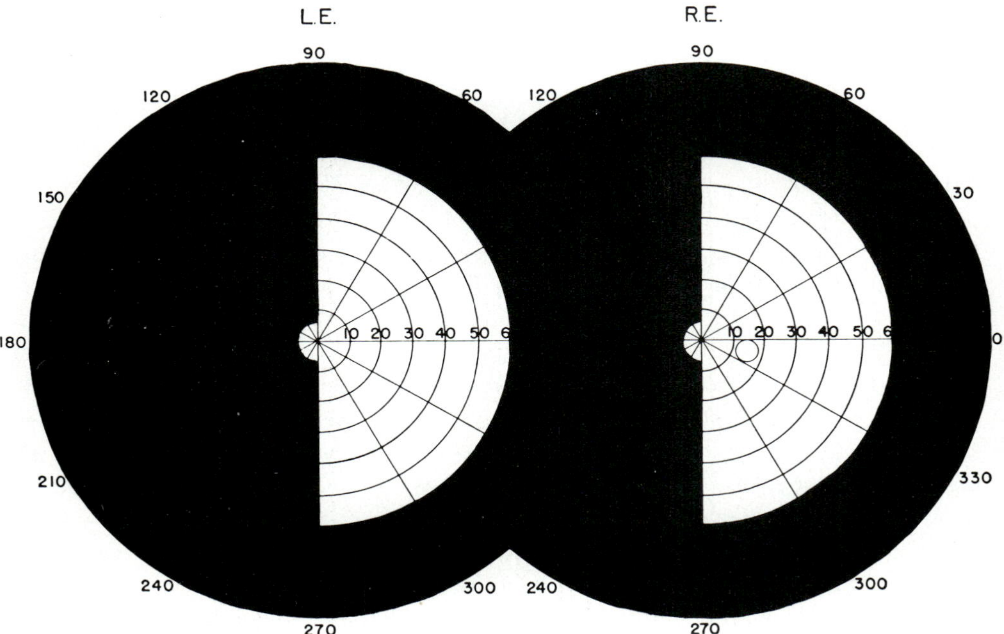

Fig. 7-6. Total homonymous hemianopsia with small area of macular sparing. Defect is same regardless of size of stimulus used.

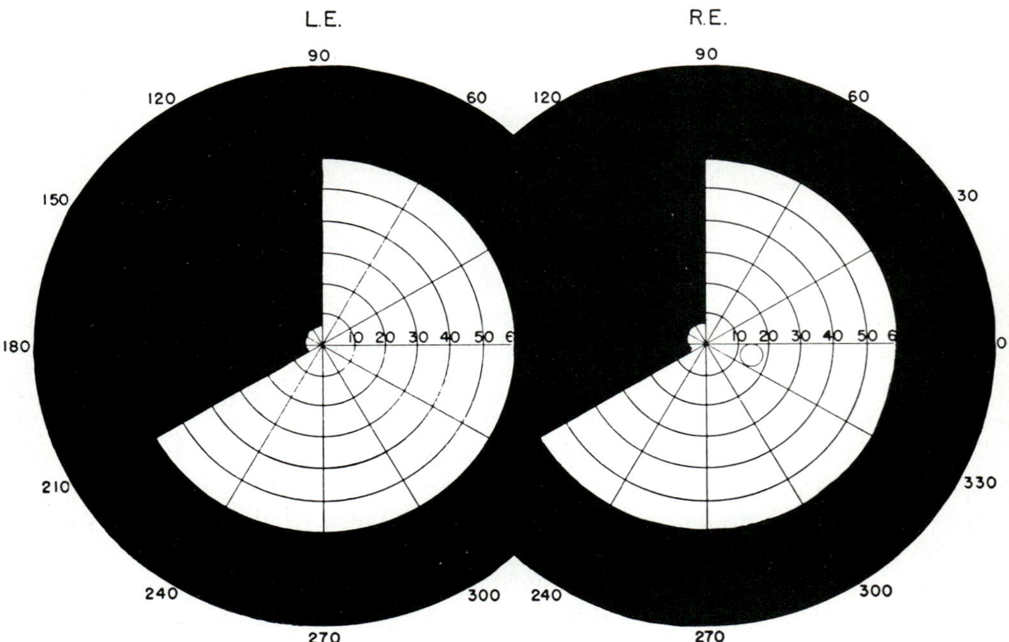

Fig. 7-7. Congruous partial homonymous hemianopsia. Margins of defect are usually steep.

postchiasmal portion. As its name suggests, it implies a partial destruction or physiologic interruption of the nerve fiber bundles at any level from the optic tract to the occipital pole. It may result from any type of lesion in this area, but it is most commonly found in patients with cerebral tumor, hemorrhage, or infarct.

Partial homonymous hemianopsia is a visual field defect in which somewhat less than one half of the visual field of each eye is blind or partially blind (Fig. 7-7). It is bilateral and right-sided or left-sided. The dividing line between the seeing and blind portions of the field is usually vertical in either the upper or the lower half of the field and horizontal or slanting in the other half.

Partial homonymous hemianoptic visual field defects may take an infinite variety of forms. The defect may involve only a small segment of one quadrant, an entire quadrant, an area within a quadrant in the form of a scotoma, or somewhat more than one quadrant. Because its margins are usually sloping, its shape will differ with the stimuli used to test it. The defect may be quadrantic in the 5/1000 isopter and total when tested with a 1-mm stimulus.

Quantitative perimetric techniques are of utmost value in examination and interpretation of these defects, and multiple isopters should always be examined, because it is only by careful analysis of such multiple isopters that the true shape, size, position, intensity, uniformity, margins, and course or progress of the defect can be studied.

For example, if a partial homonymous hemianopsia is demonstrated to have a markedly different size and shape in two or three of its central isopters, this finding indicates a sloping margin, which may point to a progressive lesion. If, in addition, the two half-fields are asymmetric or incongruous, the examiner may be able not only to localize the site of visual pathway interruption but also to make an intelligent guess as to the pathologic nature of the lesion producing the interruption.

Partial homonymous hemianopsia may be congruous or incongruous.

Congruous defect. A congruous defect is one in which both half-fields are symmetric or identical in size, shape, position, density, margins, and all other characteristics. If enough isopters are examined, absolute congruity for each stimulus is rare (if not nonexistent), except in patients with damage to the calcarine cortex.

In order to show complete congruity, each field must duplicate symmetrically its fellow field in all respects and each isopter tested in the right eye must be a carbon copy of the same isopter in the left eye, except for the difference in size of the two fields caused by the temporal crescent (Fig. 7-7).

In total homonymous hemianopsia it is not possible to determine congruity, since the dividing line between the seeing and nonseeing portions of the fields is vertical.

In partial homonymous hemianopsia, if one portion of the dividing line slants away from the vertical, it is this portion of the margin of the field defect that may determine the symmetry or congruity of the field defect.

Congruity in a defect *may* be determined by the testing of one isopter if that isopter shows a defect somewhat less than half the visual field of one eye. Congruity may show a defect somewhat less than half the visual field of one eye. Congruity

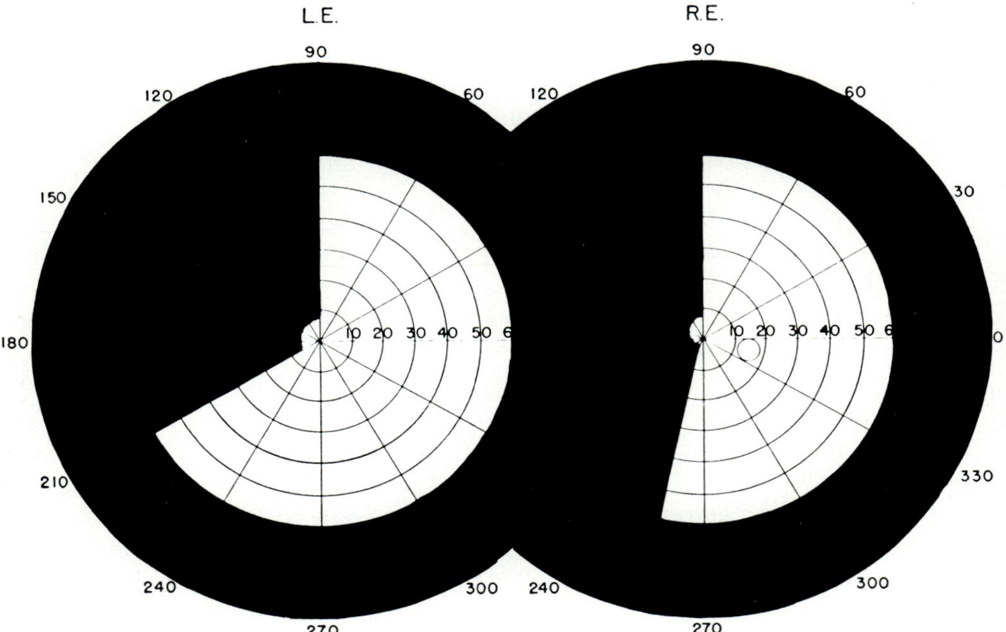

Fig. 7-8. Incongruous partial homonymous hemianopsia. Margins of defect are usually sloping, so morphology of defect varies with isopter tested. Only one isopter is shown here.

may also be demonstrated in a visual field in which the margins are more sloping in one field than the other. But unless the most careful quantitative techniques are used to study these defects, the assumption of congruity in a given visual field is not justified.

Incongruous defect (Fig. 7-8). An incongruous partial homonymous hemianopsia is one in which the two visual fields are asymmetric in size and shape or other characteristics. This definition, of course, does not apply to the inequality of the two visual fields caused by the temporal crescent, which produces a natural and constantly occurring incongruity. As noted previously, it is not possible to determine incongruity in a homonymous hemianopsia unless at least one field defect involves somewhat less than half the field.

Incongruity in homonymous hemianopsia may vary from the slightest asymmetry in the two fields, barely detectable by the most precise quantitative perimetry, to a visual field defect that shows only the faintest depression of a portion of a quadrant in one eye and total loss of the homonymous field in the fellow eye.

Minimal degrees of incongruity may be of some localizing value if associated with other neurologic signs, but they should not be allowed too much weight in diagnosis, except as they indicate the right-sidedness or left-sidedness of the lesion.

Gross incongruity or asymmetry in a homonymous hemianopsia may be of considerable localizing value and, in fact, may be the only neurologic finding that points to the anterior cerebral location of the lesion.

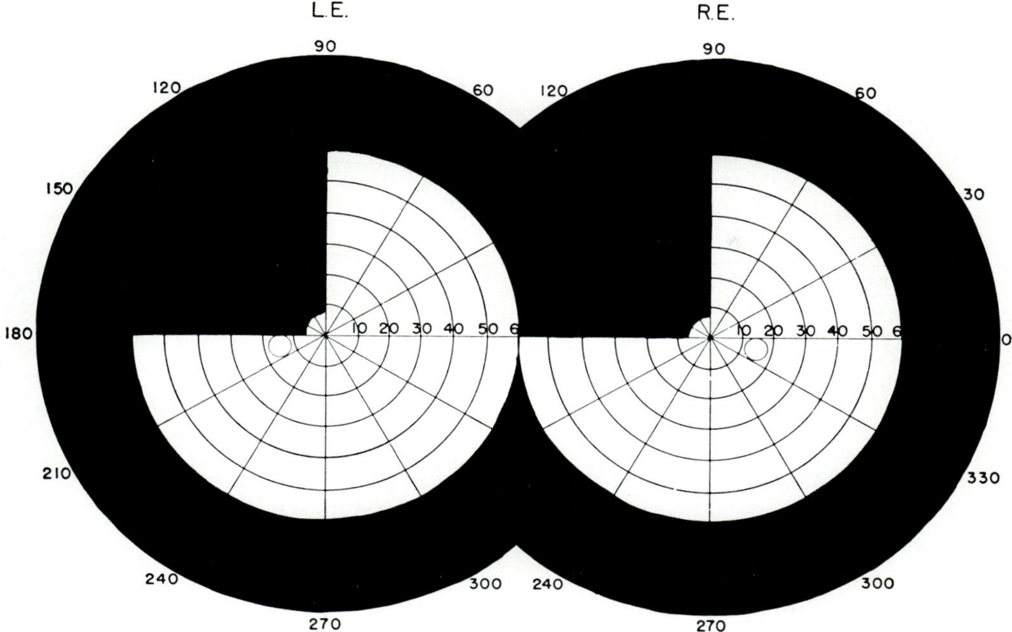

Fig. 7-9. Homonymous quadrantanopsia.

In general, the more extreme the asymmetry or incongruity in the two fields of a homonymous hemianopsia, the more anterior in the postchiasmal portion of the visual pathway is the lesion producing it.

Lesions of the temporal lobe or optic tract can therefore be separated from lesions of the occipital cortex by the character of the homonymous hemianopsia. Those showing incongruity localize the lesion anteriorly, whereas symmetric defects point to a location in the occipital cortex. In parietal lobe lesions the visual field character is less reliable; but if an inferior homonymous quadrantanopsia is associated with a positive or asymmetric optokinetic nystagmus, the lesion is almost certainly in the deeper portion of the parietal lobe (see later discussion on optokinetic nystagmus in association with lesions of the temporal, parietal, and occipital lobes).

Homonymous quadrantanopsia (Fig. 7-9). Homonymous quadrantanopsia is, in reality, a form of partial homonymous hemianopsia. It may be congruous or incongruous. It may vary in its characteristics in a great variety of ways, with steep or sloping margins. Depending on whether the upper or lower quadrants are involved in the defect, it may point to a downward or upward progression of the lesion in the opposite cerebral hemisphere or it may implicate the superior or inferior fiber bundles of the optic radiation.

Superior homonymous quadrantanopsia is said to be diagnostic of lesions of the temporal lobe but, of course, may also occur as a result of a lesion of the inferior lip of the calcarine fissure. The differentiation of these two sites may be possible if the quadrantanopsia is truly congruous, as it would be in patient with a cortical lesion, or incongruous, as it would be in a patient with a temporal lobe or optic tract lesion (see Fig. 4-12).

When a homonymous quadrantanopsia involves the inferior quadrant, it is reasonable to assume a lesion of the superior fiber bundles of the radiation in the parietal lobe or the upper lip of the calcarine fissure in the occipital lobe. Here again the symmetry or asymmetry of the two quadrant defects may assist in anteroposterior localization, although the degree of incongruity in a patient with a parietal lobe lesion is likely to be slight and difficult to elicit.

Bitemporal hemianopsia (Fig. 7-10). Bitemporal hemianopsia is a visual field defect in which part or all of each temporal field is insensitive to visual stimuli. The defect may vary from the slightest depression of the upper temporal portion of the internal isopters (1/2000) to complete blindness in each temporal field. This field defect invariably implies an interruption of the decussating nerve fibers in the optic chiasm.

The great variety of forms that the bitemporal hemianopsia may assume is largely the result of the nerve fiber arrangement and vascular supply in the chiasm and also the intimate anatomic relationship of the chiasm to many other structures in the region of the sella turcica.

The classic bitemporal hemianopsia is produced by an adenoma of the pituitary gland expanding upward from the sella turcica and compressing the central decussating fibers of the chiasm from beneath. As will be subsequently noted, this lesion

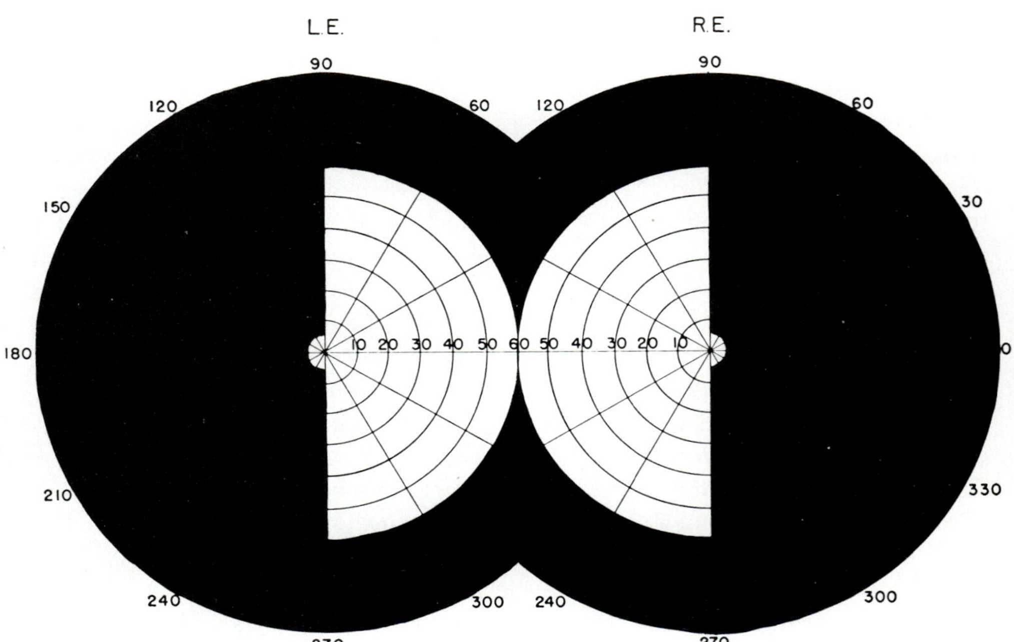

Fig. 7-10. Bitemporal hemianopsia.

first affects the visual fields in their upper temporal quadrants, with gradual extension of the defect to encompass the entire temporal field in each eye; it then finally, and in its late stages, involves the central area and lower nasal quadrants and lastly the upper nasal portion of each visual field. The progression of the defect is clockwise in the right field and counterclockwise in the left field.

Any anomaly in the suprasellar position of the chiasm or any asymmetry in the tumor or in its direction of growth usually produces an asymmetry in the defects of the visual fields. Likewise, variations in the speed of growth of the tumor, the blood supply, the secondary pressure by contiguous structures, and even the cell structure of the tumor will be reflected in the shape, size, position, margins, and other characteristics of the visual field change. Extrasellar lesions that give rise to chiasmal pressure from other directions than beneath (front, back, laterally, and above) will produce a type of bitemporal hemianopsia that is quite different from the classic defect produced by intrasellar lesions.

Binasal hemianopsia. Binasal hemianopsia is not a true hemianoptic defect. It is usually produced by more than one lesion and is irregular and asymmetric in the fields of the two eyes. It may be of some diagnostic significance.

This visual field defect implies an interruption of the uncrossed fibers in both lateral aspects of the chiasm or in both optic nerve or retinas. It therefore presupposes bilateral lesions, though they may have one etiology.

Binasal hemianopsia may be produced by symmetric lesions in the temporal halves of both retinas, such as severe retinal edema associated with diabetic retinopathy. It may be a part of the visual defect associated with postneuritic optic atrophy and with the occasional bilateral retrobulbar neuritis of multiple sclerosis. In this latter instance, it is usually the result of a very large paracentral scotoma that has involved the nasal more than the temporal field. More or less symmetrically placed lesions lateral to the chiasm, such as the adhesions resulting from opticochiasmatic arachnoiditis, may produce a binasal hemianopsia.

The nasal quadrant peripheral depression of glaucoma, when bilateral and reasonably symmetric in the two eyes, has been mistaken for binasal hemianopsia of central origin. Most binasal hemianopsias are due to intraocular disease in both eyes.

I have seen a type of binasal hemianopsia produced by a tumor of the third ventricle with extreme dilatation of the ventricle and downward pressure between the optic nerves forcing them laterally against the carotid arteries. In like manner an aneurysm of the right internal carotid artery was found to be compressing the chiasm laterally, destroying its uncrossed fibers on that side and producing a right-sided nasal field defect. At the same time the entire chiasm was shifted to the left so that the opposite normal internal carotid artery had grooved the left side of the chiasm and produced a nasal field defect on that side. This could be considered a true example of a binasal hemaniopsia from bilateral lesions with a single etiology. (See Plate 7.)

Crossed quadrantanopsia. Crossed quadrantanopsia is a rare defect in the visual field in which an upper quadrant of one visual field is lost along with the lower quadrant of the opposite visual field. It can occur as part of the chiasmal compression syndrome, wherein a lesion displaces the chiasm from beneath, compressing it against a contiguous arterial structure and thus producing simultaneous pressure above and below. It may result from wide and coincidentally crossed sector defects in the two fields and, as such, may occur in association with glaucoma or such inflammatory lesions as choroiditis juxtapapillaris. It is usually the result of asymmetric bilateral or double homonymous hemianopsia and occurs either as an incomplete bilateral hemianopsia or as its terminal stage. It is a rare phenomenon, almost certainly vascular in nature, and may be explained by a lesion of the upper lip of the calcarine area on one side and the lower lip of the opposite calcarine cortex.

Altitudinal hemianopsia (Fig. 7-11). Altitudinal hemianopsia may be unilateral or bilateral. In the former instance the lesion that causes it is necessarily prechiasmal in location. Thus thrombosis of the superior temporal and nasal branches of the central retinal artery might produce an irregular but dense inferior altitudinal hemianopsia of one eye.

Injury to the vascular supply of the optic nerve will produce an altitudinal hemianopsia, usually inferior. As has been noted, the vascular supply to the optic nerve is through a network of vessels in the arachnoidal membrane, which pass through the subarachnoidal space and enter the nerve at right angles. In its upper part the space is narrow and the vessels that traverse it from the membrane to the nerve are

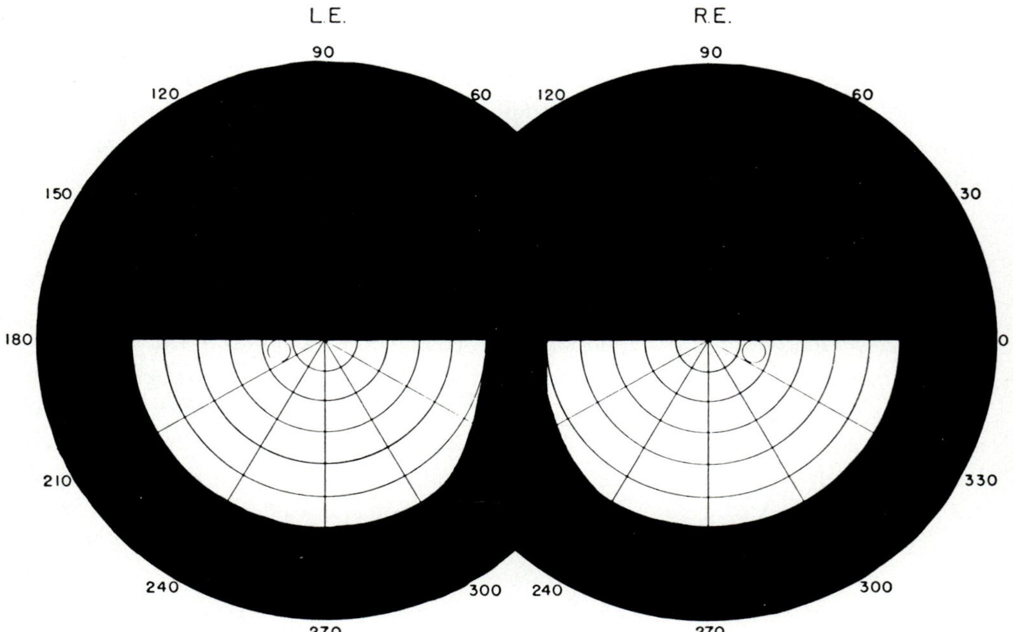

Fig. 7-11. Altitudinal hemianopsia.

short and easily damaged by torsion, edema, and other injury. This gives rise to a unilateral altitudinal field defect with horizontal border, steep edges, and great density.

A unilateral or bilateral inferior altitudinal hemianopsia may be produced by a lesion that presses the chiasm upward in its anterior portion, thus wedging the optic nerve against the superior margin of the optic foramen or against a sclerotic pair of anterior cerebral arteries.

Olfactory groove meningiomas sometimes extend posteriorly and downward, thus compressing the optic nerves in their short and vulnerable intracranial portion.

Intrinsic lesions of the optic nerves such as the atrophy in tabes dorsalis, ischemic optic neuropathy, and of course, that which accompanies advanced glaucoma will produce unilateral or bilateral altitudinal field defects of an irregular type.

Double homonymous inferior or superior quadrantanopsia may rarely result from injury or hemorrhage in the lower or upper lips of both calcarine fissures, to produce a type of altitudinal hemianopsia.

Severe hypoxia resulting from exsanguination caused by injury or massive gastrointestinal hemorrhage may produce glaucoma-like visual field defects that may simulate bilateral altitudinal hemianopsia. (See Figs. 11-18 and 15-52.)

Double homonymous hemianopsia (Fig. 7-12). Double homonymous hemianopsia is a relatively uncommon visual field defect that is always the result of lesions of the occipital area and presupposes involvement of the striate cortex of both occipital lobes. Total destruction of both occipital lobes results in total blindness. Partial destruction of the occipital cortex on both sides from severe trauma with massive brain damage (as in depressed fracture of the occiput) or from bilateral vascular lesions involving the calcarine cortex will produce bilateral or double homonymous hemianopsia with macular sparing of greater or lesser degree. This visual field de-

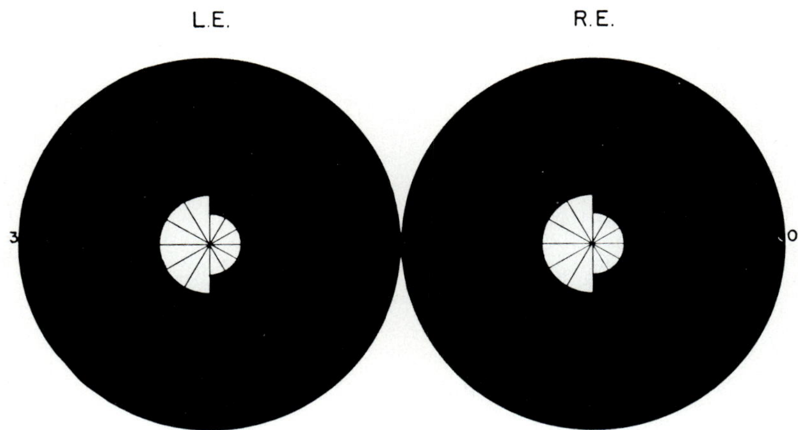

Fig. 7-12. Double homonymous hemianopsia.

fect will simulate a gross concentric contraction of the visual field with loss of all peripheral vision to all stimuli. Both hemianoptic field defects show great density and very steep margins, and the remaining small area of central vision represents the spared macular portion of both half fields. Increased intracranial pressure may cause a shift of the uncal portion of the temporal lobe downward over the edge of the tentorium, with resulting compression of the posterior cerebral arteries and infarction in the calcarine cortex.

If the area of macular sparing in one homonymous hemaniopsia is larger than that in the other homonymous hemianopsia, the spared central portion of the field will have small vertical steps above and below fixation where the two areas of macular sparing do not quite coincide. These steps may be likened to the unpaired double nasal step seen on the horizontal meridian in cases of double arcuate scotoma, in patients with glaucoma, except that they occur on the vertical instead of the horizontal meridian.

Most double homonymous hemianoptic field defects are vascular in origin, whether primary or secondary to severe trauma to the vascular supply to the striate cortex. They are always congruous, dense, and steep-margined. Bilateral or double homonymous hemianopsia may result from a stroke or infarction of one occipital lobe accompanied by complete homonymous hemianopsia with macular sparing, followed at a later date by infarction of the opposite occipital lobe, also with macular sparing. The size and shape of the remaining visual field would depend on the degree of macular sparing. On the other hand, there may be sudden and massive bilateral occipital lobe damage with cortical blindness resulting from trauma, anoxia, carbon monoxide poisoning, cerebral angiography, cardiac arrest, exsanguination, and other conditions. Partial recovery may leave a residual and permanent bilateral homonymous hemianopsia.

Macular splitting (Fig. 7-13). Macular splitting in homonymous hemianopsia is relatively uncommon. True macular splitting with absolute bisection of fixation for

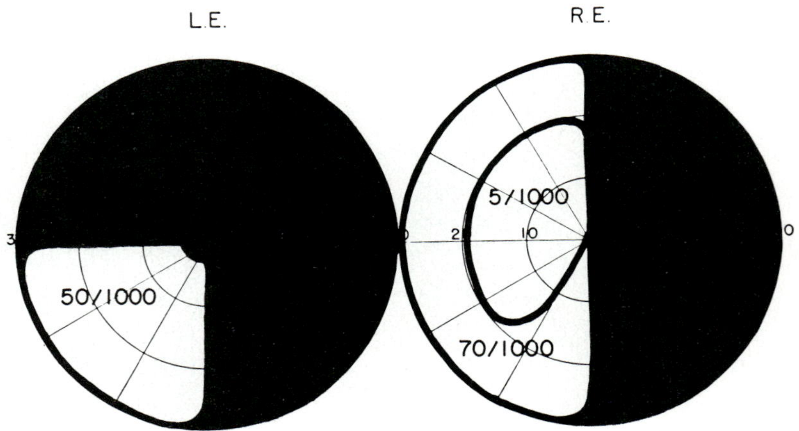

Fig. 7-13. Example of macular splitting produced by spongioblastoma of chiasm and left optic tract.

all test objects is extremely difficult, if not impossible, to elicit, because of the constant minute shifting of fixation during the test. This fixation shift occurs almost reflexly and even in the most cooperative and intelligent patients.

As might be gathered, macular splitting is more likely to occur in association with homonymous hemaniopsia produced by lesions in the anterior portion of the postchiasmal pathway, although it can occur with damage to the striate cortex.

Macular sparing. Macular sparing in homonymous hemianopsia is the rule in instances of damage to the occipital cortex. Generally, it decreases in degree the more anterior the lesion producing the hemianopsia. This is not to say that macular sparing is pathognomonic of a lesion situated in the posterior portion of the visual pathway.

The degree of sparing of the fixation area may vary from a minute area of less than one-half degree to a major portion of the affected half-field. Clinically, those lesions of the anterior portion of the calcarine fissure that produce homonymous hemianopsia are more likely to leave a wide area of macular sparing, whereas those involving the operculum will show a narrower area of retained central field (Fig. 7-14). Even in the most minute macular sparing, the central visual acuity may remain normal and normal vision may be retained with one half of the macula functioning.

Macular sparing may occur in interruption of any portion of the visual pathway in its postchiasmal portion. When the lesion is in the anterior portion of the visual pathway and when several isopters are tested, the sparing of fixation is more likely to be present for large stimuli only and the macula will appear to be split when small test objects are used. In other words the area of macular sparing produced in a homonymous hemianopsia by a lesion of the optic tract will have sloping margins, whereas that from an occipital lobe lesion will have steep margins and will be the same size regardless of the test objects used to test it.

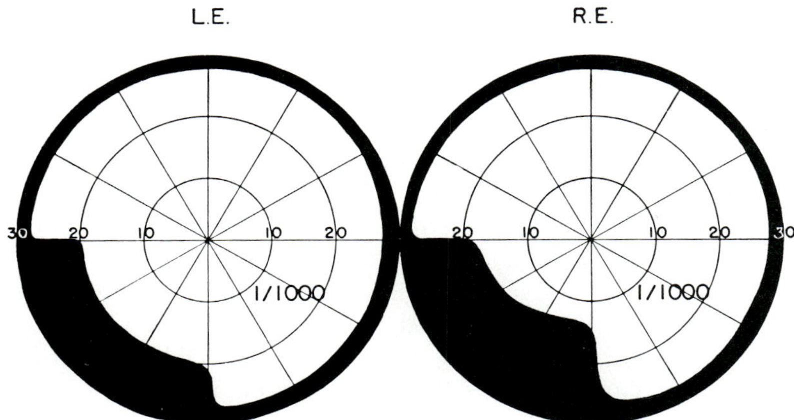

Fig. 7-14. Example of wide macular sparing in left homonymous hemianopsia produced by tumor of anterior portion of superior lip of right calcarine fissure.

The margins of an area of macular sparing may be almost perfectly semicircular, or they may be quite irregular in outline. If the irregularity is symmetric or congruous, this is further evidence of the cortical location of the lesion producing the field defect.

Macular sparing may be an initial finding in a visual field loss that may go on to progressive involvement of the central field and finally macular splitting. The late involvement of macular fibers probably results from the fact that there are so many more of them than there are peripheral fibers.

As noted in Chapter 4, each nerve fiber from the right half of each retina goes to the right occipital cortex and the left homonymous retinas send their fibers to the left occipital lobe. These fibers traverse the cerebral hemispheres in a remarkably constant pattern. In spite of this anatomic fact, it is not uncommon to find lesions producing total destruction of one visual pathway or end station in the striate cortex, with resulting homonymous hemianopsia that is total except for an area of macular sparing.

Much has been written and numerous theories have been proposed to explain this phenomenon. Each of these theories leaves some unanswered questions, and there is probably no simple answer to the problem. Some of the theories that have been proposed are briefly described next.

In some cases of total destruction of the occipital lobe with macular sparing, there, in fact, may not have been total destruction. There may remain small portions of the striate cortex even after extensive surgical procedures or trauma. Even complete interruption of the blood supply through the posterior cerebral artery may leave some cortical function.

It is probable that the occipital cortex is supplied not only by the calcarine artery branches from the posterior cerebral artery but also by the deep optic or posterior cortical branches of the middle cerebral artery and, in a fairly high percentage of cases, by branches from the posterior temporal artery. All of these arteries may supply a part of the macular area of the calcarine cortex. This is probably the most logical explanation for the high incidence of macular sparing in occipital lobe lesions. (See Chapter 5 and Fig. 5-1.)

It has been hypothecated, with valid arguments, that macular sparing is only apparent and not real, that it is due to shift of fixation toward the blind field. This fixation shift is more noticeable in the central area and can rarely be detected in the peripheral parts of the meridians, which divide normal from blind field. Overshot fields that affect the periphery are rare but are fairly commonly found in the central field.

That the macula may be truly split with retention of normal vision and production of a true overshot field is graphically illustrated in Fig. 7-15. In this patient traumatic rupture of the chiasm during infancy produced total bitemporal hemianopsia. The patient reached the age of 17 years with little or no awareness of her visual field defect until it was detected by accident in a routine vision test. She had compensated for her split macula by using half of her fovea and by rapid and uncon-

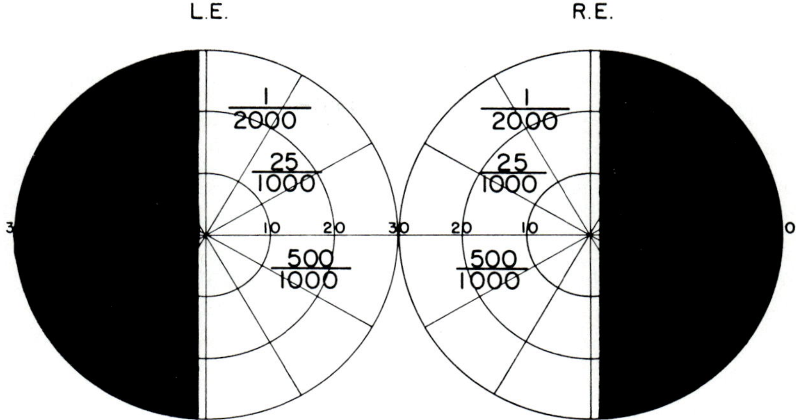

Fig. 7-15. Total bitemporal hemianopsia with split macula and overshot field in patient who as infant had sustained severe frontal head injury with chiasmal rupture. Both temporal fields were completely blind, but central visual acuity was 20/20 in each eye and patient was unaware of field defect at 17 years of age.

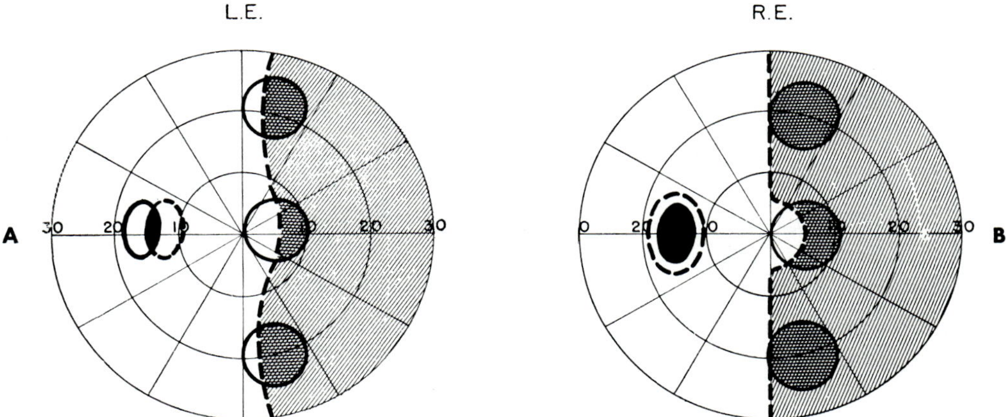

Fig. 7-16. A, False macular sparing as demonstrated by three-disc test. If three white discs are advanced from blind to seeing portion of field, all three come into view simultaneously and there is shift of normal blind spot toward blind side. **B,** True macular sparing as demonstrated by three-disc test. If three white discs are advanced from blind to seeing portion of field, central disc appears first and there is no shift of blind spot. (After Hughes.)

scious fixation shift to develop the characteristic displacement of the vertical border of the field defect.

Hughes has demonstrated a simple way in which the overshot field may be differentiated from true macular sparing (Fig. 7-16).

If three large test objects are advanced simultaneously from the blind to the seeing field and the central one appears before the peripheral ones, then the macular sparing is real. If the sparing results from fixation shift, then all three objects will appear simultaneously and at the same time a test object placed in the blind spot on the tangent screen will appear, showing that the whole field has shifted toward the blind side. This theory of macular sparing is supported by the clinical fact that the larger the occipital lesion the more likely is macular sparing. It has been found that in about 70% of cases showing macular sparing the lesion is in the dominant hemisphere and that this apparent macular sparing due to field shift may be caused by associated damage to the visual association areas resulting in disturbance in orientation.

The theory that macular vision is diffusely represented throughout the entire visual cortex has no anatomic basis and cannot be seriously considered.

Bilateral representation of the macula has been suggested by several authors as a cause of macular sparing. According to this theory, the fibers from the macula of one eye go to both occipital opercula. There is little clinical evidence to favor such a theory. For example, a surgical or traumatic anteroposterior splitting of the chiasm will produce a total bitemporal hemianopsia without macular sparing. This means that the decussation of macular fibers would have to be prechiasmal in the brain stem or callosal commissures and that these areas would be productive clinically of visual field defects; but they are not. If the maculas were bilaterally represented, than a lesion of one occipital pole should produce bilateral scotomas involving both halves of both visual fields; but this it does not do.

The theory of unilateral representation of the macula is strongly supported by anatomic evidence. Polyak failed to produce degenerative lesions in the contralateral geniculate body after removal of the occipital cortex on one side and concluded that there is no commissural tract from one geniculate body to the opposite radiation. Nor does surgical section of the corpus callosum interfere with visual fields or other ocular functions.

Regardless of the theoretical explanation of macular sparing, it remains a subject of much interest to the perimetrist; and its presence or absence and regularity or irregularity may be of considerable value.

Size

The size of a visual field defect is of less importance than its shape or position. Size is of some diagnostic value in scotomas, but in sector defects such as hemianopsia the size is largely determined by the shape of the defect. The size of a glaucomatous sector defect is, of course, of some importance in estimating the prognosis of the disease.

In quantitative examination of the visual field, the size of the defect will often be determined by the isopter tested. If the margins of the defect are sloping, the defect will be larger when small stimuli are used than for large visual angles. For this reason the size of a defect cannot be accurately determined without testing multiple isopters (Fig. 7-17).

The size of the visual field defect does not indicate the size of the lesion producing it, since very large field defects may be produced by small lesions occurring in

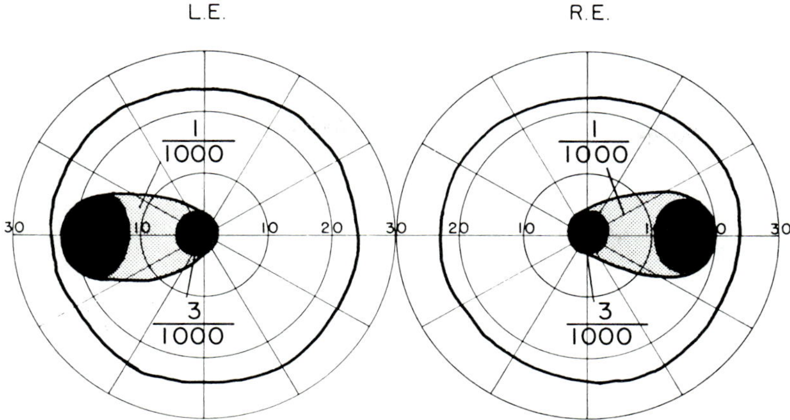

Fig. 7-17. Example of apparent difference in size and shape of bilateral central scotomas when examined with different-sized stimuli. The 3/1000 isopter shows only small central scotoma, whereas examination of 1/1000 isopter demonstrates rather large centrocecal defect. Defects are part of severe nutritional amblyopia associated with subclinical pellagra in chronic alcoholic patient.

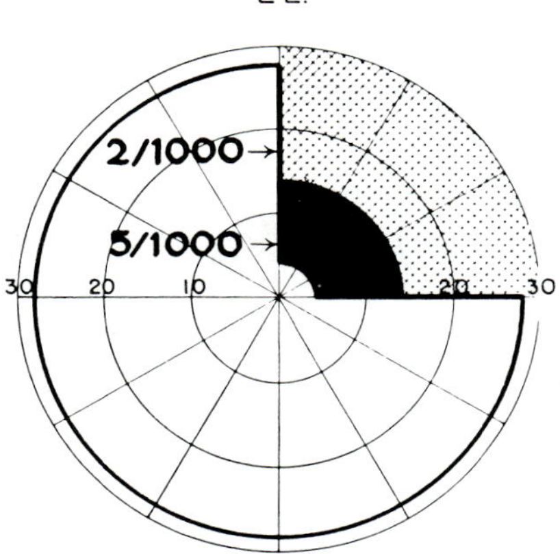

Fig. 7-18. Example of variation in intensity within area of visual field loss. Quadrantanoptic scotoma is detected in 5/1000 isopter, whereas 2/1000 isopter breaks through into periphery and shows loss of entire quadrant.

areas of the visual pathway where the nerve fiber bundles are closely packed together; and, conversely, a large lesion in the optic radiations may produce a relatively small defect in the fields.

Intensity

The intensity of a visual field deficit is determined by the visual acuity within its area (Fig. 7-18). The deficit may vary from total blindness to all stimuli, including light, to the minimum detectable visual loss within the isopter tested.

Absolute visual loss within the area of the defect is rare. If sufficient visual stimulus is presented, most defects will be found to have some visual acuity, no matter how faint. Thus a defect that appears to be of absolute intensity for the 1-mm to 10-mm test objects at a distance of 330 mm may not be present if a 20-mm object is used.

In truth, a field defect can be considered as absolute only when no stimulus is visible within its area up to the size of the area itself. Thus a scotoma with a diameter of 100 mm at a distance of 1 meter may be declared absolute only if *all* stimuli up to 100 mm are invisible within its borders. Beyond this point it is impossible to measure the intensity of the defect. The normal blind spot of Mariotte is an excellent example of absolute intensity in a visual field defect.

High intensity in a visual field defect usually indicated complete conduction interference in the nerve fibers. If the onset of the visual loss were sudden or rapid, a virulent or massive or highly destructive lesion would be indicated; and, in general, the more intense the defect, the poorer is the prognosis for complete restoration of function.

A defect may be of such low intensity as to be barely detectable within the most sensitive isopters. An example of such a defect is the earliest depression in the Bjerrum area in open-angle glaucoma. This area of visual loss is rarely observed by the patient and may require the most skillful and meticulous perimetry (including low-threshold static stimuli) for its detection.

Uniformity

The uniformity of visual loss within a visual field defect may vary considerably or it may be the same throughout the defect. Quantitative methods of perimetry are essential to analyze a defect correctly not only as to its size and intensity but also as to its uniformity. A sector defect embracing a 90-degree quadrant of a visual field in the 2/1000 isopter may show a quadrantanoptic scotoma in the 5/1000 isopter. In other words, a denser area of visual loss may lie within the sector defect close to fixation.

Lack of uniformity may merely be the result of sloping margins of the defect, as in the paramacular island of greater visual loss in the centrocecal scotoma of tobacco amblyopia.

Only by careful study of the whole area of the field loss can the true picture be ascertained, and what at first appears to be nonspecific and nondiagnostic may, with analysis of multiple isopters, prove to be a defect whose characteristics are diagnostic of a specific lesion in a precise localization.

Margins

The margins of a visual field defect are of great importance, not only in prognosticating the future progress of the disease producing it but also, in certain instances, in diagnosing specific lesions.

In a certain sense the uniformity of a field defect is determined by its margins. Thus, a bitemporal hemianopsia with sloping margins is also a defect without uniformity (Fig. 7-19).

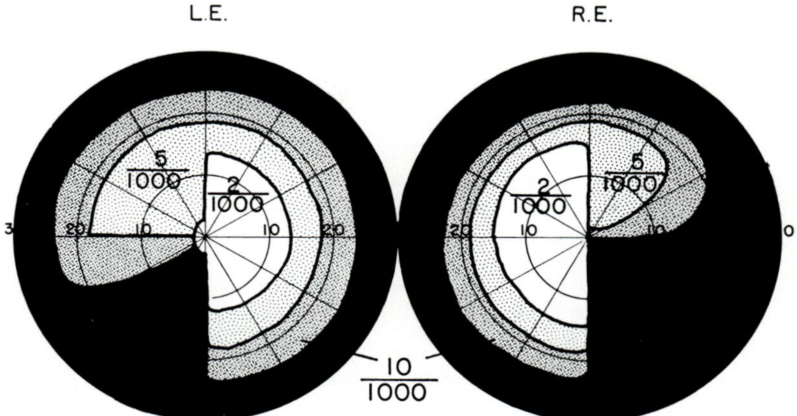

Fig. 7-19. Typical example of visual field defect with sloping margins and lack of uniformity. The 2/1000 isopter shows complete bitemporal hemianopsia, whereas isopter for 10/1000 reveals greater density in inferior temporal quadrants, thus indicating chiasmal compression from above. Patient had suprasellar meningioma.

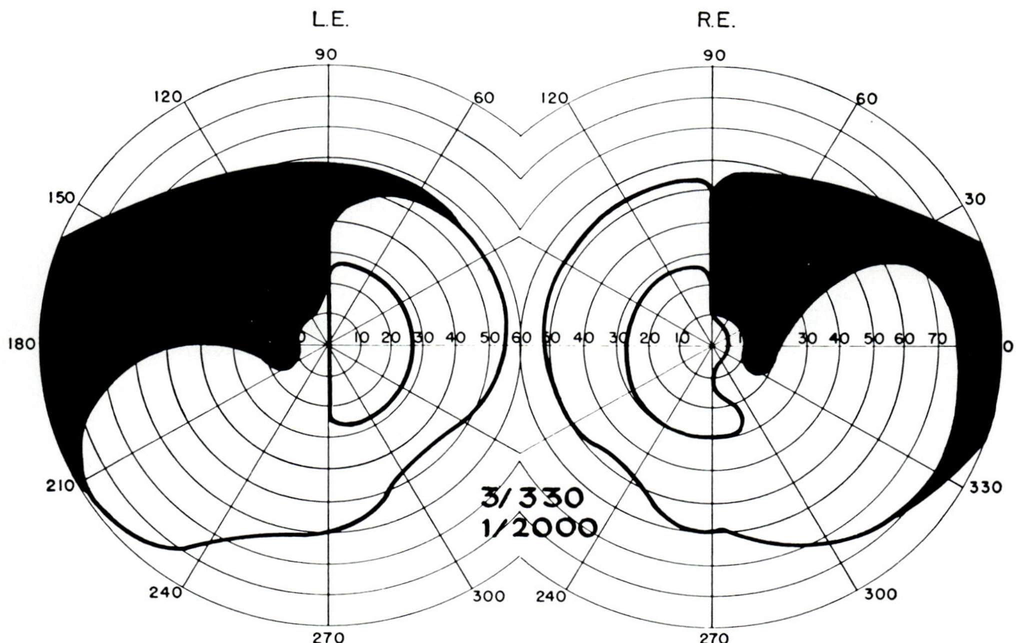

Fig. 7-20. Example of visual field defect with sloping margins. Bitemporal hemianopsia is partial in 3/330 isopter but complete in 1/2000 isopter. This pattern is from case of pituitary adenoma with visual loss, endocrine imbalance, and erosion of sella turcica.

Margins of visual field defects may be sloping or steep.

An example of the former would be a field loss in which the 5/1000 isopter is normal; the 3/1000 isopter shows a slight upper temporal quadrant depression; the 2/2000 isopter shows a complete quadrant loss; and the 1/2000 isopter shows a total temporal hemianopsia (Fig. 7-20). Such defects are commonly found when quantitative methods of examination are used (see Figs. 7-4, A, 7-19, and 7-21).

A steep-margined field defect is one in which all of the isopters would show an identical or nearly identical field loss (i.e., the isopter lines at the margin of the defect would be very close together or superimposed; see Fig. 7-5).

A classic example of a defect with sloping margins is found in the centrocecal scotoma of tobacco amblyopia. Here the isopter for 1/2000 may show a large scotoma extending from the blind spot and enveloping fixation, whereas the 3/1000 isopter reveals only a tiny island of blindness situated midway between the blind spot and fixation, within the scotoma recorded for the smaller visual angle.

One of the best examples of a defect with steep margins is the scotoma that results from a healed chorioretinitis wherein all test objects up to the size of the scotoma itself are invisible within its area.

It will be seen that these descriptions may also be applied to the definition of uniformity in a visual field defect.

Sloping margins in a field defect usually mean a lesion that is either actively pro-

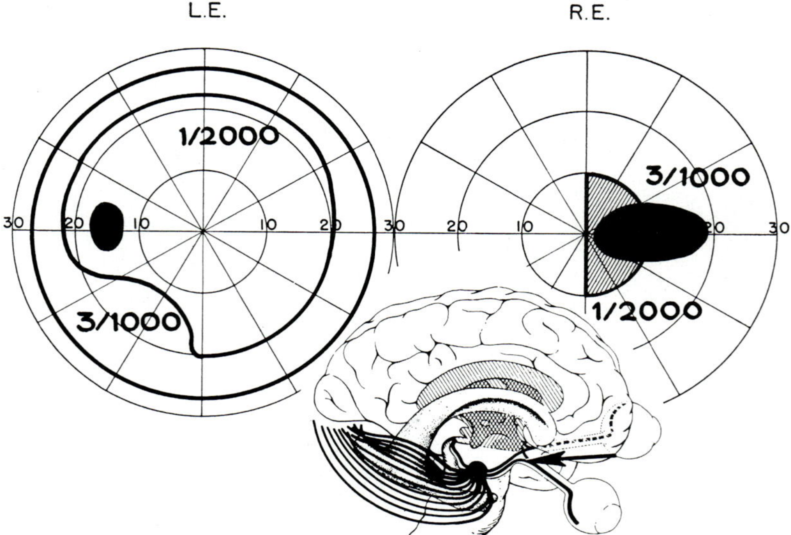

Fig. 7-21. Visual field defect with sloping margins, illustrating necessity of quantitative perimetry for correct localization, from case of meningioma of right frontal lobe with pressure on right optic nerve and anterior chiasm. Note that larger stimulus (3/1000) shows right centrocecal scotoma and normal left field whereas smaller stimulus (1/2000) shows temporal hemianoptic (junction) scotoma in right field and small inferior temporal quadrant defect in left. Bitemporal hemianoptic character of 1/2000 isopter localizes lesion correctly, whereas 3/1000 isopter implicates only right optic nerve.

gressing or regressing, whereas steep or perpendicular margins imply that the lesion producing the defect is nonactive, quiescent, or healed.

Onset and course

The onset and course of a visual field loss may be of considerable importance in the diagnosis of the pathologic process producing it. In general, sudden onset of a defect is most often produced by vascular lesions such as hemorrhage, embolism, or thrombus or by infection or trauma. Slowly expanding lesions such as tumors are more likely to give rise to a gradual onset and slow progress in the field defect. Sudden hemorrhage within a tumor may confuse the issue when only this characteristic of the field defect is considered.

The only certain way in which the course or behavior of a field defect may be traced is through repeated observations; but it is sometimes possible through quantitative methods of examination and analysis of the margins of the defect to determine in one examination the direction in which a defect is progressing. For example, the isopters for 2/1000, 5/1000, and 10/1000 may show a complete bitemporal hemianopsia, whereas a 100-mm object at a distance of 330 mm will show a loss of only the lower temporal quadrants. This would indicate that at its onset the defect was an inferior bitemporal quadrantanopsia; that it has progressed upward into each temporal field; that its margins are relatively steep; that the lesion producing it is not very active in its growth. The pathologic lesion that best fits this combination of circumstances is meningioma. Thus careful analysis of the characteristics of the field defect serves not only to localize the lesion in the visual pathway but also to indicate its pathology (see Fig. 7-19).

SCOTOMAS

A scotoma is an area of partial or complete blindness within the confines of a normal or a relatively normal visual field. In terms of quantitative measurement of visual acuity, a scotoma is an area of decreased visual acuity within an area of normal or relatively normal visual acuity for the portion of the visual field involved. Within a scotoma the vision is more depressed than in the areas of visual field surrounding it.

Utilizing Traquair's simile of the hill of vision whose apex is at the point of fixation, one can see that a scotoma is a hollow or depression on the surface of the hill, surrounded by the normal contour of the hill (Figs. 7-22 and 7-23). Thus it may be described as a lake, pit, or well, depending on its shape, depth, the steepness of its shoreline, and other characteristics. Its contour lines or isopters do not normally extend to the shoreline of the hill but surround it without interruption.

The surface of the visual hill surrounding a scotoma may be depressed or normal in height.

When static perimetry is the method of examination, scotomas are mapped as sharp or shallow dips in the profile of the hill of vision (Fig. 7-24). These may be minimal in size, or they may extend down through the depth of the hill to the sea of blindness.

Fig. 7-22. Diagrammatic representation of depression or erosion of central peak of hill of vision to produce depression-type central scotoma.

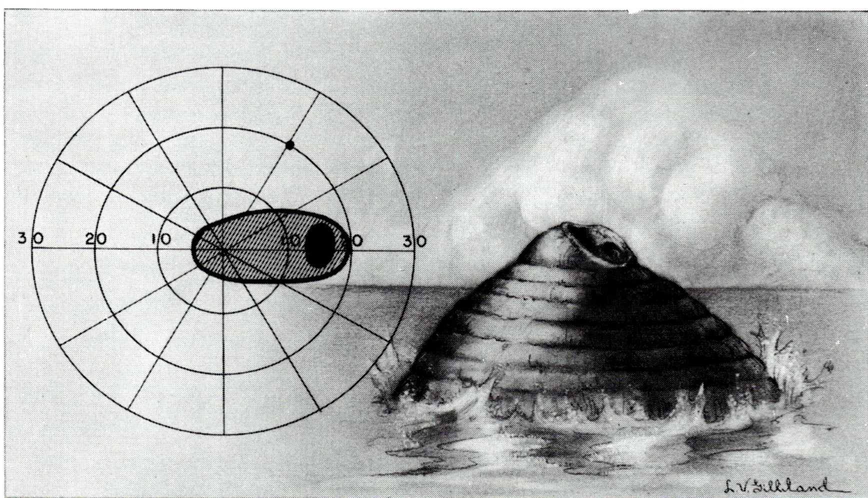

Fig. 7-23. Diagrammatic representation of formation of centrocecal scotoma by depression or erosion of peak and part of plateau of hill of vision to include pit of blind spot.

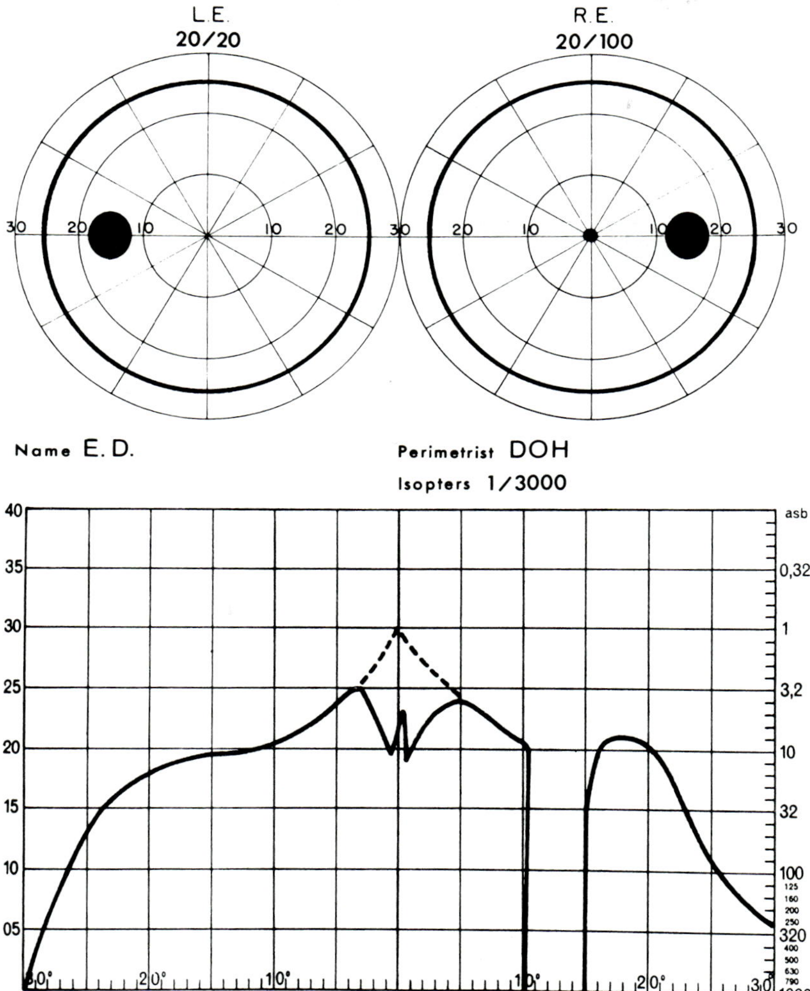

Fig. 7-24. Eclipse burn of the fovea in a 12-year-old child, unaware of decreased vision. Goldmann perimeter field was normal. Tangent screen field with 1-mm electroluminescent stimulus of 1 foot-lambert at 3 meters showed minute central scotoma. Threshold sensitivity test on Tübinger perimeter revealed a sharp dip in profile at fixation. (From Harrington, D. O.: Some unusual and difficult visual field defects, Trans. Ophthalmol. Soc. U. K. **92:**15, 1972, London, Churchill Livingstone Ltd.)

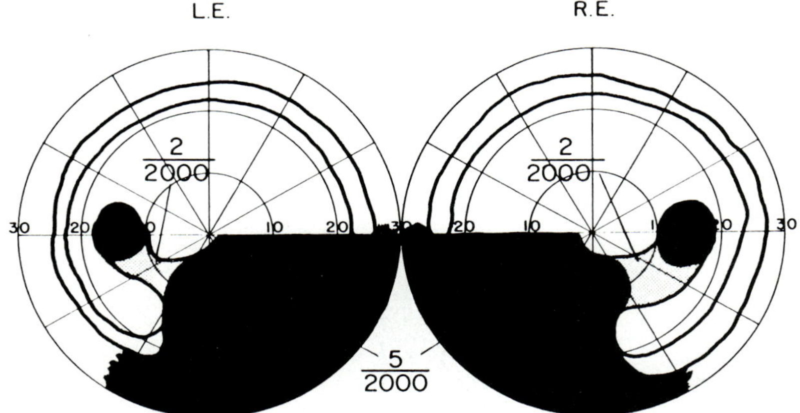

Fig. 7-25. Example of scotoma that has broken through into periphery of field from case of established open-angle glaucoma with optic atrophy and marked cupping of discs. Initial visual field loss was nerve fiber bundle defect that had coalesced with peripheral nasal depression.

When the depressed area of the scotoma extends to the periphery of the field, it is said to have broken through and may be likened to a lake with a river of varying width draining it to the sea (Fig. 7-25).

As with sector defects in the visual field, scotomas may be unilateral or bilateral and should be analyzed as to their characteristics, which are, in general, the same as those for sector defects: (1) position, (2) shape, (3) size, (4) intensity, (5) uniformity, (6) margins, (7) onset and course, and (8) unilateral or bilateral.

Position

The position of a scotoma is of considerable diagnostic importance. Scotomas are central and peripheral.

Peripheral scotomas are usually the result of localized areas of tissue destruction in the peripheral retina, most commonly from choroiditis or various forms of retinopathy or, when bilateral or hemianoptic, due to lesions of the anterior portion of the lips of the calcarine fissure (see Plate 9).

Central scotomas may be subdivided into central, pericentral, paracentral, and cecal.

Of these positions the central scotoma and the nerve fiber bundle defect are most important clinically because they are most frequent in occurrence and most destructive of visual acuity. A great variety of lesions may produce a central scotoma, and its characteristics, other than position, are diagnostically helpful in localizing the lesion and in indicating the type of pathology that produced it.

Central. Only the fixation area and the field immediately surrounding it are involved (Fig. 7-26).

Pericentral. The fixation area is relatively clear and the field immediately and equally surrounding it shows a depressed visual acuity (Fig. 7-27).

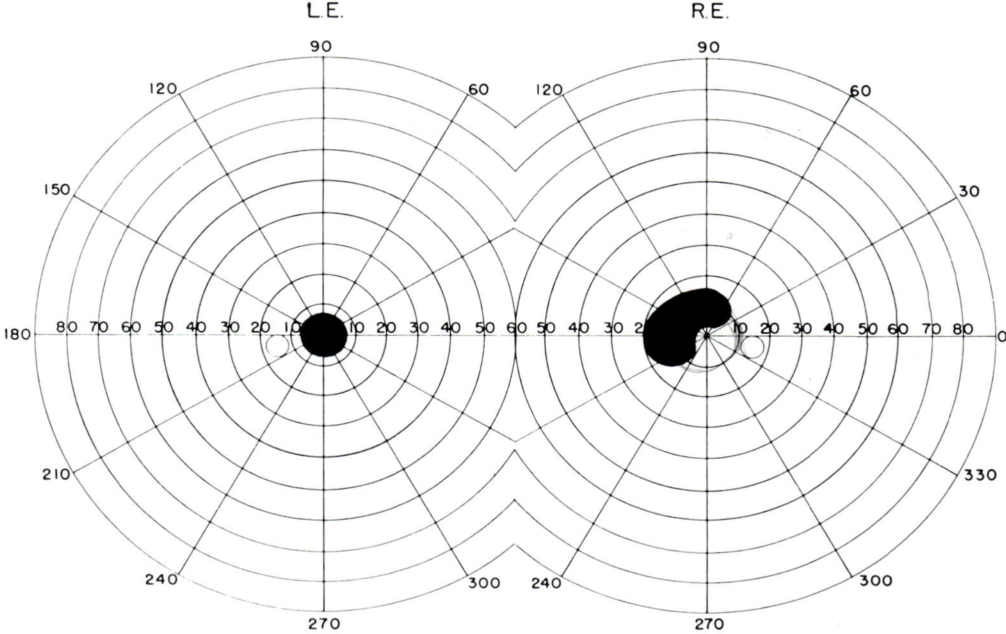

Fig. 7-26. Central scotoma, left eye. Paracentral scotoma, right eye.

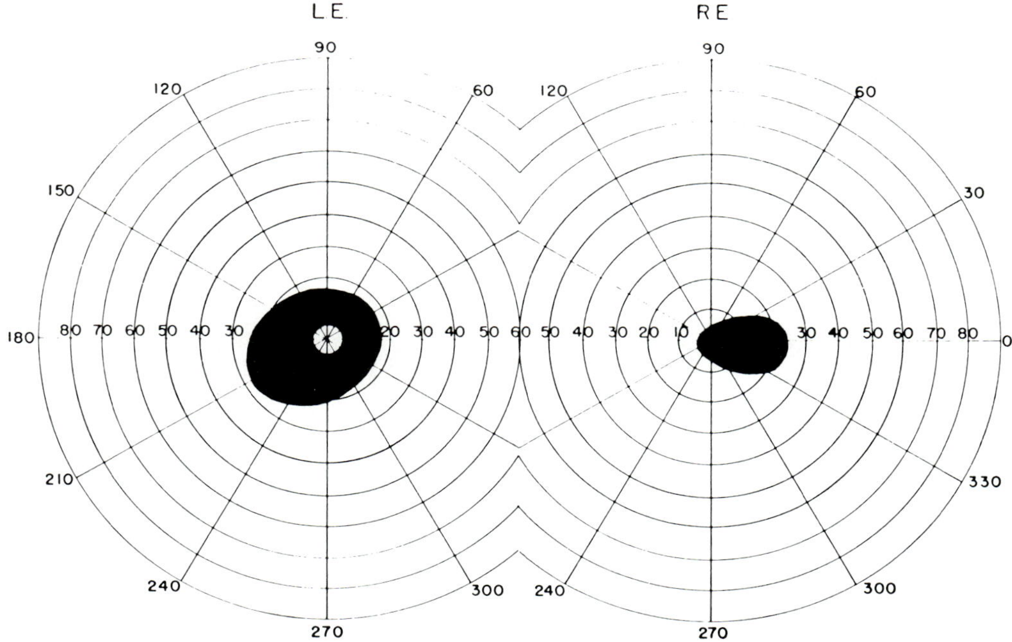

Fig. 7-27. Pericentral scotoma, left eye. Centrocecal scotoma, right eye.

Paracentral. The area of depressed visual acuity is to one side of fixation, which is not involved (Fig. 7-26). Paracentral scotomas may be further classified in terms of whether they are above, below, nasal, or temporal to fixation or in terms descriptive of the quadrant in which they lie. The normal blind spot may be considered as a paracentral scotoma.

Cecal. The area of the normal blind spot is involved. These scotomas may be simple enlargements of the blind spot or they may be pericecal or paracecal. In the latter instance they are described as occurring above, below, nasal, or temporal to the blind spot.

There are three special forms of cecal scotomas: (1) the centrocecal defect, which extends from the blind spot toward or into the fixation area and is exemplified in the important and rather common papillomacular bundle defect as seen in retrobulbar neuritis and in the scotoma of tobacco amblyopia (Fig. 7-27), (2) the angioscotoma, with its almost infinite variety of forms, and (3) the glaucomatous nerve fiber bundle defect.

Shape

The shape of a scotoma, regardless of its position, is of utmost concern. Great care should be used in the examination of a scotomatous defect to ascertain its boundaries accurately by quantitative methods of perimetry, because the clue to the disease may lie solely in the characteristic shape of the defect (see Fig. 7-29). For example, it is not unusual to find a shapeless area of relative visual loss in the upper or lower nasal field when only the 5/1000 is tested; but when this area is explored with decreasing visual stimuli, it will be seen to extend around fixation and into the blind spot as an arcuate scotoma or nerve fiber bundle defect of glaucoma (see Fig. 7-25).

A Seidel scotoma, which has limited diagnostic value, is simply a carelessly analyzed Bjerrum scotoma. (See Plate 4, *6*.)

A vaguely outlined central scotoma, which encroaches on fixation and crosses both the vertical and the horizontal meridians, may have an island of greater density within its area with a sufficiently clear-cut hemianoptic shape to be of localizing value. Here the grosser test with large visual angles is of more diagnostic value than the study of the smaller isopters.

Circular, smooth, or irregularly round scotomas. These may be peripheral, central, unilateral, or bilateral. They are usually the result of lesions within the retina, such as the irregular scotoma of chorioretinitis, but they are also commonly found in patients with optic nerve disease, especially lesions of the papillomacular nerve fiber bundle.

Oval scotoma. This is most frequently seen as the horizontal oval of a centrocecal scotoma, but it may also be seen as an incompletely analyzed sausage-shaped portion of an arcuate scotoma lying above or below fixation, one of the earliest glaucomatous field deficits.

Ring scotoma. This is an irregular circular or partially circular defect that rings

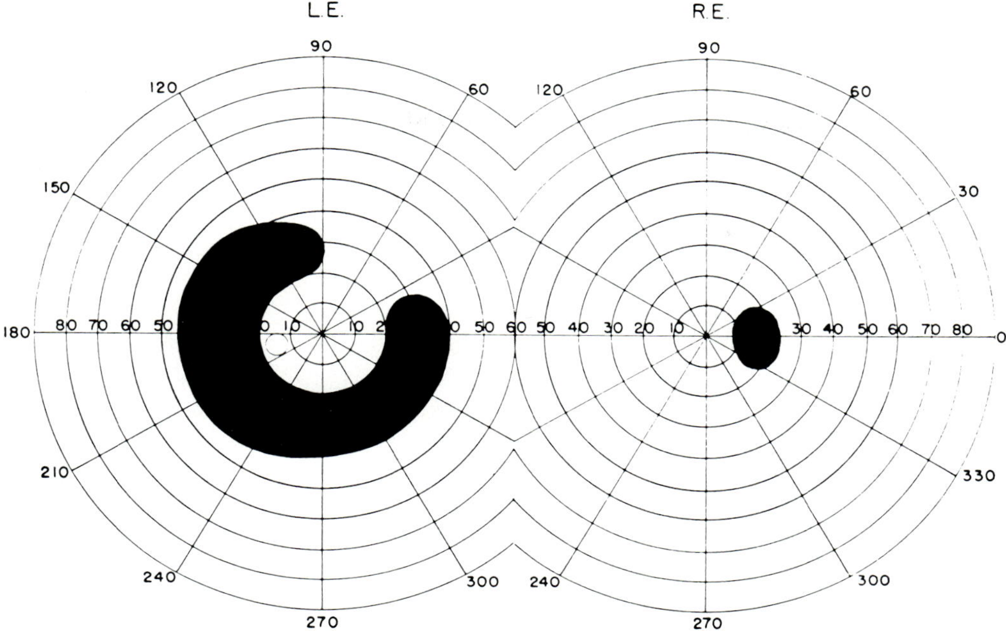

Fig. 7-28. Ring scotoma, left eye. Cecal scotoma, right eye.

the fixation point at varying distances and with more or less completeness (Fig. 7-28). It may be narrow or broad, and its most rapid expansion is usually outward until it breaks through to the periphery and leaves only a contracted field. Its shape does not conform to any nerve fiber pattern, and it may lie entirely within or outside the Bjerrum area. Its most typical example is seen in retinitis pigmentosa (Fig. 7-28).

Nerve fiber bundle scotoma (Figs. 7-29 and 7-30). This defect, variously called arcuate, scimitar, comet, Bjerrum, and Seidel scotoma, is characterized by the fact that it follows the retinal nerve fiber pattern and takes, in consequence, an arched form around fixation from the blind spot to the horizontal raphe in the nasal field, where it ends typically in a sharply demarcated horizontal or nasal step.

Arcuate defects may be incomplete, especially when examined with large visual angles. They may arise from the blind spot and follow the fiber pattern for a short distance and then fade out into areas of normal vision. They may begin at the horizontal meridian in the nasal field, at varying distances from fixation, and arch temporarily toward the blind spot but never reach it. They often appear as curved sausage-shaped defects lying directly above or below fixation, midway between the blind spot and the horizontal raphe. When their curve is projected in either direction, they will be seen always to lie in the path of the retinal nerve fiber bundles, which invariably include the blind spot in their projected pathway.

Rarely, a nerve fiber bundle defect may extend temporally from the blind spot or temporally and above or below the blind spot. These scotomas also follow the ret-

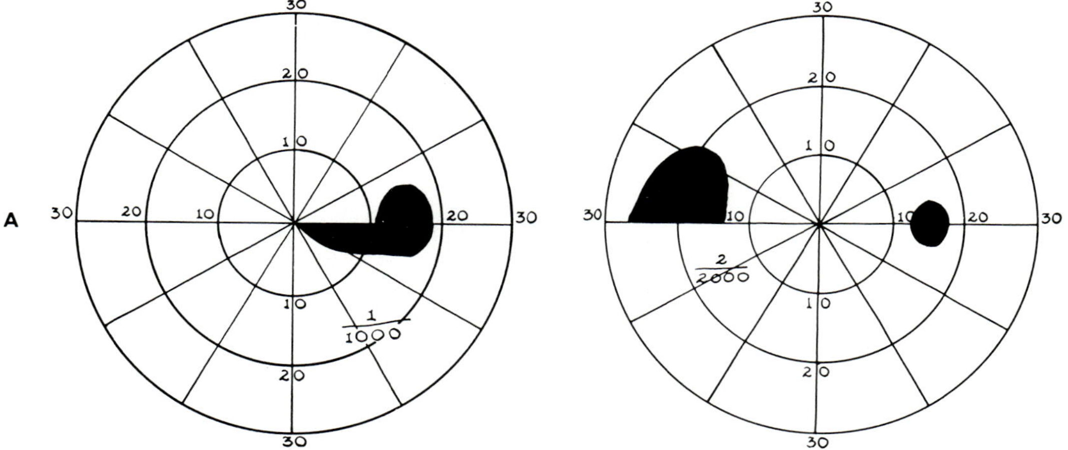

Fig. 7-29. Diagnostic importance of shape of scotoma, from case of glaucoma. **A,** Nerve fiber bundle defect involving one half of papillomacular bundle of nerve fibers to form one half of centrocecal scotoma with sharp horizontal raphe. **B,** Paracentral scotoma in nasal field with sharp horizontal border (nasal step) at raphe.

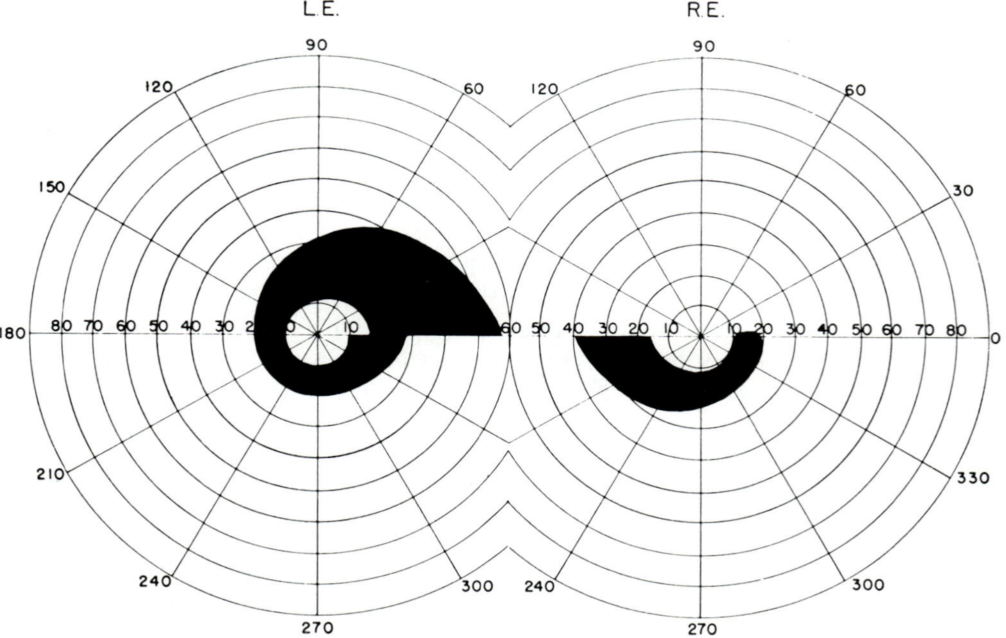

Fig. 7-30. Double nerve fiber bundle defect (double arcuate scotoma) with nasal steps, left eye, and nerve fiber bundle defect (inferior arcuate scotoma), right eye.

inal nerve fiber pattern but are straight or cuneate instead of curved and form narrow wedges of blindness extending into the temporal field.

Quite commonly a double arcuate scotoma will arise from the blind spot and arch above and below fixation to meet in the nasal field as a ring scotoma. If two symmetrically placed and equal nerve fiber bundles happen to be involved, it is sheer coincidence. Careful testing can practically always demonstrate a difference in the width and position of the superior and inferior defects, with the result that the meeting at the nasal horizontal meridian is asymmetric and a characteristic wide or narrow double nasal step is formed. This, plus the fact that the blind spot is always in the line of the ring, serves to differentiate these double arcuate scotomas from the ring scotoma of retinitis pigmentosa or other pericentral scotomas.

The nerve fiber bundle scotoma may take an infinite variety of positions and shapes, depending on the degree of retinal nerve fiber involvement, the size and intensity of visual stimulus used to test it, and the care and patience of the perimetrist. Regardless of these variables, however, there are certain constant characteristics that immediately identify the defect.

The most typical example of the defect is a scimitar-shaped scotoma attached at its temporal end to the blind spot or separated from it by a narrow gap. As the defect pushes up and nasally, it broadens in width, curving around fixation, and then abruptly curves downward to end sharply at the nasal horizontal meridian. In this form it is usually known as the Bjerrum scotoma.

Very early or incipient Bjerrum scotomas and angioscotomas may sometimes be confused but never when the angiogenetic defect is quantitatively analyzed.

The nerve fiber bundle scotoma is found most typically in patients with glaucoma.

Lesions that interfere with the vascular supply to the anterior optic nerve in the region of the ring of Zinn-Haller may also give rise to nerve fiber bundle scotomas. These may be indistinguishable from the field defect of glaucoma. They are fairly common and will be discussed later. (See Fig. 11-17.)

Hemianoptic scotoma. Hemianoptic scotomas are bounded by the vertical meridian of the field and are, in reality, central hemianoptic defects. They are usually bilateral, although, in the case of bitemporal defects (Fig. 7-31), they may be unilateral. As in peripheral hemianopsia, they may be homonymous (Fig. 7-32) congruous or incongruous, quadrantanoptic, temporal, crossed quadrant, central, or paracentral. They may spare or split the macula.

If the hemianoptic scotoma is bounded by a vertical and horizontal meridian, it is a quadrantanoptic defect, triangular in shape, with its apex at or near fixation.

A temporal hemianoptic scotoma may be associated with blindness or a temporal hemianopsia or peripheral quadrantanoptic cut in the opposite field. This is one form of the classic junction scotoma (Fig. 7-33).

Careful analysis of the margins, intensity, and uniformity of a hemianoptic scotoma is necessary to reveal its true shape, and when so studied these scotomas may be of utmost importance in indicating the localization and pathology of the lesion producing the defect.

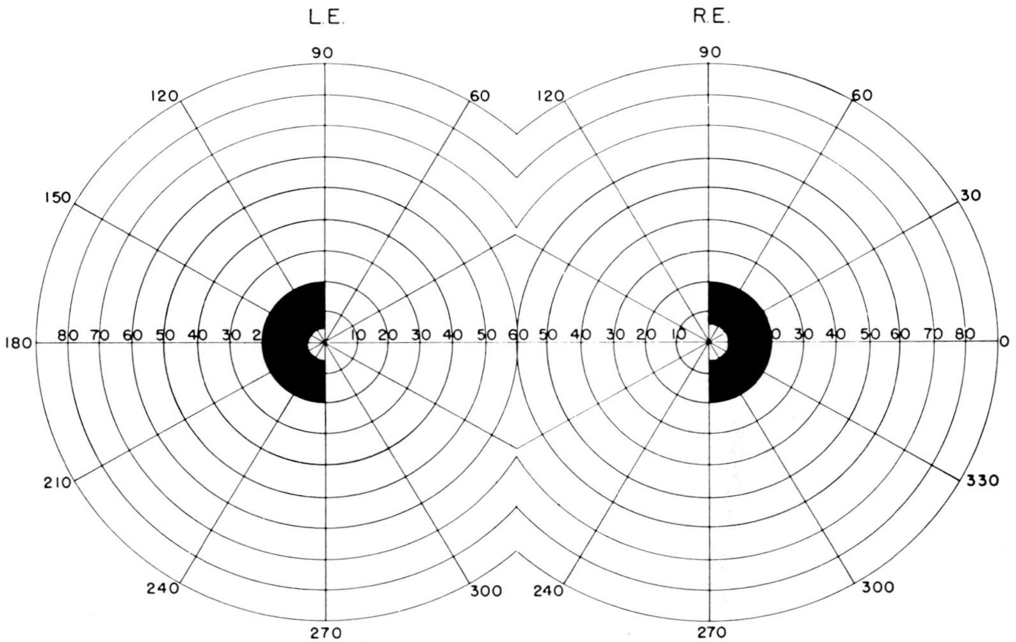

Fig. 7-31. Bitemporal hemianoptic scotomas. Macular sparing is usually minimal or absent.

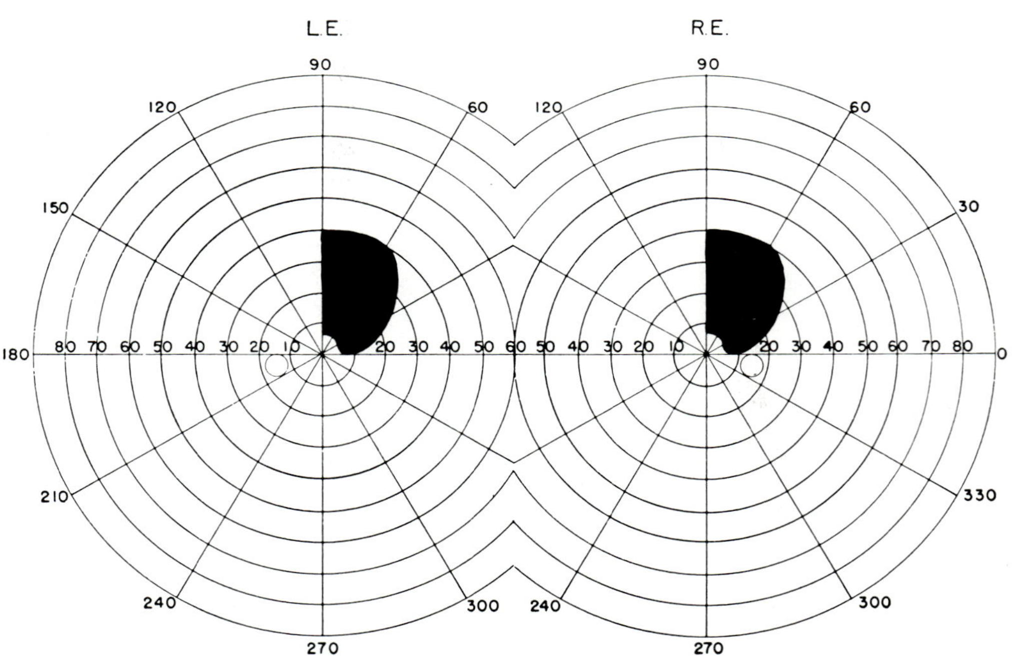

Fig. 7-32. Homonymous hemianoptic scotomas. Vascular lesion of left occipital lobe was demonstrated, involving inferior lip of posterior tip of left calcarine fissure. Note complete congruity of defects.

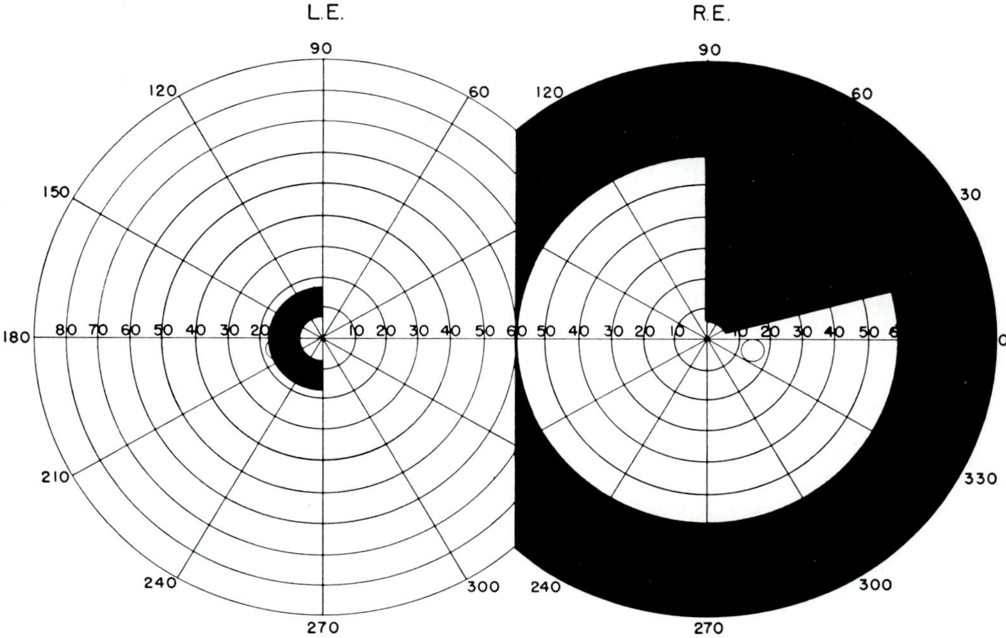

Fig. 7-33. Junction scotoma. This is from case of aneurysm of left anterior cerebral artery with compression of left optic nerve and anterior chiasm.

Size

The size of a scotoma is of less diagnostic import than the shape or position, although size may be of some value indicating the virulence of the lesion producing the scotoma. Scotomas vary in size from a minute area of slightly depressed vision, less than 1 degree in diameter, to an area of absolute blindness that encompasses almost the entire visual field. The same scotoma may vary in size from day to day, depending on progression or regression of the disease producing it. An angioscotoma may be made to vary in width and size from minute to minute by compression of the globe with its accompanying changes in retinal blood pressure and intraocular pressure. Scotomas of great intensity with steep margins may be relatively constant in size and, in general, have a poor prognosis, whereas scotomas of low intensity may vary greatly in size, depending on the stimuli used to test them. When the margins are gently sloping, the defect may appear to be quite small in the 5/1000 isopter and very large when a 1-mm stimulus is used.

Intensity

The intensity of scotomas varies from absolute blindness to a minimum detectable loss of visual acuity (Fig. 7-34). A scotoma may vary in its intensity in different portions of its area; this is spoken of as its uniformity. Scotomas of high intensity and uniformity are relatively rare and are easily demonstrated by even crude methods of perimetry. Much more common are those defects that require careful quantita-

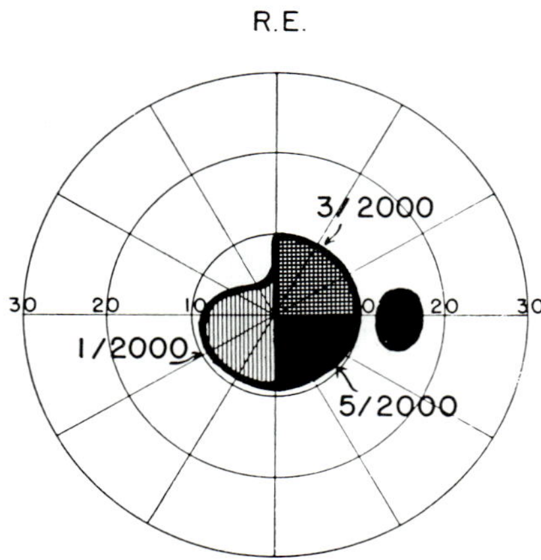

Fig. 7-34. Example of varying intensity within scotoma. Defect shows three separate shapes and sizes depending on stimulus used to test it. From case of compression of right optic nerve on medial side at orbital apex by fibrosarcoma of orbit. Scotoma regressed following removal of tumor.

tive methods to demonstrate their true size, depth, and uniformity. Not uncommonly the patient will complain of haziness of central vision or will show a corrected vision of only 20/30 on the Snellen chart and yet it will not be possible to demonstrate a scotoma by ordinary methods even though the perimetrist may be quite sure that one is present. Under these circumstances it may be necessary to reduce the stimulus considerably in order to show a defect that may have diagnostic value. This may be done in a variety of ways: (1) by decreasing the visual angle, either by increasing the tangent screen distance up to 4 meters or more or decreasing the test object size, or both, (2) by decreasing the illumination by the use of filters, as on the Goldmann and Tübinger perimeters, or by rheostatic control of floodlight or electroluminescent stimulus, (3) by decreasing the contrast between background and test object, or (4) by the use of colored test objects. It is in this situation that the method of testing the central field with luminescent monochromatic blue test objects and ultraviolet light is most useful (Fig. 7-35).

On occasion, the use of a red stimulus, sometimes of fairly large size, helps in exaggerating a bitemporal hemianopsia that may be difficult to elicit with small white targets.

The prism displacement test of Irvine is especially useful in the detection and measurement of very small scotomas at fixation.

Another method of demonstrating a minimal central scotoma is to utilize the principle of two-point discrimination. If a barely visible stimulus is chosen for fixation, the patient may see it by virtue of constantly shifting his fixation so as to bring it outside the scotomatous area. If, then, a stimulus of the same size is slowly brought in to the point of fixation, an area may be demonstrated in which one or the other of these stimuli will be seen but not both simultaneously. Such a technique may be necessary to demonstrate the minute central defect resulting from eclipse burn of the fovea or the vague foveal edema following contusion of the globe or that seen in central serous retinopathy.

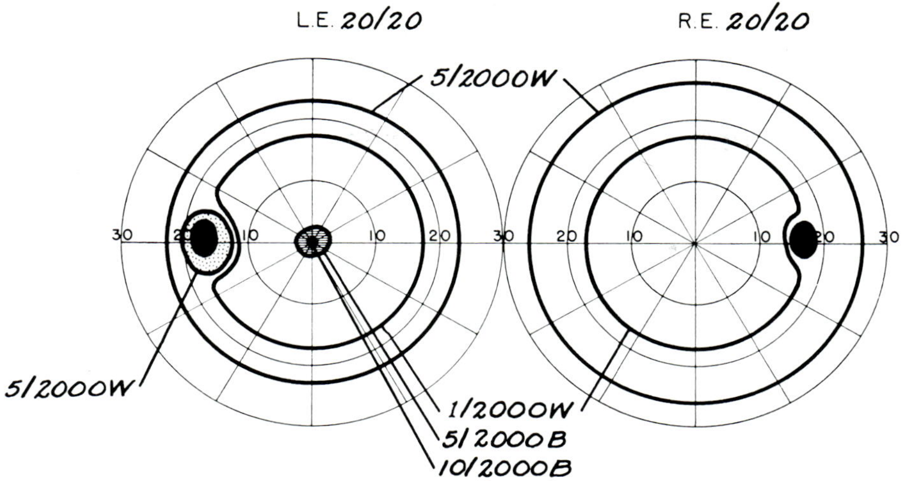

Fig. 7-35. Demonstration of minimal central scotoma with monochromatic blue stimulus. No central scotoma could be elicited even in 1/2000 isopter for white. From case of retrobulbar neuritis associated with multiple sclerosis. Patient complained of blurred vision in left eye even though visual acuity measured 20/20 in each eye.

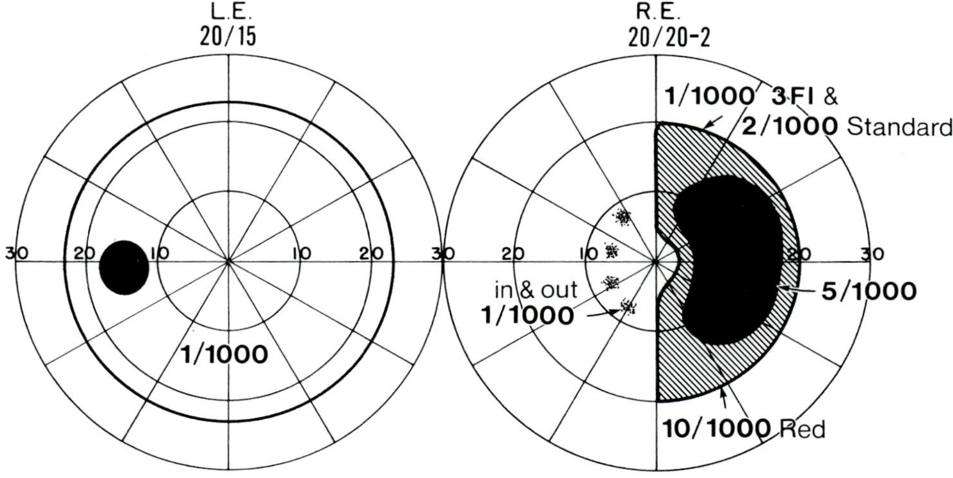

Fig. 7-36. Unilateral hemianoptic scotoma with sloping margins. Right eye shows slight retinal pigment epithelial disturbance and an optic nerve pit at the inferior nasal disc margin.

Scotomas are usually more dense in their centers than at their edges. This lack of uniformity often makes tham appear to have one or more central or eccentric nuclei when carefully examined. The analysis of uniformity within a scotoma may be of great importance in precise localization. For example, a temporal hemianoptic scotoma may show a greater density in its upper quadrant than in its lower, indicating that the pressure that produces it is directed on the macular fiber decussation from below and, by inference, giving a clue to the pathologic nature of the lesion.

Careless analysis of a typical arcuate scotoma, with large test objects and crude technique, may serve to demonstrate only its nucleus, situated as a shapeless paracentral scotoma of no diagnostic value (Fig. 7-36).

Margins

The margins of a scotoma, as would be expected, are usually sloping but may occasionally be quite steep. In general, a steep edge is indicative of little change, whereas sloping margins indicate a more active process. An analysis of scotoma margins has some prognostic value.

Onset and course

The onset and course of a scotoma may be of great importance. There is marked variation as among different diseases. Thus the onset of the scotoma of tobacco amblyopia is very gradual and its course is very slow, whereas the central scotoma resulting from multiple sclerosis may appear in a matter of hours and be gone again in a day. As in peripheral field defects, it may be generally stated that vascular lesions produce the most rapid onset of scotomas; inflammatory lesions produce the defects with the most erratic course; and defects caused by pressure of tumors are the least variable.

Angioscotomas are notoriously fleeting as to variations in their size, width, onset, density, and course. They are constant only in regard to their position.

Unilateral or bilateral

Scotomas may be unilateral or bilateral. Hemianoptic scotomas from lesions of the postchiasmal pathway are always bilateral, but it must not be inferred that all bilateral scotomas are postchiasmal in orginal. It is not uncommon for the disease that affects one retina or optic nerve to affect the other. Thus advanced multiple sclerosis may give rise to bilateral central scotoma resulting from bilateral optic nerve involvement. The scotomas of the toxic amblyopias are always bilateral.

A unilateral scotoma will indicate the pathologic process that produced it, largely because of its shape, size, density, and other characteristics. Whereas it is usually due to disease of the visual pathway anterior to the chiasm, one must not forget the scotomatous defect produced in the Foster-Kennedy syndrome and also the junction scotoma found in certain anterior chiasmal lesions.

Angioscotomas

A special word should be said regarding the angioscotoma. This characteristic defect of the visual field has been variously described by many authors, but Evans was the first to study it in exhaustive detail and attach much importance to its characteristics and variations.

Insofar as angioscotomas are extensions from the blind spot, they may be considered cecal, pericecal, or paracecal scotomas. These extensions follow the pattern of the arborizations of the retinal vascular tree, and the word *angioscotoma* is derived from the Greek *angeion* (vessel) and *skotos* (darkness), to indicate a "scotoma which the retinal vessels seem to project" (Figs. 7-37 and 7-38).

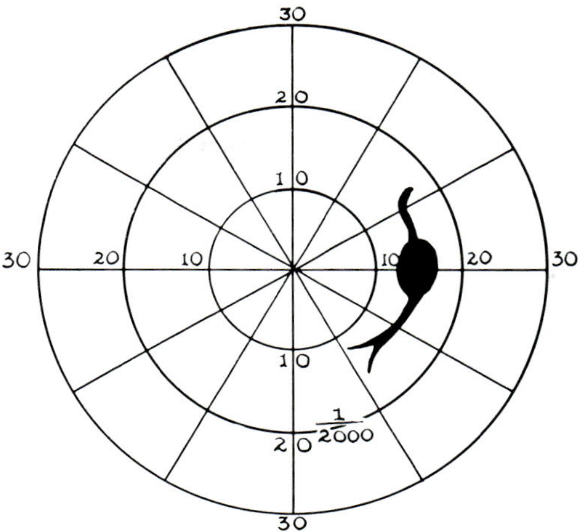

Fig. 7-37. Normal angioscotoma as plotted on tangent screen with minimal stimulus and reduced illumination.

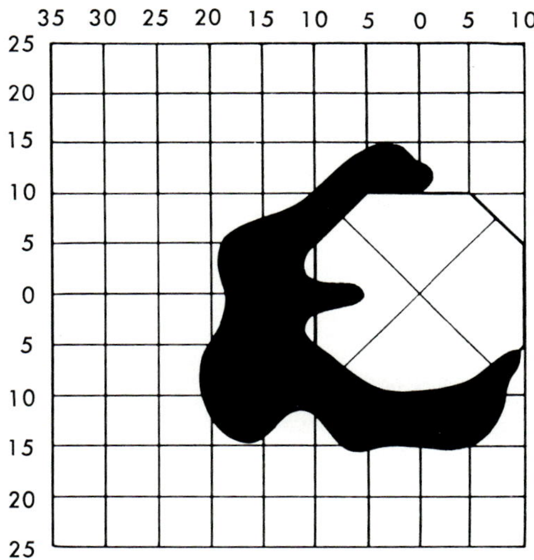

Fig. 7-38. Angioscotoma in patient with incipient glaucoma as charted on stereocampimeter.

A number of authors have confirmed Evans' work, particularly in the study of early glaucomatous field changes.

Analysis of scotomas

As indicated by the foregoing discussion, careful analysis of the characteristics of a visual field defect, whether peripheral or scotomatous, as to size, shape, position, intensity, etc., is of utmost importance. Only by such quantitative examination and analysis can one interpret the true meaning of the defects that are discovered. Correct evaluation of the characteristics of a visual field deficit makes possible the localization of the lesion producing the deficit and often allows a shrewd guess as to pathology.

It should be obvious that such analysis and interpretation must be done during the examination and not as a result of the study of a visual field defect detected and charted by another observer. In other words, the *interpreter* of the visual field must be the perimetrist, and the analysis of a field defect must be accomplished by the perimetrist *during* the examination and not from the recorded chart of the defect.

CHAPTER 8

Opacities of the media (cornea, lens, and vitreous) and their effect on the visual fields

Perimetry under conditions of reduced illumination will result in generally depressed visual fields in normal persons. Thus, if the intensity of the stimulus is sufficiently reduced by decreasing the light reflected from its surface, the isopter for a test object of any given size will be either markedly reduced in size or altogether obliterated. This reduction in light may be compensated for by the use of larger stimuli, and for some individuals with sluggish cerebral response, it is more practical to examine the field by this means than to attempt the examination of an isopter for a very small visual angle.

Visual field defects that have been detected with difficulty with small visual stimuli in the central isopters can sometimes be grossly exaggerated by a reduction in illumination. Such variation in luminance of stimuli may be obtained artificially by the use of filters (e.g., in the Goldmann and Tübinger perimeters), by rheostatic control of the illumination directed onto standard flat or spherical test objects on a tangent screen, or by rheostatic or resistance control of self-luminous stimuli such as the electroluminescent targets of the Lumiwand.

Any opacity of the media of the eye produces, in effect, a reduction in illumination of the test object, and such reduction must be taken into account in the examination of the visual fields in such patients.

Failure to attempt a visual field examination is not justified simply because the media are so opaque as to preclude the possibility with ordinary or commonly used test objects. Conversely, the interpretation of a visual field defect in an eye with opacities of the media must be approached with caution, and adequate allowance must be made for such opacities.

If the cornea, lens, or vitreous is so clouded that a 10-mm test object is virtually invisible at fixation, the perimetrist must use either more light or larger test objects. It is quite possible to obtain a reasonably accurate qualitative visual field under these conditions with 50-, 100-, or even 500-mm test objects. If this is not possible, a waving towel or flashlight may be used.

The minimum separable distance of two flashlight bulbs at 20 feet may give valuable information as to the state of the visual pathway, and especially the macula, in the presence of an almost mature cataract or a dense corneal leukoma.

In a patient with posterior uveitis with vitreous opacity and secondary glaucoma, visual field defects may be revealed by such an examination, when ordinary methods of perimetry are useless.

Much embarrassment may be avoided if, before cataract extraction, the examiner is able to detect the presence of a homonymous hemianopsia from an unsuspected cerebrovascular accident. On the other hand, a glaucomatous field defect in association with progressive cataractous changes in the lens must be assessed with great caution. The lens opacity acts to reduce the illumination, and thereby exaggerates the visual field loss, so that the glaucoma appears to be out of control. This apparent, rapid loss of visual field actually may be entirely due to the cataract and may not be indicative of the true state of the glaucoma, which may, in fact, be well controlled. Experience and careful judgment are always required to evaluate such a combination of circumstances (Fig. 8-1).

It is well known that pupillary size has some effect on the size of the visual field. In some degree, a very small pupil will constrict the visual field. In the presence of cataract or vitreous opacity, or even central corneal opacity, it is possible to obtain a more accurate estimate of the visual field with the pupils dilated than in their normal state. Because accommodation is relatively unaffected by it, the drug of choice for such dilation is phenylephrine hydrochloride (Neo-Synephrine). With the pupil dilated the visual field of a patient with central opacity of the lens may be quite normal, whereas is had appeared quite contracted before dilatation.

The commonly used estimate of the visual field obtained by the patient's ability to project a light in the peripheral field is at best a crude method, capable of detecting only the grossest defect.

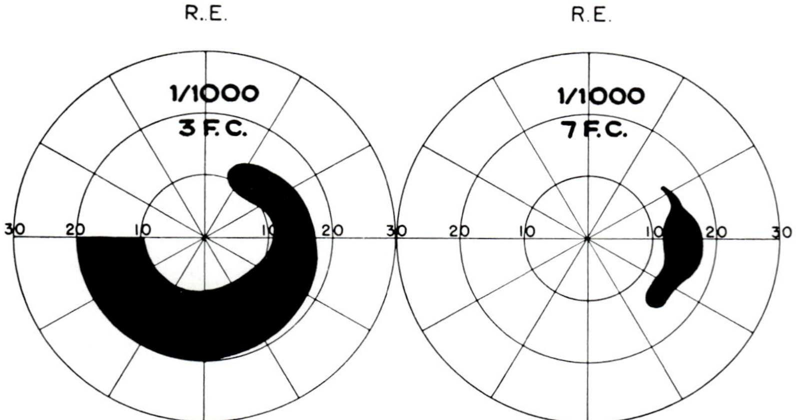

Fig. 8-1. Comparative visual field studies in case of glaucoma showing intensification of nerve fiber bundle defect produced by reduction in intensity of illumination of test object. Same effect may sometimes be obtained by increasing background illumination and reducing contrast between background and stimulus or by developing cataract.

By using a high degree of contrast between test objects and background, the examiner may, with a fairly well-advanced cataract, obtain a visual field portrait of considerable accuracy. Larger-than-average test objects must be used, and it is here that projected stimuli, both on perimeter and on tangent screen, are most useful. Self-luminous electroluminescent stimuli provide excellent contrast between stimulus and background and have proved most useful as methods of quantitative perimetry in the presence of cataract or other opacities of the media.

Because reduced illumination affects the visual fields for colors even more than it does for white, a true visual field defect in an eye with opacities of the media will be exaggerated when colored stimuli are used. Thus the central field for blue will be affected first, followed by green, yellow, and red in the more peripheral portions of the field. By means of projected or luminescent orange or red stimuli, it is sometimes possible to diagnose retinal, choroidal, or optic nerve disease, including glaucoma, when ophthalmoscopic examination of these structures is impossible because of opacification of the media.

In patients with aphakia, even though the vitreous is clear, the visual field may be considerably contracted. This normal phenomenon is further intensified by the spherical aberration produced by the thick lenses required after cataract extraction. This narrowing of the visual field is often a source of much difficulty to the patient, especially in the first few weeks after operation. Much embarrassment may be avoided if the surgeon will carefully explain the nature of the visual field contraction before surgery. Fortunately, adjustment to the contracted field is usually fairly rapid, although some patients never learn to accustom themselves to it.

Mention has already been made of Beasley's studies on visual fields in aphakia. He found that correction of the aphakis with contact lenses is the best optical device for testing both central and peripheral fields.

CHAPTER 9

Diseases of the choroid

The perimetry of choroidal lesions is of some importance both diagnostically and as a means of assessing the course and prognosis of the disease. Most choroidal disease that affects the visual pathway is visible ophthalmoscopically, and its type, location, severity, and course can usually be judged by examination of the fundus. Choroidal lesions affect the rod and cone layer of the retina by extension and the production of secondary retinitis or by depriving these structures of their vascular supply through the production of secondary retinal edema.

In early lesions the visual field defects may be disproportionate to the observable fundus lesion, and the use of blue test objects will sometimes give information otherwise unavailable as to site and extent of the disease. Care should be taken, however, not to place too much emphasis on the color fields.

Choroiditis may affect any part of the fundus. Only in special types, such as the juxtapapillary lesion of Jensen, does it commonly affect the nerve fiber layer of the retina, although the more severe forms may extend through the retina to affect the ganglion cell layer. Not infrequently the optic nerve head is affected, resulting in characteristic visual field changes. When associated with exudation into the vitreous and consequent clouding to the media, the perimetric examination may be of importance in localizing the site of the lesion.

Choroiditis of various types and location may produce a variety of visual field defects: (1) general depression of all the iopsters of the field, (2) multiple scotomas, mosaic in character, corresponding to the location of areas of choroiditis and their overlying retinal lesions, (3) enlargement or extension of the normal blind spot, (4) arcuate scotoma, (5) sector defect of Jensen, and (6) central scotoma. These defects may coexist; for instance, there may be a general depression of the smaller isopters associated with multiple peripheral scotomas, detected with larger stimuli. The sector defect of choroiditis juxtapapillaris may take an arcuate form or may involve the fixation area at the same time that it enlarges the normal blind spot.

General depression or even marked contraction of the field accompanies an acute and severe choroiditis, especially when there is vitreous exudation. This may later resolve itself into the mosaic type of multiple scotomas scattered throughout the visual field and corresponding to the pigmented patches of healed chorioretinitis seen with the ophthalmoscope. Often these scotomas follow the pattern of the retinal vascular tree and are best demonstrated and studied by the methods of angioscotometry.

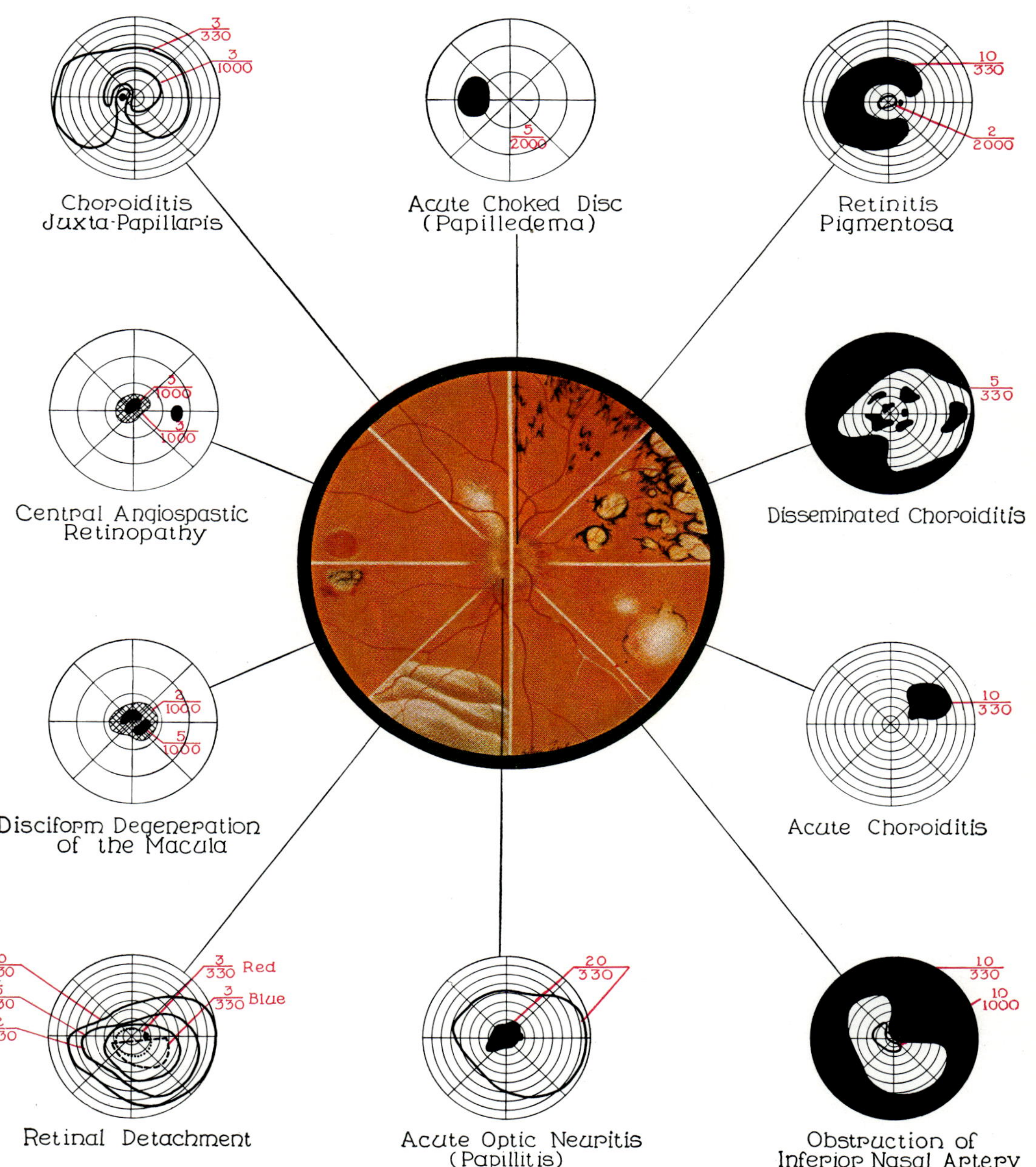

Plate 3. Visual field defects of lesions of fundus oculi.

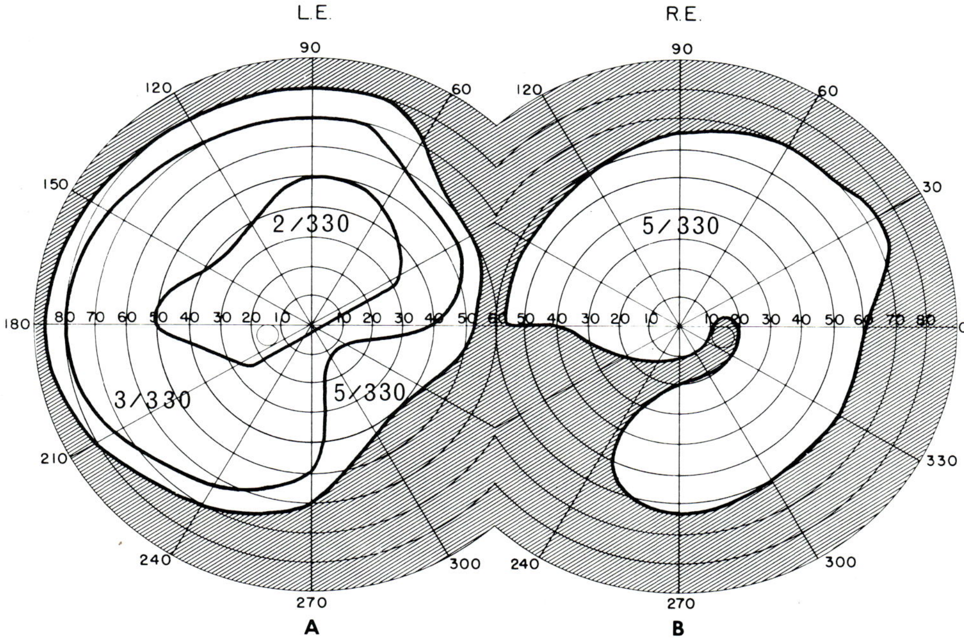

Fig. 9-1. A, Visual field defect produced by malignant melanoma of choroid with overlying retinal detachment. **B,** Nerve fiber bundle defect in visual field resulting from acute choroiditis juxtapapillaris. (From Harrington, D. O.: In Straatsma, B. R., et al.: The retina. UCLA Forum in Medical Sciences, no. 8, Berkeley, 1969, University of California Press.)

When the optic nerve head is involved in uveitis, there is an enlargement of the blind spot or a central scotoma, or both. This may vary within wide limits; it may appear as a simple overall enlargement in all its diameters, as an extension of one diameter to simulate the arculate scotoma of glaucoma (Fig. 9-1), or as the sector defect of juxtapapillary choroiditis; or when the process involves the papillomacular nerve fiber bundles, a dense centrocecal type of scotoma may appear.

The true arcuate scotoma as seen in patients with glaucoma is rare in choroiditis. When present, it implies involvement of the nerve fiber layer of the retina. What may at first appear to be a nerve fiber bundle defect will, with quantitative study, often fail to reveal the characteristic nerve fiber patterns, the nasal broadening, or the nasal step. More often the defect is irregular in shape, following only roughly the arcuate form, with steep margins and great density.

On the other hand, the specific type of choroiditis known as choroiditis juxtapapillaris can be localized exactly at the disc margin by the narrow sector type of nerve fiber bundle defect that it produces in the visual field. This defect varies greatly in size, shape, position, and other characteristics, but it always arises at the blind spot and extends in the nerve fiber pattern into the peripheral field. In the majority of cases it will break through, but in some instances it takes on the exact characteristics of the Bjerrum scotoma of glaucoma, including the nasal step. A double arcuate scotoma, common in association with glaucoma, would be a rare coincidence in juxtapapillary choroiditis. Temporal extensions of the blind spot in the form of fan-shaped defects are not uncommon in patients with this disease, whereas they are relatively rare in glaucoma. The location of the lesion is such that a small area of choroiditis involving only a few of the nerve fiber bundles may still produce an extensive visual field defect.

Central scotomas are common findings in patients with choroiditis. They vary from the most minute defect, encompassing less than 1 degree around fixation, to extensive central visual loss with little more than light perception remaining. In association with lesser degrees of macular involvement, the ophthalmoscopic appearance may be normal at first glance, but the finding of a minute scotoma may confirm the patient's rather vague symptoms of visual blurring and stimulate the examiner to search for the minimal area of retinal edema overlying the macular choroiditis.

Not infrequently the scotomas of choroiditis are positive and produce distressing symptoms out of proportion to the size of the lesion or the size of the visual field defect.

A rather common form of central scotoma in patients with choroiditis is the perimacular defect in which the central part of the scotoma is less dense than its periphery. These scotomas evolve as multiple, small paracentral defects, detectable with very small visual angles that coalesce to form a ring scotoma of considerable density and finally involve fixation. It is probable that the etiologic factor in the production of these small macular scotomas is retinal edema in the foveal area. In the case of macular choroiditis, this edema of the retina is secondary to vascular stasis in the choriocapillaris; but any instrumentality that produces foveal edema, such as trauma, or central serous retinopathy, may produce a similar visual field defect.

Another variant of the central scotoma of choroiditis is the minute paramacular defect that exists as a positive scotoma but fails to involve the fovea, with the result that central visual acuity, as tested by Snellen letters, remains good. In their early stages these lesions may produce sufficient retinal edema to involve fixation, resulting in an irregular and eccentrically placed central scotoma with defective central vision. Margins of these defects are usually sloping. As the process regresses, the central field may clear, leaving a small permanent paramacular defect in the central field.

DISSEMINATED CHOROIDITIS

The field defects in disseminated choroiditis vary greatly, depending on the stage of the disease and its intensity. Usually there is a rather marked depression of all isopters with later development of multiple peripheral scotomas. When the macula is involved, there is a central scotoma.

CHOROIDITIS JUXTAPAPILLARIS

The field defects of choroiditis juxtapapillaris have been described and are, typically, nerve fiber bundle defects that are arcuate, sector, or cuneate in form (Figs. 9-1, *B* and 9-2, *A*).

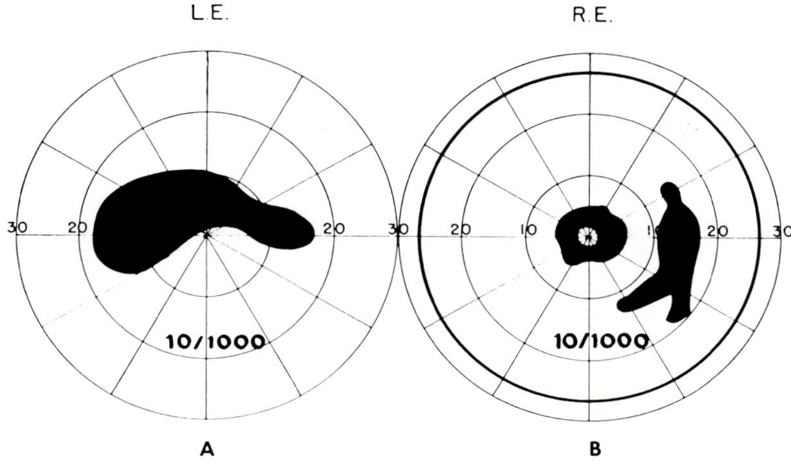

Fig. 9-2. Scotomas of choroiditis. **A,** Irregular arcuate-shaped scotoma partially surrounding fixation but not conforming to nerve fiber pattern of retina. **B,** Small perimacular scotoma with clear fixation. This was accompanied by enlargement of normal blind spot and broadening of normal angioscotoma even to gross stimuli.

MACULAR CHOROIDITIS

The common visual field defect of macular choroiditis is central, pericentral, or paracentral scotoma.

SYMPATHETIC OPHTHALMIA

The visual field loss in sympathetic ophthalmia varies with the intensity of the disease. Peripheral choroiditis is common and causes marked contraction of the field, especially in the peripheral isopters. The foveal area may also be involved in the sympathizing eye, with resulting central scotoma (Fig. 9-3).

SENILE MACULAR DEGENERATION

Senile macular degeneration may properly be classified among the diseases of the choroid, and, like most choroidal disease, it affects the visual field through secondary retinal damage. The usual visual field defect is a negative type of central scotoma of varying density. Not infrequently the fovea is affected late so that in the early stages the scotoma is paracentral.

In the early stages of the disease, the scotoma, which decreases central visual acuity, may be difficult to demonstrate. With progression of the arteriosclerotic circulatory insufficiency of the choroid, the scotoma becomes more dense and reading becomes difficult. As the condition progresses to take on the characteristics of disciform degeneration, there may be sudden visual loss with hemorrhage into the macular area of the choroid and retina with an associated dense irregular central scotoma (Fig. 9-4).

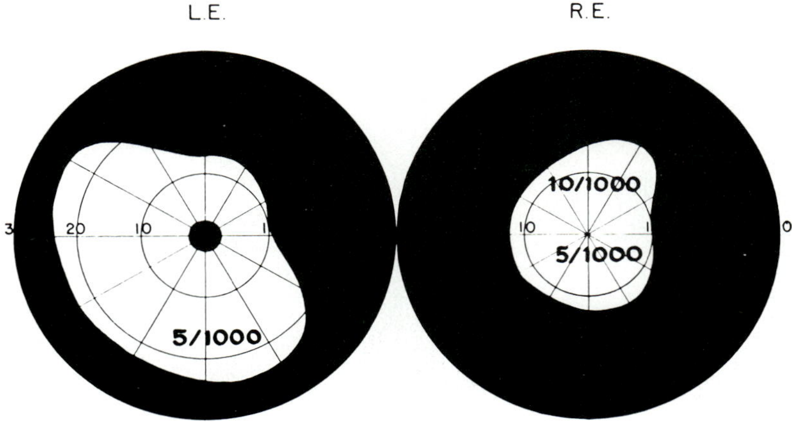

Fig. 9-3. Sympathetic ophthalmia. Left eye shows perforating injury with retained intraocular foreign body and macular chorioretinitis. Right eye shows sympathetic ophthalmia, with peripheral choroidal involvement and contraction of peripheral visual field.

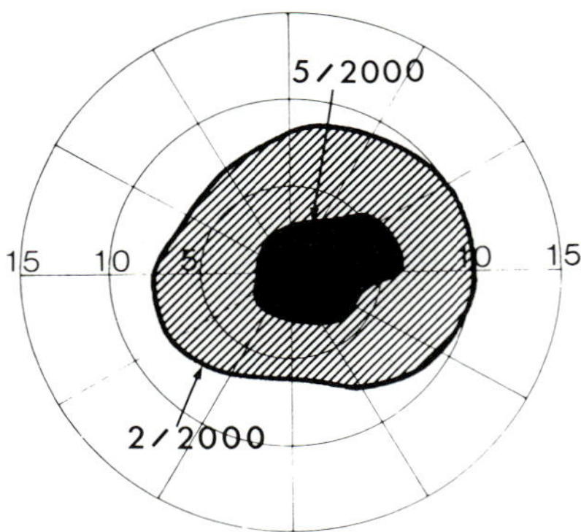

Fig. 9-4. Large, irregular central scotoma with sloping margins in typical case of disciform degeneration of macula. Other eye showed early senile macular degeneration with small paracentral scotoma. (From Harrington, D. O.: In Straatsma, B. R., et al.: The retina. UCLA Forum in Medical Sciences, no. 8, Berkeley, 1969, University of California Press.)

OPTIC NEURITIS ASSOCIATED WITH UVEITIS

As would be expected, the visual field defect in optic neuritis with uveitis is generally a central scotoma of varying size and intensity. The exact mechanism of production of papillitis in anterior uveitis is not known but is thought to be a primary dilatation of the choroidal vessels followed by retinal periphlebitis and edema of the disc.

GLAUCOMA SECONDARY TO UVEITIS

The visual field changes in glaucoma that follow uveitis are glaucomatous in type but develop late and only after prolonged and severe intraocular hypertension. These

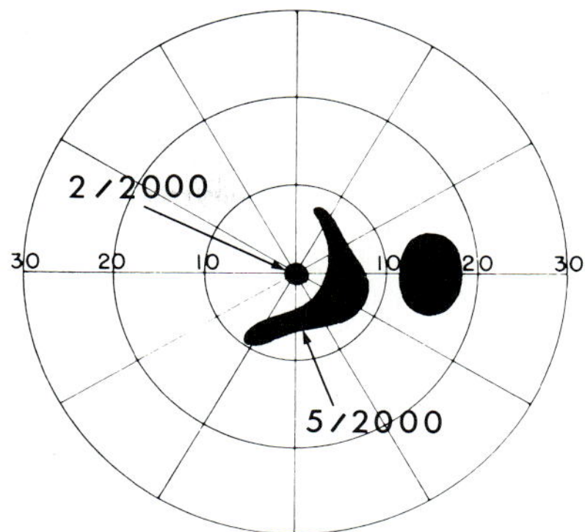

Fig. 9-5. Crescent-shaped paracentral scotoma and small central scotoma resulting from traumatic rupture of choroid. (From Harrington, D. O.: In Straatsma, B. R., et al.: The retina. UCLA Forum in Medical Sciences, no. 8, Berkeley, 1969, University of California Press.)

are peripheral (especially nasal) contraction, nerve fiber bundle scotoma, nasal step, and finally marked depression of all isopters.

DETACHMENT OF CHOROID

Visual fields are rarely examined in patients with detachment of the choroid. The defects vary with the size of the detachment. While they last, the defects are very dense, but they generally clear rapidly.

RUPTURE OF CHOROID

Rupture of the choroid is not an uncommon sequela to contusion injury of the eye. It is usually seen as a crescentic break in the choroid temporal to the optic disc. It is often accompanied by retinal hemorrhage and edema, which may involve the macula and produce a central scotoma. Sector defects may be produced by nerve fiber bundle interruption. The visual field defect may correspond to the shape, size, and location of the fundus lesion (Fig. 9-5).

TUMORS OF CHOROID

By far the most common tumor of the choroid is melanosarcoma. The visual field defects produced by these tumors naturally vary considerably with the size and position of the tumor. Anterior choroidal tumors produce peripheral depressions or sector defects, whereas those of the posterior pole may produce scotomas. The characteristics of the defect are its intensity and steep margins, in contrast to the sloping edges and varying density of the field defects in retinal detachment with subretinal fluid.

Nevus of the choroid, on the other hand, may reveal a visual field defect to the most meticulous perimetry, or it may show a scotomatous or sector defect with sloping margins and considerable variation in intensity (Fig. 9-6). When the visual field defect accompanying a nevus is clear cut, easily demonstrated, and progressive, the benignity of the lesion should be seriously questioned.

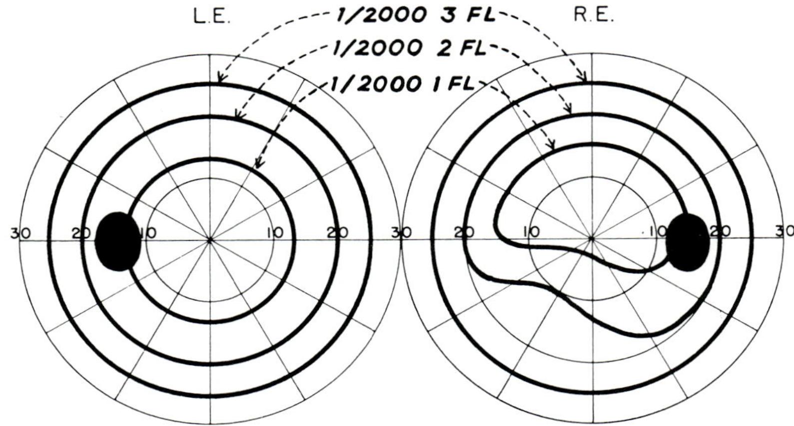

Fig. 9-6. Nevus of choroid. Standard stimulus of full luminance revealed no visual field defect, whereas sloping-margined sector defect, consistent with size and location of lesion, was demonstrated with electroluminescent stimuli of 2 footlamberts and 1 footlambert luminance.

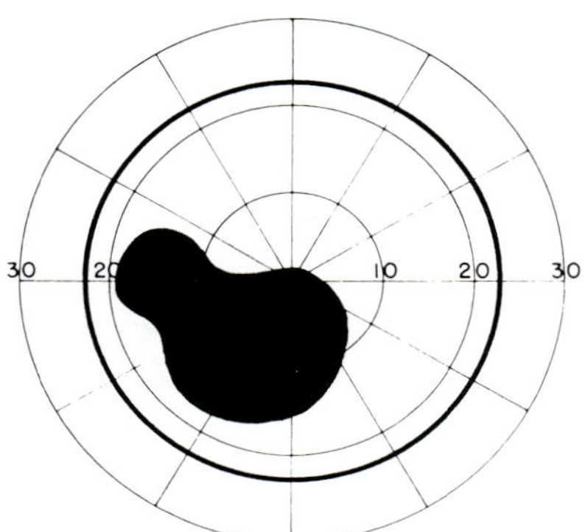

Fig. 9-7. Irregular centrocecal scotoma resulting from malignant melanoma at disc margin with overlying retinal edema and detachment. (From Harrington, D. O.: In Straatsma, B. R., et al.: The retina. UCLA Forum in Medical Sciences, no. 8, Berkeley, 1969, University of California Press.)

Flindall and Drance have studied twenty-one benign choroidal nevi with reference to corresponding visual field defects. Using the Tübinger perimeter with both static profile and kinetic techniques, they found an 85% incidence of visual field defects localized to the site of the lesion. All defects were slight-to-moderate depressions and were more readily detected with static than with kinetic perimetry. The field defects were the same size or smaller than the actual lesion.

Three eyes with malignant melanomas were studied by the same techniques (Fig. 9-7). All three had some overlying retinal detachment, and all had absolute scotomas extending into the periphery beyond the limits of the tumor itself.

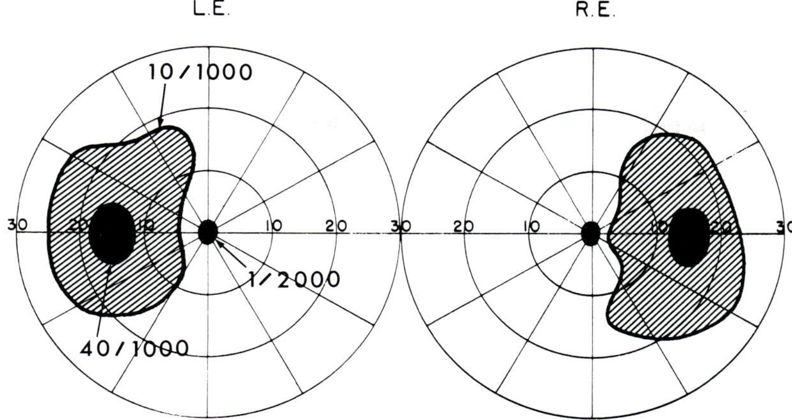

Fig. 9-8. Extreme blind spot enlargement associated with posterior staphyloma or ectasia of sclera around optic disc. Choroidal and retinal atrophy is marked. When ectasia occupies macular area, scotoma is central. This refraction scotoma may represent difference of 5 D. between two portions of retina. (From Harrington, D. O.: In Strattsma, B. R., et al.: The retina. UCLA Forum in Medical Sciences, no. 8, Berkeley, 1969, University of California Press.)

When a choroidal tumor is accompanied by an overlying serous fluid, as is not uncommon, the visual field defect may take on some of the characteristics of simple retinal detachment. Usually the denser portions of the scotoma or sector defect correspond to the area of retina in contact with the tumor, or overlying its highest point of elevation, with the area of retinal detachment more dependent and producing a sloping-edged defect indistinguishable from a simple retinal detachment.

MYOPIA

Unless there are significant choroidal changes visible with the ophthalmoscope, the visual fields in patients with myopia are usually normal. It must be remembered that only a large visual angle can be used to test a patient with myopia of high degree who is without his glasses. When visual acuity is sufficiently improved with glasses so that small test objects are visible, only the central field can be tested since the spectacle lenses produce a spherical aberration in the peripheral field. Contact lenses will overcome this difficulty.

In myopic choroidal atrophy, the visual field changes usually parallel those seen with the ophthalmoscope.

Peripheral degeneration produces general depression contraction, and perimetry of the dark-adapted eye will demonstrate a frequently occurring quadrant defect, especially involving the superior temporal quadrant.

Because most patients with myopia have a degree of night blindness, a reduction in illumination will emphasize their visual field defects and is sometimes of value in determining whether a chroidal atrophy is progressing or stationary. This is particularly true when the lesion is close to the macular and yet central vision remains good in good light. Small luminescent test objects will often show the direction of progress of the atrophy, especially if it is progressing toward the fovea.

The central visual field defects of myopia are (1) enlargement of the blind spots from extension of the myopic conus about the disc, from associated colobomas of the choroid and optic disc, and from myopic atrophy adjacent to the disc; (2) central, paracentral, and pericentral scotomas resulting from macular atrophy, degeneration, and the hemorrhages that give rise to the black spot of Fuchs; and (3) Bjerrum scotoma due to nerve fiber bundle damage at the disc (see remarks on refraction scotomas, Fig. 9-8).

CHAPTER 10

Diseases of the retina

Retinal function is measured clinically by the ability of the rods and cones to detect (1) stimuli of varying size and (2) degrees of separation and luminance within the visual field with the eye fixating a target in its visual axis.

Foveal vision, which is the function of the cones concentrated in the macular area, is measured by the recognition of standard stimuli such as Snellen letters at fixed distances and constant illumination. Macular vision is best in daylight because the cones function most effectively under photopic conditions.

Peripheral vision is the function of the rods, diffusely spread throughout the retina except for the macular area (where they are absent). They are most effective under scotopic conditions. Visual discrimination in the rod areas is low, partly because many rods are summated in a single bipolar cell and what they gain in sensitivity by such summation they lose in visual discrimination.

Any disease process that damages the receptor organs of the retina will produce a loss of function in that portion of the visual field corresponding to the retinal area affected.

The variety of visual field defects produced by retinal disease is almost limitless, and there is no completely typical defect for a specific retinal lesion. However, careful analysis of these field defects often gives sufficient information to assist in the diagnosis and prognosis of retinal disease.

The retinal lesions that result in peripheral and central visual field defects are probably best classified according to the pathology of the disease process, the layers of the retina involved, and the agents causing the disease. We should be concerned with the analysis of the various visual field defects produced by the following broad categories of retinal disease:

1. Vascular lesions affecting the arteries, veins, and capillaries of the retina and choroid
2. Inflammatory lesions of the retina and underlying choroid
3. Degenerative lesions of the various layers of the retina—hereditary, congenital, and acquired
4. Toxic retinopathy
5. Traumatic lesions of the retina
6. Tumors of the retina and of the choroid affecting retinal function
7. Miscellaneous diseases affecting retinal function

VASCULAR LESIONS

Vascular affections of the retina and choroid are most important because of their common and devastating effect on retinal function. They consist of retinal arterial occlusion, both complete and partial, with resulting retinal ischemia and ischemic infarct, capillary insufficiency, occlusion, and leakage; special retinal vascular manifestations of diabetes, blood dyscrasias, and arteriosclerotic changes without frank occlusion; choroidal vascular dsiease secondarily affecting the overlying retina and the optic papilla; damage to the retinal function from circulatory insufficiency far removed from the retina itself; and retinal venous occlusion, both partial and complete, with resulting hemorrhagic retinopathy and edema.

Retinal arterial occlusion

Because the central retinal artery with its arborizations is an end artery, its occlusion causes complete ischemia of the retina with immediate total blindness. If the eye is fortunate in having a cilioretinal artery arising from the choroid, the central area of the retina may be spared and a small island of central vision retained (Fig. 10-1). On the other hand, occlusion of a cilioretinal artery produces a total centrocecal scotoma within a normal peripheral field.

Obstructions of the retinal arterial system may be complete or may involve any part of the arterial tree from one half to a tiny macular twig. These obstructions may be embolic, atherosclerotic, ischemic, or due to vasculitis.

Embolic occlusion of the superior branch of the central retinal artery before it bifurcates into its nasal and temporal branches produces sudden loss of most of the lower visual field (Fig. 10-1, *A*), with ischemia and cloudy swelling of the affected superior retina.

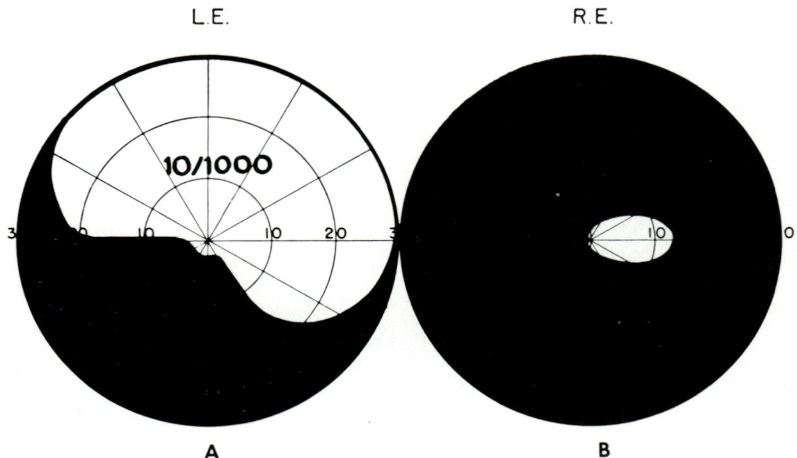

Fig. 10-1. Visual field defects produced by retinal arterial occlusion. **A,** Occlusion of superior nasal branch of central retinal artery. **B,** Total occlusion of central retinal artery. Small remnant of centrocecal visual field results from persistence of cilioretinal artery.

When the embolus (which may be a fragment of an atheromatous plaque or a fibrin-platelet microembolus from the internal carotid artery or possibly a rheumatic heart valve vegetation) lodges in an arteriole on the disc or in the anterior optic nerve, it may produce a typical or atypical nerve fiber bundle defect in the visual field (Fig. 10-2).

Occlusions of peripheral branches give rise to irregular sector defects or isolated peripheral scotomas, depending on the area of ischemic infarct in the retina. Although obstruction of minute arteriolar twigs near the macula causes very small and almost invisible areas of infarction, the visual field defect may result in considerable loss of central vision. Even if the scotoma is small, it is often positive and very annoying.

Choroidal obstruction

Embolus or obstruction of the choroidal vessels supplying the foveal area of the retina causes marked and permanent loss of central vision with an irregular, dense central scotoma. There is evidence that choroidal vascular insufficiency in the peripapillary area may be responsible for atrophy and excavation of the optic nerve head in glaucoma with resulting nerve fiber bundle defects in the visual fields.

Choroidal capillary insufficiency with secondary retinal ischemia is probably the primary cause of most macular holes. These holes or cysts are always associated with small, dense, central scotomas. Another possible result of choroidal capillary insufficiency is the loss of retinal function and consequent central scotoma in senile macu-

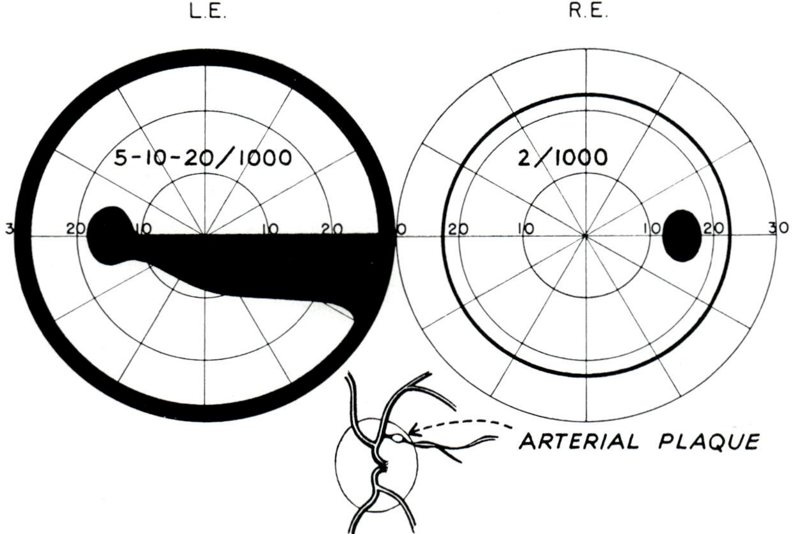

Fig. 10-2. Arterial embolus of lipid-debris type occluding small branch of superior temporal retinal artery as creamy white arterial plaque and producing localized retinal infarct. Field defect is atypical Bjerrum or nerve fiber bundle defect with steep margins and great density. Patient had left internal carotid artery occlusion with reduced ophthalmic artery blood pressure and bruit.

lar degeneration. Whether this is due to changes in the microvascular system of the macula or to deficient blood flow caused by faulty hemodynamics, resulting in blood sludging and alteration in blood lipids, is not precisely known. The characteristic scotoma is irregular in shape, with sloping margins and variable density, slowly progressing, usually unilateral in onset but eventually involving both maculas.

Retinal arterial obstruction

Atheromatous obstruction of retinal arteries is not rare. When it occurs, it produces sector defects in the visual fields corresponding to its location in the retinal vascular tree. On the other hand, death of the ganglion cell layer of the retina from atheromatous occlusion of arteries relatively far removed from the retina may cause a variety of visual field defects. Thus occlusion of small arterioles supplying the optic nerve gives rise to segmental atrophy of the nerve and corresponding visual field defects, the most notable of which are typical and atypical nerve fiber bundle defects (see Figs. 10-2 and 10-5). These Bjerrum scotomas, secondary to decreased blood flow in the nerve, are often confused with the typical scotoma of glaucoma. They are rarely bilateral. They may bisect fixation and break through into the peripheral field as a true altitudinal hemianopsia. In such cases, except that the defect is unilateral the field loss may resemble that seen in severe retinal ischemia associated with the tissue hypoxia of exsanguination or suffocation (Fig. 10-4).

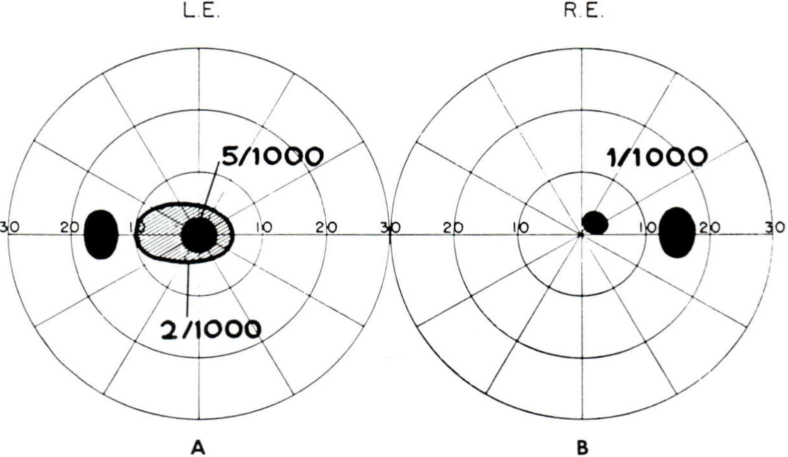

Fig. 10-3. Visual field defects produced by vascular lesions of retina. **A,** Arteriosclerotic macular degeneration. **B,** Macular hemorrhage in hypertensive retinopathy.

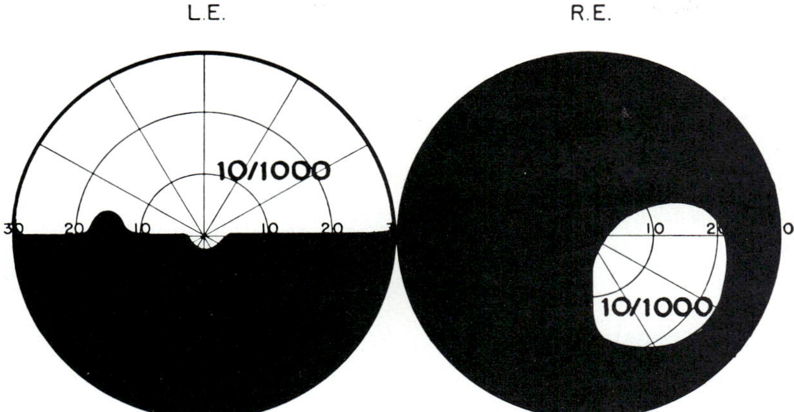

Fig. 10-4. Visual field changes secondary to exsanguination. There was sudden and severe blood loss from hemorrhaging duodenal ulcer. Optic atrophy and permanent visual loss probably resulted from hypoxia in ganglion cell layer of retina.

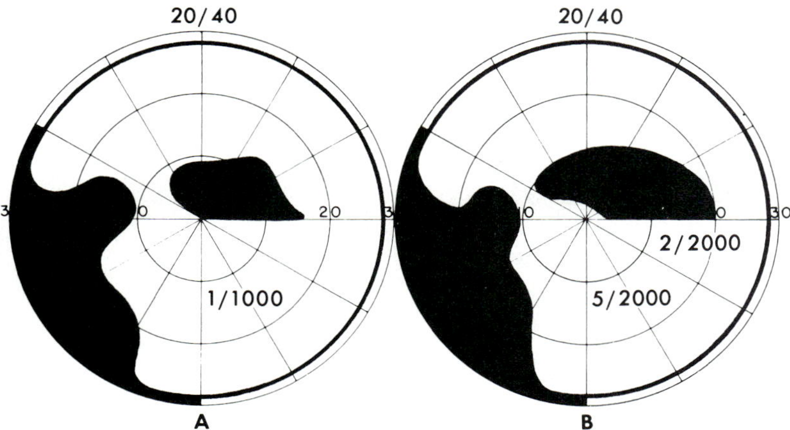

Fig. 10-5. A, Initial visual field study appeared to show paracentral scotoma and inferior temporal quadrant defect. **B,** Quantitative analysis revealed isolated nerve fiber bundle defect with nasal step and inferior temporal quadrant loss. Repeated attacks of amaurosis fugax, left eye. Creamy white fibrin platelet embolus in upper nasal artery accounts for interior temporal quadrant loss. Superior nasal scotoma in nerve fiber bundle defect due to embolization within optic nerve. Fluorescein angiography showed markedly delayed filling of entire retinal arterial tree. Endarterectomy revealed large tubular embolus of left internal carotid just above bifurcation.

The same type of arcuate scotoma, often preceded by periodic and transient blackout of one eye, may result from gradual occlusion of the internal carotid artery. These attacks of amaurosis fugax occur with increasing frequency and duration until there is a prolonged obstruction with retinal ischemia and either temporary or permanent visual field defects. The arterial emboli are usually of the platelet-fibrin type. Frequently there are other neurologic deficits such as transient contralateral hemiplegia and homonymous hemianopsia. Other signs of carotid artery occlusion may be present such as a bruit over the affected artery and lowered homolateral retinal arterial pressure as measured by ophthalmodynamometry.

Carotid angiograms will usually indicate the degree of insufficiency or stenosis; and often the opposite, asymptomatic, arterial system will show a degree of occlusion, also indicating the need for endarterectomy. Fluorescein angiography may show markedly delayed filling of the retinal arterial tree on the affected side.

Retinal arterial spasm

Arterial spasm in the retina is generally associated with hypertensive retinopathy. Localized narrowing of retinal arteries may cause ischemia and secondary retinal edema. Tangent screen studies may reveal irregular, sloping-margined scotomas and angioscotoma-like prolongations of the blind spot (Fig. 10-6). If there is associated hypertensive retinopathy with retinal hemorrhage and exudates, one may expect to find corresponding visual field deficits.

Central serous retinopathy

The condition variously known as central serous retinopathy, central serous retinal detachment, or central angiospastic retinopathy is almost certainly vascular in origin. Whether it is an exudative retinopathy due to choroidal inflammation or angiospasm is a moot point. My belief is that there may be a variety of factors capable

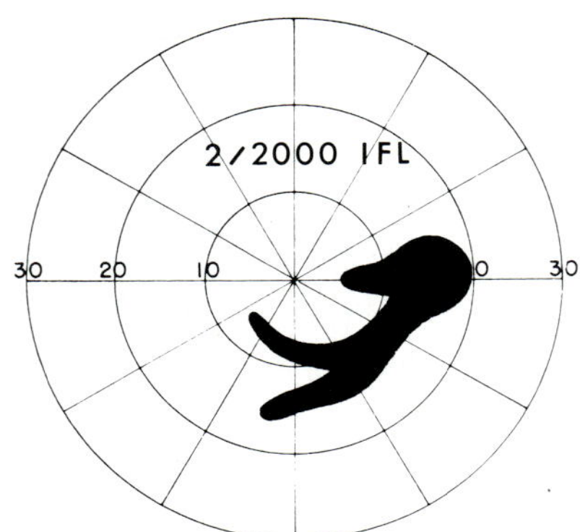

Fig. 10-6. Spasm and severe localized narrowing of superior temporal artery. Angioscotoma was easily demonstrated at 2 meters on tangent screen with 2-mm electroluminescent stimulus, 1 foot-lambert illumination. (From Harrington, D. O.: In Straatsma, B. R., et al.: The retina. UCLA Forum in Medical Sciences, no. 8, Berkeley, 1969, University of California Press.)

of producing this common and well-described clinical entity. Considerable information is being obtained from continuing studies of fluorescein angiograms, that seems to indicate that this disease is associated with small, discrete, choroidal vascular leaks.

The typical ophthalmoscopic picture is one of central retinal elevation. The area of edema is surrounded by a bright ring reflex. The entire macular area may have a deeper and darker red coloration. There is a loss of foveal reflex. Visual acuity may be reduced to a minor degree or may be less than 20/200. Metamorphopsia is frequently noticed by the patient and is demonstrable on the Amsler grid.

Visual field examination is best conducted on the tangent screen at a distance of 2 to 4 meters and shows a circular or irregular central scotoma varying in size from 2 to 5 degrees in diameter. The defect is more readily demonstrated with reduced illumination and is exaggerated when tested with 5-mm luminescent blue test objects activated by ultraviolet light (Fig. 10-7).

When such a macula is exposed to very bright light, as in the photostress test of Severin, the period of time required for vision to return to the pretest level is markedly prolonged and the size and density of the scotomas are grossly exaggerated.

The ophthalmoscopic picture and its accompanying visual depression just described may result from a variety of causes as follows.

Minute area of macular choroiditis. A minute area of macular choroiditis may cause overlying retinal edema to mask the inflammatory nature of the primary disease. As the edema subsides, the true nature of the underlying pathologic condition becomes evident. In such cases permanent scarring causes considerable loss of central vision with a dense steep-margined scotoma.

Macular edema of commotio retinae. In its early stages the macular edema of commotio retinae closely resembles central serous retinopathy. Edema and func-

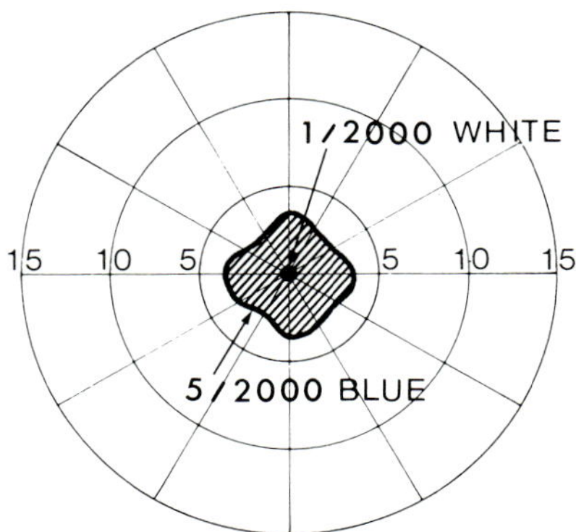

Fig. 10-7. Angiospastic retinopathy with foveal edema (central serous retinal detachment). Irregular sloping-margined scotoma is best demonstrated on tangent screen with monochromatic luminescent blue stimuli exposed to ultraviolet light. Photostress test is positive. (From Harrington, D. O.: In Straatsma, B. R., et al.: The retina. UCLA Forum in Medical Sciences, no. 8, Berkeley, 1969, University of California Press.)

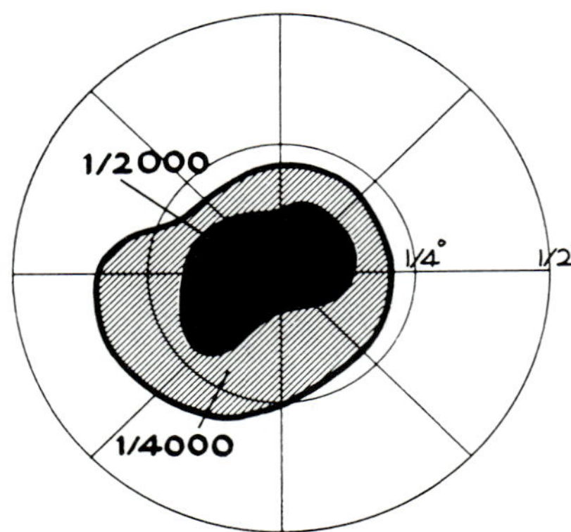

Fig. 10-8. Eclipse burn of fovea, following observation of eclipse of sun through inadequate filtering lens in boy 12 years of age. Minute irregular, central scotoma, about 0.25 degree in diameter, corresponding to ophthalmoscopically visible foveal hole. Similar permanent visual field defects have been reported after exposure to flash of atomic bomb.

tional loss are directly dependent on the severity of the contusion and the disruption of the outer retinal layers.

Thermal burn of the retina. Retinal burn or solar retinopathy, such as that seen following exposure of the inadequately protected macula to eclipse of the sun, may initially look like central serous retinopathy; but later stages reveal the minute hole in or immediately adjacent to the fovea and the tiny ragged central scotoma in the visual field. Immediately after exposure there may be marked visual loss with intense afterimage blindness, followed by the typical scotoma, which corresponds accurately to the visible retinal lesion.

These scotomas are usually fractions of a degree in size and may be difficult to detect, but careful tangent screen examination using small stimuli and two-point discrimination at 2, 3, and even 4 meters makes it possible to plot them very accurately (Fig. 10-8). They may also be mapped satisfactorily by the Irvine prism displacement test and by static perimetry with the Tübinger perimeter (see Fig. 7-22).

Because of the high density of vulnerable small fibers in the foveal outflow in the optic nerve, very small lesions of the foveal area produce a loss of up to one-fourth of all the optic nerve fibers in the eye. This accounts for the disproportionate visual loss and the dense central scotomas from these tiny lesions.

Prolonged exposure to light. There have been a number of articles on the harmful effects of excessive light on the retina and especially on the macula. Hochheimer and associates have reported visible retinal change in the monkey retina after exposure to the light from the slit lamp. Extensive retinal damage was produced in the macula of the monkey eye by a one-hour exposure to the light from an operating microscope. The damage was permanent. It has been postulated that light may be the cause of chronic cystic maculopathy.

Justification for considering central serous retinopathy as angiospastic in origin.

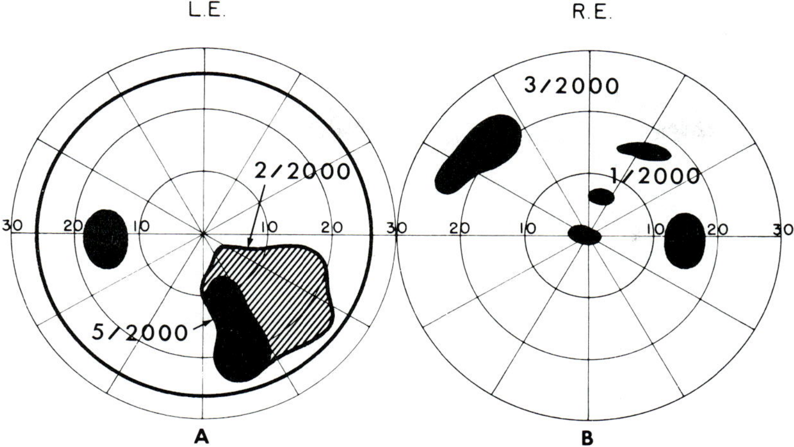

Fig. 10-9. A, Occlusion of superior temporal retinal vein with retinal hemorrhage. **B,** Hypertensive retinopathy with multiple deep and superficial retinal hemorrhages and isolated scotomas. (From Harrington, D. O.: In Straatsma, B.R., et al.: The retina. UCLA Forum in Medical Sciences, no. 8, Berkeley, 1969, University of California Press.)

From its relatively transient character, the absence of any obvious pathologic disturbance (e.g., trauma, inflammation, or arterial occlusion), and its frequent and close association with autonomic nervous system imbalance, central serous retinopathy can justifiably be considered as having an angiospastic origin.

Hypertensive retinopathy

Hypertensive retinopathy disturbs vision in many ways, and its visual field defects usually reflect the picture seen with the ophthalmoscope. There may be isolated peripheral and central scotomas resulting from outer retinal layer hemorrhage and ischemic retinal infarcts. Venous occlusion secondary to arterial compression at an arteriovenous crossing may cause severe retinal destruction and widespread visual field defects (Fig. 10-9).

Papilledema associated with hypertensive retinopathy may cause nerve fiber bundle defects in the visual field, possibly from arterial obstruction in the nerve head. More commonly disc edema produces blind spot enlargement, which may take on the character of a centrocecal scotoma if the retinal edema extends far enough into the macular region. On occasion, the blind spot enlargement may be so gross that most of both temporal fields become involved, simulating a bitemporal hemianopsia.

Retinal vasculitis

Vasculitis or inflammatory involvement of the retinal vessels may take various forms. Most typical is giant cell arteritis in which central vision and visual fields are often affected. Loss of vision may be sudden, total, and permanent. Both eyes may

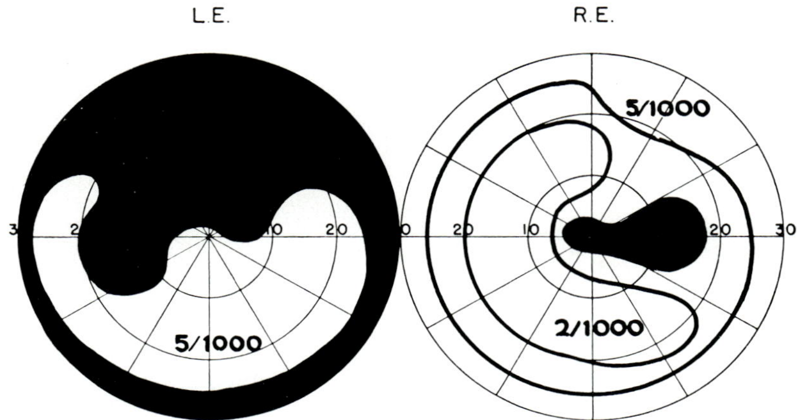

Fig. 10-10. Examples of visual field defects in patient with diabetic retinopathy. Left eye shows extensive diabetic retinopathy with retinal hemorrhages, exudates, and retinitis proliferans. Right eye shows retrobulbar neuritis with centrocecal scotoma and depression of temporal field in central isopters.

be affected, one after the other. When loss of vision is not complete, the visual fields may show a variety of defects, including central and arcuate scotomas, which may be isolated or break through into the periphery. In the case of arcuate scotomas, the defect may simulate an altitudinal hemianopsia unless carefully tested.

When vessels in the optic nerve are involved, the condition may be indistinguishable from any papillitis. Visual loss may be greater than would be expected from the appearance of the retinal vasculature. Some of these cases respond favorably to corticosteroid therapy.

Diabetic retinopathy

Diabetic retinopathy is considered here because the main cause of visual loss is vascular is origin (Fig. 10-10). In its early stages visual disturbance is uncommon. Even when there are large numbers of microaneurysms, numerous deep and superficial retinal hemorrhages, and some areas of retinal edema, there are few complaints of visual loss. If the macula is involved, especially by edema, central scotomas develop and cause defects in reading vision. Once the stage of proliferative retinopathy is reached, there will be extensive involvement of the visual fields with defects greater than might be expected from the ophthalmoscopic appearance. Such gross defects are often due to coincidental retinal detachment or arteriosclerotic and hypertensive lesions.

Retinal venous occlusion

Retinal venous occlusion occurring in the central retinal vein, usually at or just behind the lamina cribrosa, produces severe hemorrhagic retinopathy with extensive deep and superficial retinal hemorrhages. Visual loss is sudden and severe, and the visual field defect is a central scotoma of varying size and density. The scotomas are usually dense centrally but with sloping edges (Fig. 10-11).

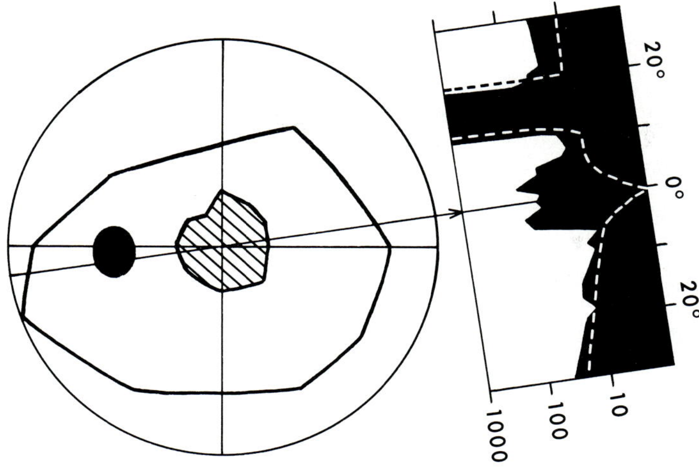

Fig. 10-11. Kinetic and static (profile) visual field in patient with partial central retinal vein occlusion.

Branch occlusion of retinal veins is more common and less destructive of central vision. Superior branch involvement will often leak hemorrhage and edema down into the macular area, however, producing large irregular sector defects in the lower peripheral fields extending upward into the macular area to cause severe central visual loss due to exaggerated macular response to edema.

Simultaneous occlusion of the central retinal artery and vein at their site of entry and exit from the optic nerve produces the picture of retinal hemorrhage, retinal edema, and engorged retinal veins. Occlusion of the central retinal vein alone produced little or no permanent visual loss. Occlusion of the central retinal artery alone produces white retinal infarction with severe visual loss and corresponding visual field defect. Combined occlusion of both artery and vein results in hemorrhagic infarction with visual loss and field defect. Resolution of a good portion of the field defect may occur if only the vein was occluded.

Mention should be made of the possible adverse effects of contraceptive pills on the retinal vasculature. It is probable that patients with a history of hypertension, retinal vein engorgement, migraine, transient neurologic deficits, and endometriosis should avoid the risk of oral contraceptives.

Chronic retinal vein occlusion or insufficiency may produce little or no visual loss, because of development of collateral circulation. There may be, however, considerable arborization and enlargement of angioscotomatous defects around the blind spot.

INFLAMMATORY LESIONS AFFECTING THE RETINA

The majority of inflammatory lesions affecting the retina are probably secondary to inflammatory disturbance of the choroid with secondary destruction of overlying retinal cells.

Harada's disease

Harada's disease may give rise to a peculiar exudative type of retinal detachment, usually bilateral, affecting the lower peripheral retina and producing irregular superior quadrant or altitudinal hemianoptic visual field defects (Fig. 10-12).

Toxoplasmosis

Toxoplasmosis is a common cause of unilateral and bilateral chorioretinal destruction with dense, irregular, steep-margined central and paracentral scotomas corresponding to the lesion as seen with the ophthalmoscope.

Choroiditis with retinitis

Choroiditis with associated retinitis, producing severe visual loss and single or multiple scotomas, may occur in diverse conditions. Sympathetic ophthalmia may produce both central scotoma and severe peripheral contraction.

Syphilitic choroiditis

The disseminated choroiditis of syphilis with overlying retinal destruction is responsible for profound visual loss when the macular area is involved. Peripheral and central island-like scotomas occur from widespread patchy retinopathy. The condition is relatively uncommon today.

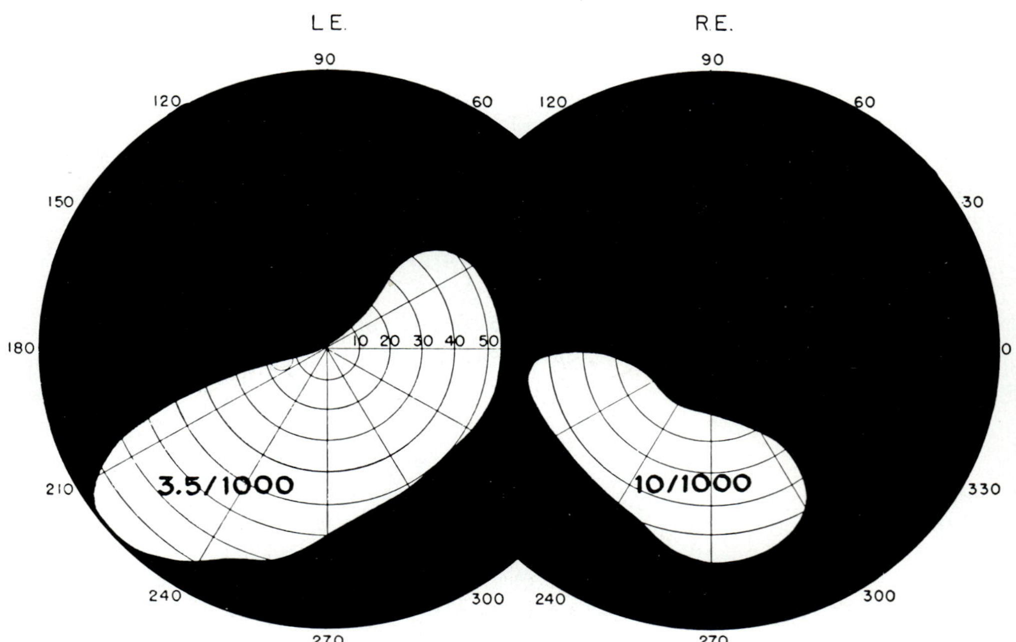

Fig. 10-12. Bilateral inferior retinal detachment in Harada's disease.

Nonspecific chorioretinitis

Nonspecific chorioretinitis is so-called because it always involves the retina. Visual loss may be severe in the acute stage, partly due to vitreous opacification but mostly to retinal edema or cellular damage. When the optic disc is involved, there is usually a dense central scotoma or at times an arcuate scotoma due to nerve fiber bundle interruption.

Minimal foveal choroiditis with overlying retinal edema may stimulate central serous retinopathy.

Degenerative lesions of the retina

Degenerative disease involving the outer retinal layers may cause marked and progressive visual loss, both central and peripheral. Except for retinitis pigmentosa, the usual visual field defect is a progressively enlarging central scotoma. The conditions are always bilateral.

Retinitis pigmentosa

Because retinitis pigmentosa initially and primarily involves the retinal rods, the earliest symptom is night blindness associated with a characteristic ring scotoma occupying the midperiphery of the visual field (Fig. 10-13). This defect usually starts as a group of isolated scotomas in the area 20 to 25 degrees from fixation. These sco-

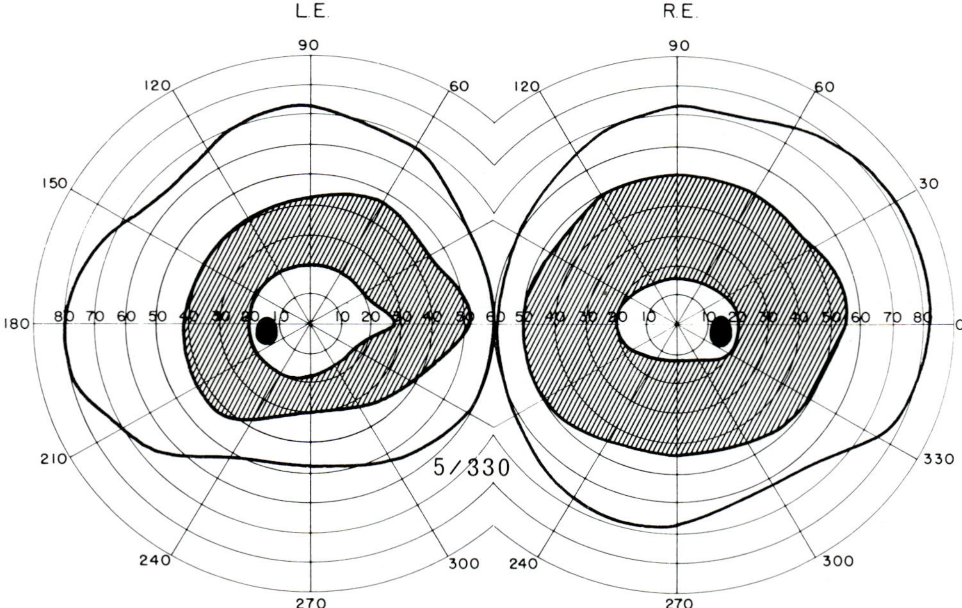

Fig. 10-13. Typical equatorial ring scotoma in early case of retinitis pigmentosa. (From Harrington, D.O.: In Straatsma, B. R., et al.: The retina. UCLA Forum in Medical Sciences, no. 8, Berkeley, 1969, University of California Press.)

tomas gradually coalesce to form a partial and finally a complete ring. The outer edge of the ring expands peripherally at a fairly rapid pace while the inner margin contracts very slowly toward fixation. Long after the entire peripheral field is gone, there remains a small oval remnant of intact central field, resembling the terminal defect of glaucoma. There are numerous variants of typical retinitis pigmentosa with occasional early macular involvement and central scotoma.

Familial or hereditary macular pigmentary degeneration

Familial or hereditary pigmentary degeneration of the macula is a fairly common condition that may affect several siblings; and, more rarely, it may affect more than one generation of a family. The condition is bilateral with gradual onset, usually in the second decade of life. Central visual loss and bilateral central scotomas with sloping margins occur early and progress slowly. Occasionally a minute area of vision is spared exactly at fixation, giving the scotoma the appearance of a doughnut.

Senile macular degeneration

Senile macular degeneration has already been discussed in connection with vascular insufficiency in the macular area of the choroid.

Disciform macular degeneration

Disciform degeneration of the macula may occur at any age but is much more common after the sixth decade of life. In its early stages vision may remain surprisingly good and scotomatous defects in the central fields may be vague and difficult to detect. The condition is always bilateral, although one eye may be seriously involved long before the other.

When hemorrhage occurs beneath or around the disc-like yellowish, elevated macular mass, the loss of central vision may be sudden and profound and the resulting central scotoma is irregular and dense (see Fig. 9-4). Visual loss and the scotoma are due to destruction of the outer retinal layers resulting from breaks in Bruch's membrane followed by hemorrhage from the choriocapillaris and proliferation of fibrous tissue from the pigment epithelium.

TOXIC LESIONS OF THE RETINA AND CHOROID

There are a few drugs and poisons that directly affect the retina and produce varying degrees of visual loss and characteristic visual field defects. These are considered separately in Chapter 12 with the toxic amblyopias.

TRAUMATIC LESIONS OF THE RETINA

Traumatic lesions of the retina include (1) contusion injury of the globe with commotio retinae, (2) traumatic rupture of the choroid, (3) thermal burn of the fovea, and (4) traumatic retinal tears. These have been considered and discussed elsewhere.

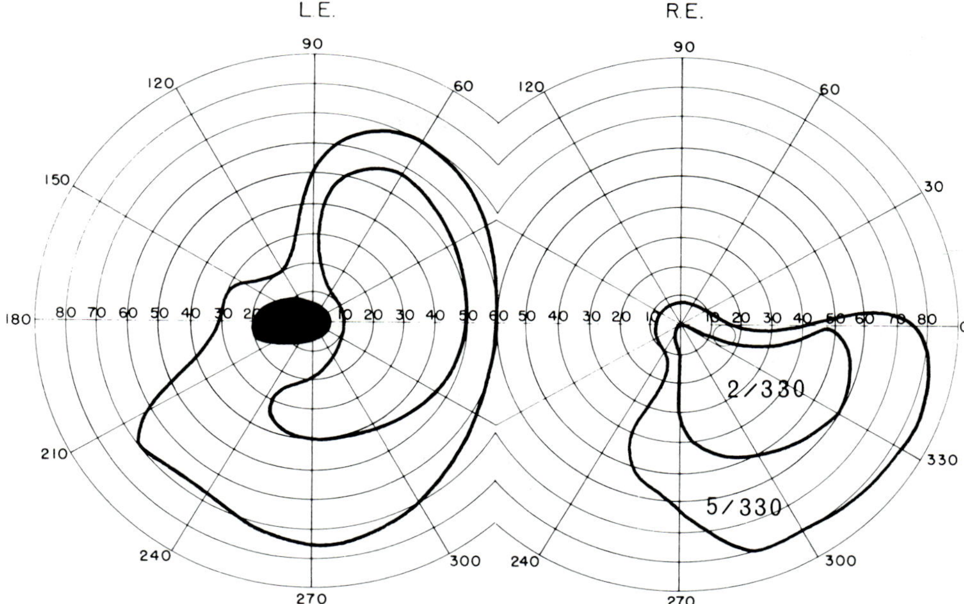

Fig. 10-14. Visual field defects in case of bilateral von Hippel's angiomatosis retinae. (From Harrington, D. O.: In Strattsma, B. R., et al.: The retina. UCLA Forum in Medical Sciences, no. 8, Berkeley, 1969, University of California Press.)

CHOROIDAL TUMORS

Tumors of the choroid with effects on the retina were discussed in Chapter 9.

Retinoblastoma is diagnosed with the ophthalmoscope. Visual field studies are of no value because of the age of the patient.

Angiomatosis retinae with or without cerebellar involvement causes severe visual loss and widespread damage to the visual fields, both central and peripheral. Both eyes are often affected. Whereas the lesions are usually in the peripheral retina and the corresponding visual field defects are also peripheral, the central retinal area is often involved, probably due to exaggerated macular response, and central scotomas are common and disabling (Fig. 10-14). Growth spread of the tumor and its vascular response eventually cause blindness.

MISCELLANEOUS DISEASES AFFECTING RETINAL FUNCTION

Among the miscellaneous diseases that affect retinal function are staphylomas, abnormal protein retinopathies, the leukemias, retinal cysts, retinoschisis, and retinal detachments.

Colobomas

Colobomas cause extensive loss of the superior field, usually involving fixation. The refraction scotoma of staphyloma of the optic nerve head has been discussed (see Fig. 9-8).

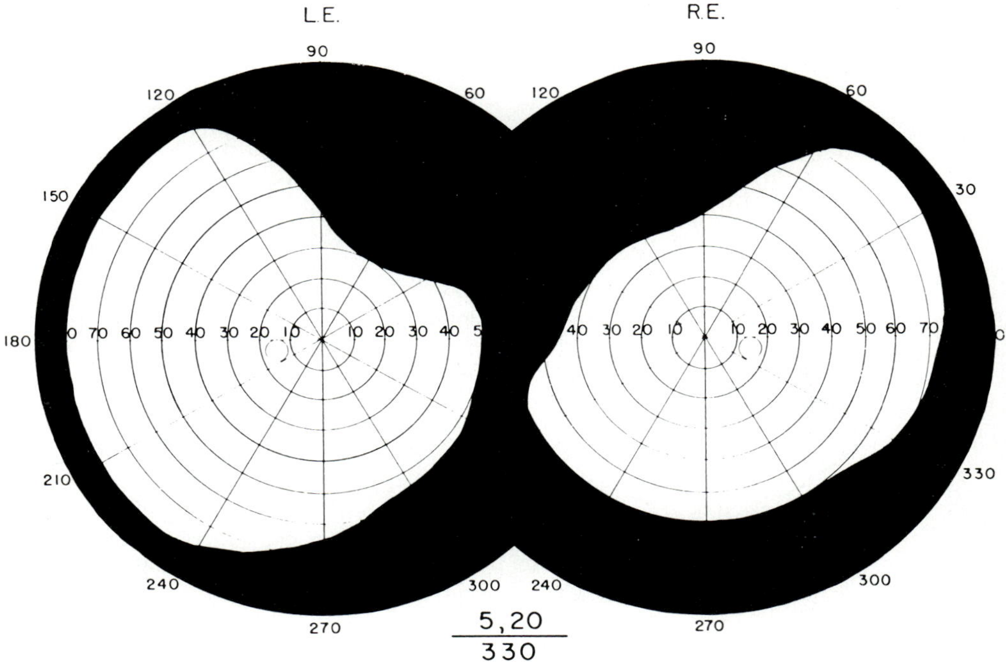

Fig. 10-15. Retinoschisis. Binasal hemianopsia of considerable extent. Note that margins are steep and field defect is same size for both 5-mm and 20-mm stimuli.

Myopia with retinal stretching and atrophy

High degrees of myopia with retinal stretching and atrophy may cause a variety of visual field defects. Central scotoma is not uncommon; a markedly enlarged blind spot secondary to abnormal conus about the nerve head is common; and, on occasion, nerve fiber bundle damage at the disc margin will produce a Bjerrum scotoma.

Retinoschisis

The visual field defect of retinoschisis is characterized by its density and steep margins, by its bilaterality, and by the fact that the nasal fields are almost always involved, more frequently above than below (Fig. 10-15). The patients may be unaware of the defect, and routine field examination with the perimeter may detect retinoschisis missed by ophthalmoscopic examination.

Retinal detachments

Detachment of the retina from whatever cause eventually destroys the outer retinal elements, with resulting loss of vision in the separated area. Visual field studies may be of considerable importance. The actual extent of the detachment may be more accurately judged by the field loss than with the ophthalmoscope, especially as it approaches the macula. When the visual field defect crosses fixation, the prog-

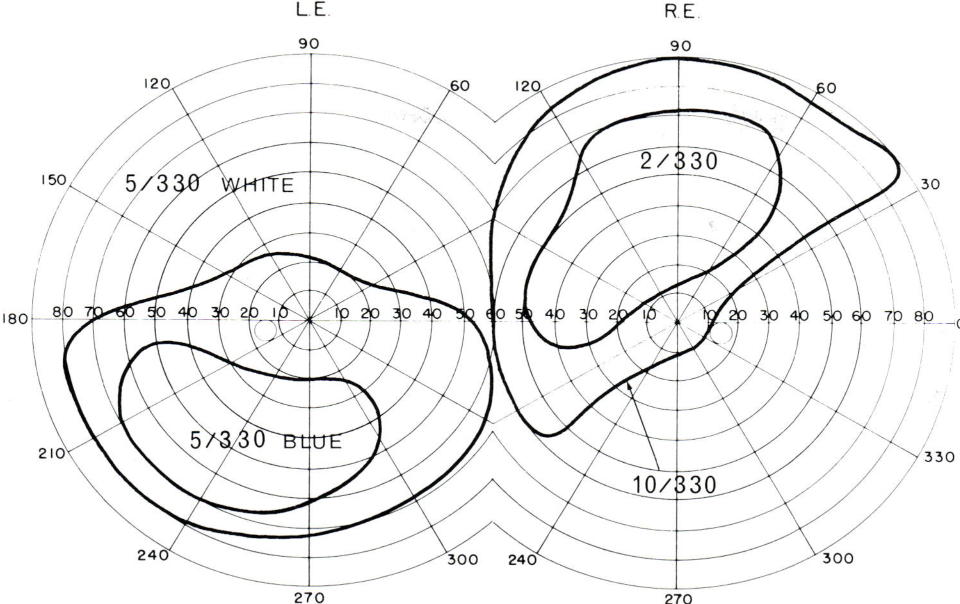

Fig. 10-16. Two eyes with typical visual field defects resulting from retinal detachment. Note that defects have very sloping margins and that most marked deficit is demonstrated with blue stimuli. (From Harrington, D. O.: In Straatsma, B. R., et al.: The retina. UCLA Forum in Medical Sciences, no. 8, Berkeley, 1969, University of California Press.)

nosis is generally poorer than when fixation is spared. When a very large bullous type of detachment of the superior retina hangs down over fixation, it may necessitate putting the patient to bed for a period of time to allow the detachment to flatten out. If the visual field is then quickly reexamined, the true area of retinal separation will be revealed.

Visual field defects in retinal detachment usually have sloping margins. They are exaggerated when the stimulus is presented under reduced illumination and also when blue stimuli are used (Fig. 10-16). Superior detachments usually have more extensive, denser, and steeper-margined defects than do those involving the inferior retina. In the early stages of retinal detachment, the field defects are more readily detected with perimeter than with tangent screen. There is no typical visual field defect in retinal detachment.

Postoperative visual field studies are necessary for evaluating progress and prognosis and for comparing with preoperative fields for medicolegal evidence.

CHAPTER 11

Glaucoma

The history of perimetry and the development of the modern techniques of visual field examination are intimately linked with the study of glaucoma. Even with the acquisition of a better understanding of the disease through gonioscopy, tonography, and increasing knowledge of the physiology and dynamics of aqueous outflow, perimetry remains of paramount importance in the early diagnosis of the disease and of even greater value in assessing its progress and prognosis.

No glaucomatous eye can be said to be fully understood until all of its many facets have been thoroughly investigated, not once but many times. A single tonometric estimate of intraocular pressure does not establish the diagnosis of glaucoma; nor does a single gonioscopic examination, no matter how characteristic the findings; nor a tonographic measurement of the facility of aqueous outflow; nor a first examination of the visual field; nor the observation of atrophic excavation of the optic nerve head. The results of all these methods of examination must be weighed and carefully correlated before the total picture of the disease begins to form. If one is to fully understand a glaucomatous eye and intelligently guide its treatment, he must first confirm these findings by repeated examination; he must estimate their degree of stability or vacillation, note their response to provocation of various types, and finally through patience and sympathy understand something of the person with the disease, his personality pattern, and his responses to external stimuli both physical and emotional.

Our primary concern with glaucoma is the loss of vision that it produces. The patient with glaucoma is disturbed not by the fact that he has an increase in his intraocular pressure but only by the possibility of impending blindness.

Measurement of the loss of function in an eye with glaucoma is accomplished by careful quantitative study of the visual field defects that are so characteristic of the disease in its established form. Because central visual acuity is rarely affected until the late stages of disease, the patient may be completely unaware of functional loss, and only measurement of the visual field defect will establish the degree of such loss and its rate of progression.

The patient may know that he has glaucoma and that glaucoma can cause blindness. He may know that he is faced with the need to use eye drops for the rest of his life or even to undergo surgery for the condition, and yet he cannot appreciate the nature of the visual loss until it is so far established as to be irreversible.

Interest in glaucoma was largely responsible for the development of quantitative methods of examination of the central portion of the visual field. Reciprocally, these careful analytic methods have revealed much about the disease and may contribute in no small measure to a better understanding of its pathogenesis.

There is no better way for the beginner in perimetry to learn finesse in the various techniques of visual field examination than to analyze thoroughly by quantitative methods an early but well-established glaucoma field deficit.

Much of our knowledge of the character of the visual field defect in glaucoma has been obtained through quantitative study of the central portion of the visual field on the tangent screen. Study of the smaller isopters at 1 and 2 meters has become the accepted method of perimetric examination in glaucoma. This is because of the importance of the Bjerrum area, which can be studied with the greatest facility by this technique, and because depressions in the peripheral isopters are reflected in similar central isopter depressions in the early stages of most glaucomatous visual field defects.

In recent years there has been a new awakening to the importance of perimetry in glaucoma, particularly in European clinics. This is largely the result of widespread adoption of the Goldmann perimeter with its precise standardization of perimetric techniques. Modifications of the Goldmann perimeter and development of the Tübinger perimeter have facilitated the investigations of static or profile perimetry and have encouraged refined experiments in perimetric examination with stimuli and background of varying luminance. All these methods have been extensively applied to the study of the visual field in glaucoma.

The exhaustive two-volume work of Ourgaud and Etienne on the functional exploration of the glaucomatous eye has greatly advanced our knowledge of the nature and cause of the loss of both central and peripheral vision in glaucoma. This monumental monograph, published by the French Ophthalmological Society in 1961, ranks with its companion volume on the visual field by Dubois-Poulsen, published by the same society in 1952.

The use of static tangent screen stimuli of varying luminance has been most helpful in the analysis of early Bjerrum scotomas.

The earliest visual field defect in glaucoma is probably an isolated scotoma in the Bjerrum area most consistently detected with minimal static threshold stimuli on the Tübinger perimeter.

Greve has used both single- and multiple-stimulus static perimetry for the early detection of glaucoma field defects and for their subsequent assessment. He uses the Friedmann visual field analyzer with its multiple static stimuli and kinetic perimetry on the Tübinger perimeter in the detection phase and assesses these detected defects by meticulous quantitative static perimetry to determine their intensity. His monograph is a most complete analysis of the methods of perimetry as used in the study of the glaucomatous field defect.

In the past decade increasing emphasis on automation of the visual field examination has spawned a variety of new perimeters and computerized perimetric systems. This has been in response to a desire for rapid, accurate detection and analysis of the visual field defects so commonly found in the glaucomatous eye. These instruments make it possible for some patients to examine their own visual fields in a constant and repeatable manner; the data are automatically recorded and can be computerized and stored for future reference and comparison with later findings. Not all glaucoma patients are suitable candidates for automated perimetry; regardless of the excellence of the instruments used to record the visual field defects, the examination must still be monitored by a technician and the defects must be carefully analyzed and interpreted. Unfortunately, as ophthalmologists become more aware of the importance of perimetry, they face the dilemma of needing more visual field assessments and having less time to devote to them. The end result is the clinician's abandonment of the examination to a paramedical technician and a computer.

TYPES OF PRIMARY GLAUCOMA

Excluding ocular hypertension due to uveitis, tumor, or other causes, there are two types of primary glaucoma that must be considered with reference to visual field changes: (1) *narrow-angle glaucoma,* which may progress to closed-angle glaucoma with acute glaucomatous crisis, sometimes known as acute congestive glaucoma, and (2) *wide-angle glaucoma,* also known as open-angle glaucoma, or chronic glaucoma, or glaucoma simplex.

Narrow-angle glaucoma

Narrow-angle glaucoma, before the onset of angle closure and acute congestive symptoms, shows little if any visual field defect. If, however, the eye has been subjected to repeated attacks of high intraocular pressure with the symptoms of glaucomatous crisis, a study of the visual fields between attacks will often reveal the following: (1) general depression of all the isopters, (2) greater depression of the peripheral than of the central isopters, (3) particular depression of the superior nasal isopters, (4) enlargement of the blind spot, (5) widening of angioscotomas, and (6) nerve fiber bundle defects.

With the development of peripheral anterior synechiae in the angle of the anterior chamber, the onset of glaucomatous crisis becomes more imminent. Under these circumstances the study of the angioscotomas may be revealing. Widening of the scotoma will be seen to parallel intermittent elevations in intraocular pressure and may presage the onset of the acute attack.

With closure of the angle and sudden extreme elevation in intraocular pressure, the eye becomes congested, painful, and often almost completely blind. Perimetric examination under theses conditions is necessarily limited to gross estimation of what little visual field remains. Frequently the minimum visible stimulus is a bright light. When some semblance of visual field examination is possible, the upper nasal periphery is usually most affected and the lower temporal quadrant the last to retain vision.

In acute narrow-angle glaucoma the extreme depression of the entire field with frequent early loss of the central field (as opposed to the persistent retention of the central field in chronic glaucoma) is evidence of a pathogenesis that is primarily vascular. It appears likely that the so-called congestive crisis is accompanied by severe edema of both the retina and the nerve head as a part of the general congestion and edema of all the structures of the globe. Occasionally this edema can be observed ophthalmoscopically, if corneal edema is not yet present, or by the use of glycerin to clear the cornea temporarily. Alterations of retinal arterial blood pressure have also been observed, and it is probable that both retinal arterial and venous circulations are severely compromised.

I have observed edema of both the macula and the optic nerve head that persisted for a period of time after the rapid reduction of intraocular pressure by the use of mannitol in a patient with angle-closure glaucoma.

If the acute attack can be controlled either by medical or by surgical treatment and the intraocular pressure again be normalized, the field may return to normal, provided the edema has not been too severe or too prolonged. Repeated attacks of short duration, however, will inevitably take their toll of vision, either central or peripheral, or both. When treatment is delayed, the vision may remain poor, with extreme depression of all isopters in the visual field or retention of only a small island of temporal vision, even though the intraocular pressure may eventually become normal. In chronic angle-closure glaucoma where intraocular pressure may be intermittently elevated to high levels or chronically elevated for longer periods of time, one may expect to find irreversible nerve fiber bundle deficits of the same type as seen in chronic open-angle glaucoma. Such visual field deficits are usually accompanied by cupping of the optic disc or atrophy or both.

In a study of visual field defects in acute and chronic angle-closure glaucoma, Douglas, Drance, and Schulzer showed that after an attack of acute angle-closure glaucoma more than half the patients retained a normal field with normal optic discs. Chronic angle-closure glaucoma presented a different picture. Increased intraocular pressure was likely to have been present for a prolonged period of time, and there was a high incidence of visual field defects of the nerve fiber bundle type. Most of these patients also exhibited optic disc pallor.

Open-angle glaucoma

The characteristic and typical visual field changes in open-angle chronic glaucoma are the insidious and gradual onset of (1) general depression of the isopters both peripheral and central, (2) widening and intensification of the angioscotoma, which may be reversible (Fig. 11-1), (3) formation of the nerve fiber bundle defect, (4) formation of the nasal step, (5) rapid peripheral contraction especially of the nasal field, (6) persistent retention of the central field until a very late stage of the disease, (7) loss of the central field and retention of a small temporal island of vision, and (8) blindness. All of these are illustrated in Plate 4.

These characteristic defects may occur singly, in pairs, or in groups. They may

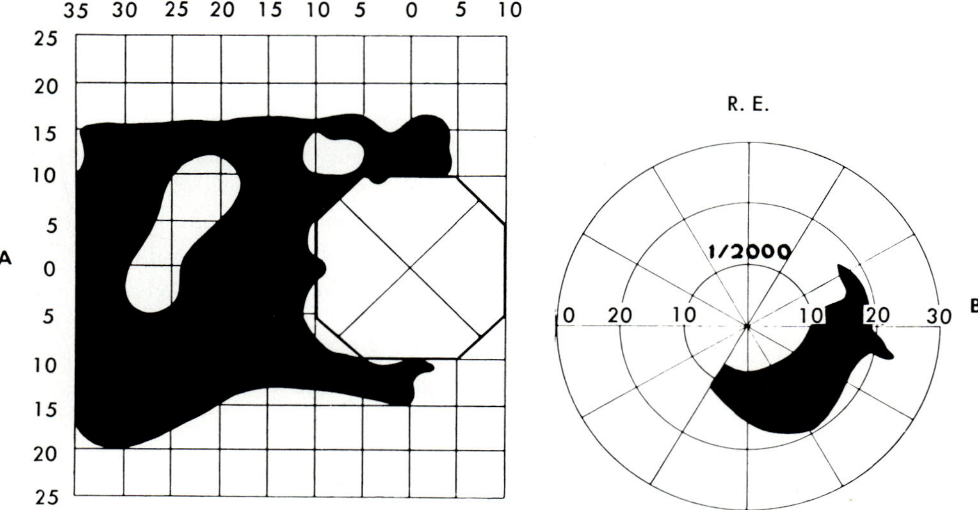

Fig. 11-1. A, Widening and coalescence of angioscotoma in case of wide-angle glaucoma as recorded on stereocampimeter. **B,** Expansion and intensification of angioscotoma in case of incipient wide-angle glaucoma as recorded on tangent screen.

develop rapidly or extremely slowly or, in some instances, very slowly at first and then suddenly or with great rapidity. They may be monocular; but when one eye is involved, the perimetrist should be scrupulously careful in this examination of the unaffected eye and should be continuously alert for incipient visual field defects indicative of glaucoma. Sooner or later the fellow eye is almost always affected with glaucoma, with the development of characteristic visual field defects. In many instances the visual field defects in the two eyes parallel each other, and often they are quite symmetric.

Many students of glaucoma have called attention to the parallel between the ophthalmoscopic appearance of the optic discs and the visual field changes; and every case of suspected glaucoma should be studied with these two findings in mind. Optic disc excavation and visual field defects should be assessed together as confirmation of the existence of glaucoma and also as part of the evaluation of the progress and treatment of the disease.

Defects in the visual fields are usually, but not always, associated with corresponding cupping of the optic discs. A vertically oval cup with narrowing of the upper or lower rim of normal nerve tissue should be viewed with suspicion as being glaucomatous in origin, and special attention should be given to the perimetric examination of the superior and inferior Bjerrum areas of the visual field.

An optic disc cup that extends downward to encroach on the inferior rim of the disc would be expected to produce a nerve fiber bundle defect in the superior Bjerrum area. This area should be meticulously searched for an actual scotoma on the 2-meter tangent screen or with the minimal stimuli of the Goldmann perimeter.

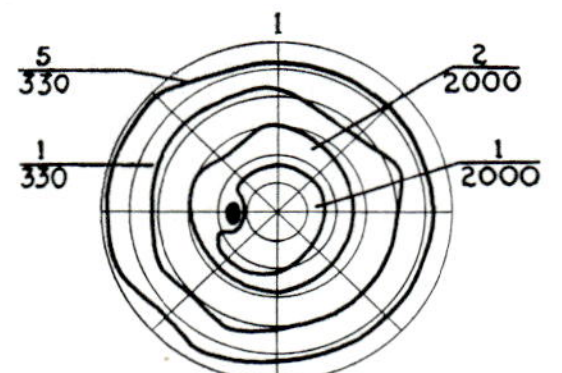

Baring of the blind spot. The earliest nerve fiber bundle defect.

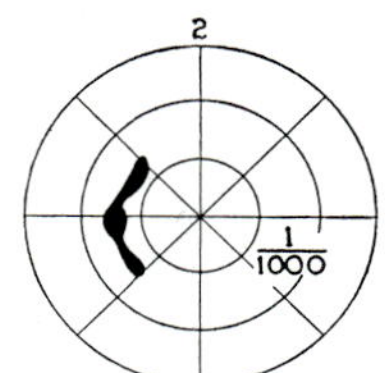

Incipient double nerve fiber bundle defect (Bjerrum Scotoma)

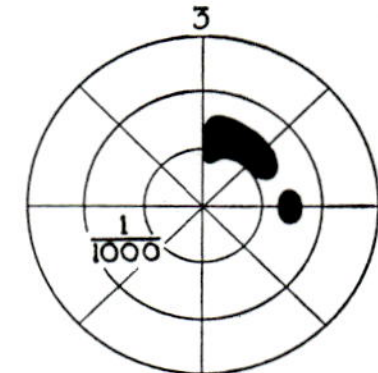

Bjerrum Scotoma isolated from blind spot.

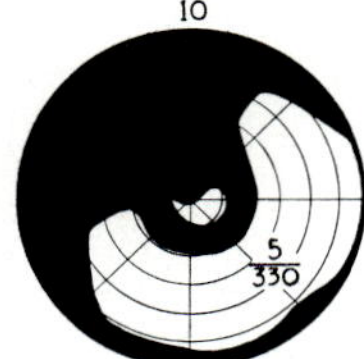

End stages in glaucoma field loss. Remnant of central field still shows nasal step.

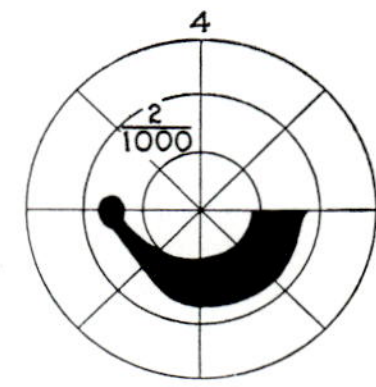

Fully developed nerve fiber bundle defect with nasal step. (Arcuate Scotoma)

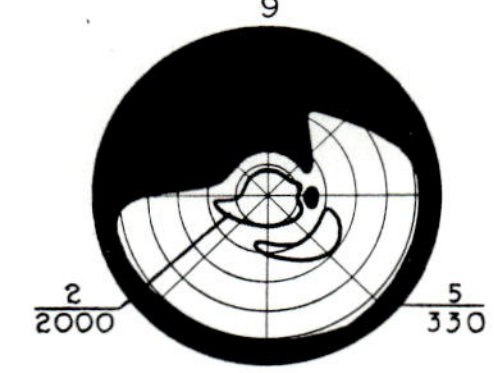

Peripheral depression with double nerve fiber bundle defect. Isolation of central field.

The basic visual field loss in glaucoma is the nerve fiber bundle defect with nasal step and peripheral nasal depression. It is here shown superimposed upon the nerve fiber layer of the retina and the retinal vascular tree. All perimetric changes in glaucoma are variations of these fundamental defects.

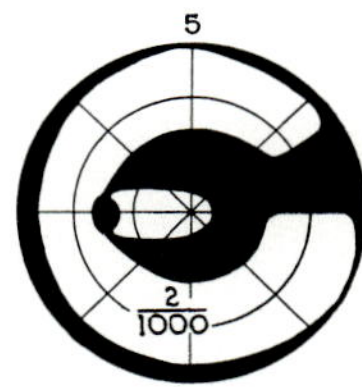

Double Arcuate Scotoma with peripheral break through and nasal step.

Nasal depression connected with Arcuate Scotoma. Nasal step of Ronne.

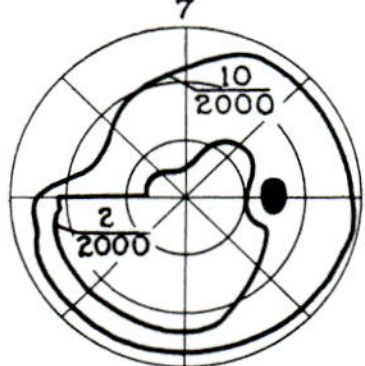

Peripheral break through of large nerve fiber bundle defect with well developed nasal step.

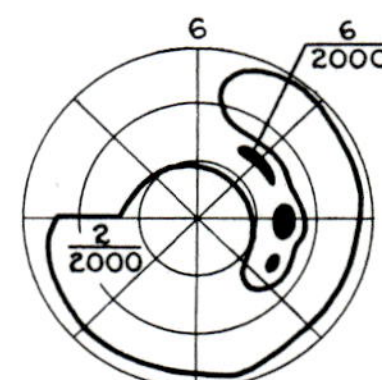

Seidel Scotoma. Islands of greater visual loss within a nerve fiber bundle defect.

Plate 4. Perimetry of glaucoma.

Careful threshold sensitivity studies of such an eye with the Tübinger perimeter will often reveal a pronounced depression of the normal profile in this area. Examination with the multiple pattern screener, the Friedmann analyzer, or one of the new automated perimeters may detect these defects as isolated paracentral scotomas, which must then be explored by quantitative methods on the tangent screen or the Goldmann or Tübinger perimeter. In the early stages of their development, such scotomas may be narrow and relative and may be completely missed by screener-type examination.

When a patient has glaucoma, Becker and Shaffer recommended routine sketching of the disc as a means of recording progressive changes in the optic cup and as a method of sharpening the ophthalmologist's powers of observation. These authors also recommend that evaluation of an optic disc include a prediction of the type and location of the probable visual field defect as a means of sharpening the examiner's eye and diagnostic acumen. Serial fundus photography is an excellent and accurate method of determining progress in the excavation of the optic nerve head. Fluorescein angiography may prove of considerable value in assessing the vulnerability of a given optic nerve to continued increase in intraocular pressure. These methods deserve intensive study and widespread use.

Occasionally visual field studies are misleading and the disc examination provides an objective check on the reliability of the subjective field study. The reverse may also be true. If a disc is normally pink in color and uncupped, the finding of an advanced visual field defect should be viewed with suspicion, or search should be made for an etiology other than glaucoma.

When repeated examination with diagrams, sketches, or photographs reveals progression in the size and depth of the optic disc cup, imminent appearance of a visual field defect may be expected and study of the field should be made at more frequent intervals and with even more than usual care. Once cupping has occurred, the nerve may not tolerate the previous level of intraocular pressure, and if visual field deficits exist the lowering of pressure becomes more and more urgent.

PHASES OF DEVELOPMENT

In the study of the visual field in the patient with glaucoma, it is convenient to consider separately the three phases of the development of glaucoma: (1) incipient, (2) established, and (3) terminal. Each of these phases in the development of glaucoma has its characteristic visual field changes, but the defects typical of one phase may overlap into another. In established glaucoma all of the classic visual field defects may be demonstrated in a single field examined by careful quantitative methods.

Incipient glaucoma

In its earliest stages glaucoma reveals its visual field defects only to the most meticulous perimetrist.

Abnormality of angioscotoma pattern

In the incipient stages of development of the glaucoma field defect, the technique of Evans is rewarding in eliciting the very early widening, intensification, and coalescence of the angioscotomas. The changes that appear around the blind spot may precede other findings that are the criteria of glaucoma (e.g., optic nerve atrophy, persistent increase of intraocular pressure, or depression of the central isopters so characteristic of the later stages of the disease). It is quite possible to demonstrate them with accuracy on the 2-meter tangent screen with 1-mm stimuli. Examination of threshold sensitivity by static perimetry with the Tübinger instrument is probably the most reliable technique for the detection of these very early defects that may be reversible and come and go from day to day.

Flicker fusion frequency fields

Another method of value in the detection of very early visual field changes in patients with glaucoma is the flicker fusion frequency field (FFF field) (Fig. 11-2). The glaucomatous eye appears to be especially sensitive to this type of vusial field examination. Here the depression of observable rates of flicker is occasionally quite marked in the areas above and below the blind spot and in the upper nasal periphery. It may precede the appearance of any frankly glaucomatous visual field defects and thereby alert the examiner to possible future changes in the fields.

Reduced illumination

The effect of reduced illumination in the exaggeration of glaucomatous visual field defects has already been mentioned. Deliberate reduction of stimulus intensity by reducing illumination may be a valuable adjunct to standard techniques in eliciting very early field changes or exaggerating and intensifying those that are vague and indefinite under standard lighting. The reduction in illumination may be ac-

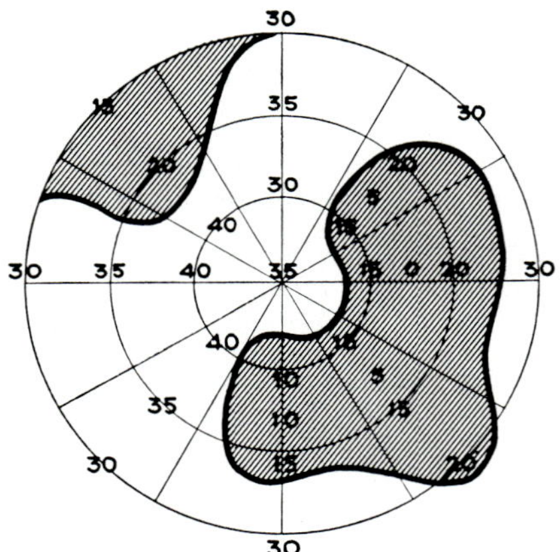

Fig. 11-2. Flicker fusion frequency field in early glaucoma. Note expansion of blind spot (analogous to widened angioscotoma) and small upper nasal field depression.

complished either with filters or a rheostat in the light circuit or by reducing the voltage to an electroluminescent stimulus.

The graded neutral filters of the Goldmann perimeter are an efficient method of varying luminance in the stimulus and its background. Modifications by Jayle and Sloan have increased the sensitivity of perimetric analysis of the Bjerrum scotoma, and the development of static perimetry by Harms and Aulhorn is a still further refinement of this principle. The Tübinger perimeter developed by them is probably the most sensitive method of detecting the earliest evidence of depression of vision in the Bjerrum area of the visual field in glaucomatous eyes.

Simple and inexpensive rheostats can be purchased for inclusion in the ordinary room light switch whereby the overall illumination of the tangent screen by floodlights can be accurately controlled and the sensitivity of standard solid stimuli increased.

Rheostatic control of the light emitted by electroluminescent stimuli is also now feasible. This allows stimuli of measured luminance to be presented in suspect areas of the visual field, and defects can thereby be discovered or exaggerated.

All of the preceding methods are particularly useful in the study of incipient glaucoma, and their proper use will lead to earlier diagnosis and hence more effective therapy.

The development of lens sclerosis and cataract in a glaucomatous eye will frequently precipitate the appearance of a glaucomatous visual field defect or will grossly exaggerate an established deficit. The glaucoma may appear to be quite out of control, and yet the only change will be the intensification of the previously existing field loss due to the light-filtering effect of the cataractous lens.

Pupillary contraction, because it decreases retinal illumination, also produces a general depression of the visual field. Miosis may therefore stimulate progression of a glaucomatous field loss in its early stages or markedly exaggerate a well-established scotoma that is in fact unchanged when tested with dilated pupils. When miosis is intensified by more vigorous therapy, the fields must be evaluated with this in mind.

Depression of central isopters and baring of the blind spot

Another valuable and early visual field change of diagnostic value is depression of the central isopters in patients with incipient glaucoma. This depression may be general, but more often it takes the form of an irregular or eccentric loss of portion of the isopters for 1/2000 or 2/2000 especially above or below the blind spot or in the upper nasal quadrant or both. When recorded on the campimeter chart, this defect is seen as the well-known baring of the blind spot. It may involve the upper or lower pole of the blind spot or both. It is, in reality, an early form of nerve fiber bundle defect, detectable in the isopters for small stimuli and having the same characteristics of depression of the upper (or lower) part of the isopter between the blind spot and the horizontal nasal raphe. It follows the arching curve of the nerve fiber bundles of the retina. The upper field seems to be more often affected than the lower. When both upper and lower fields are affected, the temporal line of the isop-

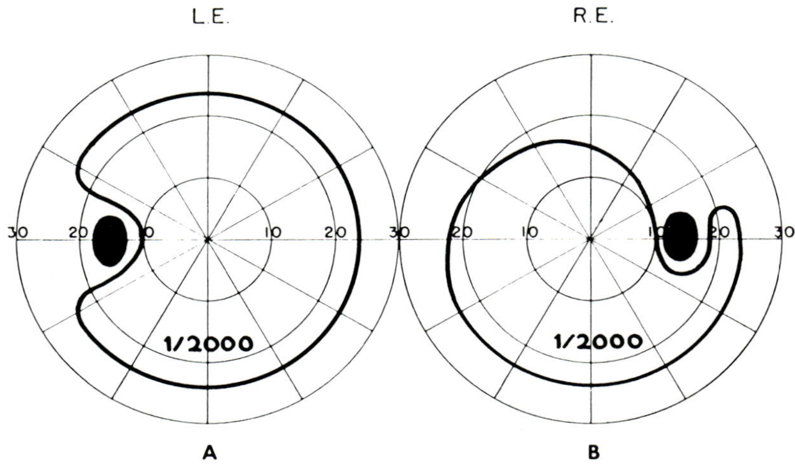

Fig. 11-3. Baring of blind spot. **A,** False baring of blind spot. This defect is not characteristic of glaucoma and is found fairly frequently with small visual angles in normal individuals. **B,** True baring of blind spot. Early visual field defect in glaucoma is, in reality, incipient Bjerrum scotoma.

ter may come down as an almost vertical line, well inside the blind spot, excluding it from an isopter that normally lies at 20 to 30 degrees from fixation on the temporal side. This is not the same defect as that occasionally found in the normal eye, wherein the isopter lies well outside the blind spot except for a small wedge-shaped sector loss immediately temporal to the blind spot, extending outward to the limits of the tangent screen, and not corresponding to any anatomic nerve fiber bundle arrangement (Fig. 11-3).

Occasionally, the true blind spot baring will arch above or below fixation to end at the nasal horizontal meridian in a small nasal step corresponding to the anatomic location of the retinal nerve fiber raphe (see Plate 4, 7).

The finding of peripheral nasal depression with nasal step with or without connection to the blind spot is a common occurrence. Slight nasal depression is suspicious, but not diagnostic. It is a common finding of automated perimetry. The presence of a clear-cut nasal step is an important finding. When studied quantitatively, it is often possible to connect such a defect with an early arcuate scotoma.

Because of the difficulty of eliciting a clear-cut baring of the blind spot in many patients, it has been said that blind spot baring is of no diagnostic importance. Drance, in fact, has shown blind spot baring to be present in a large percentage of normal eyes in aging patients when the I_2 isopter was carefully tested on the Goldmann perimeter. He feels that, with threshold targets, baring of the blind spot can be produced in everyone and is not pathognomonic of the disease.

Aulhorn and Harms have reported (and their findings are confirmed by Drance) that, when static perimetry is used, the earliest visual field deficits in eyes with open-angle glaucoma are paracentral scotomas in the Bjerrum area, separated from the

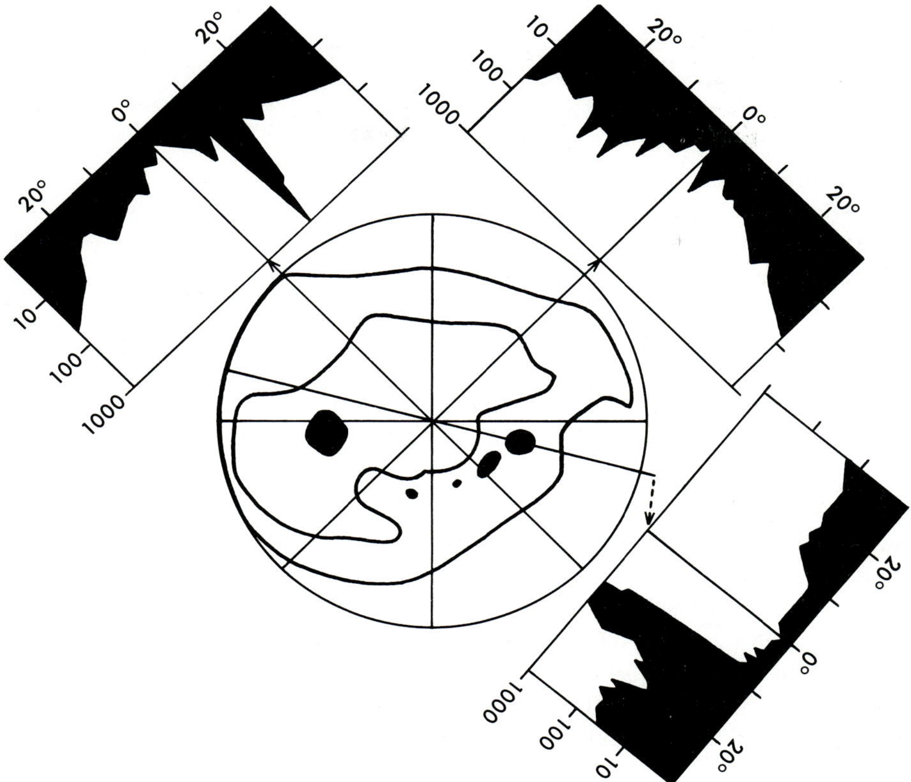

Fig. 11-4. Open-angle glaucoma with multiple small scotomas in inferior Bjerrum area. Kinetic perimetry reveals scotomas and nasal step. Static perimetry shows profiles of two absolute paracentral scotomas and small relative scotoma in three meridians. (After Drance.)

blind spot and later coalescing into an arcuate scotoma joining the blind spot (Fig. 11-4).

Seidel's scotoma

The visual field defect described by Seidel in 1914 takes the form of a crescent-shaped scotoma that includes the blind spot and arches above and below fixation in varying degrees to taper off at each end. It is, in reality, but one of many forms assumed by the typical nerve fiber bundle defect. It was detected by Seidel with rather gross stimuli (8 and 10 mm) and when carefully analyzed by quantitative methods, utilizing small test objects, it will usually reveal the classic characteristics of a glaucomatous nerve fiber bundle defect of which the Seidel scotoma is only the denser portion (see Plate 4, *6*).

Bjerrum scotoma

The scotomatous defect of the central isopters of the visual field known as the Bjerrum scotoma is the most characteristic visual field change of the glaucomatous eye (Fig. 11-5). In its typical form it is a broad area of visual loss, best elicited with small test objects, starting at or near the upper or lower pole of the blind spot and spreading nasally as a gradually widening band above or below fixation between the 10- and 20-degree circles. It conforms accurately to the anatomic nerve fiber bundle pattern of the retina; when it reaches the nasal field (temporal raphe), it ends sharply at the horizontal meridian as a nasal step. Many nerve fiber bundle defects start in the nasal portion of the Bjerrum area and spread toward the blind spot.

This classic scotoma has been variously named and described as (1) arcuate scotoma, (2) comet scotoma, (3) scimitar scotoma, and (4) Bjerrum scotoma.

It was first described by von Graefe, in 1856, as a paracentral scotoma characteristic of established glaucoma, but it was studied and analyzed in more detail by Bjerrum in 1889. Since then the defect has been the subject of intensive investigation by numerous authors, including Landsberg, Peter, Meisling, Friedenwald, Sinclair, Traquair, Rönne, Dubois-Poulsen, Aulhorn, Harrington, and Drance. Rönne called attention to the nasal step feature of the defect and did much to explain its pathogenesis. It should be designated as a nerve fiber bundle defect to distinguish it from other forms of partial ring scotomas and to indicate its etiology.

Typical nerve fiber bundle defects may occur above or below the horizontal meridian. Such superior and inferior defects may be fairly symmetrical or they may be markedly different. A superior deficit, for example, may consist of a fully developed arcuate scotoma attached to the blind spot at one end and arching across the vertical meridian above fixation to end in a steep-margined nasal step with a "breakthrough" of the defect into the superior nasal periphery. At the same time the inferior half

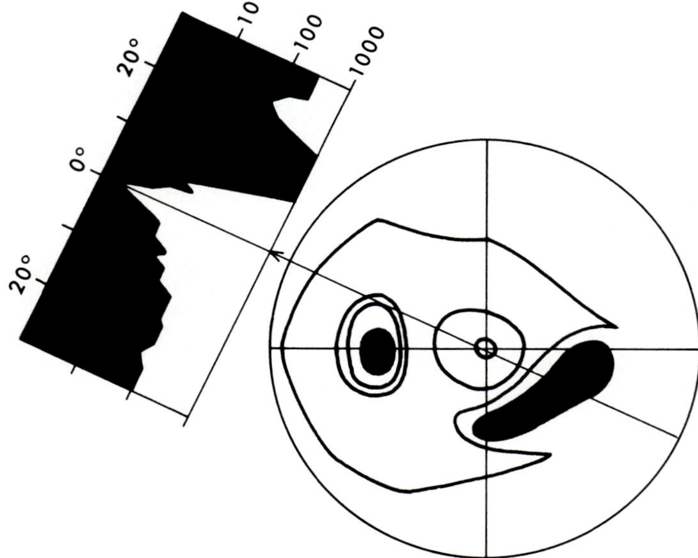

Fig. 11-5. Profile chart of static perimetric examination and conventional plot of kinetic examination of isolated arcuate scotoma in the inferior Bjerrum area on the 165-degree meridian.

of the visual field of that eye may show only a small, ill-defined paracentral scotoma in the 5- to 7-degree area with no connection to the blind spot and no nasal step.

When a glaucomatous-type visual field defect is found in one hemisphere, above or below fixation, the other hemisphere must be diligently examined for a similar deficit.

When one eye shows a glaucomatous-type field defect, the other eye should be most carefully tested. Sooner or later both eyes will almost surely develop deficits.

Nerve fiber bundle defects are rarely transient. Once established, they are usually permanent and progressive; and they are usually associated with ophthalmoscopic evidence of glaucomatous optic nerve atrophy and disc excavation of varying degree. Because of its permanence this visual field defect should rightly be considered as belonging to the diagnostic criteria of established glaucoma, although it may also be found in incipient glaucoma and in a variety of conditions not related to glaucoma.

The presence of an arcuate scotoma in the visual field is presumptive evidence of glaucomatous damage to the optic nerve until proved otherwise. But such a scotoma must be associated with other evidence of glaucoma; it is not, in itself, diagnostic of the disease any more than the isolated finding of elevated intraocular pressure establishes such a diagnosis.

Proving that a well-formed arcuate scotoma is not due to glaucoma may be a difficult task. The variety of causes of nonglaucomatous arcuate scotomas and the problem of low-tension glaucoma will be discussed later.

Established glaucoma

As noted previously, the nerve fiber bundle defect is the typical visual field abnormality of the later stages of incipient glaucoma. When the scotoma becomes per-

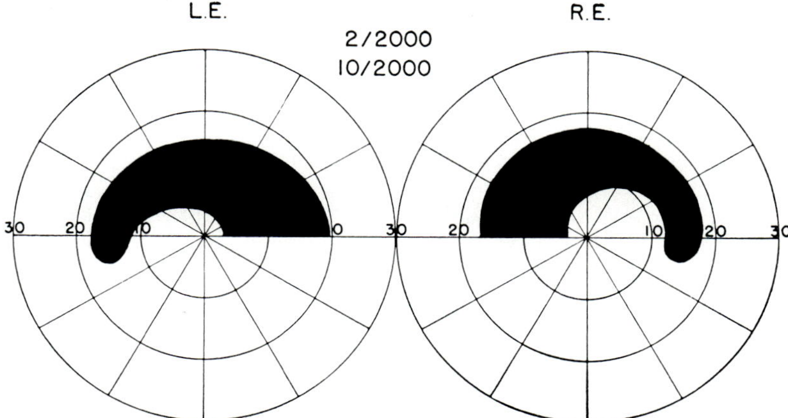

Fig. 11-6. Typical bilateral arcuate scotoma or superior nerve fiber bundle defect in chronic wide-angle glaucoma. Intraocular pressure varied between 25 and 44 mm Hg, and there was bilateral glaucomatous atrophy and excavation of optic nerve. Central vision was 20/20. Defects were dense and steep-margined, indicating stability in disease. More often scotoma lacks uniformity and has sloping margins.

manent and shows evidence of progression, associated with optic nerve atrophy, it may then be considered a sign of established glaucoma (Fig. 11-6).

The characteristics of the typical nerve fiber bundle scotoma have been described, but the defect may show many and different forms. It is more frequently found above than below fixation. The scotoma may follow any nerve fiber bundle or group of bundles. It may arch very close to fixation or well away from fixation. Theoretically, the nasal nerve fiber bundles can be affected, in which case the defect is cuneate or wedge-shaped and extends temporally into the peripheral field. The defect may start at the blind spot and progress into the nasal field; or it may begin midway between the blind spot and the horizontal raphe, in which case it will lie isolated from the blind spot, above or below fixation. The greatest depression is most often in this isolated area immediately above or below fixation. This is especially noticeable with static perimetry (Figs. 11-7 and 11-8). Occasionally, the scotoma begins in the nasal field at the horizontal meridian, forming a sharp nasal step and progressing slowly toward the blind spot along the course of the nerve fiber bundle.

When both upper and lower nerve fibers are affected, the scotoma takes the form of a double arcuate defect circling fixation, usually including the blind spot in its course and ending at the nasal horizontal meridian. If symmetric nerve fiber bundles were involved above and below the disc, the resulting ring scotoma would be a true

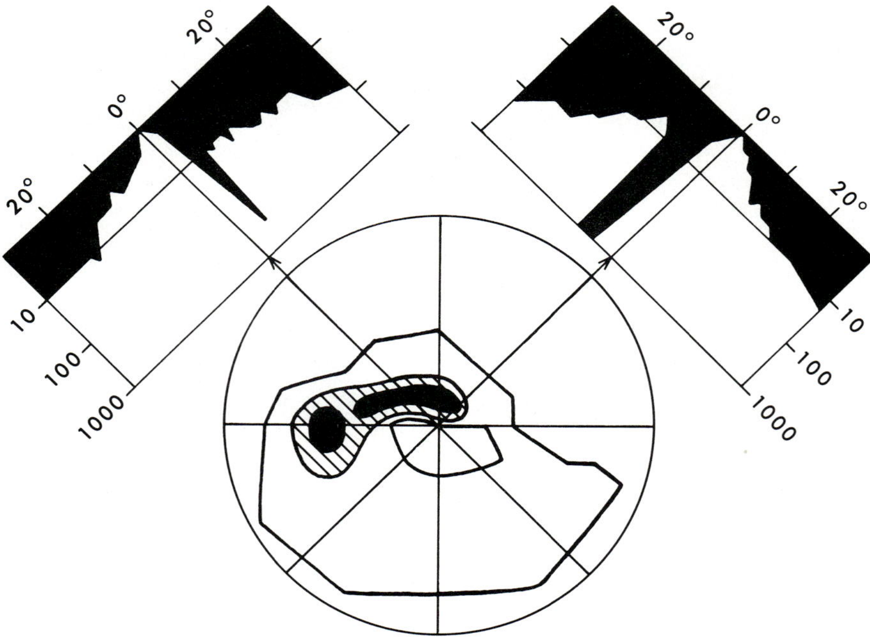

Fig. 11-7. Static and kinetic visual field in patient with typical Bjerrum scotoma and optic nerve cupping due to established glaucoma. Profile of static field taken in 45-degree and 135-degree meridians.

and complete circle. This is an extremely rare, if not impossible, coincidence. Frequently, the upper nerve fiber bundle is affected first, and by the time the inferior scotoma has developed and the ring is complete the lower portion is broader than the upper. Also, one half of the double scotoma may be closer to fixation than the other (Fig. 11-9). The result of these asymmetries is that the two halves of the ring meet at different points on the horizontal meridian or raphe, with formation of a double nasal step. Usually the inner step nearest fixation is smaller than the outer or peripheral one. Not infrequently, by the time the double nerve fiber bundle defect is complete, one half of the scotoma has broken through into the nasal peripheral field (see Fig. 11-12).

When examined by quantitative methods of perimetry, including profile perimetry and variable luminance, the nerve fiber bundle defect will be seen to be denser in its central portions with islands of absolute visual loss surrounded by a defect with sloping margins (Fig. 11-10). These islands gradually become more dense, coalesce, and expand both peripherally and centrally toward fixation. The rate of progression centrally is much slower than toward the periphery.

Even though the blind spot may be included in the nerve fiber bundle defect or lost within the ring scotoma produced by a double arcuate defect, it is not enlarged temporally or nasally until very late in the development of the terminal glaucoma field.

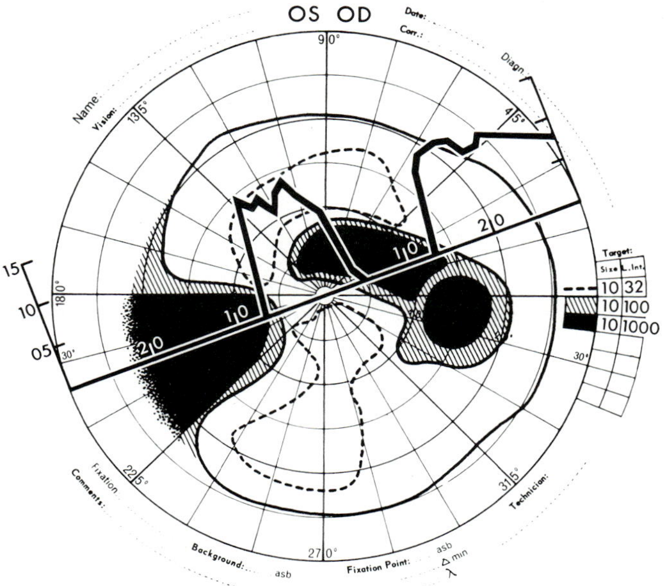

Fig. 11-8. Typical glaucomatous visual field defect measured on Tübinger perimeter. Kinetic field plotted as contour isopters shows large nerve fiber bundle defect. Static field through 200 degrees meridian plotted as profile overlay.

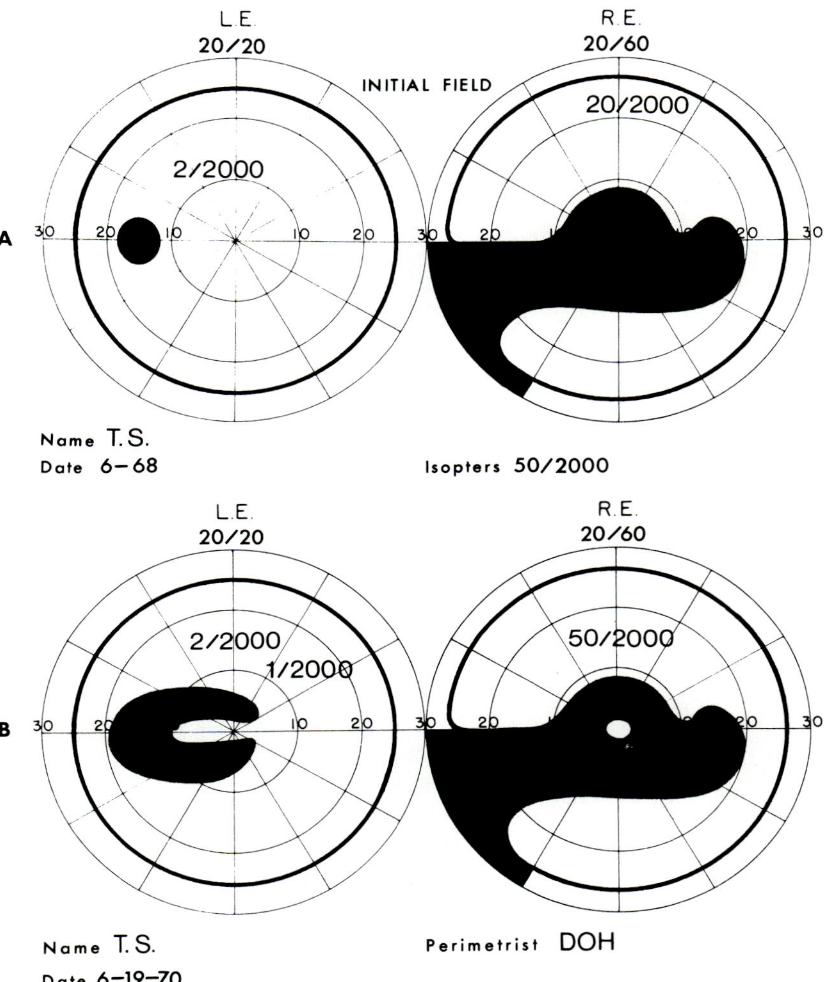

Fig. 11-9. A, Chronic open-angle glaucoma secondary to prolonged use of topical steroids in the treatment of uveitis. Initial field examination on tangent screen showed irregular centrocecal scotoma with nasal peripheral breakthrough right eye. Left field was normal. Diagnosis was retrobulbar neuritis. Goldmann perimeter field was normal in left eye. **B,** Later examination with larger stimulus showed right field defect to be a dense double nerve fiber bundle defect. Left field now shows an incomplete double arcuate scotoma. **C,** Goldmann perimeter field now shows small paracentral scotomas in Bjerrum areas of left eye. These defects were confirmed by static perimetry. (From Harrington, D. O.: Some unusual and difficult visual field defects. Trans. Ophthalmol. Soc. U. K. **92:** 15, 1972, London, Churchill Livingstone Ltd.)

C

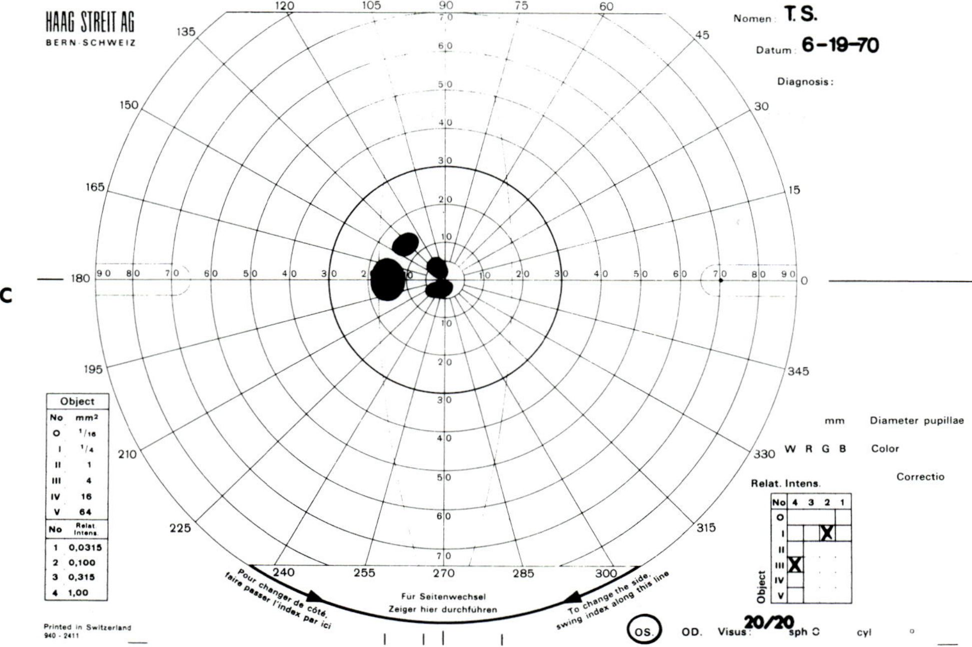

Fig. 11-9, cont'd. For legend see opposite page.

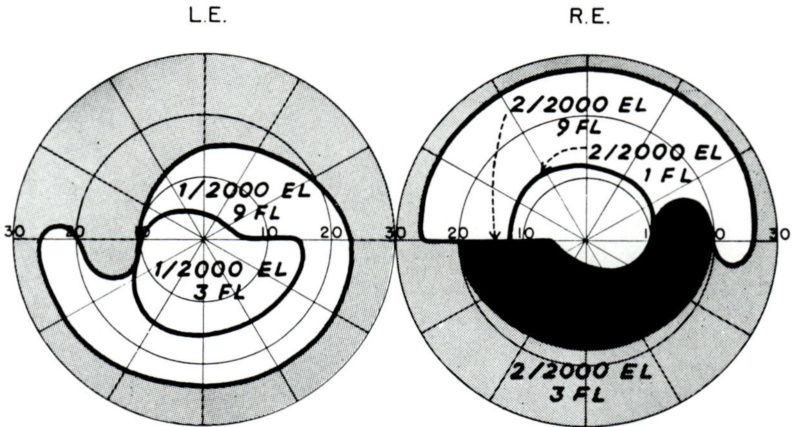

Fig. 11-10. Quantitative analysis of glaucomatous visual field defect by means of electroluminescent stimuli of variable luminance. The 2/2000 isopter when tested with 9 footlamberts of luminance reveals clear-cut inferior arcuate scotoma in right field. When only 3 footlamberts of luminance is used, entire lower field is lost, and when 1 footlambert is used, upper field is also depressed.

Rarely, the arcuate scotoma that begins in the upper pole of the blind spot will extend upward and nasally until it reaches the vertical meridian, where it appears to stop in a vertical step. Such a scotoma may be chiasmal in origin as well as glaucomatous.

Once established, the nerve fiber bundle defect progresses as follows:

1. It becomes more dense and generally more uniform so that it is easily detectable with relatively gross stimuli on either the perimeter or the tangent screen.
2. It broadens in width, expanding slowly toward fixation and more rapidly toward the periphery, especially in the nasal quadrant, where it eventually breaks through into the peripheral field or coalesces with a coexistent peripheral depression.
3. It lengthens until it connects at one end with the blind spot and terminates in a steep-margined and characteristic nasal step at the other.

Hoyt, Frisén, and Newman have demonstrated a method of visualizing nerve fiber bundle defects in the retina using ophthalmoscopy with red-free light. They studied the peripapillary nerve fiber layers in eyes with chronically elevated intraocular pressure and found that retinal nerve fiber atrophy corresponding to glaucomatous type visual field defects can be seen with the ophthalmoscope and in fundus photographs viewed with red-free light.

The nerve fiber bundle atrophy appears as multiple fine shallow grooves or slits in the arcuate bundles of the nerve fiber layer of the retina. These slits represent the effects of nerve fiber bundle degeneration (Fig. 11-11). As the glaucomatous atrophy increases, the defect in the nerve fiber layer may resemble a wedge that tapers to the disc margin. In still later stages, these wedge defects expand to sector defects in which all nerve fiber details are obliterated. There is good correlation between the ophthalmoscopic findings of degeneration and the visual field defects.

Peripheral depression

Coincident with the development of the nerve fiber bundle defect in glaucoma, a depression of the peripheral isopters occurs, especially in the nasal quadrants. When carefully examined, this nasal depression may be one of the earliest signs of functional loss in patients with glaucoma, and as such it is of considerable diagnostic importance. It may be first detected with small visual angles on the perimeter and simultaneously found to extend in to the 20-degree arc on the tangent screen. It is exaggerated in perimetry with reduced illumination. It is most easily detected in its early stages on the Goldmann perimeter with small stimuli of low intensity or in the profile of the peripheral field by static perimetry on the Tübinger perimeter. Many of these nasal depressions have a clear-cut horizontal step that may or may not be connected to an arcuate defect. When found in association with a nerve fiber bundle defect, it is almost pathognomonic of glaucoma, and its coalescence with the scotoma eventually results in the typical breakthrough into the peripheral field, which is so characteristic of the terminal stages of the disease (Figs. 11-12 to 11-15).

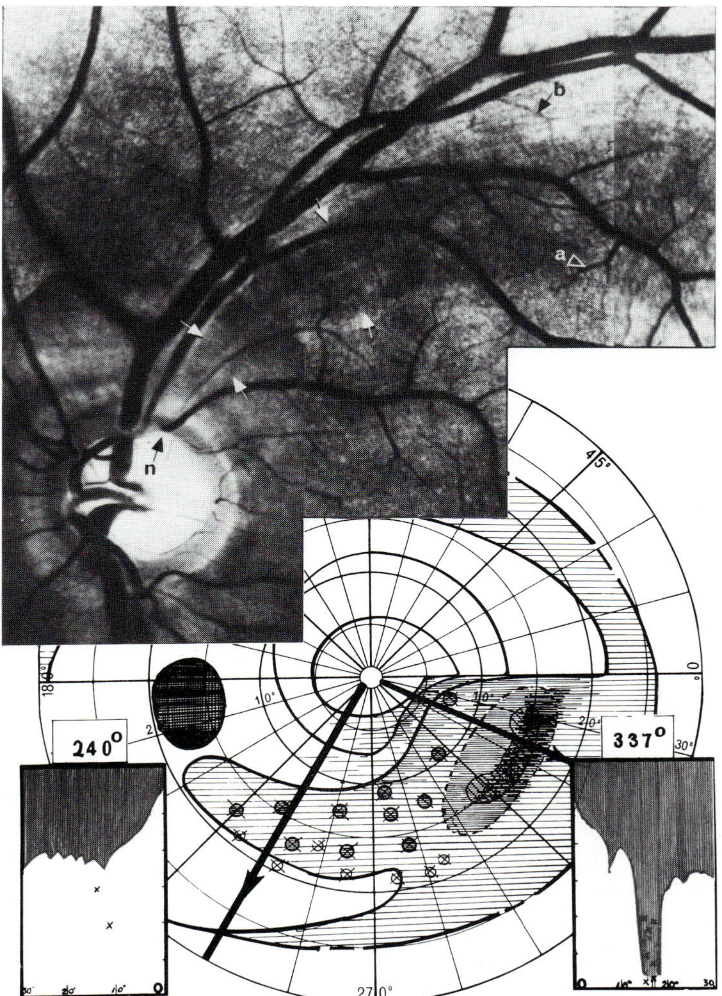

Fig. 11-11. Funduscopy of nerve fiber layer defects. Glaucomatous nerve fiber layer defect between solid white arrows and peripheral arrows **a** and **b** appears as scimitar-like wedge joining the disc margin at **n.** Borders of wedge conform to course of temporal arcuate bundles. The granular appearance throughout retina is caused by diffuse axonal attrition. Optic disc shows marked cupping with indenting of rim at **n.** Tübinger perimeter fields showed a relative scotoma in Bjerrum area with a nasal step. Static perimetry profile at the 337-degree meridian showed general depression and a dense scotoma at 15 degrees of eccentricity. (From Hoyt, W. F., Frisén, L., and Newman, N. M.: Funduscopy of nerve fiber layer defects in glaucoma, Invest. Ophthalmol. **12:**814, Nov., 1973.)

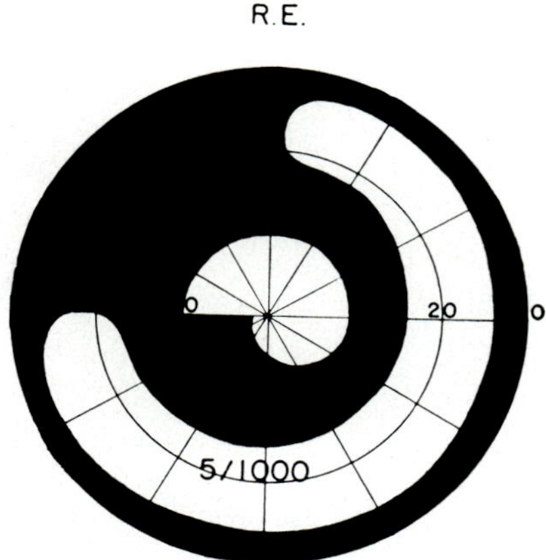

Fig. 11-12. Chronic wide-angle glaucoma of right eye. Double nerve fiber bundle defects (arcuate scotoma) with characteristic double nasal step and breakthrough into peripheral nasal field. There is unusual finding of normal visual field, normal optic nerve, and normal intraocular pressure in other eye.

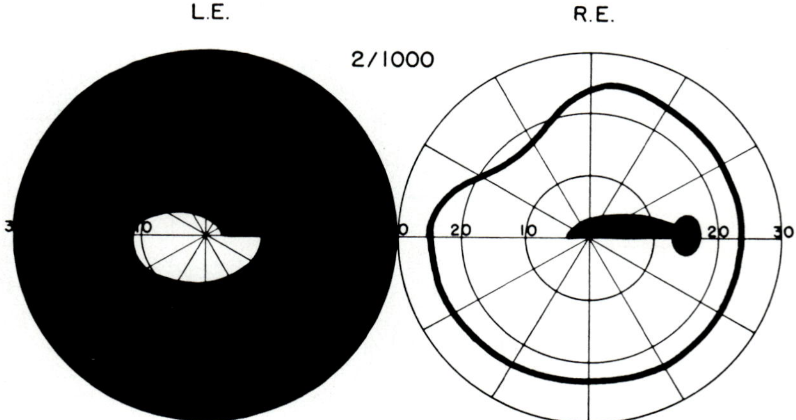

Fig. 11-13. Chronic wide-angle glaucoma with cavernous atrophy of optic nerve. Left eye shows severe general contraction with remnant of field demonstrating characteristics of double nerve fiber bundle defect and nasal step. Right eye shows narrow nerve fiber bundle defect involving portion of papillomacular bundle of nerve fibers and extending through fixation to tiny nasal step.

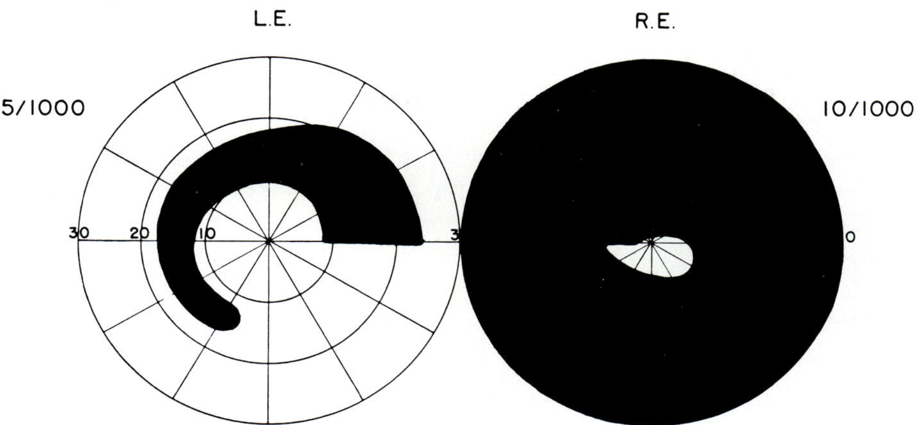

Fig. 11-14. Chronic wide-angle glaucoma. Patient was unaware of visual loss, and central vision was 20/20 in each eye. There was typical glaucomatous atrophy of both discs. Right field shows extreme contraction with tiny nasal step. Left field shows typical arcuate scotoma ending at horizontal meridian.

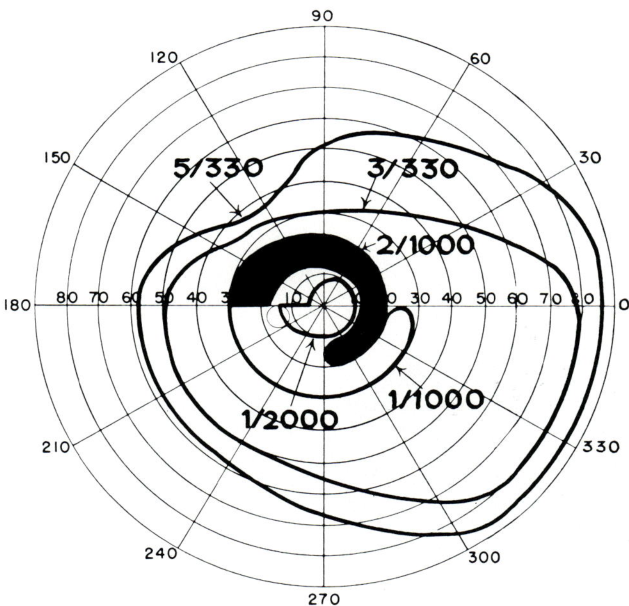

Fig. 11-15. Quantitative analysis of visual field in case of chronic wide-angle glaucoma. Each isopter shows visual field of different shape and size indicating sloping nature of margins. In this analysis of typical glaucomatous visual field defect, each isopter shows characteristic pattern. When all isopters are seen together, the pathognomonic picture of glaucoma is striking.

Although nasal depression of the peripheral field is more common in the superior quadrant, it may also occur below or in the entire nasal field. It is often a symmetric development in the two eyes.

Once established, progression of the peripheral depression is likely to be relatively rapid as compared with the changes in the central isopters, and in some instances it may simulate a quadrantanopsia, especially when it has coalesced with an arcuate scotoma. When both upper and lower nasal fields are involved and when the peripheral depression is symmetric in the two eyes, the fields take on the character of a binasal hemianopsia.

Terminal glaucoma

The transition from established glaucoma to terminal glaucoma is necessarily vague. It is marked by loss of most of the peripheral field and retention of a small island of central vision measuring only a few degrees in diameter. The retention of this tiny central area of vision is responsible for most of the neglect of treatment in glaucoma (Fig. 11-16). Central vision may remain 20/20 by Snellen test letters when the field defect has encroached to within a degree of fixation.

This central remnant of visual field will retain certain characteristics of the glaucoma field to the very last. It is oval in shape with its longest diameter horizontal and in the centrocecal area (see Figs. 11-13 and 11-14). It often shows a minute horizontal step just nasal to fixation. Thus it continues to follow the pattern of the retinal nerve fiber bundle. Final encroachment of the defect on fixation is usually from the nasal side; and when fixation is involved, the visual loss is sudden, severe, and dramatic, even though expected, because the margins are so steep and the defect so intense as to be almost total.

Associated with the central island of vision there is often a small temporal area of

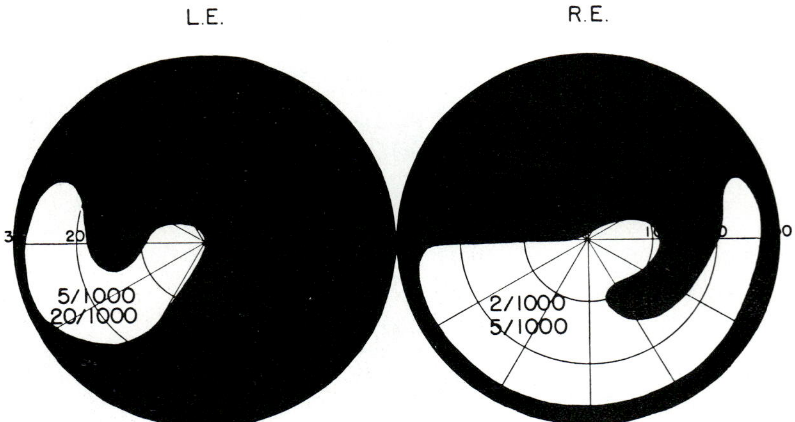

Fig. 11-16. Visual field defect in terminal stages of chronic wide-angle glaucoma. Left visual field shows only temporal remnant with vision reduced to hand movements. Right visual field defect with its nerve fiber bundle defect and wide nasal step is encroaching on fixation.

retained vision in the peripheral field. The patient may be barely aware of this area before the central defect involves fixation, at which time he immediately becomes conscious of its value as his last hope. It may remain for a long time after all other areas of vision are gone (see Fig. 11-16).

Morin, in an analysis of 3,700 central visual fields of 2,000 patients referred for glaucoma evaluation, found glaucomatous changes in 417, or 11.3%, of the tested visual fields. Each visual field was examined both statically and kinetically on the Tübinger perimeter, and the various defects were classified as to position in the field, shape, and density. The combined static and kinetic examination increases the reliability of the field analysis and especially the evaluation of peripheral field constriction.

The findings are in general agreement with the classification of glaucomatous field changes outlined above, with some minor variations. Morin feels that the dual technique of static and kinetic testing makes it possible to verify one technique with the other and is therefore superior to the tangent screen in which only the kinetic field is examined. This ignores the flexibility of the tangent screen examination and the almost limitless number of isopters that it is capable of testing.

The principal findings of the study were as follows:

1. Most Bjerrum island scotomas were in the upper temporal region, were initially circular rather than elongated, and were the same width throughout.
2. Many paracentral scotomas were isolated defects.
3. Nasal steps showed no predilection for a particular isopter. Most were curved or wedge-shaped.
4. Nerve fiber bundle defects had not originated from nasal paracentral scotomas.
5. There was no association between temporal steps and arcuate scotomas.
6. Advanced glaucoma produced absolute constriction of the visual field, and central fixation (sometimes accompanied by a temporal island of vision) is the last remnant of vision to survive.
7. Initially, the upper temporal and lower nasal fields are affected by Bjerrum scotomas, but as the field worsens absolute nasal steps appear in the upper field. Nerve fiber bundle defects are more common in the upper than in the lower half of the field.
8. Absolute circular enlargement of the blind spot was a major clue to deterioration of a visual field, often being accompanied by one or more advanced defects in another area of the field.

IMPORTANCE OF PERIMETRY IN GLAUCOMA

Visual field examination has a threefold value in glaucoma: (1) in diagnosis, (2) in prognosis, and (3) in therapy.

Diagnosis

The early changes in the visual field of patients with glaucoma have been stressed. It is a simple matter to detect the established nerve fiber bundle defect or the peripheral nasal step, since these are obvious even with crude methods of examination. It is of much greater importance to study and apply the precise methods of quantitative perimetry to the detection of early functional loss so as to forestall further damage.

The changes in the visual field are indications of established glaucoma. Strictly speaking, they are not diagnostic but rather confirmatory evidence of the disease. They must be correlated with the other signs and symptoms of the disease.

Certain visual field changes, however, may appear at a very early stage in the development of the disease and, when properly evaluated as part of the complete clinical picture, will sometimes serve to establish the diagnosis in otherwise doubtful cases. These changes are (1) modification of the angioscotoma pattern, (2) depression in the Bjerrum area, and (3) combination of these defects with early nasal depression. When it is remembered that these changes can sometimes be exaggerated in reduced illumination until they take on the characteristics of more advanced glaucoma field changes, they may assume considerable diagnostic importance.

When other evidences of glaucoma such as optic disc cupping, nerve fiber layer atrophy, increased intraocular pressure, decreased facility of aqueous outflow, and gonioscopic evidence of changes in the angle of the anterior chamber are doubtful but suspicious, the finding of early but characteristic glaucomatous changes in the visual fields takes on added significance and may be the means of establishing the diagnosis. When the examiner is in doubt about a given case, no method that will give evidence of functional loss in an eye should be neglected; and the visual field examination may be of prime importance when all available techniques of examination are used.

Prognosis

Visual field interpretation is of even greater value as a prognostic than as a diagnostic aid. In most cases the established visual field defect is associated with other signs and symptoms that are of great diagnostic value, but the progression of the field defect may tell more of the advance of the disease than any other single finding.

As in any visual field defect, a sloping margin and lack of uniformity are indicative of an actively changing process. The paracentral scotomatous areas of visual field loss, such as the nerve fiber bundle defect, are usually steep-margined, dense, and relatively uniform, whereas the gradually sloping margin of the peripheral depression is a sign of rapid change.

Repeated visual field studies with a technique that is constant will indicate the rate of progression of functional loss regardless of other findings that may appear to be relatively the same from one examination to the next.

Sudden decrease in blood pressure, even if only transient, in the vessels supplying the optic nerve head may produce rapid deterioration of the visual field, with sudden appearance of nerve fiber bundle defects or exaggeration of previously existing defects. Such a drop in blood pressure and resulting decrease in blood flow may be initiated iatrogenically by too vigorous use of blood pressure–depressing drugs or by coronary artery occlusion, cerebrovascular accident, or severe gastrointestinal or other bleeding with subsequent anemia.

Intraocular pressure may be normalized by medical or surgical means, but if the eye continues to lose field the prognosis is poor.

The gonioscopic examination and the facility of aqueous outflow may remain constant, but if the visual field shows a changing pattern the prognosis is poor.

Optic nerve pallor and cupping are likely to closely parallel the loss of visual field, but the examiner's judgment of an advancing atrophy may be most inaccurate as compared with the record of visual field changes unless photographs or sketches are available for recording it.

Extreme care must be taken in assessing visual field change in the presence of simultaneous glaucoma and cataract. The effect of any clouding of the media is to reduce the stimulus illumination and to exaggerate the field defect. Continued or increased use of miotic drugs, resulting in extreme miosis, will decrease retinal illumination and simulate progress of a field defect.

Follow-up or repeat examination of the visual field for purposes of prognostic evaluation in glaucoma must be performed under constant and carefully controlled conditions, whereas examinations for purely diagnostic purposes may vary within wide and flexible limits. The constancy of technique and the repeatibility of the test is a major advantage of automated or computerized perimetry.

Therapy

The consideration of therapy for the patient with glaucoma is closely allied to prognosis in the disease: the worse the prognosis, the more emergent must be the therapy.

To a fairly large extent the therapy of glaucoma is dictated by perimetry. Without functional loss in an eye, one is usually content with conservative medical management of the disease. With moderate functional loss or with extremely slow progression of the visual field changes, the ophthalmologist must weigh other factors against the field in making the decision as to how best to treat the eye. Thus a slowly advancing visual field loss in a very elderly person with a reasonably controlled intraocular pressure might well dictate a medical regimen, whereas the same findings in a young person would call for more radical therapy.

The case for conservatism in the management of open-angle glaucoma is presented by Shaffer and Hetherington, who reviewed the history of the various forms of therapy, reappraised the results of filtering procedures and their side effects and complications, and came to the conclusion that perhaps too many eyes have been treated too soon. The principal danger in overtreatment is the frequency with which cataract develops in both surgically and medically treated eyes. These authors pointed to the paucity of visual field defects that have turned up in hypertensive eyes found in the 10-year-old Collaborative Glaucoma Study and suggested that eyes with abnormal pressures may preserve their function and visual fields longer than was formerly believed. They further believe that since the optic nerve is not damaged—as evidenced by minimal to moderate cupping (0.3 to 0.7) and a normal visual field—no therapy is mandatory up to 30 mm Hg intraocular pressure. With larger cupping and the beginning or undoubted progression of visual field defects, especially if asymmetric in the two eyes, there is increasing responsibility to lower the pressure by one means or another to a level below that which has produced the nerve damage.

A dense arcuate scotoma proximate to the fixation area should be viewed with anxiety, and even a minor change in visual field might well indicate a poor future unless the intraocular pressure were promptly normalized, if need be, by surgical measures.

Any therapeutic measure that is followed shortly by encroachment of a visual field defect on fixation will naturally be blamed by the patient for his loss of central vision. Such a loss is not uncommon when therapy has been delayed until a dense visual field defect is perilously close to the foveal area. It therefore behooves the surgeon to carefully evaluate the progression of the field loss in its early stages and to institute medical or surgical treatment according to the early interpretation of the fields.

The sudden production of severe hypotony by fistulizing operations for glaucoma has been shown to aggravate the visual field loss until later normalization of pressure arrests this progress. Thus considerable loss in visual field may occur for a short time following such surgery, after which the field changes may become stabilized. If the preoperative field changes are severe, and especially if they are proximate to fixation, this postoperative visual field loss may obliterate the central visual area and nullify the benefits of the surgery. In other cases a rapid progression of visual field loss that obviously calls for surgical therapy is only temporarily halted by operation and later resumes its inexorable march toward blindness in spite of normalized intraocular pressure.

Occasionally, surgically induced hypotony is followed by the development of a central scotoma and loss of central vision to the distress of both patient and surgeon. In these cases macular edema associated with the hypotony is probably the causative factor.

No matter what the other findings in a glaucomatous eye, the visual field changes must always be judiciously considered in any discussion of therapy.

The greater the visual field loss, the worse the prognosis and the more difficult and urgent the therapy.

GLAUCOMA WITHOUT INCREASED INTRAOCULAR PRESSURE (LOW-TENSION GLAUCOMA)

There is some doubt that low-tension glaucoma is, in fact, glaucoma; but it simulates glaucoma so closely in so many respects that it must be considered in the discussion of glaucoma. Numerous reports on this condition are found in the literature. Its existence is difficult to explain by any of the theories of the pathogenesis of glaucoma, except by the theory of vascular insufficiency. It is one of the most difficult diagnostic and therapeutic problems to confront the clinician.

The disease is characterized by all the usual findings of well-established glaucoma, except increased intraocular pressure. The pressure is, in fact, usually hypotonic to a degree. The atrophy and excavation of the optic disc are identical to those in advanced chronic glaucoma. The visual field changes are exactly the same as those found in established glaucoma. Nerve fiber bundle defects identical to those of glaucoma are frequent. Nasal depression with rapid progress and step formation is the rule. Altitudinal hemianopsia in the late stages is common. The coefficient of outflow (C value) is usually normal and the P_0/C ratio is frequently under 100.

The applanation tonometer readings in patients with this condition are usually higher than the Schiøtz tonometer readings, and the condition is common in myopic eyes.

Nevertheless, there are many cases in which all the criteria for diagnosing glaucoma are lacking, except the findings of optic nerve atrophy and excavation and advanced visual field defects, which are glaucomatous in character.

Most authors attribute the glaucoma-like optic nerve atrophy and excavation and the nerve fiber bundle defects in the visual field, in the absence of increased intraocular pressure, to vascular changes in the optic nerve at the site of the cribriform fascia. The character of the atrophy and the frequency of altitudinal hemianopsia favor this view, since this type of visual field loss is not uncommon in association with vascular disease or trauma involving the arterial supply of the optic nerve (see Fig. 11-18).

Occasionally, an open-angle glaucoma of long standing with optic atrophy and cupping, typical visual field defects, and low outflow facility will show a gradual decrease in intraocular pressure, presumably due to decreased aqueous production. Some of these patients can even be withdrawn from miotic therapy with continued slow decrease in intraocular pressure. When such a patient is seen for the first time with normal or low intraocular pressure but gross visual field deficit, he may simulate a case of low-tension glaucoma whereas, in fact, the condition might better be termed "burned-out" glaucoma (Fig. 11-17).

Whatever the cause of the condition, its mere existence presents a challenge to all students of glaucoma, because the pathogenesis of the optic atrophy and visual field defects of true glaucoma may hinge on a more complete knowledge of this disease.

No discussion on low-tension glaucoma would be complete without reference to Drance's presentation in the 1971 William Mackenzie Memorial Lecture, published as part of a symposium on the optic nerve and edited by J. S. Cant.

In a series of 41 eyes, which fulfilled the criteria for low-tension glaucoma, 93% showed systemic abnormalities of which hemodynamic crises and low blood pressure occurred more frequently than in a carefully selected and studied control series.

A low systemic blood pressure was found to be significantly more common in subjects with low-tension glaucoma than in undamaged ocular hypertensives. The blood supply of the optic nerve head is favorably influenced by an adequate perfusion pressure (ophthalmic artery pressure less intraocular pressure) and adversely influenced by local vascular disease.

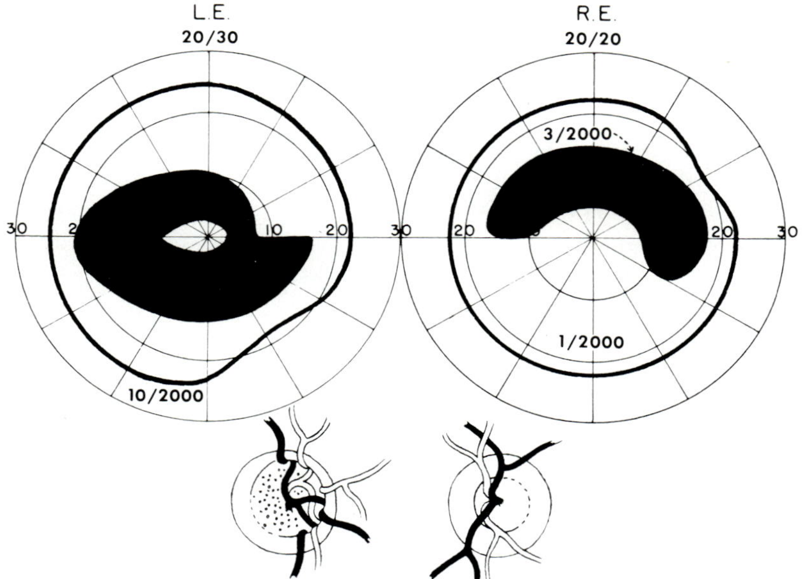

Fig. 11-17. Bilateral arcuate scotomas in case of burned-out glaucoma. Elevated intraocular pressure had been controlled with difficulty by intensive medication and had resulted in visual field defects and optic disc excavation. Gradual spontaneous decrease in pressure to low normal limits made further treatment unnecessary, and case resembled low-tension glaucoma.

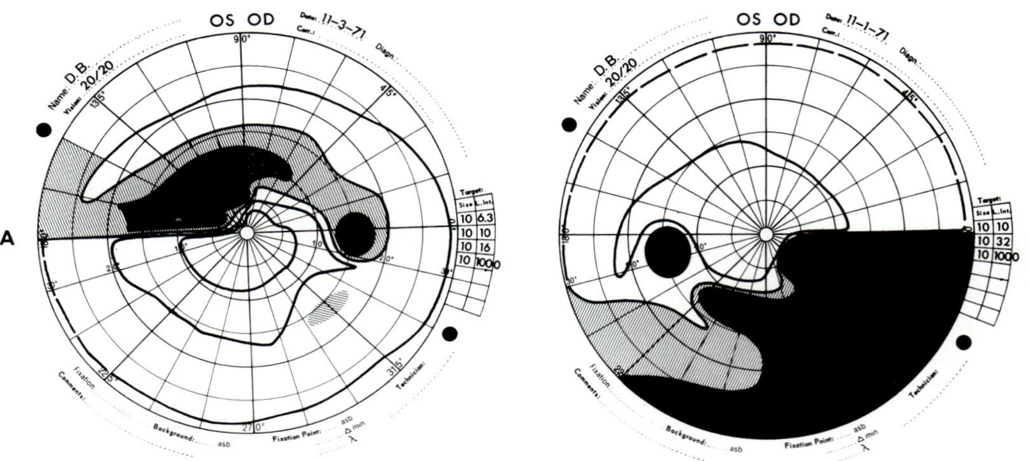

Fig. 11-18. Right eye, **A,** and left eye, **B.** Nerve fiber bundle destruction following severe exsanguination from rectal bleeding. Kinetic examination with Tübinger perimeter was very similar to tangent screen field for stimuli up to 30/2000. Both optic discs were pale. Intraocular pressure was 10 mm Hg. The field defect has remained stable for several years. Red-free ophthalmoscopy showed definite nerve fiber bundle atrophy in the areas corresponding to the field loss. (From Harrington, D. O.: Some unusual and difficult visual field defects, Trans. Ophthalmol. Soc. U. K. **92:**15, 1972, London, Churchill Livingstone Ltd.)

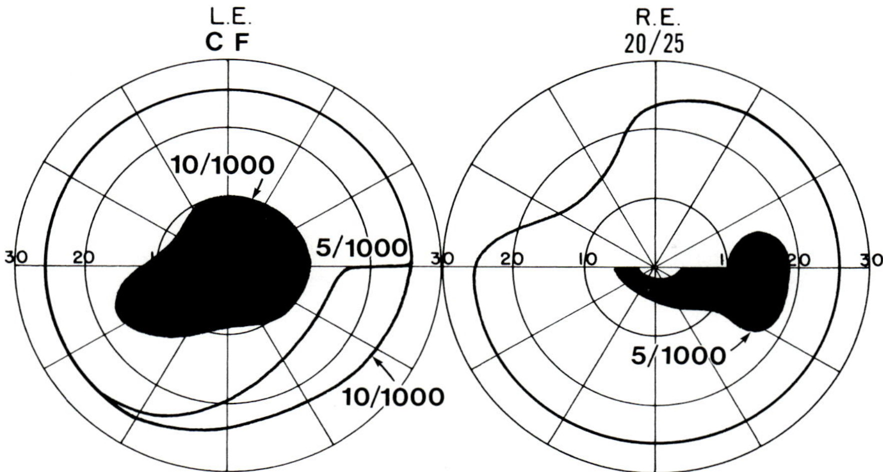

Fig. 11-19. Low-tension glaucoma. Large, deep, pale optic cups. Normal intraocular pressure. Senile macular degeneration, left eye, with dense central scotoma and nasal step. Papillomacular nerve fiber bundle defect, right field, with macular sparing.

Abnormalities in the coagulation-fibrinolytic system occurred in over half of the cases and have been shown to be associated with vessel disease.

Susanna, Drance, and Douglas have found that patients with chronic glaucoma and visual field defects had a higher prevalence of splinter hemorrhages on the optic disc than those patients with elevated intraocular pressure but no field loss.

Drance suggests that in low-tension glaucoma, one is dealing with an ischemic process of the optic nerve head that may be the result of many interacting factors and that the search for a single cause will continue to be frustrating. Both chronic open-angle glaucoma and low-tension glaucoma are most likely to be manifestations of a disease process that seriously interferes with perfusion of the optic nerve head.

Levene has published a very comprehensive review of the entire subject of low-tension glaucoma, which he defines as a condition consisting of typical glaucomatous disc and field changes in an eye with open angle and pressures within the normal range. The controversy over this entity pertains to the definition and characteristics of the condition and to the fundamental question it raises regarding the causal relationships between intraocular pressure and disc and field changes. The review is based on an exhaustive survey of the world literature and on an analysis of a large number of cases from clinic and private practice. Definitions, incidence, characteristics, differential diagnosis, and management of low-tension glaucoma are discussed as is its relationship to primary open-angle glaucoma and various other entities. Pathogenesis and possible mechanisms are also explored.

PATHOGENESIS OF THE GLAUCOMA FIELD

In 1954 Dubois-Poulsen and Magis suggested that the Bjerrum scotoma is not pathognomonic of glaucoma and showed that it may be found in association with a wide variety of lesions affecting the visual pathway anterior to the lateral geniculate body. These included vascular lesions of the retina, choroiditis, optic neuritis, and optic nerve trauma.

These authors advanced the theory that the Bjerrum scotoma is not necessarily correlated to intraocular tension or to cupping of the optic discs. They stated that they believe the Bjerrum scotoma corresponds to a well-separated nerve fiber bundle and that its cause must be vascular and extraocular. They believe that the actual lesion may be located immediately posterior to the eyeball in the arterial circle of Zinn-Haller or even further back in the optic nerve and that this "essential symptom of glaucoma" is not directly influenced by intraocular tension.

The vascular genesis of the Bjerrum scotoma (and the other visual field defects of glaucoma) was suggested by Traquair, by Lauber, and by Reese and McGavic; more recently, it has been elaborated on and confirmed by Gafner and Goldman in 1955, by me in 1958, 1959, and 1964, and by Drance in 1961, 1968, 1970, and 1977.

It is generally accepted that glaucomatous visual field defects are the result of diminished blood flow in the anterior optic nerve in the region of the lamina cribrosa, the arterial circle of Zinn-Haller, and the peripapillary choroidal circulation. This circulatory insufficiency in the anterior optic nerve may be brought about by a number of circumstances any one of which or combination will produce hypoxia in the nerve head and will result in loss of function and in the visual field deficits characteristic of glaucoma. These circumstances are as follows:

1. An increase in intraocular pressure sufficient to overcome normal arterial pressure in the arterioles of the optic nerve head and the peripapillary choroidal vessels.
2. A decrease in blood pressure in the ophthalmic artery, and secondarily in the optic nerve head arterioles, so that normal or relatively slight increase in intraocular pressure produces a stasis or back flow in the arterioles and hypoxia in the nerve.
3. Actual arterial insufficiency in the ophthalmic artery and its branches as the result of carotid artery stenosis or occlusion or atherosclerotic plaques in the small arterioles at or behind the lamina cribrosa or on the papilla (Figs. 11-20 and 11-22).

   When these atherosclerotic changes are associated with increased intraocular pressure, the resulting deterioration in the visual field may be rapid indeed.
4. Arterial insufficiency in the optic nerve resulting from embolic phenomena such as might occur in giant cell arteritis, papilledema, papillitis, and the localized retinal nerve fiber infarction associated with choroiditis or vasospasm.

Anything that upsets the normal balance between intraocular pressure and retinal or ophthalmic arterial pressure, with resulting decrease in blood flow in the nerve, will produce or exaggerate the nerve fiber bundle field defects so characteristic of disturbance in this area.

In the past decade much convincing evidence has accumulated, anatomic, physiologic, and clinical, to support this view.

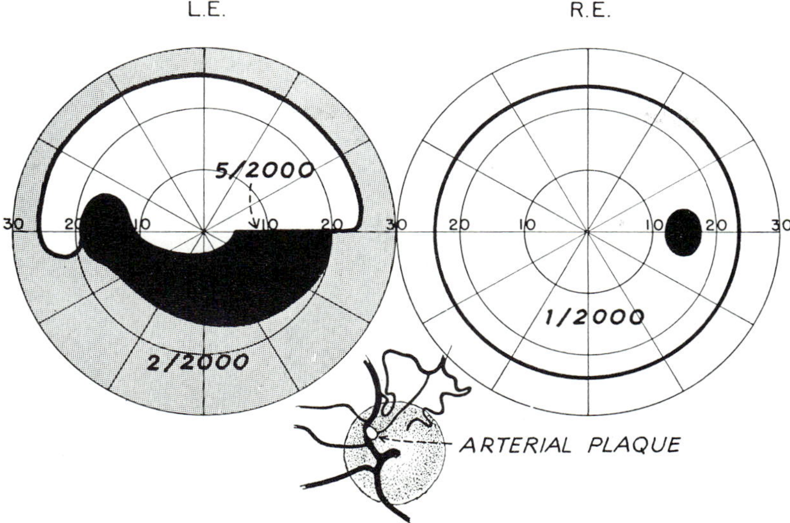

Fig. 11-20. Typical nerve fiber bundle defect with nasal step produced by atherosclerotic plaque in small arteriole on optic nerve. Drawing of retinal arterial lesion from fundus photograph. Intraocular pressure was 17 mm Hg by applanation. There was slight segmental atrophy of disc and clinical evidence of left internal carotid artery insufficiency.

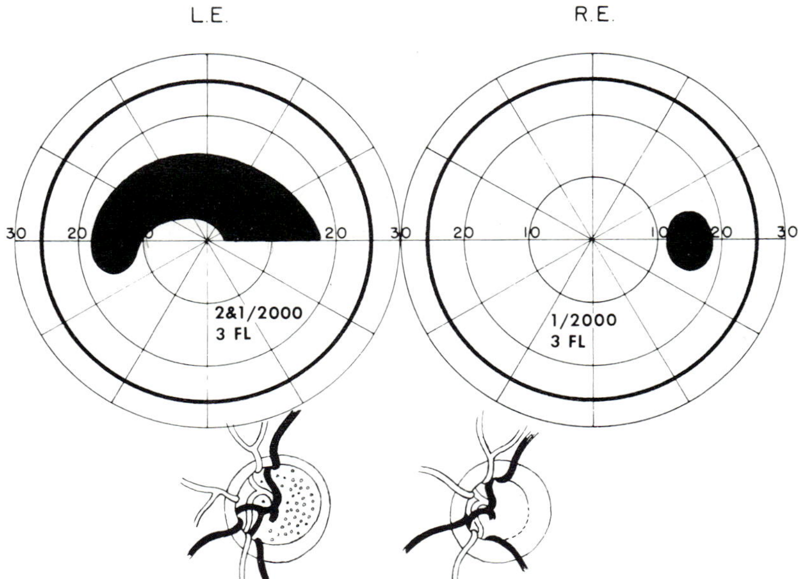

Fig. 11-21. Nerve fiber bundle defect developing rapidly in eye with well-controlled glaucoma. Patient suffered mild cerebrovascular accident with sudden marked decrease in systemic and ophthalmic artery blood pressure. Both optic discs are cupped. Left disc is partially atrophic.

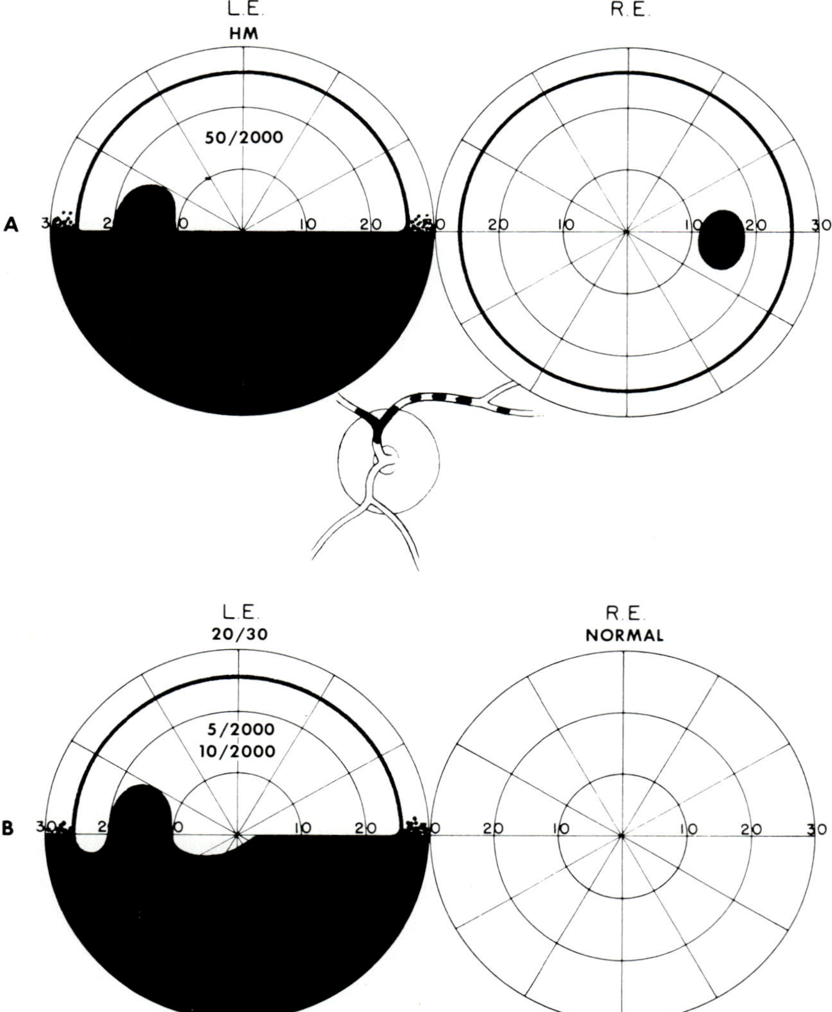

Fig. 11-22. A, Dense altitudinal hemianoptic defect in left visual field associated with visible, transient, creamy white embolus in superior retinal artery. **B,** Conversion of altitudinal defect seen in **A** into broad, dense nerve fiber bundle defect after movement of arterial embolus. Change in field defect occurred within 15-minute period. Note sparing of fixation area and marked improvement in visual acuity. **C,** Conversion of complete inferior nerve fiber bundle defect seen in **B** into typical arcuate scotoma after further clearing of arterial embolus. Defect and position of embolus are seen 90 minutes after initial visual loss. **D,** Small residual arcuate scotoma 3 days after field defect seen in **C.** Defect eventually cleared completely.

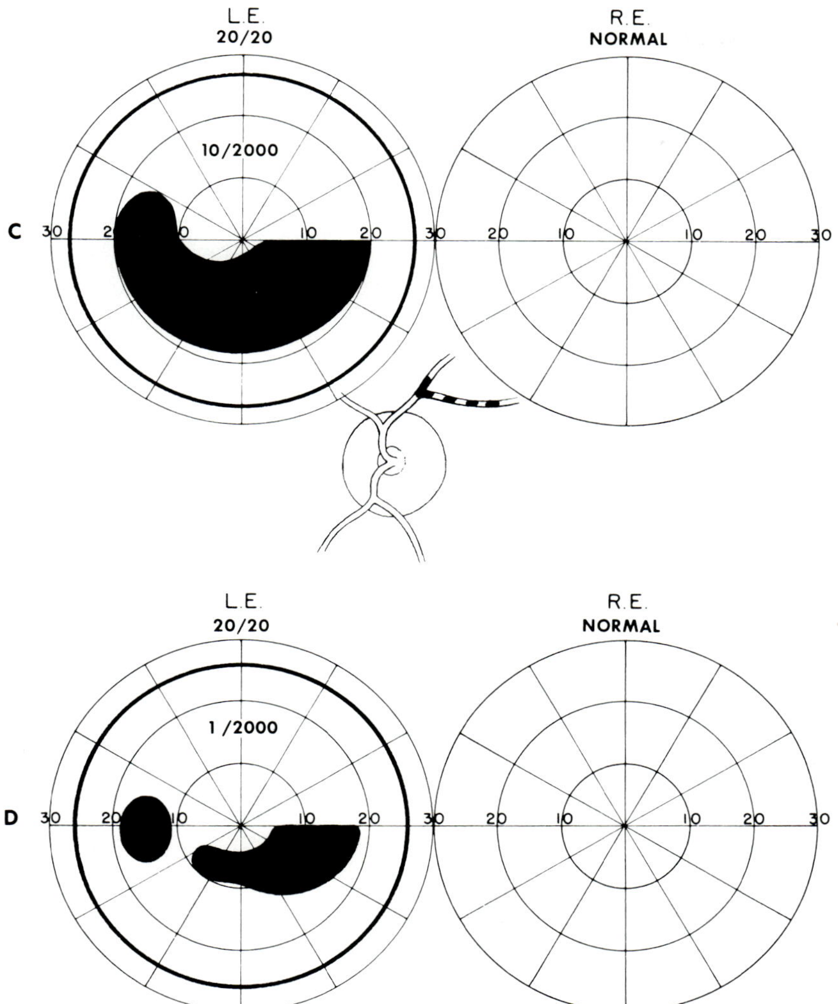

Fig. 11-22, cont'd. For legend see opposite page.

I have reported the sudden appearance of a nerve fiber bundle defect in patients with well-controlled glaucoma after their arterial hypertension had been iatrogenically lowered by excessive medication (see Fig. 11-21). I have also produced temporary nerve fiber bundle defects in the visual fields of patients with carotid artery insufficiency by artificially inducing very slight elevation in intraocular pressure through compression of the globe with an ophthalmodynamometer. Bjerrum scotomas have been produced or exaggerated in glaucomatous eyes by minimally elevating the intraocular pressure with a dynamometer, thus demonstrating that certain eyes are more vulnerable than others to increases in intraocular pressure.

Drance, Wheeler, and Pattullo studied a series of patients with uniocular glaucoma to determine which factors might influence the production of field defects. These eyes were subjected to visual field studies by kinetic and static methods of perimetry and were thoroughly studied for all possible evidences of glaucoma. Intraocular pressure, degree of optic disc cupping and atrophy, tonographic data, and ophthalmodynamometer findings varied considerably in the thirty-one eyes studied. Those patients in whom intraocular pressure was normal or slightly elevated and who showed extensive optic disc and visual field deficits had a very high incidence of vascular disease, including myocardial infarctions, which produced a transient but pronounced drop in systemic blood pressure. In the group with low-tension glaucoma, two out of four patients gave a history of massive gastrointestinal bleeding with marked lowering of blood pressure (see Fig. 11-18). In the unaffected eyes of these patients with uniocular glaucoma, visual field tests on the Tübinger perimeter revealed paracentral scotomas in fourteen eyes. All the eyes with badly damaged nerves and visual fields but with normal or very slightly elevated pressure had low diastolic perfusion pressures or had had a transient episode of very low blood pressure that would have resulted in a very low diastolic perfusion pressure at the time.

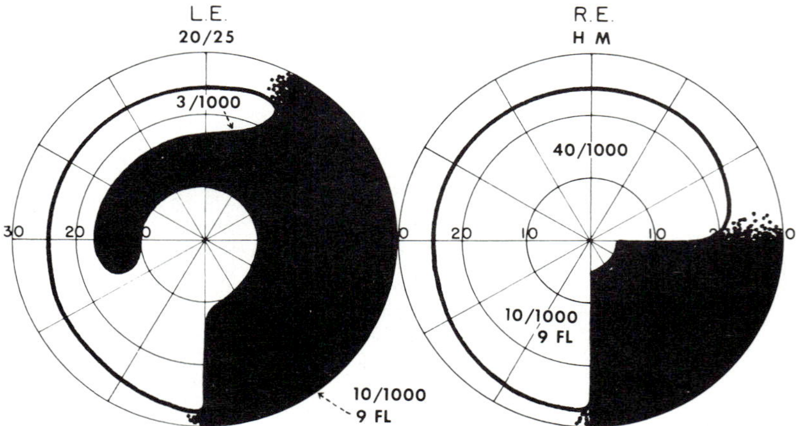

Fig. 11-23. Arcuate scotoma left eye combined with right inferior homonymous quadrantanopsia in case of left carotid artery occlusion. Retinal arterial diastolic and systolic blood pressure was markedly reduced in left eye. Right visual acuity reduced by cataract, but homonymous field loss was easily plotted with large test objects.

The authors concluded that the changes produced in chronic open-angle glaucoma can be the result, on the one hand, of markedly elevated intraocular pressure that embarrasses the circulation of the optic nerve head and retina independently of other factors and, on the other hand, of extreme circulatory events that do not require any elevation or change in intraocular pressure to cause extensive nerve and visual field damage.

Drance and Begg reported a case of chronic open-angle glaucoma with normal intraocular pressure and minimal paracentral scotomas in the visual field in which the patient sustained a sudden linear hemorrhage on the disc margin associated with enlargement of the optic cup and development of a dense new superior arcuate scotoma. They concluded that this hemorrhage occurred as a result of ischemic infarction in the nerve head, resulting from poor perfusion insufficient to maintain circulation under normal conditions of high tissue pressure at this site. The association of acute ischemic changes in the nerve head, manifested by sector hemorrhage, with the development of typically glaucomatous disc cupping and atrophy and advanced visual field defect, offers further proof of the ischemic origin of the glaucomatous defect in the field (Fig. 11-24).

Blumenthal and his co-workers investigated the effect of acute increases in intraocular pressure on the retinal, choroidal, and optic disc vessels by means of fluorescein angiography in normal human eyes. Their technique provided for controlled studies of intraocular pressure effects on the vascular bed of the eye. They demonstrated that flow ceases in the choroidal circulation at intraocular pressures significantly lower than those required to produce cessation of blood flow in the retinal vascular tree.

The optic disc capillaries were affected at the smallest increases of intraocular pressure and filled with dye only after the entire choroid had become fluorescent. In some instances the entire peripapillary choroidal area revealed a marked diminution in fluorescence. These findings imply that the peripapillary choroidal vessels and the optic disc vessels are the most vulnerable portion of the choroidal circulation when subjected to elevation of intraocular pressure.

Histologic evidence confirms the fact that the peripapillary choroidal vascular bed is the sole source of the blood supply to the pre–lamina cribrosa of the optic nerve.

In the past 10 years many additional experiments have demonstrated the vasogenic origin of glaucomatous-type visual field defects and optic nerve damage. Fluorescein angiographic studies of the optic nerve head and the peripapillary area under conditions of artificially induced ocular hypertension have implicated the retinal, choroidal, and optic nerve circulation.

Intensity of fluorescence in the optic disc capillaries was assessed. A marked decrease in capillaries is seen with increase in the cup-disc ratio, and the greater the defects in the visual fields the fewer the capillaries in the optic nerve head. It is therefore possible to predict the visual field loss from the capillary distribution in the glaucomatous optic disc.

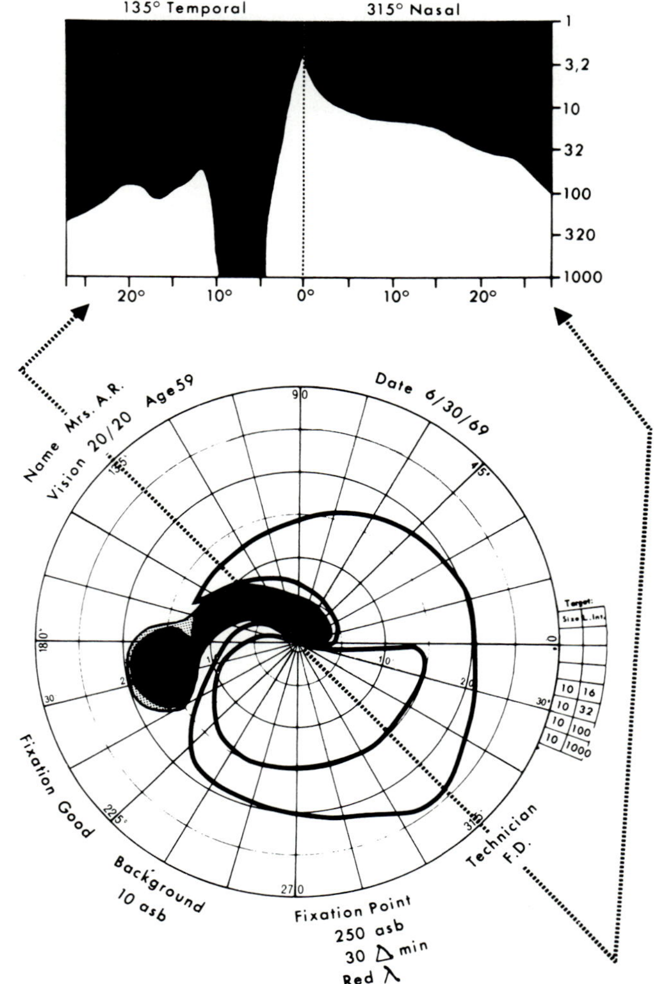

Fig. 11-24. Static and kinetic visual field examination showing absolute arcuate scotoma in eye with sector hemorrhage and acute ischemic infarct in optic disc. Patient had medically controlled chronic glaucoma with minimal relative scotoma in superior Bjerrum area until sudden appearance of capillary hemorrhage on disc. (From Drance, S. M., and Begg, I. S.: Can. J. Ophthalmol **5:**137, 1970.)

Ernest has written extensively and convincingly on the pathogenesis of glaucomatous optic nerve disease. His article carries an extensive bibiliography. Ernest's studies encompassed an elucidation of the vasculature of the distal segment of the optic nerve, measurement of the optic disc oxygen tension in monkeys, and measurement of the visual effects of induced elevations in the intraocular pressure in man. He shows that the visual threshold in the Bjerrum area is elevated with an increase in the intraocular pressure but that the eye is able to compensate with a reduction in threshold toward normal if given ample time. It is thought that glaucomatous optic nerve disease results when there is a failure of local homeostatic circulatory mechanisms to compensate for sustained elevation of the intraocular pressure.

Ernest concludes that the initiating pathogenic event in glaucomatous optic nerve disease is a breakdown in the homeostatic mechanisms responsible for normal perfusion and oxygenation of the optic disc; that the superior and inferior temporal nerve fibers are affected first, since these are in highest concentration relative to the optic disc blood supply; and that the first fibers affected in the superior and inferior nerve fiber bundles are those midway between the disc circumference and the central retinal artery, since this is the area of relatively lowest oxygen tension.

Sears has generally agreed with Ernest but seems to feel that individual susceptibility to optic nerve damage is of great import and suggests the presence of genetic markers for the development of field loss.

Drance, Maumenee, and Anderson argue the question, "Is ischemia the villain in glaucomatous cupping and atrophy?" in Brockhurst and associates' *Controversy in Ophthalmology* and present the data favoring the vascular theory, the mechanical theory, and the theory of axoplasmic flow.

Armaly and Araki found that rapid, transient elevation of ocular pressure level produces simultaneous reduction in blood flow rate in the distal 6 mm of the extraocular portion of the optic nerve of the rhesus monkey. The magnitude of this reduction was small until the intraocular pressure exceeded 50 mm Hg, after which markedly reduced blood flow rate occurred. When systemic arterial pressure was reduced, the reduction in blood flow in the anterior optic nerve was significantly greater. The results of this study demonstrate a dependence of the circulation of the distal extraocular portion of the optic nerve on ocular pressure level such that progressive increase in intraocular pressure produces a progressive reduction in blood flow rate in this region of the optic nerve.

Recent studies by Anderson and Hendrickson of rapid axoplasmic transport in monkey optic nerve reveal that it is affected by intraocular pressure. There is a selective effect deep in the optic nerve head at the lamina cribrosa, and a partial effect can be detected even at moderate elevations of intraocular pressure. When intraocular pressure is moderately elevated, there is partial obstruction of axoplasmic transport in the region of the lamina cribrosa. When intraocular pressure is elevated to within 25 mm Hg of mean blood pressure, complete obstruction of transport at the lamina cribrosa occurs. Whether the obstruction is mechanical or is secondary to reduced blood flow has not been determined and the exact relevance of these findings to the pathogenic mechanisms of glaucomatous cupping and visual field loss is not yet clear.

It seems logical to conclude, however, that such physiologic abnormalities would lead to functional deficits in the fields.

The same effect of increased intraocular pressure has been noted on slow axonal protein flow by Normal Levy. He found marked initial reduction in flow with increased pressure and a gradual recovery as pressure returned to normal.

In contrast to these findings, Phelps and Phelps have succeeded in elevating systemic blood pressure by intravenous infusion of phenylephrine while simultaneously elevating intraocular pressure by paralimbal suction. They then measured the highest level to which intraocular pressure could be raised without obliterating perception of a slowly flickering stimulus in the nasal field of vision. Elevation of systemic blood pressure was accompanied in all subjects tested by a corresponding increase in the highest "safe" level of intraocular pressure. This observation again confirms the hypothesis that pressure amaurosis is the result of pressure-induced neuroretinal ischemia.

Finally, Pederson and Anderson have studied serial disc photographs of 259 patients with elevated intraocular pressures over periods up to 15 years. Twenty-nine eyes showed progressive enlargement of the optic cup. Expansion of the optic cup was the first change observed, typically preceding visual field loss by several years. They concluded that serial disc photographs are necessary for the earliest detection of optic nerve damage in ocular hypertension and that treatment is indicated for eyes exhibiting progressive disc cupping even in the absence of visual field defects. They noted that visual field examination is important in detecting early damage, since field loss can be present even when the disc is judged normal. Moreover, visual field examination may be a better measurement to follow once a field defect is present, since cupping often is advanced by this time.

CHAPTER 12

Toxic amblyopias

The toxic amblyopias are generally classified as diseases of the optic nerve. In reality the exact location and nature of the lesion producing the visual defect are often unknown. Some, such as methyl alcohol poisoning, appear quite definitely to produce optic nerve damage, but others, such as quinine or organic arsenical poisoning, result from retinal hypoxia and damage to the ganglion cells of the retina, with secondary optic atrophy. It would appear more rational, therefore, to consider the toxic amblyopias as a separate category with the various types listed under toxic agents rather than by location of the damage.

For a detailed description of all the possible toxic agents that may affect the visual apparatus, refer to *Toxicology of the Eye,* ed. 2, the encyclopedic work of W. Morton Grant. In spite of the tremendous increase in the number of chemicals, drugs, and other noxious agents to which we are exposed, there is a surpisingly small group that affect vision and, more specifically, the visual fields. The new ones are listed and described in this edition.

In general, from a perimetric point of view, the toxic amblyopias fall into two groups: (1) those with central scotomas and (2) those with peripheral visual field loss or depression. The best known and most widely studied example of the former is tobacco amblyopia, and of the latter, quinine amblyopia.

BILATERAL CENTRAL SCOTOMAS

Scotomas of varying size, shape, density, and position, always bilateral, may be produced by the following toxic agents: (1) tobacco, (2) nutritional deficiencies, (3) ethyl alcohol, (4) methyl alcohol, (5) lead, (6) carbon disulfide, (7) iodoform, (8) thallium, (9) digitalis, (10) chloramphenicol, (11) plasmocid, (12) streptomycin, (13) sulfonamides, (14) isoniazid, (15) ethambutol, (16) disulfiram, (17) octamoxin, (18) pheniprazine, (19) emetine, and (20) chlorodinitrobenzene.

Tobacco amblyopia

No other toxic amblyopia has been so exhaustively studied and described as that produced by tobacco, and yet its pathogenesis is still poorly understood.

The visual disturbances of tobacco amblyopia occur most commonly in elderly male pipe smokers and cigar smokers. It has been reported in users of chewing tobacco and snuff. It is so rare in cigarette smokers as to be nonexistent or highly suspect.

The incidence of tobacco amblyopia varies geographically perhaps because of differences in the manner of tobacco consumption in different parts of the world. It is a common entity in the British Isles, especially in Scotland. It was much more common 40 years ago in the United States than it is today, probably because of a change in smoking habits.

In general, the more tobacco used and the darker and stronger the leaf, the higher the incidence of amblyopia, although some cases are seen in persons consuming relatively small quantities.

Tobacco amblyopia is a separate and distinct clinical entity and is unrelated to alcohol consumption. It is doubtful if ethyl alcohol, even when consumed in large quantities, gives rise to a true toxic amblyopia. The designation *tobacco-alcohol amblyopia* should be discarded.

A careful history of amounts and type of tobacco consumed, dietary habits, with particular reference to poor intake of protein and vitamin B, chronic diseases such as diabetes, increased fatigability, pernicious anemia, and alcohol consumption is important in establishing a diagnosis.

The typical visual field defect in tobacco amblyopia is a bilateral centrocecal scotoma. The shape, size, and density of these scotomas vary with the amount and duration of the patient's tobacco consumption and with his susceptibility, but certain characteristics of the defect are constant and uniform.

The scotoma is always bilateral. It may involve one eye to a greater degree than the other so that on first examination it appears to be unilateral, but when quantitative studies are performed, the fellow eye will always show a defect, however minimal (Plate 5).

The scotoma usually develops as a small area of visual loss midway between the blind spot and fixation on the temporal horizontal meridian. In its initial stages it is vague, indefinite, and detected only in the isopter for 1/2000, and the patient is rarely aware of its existence. From here the scotoma extends both nasally toward fixation and temporally toward the blind spot. Its progress may be extremely slow. Coalescence with the blind spot may take place fairly early, the loss of central vision may be quite dramatic, and the patient often insists that his visual disturbance was sudden in onset. The scotoma is negative in character.

In its early stages the centrocecal defect may extend nasally from the blind spot rather than begin in the area midway between blind spot and fixation. In these cases and also in its latter development, there is a marked widening of the arborization of the angioscotoma.

In the typical case the centrocecal scotoma increases in its vertical diameter only slightly as it extends laterally. Thus it almost always remains oval in shape, usually regular in outline, but sometimes irregular or crenated. It may, on occasion, be very slender like a bayonet pointed at fixation (Fig. 12-1).

The density of the scotoma is rarely uniform until the very late stages of an untreated case. Usually there is a central island of greater density and at times the entire scotoma appears fragmented when multiple isopters are tested. This characteristic, along with the very sloping margins of the defect, makes the accurate charting

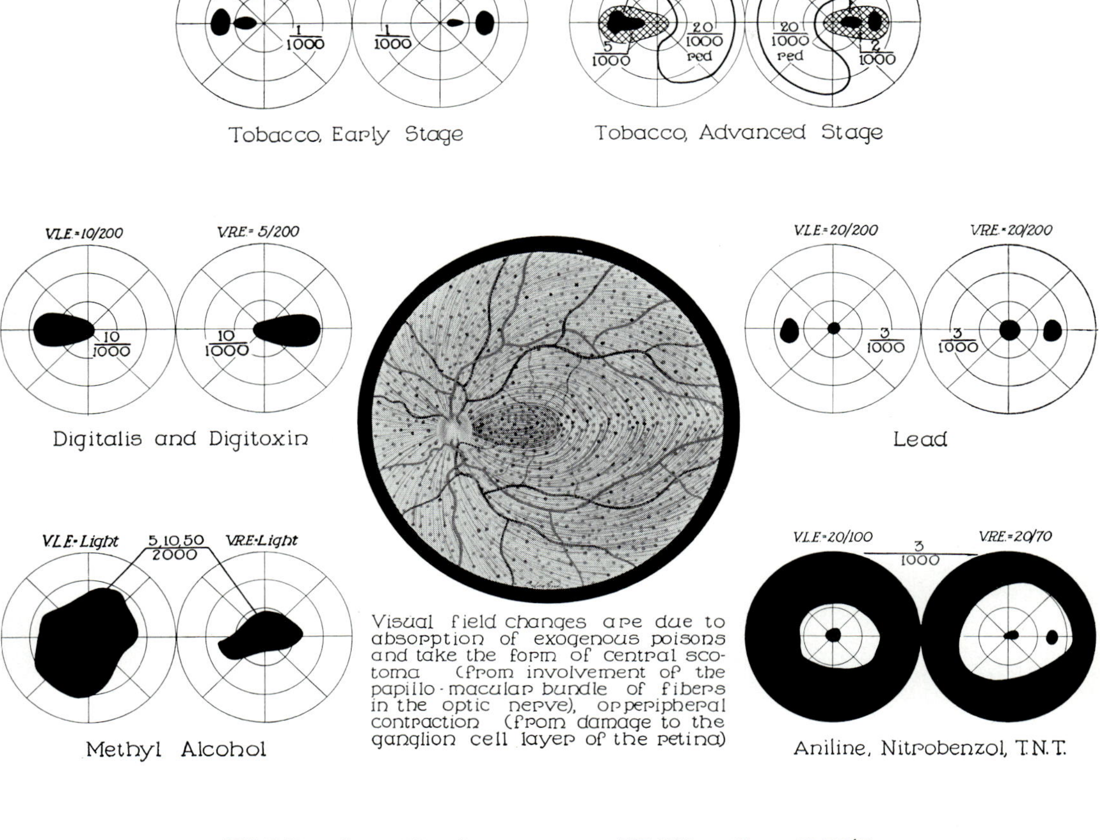

Plate 5. Visual field defects in some toxic amblyopias.

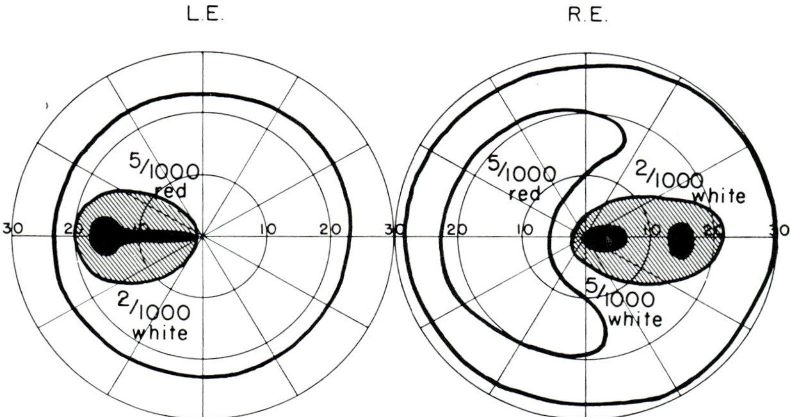

Fig. 12-1. Tobacco amblyopia. Sloping margins of bilateral centrocecal scotoma and exaggeration of defect for red stimuli are clearly demonstrated.

of the scotoma difficult, and there are times when its outline is so vague that it cannot be recorded with precision. This very vagueness may be of considerable diagnostic importance.

One of the most characteristic features of tobacco amblyopia is its effect on color vision, especially red perception. Patients are sometimes aware of this for some time before there is any actual decrease in visual acuity. Gold objects may appear silver, and friends and relatives may appear pale or even ill, to the point where the patient queries them about their health. One patient in my experience became so alarmed by the apparent pallor of his own normally ruddy complexion, as seen in the mirror, that he went to his physician. The visual field defect for red is an exaggerated form of that found with white test objects.

The centrocecal scotoma for red may become so large that it breaks through into the peripheral field and so broad in its vertical diameter that the field for red stimuli may simulate a bitemporal hemianopsia. Too much emphasis on this defect in the field for red without careful analysis of the white isopters has led to an erroneous diagnosis of pituitary adenoma.

With abstinence from tobacco and therapy with noncyanide-containing hydroxocobalamin (B_{12}), resolution of the scotoma begins in an order reverse to its formation. Usually there is a retraction of the scotoma temporally away from fixation with a consequent improvement in visual acuity, which is very encouraging to the patient. As the defect shrinks in size and density, it assumes its former position between the blind spot and fixation, and finally even this island melts away. Color vision is usually affected for a long time. Visual acuity may return to 20/20 within 6 months.

Prognosis for return of vision is good if (1) the use of tobacco is stopped, (2) the atrophy of the optic nerve is not too marked, (3) the foveal portion of the scotoma is not too dense or too long-standing, and (4) there is good response to therapy with vitamin B_{12}.

The pathogenesis of tobacco amblyopia is poorly understood. There is evidence that the primary lesion is a degeneration of the ganglion cell layer of the retina with secondary atrophy of the nerve fiber layer of the retina and the papillomacular bundle of the optic nerve. Apparently, tobacco amblyopia is a toxic optic neuropathy due to disturbance in the distribution of thiocyanate in body fluids; it is, in fact, a form of cyanide poisoning, as confirmed by its response to treatment with intramuscular hydroxocobalamin even when the patients have continued to use tobacco.

The literature on tobacco, alcohol, and nutritional amblyopia is vast and confused. Much of the confusion stems from the use of the term *tobacco-alcohol amblyopia*, and, until recently, few authors had differentiated between those cases associated with the use of tobacco and those attributed to chronic alcoholism with nutritional deficiency.

In a recent study of more than 100 cases of tobacco amblyopia, Foulds and coworkers summarized the following facts:

1. All their patients smoked tobacco.
2. The patients were often elderly and had a diet poor in protein and vitamin B.
3. Twenty percent had Addisonian pernicious anemia.
4. Forty percent had a demonstrable defect of vitamin B_{12} absorption.
5. Alcohol consumption played little or no part in the condition.

They concluded that tobacco amblyopia is a multifactorial disease in which tobacco consumption; an abnormality of vitamin B_{12} metabolism, including inadequate diet and malabsorption; and a diet low in protein are among the factors involved.

While not claiming to have discovered the cause of tobacco amblyopia, Foulds believes that a theoretical explanation can be provided by assuming that the condition is a manifestation of chronic cyanide poisoning and that the disease is the result of an abnormality of the normal detoxifying process for cyanide coupled with chronic exposure to this radical from tobacco smoke. It is known that the cyanide radical is detoxified in the body to thiocyanate and the level of thiocyanate in the blood and urine of smokers is higher than in nonsmokers. Patients with tobacco amblyopia have significantly lower levels of thiocyanate in the plasma than do unaffected smokers, suggesting an impaired ability in these patients to convert their intake of cyanide to harmless thiocyanate.

Administration of non-cyanide-containing vitamin B_{12} (hydroxocobalamin) produced a rapid improvement in visual acuity even in those patients who continued smoking.

On the basis of my experience in both European and American clinics, I firmly believe that (1) tobacco amblyopia is a recognizable clinical entity, (2) amblyopia from ethyl alcohol is nonexistent, (3) the amblyopia often associated with chronic alcoholism is a nutritional deficiency disease, probably a manifestation of subclinical pellagra, and should be so treated (see following discussion), and (4) the term *tobacco-alcohol amblyopia* is a misnomer and should be discarded.

The differential diagnosis depends on combining a detailed history with meticulous quantitative perimetric analysis of the bilateral scotomatous defects in the visual fields and a favorable response to abstinence from tobacco or treatment with non-cyanide-containing hydroxocobalamin (B_{12}).

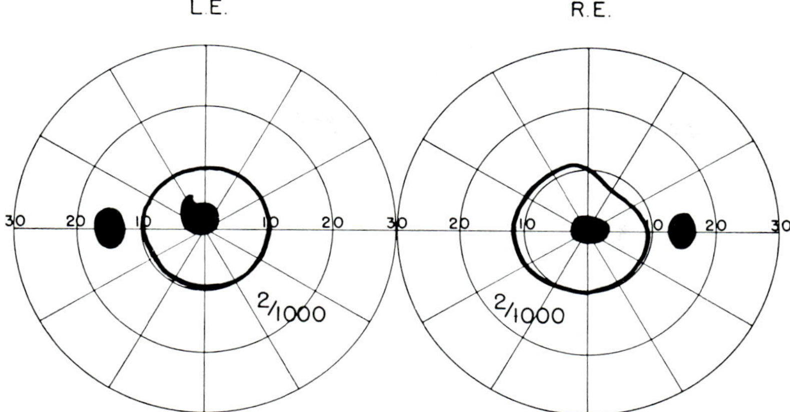

Fig. 12-2. Nutritional amblyopia. Patient was prisoner of Japanese during World War II and demonstrated optic atrophy and central visual acuity of 20/200. There is bilateral depression of 2/1000 isopter and bilateral central scotoma.

Nutritional amblyopia

Nutritional amblyopia is, in reality, a deficiency disease rather than a form of toxic amblyopia, although it has certain characteristics that seem to classify it in this group.

Some persons who were held prisoner in Japanese prison camps in World War II developed permanent visual disturbances. Most of these cases, studied after release from prison, revealed advanced bilateral optic atrophy with dense bilateral central scotomas and normal peripheral fields. The scotomas were irregular in shape with steep margins and uniform density (Fig. 12-2). In almost all instances there was severe malnutrition, but the degree of dietary deficiency could not always be correlated with the visual loss. Some of these prisoners were fairly well nourished, whereas others were in the last stages of debilitation from lack of food. There appears to have been considerable variation in susceptibility in these cases. In a few there was, in addition to the optic atrophy, a small, irregular, heavily pigmented macular choroidal lesion with central scotoma. It is not certain whether this lesion was nutritional in origin or the result of coincident central choroiditis.

Ethyl alcohol amblyopia

Although cases of ethyl alcohol amblyopia have been reported, it is difficult to establish the fact of toxic amblyopia from acute ethyl alcohol poisoning. Probably the visual symptoms that occur in association with this condition are the result of cerebral dysfunction resembling cortical blindness. Acute alcoholic amblyopia with optic atrophy and central scotoma can be produced when the ethyl alcohol is impure. Whisky and gin of low quality may contain quantities of various fusel oils sufficient to act as a toxic agent and produce this syndrome, but such poisoning should not be considered the result of ethyl alcohol ingestion.

The amblyopia associated with chronic alcoholism presents a picture identical with nutritional amblyopia but unlike tobacco amblyopia. Although the visual loss is gradual, it may be noticed by the patient in the early stages of the condition. Vision is described as hazy, but later objects in the area of the scotoma are blotted out and the scotoma may be positive.

The characteristic visual field defect is a central scotoma that is usually slightly irregular in shape, varying in size from 2 to 5 degrees and in density from a relative defect requiring a 1-mm test object for its detection to an absolute loss within the limits of the defect (Fig. 12-3). Margins are often steep, even in the early stages of development, and density is fairly uniform. The scotoma occasionally extends temporally toward the blind spot and may coalesce with it to form a centrocecal defect. When this occurs, the area of greatest density within the scotoma is at fixation rather than in the centrocecal portion as seen with tobacco amblyopia (see Figs. 7-17 and 12-1; Plate 5). The amblyopia is bilateral and the central scotomas fairly symmetric. The peripheral fields are normal or slightly depressed.

Many of these cases have no history of tobacco consumption, but a careful inquiry into dietary habits will reveal rather gross deficiencies. Anorexia is sometimes extreme, so that caloric intake is limited almost entirely to the alcohol consumed. Meals are sketchy and poorly balanced at best. Associated alcoholic polyneuritis is common and minimal, but obvious signs of pellagra are not uncommon.

This syndrome, of a nutritional type of amblyopia associated with chronic alcoholism, is confined almost entirely to the lower social classes and the abandoned drunkards of the slum areas of cities; it is rare, even in severe cases of alcoholism, in the higher social strata.

Prognosis for return of useful but not normal vision is fairly good when adequate nutrition is restored, even in those persons who persist in their alcohol consumption. Vitamin B_{12} is an important part of the therapy. Recent data suggest that zinc deficiency may also play a role in this condition.

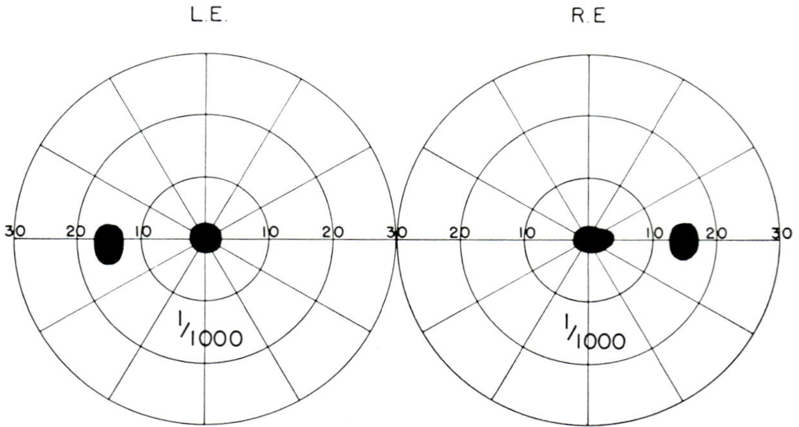

Fig. 12-3. Amblyopia from case of chronic alcoholism with severe vitamin B deficiency and some signs of pellagra. Visual field defect is due to dietary deficiency associated with alcoholism rather than to toxic effects of ethyl alcohol.

Disulfiram (Antabuse)

This rubber accelerator and vulcanizer is used in the treatment of chronic alcoholism. It has potentially serious side effects: patients who drink alcohol while taking disulfiram may develop retrobulbar neuritis with central or centrocecal scotoma. Improvement within a few weeks is the rule in those who discontinue the use of the drug.

Methyl alcohol poisoning

Methyl alcohol (methanol or wood alcohol) is a product of wood distillation widely used in industry as a solvent, antifreeze, fuel, etc. It is one of the most toxic of all substances to the eye, and there is extensive literature on its effects on vision.

Poisoning is usually the result of deliberate consumption as a beverage, by inadvertent substitution for ethyl alcohol, or by criminal adulteration of stocks of cheap gin or whisky. It may assume epidemic proportions.

As little as ⅓ ounce may cause serious poisoning, and because methyl alcohol is metabolized very slowly, significant amounts may remain in the body for days.

The symptomatology is fairly typical: nausea, vomiting, abdominal cramps, and headache developing within 6 to 24 hours. Visual symptoms vary from slight haziness to total loss of vision. Severe poisoning leads rapidly to coma and death from respiratory failure.

In the acute phase of the poisoning, vision is reduced by the development of central or centrocecal scotomas (Fig. 12-4). These scotomas may be transient but are usually permanent, the prognosis for return of vision being dependent on the density and size of the scotomas and the early appearance of the optic discs.

The optic discs are hyperemic in the early stages and later become edematous and elevated with edema extending into the adjacent retina and with venous engorgement.

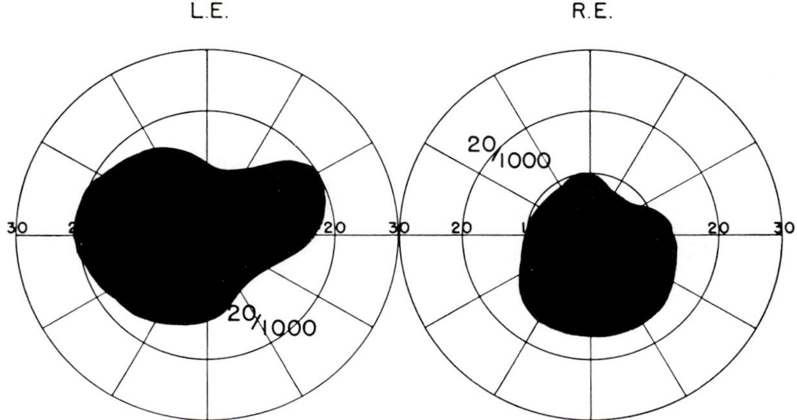

Fig. 12-4. Methyl alcohol (methanol or wood alcohol) amblyopia. There was history of ingestion of 1 ounce of methyl alcohol followed by prolonged coma, severe bilateral optic neuritis, and finally optic atrophy and dense, irregular, steep-margined central scotomas.

The subsequent course depends on the severity of the poisoning and the adequacy of treatment and ranges from complete recovery to total and permanent optic atrophy and blindness. If vision has not markedly improved within 5 or 6 days of the onset of symptoms, the prognosis is very poor and vision may continue to deteriorate for some time. With partial return of vision there is a persistence of the bilateral central scotomas, which vary in size and density. As optic atrophy develops, the peripheral field may also contract.

One of the most striking features of methyl alcohol poisoning is acidosis, manifested by dyspnea, acid urine, and reduced carbon dioxide combining power of the blood. The degree of acidosis closely parallels the severity of the poisoning, and its correction is the basis for any successful treatment of the disease.

If the carbon dioxide combining power of the blood remains more than two-thirds of normal, the symptoms are usually mild and prognosis is good; but when it is reduced below half of normal, the vision is usually very poor and return of function is doubtful. During the acute phase of poisoning, therefore, it is important to quickly measure the carbon dioxide combining power of the blood. If it is only slightly reduced, the use of sodium bicarbonate by mouth may suffice; but if acidosis is severe, intravenous sodium bicarbonate may be required in large doses.

Methanol poisoning is a threefold disease consisting of (1) narcosis, (2) metabolic acidosis, and (3) specific nervous system involvement with retinal edema, fixed dilated pupils, blindness, and basal ganglion necrosis. Ocular damage is thought to be due to the slow oxidation of methanol to formaldehyde or a formaldehyde complex. This extremely diffusible substance affects oxidative enzyme systems, resulting in tissue anoxia, edema, and varying degrees of retinal degeneration. Addition of ethyl alcohol to the therapy may prevent or lessen the degree of metabolic acidosis and ocular damage by preempting the enzymatic site of methanol oxidation and allowing methanol to be excreted as such or to be minimally oxidized.

Even with moderately severe poisoning, the patient may be too ill to cooperate in visual field examination, but a rough estimate of the state of the field is usually possible. When vision is very poor or when pupils are widely dilated, the prognosis is poor.

By the time the patient has recovered sufficiently to submit to examination, he is usually in the chronic stage of the disease. Even here the prognosis for return of vision must be very guarded. Acidosis may slowly improve but vision becomes steadily worse. The delayed visual failure may not begin for some weeks, and the central scotomas may become progressively larger while the discs become chalky white. Treatment in this stage is of no avail.

Lead poisoning

Poisoning by lead is much less prevalent today than even a few years ago, largely because of precautions against the hazard in industry. It may still occur sporadically as an occupational disease in painters, plumbers, workers in battery factories, and those who handle tetraethyl gasoline; but when such cases occur, it

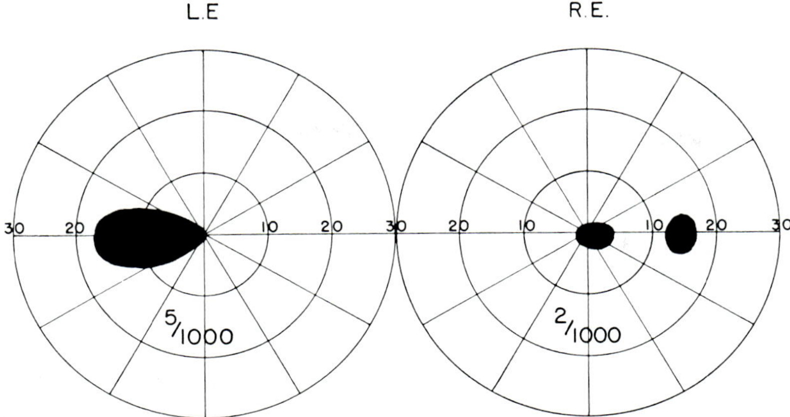

Fig. 12-5. Lead poisoning, occurring as occupational disease in man who handled storage batteries. Onset of visual loss was gradual with early involvement of fixation and gradual intensification of bilateral central scotoma. Diagnosis was confirmed by suspicious lead line in gums and finding of typical red blood cell stippling.

is usually because factory-imposed precautions have been violated. It may occur as a result of accidental ingestion (e.g., when children suck the paint off toys or cribs).

For the most part, lead poisoning is a chronic illness resulting from a gradual accumulation in the body of small amounts of the poison ingested over a considerable period of time.

All parts of the visual pathway from the retina to the occipital cortex may be affected. Increased intracranial pressure is not uncommon, especially in children, and optic atrophy may ensue from prolonged papilledema as well as from the direct effect of lead on the optic nerve.

Occasionally the onset of symptoms is acute, with sudden amaurosis from which there is later recovery. More often there is gradually increasing visual loss with generally depressed peripheral fields or bilateral central scotomas or both (Fig. 12-5). In such cases often an associated optic nerve atrophy develops and the visual field changes are permanent. In the acute cases with total or near total blindness, there is usually present a degree of papilledema secondary to increased intracranial pressure.

Diagnosis of lead poisoning is established by a history of contact with lead, a lead line on the gum margins, a basophilic stippling of red cells, lead in the blood and urine, x-ray evidence of bony deposition of lead, and the clinical signs in the nervous system (including the ocular signs) of lead intoxication.

Treatment is directed to removing the lead from the blood by parenteral administration of edathamil calcium disodium (EDTA).

Carbon disulfide

Carbon disulfide is a product of the rubber vulcanizing and rayon industry and is absorbed chiefly through inhalation and through the skin. Poisoning is uncommon.

Amblyopia of varying degrees is an early sign, and the visual fields usually show bilateral, small, oval, centrocecal scotomas. There may be concomitant peripheral field contraction. Color blindness and night blindness are frequent.

Octamoxin (Nimaol)

The monamine oxidase inhibitor octamoxin has caused optic neuritis and retrobulbar neuritis with centrocecal scotoma developing after several months' use of the drug. Vision usually returns after discontinuance, but partial optic atrophy may persist.

Iodoform poisoning

Since iodoform is rather rarely used today either as a wound dressing or by mouth, cases of poisoning by it are rare. It produces optic atrophy and an amblyopia caused by the presence of fairly large and dense central scotomas. Diagnosis is made by obtaining a history of the medicinal use of iodoform.

Pheniprazine (Catron)

Pheniprazine, a monamine oxidase inhibitor, has been used in depressive states and the treatment of hypertension. It is rarely prescribed now because of its serious side effects, consisting of loss of vision, loss of color vision, and development of bilateral central scotomas. Symptoms are usually reversible with discontinuance of the drug.

Thallium

Thallium is a heavy metal used in large quantities as a soluble salt, thallium acetate or thallium sulfate, for the extermination of insects or rodents. At one time it was also used as a depilatory. It is very poisonous.

The most common eye disturbance is optic neuritis, usually retrobulbar, occurring most often in chronic poisoning and producing bilateral central scotomas. Optic atrophy is the rule in chronic poisoning and visual loss may be marked.

Emetine

Emetine, an alkaloid extracted from ipecac, is used in the treatment of acute amebiasis by subcutaneous injection. It has been reported to cause hyperemia of the optic nerve head and retina with the production of central scotomas and occasionally with visual field constriction.

Digitalis

Ocular manifestations in patients with digitalis toxicity may be as high as 25%, and in many patients the ocular complication may occur before other symptoms of toxicity. The interval between the first dose of digitalis and the first symptom of toxicity may be as short as 1 day. More often the symptoms appear within the first 2 weeks of therapy, but they may not occur for several years after initiation of digitalis use. Symptoms usually disappear within 2 weeks of cessation of therapy and are rarely permanent. The most common ocular symptoms of digitalis poisoning are blurred vision and disturbed color vision. Objects may appear yellow (xanthopsia) or greenish or brown and may appear to be snow- or frost-covered. Photophobia, scintillating scotomas, light flashes, and sparks are common, and transient and permanent amblyopia may occur. Visual field studies will usually reveal bilateral scotomas, which account for the blurred central vision. The scotoma may be secondary to retrobulbar neuritis or to the toxic effects of digitalis on the retinal receptor cells.

Chloramphenicol

Chloramphenicol (Chloromycetin) is a widely employed chemotherapeutic agent and has caused optic neuritis with visual disturbances, edema of the optic discs, and bilateral central scotomas in a number of patients.

Plasmocid

Plasmocid and the related pamaquine naphthoate and pentaquine are used as antimalarial compounds. Plasmocid is the most toxic to the optic nerve and has caused optic neuritis and optic atrophy with impaired vision caused by central scotoma in numerous patients.

Streptomycin

Toxic effects of streptomycin on the visual pathway are probably rare but have been reported as producing a variety of visual disturbances such as xanthopsia, nerve fiber bundle–type scotomas, and central scotoma associated with optic neuritis.

Chlorodinitrobenzene (dinitrobenzene)

Chlorodinitrobenzene and related compounds used in munitions manufacture cause central scotomas from inhalation and chronic exposure. Optic neuritis and atrophy are rare.

Sulfonamide sensitivity

Widespread use of the sulfonamides in the treatment of infections has made it inevitable that there would be occasional sensitivity reactions. For the most part, these are neither serious nor severe enough to cause anxiety or even withdrawal of the drug.

Occasional cases of optic neuritis induced by sulfonamide therapy have been reported. These do not seem to be related directly to the dosage of the drug but rather to the sensitivity of the individual. Visual loss may be sudden in onset, rapid, and very severe. There is edema of the optic nerve head and large, dense, irregular central scotomas. Prognosis is good on withdrawal of the drug.

Ethambutol

Ocular toxicity caused by ethambutol is characterized by (1) loss of central vision with bilateral central or bitemporal scotomas, (2) marked decrease in color vision, and (3) peripheral visual field defects without retinal lesions. The drug is used in the treatment of tuberculosis and its toxicity is dose dependent. Ethambutol is not infrequently used in combination with isoniazid, which may also produce optic neuritis. The toxic effects of both drugs may be synergistic.

Isoniazid

Isoniazid is employed in the treatment of tuberculosis, generally in combination with *p*-aminosalicylate or streptomycin. It has produced optic neuritis and optic atrophy with bilateral central scotomas. Toxic effects are uncommon and are usually reversible on withdrawal of the drug.

PERIPHERAL FIELD DEPRESSION OR CONTRACTION

The list of poisons that produce depression or contraction in the visual field is as follows: (1) quinine, (2) chloroquine, (3) arsenic, (4) salicylates, (5) optochin, (6) filixmas, (7) carbon monoxide, (8) thioridazine, (9) methyl mercury compounds, (10) hyperbaric oxygen, (11) piperidylchlorophenothiazine, and (12) epinephrine.

Quinine

Quinine poisoning is rare. It occurs in susceptible persons from small doses of the drug or in nonsensitive persons from a large single dose. In the former instance the drug is usually given as an antimalarial prophylactic or for the relief of leg cramps. In the latter instance it is usually given in an attempt to induce abortion.

In quinine poisoning the onset of blindness is sudden and the degree of visual loss may vary greatly and may not occur for days after the ingestion of the drug. The visual loss may be transient or permanent. Total blindness is rare and almost never permanent. Partial blindness is common and is often permanent.

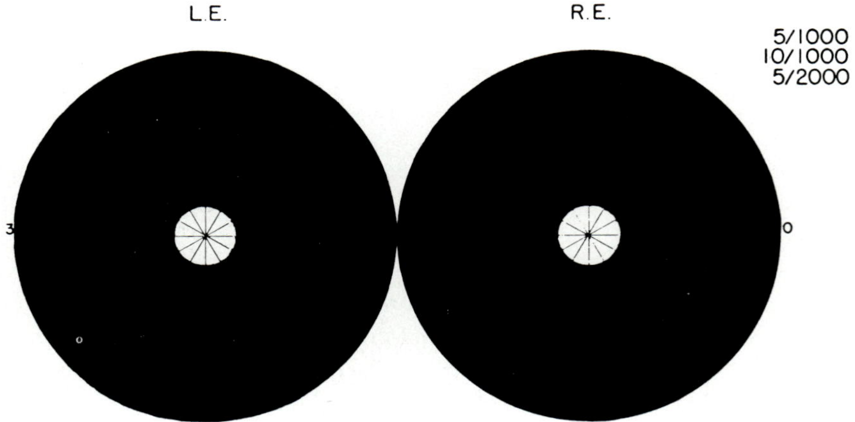

Fig. 12-6. Quinine amblyopia. Visual loss was sudden after ingestion of approximately 40 grains of quinine in attempt to abort pregnancy. Contraction of visual fields is organic in type as opposed to tubular or cylindric visual field contraction of hysteria. There is partial optic atrophy and marked attenuation of retinal arteries.

Quinine affects the ganglion cells, nerve fibers, and rods and cones of the retina. There is marked attenuation of the retinal vasculature. Optic atrophy of marked degree results from this degeneration.

The visual field changes are constriction or contraction of the peripheral field, varying from slight depression of the peripheral isopters to contraction of the field to within a few degrees of fixation in all quadrants. This visual field loss is usually permanent, although partial recovery may occur (Fig. 12-6).

Quinine-induced hypoplasia of the optic nerve has been reported in infants whose mothers ingested large amounts of quinine early in the first trimester of pregnancy. Side effects in the mother included severe dizziness, headache, blurred vision, and nausea. The drug failed to produce abortion.

Differentiation of the ganglion cell layer of the retina, whose axons extend into the optic stalk to form the optic nerve, occurs in the seventh to eighth week of gestation. This corresponded closely to the time of maternal quinine ingestion.

Chloroquine

Among the synthetic antimalarial drugs, chloroquine compounds have been the most widely used in the treatment of lupus erythematosus and rheumatoid arthritis. Dosage of the drug for treatment of these conditions is considerably in excess of that used for malaria. Numerous cases have been reported with corneal deposits and severe visual loss. These visual disturbances result from retinopathy that may involve the macular area, the midperipheral retina, or both. It is associated with marked narrowing of the retinal arterioles and eventually with pigmentary degeneration of the retina and optic atrophy somewhat resembling retinitis pigmentosa.

Visual field defects vary from central scotoma to ring scotoma to peripheral contraction. The most characteristic field deficit is probably a large central scotoma with

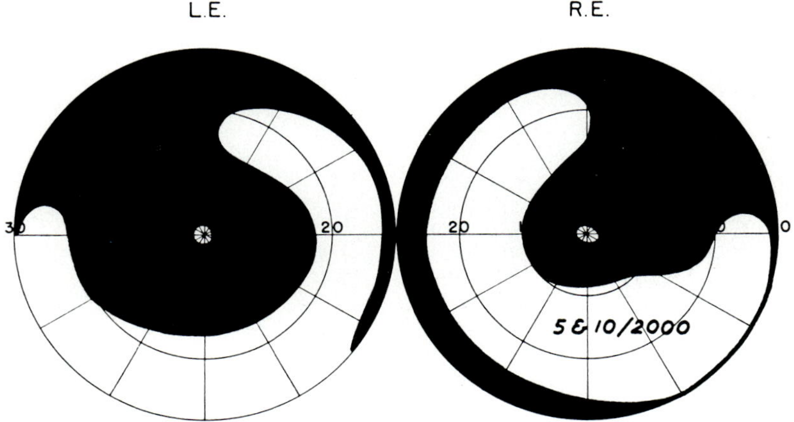

Fig. 12-7. Chloroquine toxicity. Pigmentary degeneration of retina following 4 months' use of chloroquine in patient with lupus erythematosus. Minute islands of central vision are retained surrounded by dense ring scotomas.

a small island of slightly lesser visual loss in its center. When tested with large stimuli, the defect is a large, dense ring scotoma, sometimes breaking through into the periphery (Fig. 12-7); when small test objects are used, the defect appears as a large central scotoma.

The dose of chloroquine usually required to produce retinopathy is 0.1 to 0.6 gram per day for 2 to 3 years, although damage may occur in a much shorter time.

The symptoms of chloroquine retinopathy are reading difficulties, photophobia, blurred distance vision, and light flashes. Color vision testing with the Hardy, Rand, Rittler pseudoisochromatic plates may be useful in early detection of the condition. The effects of chloroquine toxicity may not appear until some time after use of the drug has been stopped. The finding of a central scotoma for red stimuli is an early sign of retinal damage.

Chloroquine is stored in the pigmented uvea and may be retained in the retinal pigment epithelium for long periods after discontinuance of the drug. This would account for the retinopathy and the permanence of visual field defects.

The incidence of chloroquine retinopathy is dose related; it is most likely to occur when the total dose exceeds 300 grams over a 2- to 3-year period.

Fluorescein angiography dramatically demonstrates the area of retinopathy.

Arsenic

Inorganic arsenicals, used in industry and in various pest poisons, are capable of producing severe poisoning and death, but they rarely if ever affect the optic nerve or retina.

Organic arsenicals, which a few years ago found their greatest usefulness in the treatment of syphilis, are capable of initiating severe toxic amblyopia of a specific type.

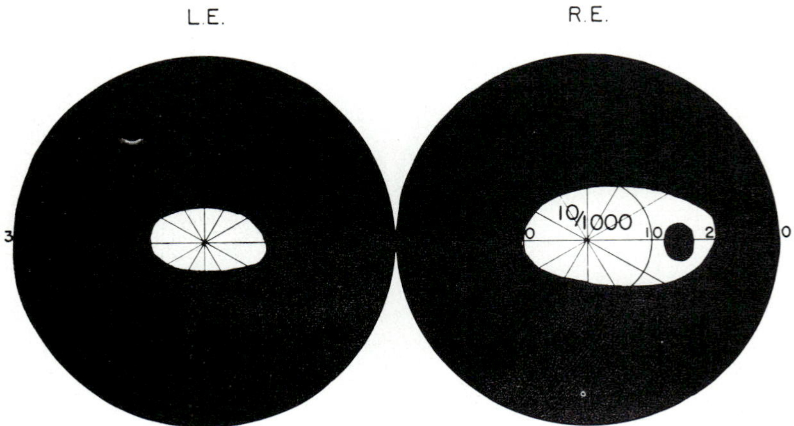

Fig. 12-8. Tryparsamide poisoning. Sudden loss of peripheral vision shortly followed first injection of tryparsamide. There was probable sensitivity to drug with destruction of ganglion cells of retina.

Trivalent arsenicals, such as arsphenamine and neoarsphenamine, may produce optic nerve damage and visual field contraction in susceptible persons on rare occasions. The pentavalent arsenicals, atoxyl and tryparsamide, are most dangerous. These latter drugs have been known to produce acute degeneration of the ganglion cell layer of the retina with severe contraction of the visual field, especially in the vertical diameter, and a permanent loss of vision (Fig. 12-8).

It is difficult at times to determine which is the cause of the visual loss, the syphilitic process in the optic nerve or the arsenical therapy. Care must be taken to make this distinction. Since the advent of penicillin, these drugs are rarely used.

Salicylates

Salicylate poisoning resembles that induced by quinine in most respects. There is usually an individual sensitivity to the drug (sodium salicylate, salicylic acid, aspirin, methyl salicylate), but overdosage has been reported as a cause of amaurosis.

The pupils are dilated and fixed, and the visual fields may show marked concentric contraction.

Large doses of the salicylates for treatment of rheumatism may produce total amaurosis, but in the less severe cases the prognosis is good.

Filixmas

In filixmas, again, the ocular symptomatology of poisoning resembles that from quinine. Filixmas was formerly used in the treatment of tapeworm infestation. Individual sensitivity to the drug, more than dosage, is responsible for toxic effects. Amaurosis may be extreme following ingestion of moderate doses.

The visual field changes may be unilateral or bilateral and consist of concentric contraction of the peripheral and central fields. There is gradually increasing pallor of the optic disc and narrowing of retinal arterioles.

Methyl mercury compounds

Methyl mercury compounds are used for the protection of wood or seeds. Poisoning may result from inhalation in manufacture and in industrial application and from eating treated seeds and contaminated fish or meat. Poisoning results in extreme contraction of the visual fields due to atrophy of the visual cortex, greatest at the anterior end of the calcarine fissure, with relative sparing of the occipital poles. Blindness may result from extensive atrophy of the entire cerebral cortex. No recovery of the field loss has been reported.

Oxygen

Hyperbaric oxygen has been shown to produce peripheral constriction of the visual fields in young healthy males after prolonged breathing of pure oxygen at 3 atmospheres of pressure. After 4 hours there was progressive contraction of the fields, impaired central vision, and mydriasis, all of which were reversible after discontinuance of the oxygen or return to normal pressures.

Carbon monoxide

Poisoning from carbon monoxide, a colorless, odorless gas, may result from attempted suicide or from inadvertent inhalation of automobile exhaust fumes or manufactured heating or cooking gas.

Toxic signs and symptoms and death are caused by conversion of a portion of the hemoglobin of the blood to carbon monoxyhemoglobin, with reduction in the amount of normal hemoglobin available for oxygen transport. Small concentrations of carbon monoxide in air may cause great reduction of the oxygen-carrying capacity of the blood.

When exposure is severe enough to produce unconsciousness, permanent damage to the central nervous system may result.

When consciousness is regained, blindness may immediately be noted. Pupils react to light and convergence, suggesting that the blindness is cortical in origin. Visual hallucinations and agnosia may occur. If cerebral hypoxia is not too severe, complete or partial recovery of vision will occur. When recovery is partial, the resultant visual field defect may be a double or bilateral homonymous hemianopsia with a small central island of vision determined by the area of macular sparing in the two half-fields (see Fig. 7-12).

Thioridazine

Thioridazine, a phenothiazine derivative employed in psychotherapy, has been found to cause decreased visual acuity and pigmentary degeneration of the retina when used in high dosage. Visual loss may vary from slight and transient to severe and permanent. Visual fields may show contraction or central scotoma or both. Electroretinograms are grossly abnormal.

Piperidylchlorophenothiazine (NP 207)

Piperidylchlorophenothiazine is a major tranquilizer that has been used in the treatment of psychoses such as schizophrenia. In fairly large dosages of 0.4 to 0.8 gram per day for 2 to 3 months, patients have developed visual disturbances with contracted fields especially in dim light due to development of abnormal retinal pigmentation, resembling retinitis pigmentosa with damage to both rods and cones. Recovery is only partial with discontinuance of the drug.

Epinephrine (Adrenalin)

When used in the treatment of glaucoma in aphakic eyes, epinephrine has been found to produce a maculopathy in a significant percentage of such eyes. Central visual acuity is reduced, the maculae show a definite though slight edema, and visual fields demonstrate a central scotoma. Although this is not a true toxic amblyopia, it is certainly an abnormal drug response.

Oral contraceptive pills

There is some question as to whether the ocular and cerebrovascular disturbances associated with ingestion of oral contraceptives should be considered as a form of toxic amblyopia. The drug appears to be toxic to some individuals and very rarely may initiate retinal or cerebrovascular occlusion that causes visual loss and visual field deficits depending on the location of the vascular lesion. The pills frequently precipitate migraine attacks in young women without previous history of migraine and the attacks cease when the medication is discontinued.

CHAPTER 13

Optic nerve

Except for visible changes in the optic disc and the nerve fiber bundles of the retina that are observable ophthalmoscopically, we are largely dependent on perimetric examination for knowledge of the pathologic processes that affect the optic nerve. Here is the first portion of the visual pathway that cannot be seen and whose abnormalities must be diagnosed and localized on the basis of a subjective rather than an objective examination. It is obvious, therefore, that since we are deprived of the use of the ophthalmoscope, the perimeter and tangent screen assume increasing importance.

Even when there are visible changes in the nerve head, their appearance is likely to be so nonspecific that visual field examination is necessary for correct interpretation. Thus the morphologic difference between papilledema and papillitis may be so slight that a perimetric examination is essential for diagnosis.

Not only is the visual field examination of primary importance in localization of the lesion within the nerve, but it is also of value in indicating the nature of the pathologic process, the prognosis, and the treatment.

Perimetric studies that localize a lesion in the intracranial portion of the nerve must be correlated with other clinical and radiologic findings and may be the most important consideration in the neurosurgeon's decision to explore the region in question.

The most frequent visual field defect in patients with optic nerve disease is the central scotoma due to the predilection of these lesions for the papillomacular bundle of nerve fibers. Scotomas may be bilateral, as in certain systemic disease and the toxic amblyopias, but more often they are unilateral. There may be many clues indicating the presence of a scotoma, such as a positive defect noticed by the patient, a severe deficiency in vision without noticeable curtailment of the ability to get about, walk, or even drive a car, a characteristic manner of reading the Snellen chart in which letters are skipped over, or the observation that a letter can be seen only if the patient looks at the one next to it plus an inability to see the fixation target on the tangent screen. Color vision, as tested with the HHR color charts, may be markedly affected. The afferent pupillary reflex or Marcus Gunn pupil is a valuable sign of optic nerve conduction disturbance.

The tangent screen is the instrument par excellence for detection and analysis

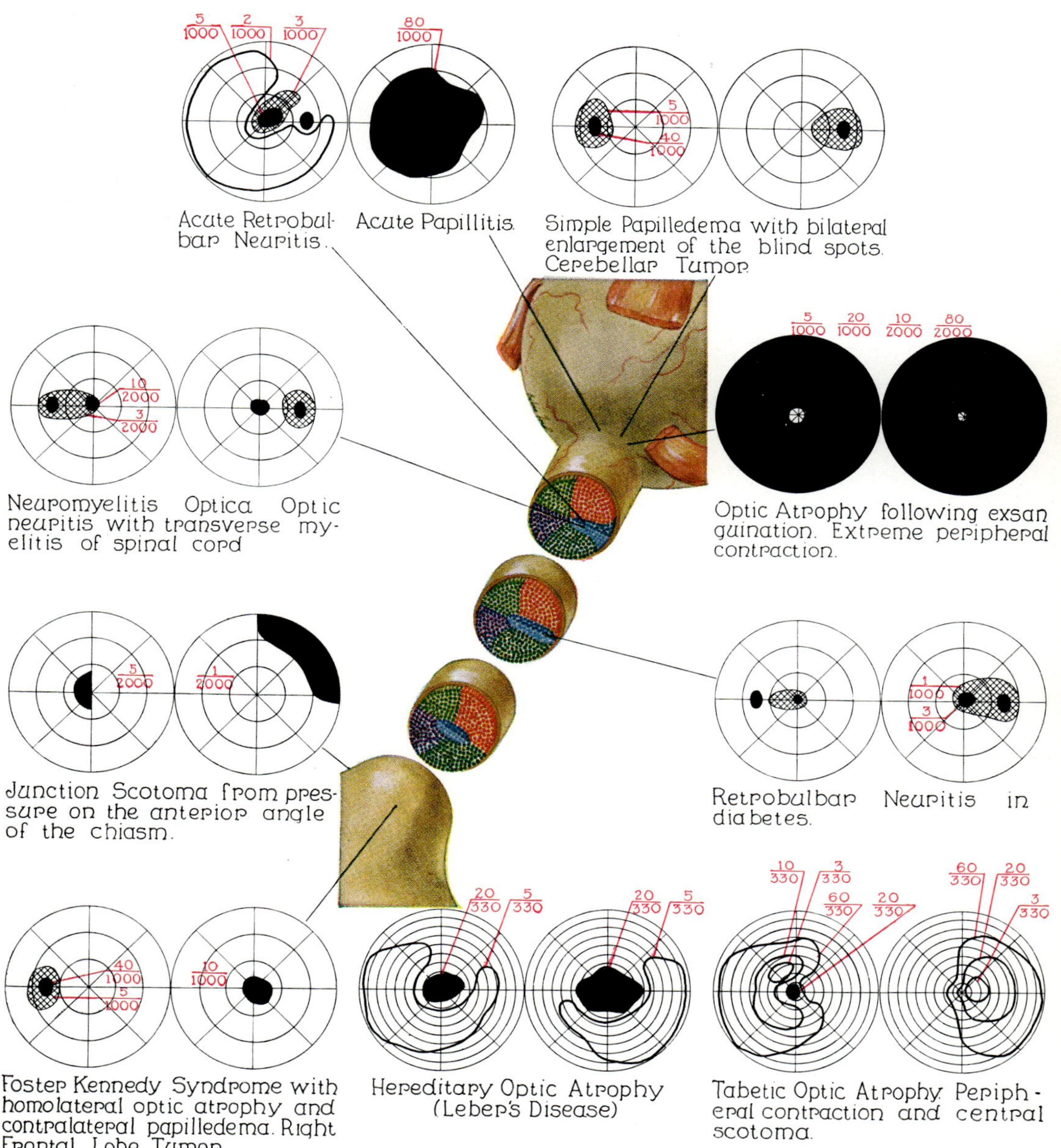

Plate 6. Perimetry of optic nerve lesions.

of scotomas. The greater the distance used, the larger is the defect and the more readily its characteristics can be studied.

CLASSIFICATION OF LESIONS OF OPTIC NERVE

It is customary to consider the optic nerve lesions that produce visual field defects according to their anatomic localization within the nerve. To this end the nerve is arbitrarily divided into three parts: optic nerve head or papilla, retrobulbar optic nerve, and intracranial optic nerve. Each of these portions may be further divided into (1) axial portion of the nerve and (2) peripheral portion of the nerve. Within each of these divisions the nature of the lesion producing the defect must then be considered. These are generally classified as (a) inflammatory, (b) pressure, (c) vascular, (d) traumatic, or (e) toxic (considered separately in the discussion of toxic amblyopias, Chapter 12). With this anatomic and pathologic classification in mind, we now consider the various visual field changes associated with diseases of the optic nerve.

OPTIC PAPILLA, NERVE HEAD, OPTIC DISC

Abnormalities of the optic disc that are directly observable ophthalmoscopically are usually diagnosed by this means. Visual field changes, however, may confirm such diagnosis and in some instances may be the only means of differentiating two morphologically similar fundus pictures.

Myelinated nerve fibers

Myelinated nerve fibers at the nerve may be mistaken for choroiditis juxtapapillaris or even papilledema from increased intracranial pressure. Even in extensive myelinization, however, the field is usually normal, or when defective, it is static. The most frequently encountered visual field defect results from a nerve fiber bundle interference (i.e., an arcuate defect resembling that in glaucoma). Occasionally there will be an irregular enlargement of the blind spot, and rarely, when the myelinated nerve fibers extend well out into the retina, a paracecal scotoma of indefinite outline. The visual field changes correspond to the anatomic location of the myelinated fibers and to their density and thickness.

Colobomas of optic nerve

Colobomas of the optic nerve (Fig. 13-1) are readily demonstrable with the ophthalmoscope. Their associated visual field defects cannot be strictly correlated with their appearance. Often large colobomas will show surprisingly little visual loss, and at times a minimal nerve head lesion produces extensive damage to the visual field.

Most commonly the visual field changes associated with the condition resemble those of glaucoma, with dense nerve fiber bundle defects and superior nasal depression and contraction. When associated with deeply cupped optic discs, the differentiation from glaucoma may be difficult indeed. Both the appearance of the discs and the visual field changes, however, are stationary as compared with the progres-

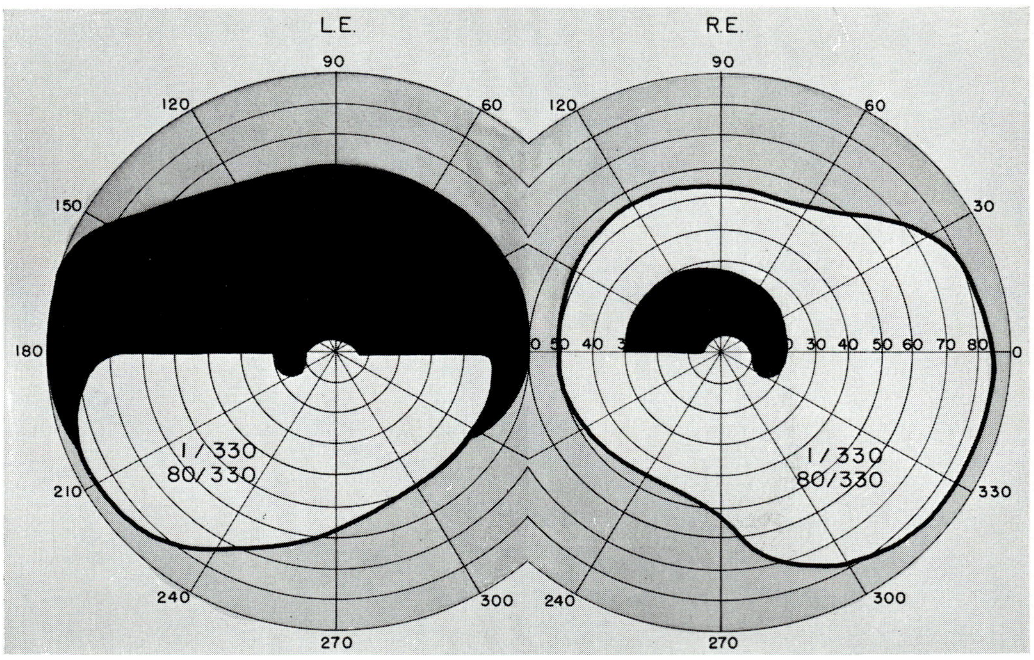

Fig. 13-1. Colobomas of optic nerves. There was history of defective vision from childhood. Central vision was 20/20 in each eye. Visual field defects resembled those of glaucoma but remained unchanged in 5 years of observation. Intraocular pressure was repeatedly normal.

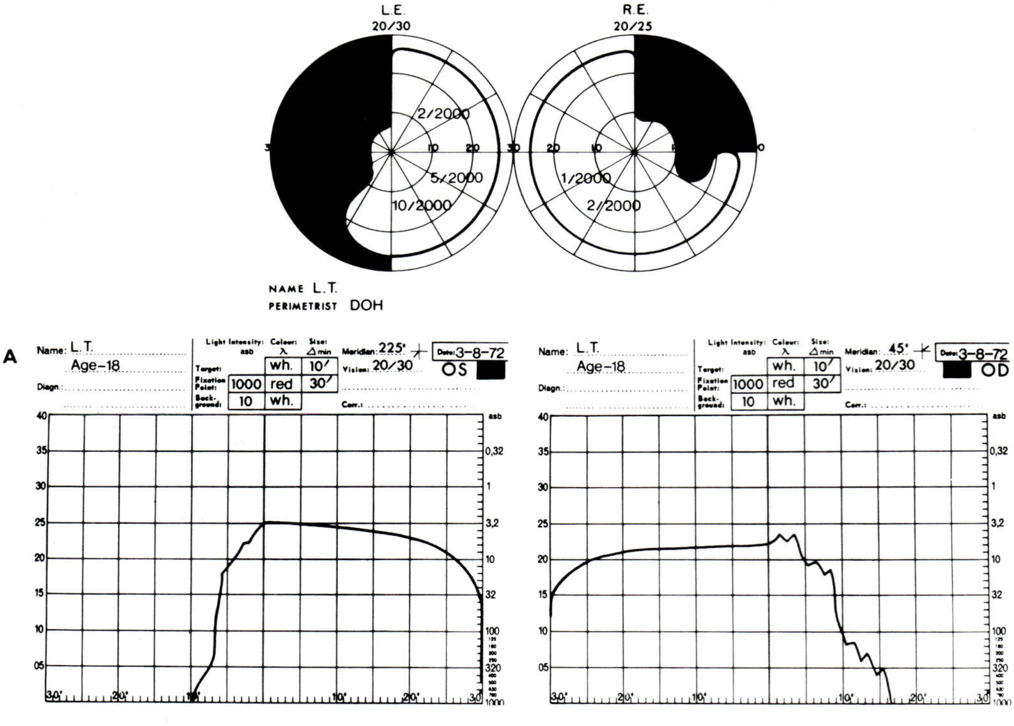

A

Fig. 13-2. For legend see opposite page.

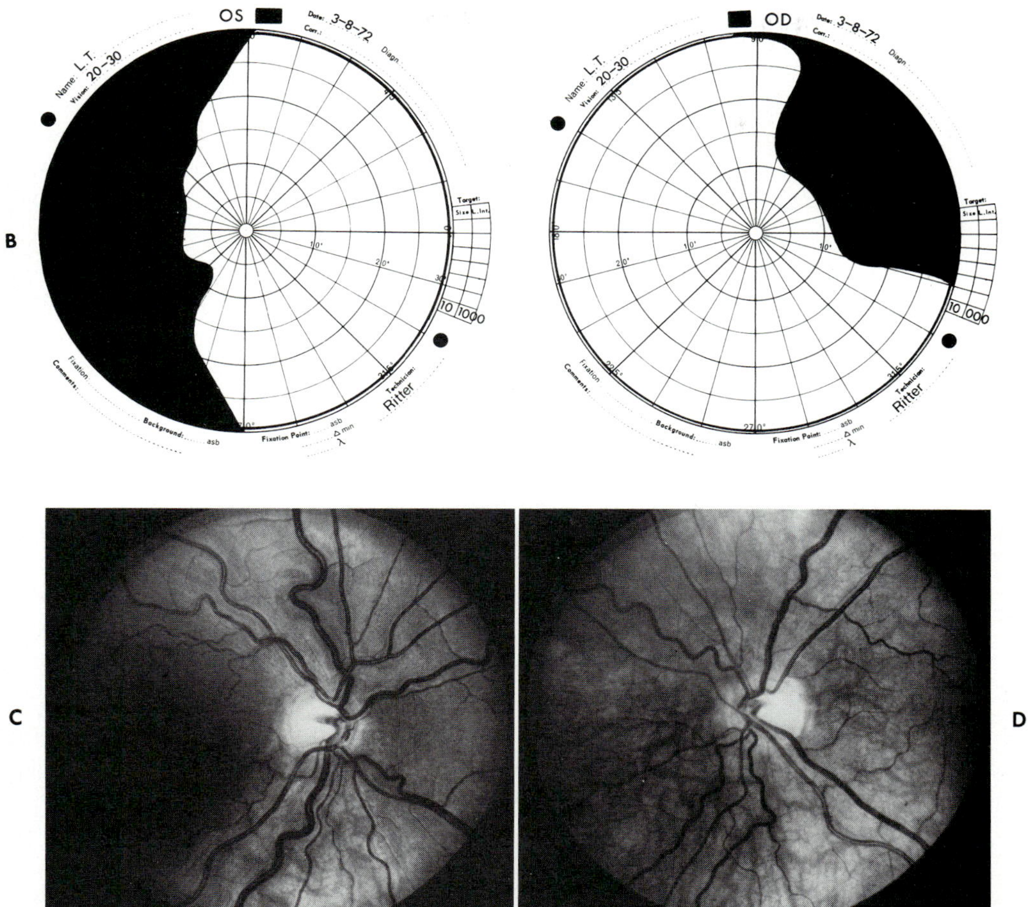

Fig. 13-2. A, Bilateral congenital optic nerve hypoplasia with irregular bitemporal hemianopsia. A visual field deficit associated with vertical and lateral nystagmus and complicated vertical and lateral extraocular muscle imbalance. In spite of its density, the patient was unaware of field deficit when examined on tangent screen and by static perimetry. Field defect has remained stable since time of discovery. **B,** Goldmann perimeter field of patient shown in **A. C,** Right and **D,** left eye of patient seen in **A.** Fundus photography with red-free light reveals bilateral optic nerve hypoplasia with sector atrophy. Degeneration of ganglion cells and nerve fiber layer of nasal hemiretinae produced congenital bitemporal hemianopsia. (From Harrington, D. O.: Some unusual and difficult visual field defects, Trans. Ophthalmol. Soc. U. K. **92:**15-34, 1972.)

sive field loss in glaucoma. Occasionally, with very large inferior colobomas, the entire upper field will disappear in a superior altitudinal hemianopsia.

Congenital optic nerve hypoplasia

Optic nerve hypoplasia is a congenital disturbance that has been recognized for many years.

Visual field defects associated with this condition vary widely from total blindness of one or both eyes to a minimum paracentral scotoma or a binasal or bitemporal hemianopsia (Fig. 13-2). The condition is either a single ocular abnormality or in association with anterior midline central nervous system defects such as chiasmal malformation and agenesis of the anterior commissure and septum pellicidum. In the latter case, the result is a monocular temporal field loss or a bitemporal hemianopsia.

Many optic nerve hypoplasias that appear to be unilateral may, on closer study, be bilateral. The disc changes are often very subtle, and, unless there is a field deficit or some decrease in central visual acuity, it is easy to miss the diagnosis. In many cases, the condition is frankly bilateral and in these patients the field loss may be binasal or bitemporal.

Associated extraocular muscle imbalance and nystagmus are common.

There is a sparsity or absence of the ganglion cell and nerve fiber layer of the retina, which may be seen quite clearly when examined or photographed with red-free light (Fig. 13-2, *C-D*).

The optic nerve hypoplasia may be misdiagnosed as optic atrophy and yet visual acuity, while not normal, may be quite good. In such a situation, the patient may be completely unaware of even a dense visual field deficit, as is often the case with congenital defects, and the extent of the field loss will be discovered by accident or during routine examination. Temporal visual field defects are less common than inferior deficits. Functional loss may be closely correlated with visible defects in the retinal nerve fiber layer. Maternal phenytoin (Dilantin) ingestion appears to be a significant etiologic factor in optic nerve hypoplasia (Fig. 13-3).

Drusen of optic disc

Drusen, or hyaline bodies, on the optic disc may produce extensive and slowly progressive visual field defects; these may take decades to develop. The ophthalmoscopic appearance may give little indication of the visual loss to be expected. In most cases vision is good and field changes do not occur until the drusen are extensive. In many such cases a diagnosis of pseudopapilledema is made and there is gross enlargement of the blind spot. Occasionally the condition is mistaken for true papilledema. A number of cases have been reported with hemorrhage into or adjacent to the drusen, and these may adversely affect the visual field by leakage into the macular area or pressure on the nerve fiber bundles or their vascular supply at the disc margins or both (Fig. 13-6).

Visual field changes usually take the form of irregular peripheral contraction, blind spot enlargement, or nerve fiber bundle (arcuate) scotomas that may closely resemble the typical glaucomatous visual field defect (see Figs. 13-4 and 13-6).

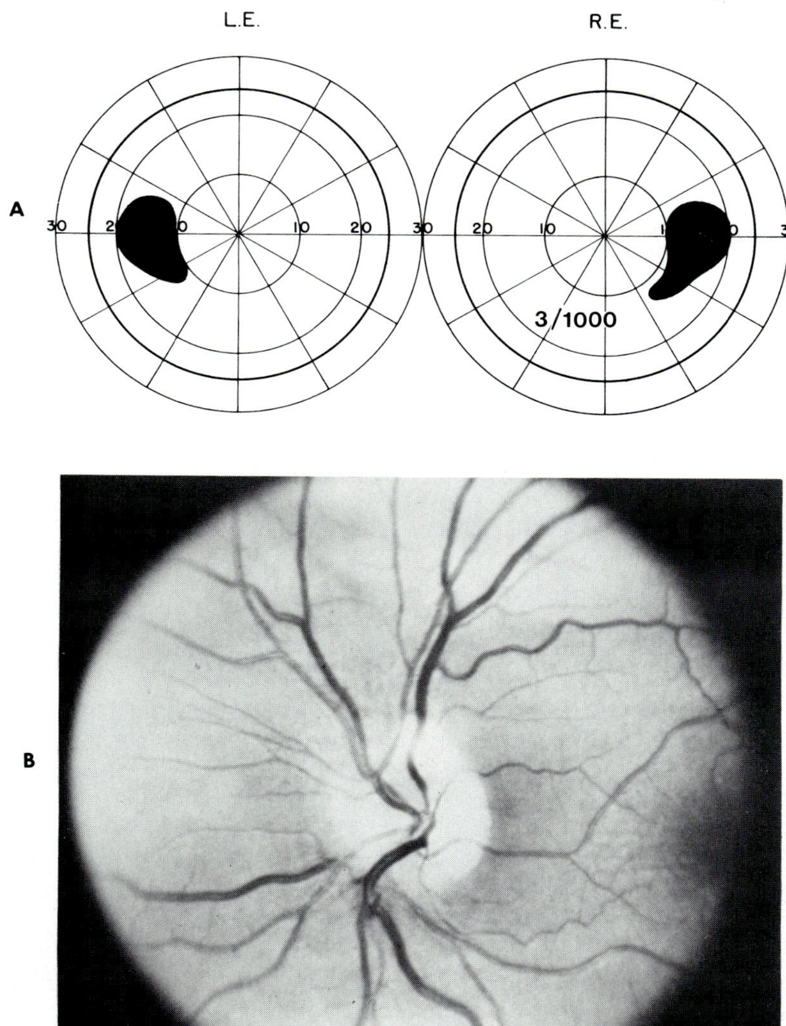

Fig. 13-3. A, Congenital optic nerve defect. Moderate optic nerve hypoplasia with bilateral inferior extension of blind spot. **B,** Optic nerve abnormality responsible for field defect shown in **A.** Identical finding in both optic nerves.

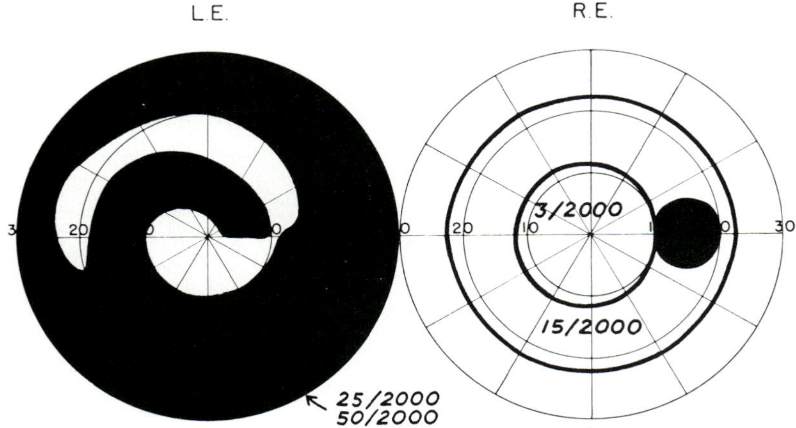

Fig. 13-4. Drusen of both optic discs, more marked on left, with double nerve fiber bundle defect and nasal step. Defect is steep margined and dense, indicating its static nature. Right field shows central depression and gross blind spot enlargement.

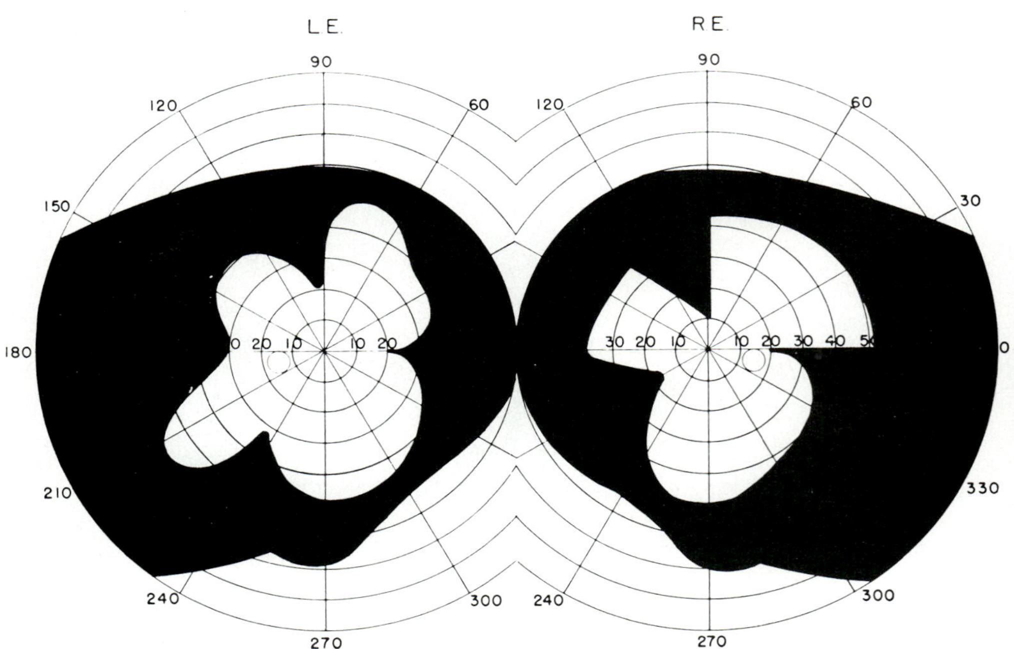

Fig. 13-5. Drusen on optic disc. Slowly progressive irregular contraction of the visual fields was associated with increasing optic atrophy. In some cases, contraction is more regular, whereas in others only single sector may be involved. Nerve fiber bundle defects are not uncommon.

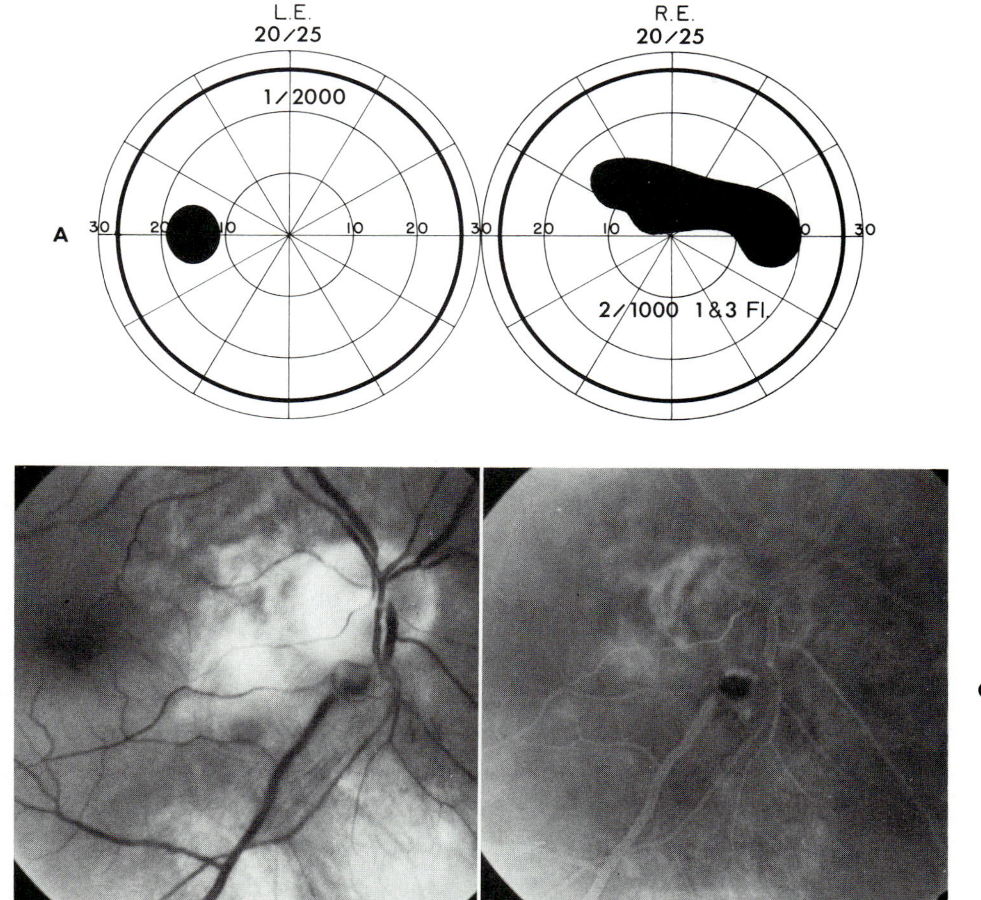

Fig. 13-6. A, Retinal vein aneurysm at lower margin right optic disc. Sudden loss of entire superior field in right eye associated with marked rise in systemic blood pressure. Gradual partial resolution of field deficit with resulting atypical, permanent, nerve fiber bundle defect. The lesion producing this field loss is seen in **B** and **C. B,** Aneurysm of inferior retinal vein, right eye, photographed with red-free light and giving rise to superior nerve fiber bundle defect seen in **A. C,** Fluorescein angiography, full venous phase.

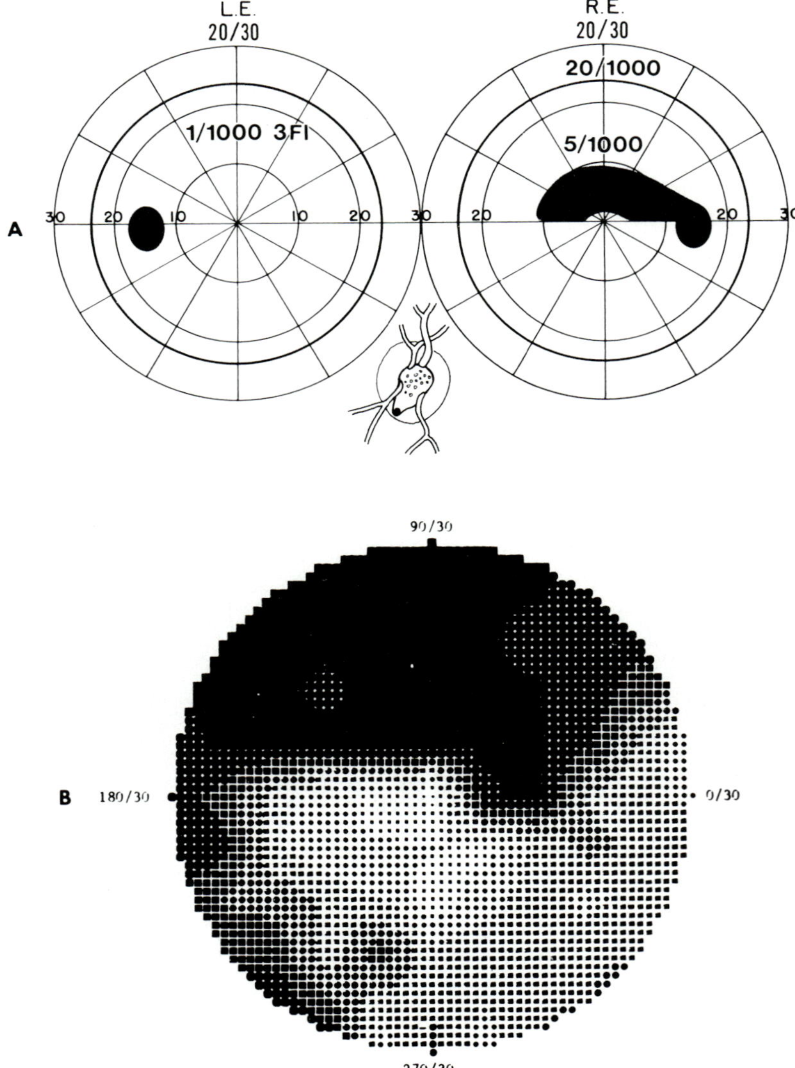

Fig. 13-7. A, Optic nerve pit plus ocular hypertension, right eye. Dense, steep-margined nerve fiber bundle scotoma. Scotoma later expanded into superior nasal periphery. **B,** Octopus perimeter system visual field defect of case in **A** showing expanded and very dense scotoma.

Drusen may be deeply embedded in the nerve and not be visible to the ophthalmoscope and yet may give rise to extensive visual field defects. Such cases constitute a considerable diagnostic problem (see Fig. 13-5).

Visual field loss may progress very slowly and loss of central vision is rare except in those cases with vascular damage at the disc edge.

Optic nerve pits

Pits of the optic nerve head are a fairly common congenital abnormality. They appear as small gray, black, or yellow depressions of the disc, most frequently located at the inferior or inferotemporal border of the nerve head. The defect is congenital but, because it may not cause any visual loss, it may not be noticed until late in life either as part of a routine ophthalmoscopic examination or because of the development of a retinal detachment or a visual field defect.

When viewed stereoscopically the pit is deep and steep sided.

Central visual loss in the form of an irregular sloping-margined scotoma occurs in 50% of cases as a result of serous macular detachment due to leakage of liquefied

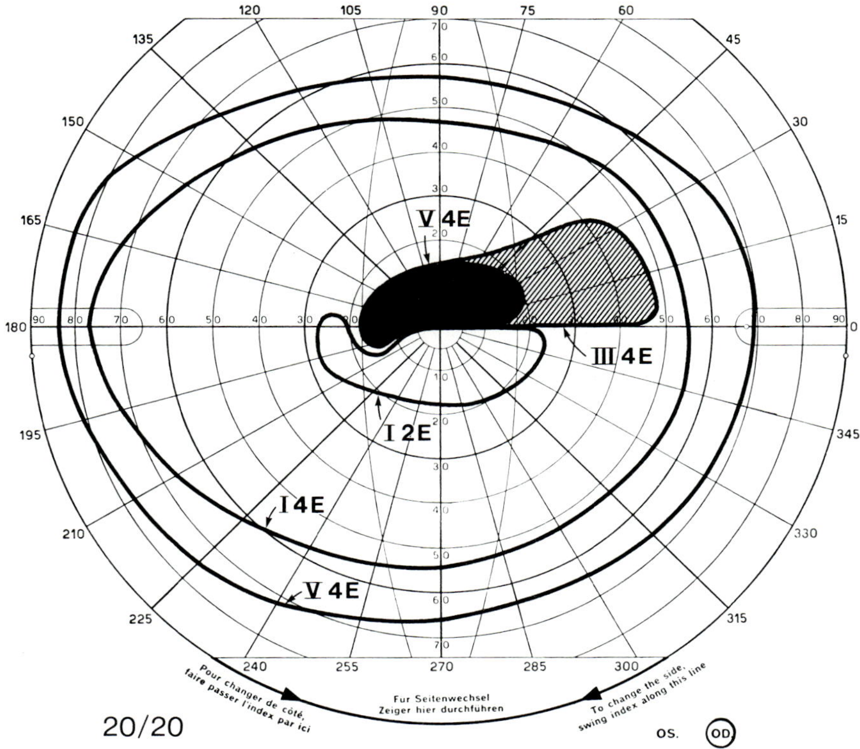

Fig. 13-8. Atypical nerve fiber bundle visual field defect from congenital optic nerve pit at inferior margin right optic disc. Note retention of 20/20 vision in spite of apparent macular splitting.

vitreous through the pit and into the subretinal space. The incidence of macular detachment is greater when the pit is located on the temporal disc margin.

Visual field defects vary considerably depending on the location and size of the pits and the presence or absence of retinal detachment. Gross enlargement of the blind spot may occur, with or without macular involvement (see Fig. 13-9). Isolated paracentral scotomas in the form of steep-margined nerve fiber bundle defects or Bjerrum scotomas may occur and remain stable throughout life. They usually are attached to the blind spot, are readily detected on tangent screen examination, have a clear-cut nasal step, and are indistinguishable from the scotomas of glaucoma (see Fig. 13-6).

A third type of field deficit is a broad, dense, nerve fiber bundle scotoma that has a steep-margined nasal step, a peripheral nasal breakthrough, and close encroachment on fixation, so that it may be mistaken for an altitudinal hemianopsia (Fig. 13-7).

Papilledema or choked disc

Edema of the optic nerve head, secondary to increased intracranial pressure, hypertension, or other causes, produces generalized enlargement of the blind spot with certain characteristic features. In the majority of instances, it is probable that the changes in the nerve head are ophthalmoscopically visible by the time the visual field defect is detectable.

Mild or moderately severe edema of the nerve head from increased intracranial pressure causes generalized enlargement of the blind spot in all directions. In more severe edema of the disc there will often be some exudate and hemorrhage on the nerve; and in chronic papilledema there may be considerable gliosis. These will affect the blind spot enlargement (Figs. 13-9 and 13-10).

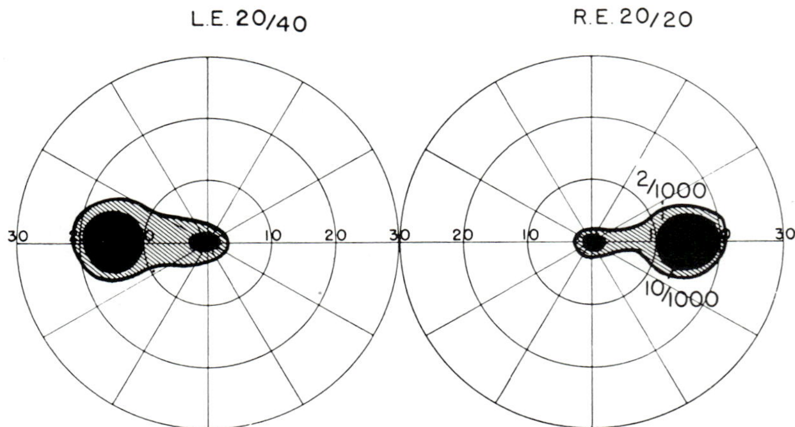

Fig. 13-9. Papilledema. Bilateral disc edema of 5 D in case of cerebellar tumor showing absolute blind spot enlargement and relative scotoma extending toward fixation. Involvement of fixation area is probably caused by extension of edema into macula.

Because of the crowding of the nerve fibers from the papillomacular bundle in the temporal part of the disc and their sloping course into the nerve, there is a strong tendency for disc edema to spread into the retina toward the macula. This enlarges the blind spot toward fixation in the form of a centrocecal-type scotoma with sloping edges and variable density. The area immediately adjacent to fixation will sometimes show a small island of increased density joined to the enlarged blind spot by a narrow neck of relative scotoma. This type of visual field defect is sometimes difficult to distinguish from the papillomacular bundle involvement in optic neuritis, although central visual acuity is usually much worse in the latter condition.

Pseudotumor cerebri, or benign intracranial hypertension, may produce a variety of visual field defects in approximately half of the cases. Transient visual loss is common. Papilledema is the rule, and enlarged blind spot, arcuate scotomas, and generalized depression of peripheral isopters are not uncommon. Severe chronic papilledema may result in ischemic optic neuropathy with sudden visual loss and altitudinal visual field defects.

The most severe papilledema with the grossest blind spot enlargement is found in patients with space-consuming lesions of the posterior fossa and tumors of the third and fourth ventricles.

Secondary optic atrophy

When papilledema is prolonged, gliosis takes place in the nerve head and there is a gradual development of optic atrophy known as secondary or consecutive atrophy. The visual field change associated with this condition is peripheral contraction, especially in the nasal field, due to destruction of the peripheral nerve fibers by the progressive gliosis. Eventually the entire nerve is involved and blindness ensues. The peripheral field defect is absolute and slowly progressive (see Fig. 13-10).

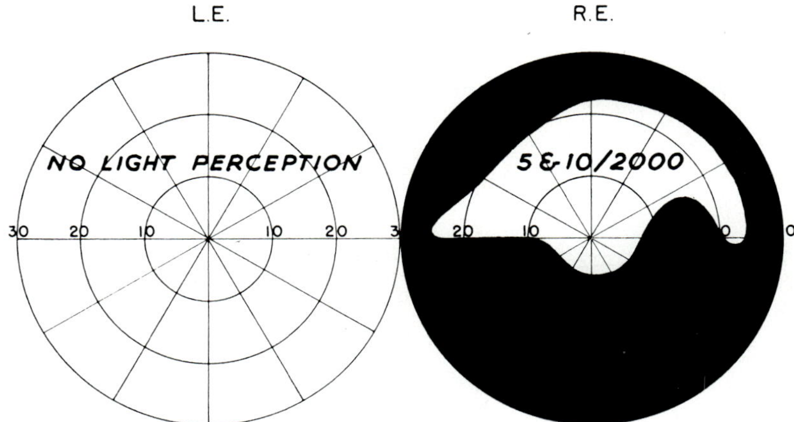

Fig. 13-10. Chronic papilledema with gliosis and optic atrophy resulting from left acoustic neuroma. There was involvement of eighth, seventh, sixth, and fifth cranial nerves on left, along with almost total left optic atrophy and partial atrophy of right optic disc. Altitudinal field loss is caused by peripheral breakthrough of nerve fiber bundle defect.

Compression of nerve fiber bundles and their arterial supply may produce glaucoma-like nerve fiber bundle defects, altitudinal hemianopsia, irregular constriction of the peripheral field, and finally blindness.

Once visual field contraction has become well established, the prognosis for return of vision after removal of the intracranial lesion is poor. Gliosis often proceeds apace even after removal of pressure.

Papillitis or optic neuritis

The term *papillitis* refers to inflammation of the optic disc. Strictly speaking, it confines the lesion to the intraocular portion of the nerve, and because this is a rare if not impossible condition, the term is inaccurate. Optic neuritis, on the other hand, is too all-inclusive a term, embracing as it does the entire nerve. For practical purposes papillitis is an inflammation of the optic nerve involving the anterior portion of the nerve and with ophthalmoscopically visible changes in the disc in the form of edema, exudate, venous engorgement, and sometimes hemorrhage (Fig. 13-11).

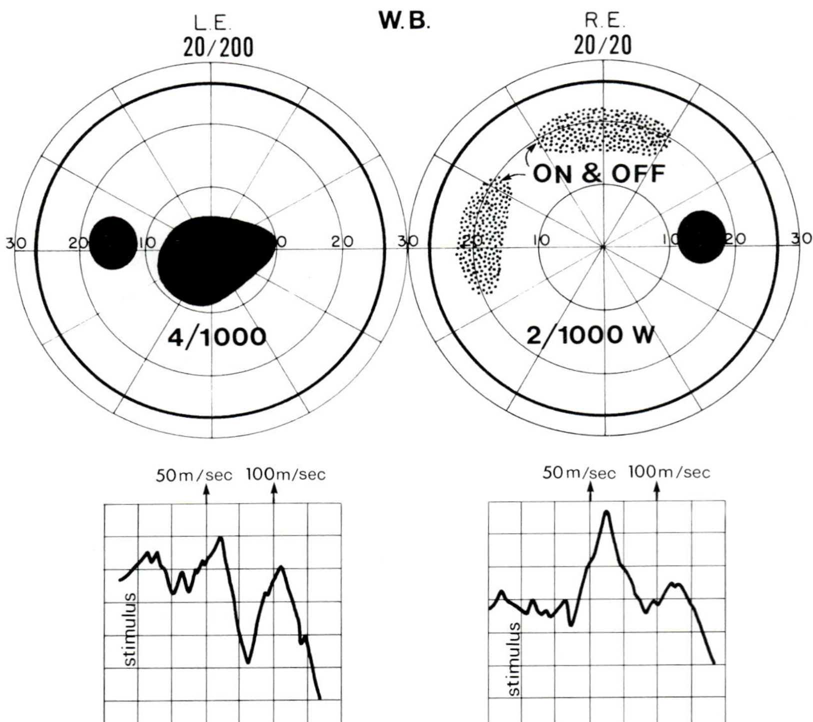

Fig. 13-11. Acute optic neuritis in a 25-year-old white male. Right field shows vague paracentral scotomas with 20/20 vision. Left field shows dense central scotoma with 20/200 vision. Marcus Gunn pupil reaction left eye and absent-to-poor color vision both eyes. Visual-evoked response (VER) shows bilateral symmetrically delayed initial peaks. Diagnosis, probable multiple sclerosis.

The visual field changes in papillitis are the same as those of inflammation anywhere in the optic nerve, that is, a central scotoma with or without peripheral depression or contraction depending on whether or not the axial or peripheral portions of the nerve head are involved (Fig. 13-12).

The neuritis is usually unilateral but may be bilateral, as in Leber's disease (see Fig. 13-19) in its initial stage of development, neuromyelitis optica (Devic's disease; see Fig. 13-18), syphilitic, meningococcic, or tuberculous meningitis, and other systemic diseases.

When nerve head edema is severe, there is a corresponding enlargement of the blind spot (Fig. 13-13). Not infrequently the scotoma will be arcuate in shape as a result of involvement of a nerve fiber bundle at the periphery of the disc; I have seen patients in whom both central and arcuate scotomas were found in the same field.

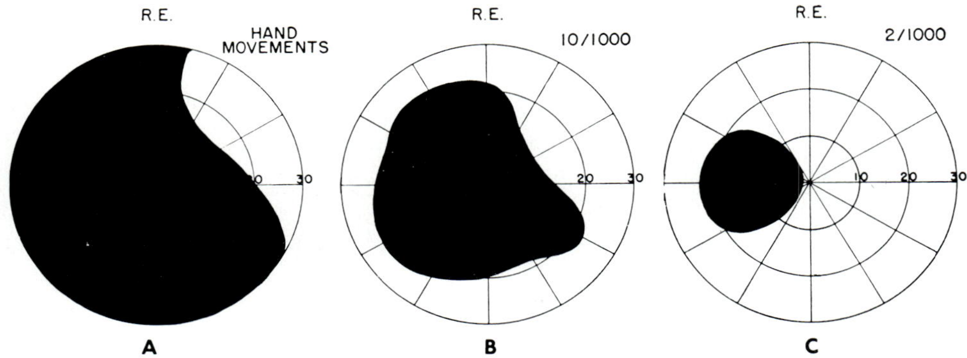

Fig. 13-12. Optic neuritis. **A,** Sudden onset of severe visual loss with destruction of most of central field. **B,** Gradual regression of scotoma. **C,** Scotoma recedes from fixation with restoration of 20/30 vision. Optic nerve was edematous. There was history of similar attack 3 years before.

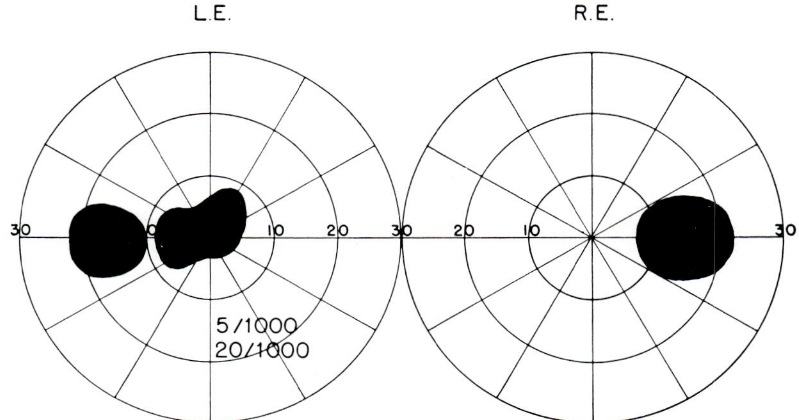

Fig. 13-13. Papillitis in left eye with central scotoma and diminished visual acuity. There was increased intracranial pressure with papilledema in right eye, accompanied by enlargement of blind spot and retention of normal vision.

It is quite possible that these nerve fiber bundle defects are caused by extension of the inflammation into the juxtapapillary choroid with a resultant visual field defect of the Jensen type.

When peripheral depression occurs, it often has steep margins and progresses rapidly. The combination of dense central scotoma coalescing with a peripheral contraction gives a poor prognosis.

Pressure on optic nerve head

Pressure on the optic nerve head occurs classically in glaucomas, described elsewhere (see Chapter 11). Other forms of pressure on the optic disc may occur from intrinsic tumor, disc drusen, as mentioned previously, or extreme orbital swelling as seen in severe hemorrhage or cellulitis, and in malignant exophthalmos. All of these conditions might be expected to produce circulatory changes in the optic disc with visual field defects, depending on whether the axial or peripheral nerve fibers were involved.

Vascular lesions of optic disc

Vascular lesions of the optic disc usually take the form of hemorrhage associated with venous thrombosis, severe papilledema, spontaneous subarachnoid hemorrhage, and trauma.

In arteriosclerotic optic atrophy with cupping of the disc and all the findings of low-tension glaucoma, the visual field changes are usually a peripheral depression and a glaucoma-like nerve fiber bundle defect. These are thought to be caused by atherosclerotic closure of the small arterial twigs to the periphery of the nerve.

Arterial emboli from atherosclerotic material in the vessels of the neck may occlude small arterioles in the optic nerve or on the disc, giving rise to sectorlike defects in the visual fields or to typical Bjerrum scotomas. These arterial plaques may sometimes be seen ophthalmoscopically on the optic disc (see Figs. 10-2 and 11-20), or they may occur deeper in the vasculature of the nerve and only become manifest through the field changes that they produce.

Ischemic optic neuropathy may occur, usually in elderly patients, with sudden onset of complete or partial visual loss and edema of the optic disc. When partial, the visual fields may show central scotoma, sector defects, or large and dense arcuate defects simulating altitudinal hemianopsia. These field defects are dense, steep-margined, and permanent. Later the optic disc will show sector-type atrophy, which is characteristic. The majority of such patients will have an elevated blood sedimentation rate, and some will show positive evidence of arteritis on biopsy of the temporal artery. Early treatment with corticosteroids is mandatory to prevent further visual loss. In others the optic nerve disease will be secondary to arterial occlusion from carotid arterial stenosis.

Trauma to papilla (Fig. 13-14)

Direct trauma to the nerve head would occur as a result of avulsion of the nerve secondary to extreme compression of the globe. I have seen a partial avulsion of the

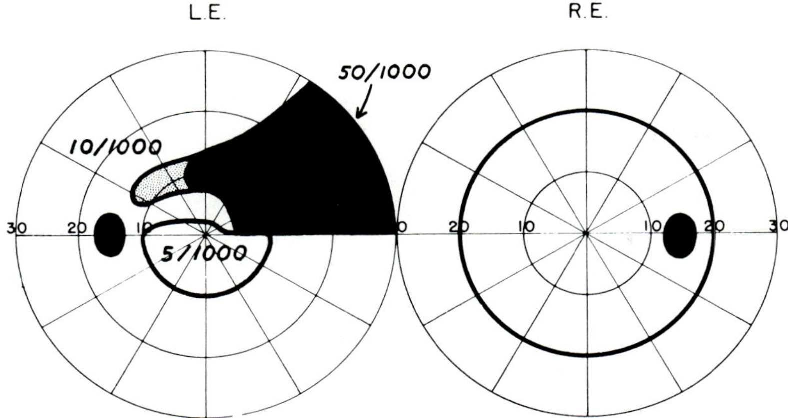

Fig. 13-14. Nerve fiber bundle type defect with peripheral nasal breakthrough secondary to optic atrophy following severe shock from high tension wire. Patient fell 10 feet but was not unconscious. Field defect may be secondary to vascular lesion in nerve resulting from either trauma of fall or electric shock.

nerve in which only a remnant of temporal field remained, corresponding to a few nasal fibers left intact by the injury.

Another form of trauma is from perforating foreign bodies, such as small bird shot. I have also seen a case of penetration of the globe by a spicule of steel, which buried itself in the optic disc with a resulting wide-sector defect in the visual field.

RETROBULBAR OPTIC NERVE

Lesions within the trunk or orbital portion of the optic nerve present no ophthalmoscopic evidence of their presence until atrophy appears in a late stage of the disease. Their diagnosis, localization, pathology, prognosis, and indications for therapy are therefore largely dependent on the findings of careful quantitative perimetry and an analysis of the characteristics of their visual field deficits.

Depending on whether the disease affects the axial or peripheral portions of the nerve, the visual field defects are central, paracentral, or centrocecal scotomas, or peripheral depression or contraction of the visual field, or both.

The pathologic processes that affect this section of the optic nerve are (1) acute axial neuritis, (2) acute peripheral optic neuritis, (3) total transverse neuritis, (4) multiple sclerosis, (5) neuromyelitis optica (Devic's disease), (6) hereditary optic atrophy of Leber, (7) syphilitic optic neuritis and atrophy, (8) hereditary cerebellar (Friedreich's) ataxia, (9) trauma to the optic nerve, (10) vascular lesions of the optic nerve, and (11) compression of the optic nerve.

Acute axial neuritis

Acute axial neuritis is characterized by rapid onset of severe visual loss with production of a large and very dense central or centrocecal scotoma. Movement or rotation of the globe is often painful. The ophthalmoscopic examination is normal. The condition is commonly unilateral. Diagnosis is made upon the finding of a central scotoma. Return of vision is slow, and frequently there is a permanent central scotoma and loss of central vision. In the later stages of the disease, optic atrophy may ensue and peripheral contraction of the visual field takes place in addition to the central scotoma. Rarely, the scotoma takes an arcuate form, but whatever its form margins are steep and the density uniform.

Occasionally, when involvement of the axial portion of the retrobulbar optic nerve is minimal, the scotoma will be very small and visual acuity almost normal. Here use of the 2-meter distance in tangent screen examination is useful as is also a field taken with ultraviolet light and luminescent blue test objects (Fig. 13-15).

In many instances the causative agent is never known. Careful but fruitless search may be made for foci of infection, and occasionally the nasal accessory sinuses are implicated, especially the sphenoid and ethmoid sinuses. In younger persons exhaustive neurologic examination may or may not reveal evidence of multiple sclerosis.

Prognosis must be guarded, because the smallest scotoma may persist, whereas the massive scotoma, involving two-thirds of the central field, may melt away.

The effectiveness of therapy, such as intensive corticosteroid therapy, must be judged by its effect on the scotoma. Central visual acuity may remain poor in spite of shrinkage of the scotoma. Complete recovery is relatively rare.

Acute peripheral optic neuritis

When acute inflammation involves the peripheral fibers of the optic nerve either as a primary process or secondary to disease of the pial sheath of the nerve, the resulting visual field defect is a peripheral depression or contraction. Central vision

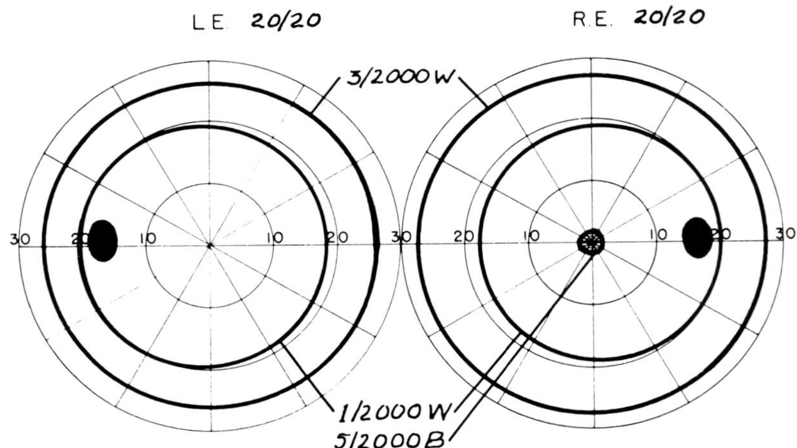

Fig. 13-15. Retrobulbar neuritis associated with chronic ethmoiditis accompanied by fistulous tract into posterior orbit. Central scotoma was demonstrated with luminescent monochromatic blue test object even though visual acuity was blurred 20/20 in right eye. Two-point discrimination was shown to be defective when two 1-mm targets were brought together on 2-meter tangent screen. Color vision was deficient.

remains intact until the onset of optic atrophy. Both eyes may be involved, but usually unequally, and the neuritis is more often unilateral. Peripheral neuritis with concentric contraction of the field usually localizes the lesion in the posterior portion of the nerve behind the point of entry of the central retinal artery. Differential diagnosis from tabetic optic atrophy may be difficult except that the tabes is usually slow in onset, never regresses, is usually bilateral, and is accompanied, rather than followed, by optic nerve atrophy.

Total transverse neuritis

Fortunately, total transverse neuritis is rare. It may accompany nonspecific or influenzal acute encephalitis and gives rise to total amaurosis of sudden onset or to very large and dense central scotomas with almost complete loss of vision. The prognosis is poor.

Multiple sclerosis

Multiple sclerosis is probably the most common cause of acute retrobulbar neuritis. It has been reported in from 8% to 75% of all cases of multiple sclerosis, with an average incidence of 50% in the statistical analyses of different authors.

The characteristic visual field defect is a scotoma in the central field (Fig. 13-16). This scotoma may take an almost infinite variety of forms such as arcuate, paracentral, pericentral, annular, or centrocecal. It is most frequently central. It may be bilateral or unilateral, with sloping or steep margins, large or small, round, oval, or irregular. When the lesion extends into the chiasm or even into the tract, the field changes may take on the characteristics of other disturbances of the visual pathway in those areas, namely, bitemporal or homonymous hemianopsia or hemianoptic scotomas (Fig. 13-17).

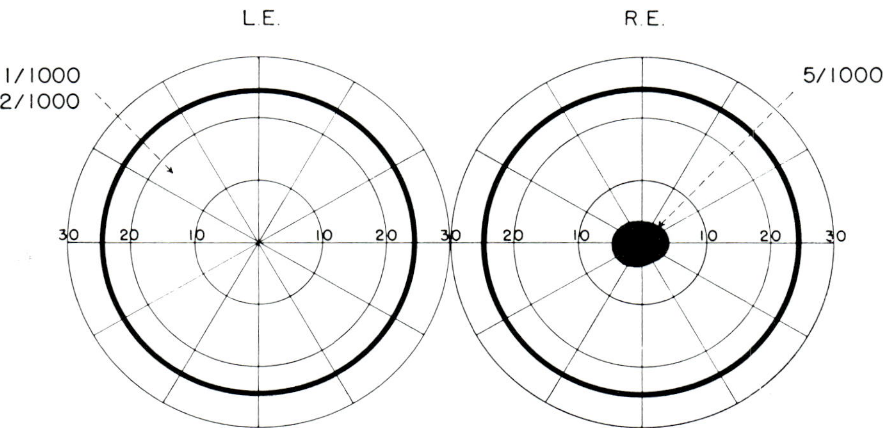

Fig. 13-16. Retrobulbar neuritis associated with multiple sclerosis. Visual loss was sudden in onset and accompanied by pain on rotation of eye. Scotoma cleared completely in 10 days. There was later attack of transient vertical diplopia and some peripheral motor and sensory disturbance.

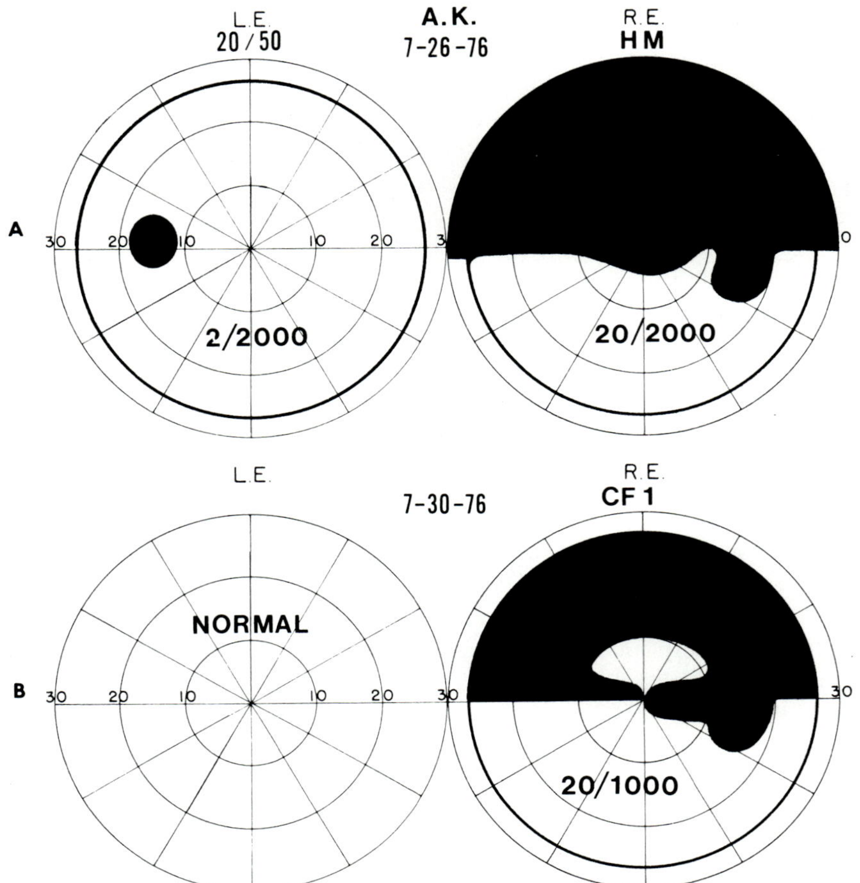

Fig. 13-17. A, Retrobulbar neuritis of right eye in a 26-year-old white male. Sudden visual loss with altitudinal hemianopsia, Marcus Gunn pupil, and markedly delayed visual-evoked response (VER) both eyes. **B,** Beginning resolution of visual field defect within 4 days with return to completely normal field and vision in 1 month. VER remained abnormal in both eyes. Diagnosis, probable multiple sclerosis.

Frequently the scotomas are vague, relative, and ephemeral or fleeting in appearance, present on one examination and absent a few days later. Because of this characteristic, the evaluation of therapy is extremely difficult, and great caution must be exercised in attributing a cure to any current form of treatment.

In many patients the visual acuity and the size and the depth of a scotoma may be directly affected by exposure to heat. A hot bath or even prolonged sunbathing causes noticeable transient decrease in vision.

In well-established multiple sclerosis, a characteristic thinning and atrophy of the nerve fiber bundles of the retina may be seen with red-free ophthalmoscopy.

An inconstant central scotoma that fades after a few days only to reappear days, weeks, months, or even years later is highly suggestive of multiple sclerosis. If, in addition, there is a history of transient diplopia or evidence of other cranial nerve involvement, the diagnosis is more certain. When details of history or neurologic examination reveal peripheral motor or sensory involvement, abnormal deep and superficial reflexes, emotional instability, and finally an optic atrophy, the diagnostic criteria are complete.

Quite probably there are patients with multiple sclerosis in whom the only finding is a transient and recurrent scotoma in the central field of one or both eyes. There may be lengthy remissions between attacks of retrobulbar neuritis, and optic atrophy with bitemporal pallor of the nerve heads may or may not ensue. After many years there may be a concentric contraction of the peripheral field, usually associated with optic atrophy.

In other cases the retrobulbar neuritis with its typical transient scotoma may precede the general neurologic findings of multiple sclerosis by 10 to 20 years.

When the central scotoma is progressive from its onset, it is usually quickly followed by optic atrophy and the prognosis for visual return is very poor.

Visual perception is delayed after an attack of retrobulbar neuritis. In addition to delayed visual-evoked response (VER), critical flicker fusion frequency is reduced in a high proportion of multiple sclerosis patients. Demyelination also impairs a patient's ability to detect that two closely following lights flashes are double rather than single, and the time interval between the two flashes must be increased to restore the patient's perception of double. The abnormality is large and easily detected, may be present long before the development of visual field defects, and remains after return to normal vision.

In many cases the only finding may be a delayed VER in one eye or, more often, both eyes. This abnormal latency may precede the onset of a frank and measurable visual field deficit, or it may persist for a long period after the resolution of a scotomatous field defect and return of vision to normal.

The reliability of the VER, especially its latency, makes it particularly sensitive to alterations in conduction velocity in the visual pathway, so that it has gained diagnostic value in the evaluation of patients suspected of having demyelinating disease. The usefulness of the VER is enhanced by the fact that the optic nerves are among the earliest and most frequently involved sites in multiple sclerosis.

On the other hand, Patterson and Heron examined the visual fields with a 2-meter tangent screen and found that a high percentage of patients with definite or suspected multiple sclerosis had abnormal visual fields. The commonest defect found was an arcuate or nerve fiber bundle defect even though many patients had no visual symptoms.

The authors compared their visual field findings with those of VER and concluded that visual field examination with a traditional tangent screen is a widely available, simple, and sensitive method of demonstrating visual pathway damage in multiple sclerosis and compares favorably with more sophisticated methods.

Neuromyelitis optica (Devic's disease)

Devic's disease is a severe bilateral optic neuritis. It is associated with transverse myelitis and is accompanied by the production of central scotomas and paraplegia

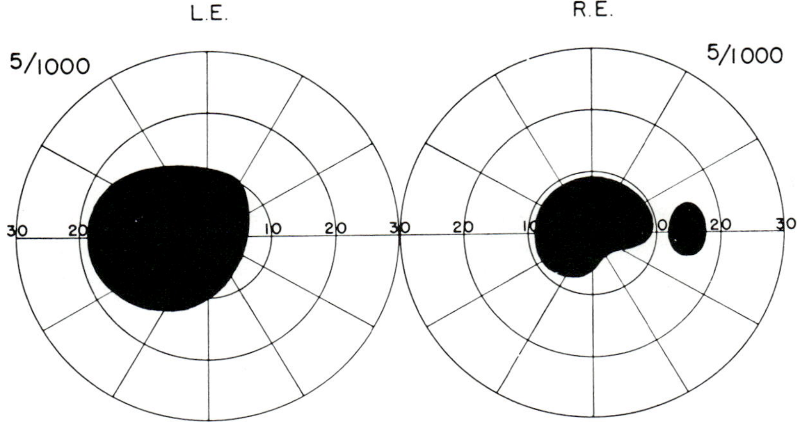

Fig. 13-18. Neuromyelitis optica (Devic's disease). There was bilateral optic disc edema with poor vision and central scotomas. Visual disturbances were sudden in onset and followed in 2 weeks by complete paraplegia. Both optic neuritis and myelitis partially cleared after 4 months.

(Fig. 13-18). It occurs most frequently in adolescents or young adults, but I have seen one case in a man 65 years of age.

In about one half of the cases, the myelitis precedes the appearance of the scotomas. In about one-fourth of the cases, onset is with retrobulbar neuritis followed by the paraplegia. The remaining cases show a simultaneous onset of myelitis and ocular signs.

The optic neuritis may involve the papilla or may be entirely in the axial portion of the retrobulbar nerve. The scotomas are usually large and very dense in the central portion with somewhat sloping margins. Occasional peripheral field involvement is seen, and rarely the lesion extends into the chiasm or the optic tracts with the production of bitemporal or homonymous hemianopsia. The prognosis is poor. The disease may be confused with, and is perhaps related to, the acute disseminated encephalitis of Schilder.

Hereditary optic atrophy of Leber

Leber's disease is a familial bilateral optic atrophy with a predilection for males. Its onset is usually in the second or third decade, and there is acute loss of central vision, large, dense, steep-margined, bilateral central scotomas, and finally optic atrophy (Fig. 13-19). The changes in the disc and in the visual fields are permanent. The condition may affect four out of five males in a family and an occasional female, acting as a sex-linked recessive trait.

In the acute stage of the optic neuropathy in Leber's disease Smith and coworkers have found three characteristic fundus changes:

1. Swelling of the nerve fiber layer around the disc
2. Circumpapillary telangiectatic microangiopathy
3. Absence of staining on fluorescein angiography

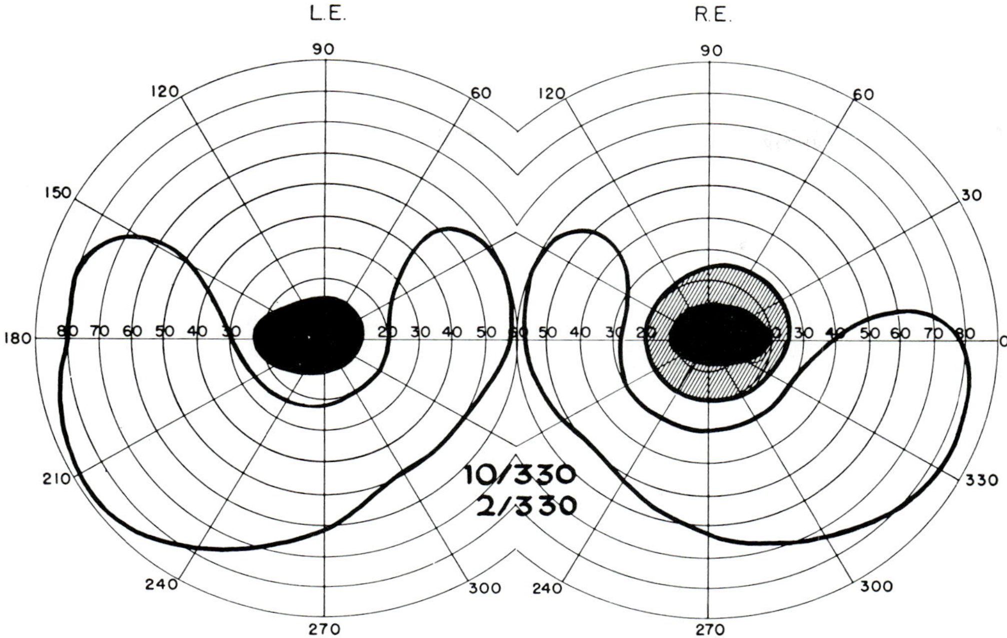

Fig. 13-19. Hereditary optic atrophy (Leber's disease). This affected four male members of family, all of whom developed visual loss and bilateral central scotomas.

The initial changes mimic edema of the disc, but the rapid visual loss and the finding of scotomas in the visual field coupled with the inheritance pattern should make such a diagnostic error unlikely.

The scotoma may assume many different forms, but it is always central in postion and usually quite large and very dense. Occasional cases show some regression in the scotomas, but in most the visual loss is permanent although blindness is extremely rare. Peripheral depression or contraction of the field is common in the later stages.

Infantile optic atrophy

Aside from the hereditary optic atrophy of Leber, Kjer and C. S. Hoyt have described a number of cases of infantile optic atrophy with an autosomal dominant mode of inheritance.

Visual acuity is not severely affected unless nystagmus is present. Age of onset is early in life and often goes unnoticed until detected in a school screening program. The optic atrophy varies in degree.

The characteristic visual field defect is a centrocecal scotoma, and its density varies greatly. Some cases show a nerve fiber bundle defect. The centrocecal defect may enlarge to encompass a large area of temporal field and simulate a bitemporal hemianopsia. Tests with colored stimuli exaggerate these deficits.

Syphilitic optic neuritis and atrophy

Diagnosis of syphilitic optic neuritis and atrophy depends on correlating a number of findings: appearance of the optic disc, visual field changes, and clinical and serologic evidences of syphilis.

In its acute stages the disease should more properly be called syphilitic optic neuritis, whereas its more chronic and familiar form is an optic atrophy. The degenerative changes may involve the axial portion of the nerve, but they are more commonly found in the peripheral nerve fibers, and they are secondary to syphilitic inflammation. Papillitis is rarely present. In most cases the nerve is affected in its posterior orbital or its intracranial portion. The same pathologic process may be seen in tabes dorsalis and in general paresis.

Visual field defects in association with syphilitic optic atrophy are dependent on the portion of the nerve involved by the degenerative process:

1. Peripheral or concentric inflammation is followed by nerve fiber degeneration that slowly advances toward the center of the nerve and gives rise to a gradually contracting visual field with steep margins of the coast-erosion type. Central vision may be maintained for some time, but eventually fixation is involved and ultimate blindness is the rule. The contraction may not be concentric but may spare one quadrant long after the rest of the visual field is gone. Occasionally the shape of the visual field is bizarre (Fig. 13-20).
2. Sector-like degeneration may occur with wedge-shaped areas of visual field

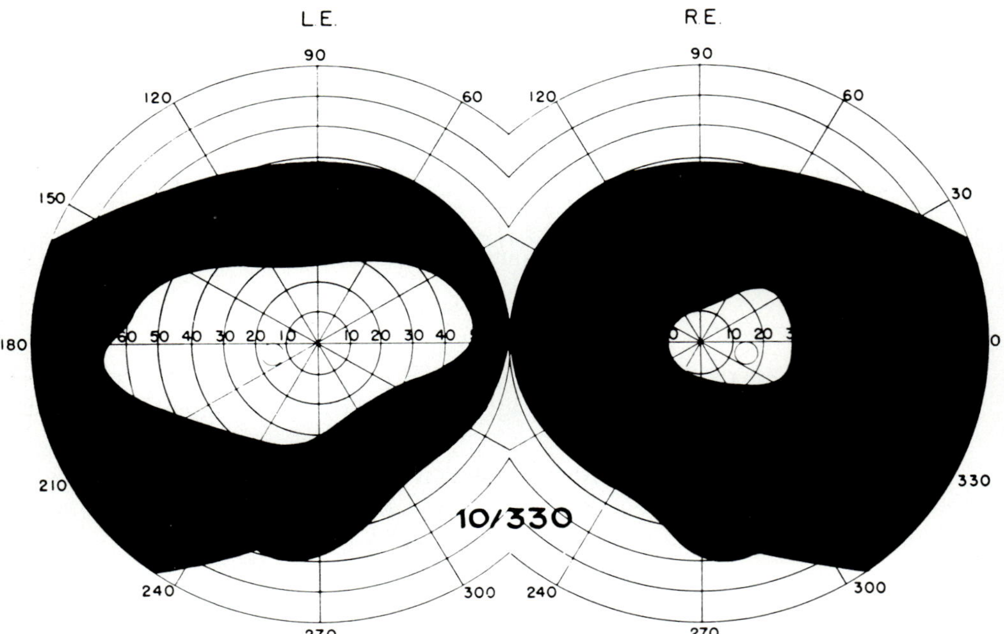

Fig. 13-20. Tabetic optic atrophy. Note general contraction of visual fields.

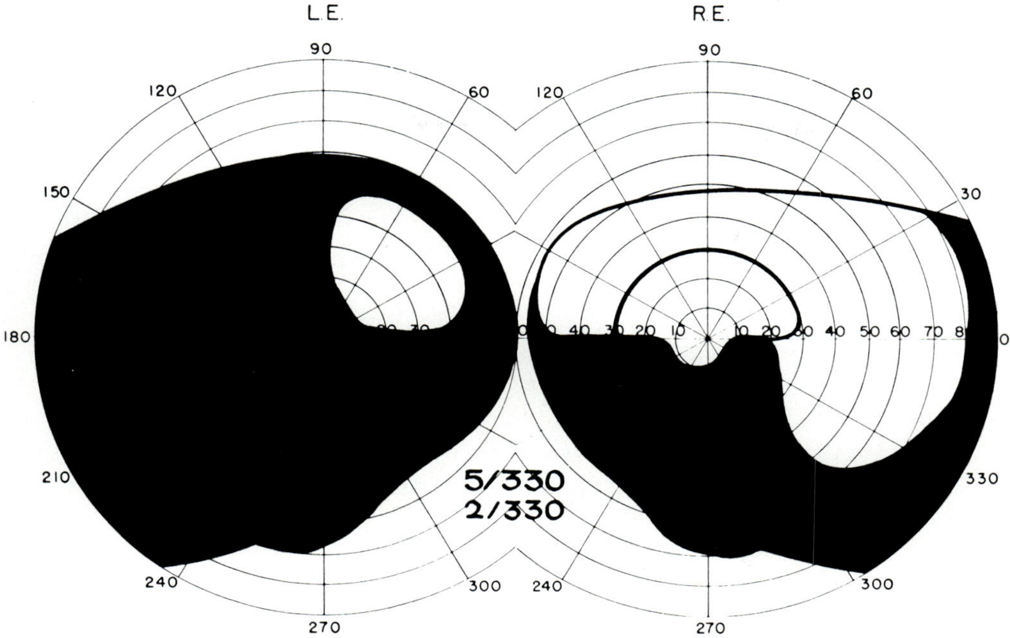

Fig. 13-21. Tabetic optic atrophy. Note sector-type defects of visual fields.

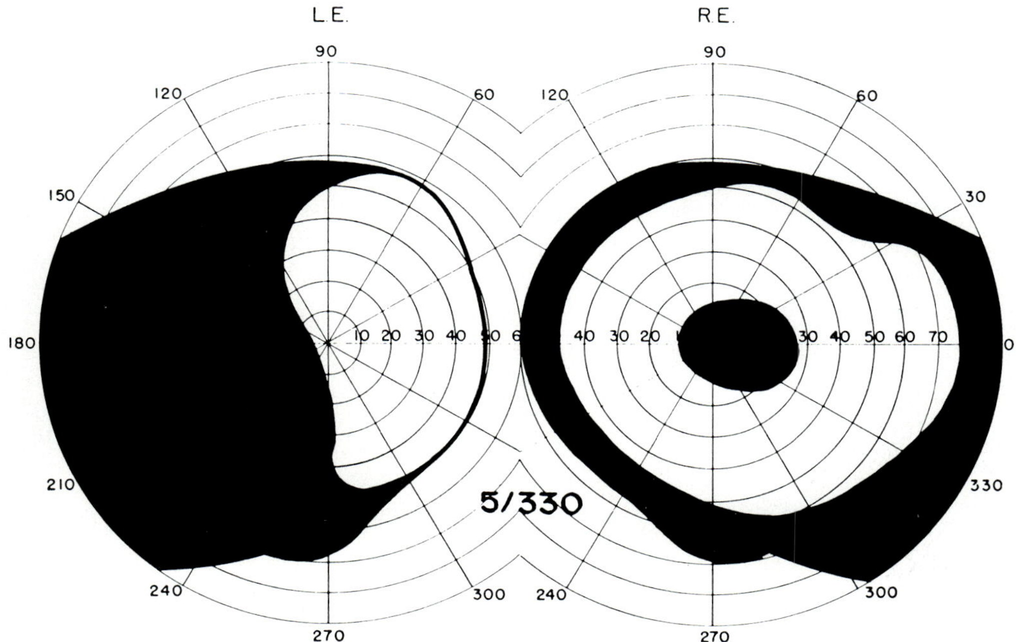

Fig. 13-22. Tabetic optic atrophy. Scotomatous-type defect was demonstrated in right field and hemianoptic loss in left field.

loss pointing their apices at fixation. Optic atrophy in these patients may appear to involve the entire disc; when both eyes are about equally involved, the visual field defects sometimes take on hemianoptic characteristics, which make them difficult to differentiate from chiasmal and postchiasmal lesions (Figs. 13-21 and 13-22).

3. Syphilitic retrobulbar neuritis followed by degeneration of the axial portion of the nerve gives rise to central scotomas. These may be sudden or gradual in onset. They are of various forms and are progressive. The peripheral visual field may remain unaffected for a long time but is usually involved eventually in one or both eyes.

The visual field defects of tabetic optic atrophy may simulate those of almost any disease of the visual pathway. Since the advent of penicillin, optic nerve damage is less common than formerly.

The diagnostic criteria are the bilaterality of the condition, the optic atrophy, the prolonged course, and the inexorable advance of the visual field loss toward blindness.

Hereditary cerebellar (Friedreich's) ataxia

Visual field changes are not uncommon in Friedreich's ataxia and have been variously described by different authors as concentric contraction, annular scotoma involving the blind spot, and central scotoma, all in association with optic atrophy.

Injury to optic nerve

Direct injury to the optic nerve, such as may occur in avulsion of the nerve or in gunshot wounds of the head, usually causes immediate, total, and permanent visual loss. Indirect injury may be of varying degrees of severity and produces visual field defects in keeping with the nerve damage.

Walsh has classified the lesions of the optic nerve and chiasm associated with indirect trauma as follows:

PRIMARY LESIONS

1. Hemorrhages in the nerve, dura, and sheath spaces
2. Tears in the nerve or chiasm
3. Contusion necrosis of optic nerves and chiasm

SECONDARY LESIONS

1. Edema and swelling of optic nerves and chiasm
2. Necrosis from systemic circulatory failure or local vessel compression
3. Softening (infarction) in the optic nerve or chiasm related to vascular obstruction from thrombosis

This classification was based on microscopic studies and is not concerned with visual defects resulting from such lesions. In most instances, lesions were of such severity as to preclude evaluation of visual field deficits.

During World War II, I saw a number of interesting cases of this type in which gunshot wounds of the temporal region had damaged the optic nerve by the con-

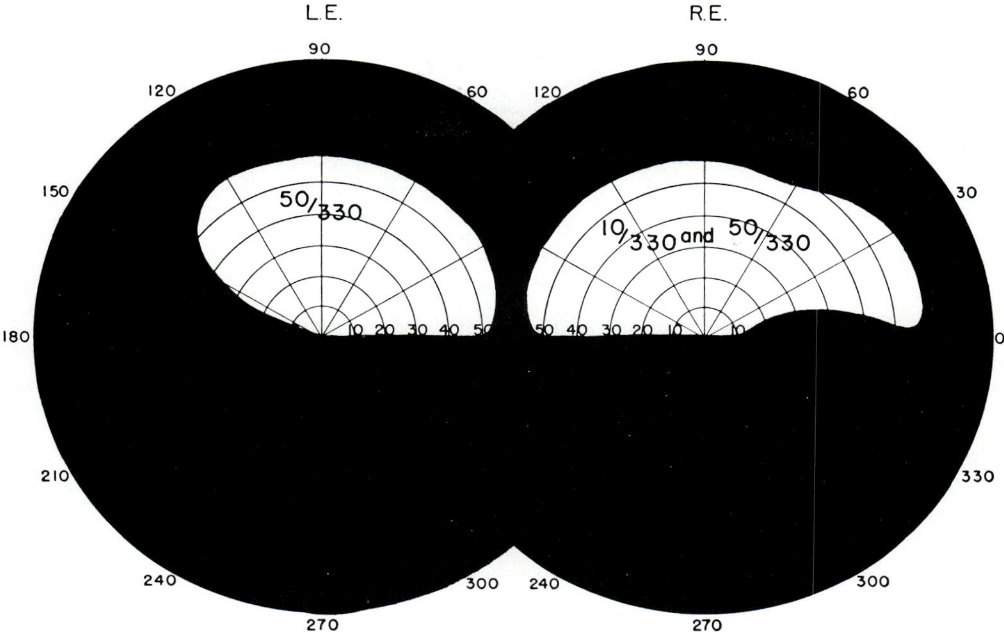

Fig. 13-23. Concussion injury to optic nerve. Rifle bullet passed through right frontal lobe above and anterior to orbital apices. Path of bullet was obliquely upward from right to left, at considerable distance from optic nerve. Retina was normal.

cussive effect of the bullet's passing near but not through the nerve (Fig. 13-23). In each case the damage was greatest on the side where the bullet made its exit because of the greater concussion on that side. In one instance, operative exploration of the frontal area and decompression of the orbit and the intracanalicular portion of the nerve from above failed to reveal any direct injury to the canal, the optic nerve, or its dural sheaths; in fact, the tract of the bullet was a considerable distance from these structures.

In each of these patients, the visual fields showed an altitudinal type of defect with complete loss of the lower field and in one patient a partial loss of the upper temporal field as well. The margins of the hemianopsia were very steep.

In another patient a small bird shot entered the right orbit through the upper lid and passed along the roof of the orbit into the apex, where it lodged against the superior aspect of the optic nerve as it passed into the optic foramen (Fig. 13-24). The other eye was blind from multiple wounds of the globe. Because there might have been hemorrhage at the orbital apex with compression of the nerve, a decompression was performed through a frontal osteoplastic flap. No gross hemorrhage was seen, but the small lead shot was removed from the orbital entrance of the optic canal. The visual field showed an altitudinal type of defect with major loss in the lower field.

Severe skull fracture with possible basilar fracture in the area of the optic foramen

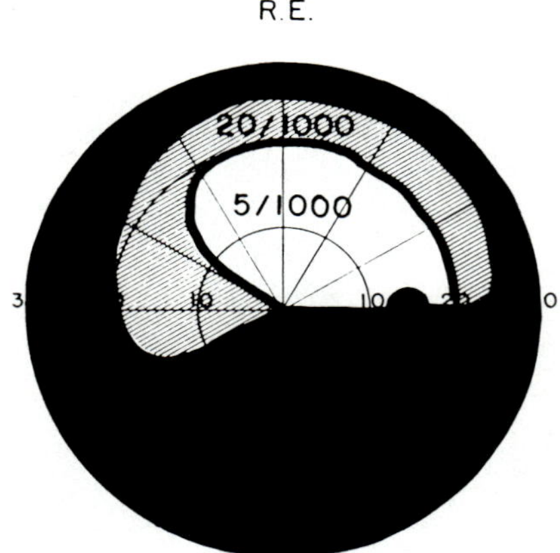

Fig. 13-24. Direct injury to optic nerve. Small bird shot entered right orbit through upper lid and passed backward along orbital roof, without injury to globe, to lodge against superior aspect of optic nerve in orbital apex. It was removed in course of orbital and optic canal decompression from above.

may give rise to optic nerve injury with unilateral or bilateral altitudinal hemianoptic field defects. Occasionally, only a small portion of the lower visual field will be depressed, and in some instances this slight peripheral depression will be accompanied by a nerve fiber bundle defect.

The type of visual field defects, the nature of the injuries producing them, and the evidence of operative exploration of the orbit all indicate that the lesion that produces these defects is in the optic canal and is probably caused by damage to the vascular supply of the nerve rather than damage to the nerve fibers directly.

The nerve at this point is movable within its dural sheath, which is firmly attached to the periosteum of the optic canal. Slight torsion or pulling of the nerve in any direction would tend to shear the tiny vascular twigs that enter the nerve at right angles from the pial sheath. The blood vessels supplying the upper half of the nerve are shorter than those to the inferior portion and are more vulnerable to this shearing action, thus giving rise to the inferior visual field defects.

Fractures into the optic canal are extremely rare and difficult to diagnose radiologically. I have seen one case of fracture of an anterior clinoid, demonstrated by roentgenography, associated with permanent visual loss in one eye and a visual field defect in which only a small island of vision was spared in the upper temporal quadrant.

Vascular lesions of optic nerve

Arteriosclerotic disease of the small arterioles that supply the optic nerve may give rise to circulatory embarrassment and chronic hypoxia with resulting defects in the visual fields. These may take the form of gradual peripheral depression or, when the axial portion of the nerve is involved, vague and irregular scotomas in the central field. Frequently there are nerve fiber bundle defects as described in the discussion of low-tension glaucoma.

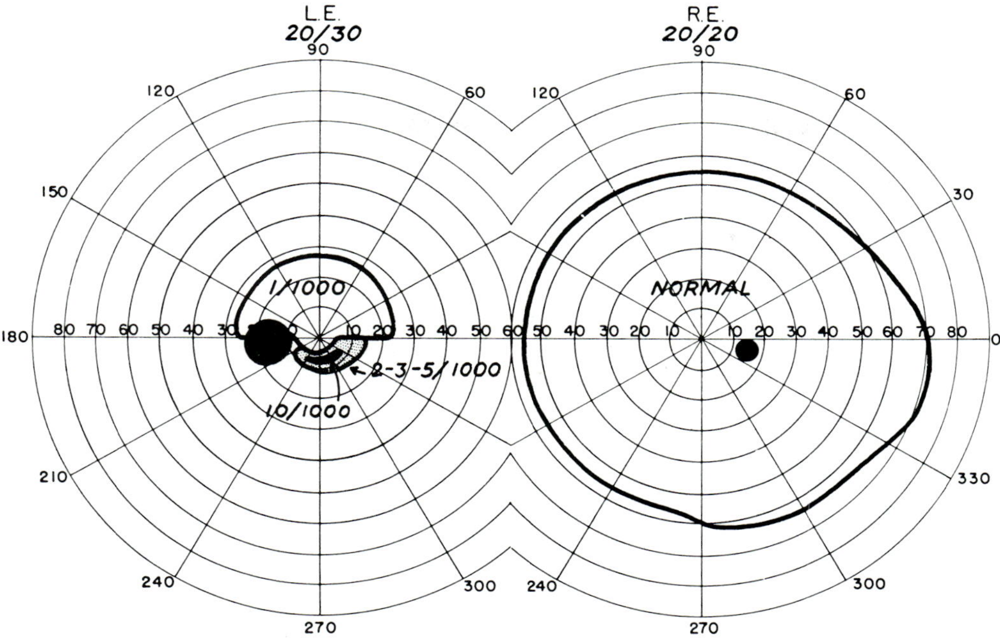

Fig. 13-25. Nerve fiber bundle defect, left eye, associated with partial optic atrophy and marked attenuation of retinal arterioles. There was history of amaurosis fugax. Roentgenograms showed dense calcification of siphon of left internal carotid artery. Intraocular pressure was 12 mm Hg.

When the arterial occlusion is more acute, as in thrombosis or embolism, sector defects or large dense central scotomas may develop.

As mentioned previously, the visual field defects associated with indirect injury to the optic nerve are probably vascular in origin; and, quite probably, those produced by compression of the optic nerve are also due, at least in part, to circulatory failure.

The type of visual field loss most frequently produced by vascular disturbance in the optic nerve is horizontal or altitudinal hemianopsia. Another type of field defect commonly found in association with vascular disease is the nerve fiber bundle defect similar or identical to that of glaucoma (Fig. 13-25). The pathogenesis of these defects is discussed in Chapter 11.

Compression of optic nerve

The orbital portion of the optic nerve may be compressed by tumors impinging on it from four sides and from within the nerve itself. Visual field defects may arise from direct pressure on the nerve fibers or from interruption of the vascular supply by compression of the arterioles supplying the various portions of the nerve. These tumors may involve the nerve in the anterior, middle, or posterior part of the orbit. Tumors in the anterior and middle parts of the orbit rarely give rise to visual field defects, whereas posterior orbital tumors compressing the nerve in its more fixed portion, as it enters the optic canal, give rise to characteristic visual field defects.

When the field defect is unilateral and remains so, the pressure is probably intraorbital; but when the defect is bilateral, the lesion is more likely to be intracranial.

The commonest visual field defect produced by compression of this portion of the nerve is a central scotoma, often with certain hemianoptic features. The scotoma may involve an area of 10 to 20 degrees around fixation; but when quantitatively examined with multiple isopters, it will be seen to have areas of greater density in the portion opposite the direction of pressure. These areas of greater density are limited by the vertical or horizontal meridians so that the densest area of the scotoma assumes a quadrantic or hemianoptic character. Thus pressure exerted on the upper temporal portion of the nerve just before its entrance into the optic foramen is likely to produce an irregular central scotoma whose area of greatest density is a quadrantic sector in the inferior nasal portion of the scotoma. Pressure on the medial side of the nerve gives rise to a unilateral hemianoptic scotoma on the temporal side of fixation.

Frequently the central scotoma extends toward the blind spot, but it rarely extends into the peripheral field. Peripheral depression of the field is a late development and is usually associated with advanced atrophy of the nerve, exophthalmos, and limitation of motion of the globe.

Tumors within the optic nerve, usually gliomas, give rise to visual field defects through a combination of pressure, nerve fiber destruction, and vascular occlusion. As would be expected, the field defects are larger, denser, and more variable than with external compression.

The initial visual field defect in glioma of the optic nerve is usually a central sco-

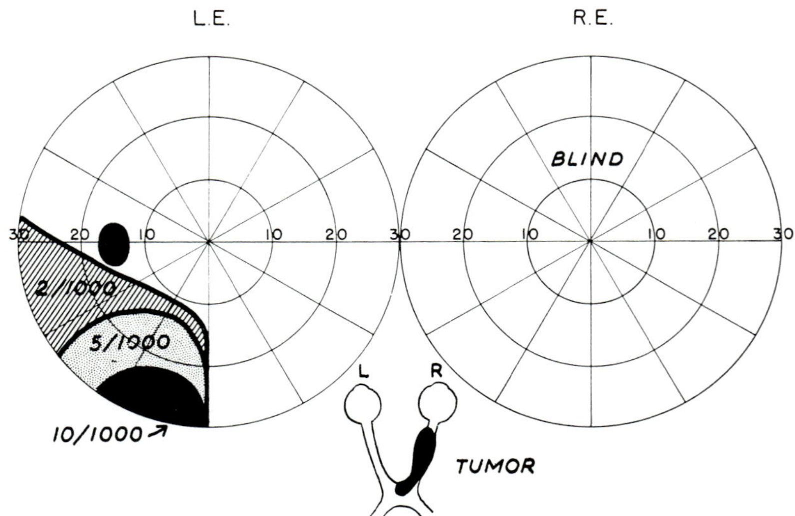

Fig. 13-26. Total amaurosis of right eye with contralateral inferior temporal quadrant loss. Patient had glioma of right optic nerve extending through optic foramen and invading chiasm. Tumor was slow growing and had produced exophthalmos of considerable degree.

toma that is rather steep-margined and of uniform density. This scotoma enlarges with the tumor growth and breaks through into the periphery in the form of irregular sector defects, which may occur in any area of the field. Eventually the chiasm may be invaded, with resulting involvement of the contralateral visual field (Fig. 13-26).

INTRACRANIAL PORTION OF OPTIC NERVE

Precise localization of lesions affecting the intracranial portion of the optic nerve may sometimes be attempted because of the anatomic characteristics of the nerve and its surrounding structures. As the lesion progresses, however, it invades the anterior angle of the chiasm and should rightfully be considered with the diseases affecting that structure.

The classic example of a lesion of this part of the nerve is seen in the Foster-Kennedy syndrome, in which there is visual loss, central scotoma with hemianoptic characteristics, optic atrophy on the same side as the tumor, and papilledema in the opposite optic nerve (Figs. 13-27 and 13-28). The tumor is usually an olfactory groove meningioma, but the syndrome may be caused by tumors of the frontal lobe, cerebellar tumor with extreme third ventricle dilatation, aneurysm of the ophthalmic artery (Fig. 13-29), internal carotid artery, or anterior cerebral artery, arachnoidal cysts, or even intrinsic gliomas of the nerve that have not yet extended into the chiasm.

Figs. 13-31 and 13-32 are examples of differential diagnosis and precise localization of a lesion involving the optic nerve in its intracanalicular portion by quantitative analysis of the visual fields. The initial defect was a small scotoma below and paracentral to fixation. This expanded to involve the inferior temporal quadrant and finally to become an inferior altitudinal loss in one eye. The horizontal margin of the defect and its manner of progression suggested a lesion compressing the nerve from above. Roentgenograms of the optic foramina were normal. On the basis of the field defect, a frontal craniotomy was performed, disclosing a small meningioma within the left optic canal that was compressing the optic nerve from temporally and above. The tumor lay on the left carotid artery and extended well into the optic canal, causing erosion of the canal with a small sequestrum of bone from the posterior lip of the canal. Complete removal of the tumor was accomplished.

Figs. 13-33 to 13-35 are similar examples of precise tumor localization by careful quantitative perimetry. All three meningiomas initially involved one optic nerve and later, by extension, involved the chiasm. They initially affected vision and the visual field in one eye only. The hemianoptic character of the field loss indicates early chiasmal compression, which may be missed without the most meticulous perimetry. Color perception may be impaired as an early sign and the field defects are exaggerated for red stimuli.

Knight, W. F. Hoyt, and Wilson have described the characteristics of the monocular syndrome of incipient prechiasmal optic nerve compression as slowly progressing dimming of vision, poor color perception, positive Marcus Gunn pupillary sign, and normal-looking optic disc. Their visual field studies showed slowly progressive

Text continued on p. 266.

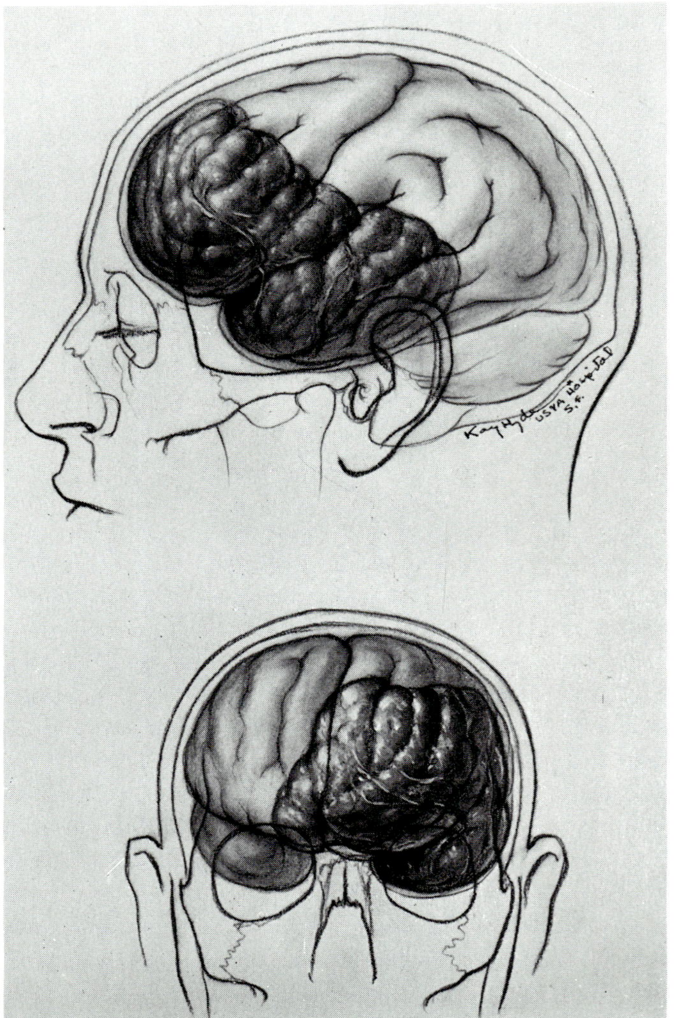

Fig. 13-27. Very large and slowly growing meningioma of left frontal lobe. Anteroposterior and lateral views, as sketched at operation, showed backward extension of tumor over optic nerve and chiasm.

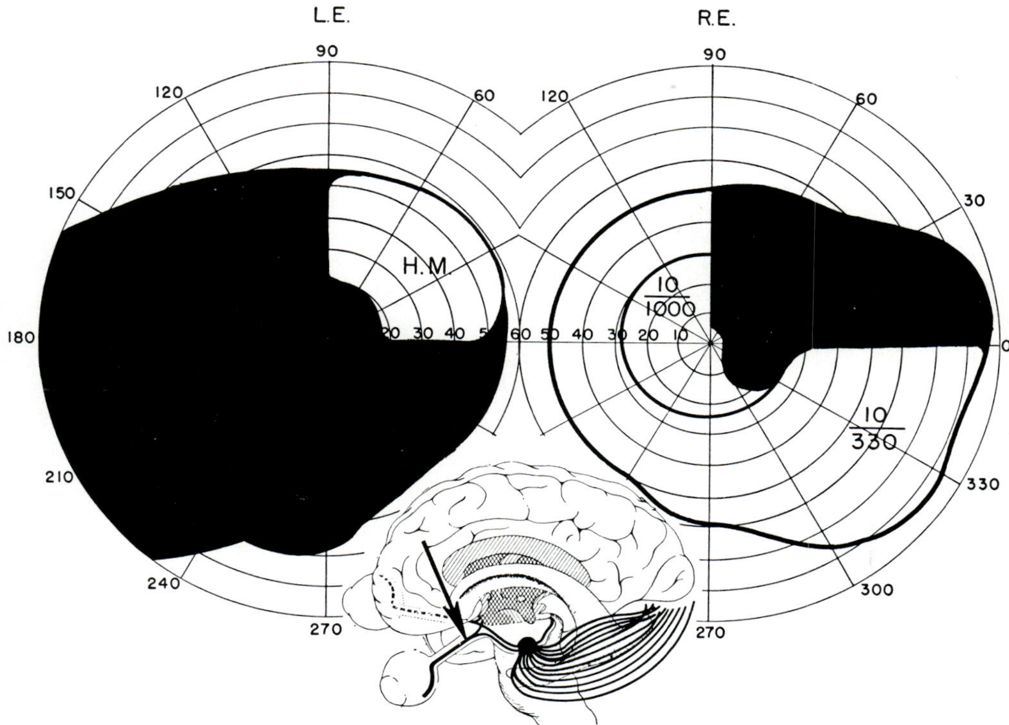

Fig. 13-28. Visual fields in case illustrated in Fig. 13-27 with schematic representation of site and direction of pressure on nerve and chiasm. Left eye was almost blind with advanced optic atrophy and small remnant of nasal field. Right eye showed temporal field loss and papilledema (Foster-Kennedy syndrome).

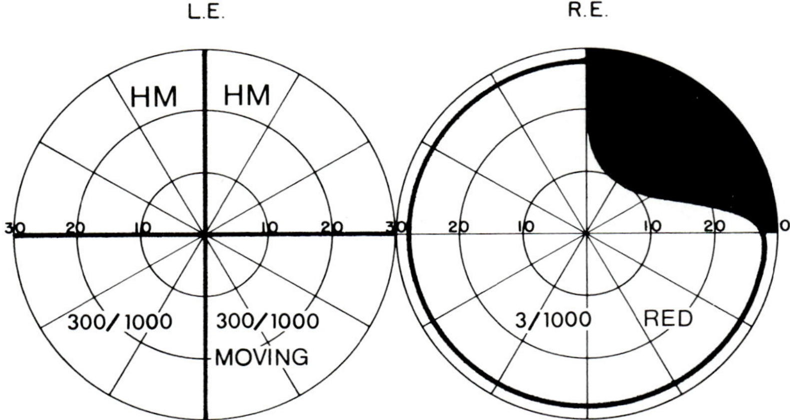

Fig. 13-29. Aneurysm of ophthalmic artery. Left vision reduced to moving objects. Right field shows superior temporal defect for red stimulus. Color vision is also deficient with color charts. Left optic disc atrophic. Arteriography revealed huge aneurysm of left ophthalmic artery with extension across midline to right perichiasmal region.

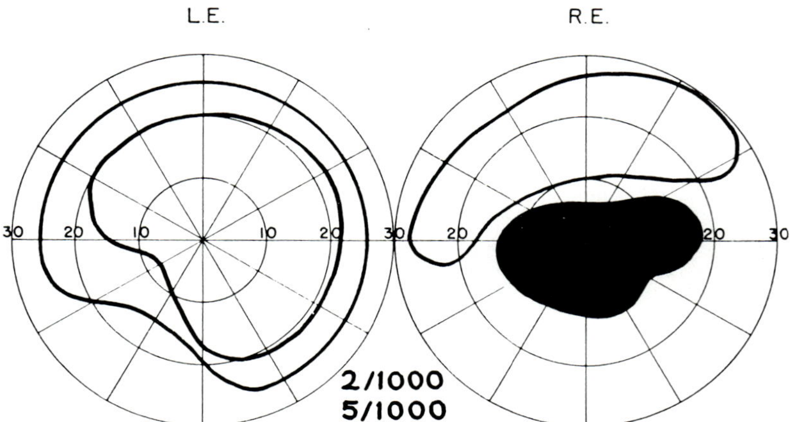

Fig. 13-30. Meningioma of lesser wing of sphenoid on right side. Visual fields show loss of central vision with dense central scotoma on right and minimal inferior temporal defect on left. There was exophthalmos and limitation of motion of right globe.

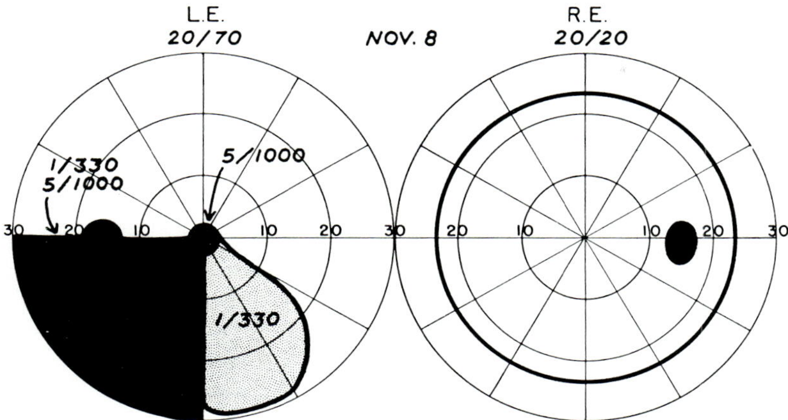

Fig. 13-31. Inferior temporal quadrant defect with slight extension into inferior nasal field. Patient had small meningioma of posterior superior lip of optic canal.

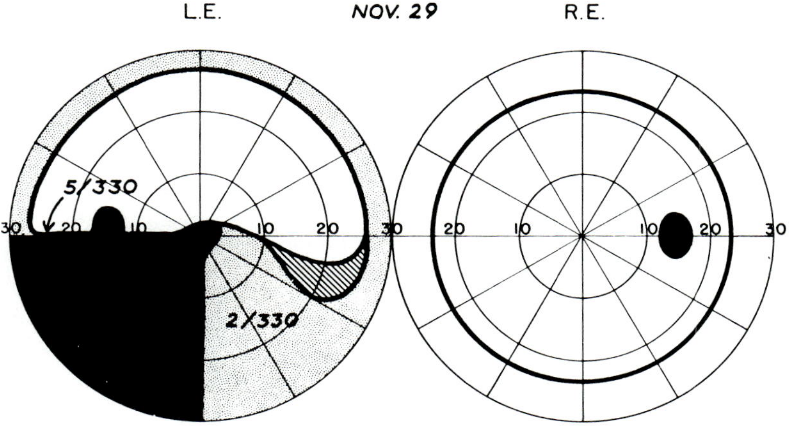

Fig. 13-32. Extension of inferior field defect shown in Fig. 13-31 to become altitudinal loss. Progression occurred in 3 weeks.

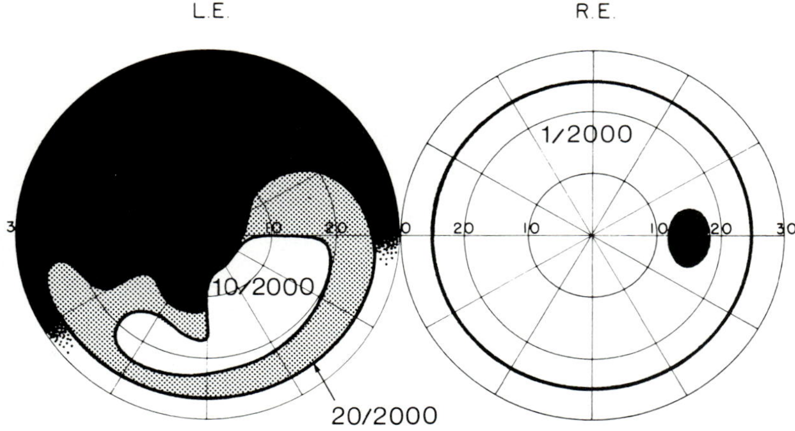

Fig. 13-33. Superior temporal quadrant defect resulting from small meningioma arising from lip of left optic foramen under optic nerve and encroaching on chiasm and internal carotid artery. Advanced optic atrophy continued to progress after removal of tumor.

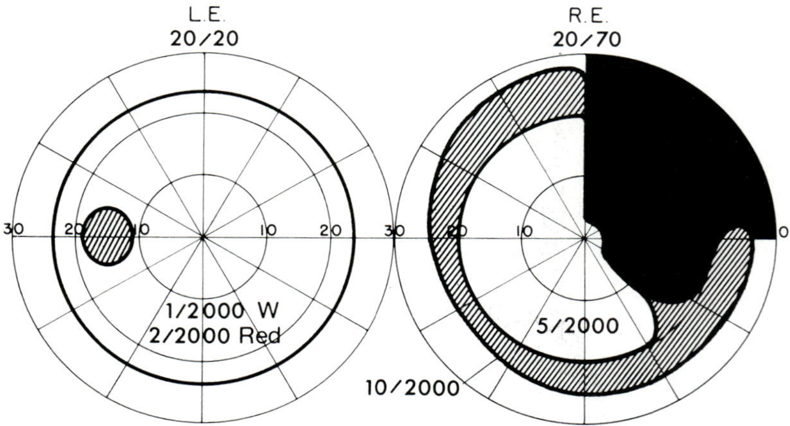

Fig. 13-34. Suprasellar meningioma. Very gradual visual loss in the right eye with hemianoptic superior temporal field deficit. Arteriogram and pneumoencephalogram showed large tumor impinging on tuberculum sellae. Tumor had invaded pial sheath of right optic nerve and markedly deformed left optic nerve. The tumor was successfully removed.

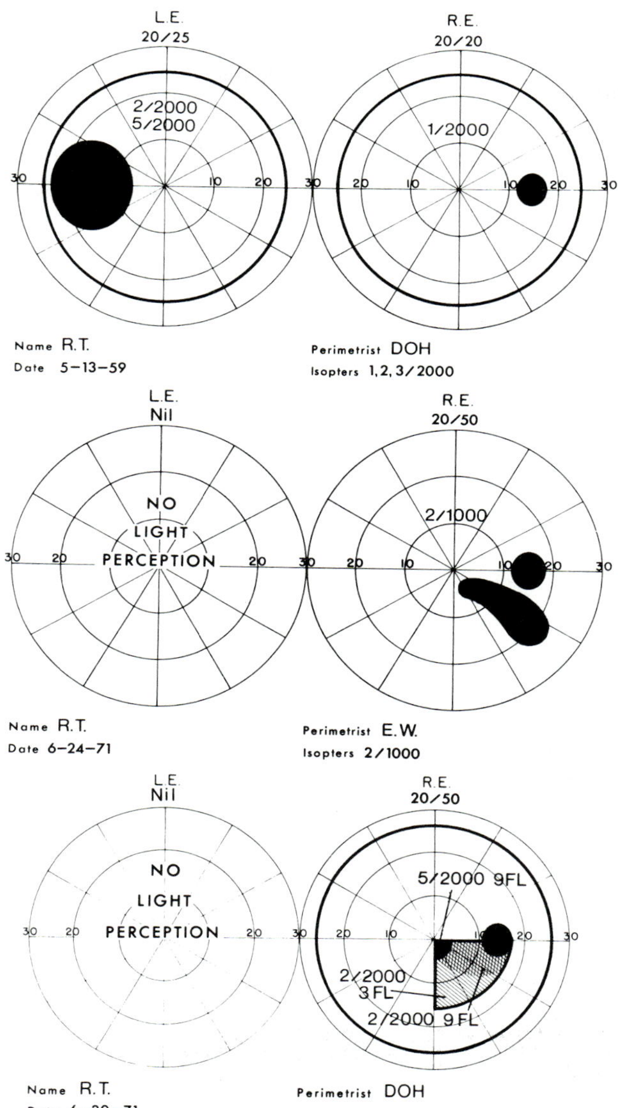

Fig. 13-35. Prechiasmal pressure by a meningioma involving the left optic nerve caused complete blindness in the left eye. The tumor was then extended across the midline to compress the right optic nerve at the intracranial optic foramen. Note the quadrantic nature of the right hemianoptic scotoma when tested with multiple stimuli. Note 12-year lapse between first and last examination. The tumor was removed, with restoration of vision in right eye. (From Harrington, D. O.: Some unusual and difficult visual field defects, Trans. Ophthalmol. Soc. U.K. **92:**15, 1972, London, Churchill Livingstone Ltd.)

monocular quadrantic defects similar to those seen in Figs. 13-31 and 13-35. Even very small tumors in this area can now be detected by modern neuroradiologic techniques. Microsurgical resection of these lesions ensures a chance for prompt restoration of vision.

I have seen one case in which an intrasellar tumor (chromophobic adenoma of the pituitary gland) had tilted the chiasm upward and kinked the optic nerve against the superior edge of the optic foramen, giving rise to a unilateral inferior altitudinal hemianopsia. The chiasm was postfixed and freely movable. This probably accounted for the lack of signs of inferior chiasmal pressure, even though the tumor was large and had produced roentgenographic evidence of erosion of the sella turcica. The opposite field was normal to the most careful quantitative examination.

Even before the contralateral visual field becomes involved, the disease may involve the chiasm. As in all tumors of this area, signs of involvement of contiguous structures are of utmost importance. Radiologic evidence of calcification within the tumor or of unilateral enlargement of the optic foramen should be obtained when possible, and computer-assisted tomography is of great value in precise localization of such tumors.

CHAPTER 14

Chiasm

No other portion of the visual pathway offers a better opportunity for exact correlation between anatomy and function than the chiasm. The architecture of the nerve fiber pattern in this structure is responsible for characteristic changes in the visual fields that are pathognomonic of lesions in this area and this area alone.

Binocular vision begins in the chiasm, which is the first portion of the visual pathway where a single lesion produces a simultaneous defect in both visual fields. This double or hemianoptic visual field defect is seen typically in lesions of the chiasm as a bitemporal hemianopsia.

Although the nerve fiber pattern of the chiasm is remarkably constant, there are other factors that must be taken into account in the interpretation of the visual field changes associated with chiasmal affections. These factors give rise to an extraordinary number of possible variations in hemianoptic morphology. At first glance they are very confusing, but in many instances they may be adequately explained by a knowledge of the chiasmal fiber architecture, its vascular supply, and its contiguous structures. We must therefore consider (1) normal variation in chiasmal position, (2) normal variations in body structure in the chiasmal area, and (3) the close anatomic relationship between the chiasm and (a) the vessels of the circle of Willis, (b) the pituitary body, (c) the pituitary stalk, (d) the third ventricle, and (e) the tuberculum sellae and the sphenoid ridge.

Study of the complicated nerve fiber pattern within the chiasm makes it obvious that pressure at different points and from different directions will give rise to varying hemianopsias, most of them bitemporal, some of them peripheral, and some scotomatous; but some homonymous, some binasal, and some altitudinal.

Further consideration of the large number of contiguous structures that may directly compress or give rise to indirect pressure on the chiasm makes it clear that a thorough knowledge of the area is essential for reasonably accurate interpretation of the visual fields. (See Chapters 4 and 5.)

Although perimetry is the most valuable single method of examination for diagnosis of lesions of the chiasm, the neuro-ophthalmologist should take full advantage of any other diagnostic procedures that might clarify the clinical picture and perhaps support the interpretation of the visual field studies. Some of the more important of these clinical examinations are as follows:

1. Endocrinologic studies, both clinical and laboratory, for the detection of pituitary dysfunction
2. Neurologic examination with particular reference to the function of the other cranial nerves
3. Radiologic examination of the skull with special reference to the sella turcica, the optic foramina, the sphenoid ridge, and the tuberculum sellae

   Important advances in neuroradiologic techniques make it possible to localize very accurately even small tumors that have produced visual field defects by chiasmal compression. These techniques include hypocycloidal polytomography combined with fractional pneumoencephalography, cerebral angiography with or without subtraction techniques, the use of radioactive mercury in brain scanning, and the very effective technique of computer-assisted tomography (CAT scan).
4. Electroencephalography
5. Ophthalmoscopy should include examination of the retinal nerve fiber layer with red-free light. (See Fig. 13-2, *D*.)

   Evaluation of optic nerve pallor is often difficult. One cannot judge the depth of a visual field defect by the appearance of the optic disc in chiasmal lesions, and discs may appear quite normal in the face of advanced bitemporal hemianopsia.

When all these methods have been utilized, perhaps with negative results, the perimetric examination alone may provide the only positive finding that implicates the chiasm or the chiasmal region.

Not infrequently the first symptom of chiasmal disturbance is visual and the first physician consulted is the ophthalmologist. In other instances, vague signs and symptoms of endocrine dysfunction may implicate the pituitary gland and the endocrinologist may request the assistance of visual field examination to support his impression of disease in this organ. In either situation, careful quantitative examination of the visual field is of utmost importance.

PERIMETRIC TECHNIQUES FOR CHIASMAL LESIONS

Except when there is a scotomatous element in the visual field defect, the patient may be completely unaware of an advanced bitemporal hemianopsia. When the macula is spared, the nasal field of one eye overlaps the defective temporal field of the other eye, so that even tasks requiring excellent vision are performed with ease. (See Figs. 7-15 and 13-2.)

Gross methods of examination of the field, such as confrontation, are frequently useless in early involvement of the chiasm. The relatively crude stimulus of the 3/330 isopter is insufficiently sensitive. The peripheral field, as tested on the perimeter, may be normal.

The multiple pattern method of visual field examination may be very sensitive in the detection of an early bitemporal hemianopsia. This is probably due to the qualitative depression in the superior temporal quadrants, which are less sensitive to the

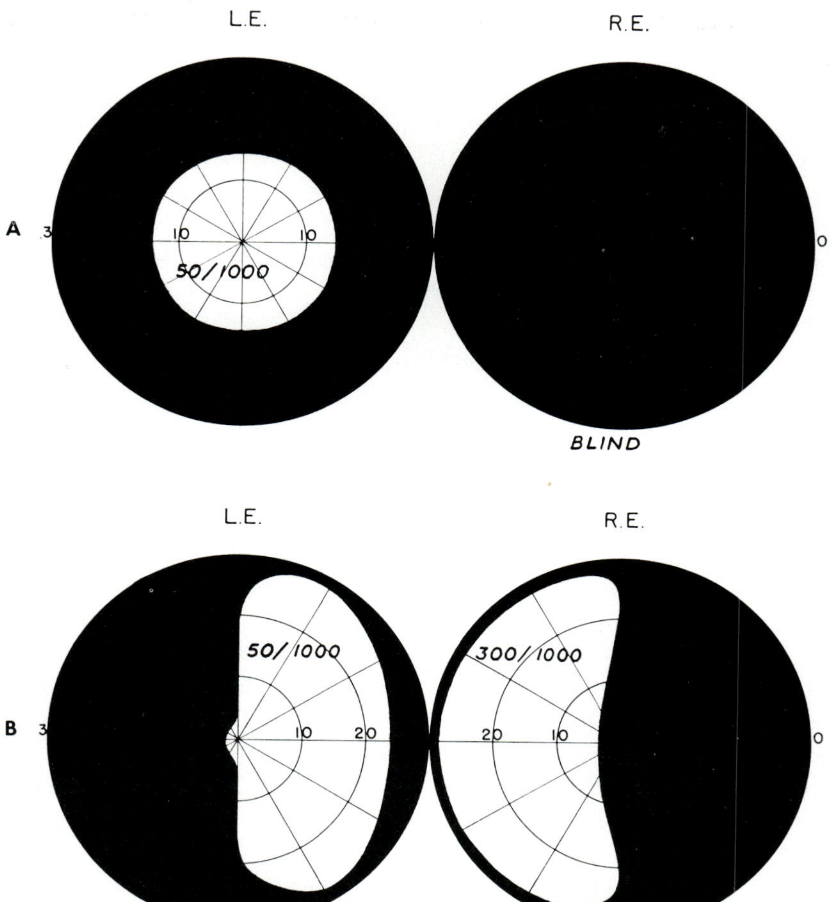

Fig. 14-1. A, Initial field of patient with suprasellar chordoma. Patient's statement that she was blind in right eye was discounted when her pupillary reactions were found normal. Left field was considered hysterically contracted, and diagnosis was hysterical amblyopia. Bilateral optic disc pallor indicated need for quantitative reevaluation of visual fields. **B,** Visual field defect when tested quantitatively with larger stimuli. Deficit was shown to be bitemporal in character, and pneumoencephalography revealed large, lobulated, suprasellar mass with eroded posterior clinoids.

flash presentation of the stimulus. For the same reason the light threshold sensitivity test used in static perimetry is very likely to detect the earliest indications of chiasmal interference.

The earliest field changes in chiasmal interference are found in the 1/2000 white and 3/2000 red isopters in the central portion of the visual field. Perimetric techniques that quantitatively analyze this area are therefore of most value if early diagnosis is to be made. These techniques are as follows:

1. Examination with the tangent screen using small white stimuli and standard illumination or reduced illumination
2. Examination with the tangent screen using electroluminescent stimuli, especially those of low luminance
3. Examination of the central field with static perimetry (30-degree field)
4. Tangent screen examination with 3-mm and 5-mm red stimuli (20-degree field)
5. Flicker fusion frequency (FFF) fields
6. The multiple pattern method of visual field examination

When visual field defects are found, their analysis as to character, through testing of multiple isopters, is most important. Examples of such analysis are as follows:

1. A hemianoptic scotoma is usually associated with a peripheral temporal cut in the field of the same or opposite eye. One may be forced to search most diligently for this second defect in order to differentiate a chiasmal from an optic nerve lesion.
2. In a total bitemporal hemianopsia, present for all stimuli up to 100 mm, it may be necessary to use a stimulus of 400 or 500 mm diameter, or even a small light, to demonstrate that the densest portion of the anoptic field is in the lower quadrant, thus indicating that the initial field loss was in this area and the probable direction of pressure on the chiasm was from above.
3. Sloping margins in a bitemporal defect usually indicate a progressive visual field change, whereas steep margins and uniform density are signs of a static lesion.
4. Occasionally a nerve fiber bundle type of scotoma is found in association with disease of the chiasm. Only careful examination of the vertical meridian will determine whether this defect crosses or stops at the midline and is truly hemianoptic.
5. When a temporal defect of hemianoptic shape is found in one field, whether scotomatous or nonscotomatous, the contralateral field should be searched most thoroughly for a similar defect.
6. In view of the extraordinary variation in the morphology of bitemporal hemianopsia, numerous errors and misinterpretations of these visual field defects are possible. Only through the most careful attention to the details of quantitative technique in perimetry can these errors be avoided. By these techniques, a confused and apparently atypical visual field defect can often be resolved into a diagnostic sign of utmost importance, localizing the lesion that produced it and even indicating its probable pathology.

TYPES OF VISUAL FIELD DEFECTS PRODUCED BY CHIASMAL LESIONS

The typical visual field defect, most often produced by pituitary adenoma, is bitemporal hemianopsia. Binasal, altitudinal, and homonymous hemianopsia are also seen in lesions of the chiasm.

Bitemporal hemianopsia

In its classic forms bitemporal hemianopsia may be of two types: scotomatous and nonscotomatous.

Scotomatous bitemporal hemianopsia. Hemianoptic scotomas occur infrequently in association with disease affecting the chiasm. Such defects may be explained by the "little chiasm within the chiasm," formed by macular fibers and described by Traquair. They are usually associated with a hemianoptic scotoma of the opposite field, or with a temporal peripheral defect in the same or opposite field, or both. Almost any combination of scotoma with peripheral depression is possible. The scotoma may be quadrantic or it may be hemianoptic. It may be uniformly dense or may have sloping edges. It may be isolated or may break through into the periphery. It may extend toward the blind spot or even engulf the blind spot. Its one constant characteristic is that it stops at the vertical meridian.

When the chiasm is flattened and tilted upward causing traction on the optic tracts, a bitemporal hemianoptic scotoma may result, signaling the presence of an intrinsic lesion within the third ventricle such as a cystic craniopharyngioma or a small and invasive metastatic tumor, or, as in Fig. 14-2, a pituitary apoplexy.

As might be expected, these defects are most readily detected in the internal isopters of the field. They may split or spare the macula, usually the former.

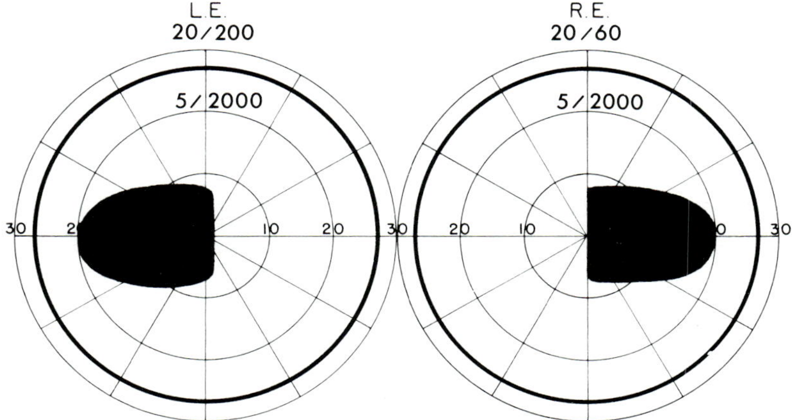

Fig. 14-2. Pituitary apoplexy. Hemorrhage into large pituitary tumor. Sudden onset of bitemporal hemianoptic scotomas with macular splitting and decreased central vision. Analysis of bilateral centrocecal scotomas revealed steep vertical hemianoptic borders characteristic of chiasmal involvement. Large hemorrhagic cyst evacuated with restoration of vision.

Bitemporal hemianoptic scotomas usually indicate a rapidly progressing lesion with the site of interference in the posterior chiasm (Fig. 14-3).

When the scotoma is quadrantic or when the upper field is implicated to a greater extent than the lower, the direction of pressure is from below. In this circumstance the progression of the scotoma is from the upper temporal quadrant, across the horizontal meridian, into the lower temporal field. At the same time it may expand outward slightly and may fuse or break through into a gradually progressing peripheral temporal defect.

Having reached the inferior temporal quadrant, the hemianoptic scotoma may remain relatively static for some time before beginning the next stage of progression into the lower nasal field and finally into the upper nasal quadrant or across the midline into the nasal field, with macular involvement and resulting loss of central vision. By this time there is usually some optic atrophy and general depression of the peripheral isopters of the field, especially in the upper temporal quadrant.

Progression of the bitemporal hemianoptic scotoma, then, is typically clockwise in the right eye and counterclockwise in the left eye.

The two visual fields may show symmetric or nearly symmetric defects, but more often the changes in one field are considerably in advance of the other. In some instances the asymmetry is extreme. When one field presents a temporal hemianoptic scotoma and the other shows a peripheral defect, the scotoma is designated a junction scotoma (Traquair) and indicates a lesion involving the anterior portion of the chiasm with the scotoma on the side of the lesion (see Fig. 7-33). The scotoma has the same characteristics as those resulting from optic nerve compression, but the temporal depression of the opposite field indicates involvement of the chiasm. This peripheral temporal loss is caused by compression of the fibers from the contra-

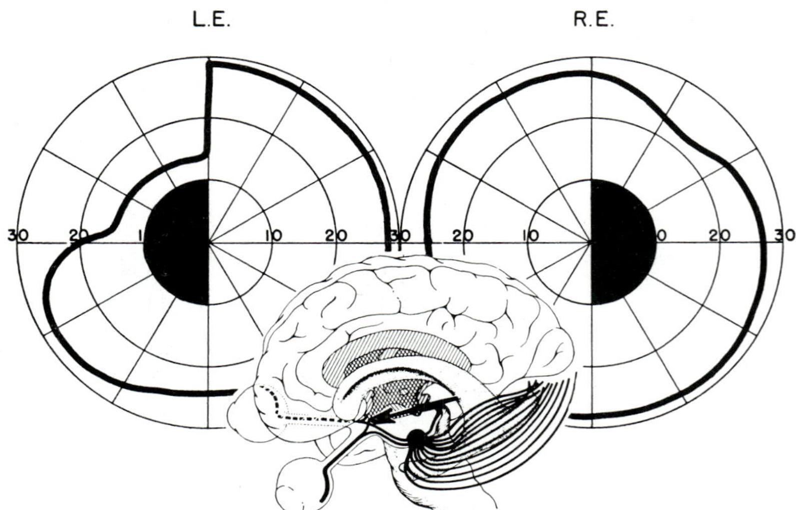

Fig. 14-3. Bitemporal hemianoptic scotomas with superior temporal peripheral defects in case of pituitary adenoma. Subjective visual disturbance was rather sudden in onset, although other signs and symptoms of endocrine imbalance had existed for at least 6 months.

lateral optic nerve as they loop into the ipsilateral nerve before passing backward into the body of the chiasm. The lesion is usually medial to the nerve, arising between the two optic nerves and pressing backward and laterally.

Nonscotomatous bitemporal hemianopsia. The nonscotomatous type of bitemporal hemianopsia is in every way like the scotomatous, except that the changes are largely in the peripheral isopters and no scotoma is present. Central visual acuity is good, and in the early stages the defect is usually detectable only with small stimuli in the area beyond 10 degrees.

In its typical form, resulting from median chiasmal pressure from below, the upper temporal quadrants of the field are symmetrically depressed and the defects slowly progress into the lower temporal quadrants and finally cross the vertical meridian into the lower nasal field and thence into the upper nasal quadrant. As in the scotomatous type, great variation may occur and also marked asymmetry in the two fields.

The typical progression of a bitemporal hemianopsia may be studied in two ways: (1) by periodic examination of the visual field using the same test object and illumination, which usually requires many months or even years; (2) by quantitative analysis of an advanced visual defect—smaller test objects will show late changes in the field with earlier loss being demonstrated by progressively increasing stimuli (Fig. 14-4).

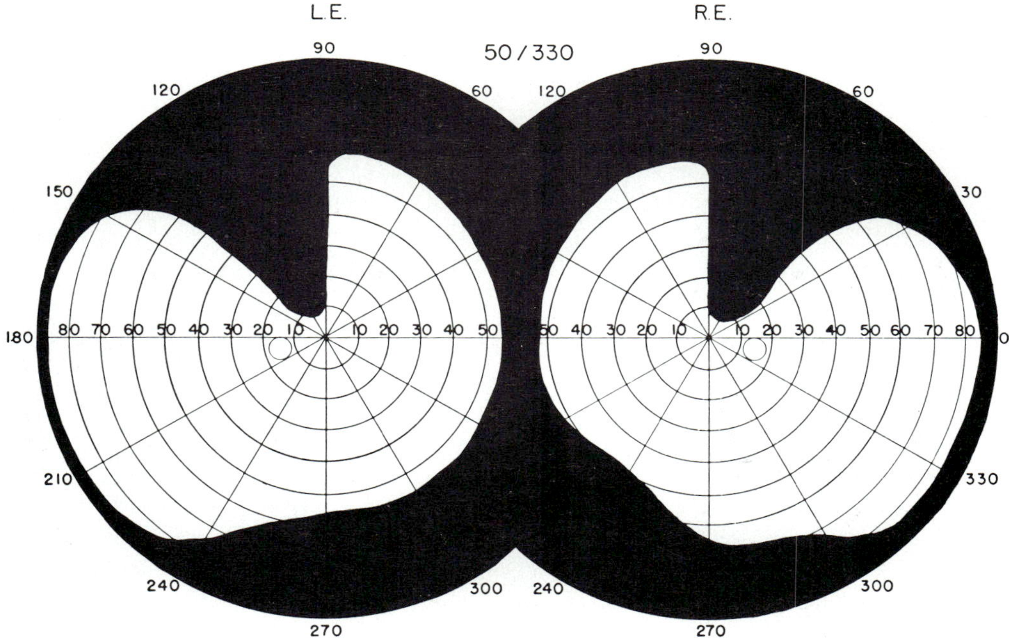

Fig. 14-4. A, Progress in development of bitemporal hemianopsia from pituitary adenoma. This was demonstrated by visual fields taken on same day using multiple stimuli subtending different visual angles (multiple isopter technique of quantitative perimetry). Field for the 50/330 isopter shows only small superior bitemporal sector-type defect. (See also **B** to **E.**) Same mode of progression may be demonstrated by visual field examinations at regular intervals over period of time.

Continued.

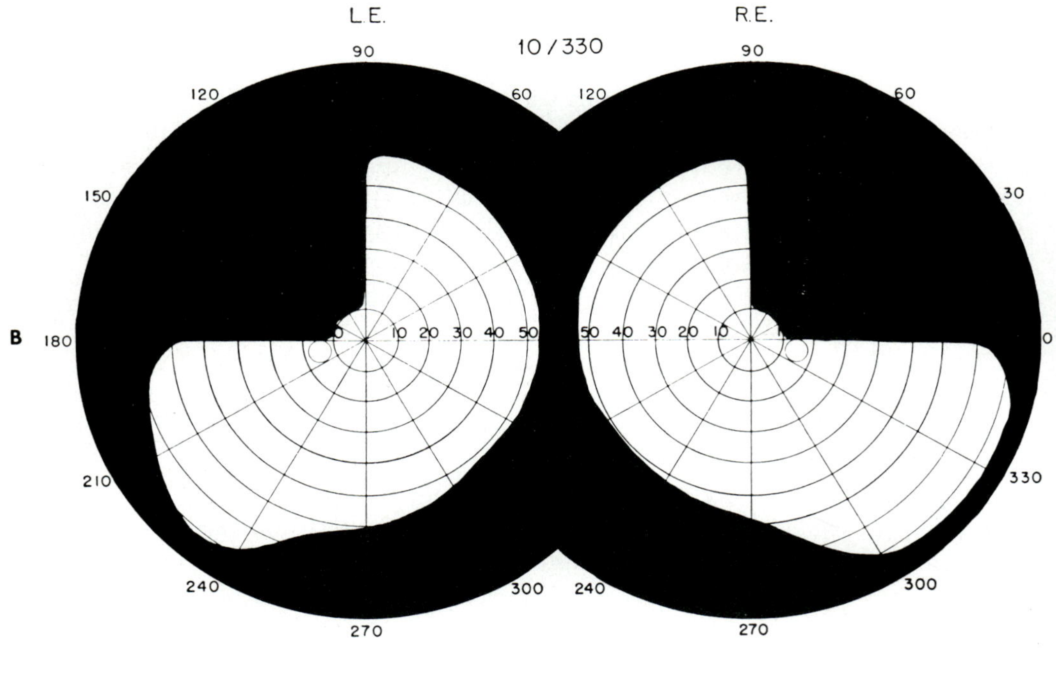

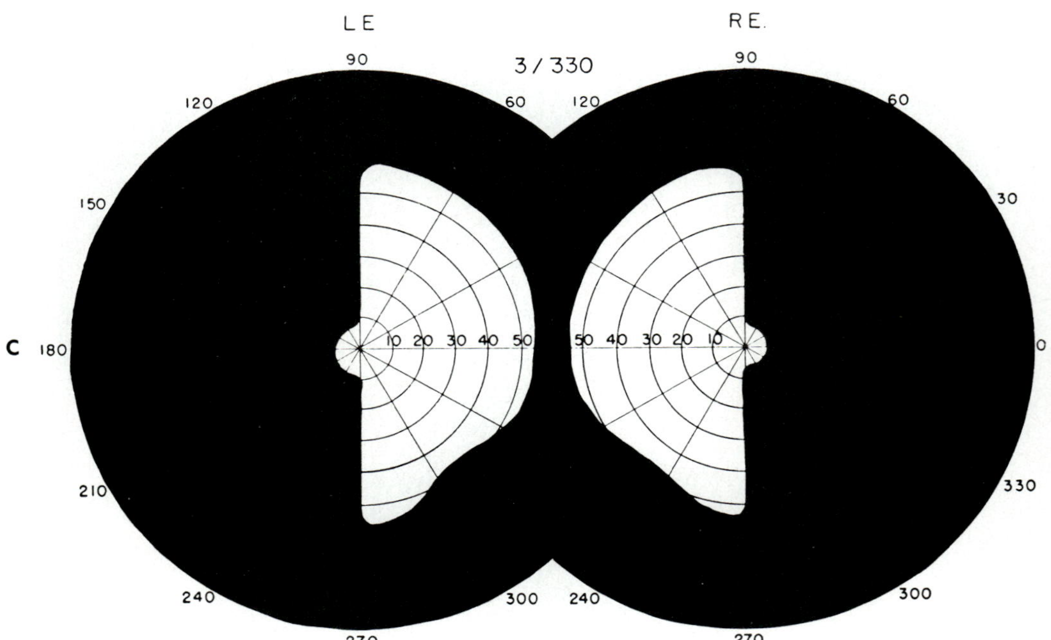

Fig. 14-4, cont'd. B, Field for 10/330 isopter shows superior bitemporal quadrantanopsia. **C,** Field for 3/330 isopter shows total bitemporal hemianopsia.

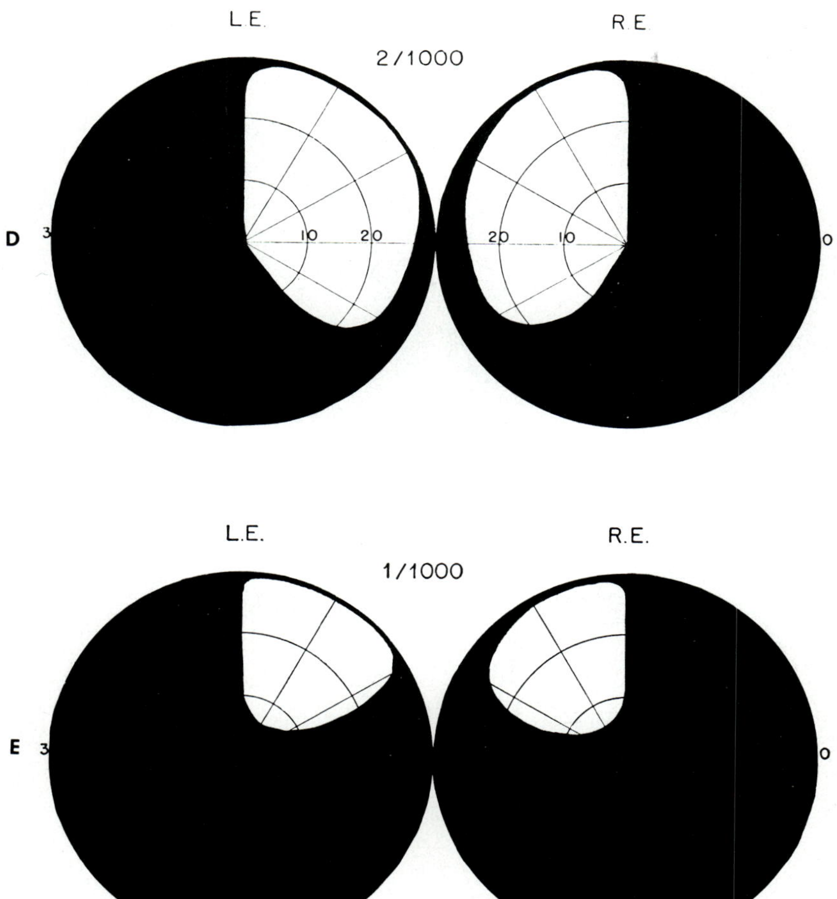

Fig. 14-4, cont'd. D, Field for 2/1000 isopter shows early involvement of both inferior nasal fields. **E,** Field for 1/1000 isopter shows only remnant of two superior nasal fields. Mode of progression of visual field defect is well demonstrated by use of diminishing stimuli in visual field examination.

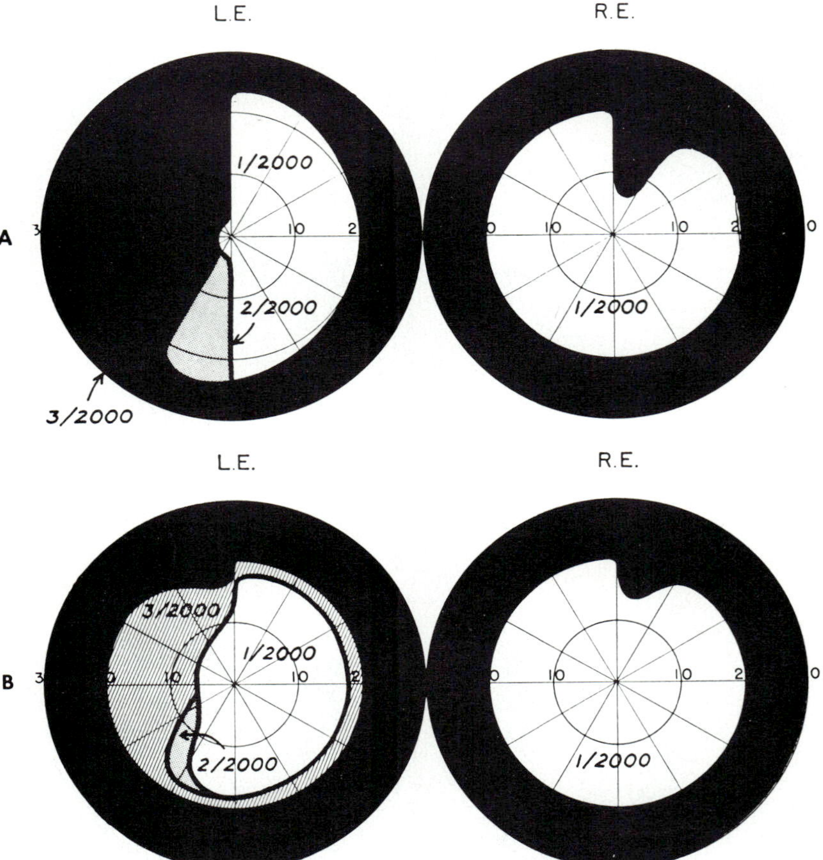

Fig. 14-5. A, Preoperative visual field in typical case of chromophobic adenoma of pituitary. Left field shows loss of most of temporal field in 3/2000 isopter, whereas right field shows minimal defect for 1/2000 stimulus. **B,** Postoperative visual field defect 3 weeks after removal of chromophobic adenoma that produced field defect in **A.** The 3/2000 isopter is now almost normal in left eye, and even 1/2000 isopter shows marked improvement. Right field has returned to almost normal.

Resolution of the visual field defect, after surgical removal of the tumor, is in the opposite direction from the field loss. When nerve fiber atrophy is incomplete, the return of function is first noted in the lower nasal field, then in the lower temporal quadrant, and finally in the superior temporal field. Generally, if the temporal field loss is absolute, restoration of the visual field does not occur or, at best, is incomplete. In these patients the defect becomes static with steep margins and uniform density (Fig. 14-5).

The mere fact that there is such wide variation in visual field morphology in lesions of the chiasm makes more accurate localization of the lesion possible. Thus a tumor that is compressing the chiasm from the right anterosuperior direction is likely to produce quite a different type of bitemporal hemianopsia from what a tumor pressing upward in the midline would produce.

The ability to localize the site of pressure with some accuracy in the anterior, middle, and posterior portions of the chiasm, as well as laterally and to some extent obliquely, may make possible a reasonably intelligent estimate of the pathologic process producing the pressure. This is so because certain types of lesion are known to arise from certain structures adjacent to the chiasm, and when pressure is exerted from the direction of these structures they and their more common pathologic conditions become suspect.

Mention should be made here of theories of the pathogenesis of field defects in lesions of the chiasm. Those theories that hypothecate the action of toxins or that attribute the visual field changes to traction or even to direct pressure on the nerve fibers have little to recommend them. It is incomprehensible that blunt pressure of a tumor impinging on the nerve fibers could produce the sharp-margined vertical borders so often found in bitemporal hemianopsia.

It has been shown that, in other portions of the nervous system, the pressure that produces motor or sensory loss does so not by direct compression of the nerve fibers but by vascular compression, giving rise to venous stasis or arterial ischemia. The nerve fibers are secondarily affected by edema and anoxia caused by disturbance in their blood supply. With this in mind, one can easily see that too precise localization of pressure is not desirable. What is being localized is not a point of pressure on the nerve fibers but the point at which its blood supply has been interrupted. Fortunately, these areas are rarely far removed from each other and clinical localization of the lesion may be accomplished in most instances almost as though the nerve fiber dysfunction were the result of direct compression.

Actual invasion of the chiasm, optic nerves, or optic tracts may take place with certain tumors. Irregular and bizarre visual field defects result from such infiltration, which may occur in craniopharyngioma or in certain gliomas and metastatic tumors of the chiasm.

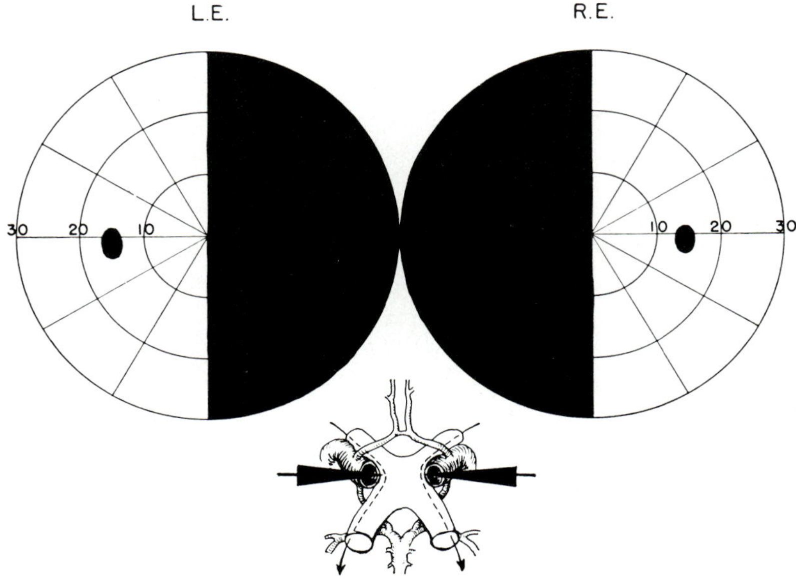

Fig. 14-6. Binasal hemianopsia. Note direction of pressure lateral to chiasm. This may be produced by calcified and sclerotic internal carotid arteries or by aneurysm of one internal carotid artery with shift of chiasm against normal opposite carotid artery. (See also Plate 7.)

Binasal hemianopsia

Binasal hemianopsia implies two lesions compressing the chiasm from each side, and such situations are obviously rare (Fig. 14-6). It must be remembered, however, that certain diseases characteristically involve both optic nerves and may produce visual defects that are predominantly binasal. Among these are (1) glaucoma, (2) tabetic optic atrophy, and (3) multiple sclerosis with degenerative plaques in both optic nerves or in the chiasm. Other conditions that produce binasal hemianopsia, either symmetric or irregular, and (4) aneurysm of one internal carotid artery with displacement of the chiasm against the normal artery on the opposite side (Figs. 14-7 to 14-9), (5) opticochiasmatic arachnoiditis (Fig. 14-10), (6) infratentorial tumors with ventricular dilatation and hydrostatic compression of the chiasm (always accompanied by papilledema), (7) intraventricular tumors, especially those involving the third ventricle, and (8) meningiomas, especially those arising from the lesser wing of the sphenoid bone.

O'Connell and Du Boulay report three patients with binasal lower field defects produced by tumor displacement of the optic nerves against the anterior cerebral or internal carotid arteries. Two tumors were meningiomas and the third was a chromophobe adenoma.

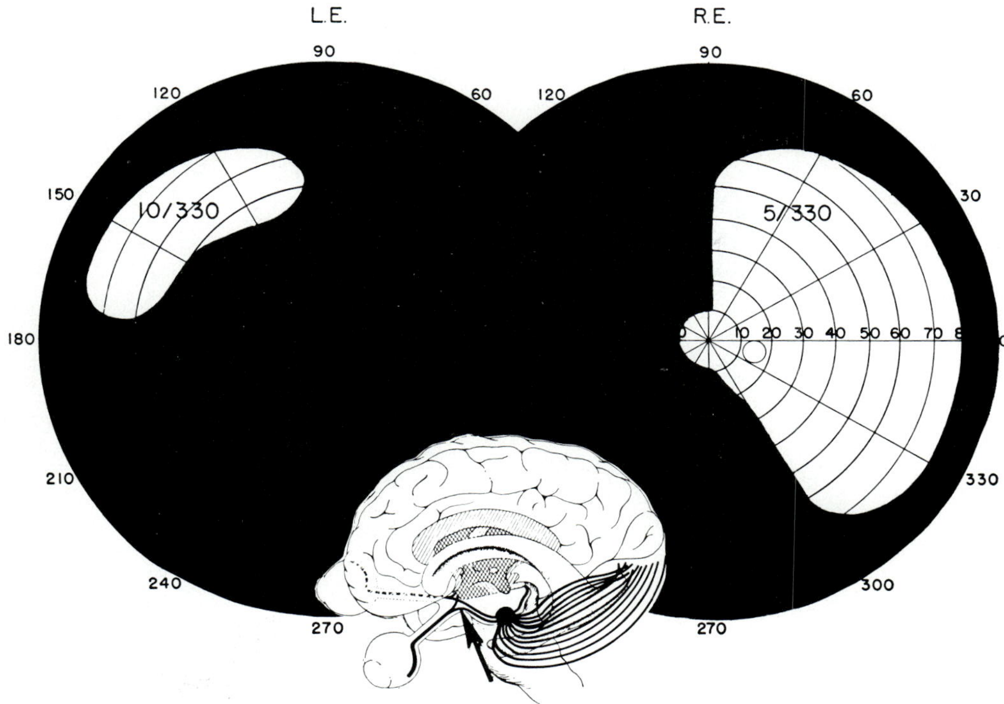

Fig. 14-7. Binasal hemianopsia produced by large aneurysm of left internal carotid artery. Left eye was blind for 1 year before visual field defect was noted in roght eye. Aneurysm was demonstrated by arteriography, and subsequent operation revealed shift of chiasm to right side against normal right internal carotid to produce right nasal field loss. Note site and direction of pressure lateral to chiasm.

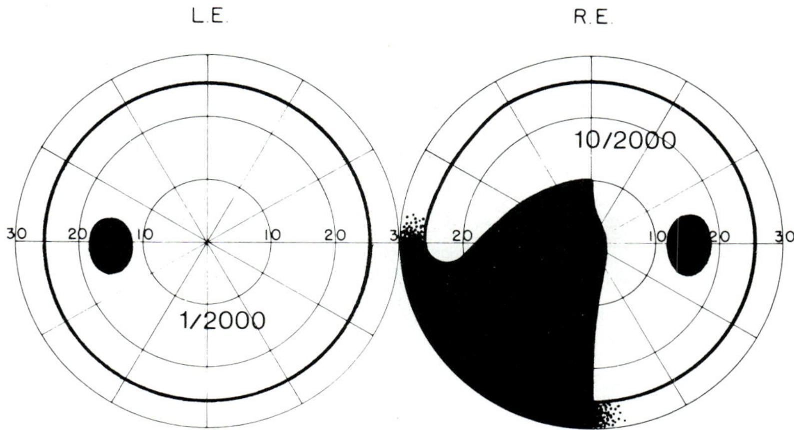

Fig. 14-8. Inferior nasal quadrant defect produced by large aneurysm of right internal carotid artery. Visual loss was gradual. Arteriogram confirmed diagnosis of aneurysm lateral to chiasm. Artery gradually occluded, with return of visual field to normal.

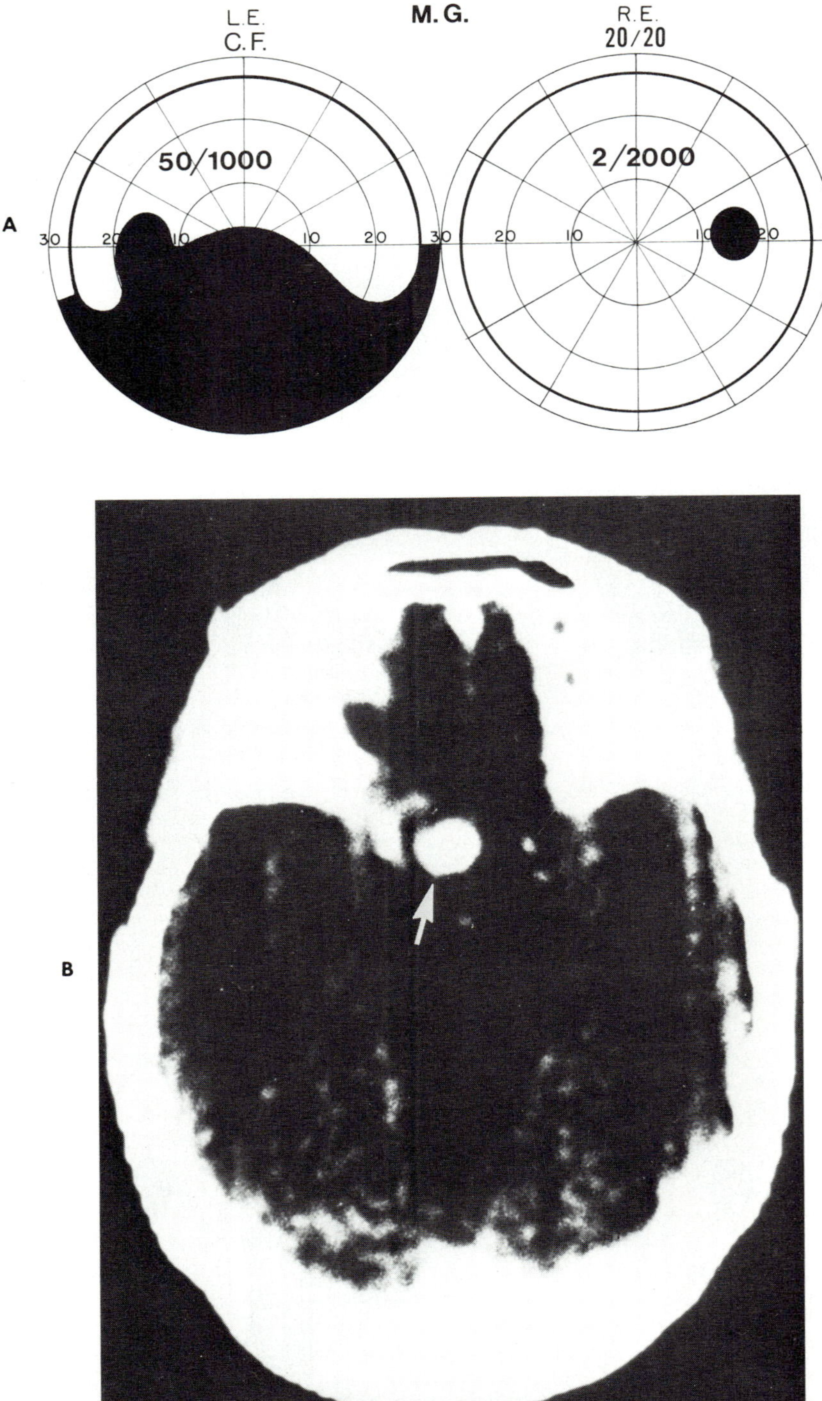

Fig. 14-9. A, Steep-margined left inferior altitudinal hemianopsia resulting from chiasmal pressure by a giant supraclinoid left internal carotid aneurysm. Complaint of severe headache and rapid loss of vision. **B,** Computerized tomography of lesion in **A** shows giant aneurysm *(arrow)* next to clinoid and slightly to left. Findings confirmed by cerebral angiography.

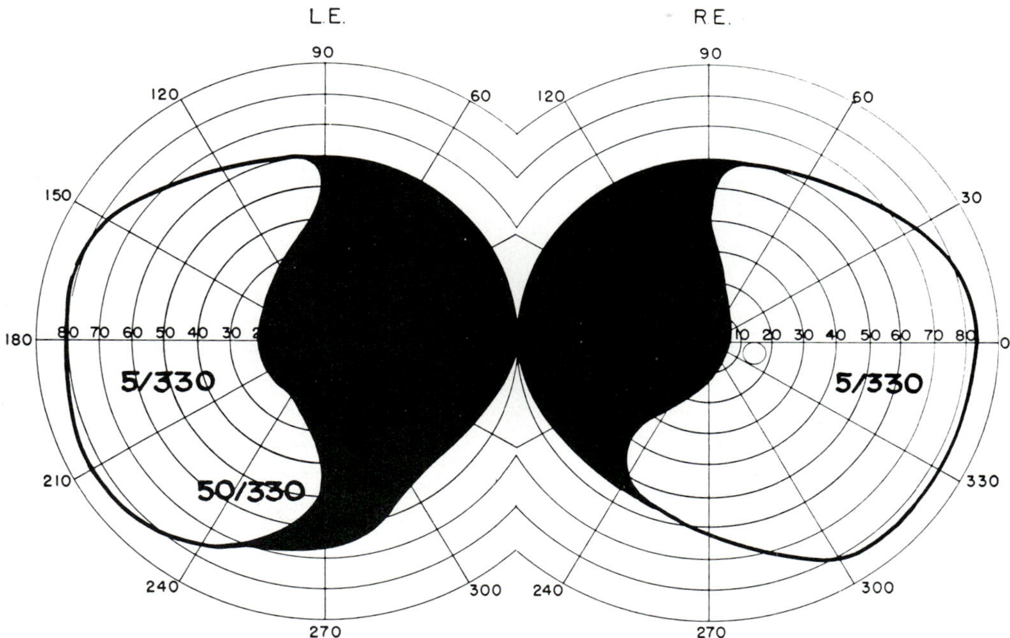

Fig. 14-10. Binasal hemianopsia resulting from chiasmal adhesions in case of opticochiasmatic arachnoiditis.

Altitudinal hemianopsia

Altitudinal hemianopsia may rarely occur as the result of a lesion of the chiasm. This visual field defect, which involves both upper and both lower quadrants with the hemianoptic border of the field on the horizontal line, has been dealt with elsewhere. Its etiology is often obscure, but it more often results from inflammatory or vascular lesions than from tumors.

Homonymous hemianopsia

Homonymous hemianopsia, which again may be scotomatous or nonscotomatous, is encountered in chiasmal affections when the lesion is in the posterior portion or angle and involves the beginning of one or both optic tracts (Plate 7 and Fig. 14-11).

If the lesion compresses the inner side of the tract, it produces a temporal field loss in the opposite field and a nasal field loss on the side of the lesion (Fig. 14-12). If compression is from the lateral side, the nasal field loss occurs first on the side of the lesion and is later followed by loss of both temporal fields, so that there is blindness on the side of the lesion, with temporal hemianoptic defect in the contralateral field (Fig. 14-13).

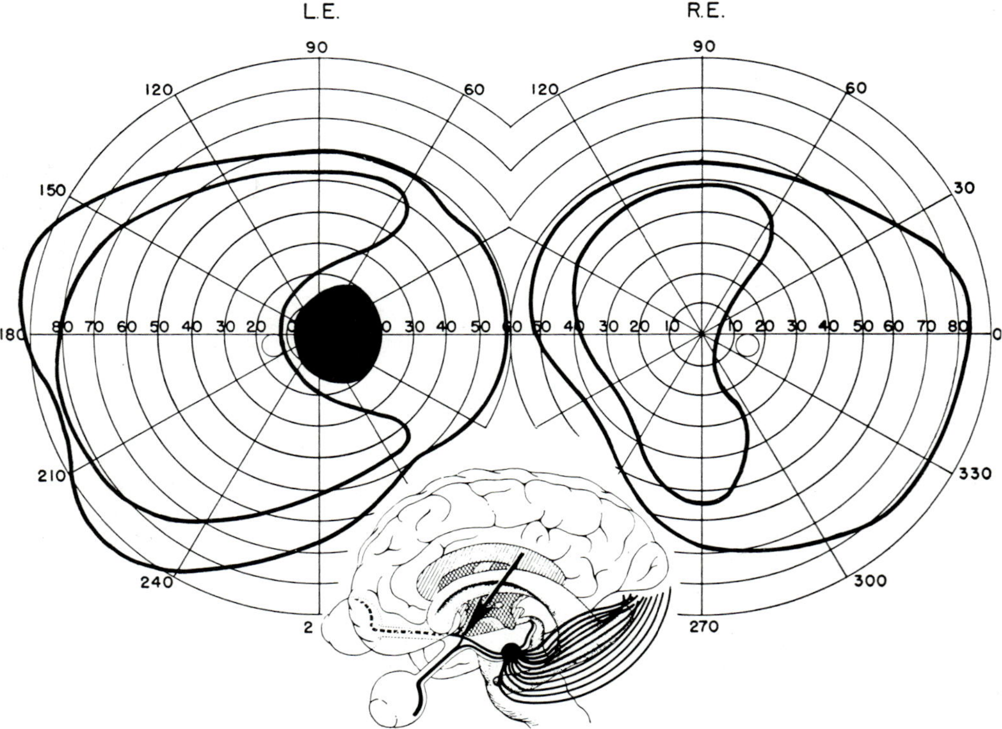

Fig. 14-11. Nasal scotoma and homonymous hemianopsia from tumor of third ventricle. Note site and direction of pressure in posterior chiasmal angle.

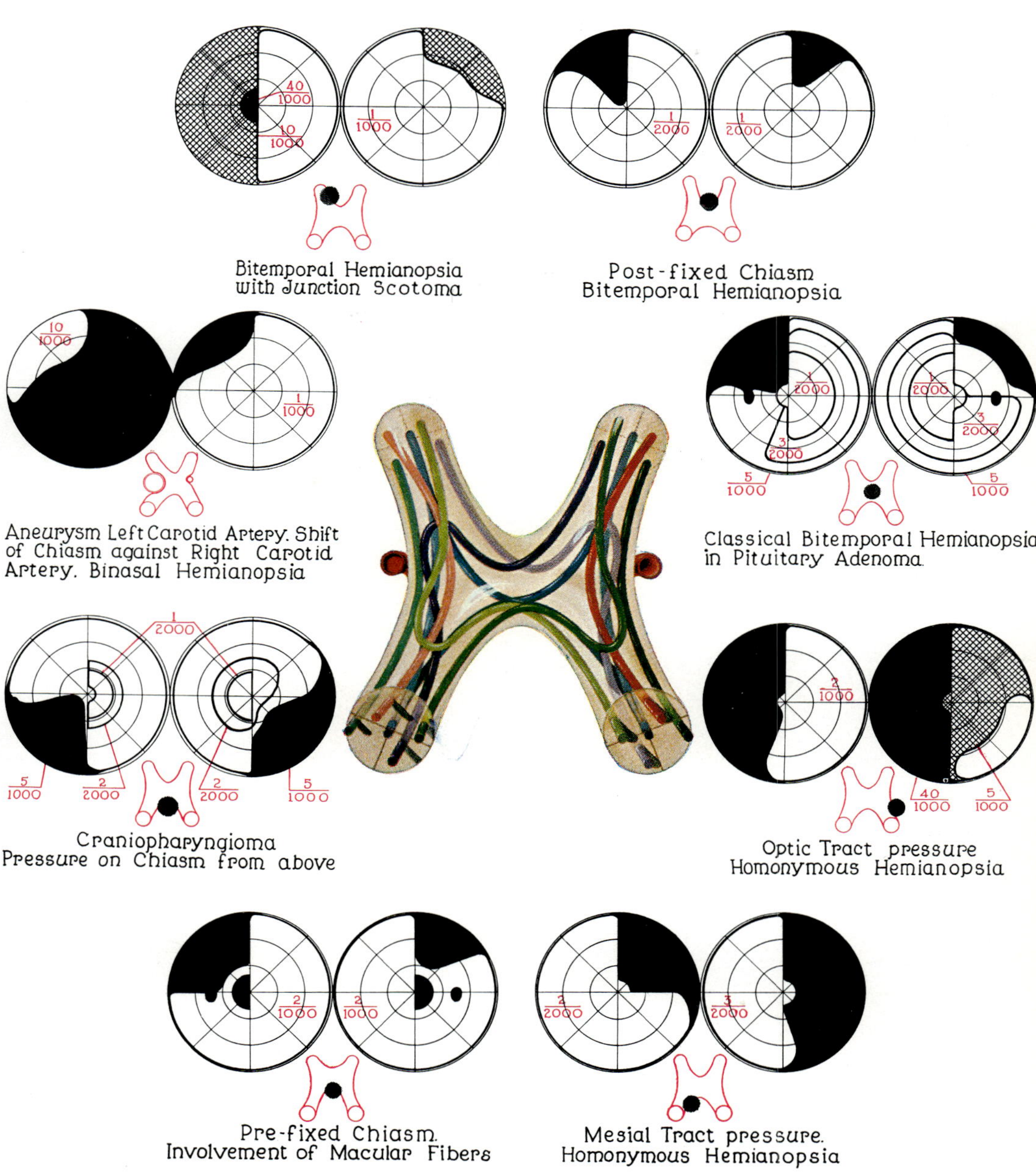

Plate 7. Perimetry of chiasmal lesions.

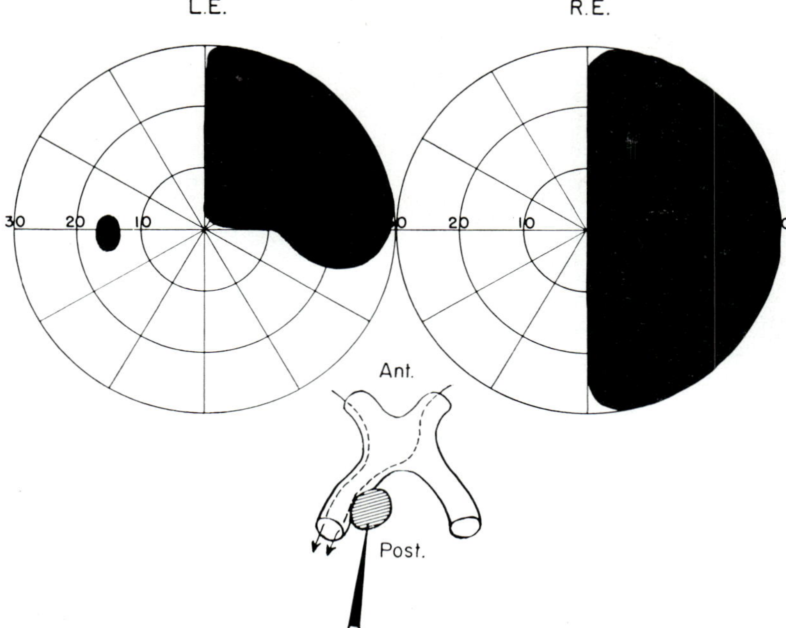

Fig. 14-12. Homonymous hemianopsia produced by pressure mesial to left optic tract in posterior chiasmal angle. Major field loss is contralateral to lesion.

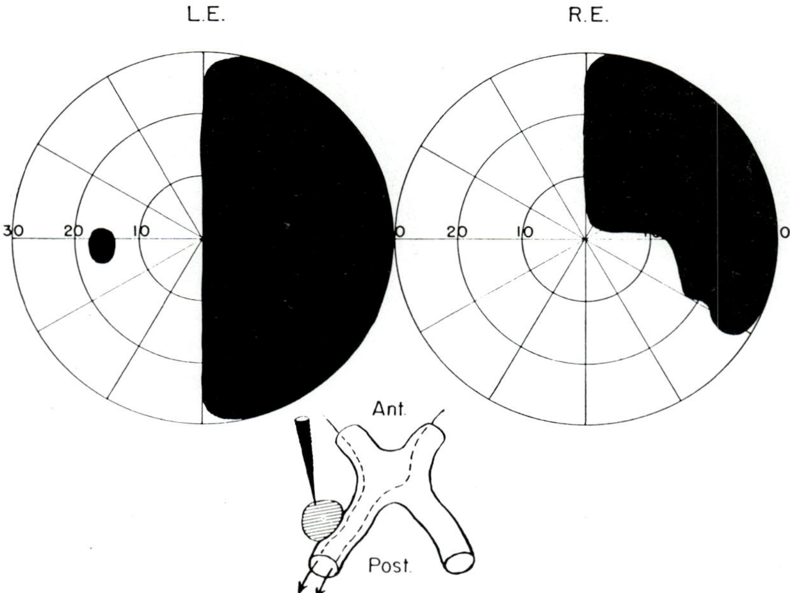

Fig. 14-13. Homonymous hemianopsia produced by pressure lateral to left optic tract at chiamsal junction. Major field loss is on side of lesion.

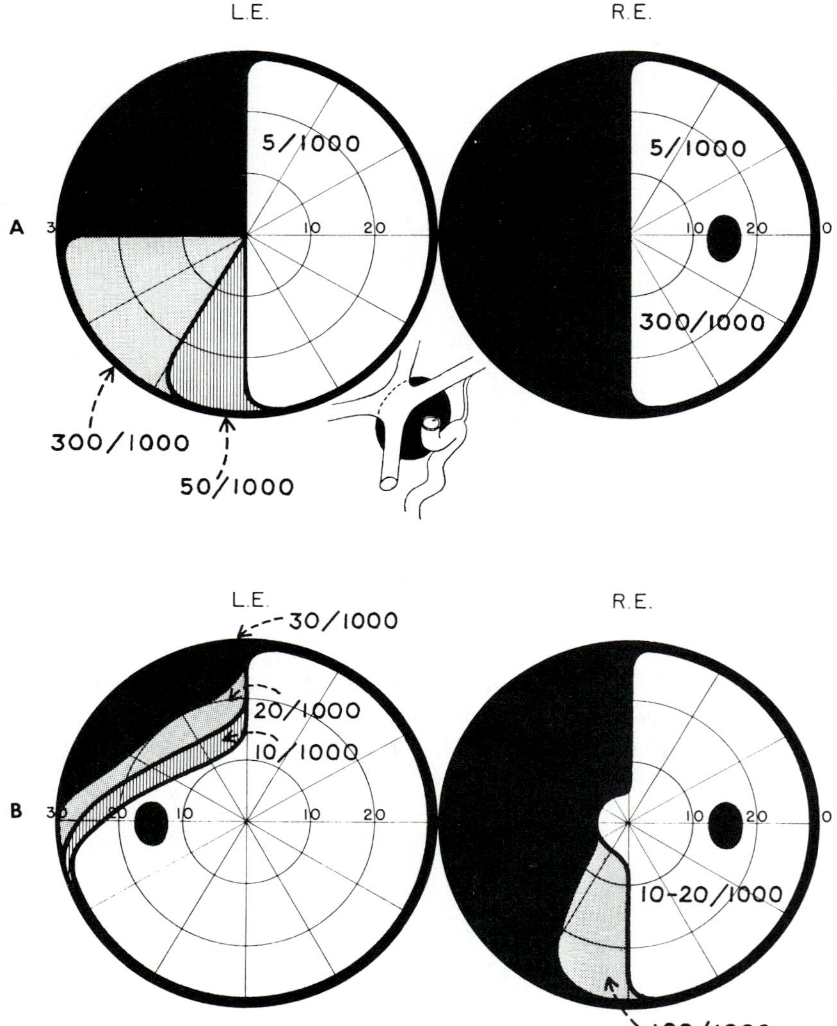

Fig. 14-14. A, Typical incongruous homonymous hemianopsia resulting from pressure on right optic tract from large chromophobic adenoma of pituitary. Tumor was found protruding between two optic nerves as well as laterally between right optic tract and carotid artery. **B,** Visual field 16 days after surgical removal of pituitary tumor causing defect in **A.** Rapid recovery, sloping margins, and increased area of macular sparing all indicate lack of permanent nerve fiber damage.

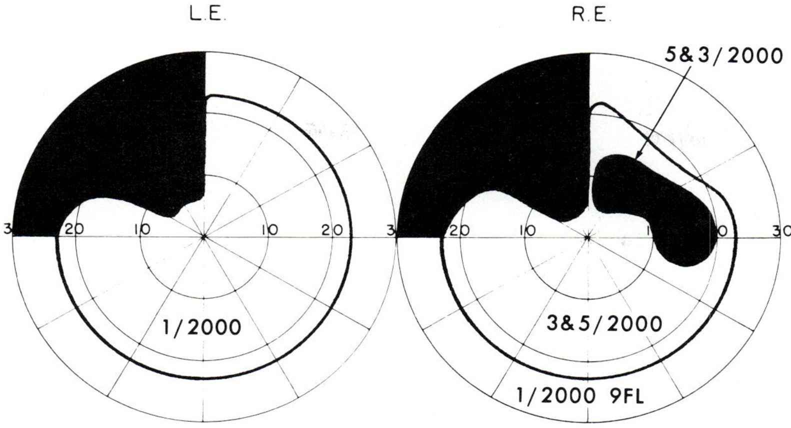

Fig. 14-15. Left upper homonymous quadrantanopsia with right superior arcuate scotoma in patient with recurrence of chromophobic adenoma of pituitary. Ten years previously patient had typical superior bitemporal quadrantanopsia. Fields returned to normal after surgical removal of tumor. Recurrent tumor involved right optic tract, causing homonymous quadrantanopsia. This defect improved with radiation therapy.

If, in cases of medial tract pressure, there is simultaneous involvement of the body of the chiasm, there will be a loss of temporal as well as nasal field on the side of the lesion. It is therefore not always possible to localize the lesion medially or laterally to the tract since both may give rise to blindness on the side of the lesion with temporal loss in the opposite field.

Although these homonymous hemianopsias should rightfully be considered in the discussion of the postchiasmal pathway, they are frequently found in affections of the chiasmal area and rarely in diseases of the posterior portion of the optic tracts (Plate 7).

INTERPRETATION OF VISUAL FIELD DEFECTS ASSOCIATED WITH AFFECTIONS OF CHIASM

The clinical importance of careful examination and interpretation of the visual fields appears obvious from the preceding discussion. Perimetry may be of value as a supplemental method of examination to support the findings of endocrinologic, neurologic, and radiologic study; or it may be the only method that reveals disease in the area of the chiasm. Not infrequently the neurosurgeon must rely on the results of perimetry for information as to diagnosis, localization, prognosis, and the effects of surgery or radiation therapy.

Having considered the general characteristics of the visual fields in lesions of the chiasm, we should now study the changes associated with more specific localization and pathology.

The clinician centers interest not only on the sites of fiber interruption but also on the probable pathology of the lesion producing the dysfunction. Because they

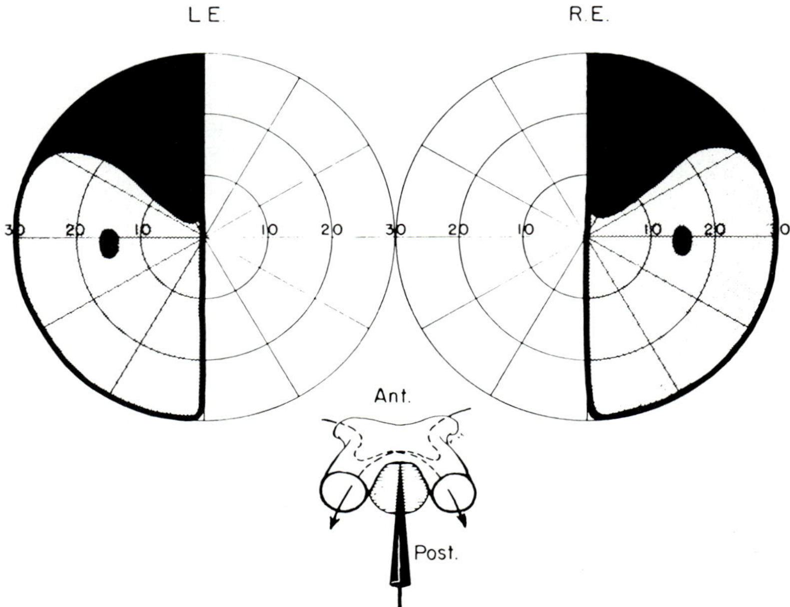

Fig. 14-16. Bitemporal hemianopsia produced by pressure from directly beneath chiasm in midline. This is typical visual field defect associated with chromophobic adenoma of pituitary. Field defect begins in superior temporal quadrants and progresses downward.

are closely interrelated, the localization, direction of pressure, and probable pathology of these specific lesions are discussed as a group.

Infrachiasmatic lesions

Infrachiasmatic lesions comprise the pituitary adenomas, which typically exert their pressure in the midline from below (Fig. 14-16). They may vary in their exact sites of nerve fiber compression, depending on whether the chiasm is prefixed (with short optic nerves), in the middle position, or postfixed (with long optic nerves). (See Fig. 4-6.)

Their classic visual field defect is a symmetric bitemporal hemianopsia of either the scotomatous or the nonscotomatous variety. When the defect is scotomatous, either a rapidly growing tumor is indicated, or a prefixed chiasm with pressure on the posterior angle, or both.

I have seen a patient with a slowly progressing bitemporal upper quadrant field defect who suddenly developed bitemporal hemianoptic scotomas. Surgical exploration revealed a cystic tumor filled with hemorrhage that had broken out of the sella turcica in the posterior chiasmal angle (see Fig. 14-2).

The three types of pituitary adenoma are chromophobic, acidophilic, and basophilic.

Chromophobic adenomas. Chromophobic adenomas are by far the most frequent

A

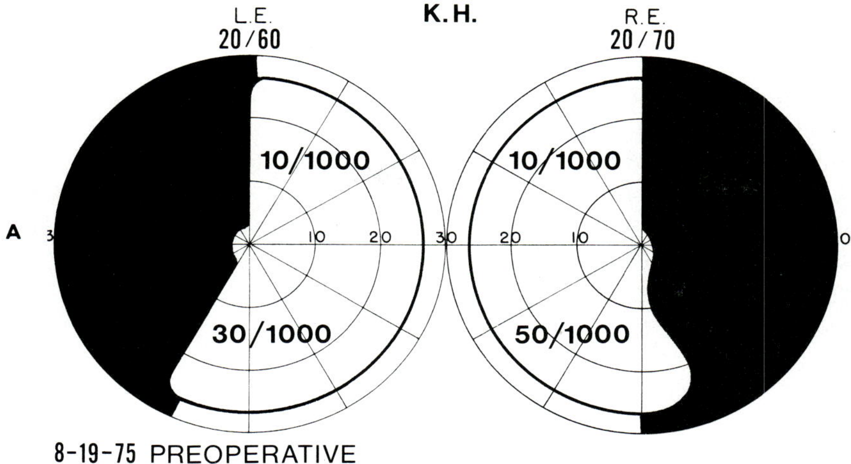

B

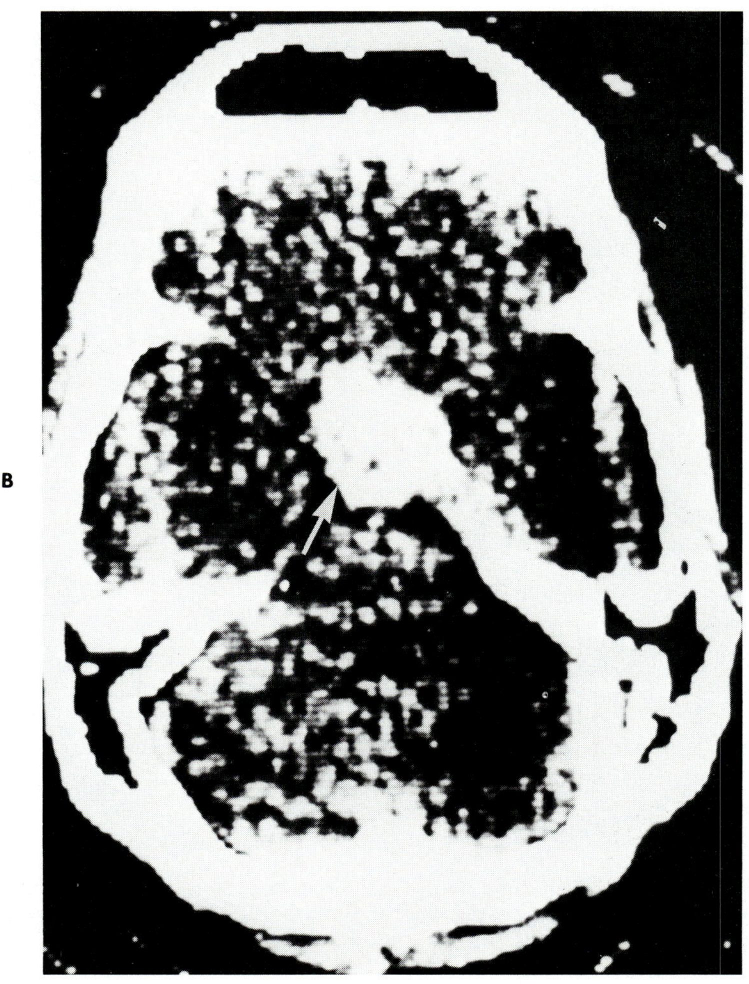

Fig. 14-17. A, Chromophobic adenoma of pituitary. Preoperative field shows dense bitemporal hemianopsia with minimal macular sparing. Roentgenograms showed enlarged and eroded sella turcica. **B,** CAT scan shows large tumor within sella turcica *(white arrow).* Marked improvement of vision and visual field defects followed surgical removal of tumor followed by x-ray therapy.

infrachiasmatic tumors (about 75%). They are characterized by enlargement of the sella turcica, erosion of the clinoids, depression of libido and sexual function, alterations in skin and hair, adiposity, and midline chiasmal compression. Their growth is slow and inexorable, and the visual defects begin in the upper temporal quadrants and usually progress slowly. The multiple pattern method of visual field examination seems to be unusually sensitive in its ability to detect the early bitemporal notching caused by chromophobic adenoma (Figs. 14-17 and 14-18, *A*).

Acidophilic adenomas. Acidophilic adenomas account for gigantism in the child and acromegaly in the adult. They produce extreme enlargement and erosion in

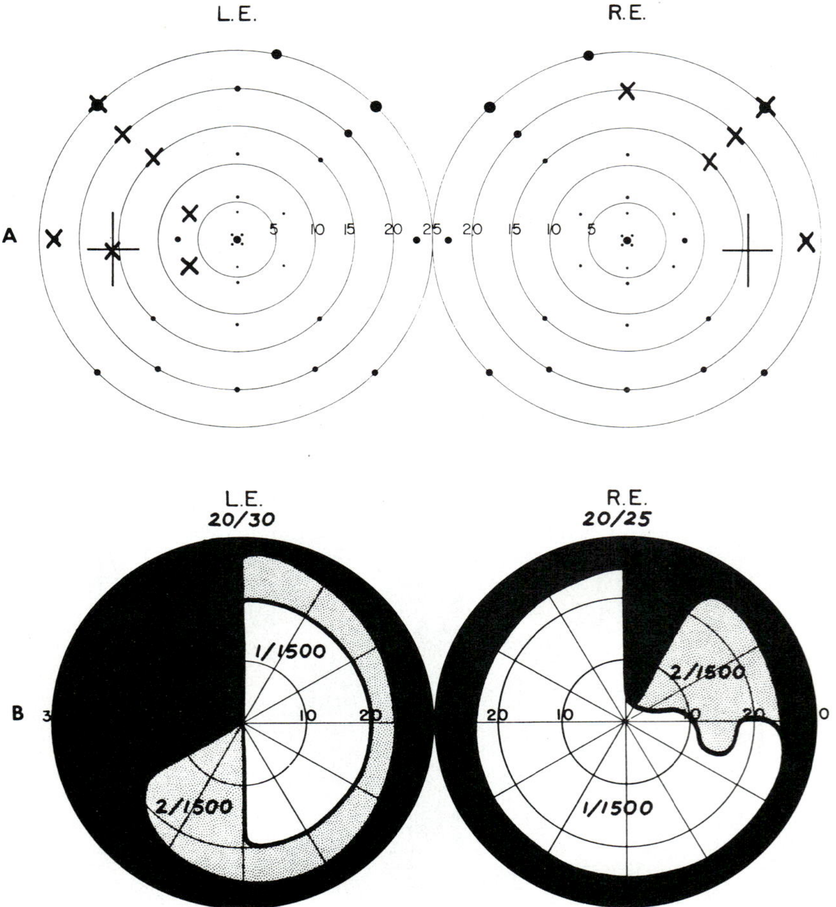

Fig. 14-18. A, Bitemporal upper quadrant defect of chiasmal pressure as shown by multiple pattern method of examination. **B,** Early bitemporal hemianopsia revealed with small test objects in case of chromophobic adenoma of pituitary.

the sella turcica, and the tumor often breaks out of the sella turcica below and does not involve the chiasm until very late. When it does so, the visual field defects are typical of midline compression from below.

Basophilic adenoma. Basophilic adenoma is a rare form of pituitary tumor that gives rise to adiposity, hypertrichosis, acrocyanosis, amenorrhea, hyperglycemia, and arterial hypertension. Its visual field changes are rare but, when present, are the same as in the more common chromophobic type. The sella turcica is usually normal in size.

These tumors characteristically grow slowly; they arise beneath the chiasm and elevate and stretch this body over their superior surface. They may attain enormous size, and the chiasm may be slowly stretched until it is little more than a thin ribbon spread across the top of the tumor.

As the chiasm is pushed upward, its anterior portion with the two optic nerves may be squeezed between the tumor and the two anterior cerebral arteries, giving rise to visible notching of the nerves on their upper surface and complicating the visual field changes by producing simultaneous upward pressure on the body of the chiasm and downward pressure on the optic nerves (Figs. 14-19 and 14-20).

Rovit and Duane have pointed out that diagnosis of Cushing's disease should be restricted to instances where the endocrinopathy is associated with a proved basophilic pituitary adenoma. In Cushing's syndrome the endocrinopathy is present but the pituitary neoplasm is absent or at least not clinically apparent.

Pituitary tumors are demonstrated in only about 10% of patients with Cushing's syndrome, but, when present, they may cause gross distortion of the chiasm and consequent dense visual field defects. Because the ACTH-producing cells of the anterior hypophysis are being driven by excess corticotropin-releasing factor, the pituitary tumors that develop with Cushing's syndrome display an exaggerated

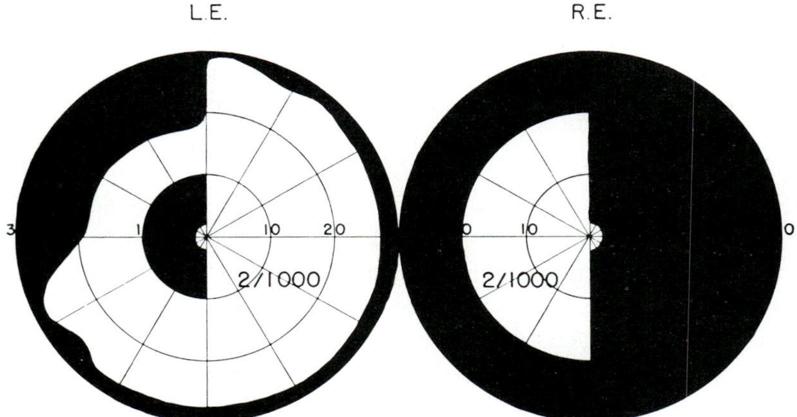

Fig. 14-19. Bitemporal hemianopsia and hemianoptic scotoma produced by compression of chiasm between pituitary adenoma and overlying anterior cerebral arteries. Grooving of nerve was demonstrated at surgical removal of tumor.

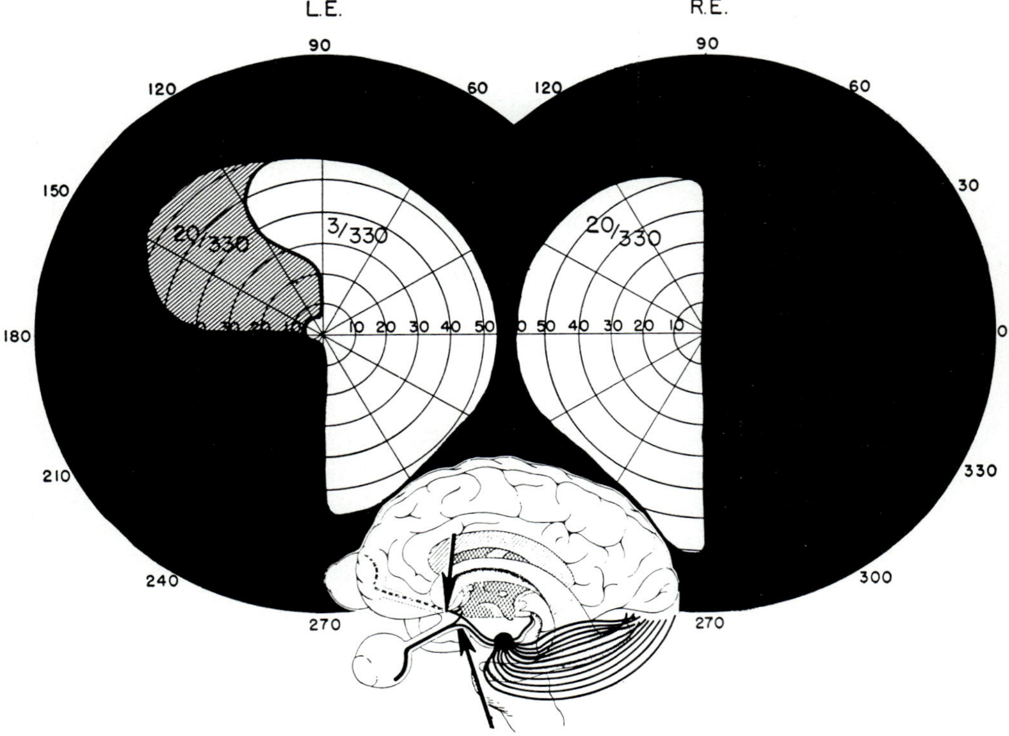

Fig. 14-20. Asymmetric bitemporal hemianopsia resulting from pressure on chiasm from beneath and on right with tilting of chiasm up and to left against overlying left anterior cerebral artery. Note macular splitting in right field and interior quadrant depression in left field. Note also simultaneous superior and inferior compression of chiasm as illustrated in anatomic sketch.

growth potential with a high incidence of ocular muscle palsies and pituitary apoplexy along with bilateral cavernous sinus compression and very rapid field loss. The tumors in Cushing's syndrome are usually composed of ACTH-secreting chromophobic cells rather than basophilic cells as originally described in Cushing's disease.

Suprachiasmatic lesions

A variety of lesions attack the chiasm from above. Their salient feature as regards the visual field is production of bitemporal hemianopsia, usually beginning in the inferior temporal quadrants and unaccompanied by signs of pituitary dysfunction or radiographic evidence of erosion of the sella turcica (Fig. 14-21).

The visual field changes show great variation, and some idea of the pathologic nature of the lesion and its direction of growth or pressure may be gained by analysis of these variations.

Suprachiasmatic lesions may be conveniently divided into two main groups: (1) those that impinge on the chiasm from the anterosuperior direction (Fig. 14-22) and (2) those that attack the chiasm from the posterosuperior direction (Figs. 14-23 and 14-24).

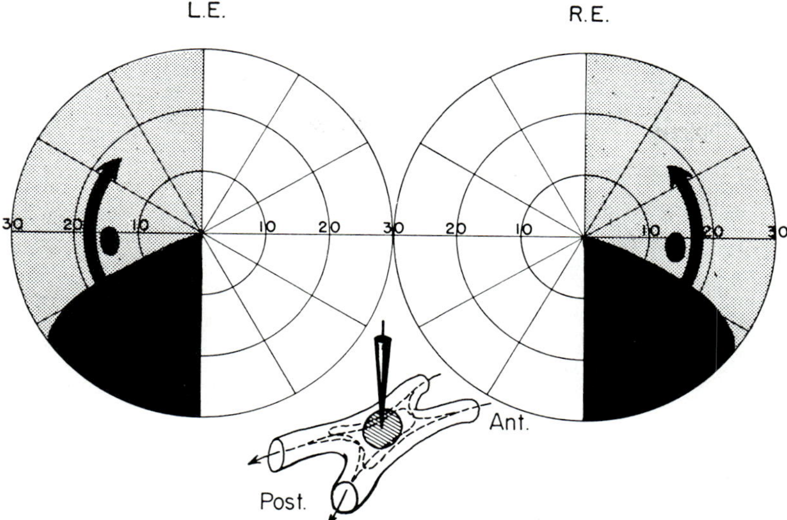

Fig. 14-21. Pressure from above downward on center of chiasm producing bitemporal hemianopsia with initial loss in inferior temporal quadrants, later expanding upward.

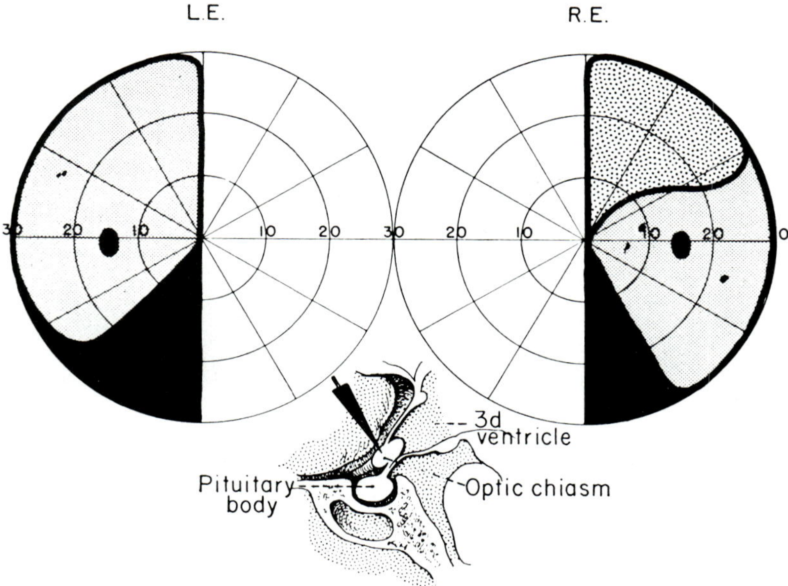

Fig. 14-22. Inferior bitemporal hemianopsia resulting from pressure on chiasm from above and in front. Direction and site of pressure are shown in sagittal section.

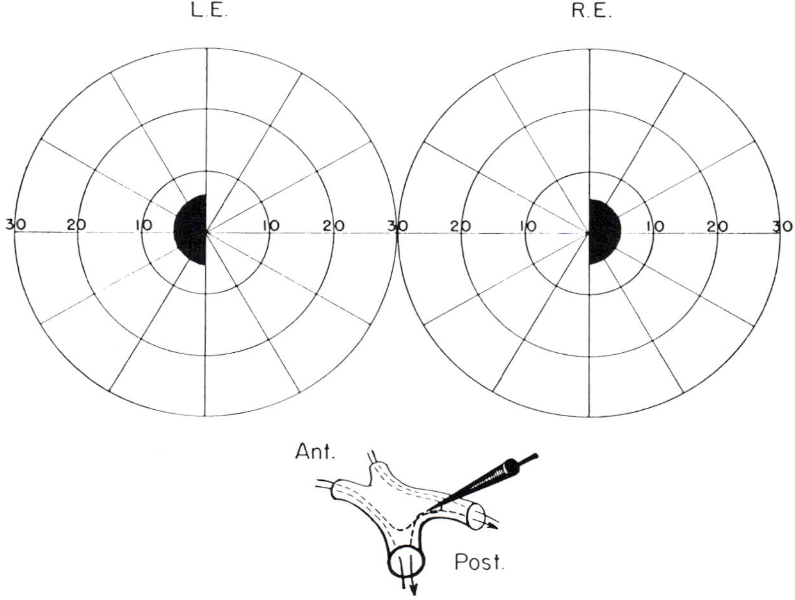

Fig. 14-23. Bitemporal hemianoptic scotomas resulting from pressure on decussating macular fibers from posterior and above. Scotomas are rarely as symmetric as shown.

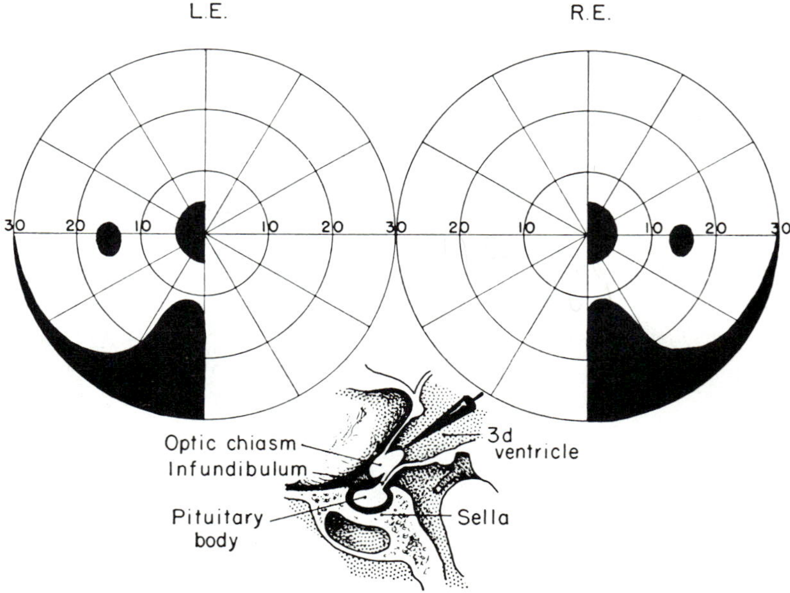

Fig. 14-24. Inferior bitemporal quadrantanopsia and bitemporal hemianoptic scotomas resulting from pressure on chiasm from region of third ventricle. Direction of pressure from above and behind is illustrated in sagittal section.

Anterosuperior aspect

The most frequent and important tumors affecting the anterosuperior aspect of the chiasm are the meningiomas. They arise from the olfactory groove, the tuberculum sellae, or the lesser wing of the sphenoid bone. Gliomas and meningiomas of the frontal lobe also compress the chiasm from above in its anterior portion. Small meningiomas may arise from the intracranial lip of the optic foramen and give rise to unilateral optic nerve compression and bizarre visual field defects (see Fig. 13-35). Pressure may be directed to the nerve from above, below, or laterally.

Meningiomas often give radiographic evidence of their presence by calcification within the tumor, bone changes, ventricular displacement, characteristic angiograms, fractional pneumoencephalograms, and computer-assisted tomography. Other symptoms and indications that may assist in localization are neighborhood signs with involvement of the third, fourth, fifth, and sixth cranial nerves and unilateral exophthalmos.

Another rather frequent pathologic process that may produce visual field changes indicative of anterosuperior chiasmal pressure is aneurysm of the anterior cerebral arteries or the anterior communicating artery.

Olfactory groove meningiomas. Olfactory groove meningiomas are relatively common. They arise in the midline and tend to extend straight back into the anterior chiasmal angle, where they may give rise to symmetric bitemporal hemianopsia beginning in the lower visual field. Quite commonly they will grow eccentrically and encroach on one optic nerve long before they reach the chiasmal angle or involve the other nerve (Fig. 14-25). In these cases the visual field defects are very asym-

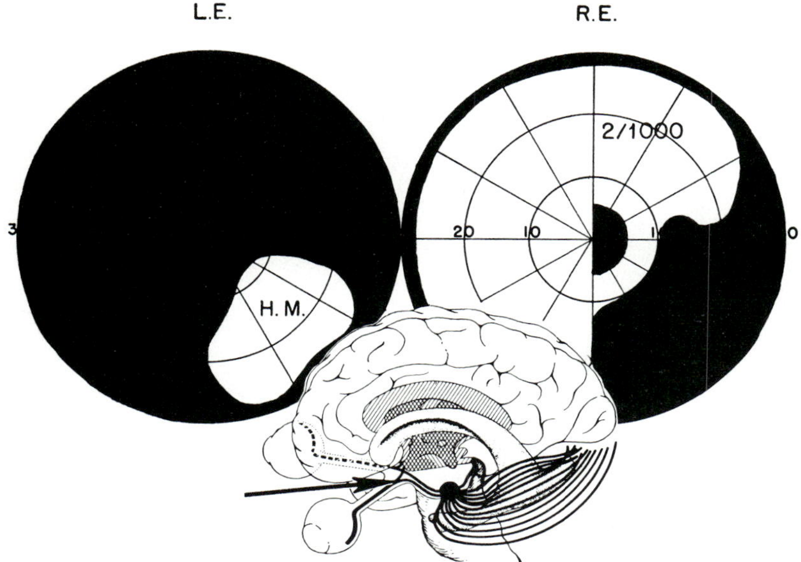

Fig. 14-25. Bitemporal hemianoptic field defect from case of olfactory groove meningioma. Left eye was blind for several years before visual field defect appeared in right. Point and direction of maximum pressure on optic nerve and chiasm are shown in anatomic sketch.

metric and begin with a central or hemianoptic scotoma on the side of the tumor. This central defect may expand and increase in density until the eye is nearly or entirely blind. Further extension of the tumor into and over the chiasm will finally involve the crossing fibers and the temporal field of the opposite eye. Varying degrees of asymmetry in the fields are more common than the theoretically typical bitemporal inferior quadrantanopsia.

The classic Foster-Kennedy syndrome of optic atrophy in the eye on the side of the tumor and papilledema in the contralateral eye may occur in these cases.

Meningiomas arising from tuberculum sellae. Meningiomas from the tuberculum sellae (Fig. 14-26) produce visual field defects that may be similar to those of the olfactory groove meningioma. The tumor, arising close to the chiasm, may compress its anterior angle whilte still quite small. In the theoretically typical case, it impinges on the anterior edge of the chiasm in the midline, producing bitemporal inferior quadrantanopsia with symmetric fields (Figs. 14-27 and 14-28). In actual fact this is rarely the case, and asymmetrically placed tumors give rise to equally asymmetric visual field defects (Fig. 14-30). Junction scotomas with contralateral temporal field loss are not uncommon. These are caused by optic nerve pressure. Bitemporal hemianoptic scotomas, altitudinal hemianopsia, and homonymous hemianopsia are rare.

Visual field progression is slow, and the margins of the temporal defects may be fairly steep.

Text continued on p. 299.

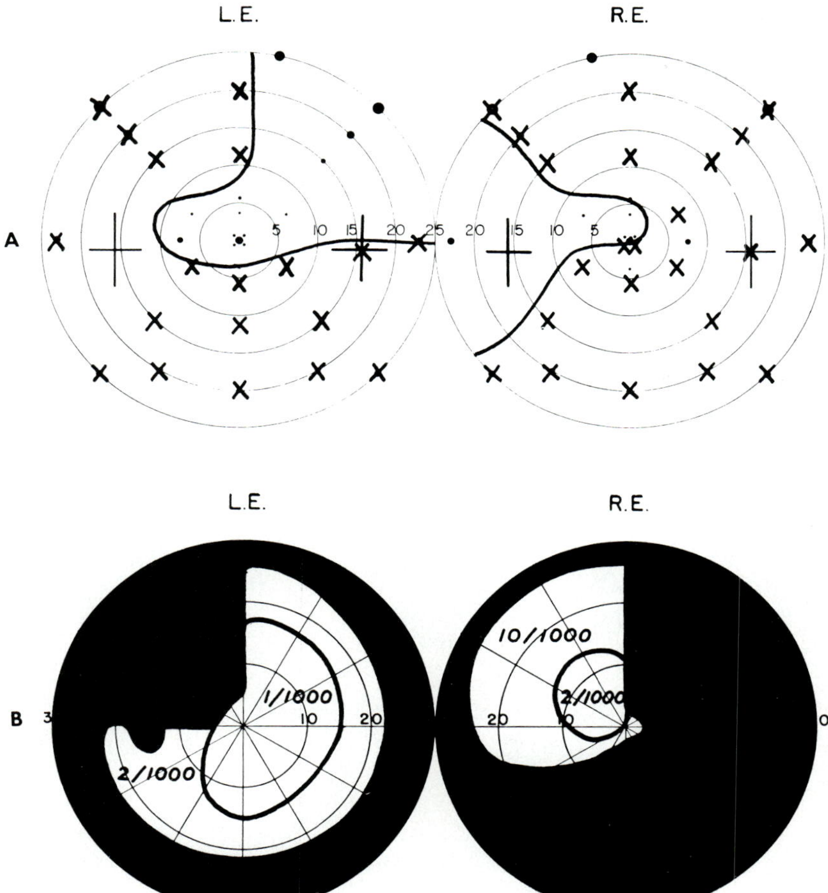

Fig. 14-26. A, Multiple pattern visual field chart of patient with meningioma of tuberculum sellae. Note major loss of lower field and greater loss for this test than conventional tangent screen examination. **B,** Tangent screen field in case of tuberculum sellae meningioma, as in **A.** Tumor compressed right optic nerve and extended across to attach to medial side of left optic nerve and anterior cerebral artery. It was size of golf ball.

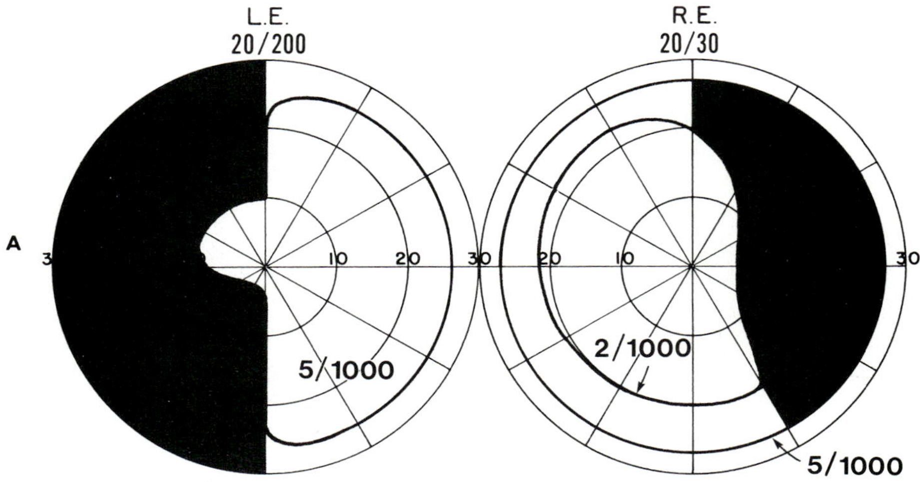

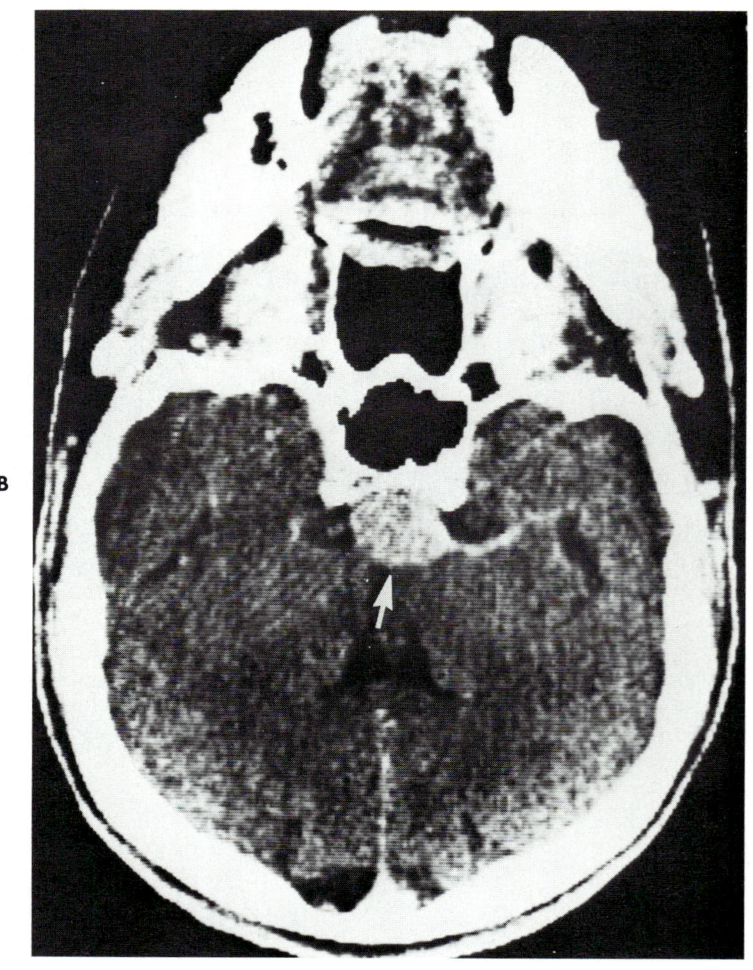

Fig. 14-27. A, Suprasellar meningioma with bitemporal hemianopsia. Temporal pallor both optic discs. Defective color vision. **B,** CAT scan of case shown in **A.** Suprasellar mass strongly enhanced with contrast *(white arrow).* Marked improvement in visual field defects after tumor removal.

A

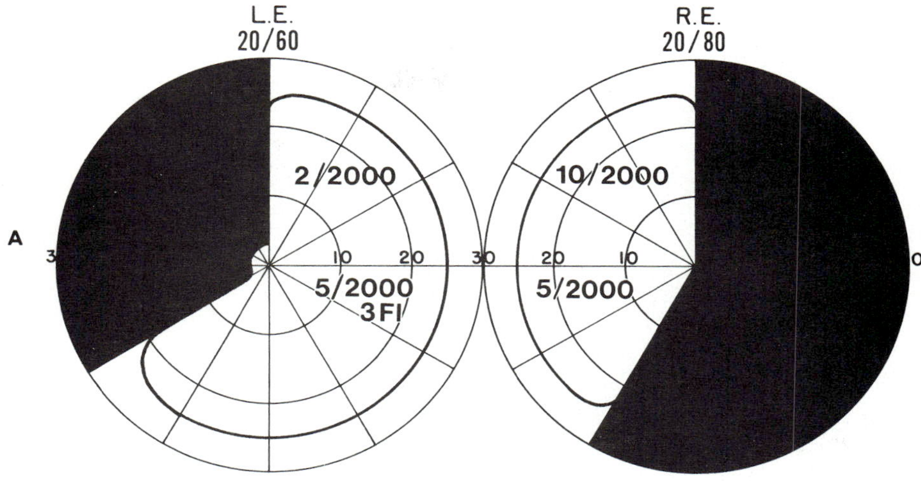

B

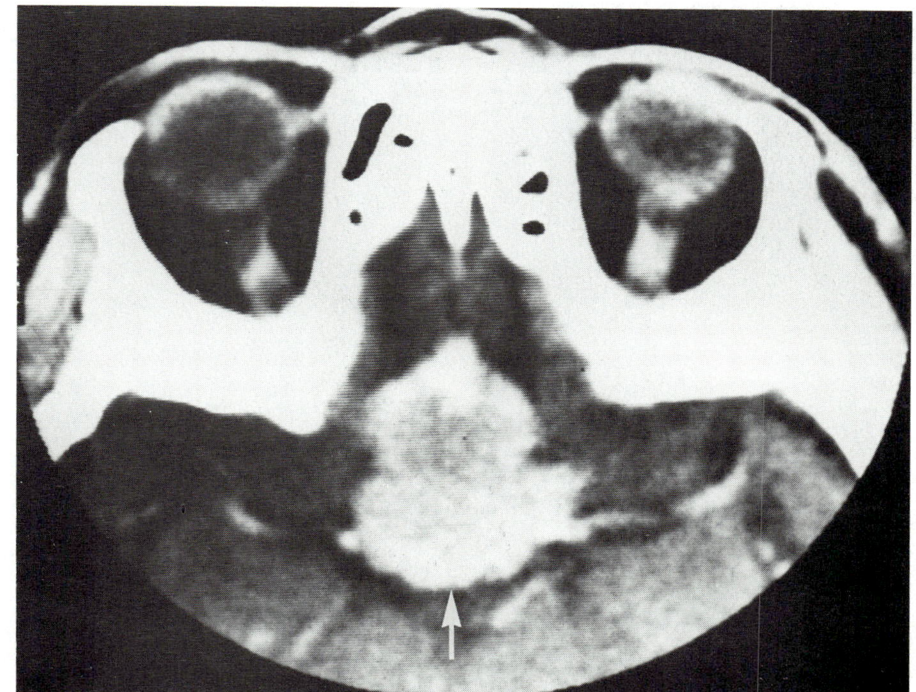

Fig. 14-28. A, Bitemporal hemianopsia in a patient with very large suprasellar meningioma. Field defect much denser in right eye. Left field quite normal on Goldmann perimeter. Skull roentgenograms and tomograms of sella turcica were normal. **B,** CAT scan of case shown in **A.** Enlarged and enhanced computerized tomography shows enormous tumor overlying sella *(white arrow).*

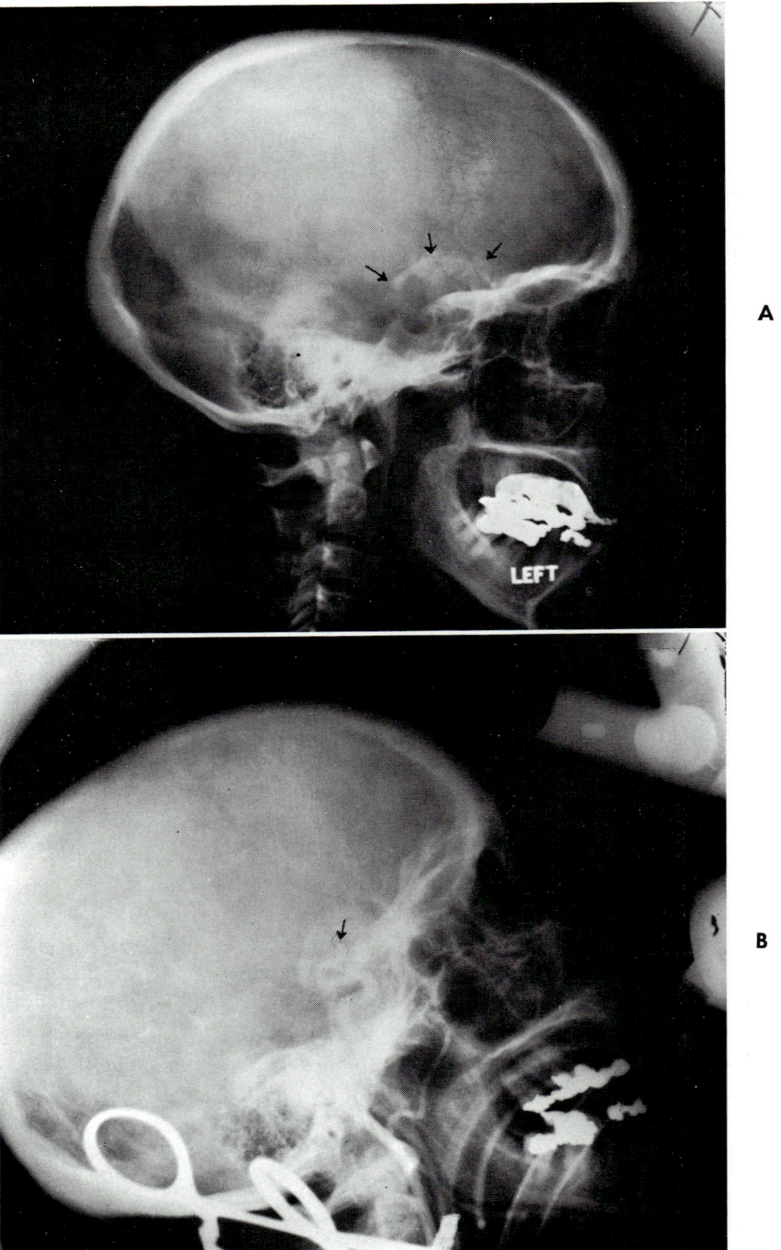

Fig. 14-29. A, Lateral roentgenogram of skull showing calcified meningioma of tuberculum sellae. **B,** Angiogram of same tumor. Point of entrance of external carotid artery into tumor can be seen in sudden vessel arborization, resulting in blush of tumor area. **C,** Visual field defects produced by same tumor. It was meningioma arising from tuberculum sellae, anterior to right clinoid process. It compressed right optic nerve from below and spread through anterior chiasmal notch to compress anterior aspect of chiasm and encroach inferiorly on left optic nerve. (**A** and **B** courtesy Thomas Fullenlove, M.D.)

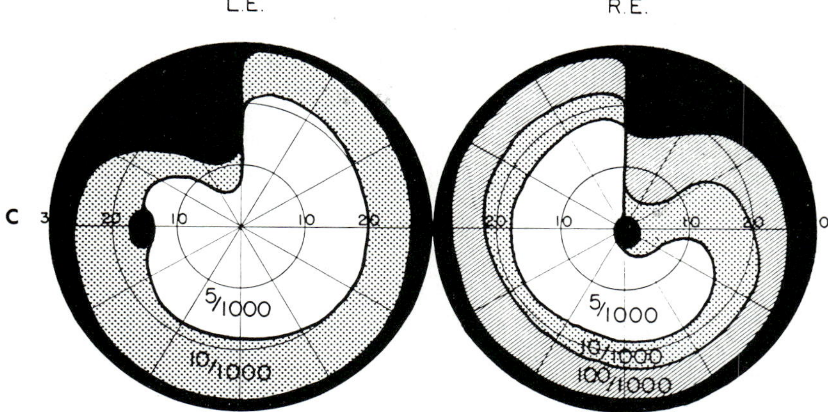

Fig. 14-29, cont'd. For legend see opposite page.

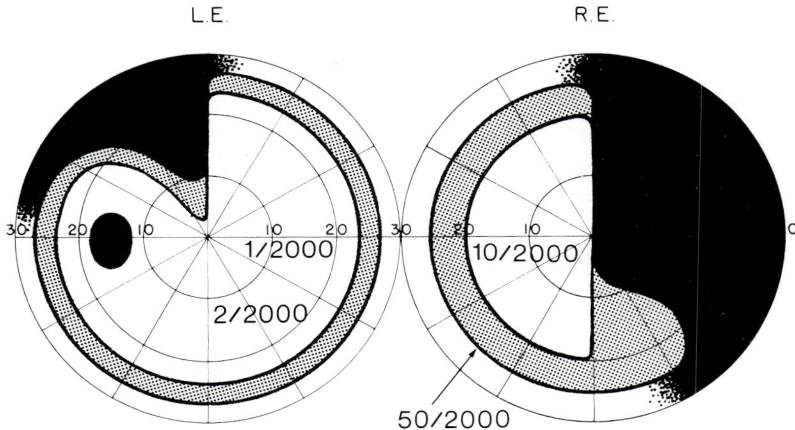

Fig. 14-30. Asymmetric bitemporal hemianopsia produced by slow-growing benign psammomatous-type meningioma arising under right optic nerve and extending backward and down into sella turcica and laterally toward right internal carotid artery.

Meningiomas of lesser wing of sphenoid bone. Meningiomas of the lesser sphenoid wing (Figs. 14-31 and 14-32) are laterally situated with respect to the chiasm and, as a result, produce the most irregular and symmetric of all the visual fields from chiasmal compression in this area (Fig. 14-33). A scotoma on the side of the lesion is common. It may be large, dense, and central, with or without hemianoptic characteristics. Bitemporal hemianopsia, much more advanced in one field than in the other, occurs when the tumor is more nearly midline. Binasal hemianopsia has been frequently reported in patients with these tumors, probably resulting from displacement of the chiasm.

Other diagnostic signs in tumors of the lesser wing of the sphenoid bone are unilateral exophthalmos, occasional third nerve paralysis (see Fig. 13-30), and occasional Foster-Kennedy syndrome. Roentgenograms may show bony erosion of the sphenoid.

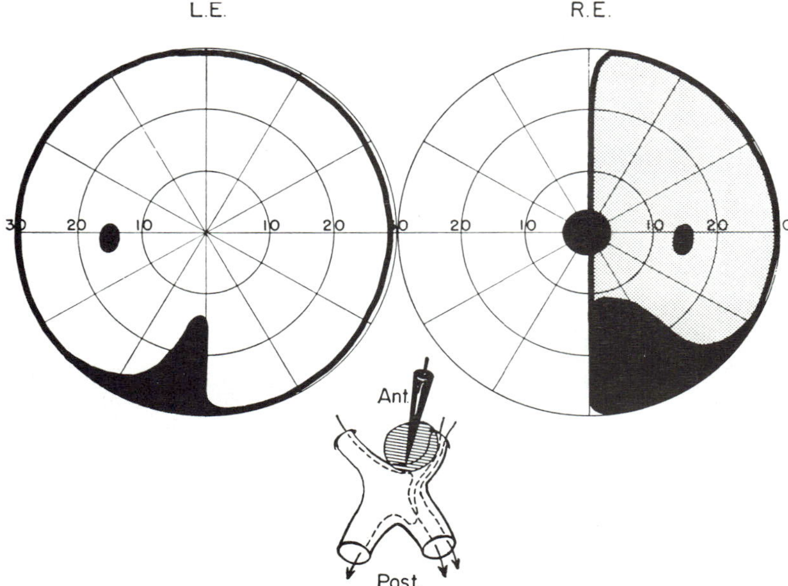

Fig. 14-31. Visual field defect resulting from pressure on chiasm from in front, above, and on right. There is loss of central vision and temporal field in right eye, with inferior temporal quadrant loss in left eye. This field might be produced by meningioma of frontal lobe or sphenoid ridge, or by aneurysm of anterior cerebral or anterior communicating artery. Central scotoma in ipsilateral field is usually larger, more irregular, and more temporal in location. Tiny inferior sector defect in contralateral temporal field implicates anterior loop of decussating fibers as shown in anatomic sketch.

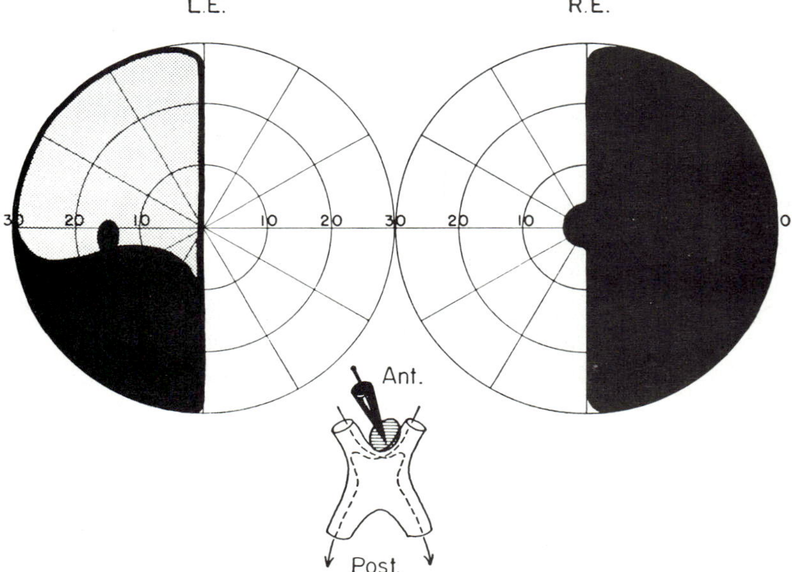

Fig. 14-32. Pressure on chiasm from in front and above with involvement of right optic nerve, loss of right temporal field, and beginning defect in left inferior temporal quadrant. This was caused by meningioma of sphenoid ridge.

A

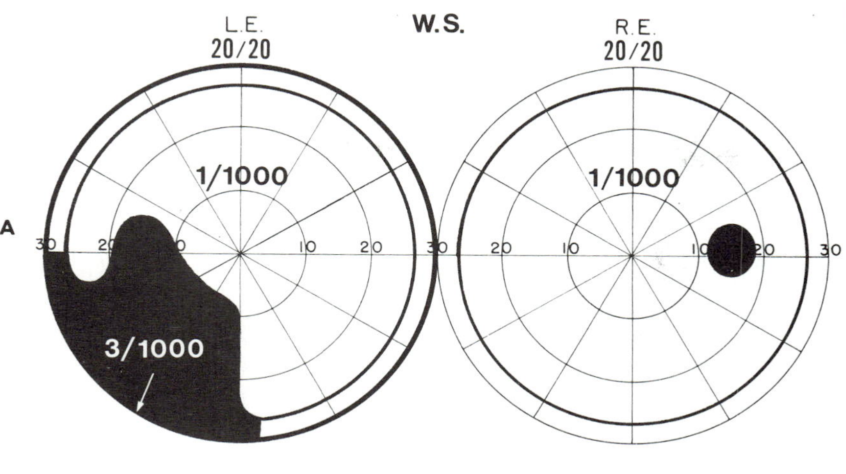

B

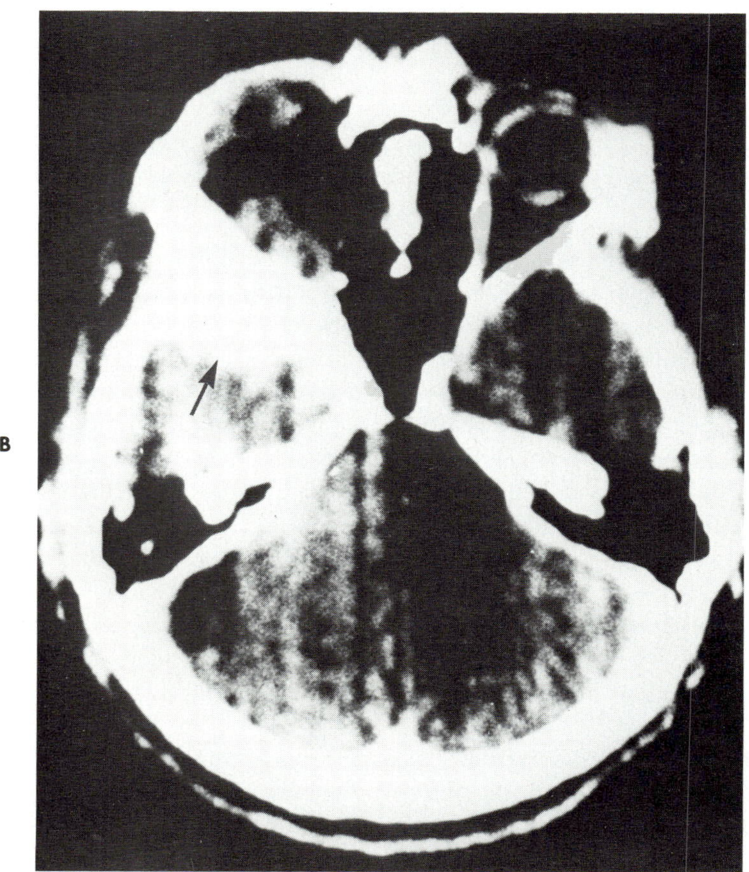

Fig. 14-33. A, Recurrent meningioma of left orbit and middle fossa with proptosis of left eye and inferior quadrant field loss. Note sharp vertical border to field defect. **B,** CAT scan shows marked thickening and hyperostosis of lateral wing of left sphenoid bone *(arrow)*.

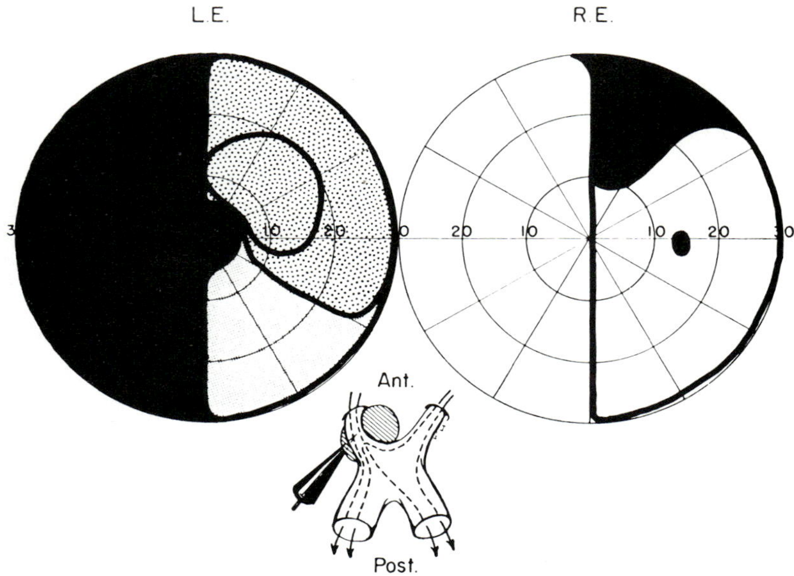

Fig. 14-34. Pressure on chiasm from in front on left side with involvement of left optic nerve and later compression of anterior decussating loop of fibers from right optic nerve. Left eye was blind and showed advanced optic atrophy for considerable time before right field defect could be demonstrated.

Glioma or meningioma of frontal lobe. Glioma or meningioma of the frontal lobe may compress one optic nerve in its intracranial portion or may extend posteriorly to compress or almost engulf the chiasm from above (Fig. 14-34).

The classic symptom complex with these tumors is the Foster-Kennedy syndrome, but scotoma is not always present and the field not uncommonly assumes the form that might be expected, that is, a bitemporal hemianopsia with greatest density in the lower temporal fields and with sloping edges and slow progression.

Perimetry may be very difficult in these patients because of psychic disturbance, euphoria, inability to comprehend instructions, and belligerence. The use of gross stimuli, double stimulation, and a technique of perimetry that makes use of sharp command is often indicated. Other signs that are of value in diagnosis are the findings of anosmia, ventricular displacement, occasional oculomotor palsy, and occasional unilateral exophthalmos. If a meningioma is present, roentgenography may show calcification in the tumor or a distinct blush in the angiogram. CAT scan is usually revealing.

Aneurysm of anterior cerebral artery or anterior communicating artery. Aneurysm of either the anterior cerebral or the anterior communicating artery may give rise to visual field changes that closely simulate tumors of this area.

The typical visual field defect is unilateral blindness or advanced visual field loss in one eye with or without central scotoma and a lesser inferior temporal field defect in the other eye. Optic atrophy is common. Pain or severe paroxysmal headache is the rule, with marked fluctuation in symptoms. Angiograms are of utmost value as is CAT scan (see Fig. 14-9).

Symptoms associated with aneurysm are often sudden in onset and are probably caused by leakage rather than direct pressure.

Posterosuperior aspect

The important lesions that compress the chiasm in its posterosuperior aspect are Rathke's pouch tumor (craniopharyngioma) and dilatation of the third ventricle. Other rare tumors of this area are cholesteatoma, osteoma, and osteochondroma.

All of these affections produce varieties of bitemporal hemianopsia, frequently with central or bitemporal hemianoptic scotomas caused by compression of the posterior chiasmal angle. Homonymous hemianopsia caused by tract pressure is not infrequent.

Craniopharyngioma or Rathke's pouch tumor. Craniopharyngioma is notoriously erratic in its growth and effect on the chiasm (see Figs. 14-35 and 14-41).

The hypophyseal duct runs from the anteroinferior wall of the third ventricle down between the posterior legs of the chiasm (optic tracts) to the pituitary body.

Tumors of this structure are in close contact with the posterior portion of the chiasm in the initial stages of their growth. Visual complaints are therefore an early sign of their presence. They occur most often in childhood or youth and may reach considerable size, compressing the chiasm without giving evidence of endocrine

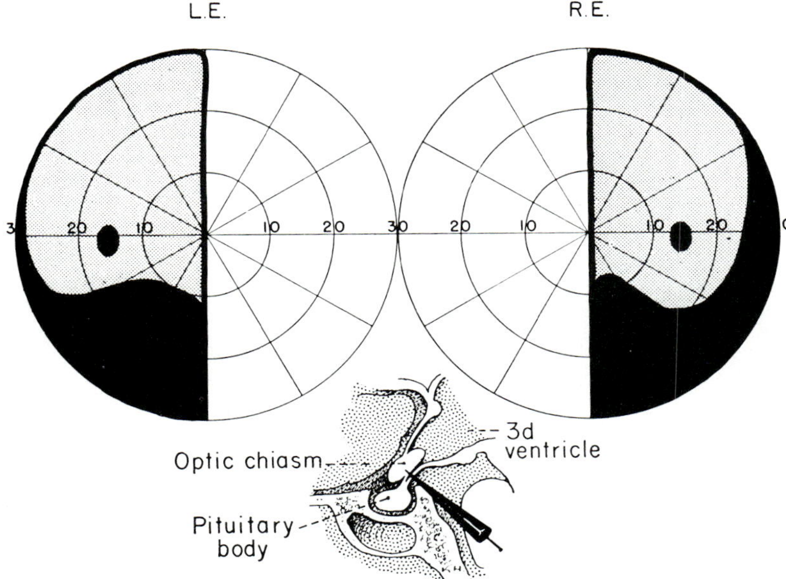

Fig. 14-35. Inferior bitemporal hemianopsia from pressure on chiasm from behind in case of craniopharyngioma. Visual field defects in this tumor are rarely as regular as shown here. Site and direction of pressure are demonstrated in sagittal section.

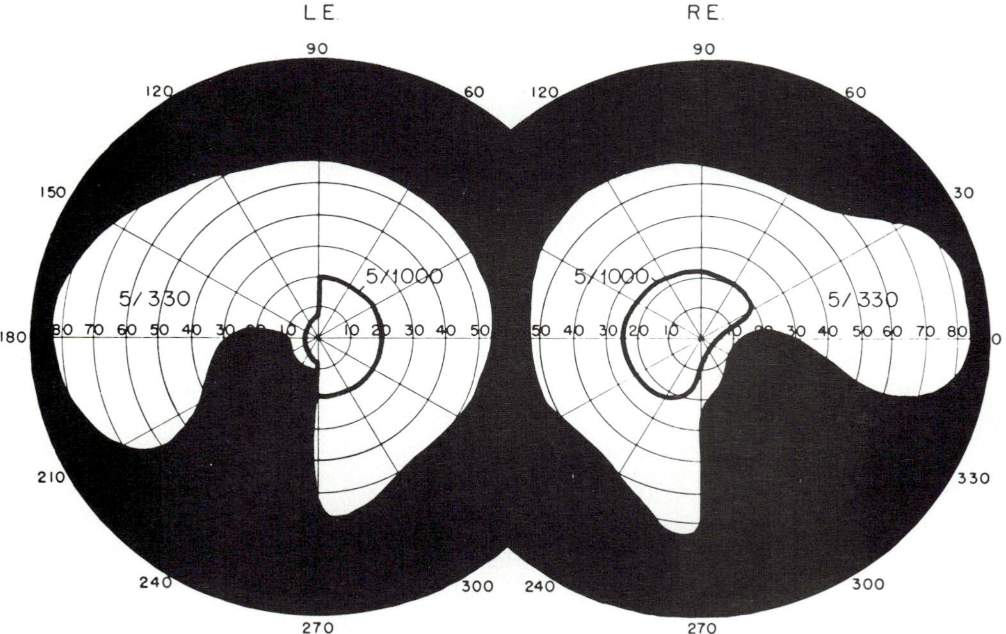

Fig. 14-36. Craniopharyngioma. Large cystic tumor mass was demonstrated in 13-year-old boy with suprachiasmal pressure and inferior bitemporal quadrantanopsia. Macular sparing, as seen here, is uncommon.

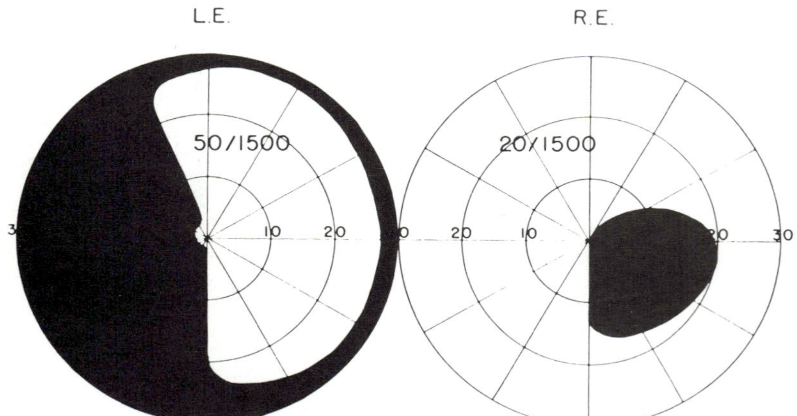

Fig. 14-37. Craniopharyngioma. There was dense temporal field loss in left eye with temporal hemianoptic scotoma on right. Both clinoids were eroded, and calcium flecks were seen in suprasellar region. Ventriculograms showed mass protruding into third ventricle. Large Rathke's pouch cyst (craniopharyngioma) was found at operation. Patient was 55 years of age. Most of these tumors occur in first two decades of life.

disturbance (Fig. 14-36). They are occasionally seen in adults in the fifth and sixth decades of life (Fig. 14-37).

A fairly high percentage of cases shows roentgenographic evidence of suprasellar calcification and, in the very young patient, a widening of the suture lines with finger-like areas of radiolucence in the cranial vault. The sella turcica may be flattened from above with erosion of the posterior clinoids. Intrasellar craniopharyngioma produces ballooning of the sella with extension into the sphenoid sinus. Pneumoencephalography and CAT scan are important to determine the size of the tumor, especially when it is situated posteriorly.

Increased intracranial pressure with papilledema is common. Secondary optic atrophy often ensues with general depression of all the isopters of the visual field, somewhat complicating the interpretation of visual field defects. Rupture of Rathke pouch cyst may give rise to meningeal irritation simulating bacterial meningitis.

The classic visual field change is a bitemporal hemianopsia, irregular and asymmetric, and often beginning in the lower temporal quadrants (Figs. 14-39 to 14-42). Central scotomas are frequent and early changes. In some patients the initial field changes are in the superior temporal field. The scotoma may show a tendency to bitemporal morphology, but the vertical division between the temporal and nasal field is rarely sharp.

Blind spots are usually large.

Because of the youth of many patients with craniopharyngioma, perimetric examination may be difficult. The multiple pattern method of visual field examination may be especially useful in these instances, and in every case field examination

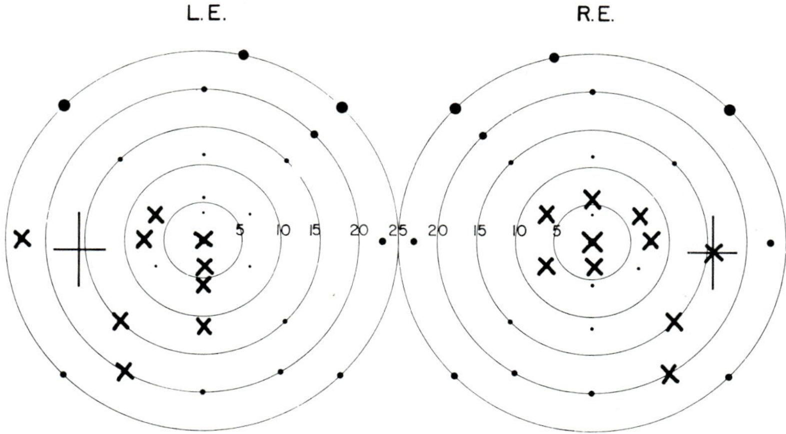

Fig. 14-38. Multiple pattern field chart of patient with craniopharyngioma. (See also Fig. 14-39.)

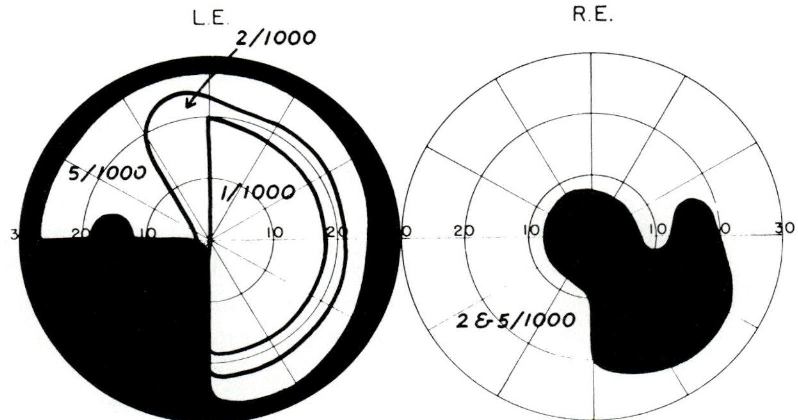

Fig. 14-39. Typical visual field defect seen in 16-year-old girl with large, cystic craniopharyngioma lying on chiasm and right optic nerve. Visual loss was gradual and endocrine imbalance was severe. (See also Fig. 14-38.)

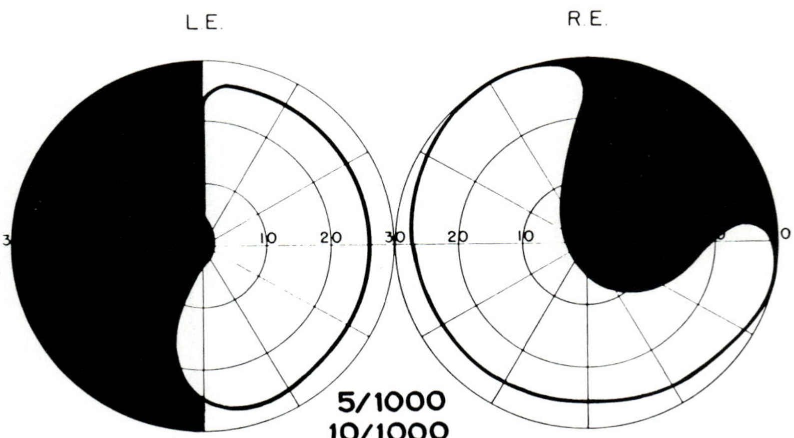

Fig. 14-40. Craniopharyngioma. There was marked loss of central vision with asymmetric bitemporal hemianopsia and optic atrophy. Partial restoration of vision occurred after removal of tumor.

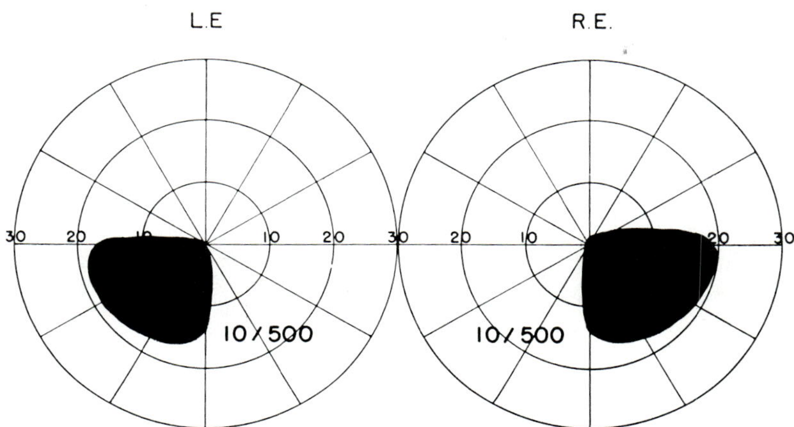

Fig. 14-41. Bitemporal inferior quadrantanoptic scotoma in case of Rathke's pouch cyst in man 42 years of age. Defects are dense and steep margined.

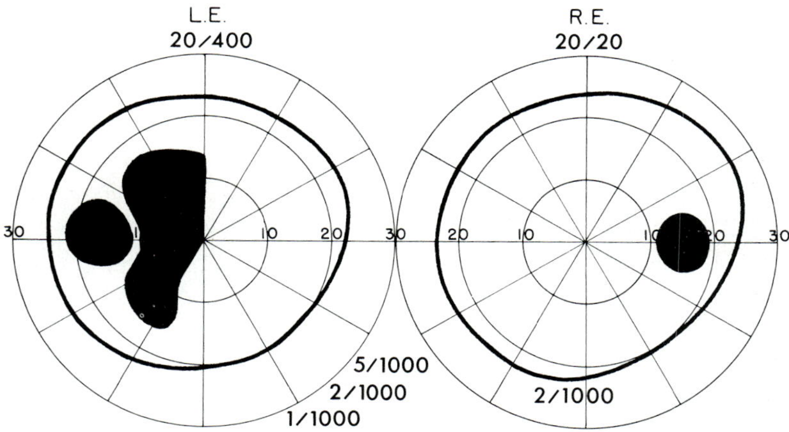

Fig. 14-42. Craniopharyngioma. Initial diagnosis was retrobulbar neuritis. Goldmann perimeter fields were inconclusive. Tangent screen field revealed left temporal paracentral junction-type scotoma with steep hemianoptic margin. Roentgenograms showed a large tumor with calcification and erosion of sella.

should be attempted; sometimes it is surprisingly informative. (See discussion of pediatric perimetry.)

Dilatation of third ventricle. Dilatation of the third ventricle with downward and forward pressure on the posterior aspect of the chiasm may be the result of tumor growth far removed from the chiasm itself. The most frequent location of these tumors is in the third ventricle. Other such growths are the infratentorial cerebellar tumor and acoustic neuroma, and rarely a pinealoma and tumor of the fourth ventricle; all of these produce obstructive hydrocephalus (see Figs. 14-11 and 14-24).

Papilledema is severe, and secondary optic atrophy sets in early; both of these affect the visual fields.

The chiasm actually forms the lowest part of the anterior wall of the third ventricle. Behind the chiasm the cerebrospinal fluid is in contact with the posterior surface of the chiasm.

The visual field defects associated with third ventricle dilatation are what might be expected from uniform midline pressure against the posterior border of the chiasm from above. The earliest visual field defect is likely to be a small, vague, bilateral inferior quadrant scotoma close to fixation. This scotoma advances toward the periphery, and at the same time a peripheral depression of the inferior temporal quadrants is noted. The defects progress into the upper temporal quadrants, and the central scotoma fuses with the peripheral depression until a complete bitemporal hemianopsia results. Margins are usually sloping, and the scotomatous area usually remains more dense than the periphery.

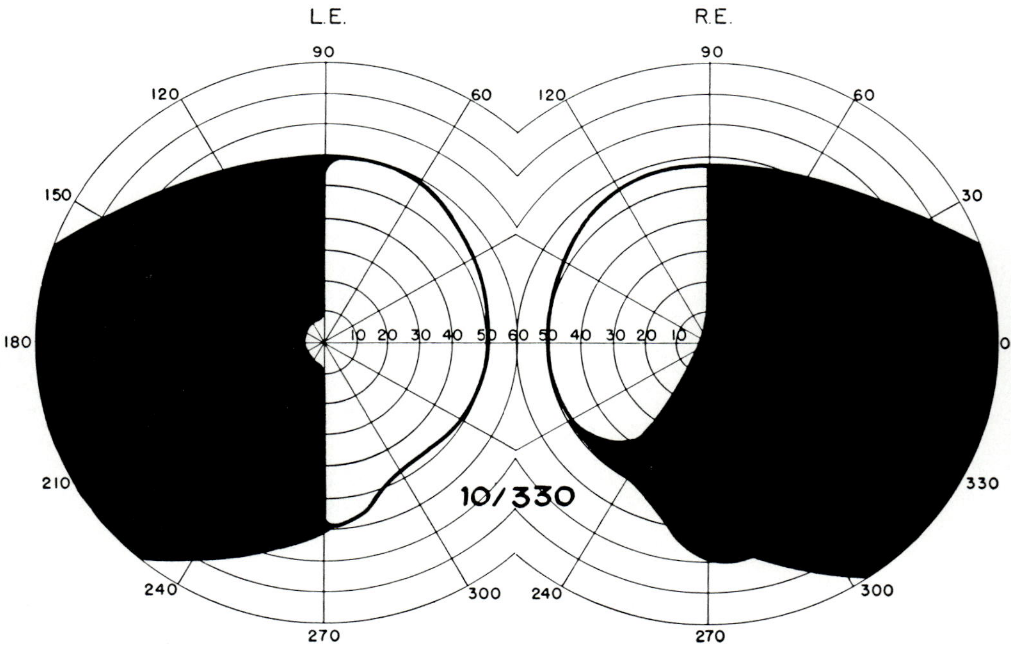

Fig. 14-43. Suprasellar cholesteatoma with bitemporal hemianopsia and bilateral optic atrophy.

The manner in which the field changes progress and the associated papilledema and other neurologic symptoms develop should simplify the diagnosis. It is important that the perimetrist be aware of the fact that tumors far removed from the chiasm may nevertheless produce chiasmal pressure.

Cholesteatoma. Cholesteatoma (Fig. 14-43) is a rare tumor that may give rise to optic atrophy and bitemporal hemianopsia in young persons. It is a type of craniopharygioma. The visual field changes are usually grossly asymmetric, and one case has been reported with bitemporal crossed quadrantanopsia.

Perichiasmatic lesions

Perichiasmatic lesions are largely inflammatory in nature. Most of these infections attack the chiasm from the anteroinferior direction.

The chiasm is covered inferiorly by the pia mater. The subarachnoid space below and anteriorly is expanded into the cisterna chiasmaticus. Infections often start here, especially syphilitic basilar meningitis. Purulent infiltration of the arachnoid is accompanied by involvement of the nerves with necrosis, thrombosis, and abscess formation. Traumatic basal meningitis also involves this area. All of these infections may lead to chronic arachnoiditis and the so-called opticochiasmatic arachnoiditis.

The role played by arachnoidal adhesions around the chiasm is still debated. Numerous case reports attest to the presence of bitemporal or other visual field defects, which retrogressed after removal of these opticochiasmatic arachnoidal adhesions. Many patients have been operated on for suspected pituitary adenoma, and the arachnoidal adhesions were an accidental finding in an otherwise normal chiasmal area.

Arachnoidal adhesions and cysts may result from a variety of inflammatory reac-

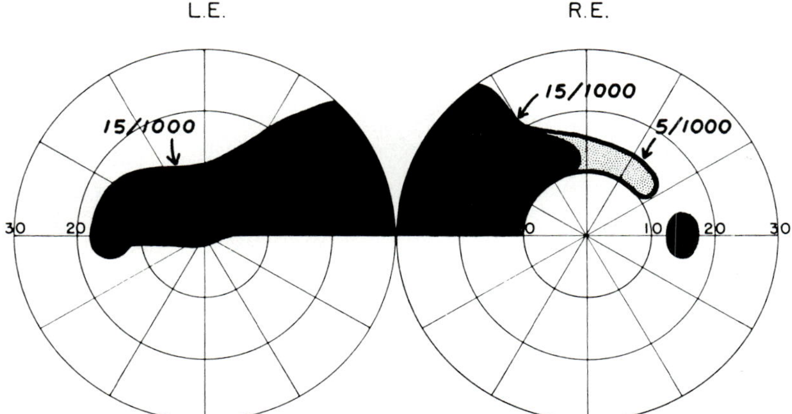

Fig. 14-44. Irregular binasal hemianoptic visual field defects simulating Bjerrum scotomas with peripheral breakthrough in case of opticochiasmatic arachnoiditis. Intracranial optic nerves, anterior chiasm, and left carotid artery were enveloped in dense adhesions. Surgical exploration and interruption of these adhesions resulted in regression of right field defect. Examination 20 years later revealed almost normal right visual field but no change in left field defect.

tions from infections or trauma. Cyst formation in the sella is not uncommon and may be associated with the "empty sella syndrome" and pituitary atrophy. Cyst formation is also common in perichiasmal opticochiasmatic arachnoiditis and these arachnoidal cysts may invade the sella, thus severely affecting vision.

Cystic suprasellar and retrosellar arachnoiditis with bitemporal hemianopsia has been reported and confirmed at autopsy.

Cushing called attention to the mild meningeal reaction produced in the cerebellopontine cisterna by an inflammation in the middle ear and saw no reason why a

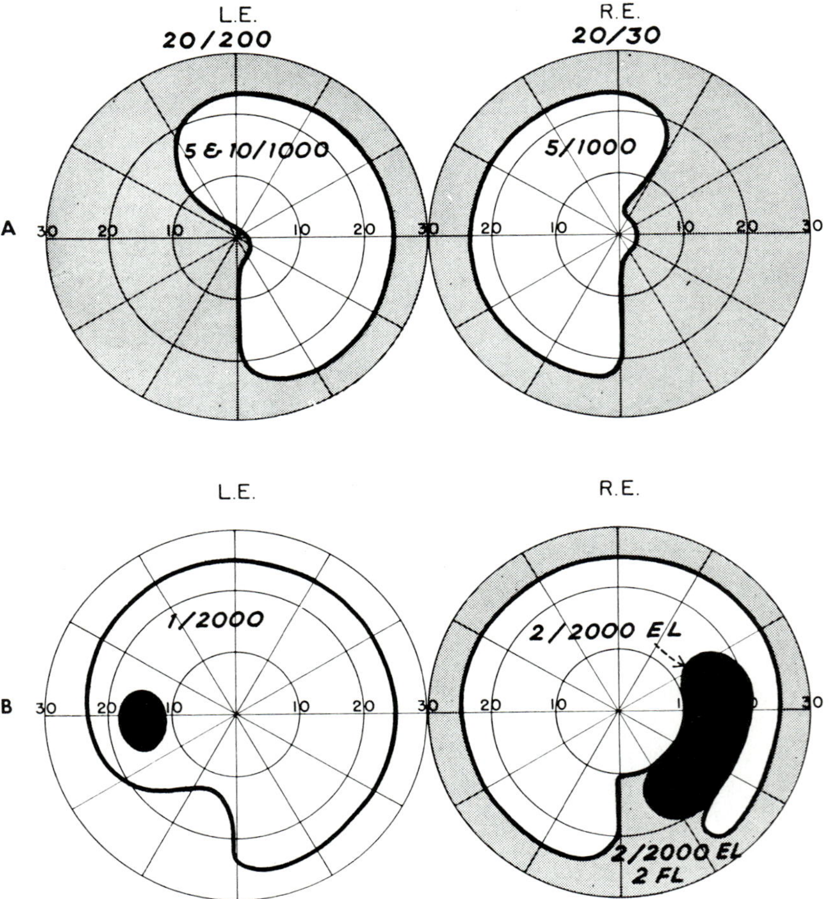

Fig. 14-45. A, Opticochiasmatic arachnoiditis with bitemporal hemianopsia in 20-year-old girl. Preoperative diagnosis was craniopharyngioma. Surgical exploration of chiasmal region revealed dense adhesions involving optic nerves, chiasm, right anterior communicating artery, and internal carotid artery. Also, tough band from sphenoid ridge over left optic nerve and chiasm was discovered. **B,** Postoperative visual field of same patient. There has been marked improvement in visual acuity, especially in left eye. Right field defect shows quantitative analysis of deficit with electroluminescent stimuli of 9.5 footlamberts and 2 footlamberts luminance.

similar process might not occur in the chiasmal cisterna with an inflammatory process in the paranasal sinuses.

With the widespread use of potent and specific antibiotics, the condition sould become rarer.

The visual field changes in this condition are extremely variable, as would be expected, since the lesion may attack only a small part of the chiasm or may envelop it. The following field changes have been reported:

1. Classic bitemporal and homonymous hemianopsia (see Fig. 14-45)
2. Central scotoma and hemianoptic scotomas (see Fig. 14-46)
3. Concentric contraction of the peripheral field
4. Binasal hemianopsia (Fig. 14-44)

The hemianopsias are usually partial and asymmetric. Numerous binasal hemianopsias and a few altitudinal defects have been found.

The association of a central scotoma with a peripheral hemianoptic defect is most suggestive of a possible opticochiasmatic arachnoiditis, especially when both defects are irregular and atypical.

Postoperative improvement in the visual field defects, after separation of the adhesions from the chiasm, is the best argument for the role of these adhesions in the production of the defects (Figs. 14-45 and 14-46).

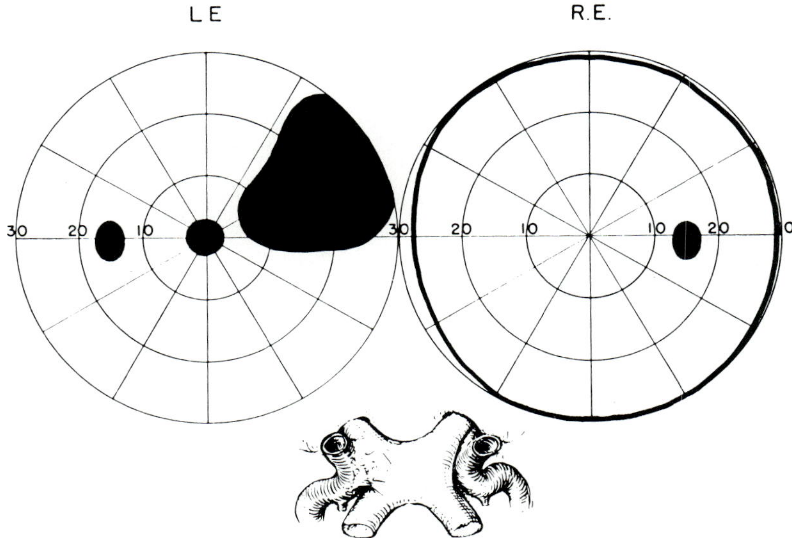

Fig. 14-46. Nasal hemianoptic scotoma in 11-year-old girl resulting from adhesions between left optic nerve and left internal carotid artery in opticochiasmatic arachnoiditis exposed through left frontal osteoplastic flap. Location of major area of adhesions is shown in anatomic sketch. There was some return of vision and restoration of visual field following operation.

Vascular lesions

The intimate relationships between the chiasm and the basilar arteries of the brain in the circle of Willis make these structures important potential causes of pressure on the chiasm and its blood supply.

Aneurysms may arise at almost any point in the circle and give rise to chiasmal compression simulating that produced by tumors. The variability of the visual field defects is in itself an important diagnostic sign of aneurysm.

The most frequent visual field defects suggesting aneurysm are (1) nasal defect with a scotoma on the side of the lesion and a temporal defect in the contralateral field, (2) inferior bitemporal quadrantanopsia, (3) unilateral nasal hemianoptic defect, and (4) homonymous hemianopsia (Fig. 14-47).

Many combinations of bilateral visual field defect that do not conform to usual

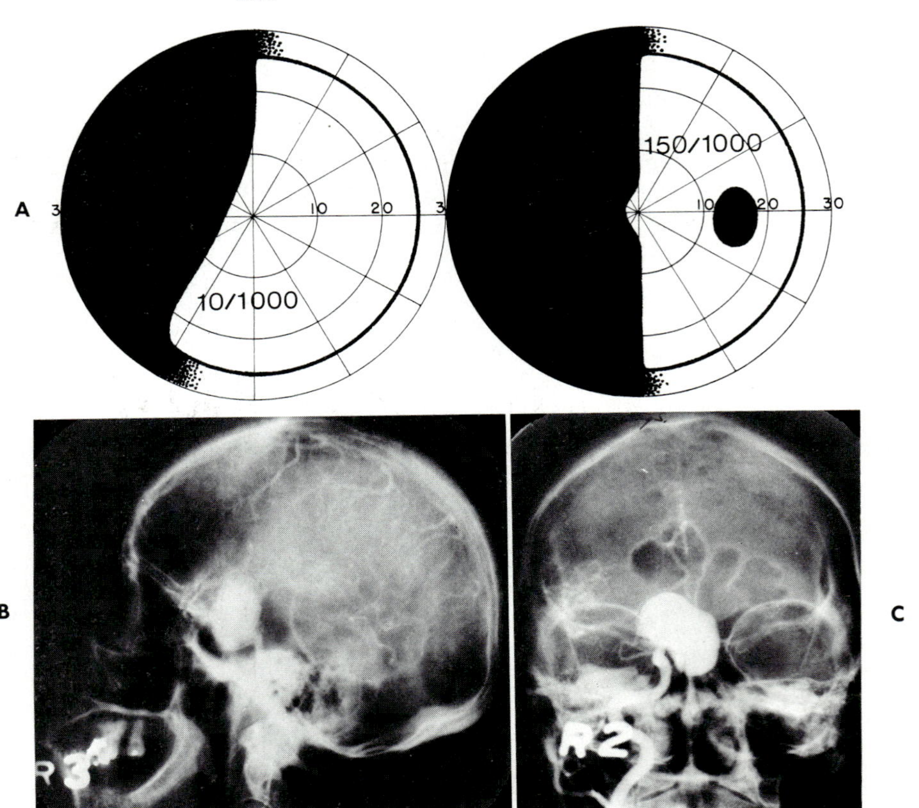

Fig. 14-47. A, Homonymous hemianopsia resulting from large aneurysm of right internal carotid artery. Dense nasal field defect with optic atrophy right eye indicated lateral pressure on chiasm and nerve and suggested diagnosis of aneurysm. Left field defect cleared after ligation of aneurysm. **B,** Arteriogram, lateral view, showing big lobulated aneurysm that produced field defect in **A. C,** Arteriogram, anteroposterior view, of same aneurysm. It was at take-off of ophathlmic artery from right internal carotid artery and extended toward midline to completely fill sella turcica and produce field defect seen in **A.**

patterns explained by the fiber architecture of the chiasm are suggestive of aneurysm.

The most frequent aneurysm encountered in this area is aneurysm of the internal carotid artery. This gives rise to lateral pressure on the chiasm. Aneurysms of the internal carotid artery are of two types: (1) subclinoid aneurysms, which occur within the cavernous sinus and are associated with oculomotor and trigeminal palsy and later with visual field loss; and (2) supraclinoid aneurysms, which occur above the cavernous sinus and exhibit visual field loss as an early sign (see Fig. 14-9).

Visual field changes resulting from pressure of these aneurysms on the chiasm are typically scotomatous with early and severe visual loss on the side of the lesion and temporal field loss in the opposite eye (Figs. 14-48 and 14-49). Finally, there is blindness in the opsilateral field and temporal loss in the contralateral field (see Figs. 14-7 and 14-8).

Disturbances in ocular motility are very common with unruptured aneurysms. Total ophthalmoplegia with homolateral 5th nerve damage is characteristic of an aneurysm of the internal carotid artery in the cavernous sinus. There may be simultaneous involvement of the 3rd, 4th, and 6th cranial nerves.

Isolated 3rd nerve paresis may result from aneurysm of the internal carotid artery at the junction of the posterior communicating artery.

Unilateral optic nerve lesions may be caused by intracranial aneurysms of the ophthalmic artery. (See Fig. 13-29.)

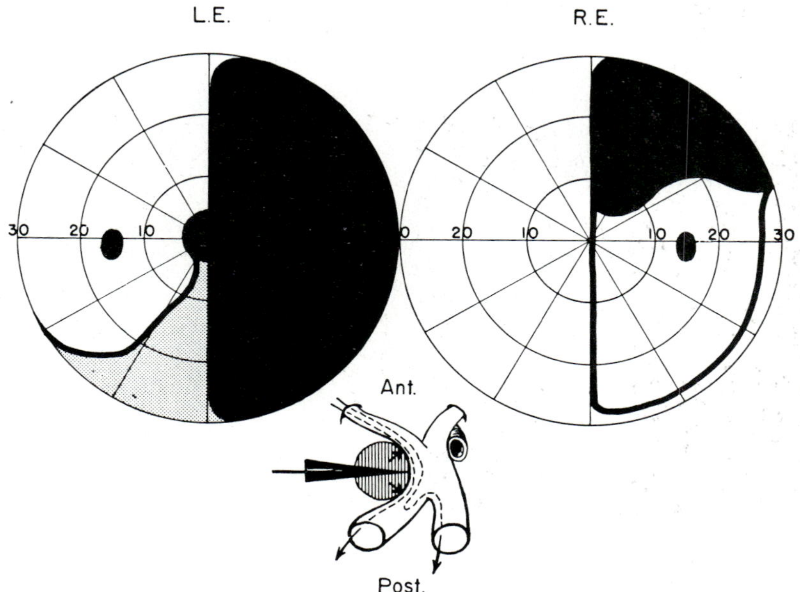

Fig. 14-48. Aneurysm of left internal carotid artery with pressure on left optic nerve and chiasm, accompanied by left nasal and central field loss. Upper temporal field loss on right is from involvement of anterior decussating fibers from right optic nerve, as they loop into left optic nerve before passing backward through chiasm and into optic tract.

A

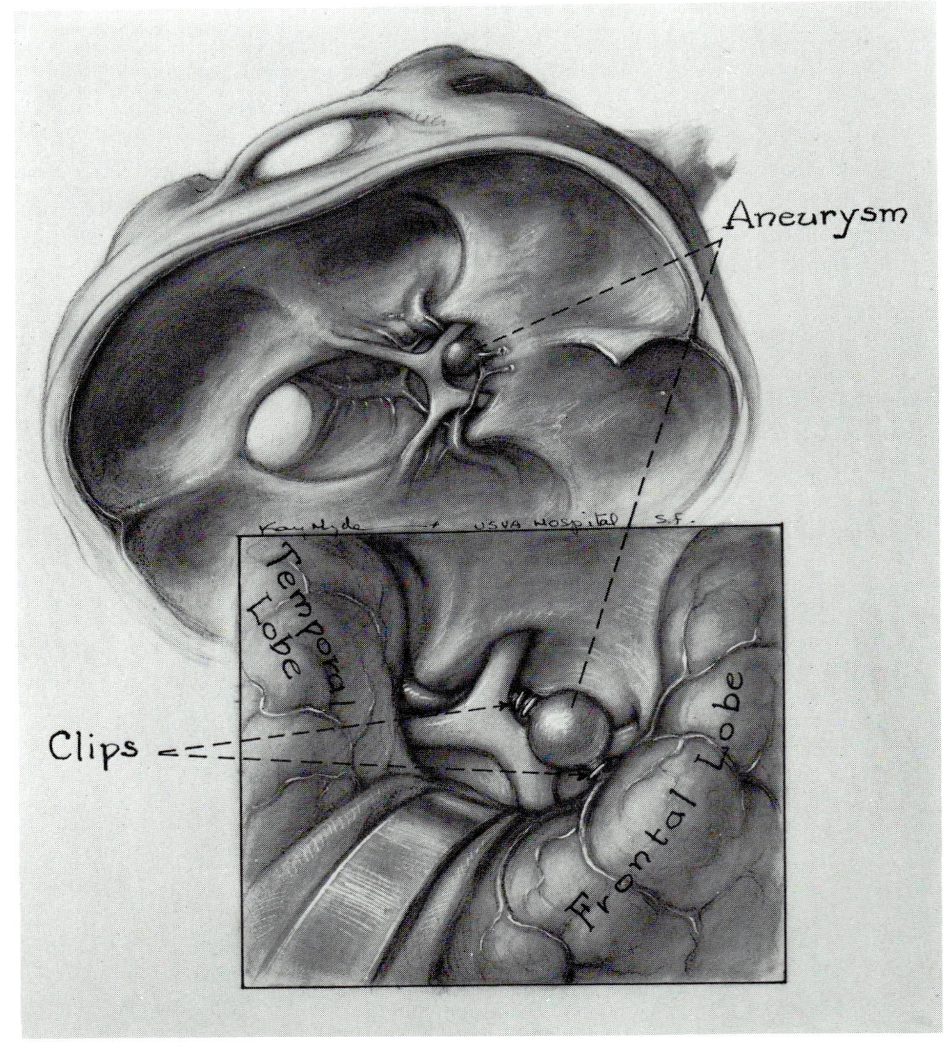

Fig. 14-49. A, Aneurysm of left anterior cerebral artery. This was diagnosed by angiography and exposed and clipped through left frontal osteoplastic flap. Note relationship of aneurysm to left optic nerve and chiasm.

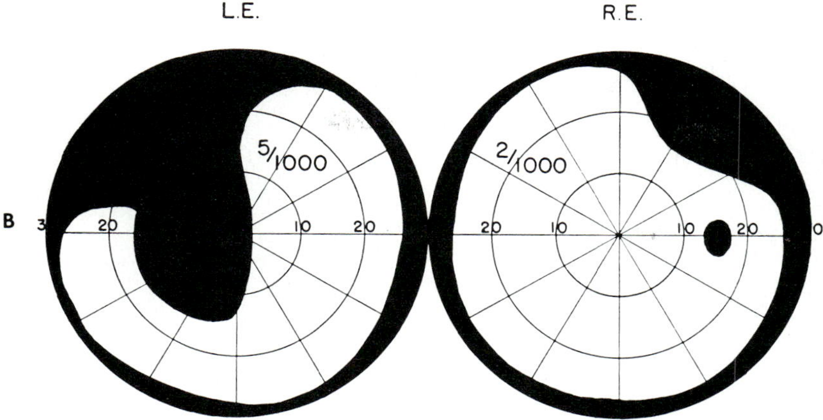

Fig. 14-49, cont'd. B, Visual field defect from same aneurysm. Temporal hemianoptic (junction) scotoma on left is from optic nerve pressure, with minimal superior temporal loss in right field due to involvement of decussating anterior nerve fiber loop from right optic nerve.

When these neurologic signs are associated with irregular bitemporal field defects, the aneurysm may be localized in close proximity to the chiasm. When the field deficit is an incongruous homonymous hemianopsia, the aneurysm may be localized in the middle cerebral artery. The occurrence of retinal hemorrhages in association with hemianoptic field loss and extraocular muscle palsies indicates aneurysmal rupture and subarachnoid hemorrhage and carries a poor prognosis.

Trauma

Direct trauma to the chiasm is rare. Surgical splitting of the chiasm was reported by Cushing, and I have seen one such case, in which total bitemporal hemianopsia resulted.

Indirect trauma to the chiasm is less rare. Numerous cases have been reported. The responsible injury has usually been direct and severe trauma to the frontal region of the skull. Because of this relationship to frontal head injury, it has been assumed that contrecoup basilar skull fracture is responsible for the chiasmal damage. Roentgenograms of the skull fail to reveal evidence of fracture, however, in a considerable portion of the cases.

The manner in which the chiasm is injured is not certain. Some authors have thought that direct splitting of the decussating fibers occurs. I am in agreement with those who believe that, in the majority of cases, the nerve fiber damage and ischemic necrosis result from injury to the nutrient vascular system of the chiasm, which is very vulnerable. Quite probably, sudden and severe shifting of the chiasm shears off the vessels that enter it from the overlying pia mater in much the same manner as the vascular supply to the optic nerve may be injured in its passage through the optic canal.

Whatever the mechanism, the end result is usually a total bitemporal hemi-

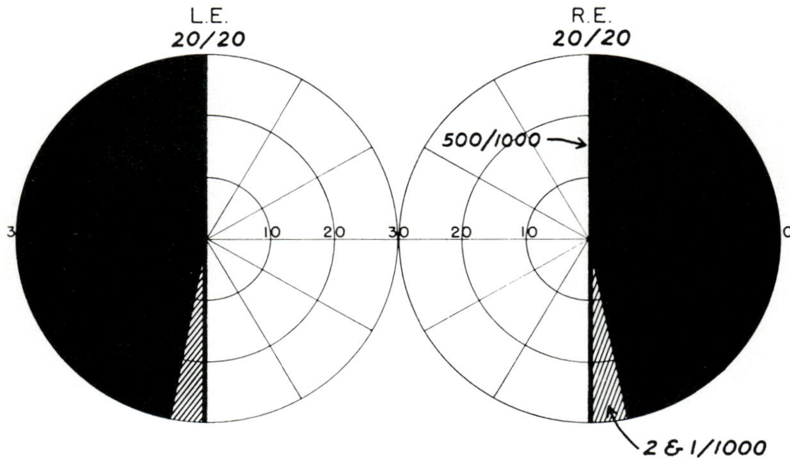

Fig. 14-50. Traumatic bitemporal hemianopsia resulting from severe frontal head injury (automobile collision) with rupture of chiasm or injury to its blood supply. Defects are total to all test objects except for narrow inferior wedge detected only with small stimuli. Note that vision is 20/20 in spite of macular splitting. (See also Fig. 7-16.)

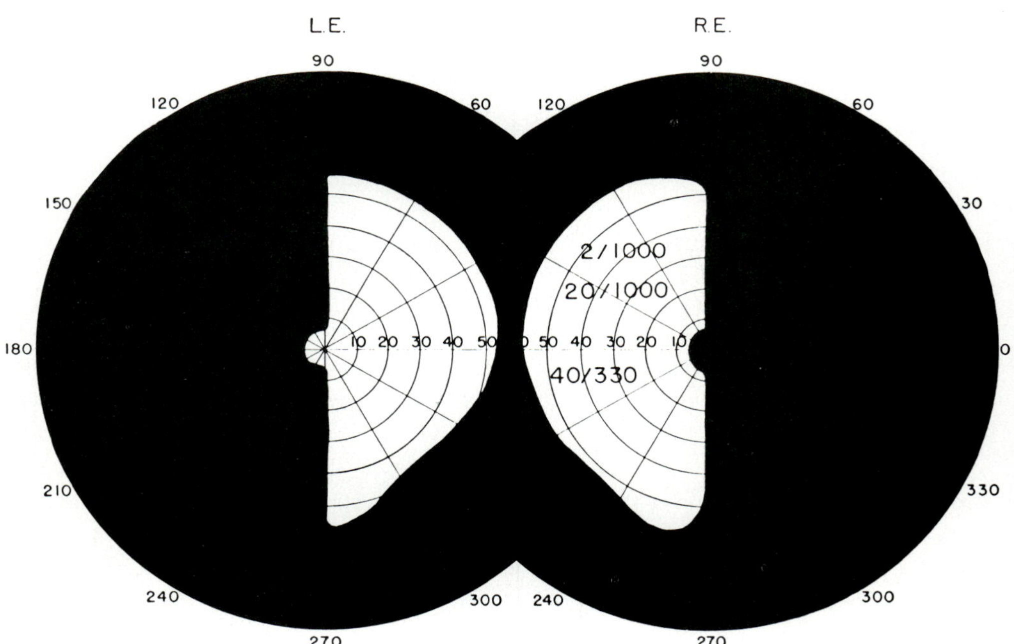

Fig. 14-51. Traumatic rupture of chiasm with total bitemporal hemianopsia resulting from blow to frontal region of skull in automobile accident. There was skull fracture in frontal area and contrecoup fracture of base of skull.

anopsia with macular splitting. The deficit is permanent (see Figs. 7-15, 14-50, and 14-51). Partial bitemporal hemianopsia is rare but has been reported. The margins of the defect are steep. In most patients the visual field loss is recognizable as soon as it can be searched for; but cases have been reported in which the bitemporal field loss did not develop for some time after injury, presumably because of slowly developing adhesions around the chiasm and optic nerves.

Even in the face of absolute amaurosis in the temporal fields and apparently split maculas, as determined by use of the finest test objects, central visual acuity may be 20/25 or even 20/20.

I have seen several cases of traumatic bitemporal hemianopsia that resulted from head-on automobile collisions in which the patient was catapulted into the windshield or the instrument panel. Two cases resulted from having been thrown from a moving car onto concrete. By roentgenography one patient demonstrated a frontal skull fracture and one a basilar fracture. All of these patients gave evidence of severe concussion and general brain damage with prolonged periods of unconsciousness.

Intrachiasmatic lesions

Intrachiasmatic lesions may be subdivided into tumors and infections. Both are rather rare but must be kept constantly in mind when attempting interpretation of bitemporal visual field defects.

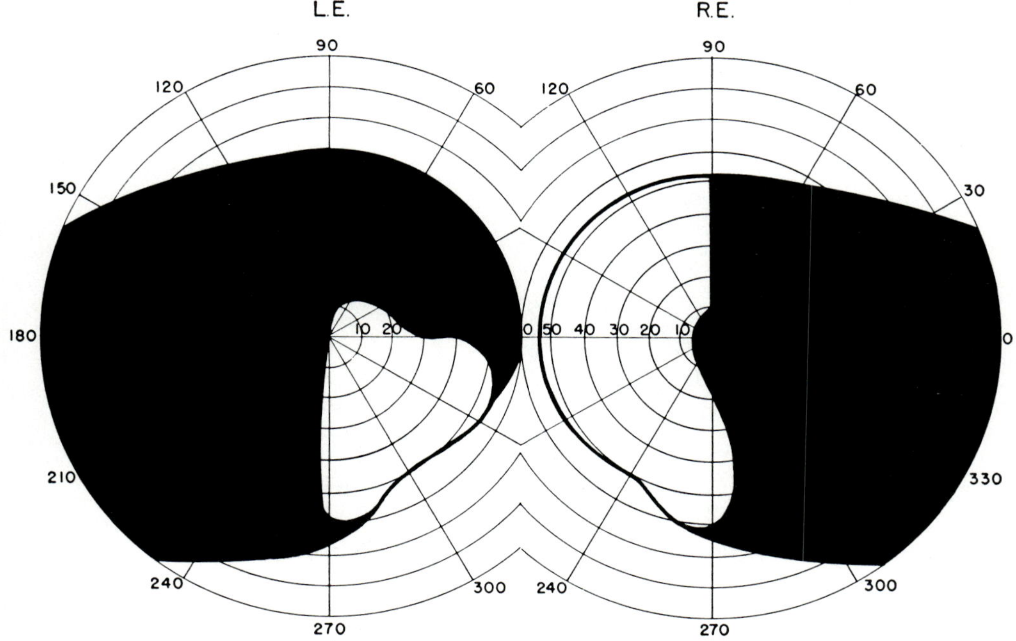

Fig. 14-52. Asymmetric bitemporal hemianopsia in case of intrachiasmal glioma.

Glioma of chiasm

Glioma of the chiasm usually develops during the first two decades of life. The principal visual field change is a bizarre form of bitemporal hemianopsia, frequently with some scotomatous element (Fig. 14-52).

These tumors may grow erratically within the chiasm, either superiorly or inferiorly. They may extend forward to invade the optic nerves or posteriorly into the tracts, and their visual field changes correspond to their direction of growth. Thus the visual fields may show central or peripheral bitemporal hemianopsias (Fig. 14-53), or combinations thereof, or they may develop as blindness of one eye with subsequent temporal field loss in the other. They may begin as bitemporal hemianopsias and change over to homonymous hemianoptic defects.

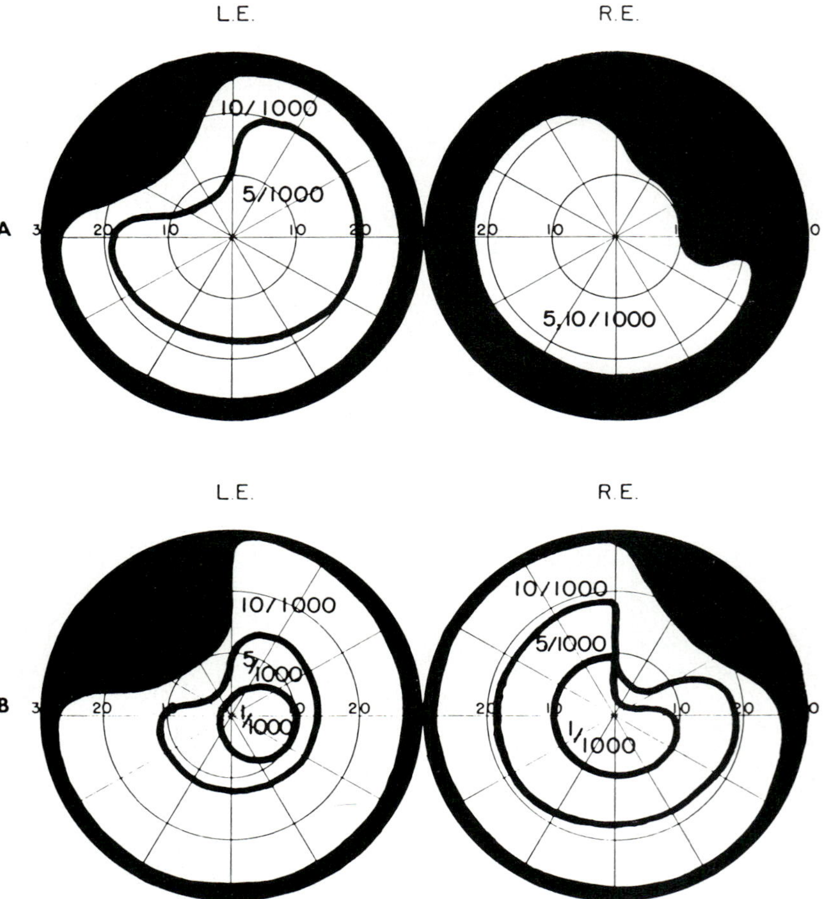

Fig. 14-53. A, Superior bitemporal quadrantanopsia in 8-year-old girl with polar spongioblastoma of chiasm. There were no symptoms or signs except moderate reduction in central visual acuity. **B,** Same visual field defect, after lapse of 19 months. Tumor arose from posterior portion of chiasm, slightly to left side.

If the tumor growth is downward into the sella, the optic atrophy and visual field defects may be associated with roentgenographic evidence of enlargement of the sella. Endocrine disturbances may be present, such as diabetes insipidus, obesity, infantilism, and hair and skin changes.

Hemianopsias are usually irregular and asymmetric, and there is frequent involvement of the macular fibers with loss of central vision and central scotoma.

Von Recklinghausen's disease may occur concomitantly with chiasmal glioma.

Invasion of the third ventricle by the tumor mass gives rise to signs of increased intracranial pressure with papilledema instead of optic atrophy.

Craniopharyngioma may invade the body of the chiasm, thereby giving rise to very irregular and asymmetric bitemporal hemianopsia (see Figs. 14-40 and 14-41).

Not infrequently the field changes are so bizarre as to make exploration of the chiasmal area necessary to establish a diagnosis.

Glaser, Hoyt, and Corbett studied twenty cases of chiasmal glioma to determine the natural history of visual field changes in long term follow-up examinations and the efficacy of irradiation versus no treatment on the visual fields. They found the field defects to be nonspecific and variable. Central scotoma or depression of the central field occurred in 70% of these forty eyes. Peripheral defects were common and occurred as quadrantic, hemianoptic, or diffuse depression of the field, sometimes quite dense.

Typical bitemporal hemianopsia was not found. When the field loss had a unitemporal or bitemporal pattern, the defects often extended irregularly across the midline, involved fixation, and were more characteristic of unilateral or bilateral intrinsic disease of the optic nerves rather than the chiasm.

The field defects were static with little or no progression over a long period of time.

Over prolonged follow-up periods, nonirradiated patients fared as well as patients receiving treatment, and there was no evidence to support the efficacy of radiation therapy for optic glioma.

Neuritis of chiasm

Extension of retrobulbar neuritis from the optic nerve into the chiasm is quite rare, but it does occur and I have seen several such cases.

A central scotoma that starts on one side and subquently involves the second field as a temporal hemianoptic scotoma should suggest this lesion. Bitemporal hemianoptic scotoma of sudden onset in young persons, with no neighborhood signs, is suggestive of chiasmal neuritis. The more frequent cause of these lesions is multiple sclerosis. (Fig. 14-54).

Bilateral central scotomas should be most carefully analyzed for hemianoptic characteristics to differentiate them from ordinary bilateral retrobulbar neuritis or toxic amblyopia. If there is associated peripheral temporal field loss in one or both fields, the diagnosis is somewhat simplified.

Other neurologic symptoms and signs of multiple sclerosis may or may not be present.

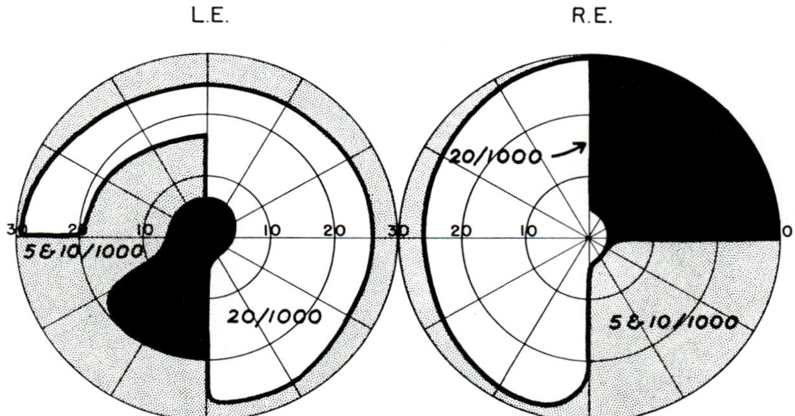

Fig. 14-54. Bitemporal hemianopsia from multiple sclerosis with chiasmal involvement. There was history of transient visual loss and extraocular muscle palsies at age 27 years. Later, pyramidal tract signs, speech impairment, emotional instability, characteristic reflex changes, and visual field defects developed.

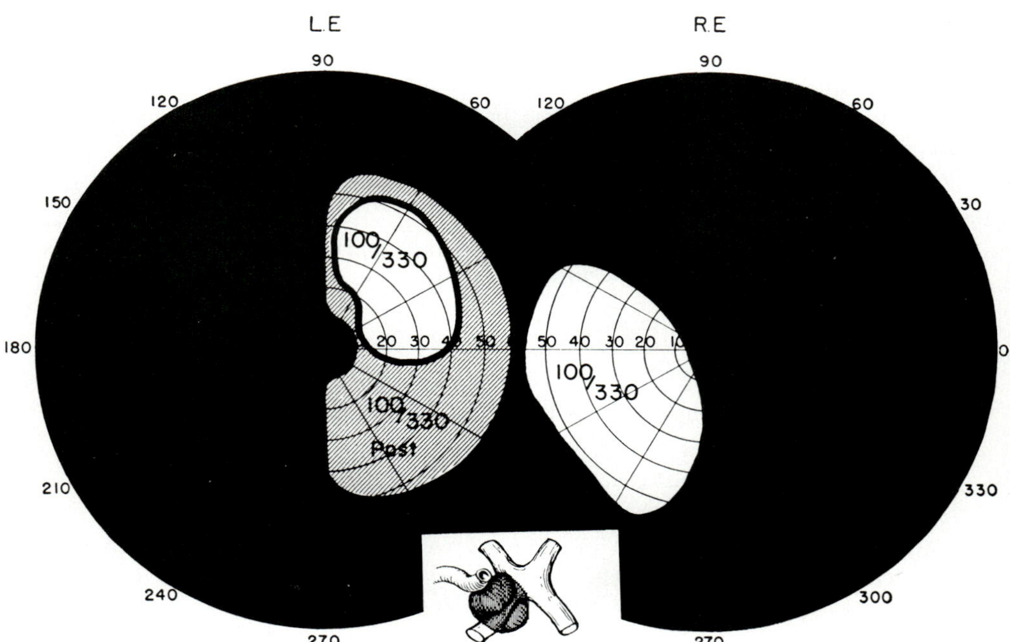

Fig. 14-55. Displaced pinealoma with bitemporal hemianopsia demonstrated with large visual angles in 19-year-old boy. There was marked sexual immaturity and height of only 4½ feet. Optic atrophy was progressive and severe. Neurologic examination and roentgenograms were normal. Operative exploration revealed displaced pinealoma growing up from sella turcica on left side and enveloping and compressing chiasm and anterior optic tract from beneath, laterally, and above.

When central visual acuity varies or the bitemporal visual field defect fluctuates or appears and disappears, the diagnosis of inflammatory etiology is virtually certain. Prolonged exposure to heat, such as a hot bath or sunbathing, may aggravate the visual loss.

In instances of multiple sclerosis involving the chiasm, the prognosis for return of vision may be good, just as in the case of retrobulbar neuritis from the same cause.

Other infections may also involve the chiasm and give rise to bitemporal field defects. These are neuromyelitis optica and possibly severe sphenoidal or ethmoidal sinus infection.

PROGNOSTIC AND THERAPEUTIC INDICATIONS OF PERIMETRY IN LESIONS OF CHIASM

Careful study and analysis of characteristics of the visual field defects in affections of the chiasm are important in indicating prognosis. It may be said in general that the more static the defect, the steeper the margins, and the more absolute the visual field loss, the worse the prognosis. Removal of compression in such cases may accomplish little to restore the field. Conversely, if the central field is spared and the margins of the defect are vague and gently sloping, the outlook for visual return following removal of the lesion is excellent.

If a pathologic diagnosis can be made with reasonable certainty, the prognosis may be established more surely. Some tumors are impossible to remove in toto, whereas others may be largely extirpated. Preoperative knowledge of the nature of the tumor producing the visual field loss will naturally affect the prognosis.

Localization of the lesion may have considerable prognostic value. A lesion anterior to the chiasm generally has a better outlook than does a posterior lesion. This is true not only because its removal may be technically easier but also because it is not so near to vital centers in the midbrain.

Perimetric evidence of involvement of the chiasm is of utmost value to the neurosurgeon in the assessment of treatment. The more exact the localization, the more valuable is the visual field study, especially when it tends to confirm other less definite clinical signs and symptoms.

A normal visual field may be present in the face of otherwise strong evidence of chiasmal interference, but even in such cases the very negative character of the field may be of some value in indicating the type and position of the lesion.

When transfrontal approach to the chiasm is contemplated, it may be of some value if the perimetric evidence points fairly definitely to the right or left side.

Finally, regression of the visual field defect following surgery of x-ray therapy is at least a partial indication of success of the therapy.

CHAPTER 15

Postchiasmal visual pathway

The division of the visual pathway into prechiasmal and postchiasmal portions is clinically, although not anatomically, sound. It is based on the following classification of the visual field defects produced by lesions of these areas:

1. Prechiasmal lesions give rise to monocular visual field defects, except when there are two separate lesions or in toxic amblyopia.
2. Chiasmal disease gives rise to bitemporal visual field defects from a single lesion.
3. Postchiasmal interference in the visual pathway produces homonymous hemianopsia in the visual fields from a single lesion.

Anatomically the postchiasmal visual pathway is made up of four parts: (1) the optic tracts, (2) the external geniculate ganglion, (3) the optic radiations, and (4) the striate cortex of the occipital lobe.

The first of these, the optic tract, is simply a continuation of the second neuron; and, although its fibers have decussated and represent the corresponding halves of the two retinas, it is indistinguishable from the nerve fiber bundles of the chiasm and optic nerve, except in the architectural arrangement of these fibers. Injury to any fiber within the optic tract will produce degeneration of that fiber from the point of injury forward through the chiasm and optic nerve to the ganglion cell layer of the retina.

The external geniculate body is a true ganglion, and as such it represents the end station of the second neuron and is an anatomic part of it.

Anatomically, then, the optic tract and external geniculate ganglion should be included in the discussion of the chiasm and optic nerves.

The optic radiation and its end station, the striate cortex of the occipital lobe, are the neuron of the third order and should properly be considered separately from the optic tracts and external geniculate ganglion. That they are not is due to practical considerations, because lesions affecting all four of these areas produce the same type of visual field loss (i.e., homonymous hemianopsia).

Homonymous hemianopsia is bilateral and consists of loss of vision in the two right halves or the two left halves of the visual fields. Thus a temporal portion of the field of one eye is destroyed simultaneously with a nasal portion of the field of the other eye.

As in the case of the bitemporal hemianoptic field loss in association with lesions of the chiasm, the homonymous hemianopsias exhibit extreme variation in morphology. This variation may be of diagnostic importance not only in localizing the lesion that produces it but also in indicating its pathology.

Because of the partial decussation of the nerve fibers of the visual pathway in the chiasm, the homonymous hemianopsia produced by a lesion of the right side of the postchiasmal pathway is located in the left visual field and vice versa.

Although the precise relationship of fibers from corresponding retinal points throughout the visual pathway has not been anatomically established, it seems probable, on clinical grounds, that the fibers are more widely separated in the anterior portion of the postchiasmal pathway than they are in the middle and posterior portions. By the time they reach the end organ of vision in the cells of the area striata of the occipital lobe, these fibers appear to correspond exactly to their counterparts in the retina.

The alignment of fibers from corresponding points in each retina is imperfect in the anterior part of the retrochiasmal pathway and becomes more ane more perfect as the fibers run backward until they reach the cortical cells, where the alignment is quite exact.

In each pathway, right and left, there is a group of fibers from the extreme nasal portion of the contralateral retina that have no counterpart in the opposite pathway. These fiber bundles are responsible for the temporal crescent in the visual field and give rise to a form of incongruous homonymous hemianopsia when they are spared by lesions of the visual pathway.

Variations in the morphology of homonymous hemianoptic visual field defects may result, at least in part, from this asymmetry in the fiber patterns from corresponding retinal points.

Careful investigation, analysis, and interpretation of these variations may be of value in localizing the lesions that produce them; thus it becomes possible not only to place the lesion on the right or left side, but also, within certain limits, to estimate the anteroposterior position of the lesion in the brain. Visual field examination, then, is an important tool in the localization of intracerebral lesions in the course of the postchiasmal visual pathway, but, as in affections of the chiasm, it is only one method of examination and should be supported by all possible data obtainable from clinical, laboratory, and radiographic examination (Fig. 15-1).

The postchiasmal visual pathway comprises about two-thirds of the entire visual system. All of it is intracranial. It passes in intimate juxtaposition to numerous vital centers of the brain, and its vascular supply in many places is the same as that which supplies other sensory and motor areas of the brain. The pathway is long, and the localization of lesions that interrupt it is complex and difficult; but because of its intimate relationship to other structures, this difficulty is partly resolved.

I cannot emphasize too strongly that visual field studies and interpretation are only a part of the complete clinical investigation. It is true that, at times, they give the only positive sign of brain disease and should be accorded due weight in the whole examination. For the most part they are of greatest value in confirming the

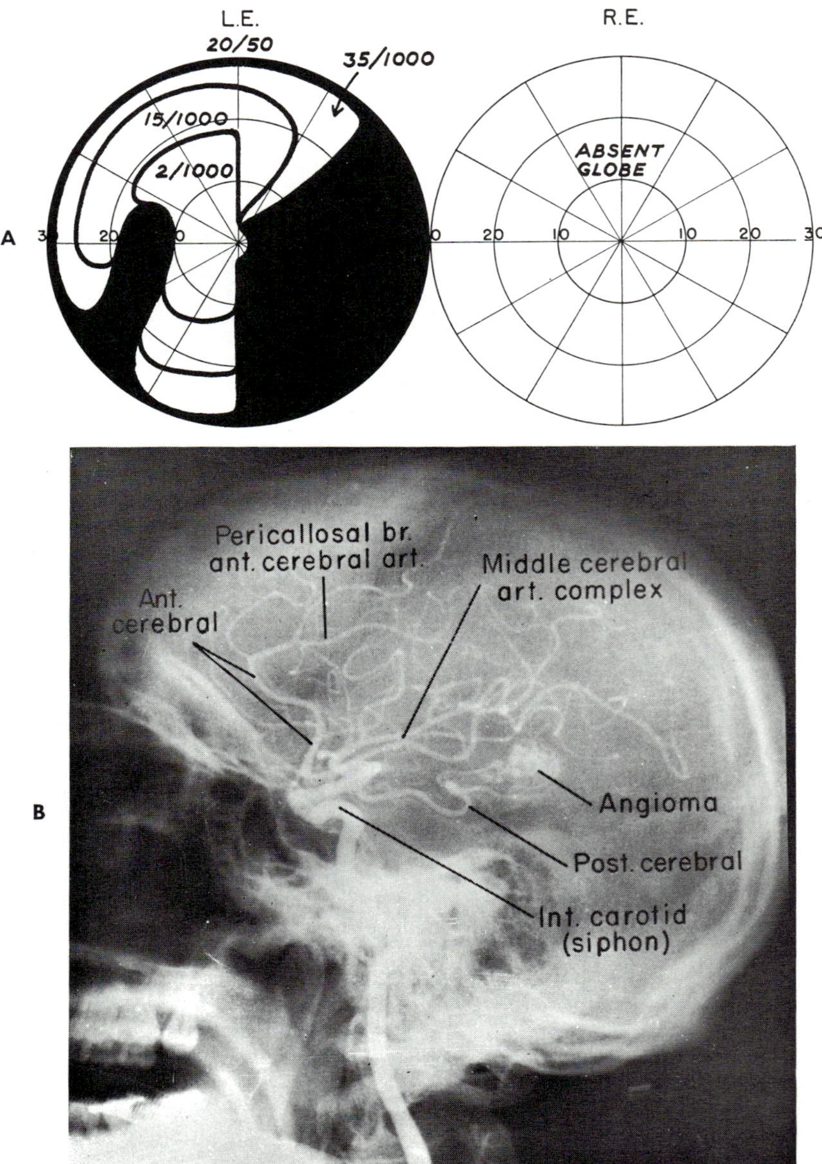

Fig. 15-1. A, Example of analysis of character of monocular visual field defect to implicate postchiasmal visual pathway. Patient had lost right eye in war injury. Left eye had also been injured and was initially blind but recovered. There was area of traumatic juxtapapillary choroiditis. Recent visual change, after 12 years quiescence, shows nasal hemianoptic loss in left field with sloping border and major inferior quadrant deficit. Parietal lobe lesion was diagnosed on basis of this monocular field defect with hemianoptic characteristics. Angiograms revealed hemangioma in pareital lobe. **B,** Angiogram showing parietal lobe hemangioma producing visual field defect in **A.**

findings of other types of examination. Thus a right homonymous hemianopsia implies a left-sided intracerebral lesion. Certain characteristics of this binocular field defect may indicate whether it is the result of a lesion in the anterior or posterior portion of the postchiasmal pathway, but a more important and exact localizing sign would be some other neurologic disturbance that, in conjunction with the field defect, would pinpoint the site of the lesion. A classic and rather obvious example of this is the association of homonymous hemianopsia with hemiplegia in lesions of the posterior limb of the internal capsule.

Precise localization often makes possible a more exact etiologic diagnosis.

In addition to neurologic, radiologic, and laboratory evidence, there are certain ocular signs and symptoms, other than visual field defects, that may be of value in the localization of intracranial lesions:

1. Symptoms of visual loss noted by the patient usually indicate a macular splitting, which in turn in more indicative of an anterior than a posterior lesion. But it must be remembered that 20/20 vision is possible when only half the macula is functioning.
2. Diplopia, with bilateral sixth nerve involvement, may indicate only an increase in intracranial pressure and may be of little localizing value. When the third or fourth nerves are involved, the possible sites of interference are decreased considerably.
3. Monocular diplopia with homonymous hemianopsia originates in the calcarine cortex.
4. Lightning streaks, colored lights, and other abstract visual hallucinations are usually evidence of visual cortex irritation. Most patients describe these light flashes as though they were in one eye only and are unaware of their hemianoptic character. The flashes are thus often confused with similar scintillations that occur monocularly in incipient vitreous or retinal detachment.
5. Formed visual hallucinations, such as people, familiar faces, landscapes, and animals, occur with lesions of the temporal and parietal areas.
6. Homonymous hemianopsias without other signs and symptoms usually indicate a temporal or occipital lobe lesion. Complete unawareness of the defect usually indicates a lesion in the parietal lobe, especially when the hemianopsia is elicited only with simultaneous double stimulation.
7. Papilledema with homonymous hemianopsia generally points to a space-consuming lesion of the suprageniculate pathway.
8. Optic atrophy with homonymous hemianopsia implies a lesion in the geniculate body or optic tract. It is slow in development.
9. Hemianoptic pupillary reactions are theoretically valuable because the optic tracts carry pupillomotor fibers whereas the optic radiations do not. The test is so difficult to perform and so unreliable that it is rarely used.
10. Optokinetic nystagmus is a basic ocular reflex in which the eye fixates in turn a series of objects moved before it. When objects are brought into the visual field in some homonymous hemianopsias, the reflex is disturbed.

An abnormal optokinetic response is of value in differentiating a homonymous hemianopsia of tract or temporal lobe origin from one produced by a lesion of the partietal lobe.

When the patient views a series of moving stripes on a rotating drum, a resultant nystagmus is produced in his eyes that is normally symmetric to the two sides. It is also symmetric in lesions of the tracts or anterior optic radiations in the temporal lobe and in some occipital lobe lesions. With parietal lobe involvement, however, the optokinetic response is characteristically asymmetric to the two sides. There is a diminished or absent response with rotation of the drum toward the side of the lesion, whereas rotation of the stripes toward the opposite side elicits a normal nystagmic response.

Cogan's rule, cited by J. Lawton Smith, states that an occipital lobe field defect (congruous homonymous hemianopsia), associated with a negative (normal symmetric) optokinetic nystagmus sign, usually indicates a vascular lesion, whereas a positive (asymmetric) optokinetic nystagmus sign indicates a space-occupying mass in the occipital lobe.

11. Associated signs of aphasia, agnosia, astereognosis, and other evidences of involvement of the temporal and parietal lobes in the dominant hemisphere are indication of disturbance of the anterior portion of the optic radiation. It is well to remember that aphasia may complicate the examination of the visual field by making it necessary for the patient to indicate his responses in sign language.

The methods of examination of the visual fields in patients with homonymous hemianopsia differ in no way from the field examination in patients with disease of other areas. Careful quantitative methods of perimetery are essential if the visual field changes are to be of any diagnostic value.

Although it is often possible to detect a gross homonymous hemianopsia by confrontation examination, a negative confrontation test does not rule out the presence of a defect. Whenever a defect is found, it must be explored with the same care as would be used in the study of a glaucomatous field defect or a bitemporal hemianopsia from an affection of the chiasm.

Because most homonymous hemianopsias are the result of cerebral disease, the method of simultaneous double stimulation is sometimes of great value in detecting them. The test may be performed with both eyes open, and at times a homonymous hemianopsia that cannot be found on a perimeter or tangent screen even with small, single, stationary stimuli can be demonstrated with two moving hands. Often the only test that can be performed is a crude analysis of the binocular fields by the confrontation method, because of the patient's illness or disorientation. If use is made of simultaneous double stimulation and the extinction phenomenon, it will in many instances demonstrate a homonymous field defect that would otherwise have been missed.

Because the multiple pattern method of visual field examination makes use of double stimulation, it seems to be of special value in detecting homonymous hemianopsia of parietal lobe origin.

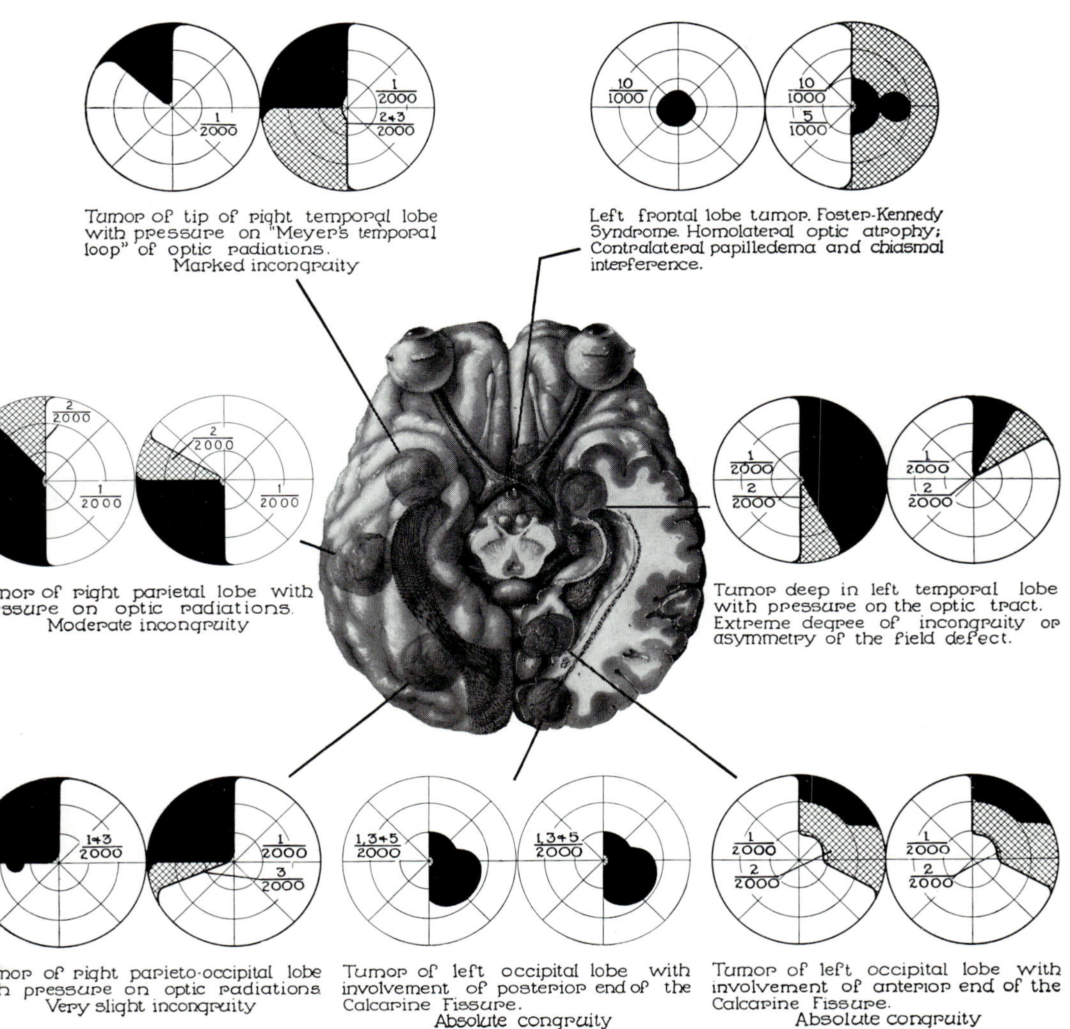

Plate 8. Localizing value of incongruity in visual field defects.

As in all visual field defects, the quantitative examination of the margins between seeing and nonseeing field is of most importance. This is especially true of the vertical meridian and more particularly of any oblique meridian in an incomplete hemianopsia. Only in this way can full diagnostic use be made of congruity or incongruity in visual field defects.

The diagnostic value of congruity and incongruity in incomplete homonymous hemianopsia is still debated. Some authors seem to believe that all homonymous hemianopsias caused by lesions of the postgeniculate pathway are congruous, and yet even a superficial perusal of the literature will show that this is not the case.

My own studies clearly demonstrate the actuality of incongruity in the partial homonymous hemianoptic visual field defects produced by lesions of the optic radiations in the temporal lobe (Plate 8) and the exquisite symmetry that characterizes the visual field defects resulting from lesions of the visual cortex in the occipital lobe (Plates 8 and 9).

When careful quantitative perimetric examination using multiple stimuli is applied to the study of the partial homonymous hemianoptic visual field defects produced by lesions of the postgeniculate visual pathway, it will be found that interruption of the anterior portion of the optic radiation gives rise to incongruous homonymous hemianopsia in all cases. Lesions of the visual end station in the calcarine cortex, on the other hand, always produce precisely symmetric or congruous defects in the two fields.

These differences in the character of the visual field defects resulting from lesions in these two cerebral areas are of obvious diagnostic value and clinical importance.

The most logical explanation for these variations in symmetry in homonymous hemianoptic field defects is that there is a dissociation of homologous fibers from corresponding retinal points in the optic tract and radiation with coalescence of these fibers again in the visual cortex.

In the absence of conclusive transsynaptic degeneration studies, the perimetric examination of persons with precisely localized cerebral lesions is the only method of arriving at an understanding of the architecture of the optic radiations and the area striata.

The clinical evidence for separation of homologous fibers in the anterior portion of the optic radiation is in accord with Spalding's postulated arrangement of the visual fibers in this area.

The complete symmetry of the field defects produced by lesions of the occipital cortex in the calcarine fissure and at the occipital pole is the best evidence that the retina is represented in the striate cortex in a precise point-to-point manner. This has been amply illustrated by Holmes, Spalding, and in my own cases.

TYPES OF HOMONYMOUS HEMIANOPSIA

It should be clear that there are many types of homonymous hemianopsia; in fact, the variety is almost infinite.

Homonymous hemianopsia may be partial or complete, relative or absolute; it may have steep or sloping margins; its intensity may be uniform or variable. All of these variations depend in part on the anatomic location of the lesions producing them and are therefore of diagnostic value.

The basic types of homonymous hemianopsia are as follows:

1. Sector defects that are homonymous but less than a full quadrant
2. Homonymous quadrantanopsia
3. Partial defects that are homonymous but more than a quadrant and less than total hemianopsia
4. Total homonymous hemianopsia
5. Congruous sector or partial homonymous hemianopsia
6. Incongruous sector or partial homonymous hemianopsia (Fig. 15-2)
7. Homonymous hemianopsia with macular sparing
8. Homonymous hemianopsia with macular splitting
9. Unilateral homonymous hemianopsia with involvement of the temporal crescent
10. Homonymous hemianopsia with sparing of the temporal crescent
11. Homonymous hemianoptic scotomas
12. Double homonymous hemianopsia

Each of these types may vary in numerous ways, and each variation may indicate some slight difference in localization and possible etiology (see Plate 8).

Sector defects

Sector defects that encompass less than a quadrant are relatively rare. They occur in one field of a markedly incongruous homonymous hemianopsia, the other

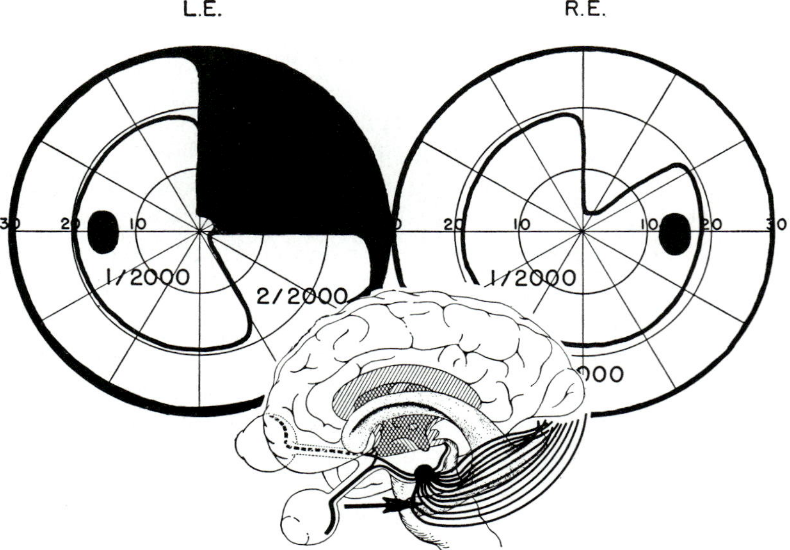

Fig. 15-2. Tumor of tip of left temporal lobe with markedly incongruous homonymous hemianopsia. Major field loss is on same side as tumor. Note that right field was apparently normal to all stimuli larger than 1/2000. Site and probable direction of pressure are shown in anatomic sketch.

field of which shows a quadrant or greater than quadrant loss. They are usually depressional-type defects whose margins are sloping. They are most often detected in the central isopters with small test objects and only by careful quantitative perimetry.

When perimeter or tangent screen examination reveals an apparent unilateral hemianoptic field defect involving a quadrant or slightly more than a quadrant loss in one eye only and a normal field in the other eye, a careful search of the central isopters of the normal field with minimal stimuli will often reveal a sector defect that is homonymous with the other field. This is in reality a grossly incongruous homonymous hemianopsia and indicates a lesion in the anterior portion of the postchiasmal pathway in the optic tract, geniculate body, or the anterior part of the optic radiation.

Homonymous quadrantanopsia

Homonymous quadrantanopsia may occur as a depression type of field loss with sloping margins and varying intensity, mainly found in the central isopters. In this type the defects are likely to be slightly asymmetric or incongruous. They may occur in lesions of the anterior radiation because of the wide separation of the upper and lower quadrant fibers (Fig. 15-3). When the upper quadrants are involved, the lesion is usually in the lower part of the temporal lobe. This is the upper homonymous quadrantanopsia referred to by Cushing in his articles on tumors involving the temporal loop of Meyer (Fig. 15-4). Lower homonymous quadrantanopsia of depressional type most often indicates a lesion high in the temporoparietal or parietal lobe. (See Fig. 4-12.)

When the quadrantanopsia is sharp margined, dense, and congruous, the lesion usually is in the striate cortex of the occipital lobe (Fig. 15-5). Loss of the upper

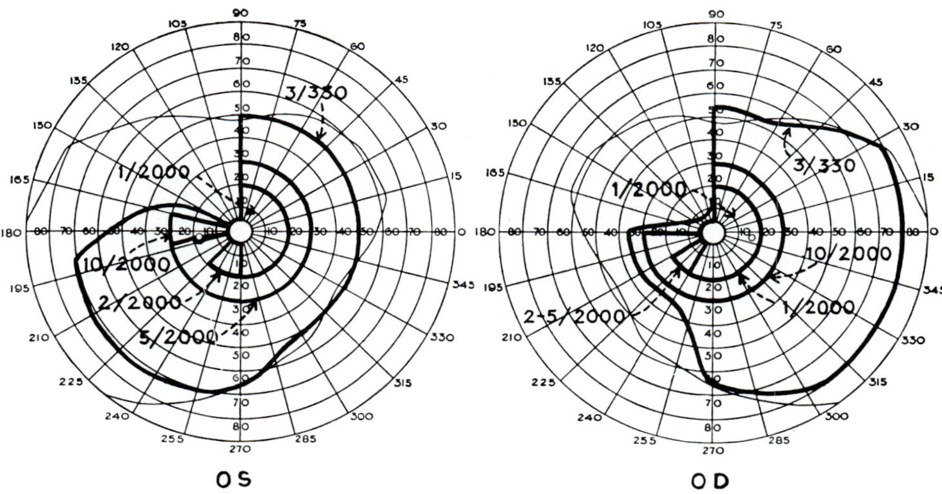

Fig. 15-3. Quantitative analysis of incongruous left upper homonymous quadrantanopsia resulting from glioma of anterior portion of right temporal lobe. Defects are most markedly asymmetric in larger isopters.

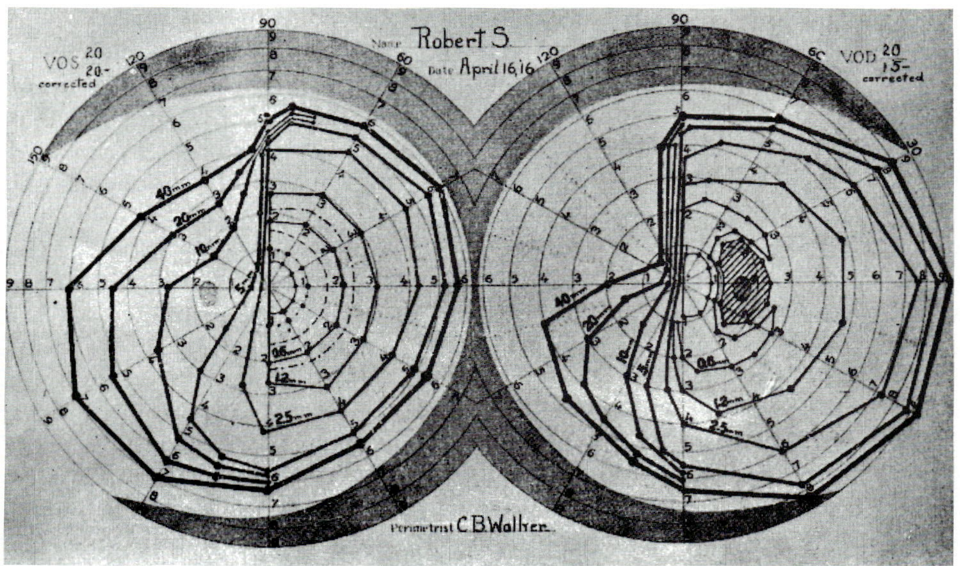

Fig. 15-4. Example of demonstration of incongruous homonymous hemianopsia in case of gliomatous cyst of right temporal lobe. Note that greatest degree of asymmetry is shown in isopters for largest stimuli and that larger defect is on side of lesion. Case is Cushing's with precise quantitative perimetry performed by C. B. Walker in 1916. (From Cushing, H.: Brain **44:**341, 1922.)

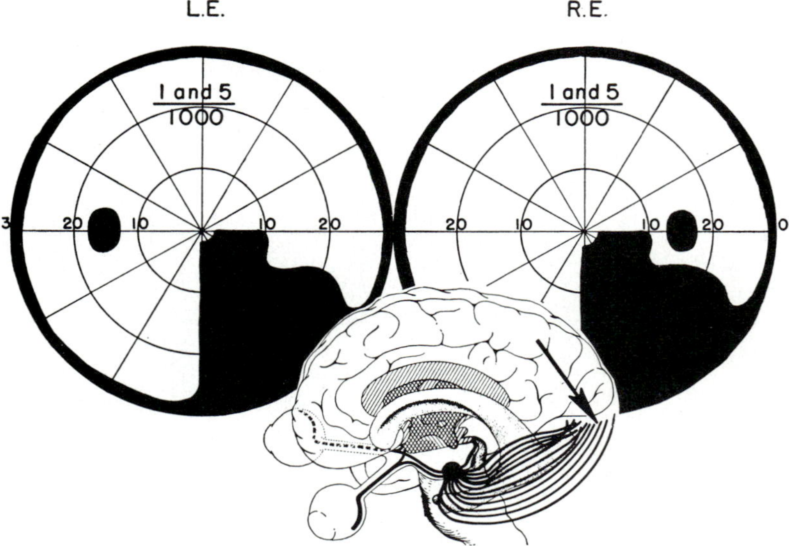

Fig. 15-5. Completely congruous but irregular right inferior homonymous quadrantanopsia. Note that congruity extends even to irregularities of horizontal margin. This arose from vascular lesion of upper lip of left calcarine fissure with site of calcarine cortical damage illustrated in anatomic sketch.

quadrant implies a lesion of the lower lip of the calcarine fissure, and vice versa. Sparing of the macula is the rule in this type of quadrantanopsia, and, when the lesion is far forward in the fissure, the macular sparing may be very wide.

In the homonymous quadrantanopsia from lesions of the optic radiation, the horizontal margin is usually straight or slightly curving. Those resulting from cortical lesions may have an irregular horizontal margin that is completely symmetric in the two fields, even to minute irregularities. This is especially true in traumatic and vascular lesions.

Upper homonymous quadrantanopsia is more common in lesions of the radiations due to more frequent involvement of the temporal loop, whereas lower homonymous quadrantanopsia is the rule in occipital lobe lesions, especially traumatic, since the upper calcarine area is more exposed to injury.

Partial homonymous hemianopsia

In partial homonymous hemianopsia, as in the case of quadrantanopsia, we are dealing with an incomplete homonymous hemianoptic defect that may be either congruous or incongruous (Figs. 15-6 and 15-7).

Asymmetric field defects are most frequently the result of compression of the

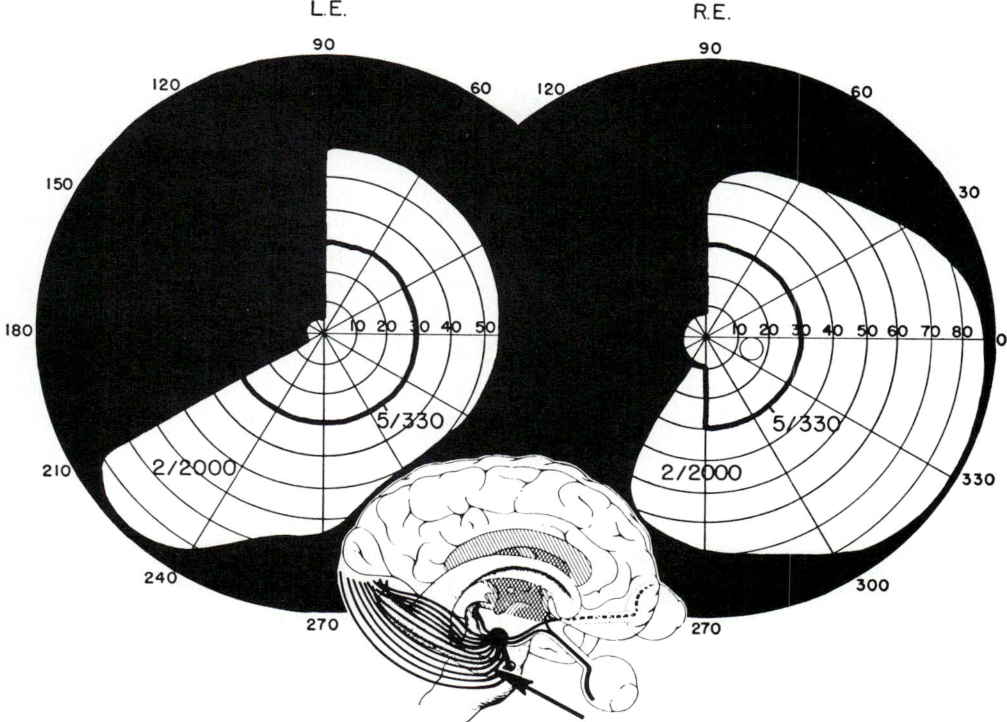

Fig. 15-6. Incongruous partial homonymous hemianopsia resulting from spongioblastoma of right temporal lobe. Patient had headache, blurred vision, hallucinations of smell, and papilledema. Ablation of right temporal lobe resulted in total left homonymous hemianopsia.

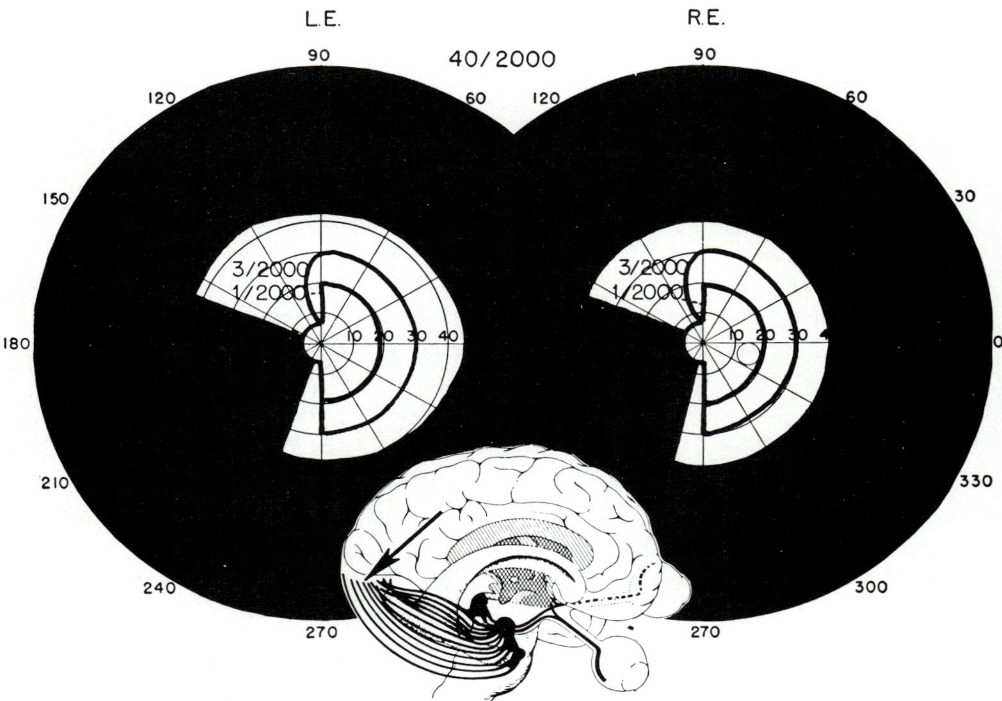

Fig. 15-7. Congruous partial homonymous hemianopsia resulting from trauma to right occipital lobe in area shown by arrow in anatomic drawing.

nerve fiber pathway or its vascular supply in the optic tract or radiation. They have sloping, straight, or slightly curved margins and may involve a quadrant or slightly more than a quadrant area of one field and a complete loss of the homonymous area in the other field in the same isopter.

When multiple isopters are tested, a different morphology may be evident. Thus the 1/2000 isopter may show an apparent total homonymous hemianopsia, whereas the 5/1000 isopter will reveal a less than total loss, with one field being more involved than the other.

When the two fields show symmetric but still incomplete hemianoptic defects, their interpretation usually implicates the occipital cortex. Again, as in the quadrantanopsias, this is more surely so if the margins are steep, the density uniform, and the area of macular sparing relatively large. Except for the mode of onset, the occipital type of incomplete hemianopsia is the same whether produced by tumor, injury, or vascular lesion.

When the isopters are widely spaced so that the visual field defect is morphologically different in the various isopters, it is a depression-type field loss. This kind of incomplete homonymous hemianopsia most often results from an active lesion compressing the geniculocalcarine pathway fibers in a progressive manner, and the most likely cause is a tumor.

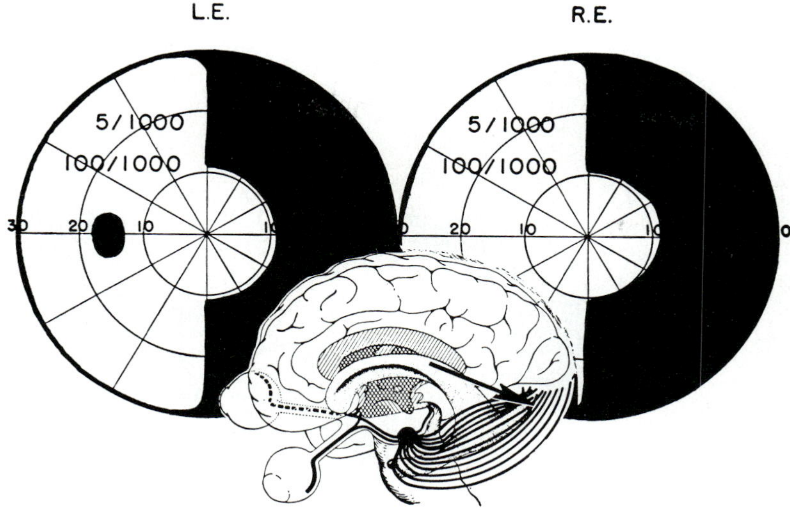

Fig. 15-8. Total homonymous hemianopsia with wide macular sparing. Almost entire left occipital lobe was involved in carcinoma that had metastasized from breast. Location of tumor, as determined at operation, is indicated in anatomic drawing.

Total homonymous hemianopsia

Absolute loss to all stimuli of the complete homonymous halves of both visual fields may be interpreted as due either to a very extensive lesion in that portion of the postchiasmal pathway where the fibers are widely dispersed or to a very destructive smaller lesion in those areas where the fibers are concentrated in a narrow bundle. Such a visual field defect might occur from a lesion in the optic radiations as the result of a relatively small hemorrhage in the knee of the internal capsule or as a widespread infiltrative or compressive lesion in the temporal, parietal, or occipital lobe (Fig. 15-8).

Involvement of the optic tract or external geniculate body may produce such a field loss with complete interruption of the fibers, such as can occur in association with intrinsic tumor, multiple sclerosis, or injury. Lateral or medial pressure on the tract from a tumor in the posterior chiasmal angle rarely gives rise to total homonymous hemianopsia.

With total loss of the homonymous half-fields, there can, of course, be no demonstration of congruity or incongruity in the visual fields.

Congruous sector or partial homonymous hemianopsia

When the visual field defects in each eye are completely symmetric in every respect, so that they appear to be carbon copies of each other, they are said to be congruous.

To fulfill the criteria for complete congruity, the two half-field defects must be less than complete, and they must correspond in every detail, even to minute irregularities of their hemianoptic borders.

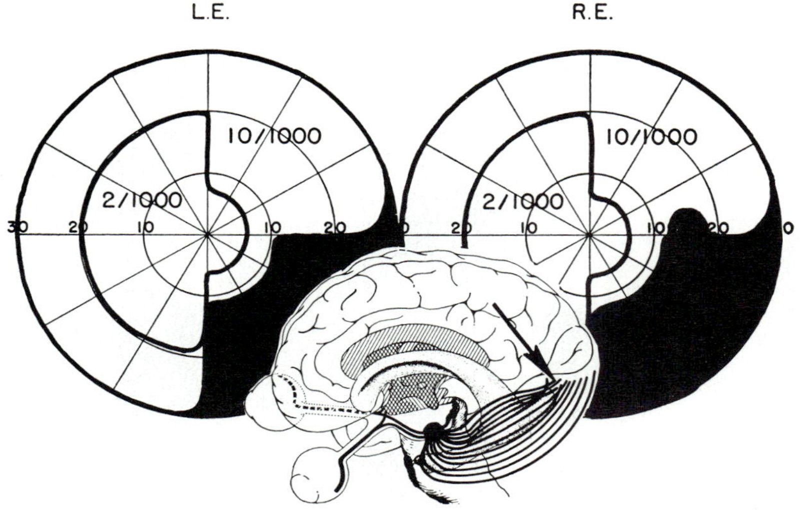

Fig. 15-9. Congruous right inferior homonymous quadrantanopsia produced by meningioma arising from falx and compressing upper lip of left calcarine fissure in its anterior portion. There were unformed visual hallucinations. Note wide area of macular sparing and apparent asymmetry of defect resulting from inclusion of blind spot in right visual field loss.

The fields should be examined in each eye separately and then binocularly, and the hemianoptic border between seeing and nonseeing areas must be exactly the same for all three examinations for each isopter. In a field with sloping margins, the defect for the 1/1000 isopter may be quite different from that for the 5/1000 isopter, but in each eye the defect should be identical for the same stimulus.

Allowance must, of course, be made for the fact that the temporal field is larger than the nasal field, which gives a spurious asymmetry to all homonymous hemianopsias. It must also be remembered that one visual field will have a blind spot in its seeing area whereas the other will not. In the case of a quadrantanopsia, this blind spot may give rise to an apparent indentation of the horizontal margin of one visual field that is not present in the other (Fig. 15-9).

Congruence is measured primarily in the oblique and near-vertical meridians and is seen most clearly in the central isopters. When the margins of the field defect are sloping, great care must be exercised in measurement and analysis of congruity or incongruity in the visual field. Under these circumstances the point of emergence or disappearance of the test object may be vague and subject to error. Unless the degree of symmetry or asymmetry is marked, it should not carry too much weight in the interpretation of the field loss. On the other hand, when the hemianoptic border of each field is steep, the response of the patient to the test object will be accurate and consistent, and congruity or incongruity may be easily established.

Congruous homonymous hemianopsia is best and most frequently seen in lesions of the striate cortex in the occipital lobe. The classic example of this type of field loss occurs with injury to the posterosuperior lip of one calcarine fissure, resulting in irregularly shaped but completely symmetric inferior homonymous quadrantanoptic scotomas (see Plate 9, *3*, *4*, and *6*).

Incongruous sector or partial homonymous hemianopsia

An incongruous or asymmetric homonymous hemianopsia is the opposite of the congruous defect already described. It must be an incomplete hemianopsia in order to measure the degree of asymmetry present. Not uncommonly this type of visual field defect will show a quadrant or sector loss in one field, whereas the other eye reveals a complete half-field loss for the same stimulus.

Because incomplete hemianopsia is now a relatively common finding as a result of earlier diagnosis of cerebral lesions, measuring the congruity or incongruity of the field defect becomes important.

When true incongruity is present, especially when it is fairly marked so that errors in stimulus response cannot be blamed, a lesion in the anterior portion of the postchiasmal pathway is indicated. The same type and degree of incongruity may be found in lesions of the tract and in the anterior optic radiations in the temporal lobe. The more posterior the lesion, the more symmetric will be the field loss in the two eyes (see Plate 8).

Homonymous hemianopsia with macular sparing

Numerous attempts have been made to explain the sparing of the macula that occurs in most cases of homonymous hemianopsia. None of them has been completely successful, whether from the anatomic, physiologic, or clinical point of view.

Some observers have maintained that there is a widespread macular representation in the occipital lobe, whereas others, on the basis of anatomic studies, emphatically deny this. These investigators point out that when the macular fibers reach the occipital lobes they arborize and make wide and intricate associations with different parts of the cortex. In his discussion of the point-to-point relationship in the visual system, Lorente de Nó stated that "each point of the retina is projected into a larger area of cortex because arborizations, protoplasmic as well as axonal, are extensive and therefore impulses set in any point of the retina may be transmitted to a larger area of the cerebral cortex. However, assuming that the neuron is a summation apparatus that reaches threshold excitation only when a certain number of its synapses are active, it becomes evident that, physiologically, the projection of the retina on the cerebral cortex may be point-like."

Bender and Kanzer concluded that "there may well be a wide representation of the macula in the occipital cortex in which the predominant number of impulses of macular origin reach the most posterior part of the striate area while the remainder enter other parts of the cortex. At the same time fibers from the peripheral retina are predominantly represented in the anterior part of the area striata, and a much smaller number connect with the occipital pole or cortical macula." These authors believe that the preservation of central vision or macular sparing in lesions of the occipital pole results from a shifting of function to another part of the calcarine cortex or to a widespread representation of the macula in the cortex, or both. They do not believe that there is bilateral representation of the cortical macula, and they agree with the anatomic studies of Brouwer and Zeeman, Putnam and Putnam, and Polyak that in the optic radiations the macular fibers are arranged in the middle bundle between the upper and lower peripheral retinal fibers.

Macular sparing may, in some cases, be merely a stage in the development of a homonymous hemianopsia. When field loss begins in the periphery and progresses toward fixation, the macular area is the last to be involved. Bender and Strauss have suggested that the reason for this is that the central area of the field represents a greater concentration of fibers than does the peripheral field. In the case of a uniform lesion, removal of function in a certain proportion of fibers of the pathway at one level would preserve proportionately more macular than peripheral fibers.

Conclusive evidence in support of the theory of bilateral macular representation has not been forthcoming. A number of authors have described cases in which total occipital lobectomy has produced macular sparing whereas other cases of similar type showed macular splitting.

The concept that macular preservation is the result of careless perimetric technique has been repeatedly disproved.

The theory that macular sparing results from shift in in fixation, and is therefore more apparent than real, deserved careful consideration and is undoubtedly responsible for preservation of a small area of central vision in some cases. It would not, of course, account for those homonymous hemianopsias with 10 degrees or more of macular sparing. In fixation shift, the patient unconsciously swings his field to the blind side and finds a new point of fixation. Such overshooting can be readily checked by the three-disc test of Hughes (see Fig. 7-16). The effect of such a macular shift is more apparent in the macular area where acuity is highest and the peripheral hemianoptic border may still appear to be midline. Hughes points out that this theory of macular sparing is strongly supported by the fact that small lesions at the occipital pole do not show macular sparing whereas larger lesions are must more likely to preserve central vision. It is also true that about 70% of cases of macular sparing are found in lesions of the dominant hemisphere. Field shift may therefore be caused by damage to the visual association areas and consequent disturbance in field fixation and orientation.

The most logical theory to account for macular sparing in lesions of the occipital cortex is the effect of overlapping blood supply to this area of the brain (see Fig. 5-1). While the major blood supply to the occipital lobes is from the posterior cerebral and calcarine arteries, the macular area of the occipital lobe is also frequently supplied by the posterior cortical or deep optic branches of the middle cerebral artery, branches of the posterior temporal artery, branches from the parieto-occipital artery, and a direct contribution from the middle cerebral artery.

Whatever the explanation for the phenomenon of macular sparing, it is a clinical fact that most homonymous hemianopsias, regardless of their varying morphology, show some degree of preservation of central vision. This is usually manifested as a

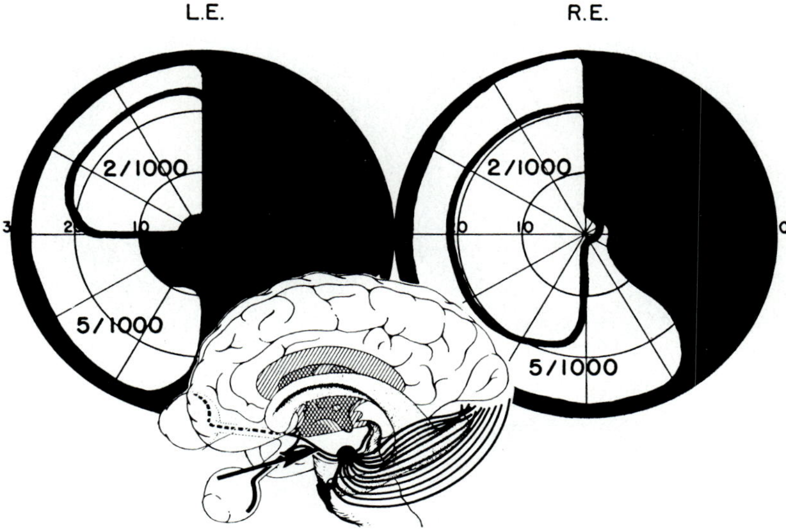

Fig. 15-10. Incongruous right partial homonymous hemianopsia, from case of arachnofibroblastoma of left petrous ridge and left temporal lobe with pressure on optic tract.

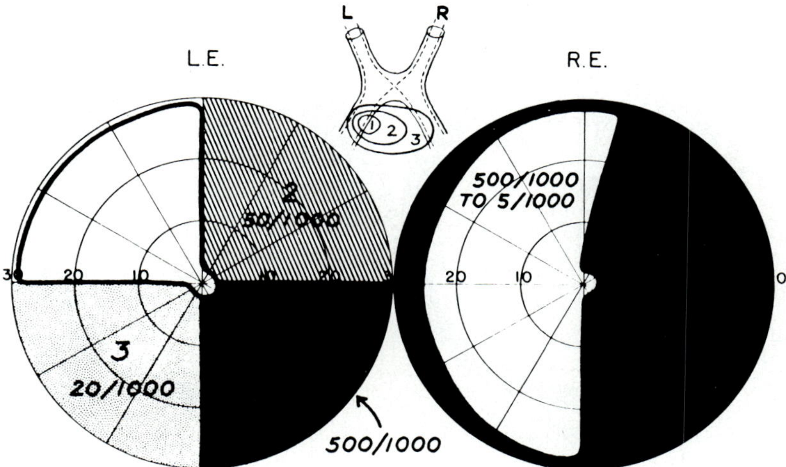

Fig. 15-11. Quantitative analysis of grossly incongruous homonymous hemianopsia produced by progressive expansion of craniopharyngioma medial to left optic tract. Study of multiple isopters reveals initial (and most dense) field loss in right temporal field and in area of left field marked *1*. Area of tract compression *(1)* is shown on anatomic sketch. As tumor expanded to area *2*, it caused loss of superior nasal quadrant in left field *(2)*. Further growth involved opposite tract and loss of lower temporal quadrant of left field *(3)*.

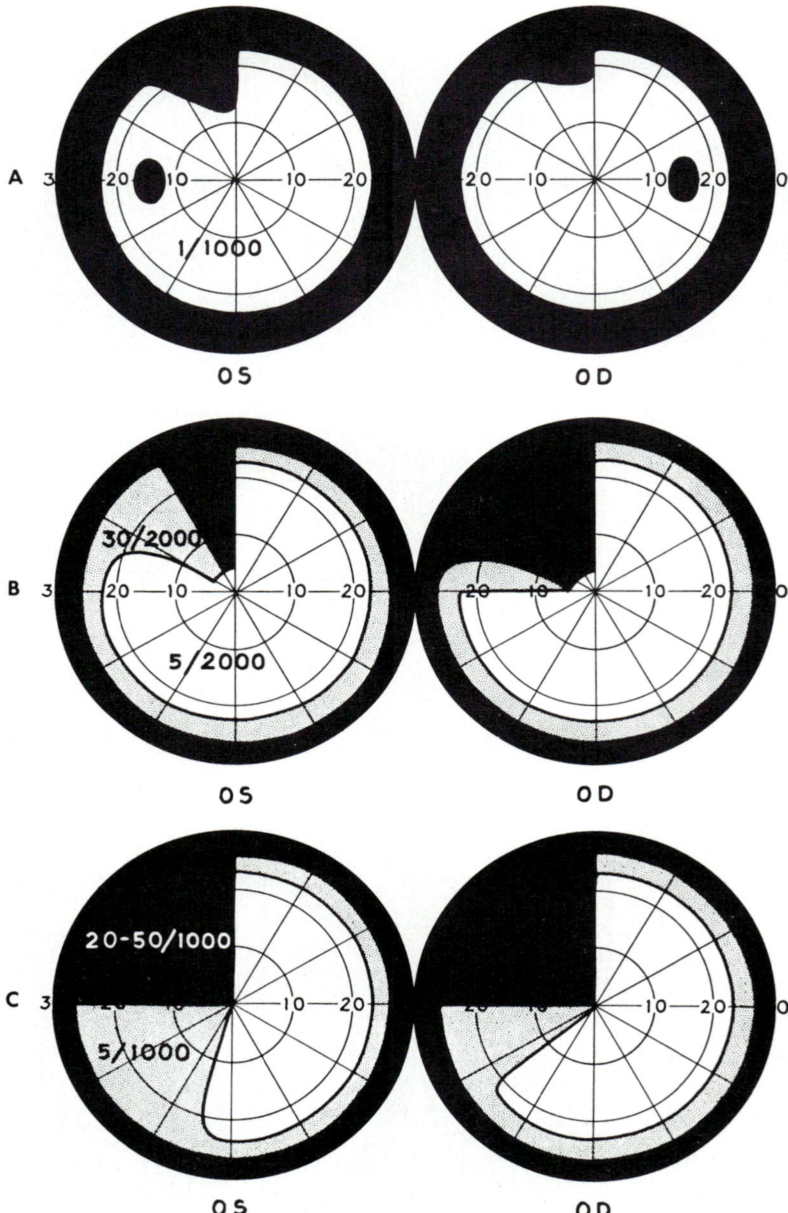

Fig. 15-12. A, Preoperative slightly incongruous minimal left upper homonymous quadrantanopsia resulting from astrocytoma of right temporal lobe. There were uncinate fits; arteriograms revealed tumor. **B,** One month later. Most of temporal lobe was removed at operation, including hippocampus and uncus. There was no evidence of optic tract damage. Homonymous quadrantanopsia is grossly incongruous with asymmetry most marked in isopters for large stimuli. **C,** Three years later. Increased field loss indicates extension of tumor into parietal lobe. Homonymous hemianopsia is still slightly incongruous. Six months later, homonymous hemianopsia was total and patient died.

deviation of the vertical hemianoptic border a few degrees around the fixation point. Rarely, the area of sparing extends along the entire vertical meridian as a narrow band of the seeing field encroaching on the anoptic field. This has been called the overshot field (see Figs. 7-15 and 7-16, *A*).

True macular sparing may show enormous variation, with the area extending from 0.5 to 30 degrees into the blind field. The areas of sparing may be congruous or incongruous, and they may be perfect hemispheres or irregular in outline. In the average homonymous hemianopsia, the area of sparing is approximately 3 degrees in size.

The general statement may be made that the more anterior the lesion in the postchiasmal pathway the smaller the area of macular sparing is likely to be (Fig. 15-11). Thus, although it is quite possible for a lesion of the posterior chiasmal angle to produce a homonymous hemianopsia with 5 degrees of macular sparing, a more common finding would be an area of sparing of 2 degrees or less. Conversely, lesions of the area striata most commonly give rise to relatively large areas of macular sparing,

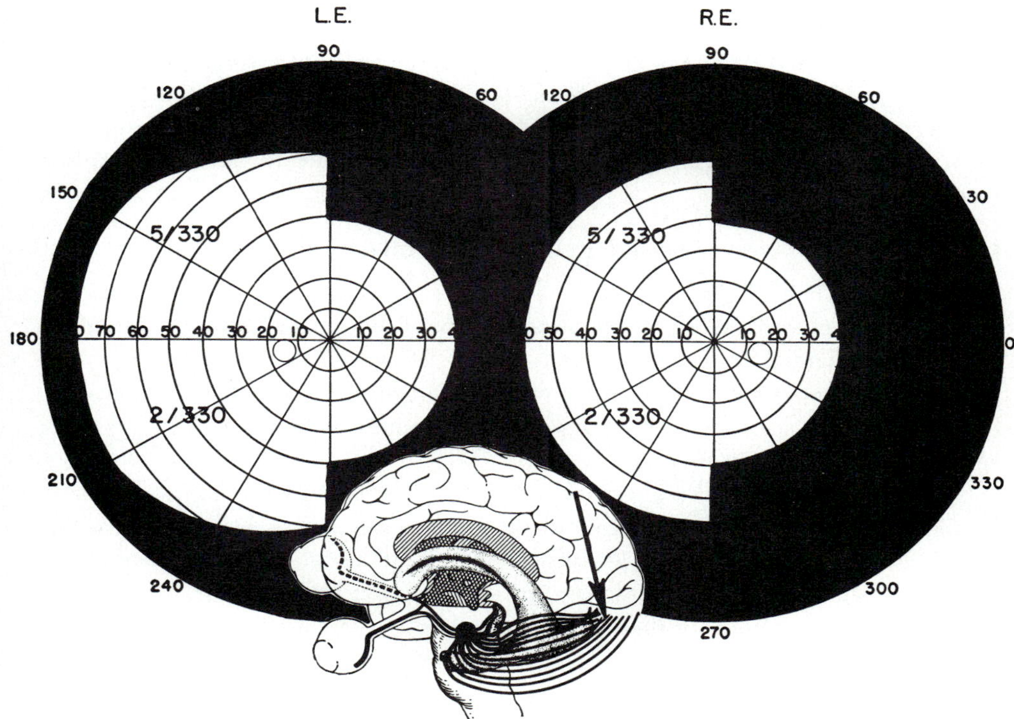

Fig. 15-13. Example of extremely wide macular sparing in homonymous hemianopsia. There were unformed hallucinations of "wisps of smoke," but patient was unaware of visual field defect, which was detected only on examination with perimeter beyond 30-degree circle. Operative diagnosis was meningioma of right calcarine fissure arising from falx in its anterior portion, as schematically shown in anatomic sketch.

often measuring 5 degrees or more. A tumor near the anterior end of the calcarine fissure may produce a homonymous hemianopsia in which only the peripheral field is involved and the area of central field is preserved out to 30 degrees or more from fixation (Fig. 15-13). A minute injury or vascular lesion at the tip of the occipital lobe may, on the other hand, cause a tiny hemianoptic scotoma with splitting of the macula or an extremely small area of sparing (see Figs. 15-16 to 15-20).

Therefore, careful quantitative examination of the central area in homonymous hemianopsia may have sufficient diagnostic value to warrant the effort expended on it. Macular sparing, especially when combined with other characteristic features in a hemianoptic field loss, is often a localizing sign of some importance.

Homonymous hemianopsia with macular splitting

True macular splitting is probably rather rare in lesions of the postchiasmal pathway. It is certainly uncommon in lesions of the area striata, where, as already noted, rather wide macular sparing is the rule, although it can occur under these conditions. It is common in affections of the posterior chiasmal angle and the beginning of the optic tracts (see Fig. 15-10). The question of macular sparing is discussed at length by Walsh and Hoyt. Cogan feels that it has assumed, by force of repetition, a prominence out of proportion to its actual importance. Interestingly, in this connection, visual acuity, as tested with Snellen test letters, is not affected by hemianoptic visual field defects, even in those patients with macular splitting (see Fig. 7-15). The resolving power of one-half the macula is equal to that of the entire macula.

Unilateral homonymous hemianopsia with involvement of the temporal crescent

Interference with the unpaired peripheral nasal fibers is the only explanation for a truly unilateral field defect resulting from a lesion of the postchiasmal visual pathway. The temporal field is larger than its homonymous nasal field because of the presence of these unpaired nasal fibers. In the normal field this accounts for a spurious type of incongruity.

According to Polyak, the fibers for the superior unpaired nasal fibers and those for the inferior fibers separate in the radiation and continue straight backward at the upper and lower borders of the pathway, coming together at the anterior tip of the calcarine fissure in its upper and lower lips. When either this upper or lower mesial bundle of fibers, or both, or their termination in the calcarine cortex is involved, a scotomatous defect in the upper, lower, or entire extreme peripheral crescent of the temporal field of the opposite side results, thus giving the effect of a unilateral field defect. Later this unilateral defect may develop into a homonymous hemianopsia, and, in fact, it is usually not recognized until it does so (Fig. 15-14).

Unilateral temporal crescentic scotoma in the visual field may indicate early disease of the posterior optic radiation or anterior striate cortex.

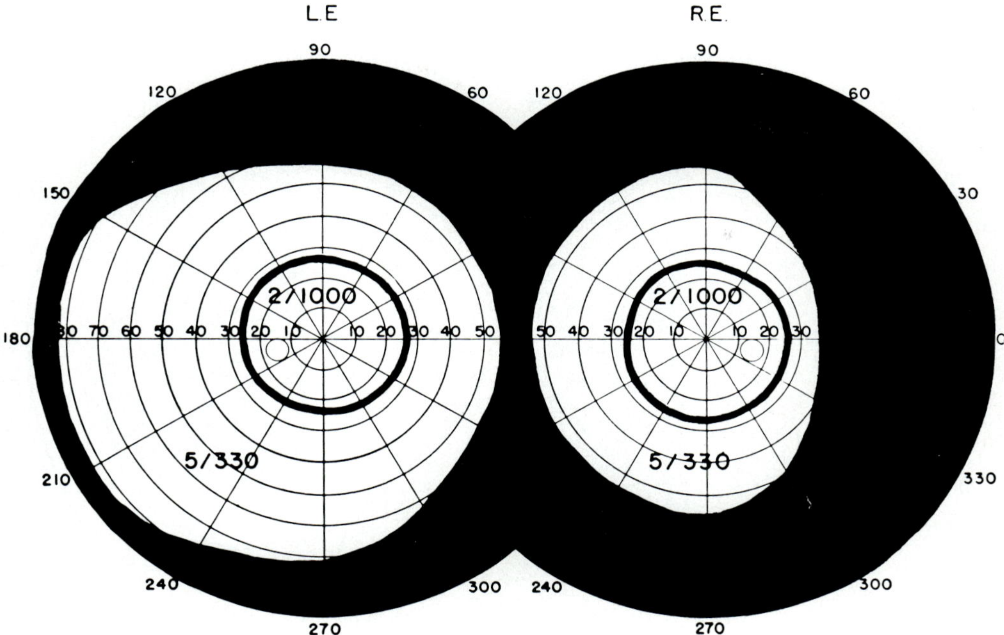

Fig. 15-14. Apparent unilateral hemianopsia due to involvement of right temporal crescent.

Homonymous hemianopsia with sparing of the temporal crescent

Homonymous hemianopsia with temporal crescent sparing is a much more common visual field defect, in which the temporal crescent plays a diagnostic role (Fig. 15-15). It results from involvement of the occipital lobe and may be a valuable localizing sign. The crescent may be completely spared or only its upper or lower portion may be spared. The resulting field may thus give the appearance of a complete hemianopsia in the ipsilateral nasal field with a large homonymous hemianoptic scotoma in the contralateral temporal field.

Benton, Levy, and Swash have reported on four patients with hemianopsias due to occipital infarction, well documented with visual field studies on the Goldmann perimeter and computer-assisted tomography (CAT scan), in whom there was useful residual vision in the unpaired temporal crescent. Moving stimuli were particularly well perceived in this part of the field. In each case preservation of the temporal crescent resulted in strikingly incongruous fields. The significance of this part of the visual field is discussed in relation to perception of movement and to the fixation reflex and also with regard to reports of residual visual ability in patients with lesions of the striate cortex and to the role of the monocular temporal field in striate and tectal visual systems.

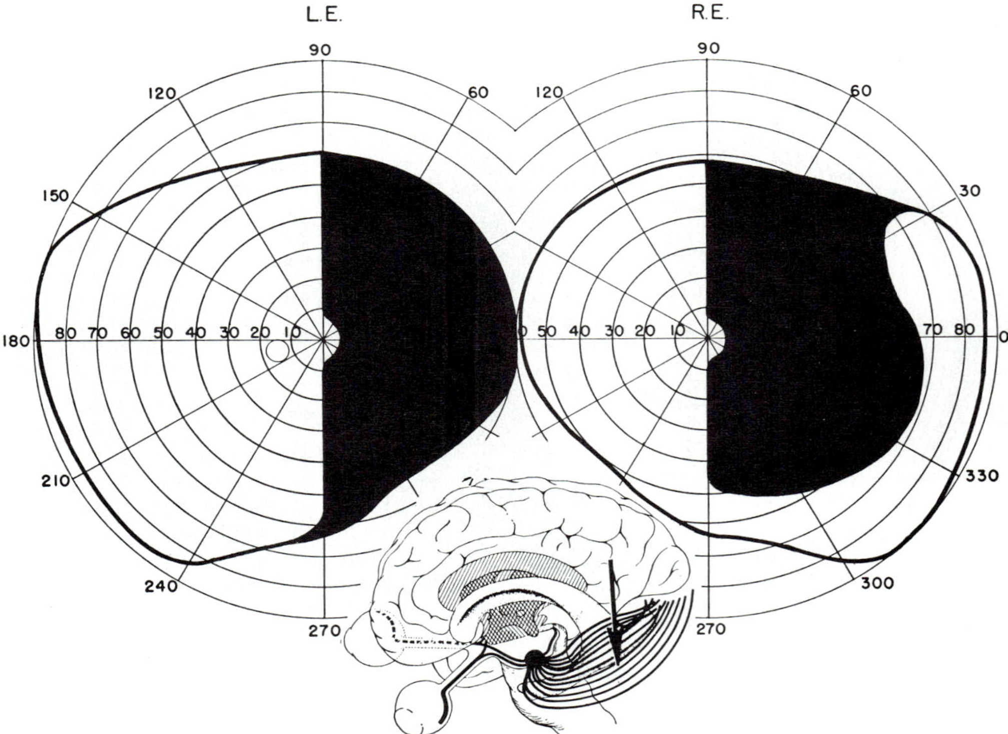

Fig. 15-15. Right homonymous hemianopsia with preservation of temporal crescent from cerebrovascular accident. Location of lesion in central portion of left parietal lobe is shown in sketch.

Homonymous hemianoptic scotomas

Homonymous hemianoptic scotomas have been generally considered as extremely rare. In my own experience they are not uncommon. There are two main types of lesions capable of producing such a field defect, the vascular and the traumatic. All of my own cases showed completely congruous paracentral homonymous hemianoptic scotomas. They were irregular in outline, steep-margined, and dense. None resulted from compression of the visual pathway by tumor, and all were static and permanent.

All these characteristics implicate the occipital cortex as the site of the lesion, and in the traumatic cases this was easily verified.

Vascular lesions are probably caused by occlusion of small arterial twigs supplying the calcarine cortex. They are sudden and spontaneous in onset and are noticed early by the patient because they interfere with reading, especially when they are in the right homonymous fields.

Traumatic lesions are often the result of war wounds of the occiput, with depressed fracture, cortical injury from bone spicules, and minute intracranial foreign bodies (Figs. 15-16, 15-18, and 15-19). These cases also show small, irregular,

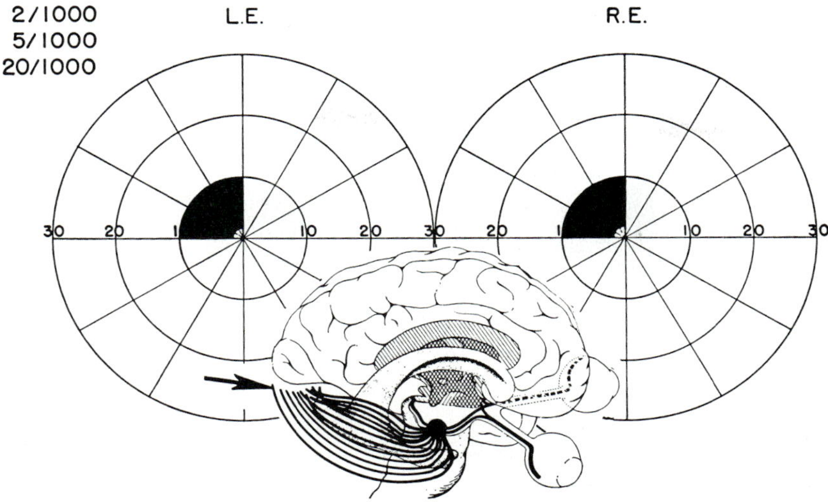

Fig. 15-16. Homonymous quadrantanoptic scotoma from shrapnel wound of skull with depressed fracture over occiput. Debridement of wound revealed spicule of bone penetrating dura over tip of right occipital lobe with brain damage and hemorrhage in inferior lip of right calcarine fissure. Vision was 20/20 in each eye.

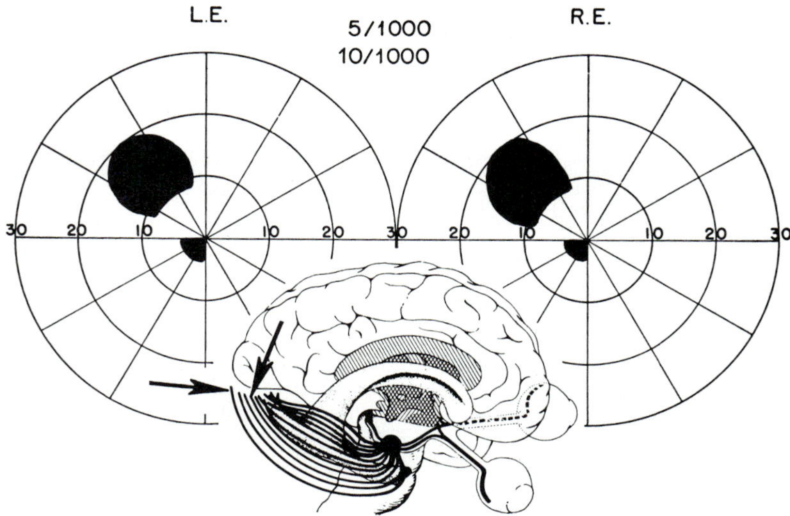

Fig. 15-17. Double homonymous hemianoptic scotomas. Visual loss was sudden. Neurologic examination was normal. The scotomas resulted from presumed vascular lesion of right occipital lobe with one small lesion in posterior tip of right superior calcarine lip and another in middle portion of lower lip of fissure. Note absence of macular sparing in inferior quadrantanoptic scotoma and rather wide macular sparing in superior paracentral homonymous hemianoptic scotoma.

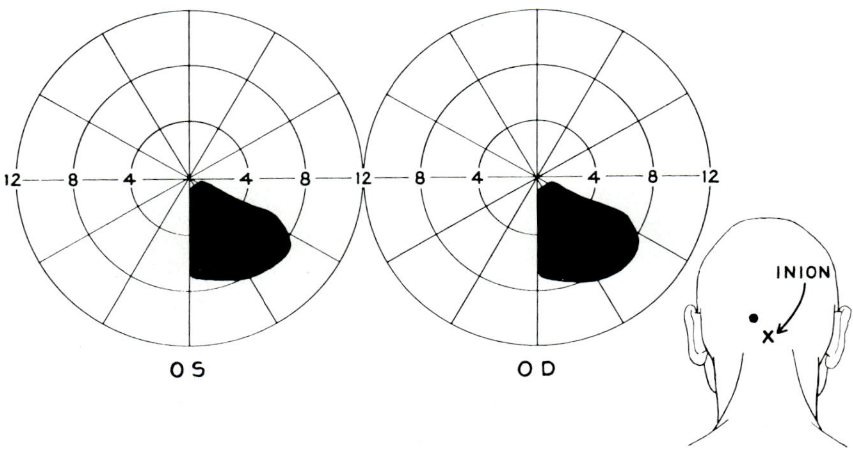

Fig. 15-18. Absolute congruity in paracentral right inferior homonymous quadrantanoptic scotoma produced by small depressed fracture of skull above and to left of external occipital protuberance. (Redrawn from Holmes, G., and Lister, W. T.: Brain **39:**34, 1916.)

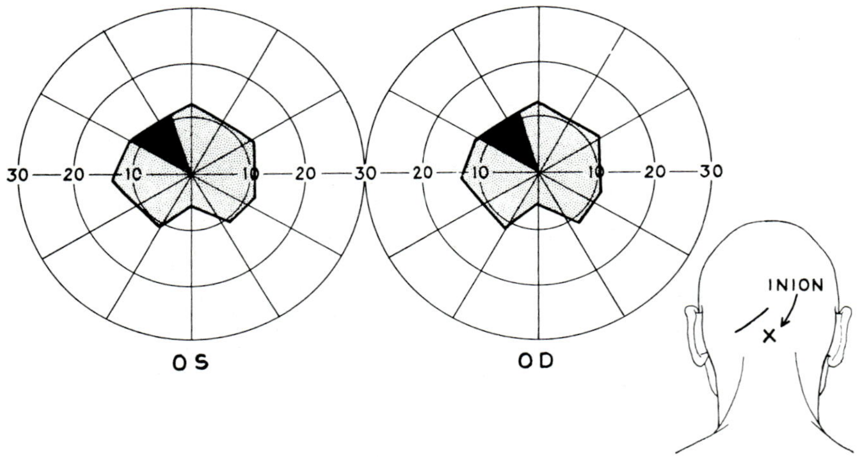

Fig. 15-19. Visual field defects produced by small area of injury to both occipital poles. Note complete symmetry in scotomas as to size, shape, and density. (Redrawn from Holmes, G., and Lister, W. T.: Brain **39:**34, 1916.)

completely congruous, steep-margined, and dense homonymous hemianoptic scotomas. In several patients with retained intracerebral foreigh bodies (shrapnel fragments), it has been possible to localize accurately the site of brain damage in the area striata by careful perimetry and then confirm the localization by means of measurement on stereoscopic roentgenography.

A few cases of incongruous homonymous hemianoptic scotomas have been re-

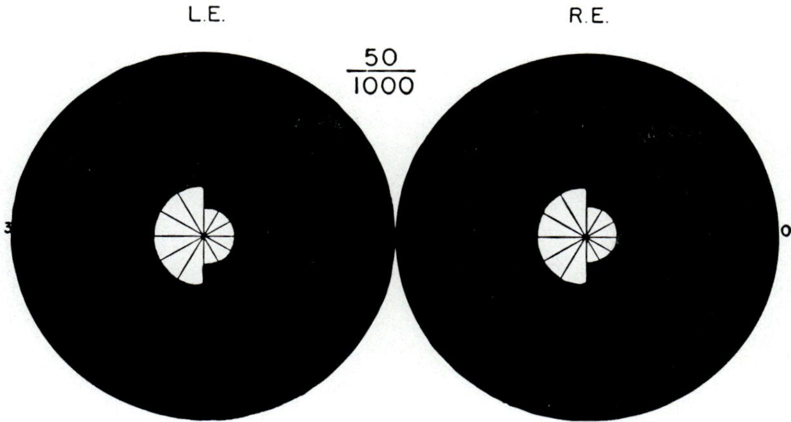

Fig. 15-20. Double homonymous hemianopsia, caused by injury to occipital pole from falling weight. Remnant of visual field is result of bilateral macular sparing, area of left field being slightly larger than that on right. Note small vertical steps produced by this difference in size of spared areas.

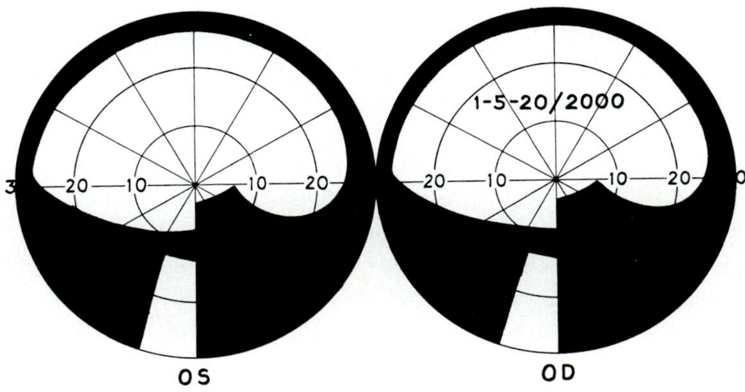

Fig. 15-21. Congruous bilateral inferior homonymous quadrantanopsia resulting from vascular insufficiency and infarction in upper lips of both calcarine fissures.

ported. The site of the lesion in such cases is not known, but it might be in the optic tract as the result of a minute vascular, demyelinating, or inflammatory disturbance.

Double homonymous hemianopsia

Bilateral lesions of both area striata are not uncommon. Some are the result of injury, but most are vascular (Figs. 15-17 and 15-20). Severe injury to the occiput in automobile accidents is not uncommon. Falling objects striking the head also cause such brain damage.

The sudden, spontaneous development of double homonymous hemianopsia associated with signs of brain stem damage, such as nystagmus and internuclear oph-

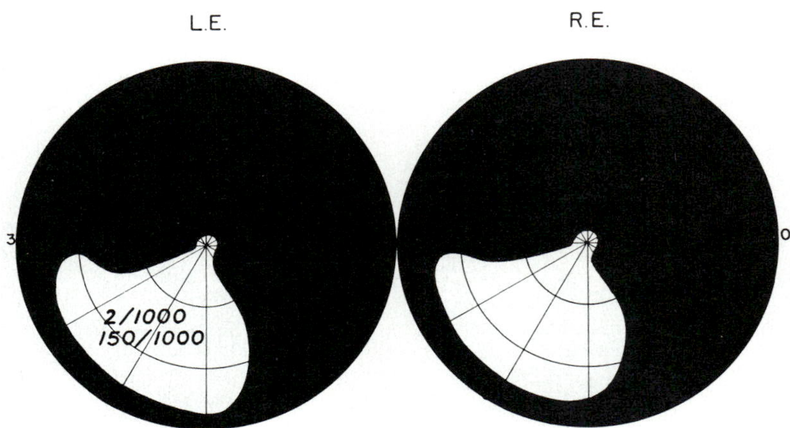

Fig. 15-22. Double homonymous hemianopsia associated with thrombosis of basilar, vertebral, and posterior cerebral arteries. Note absolute congruity of defect margins for large and small stimuli.

thalmoplegia, is almost certain evidence of occlusion of the basilar artery (see Fig. 15-22).

The visual field defects in these cases vary widely in morphology. If the upper lips of both calcarine fissures are damaged, the resulting field will be an inferior altitudinal hemianopsia with a downward preservation of the macular area (Fig. 15-21).

If both calcarine fissures are extensively involved, the visual field will look like the end stages of a bilateral glaucoma field, with only central vision remaining due to the bilateral macular sparing. The loss may be unequal in the two fields, resulting in somewhat wider macular sparing on one side than the other and steplike defects on the vertical meridian (see Fig. 15-20). Central vision may remain normal so that reading is possible if the area of sparing is sufficiently wide, but locomotion with such narrowed fields is very difficult.

A related but rare type of visual defect is crossed quadrant hemianopsia, which is in reality a partial bilateral homonymous hemianopsia with the site of the lesions in the upper lip of one calcarine fissure and the lower lip of the other.

ANATOMIC DIVISIONS OF POSTCHIASMAL VISUAL PATHWAY

Having considered the general morphology of the homonymous hemianopsias resulting from lesions of the retrochiasmal visual pathway, we will now discuss the visual field changes associated with each of its four anatomic divisions: (1) the optic tracts, (2) the external geniculate body, (3) the optic radiations or geniculocalcarine pathway, and (4) the occipital cortex or the area striata.

In each case detailed knowledge of the anatomy of the area is essential, not only of the fiber pathway but also of contiguous structures, vascular supply, and the more common pathologic lesions affecting the area in question. Only in this way will analysis of the visual field defects lead to reasonably correct interpretation of the localization and etiology of the lesions causing them.

Optic tracts

The characteristic visual field defect produced by lesions of the optic tract is a homonymous hemianopsia that is incomplete, incongruous, of variable density, and with sloping margins. The defect often begins with loss of a quadrant, and there is a small area of macular sparing. As the field change progresses, it encroaches on the fixation area and involves more of the peripheral field, until finally there is a total homonymous hemianopsia with splitting of the macula (see Fig. 7-13).

In early lesions the asymmetry of the hemianopsia may be so marked that the defect may at first appear to be unilateral; and only after careful search will the homonymous loss in the opposite field be detected.

Primary lesions of the optic tract are relatively rare, although the tract is occasionally the site of a glioma and may be affected in multiple sclerosis.

Chiasmal and retrochiasmal involvement in patients with multiple sclerosis is rare but would probably be encountered more frequently if searched for. I have seen several instances of bitemporal hemianopsia (see Fig. 14-54) produced by extension of retrobulbar neuritis into the chiasm and of homonymous hemianopsia (see Fig. 15-25) from tract lesions associated with well-advanced multiple sclerosis. Boldt reports five (1.4%) such examples in a series of 365 cases of multiple sclerosis studied perimetrically. The lesions that most frequently affect the optic tract are tumors of adjacent structures and aneurysms of the posterior arteries of the circle of Willis (i.e., the posterior communicating, posterior cerebral, internal carotid, and middle cerebral arteries).

The intimate relationship of the optic tract to the pituitary body, the ventricular system, the basilar vessels and meninges, the temporal lobe, and the basal ganglia may cause the tract to become involved in a multitude of lesions arising from neighborhood structures.

Aneurysms may give rise to acute symptoms with rapid field loss associated with pain from involvement of the fifth nerve.

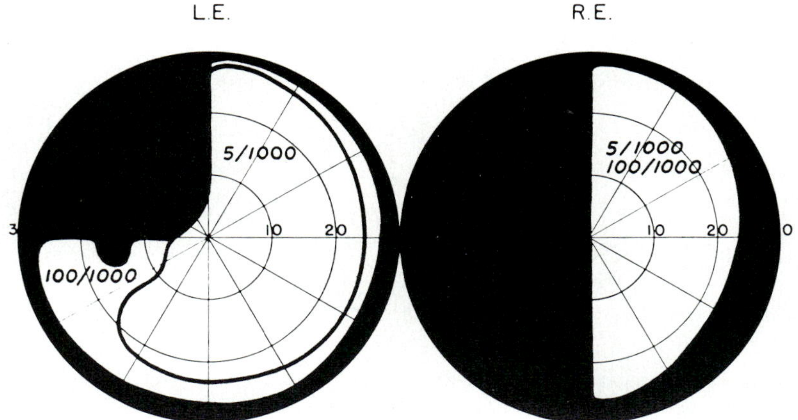

Fig. 15-23. Incongruous homonymous hemianopsia resulting from mesial pressure on right optic tract from carcinoma of pituitary gland. Associated neurologic signs were paralysis of conjugate gaze to right, fixed right pupil, and ptosis.

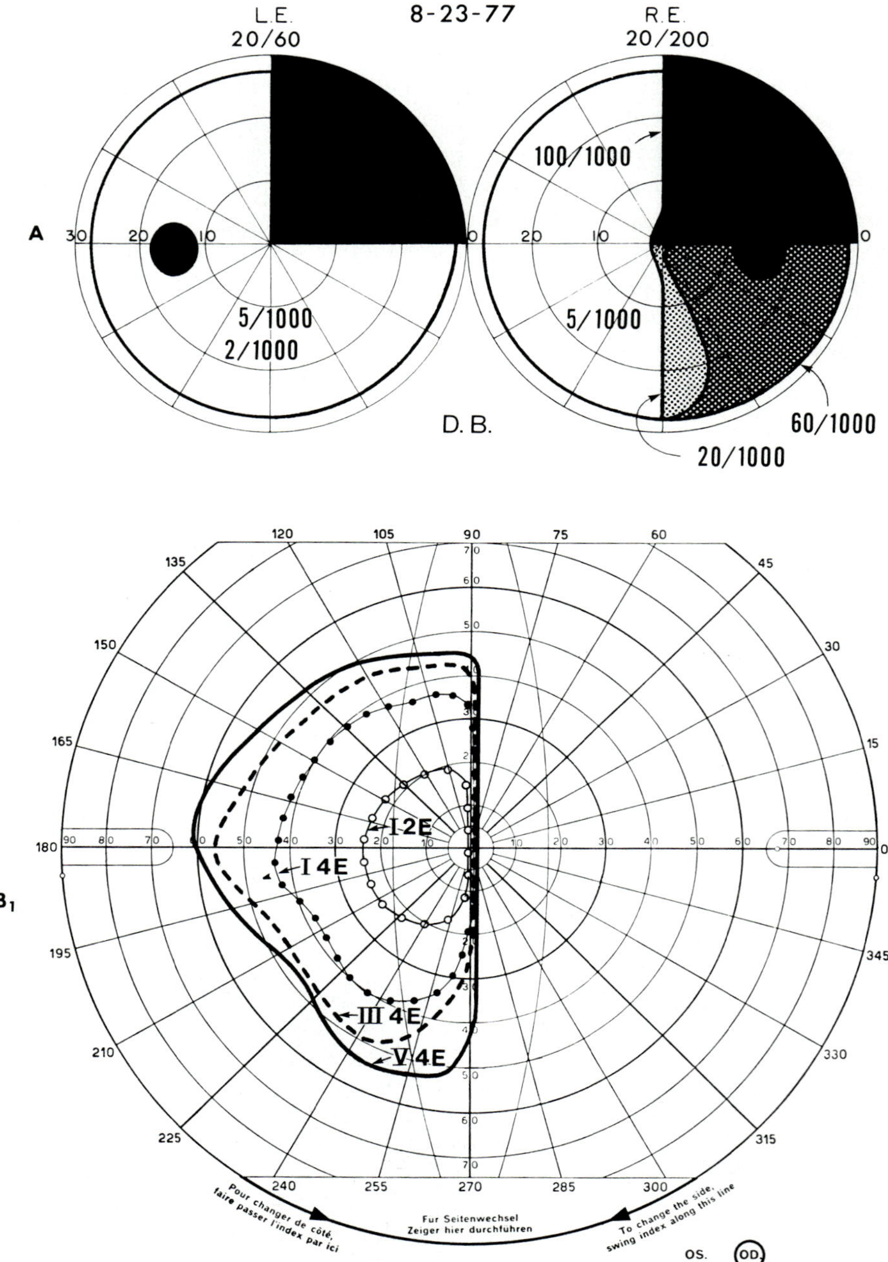

Fig. 15-24. A, Intracranial sarcoidosis. Tangent screen field showing markedly incongruous right homonymous hemianopsia with macular splitting. **B_1 and B_2,** Goldmann perimeter field of case shown in **A.** Markedly incongruous right homonymous hemianopsia due to intracranial sarcoidosis involving left optic tract. **C,** CAT scan of case shown in **A.** Intracranial sarcoidosis involving left optic tract. Chest roentgenograms show extensive hilar adenopathy. Lymph gland biopsy positive for sarcoid, and slit lamp shows evidence of chronic anterior uveitis.

B2

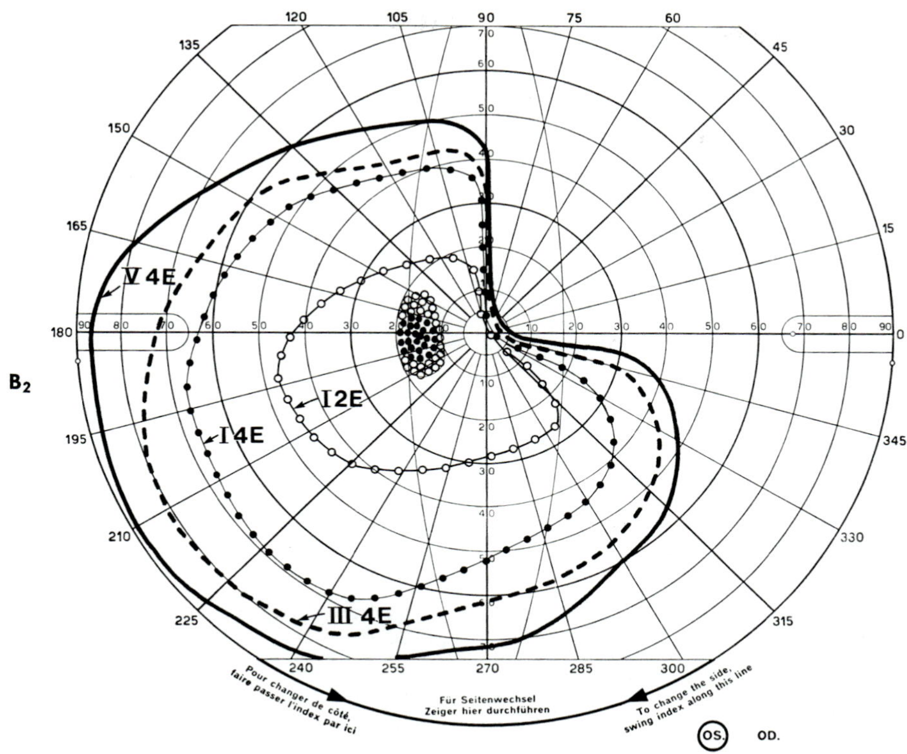

C

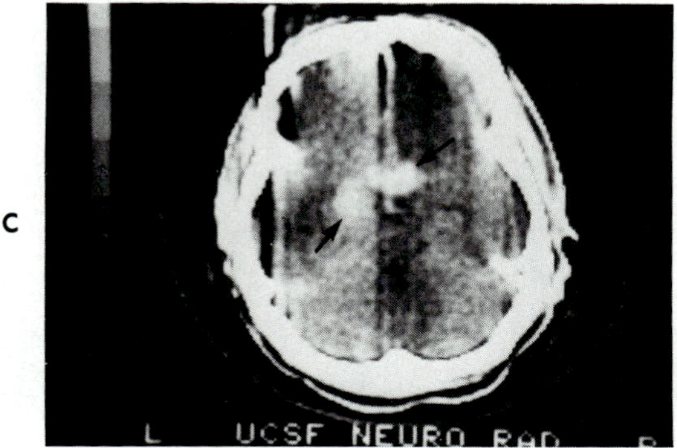

Fig. 15-24, cont'd. For legend see opposite page.

Tumors affecting the tracts are more common, with pituitary tumor by far the most frequent (Fig. 15-23). Parasellar tumor, tumor of the third ventricle, basal ganglion, and transverse fissure may also affect the optic tracts.

Tumors of the medial portion of the temporal lobe may occasionally be responsible for pressure on the lateral aspects of the optic tracts. It cannot be said with certainty whether the visual field defects associated with these tumors are the result of pressure on the optic tracts or on the fibers of the optic radiation within the temporal lobe (see Fig. 15-10).

Anterior tract lesions are usually caused by pituitary tumor or lesions closely associated with the posterior chiasmal angle. They are frequently accompanied by signs and symptoms of pituitary disease.

Midtract lesions may be accompanied by pyramidal tract signs and hemianesthesia on the same side as the hemianopsia or by involvement of the third, fourth, fifth, and sixth cranial nerves on the opposite side.

Sarcoidosis involving the nervous system has been reported by a number of authors. It is a rare manifestation of the disease. McLaurin and I have recently examined a patient with intracranial sarcoidosis involving the left optic tract and temporal lobe, with incongruous homonymous hemianopsia and a positive CAT scan (see Fig. 15-24). The diagnosis was substantiated by radiologic evidence of bilateral

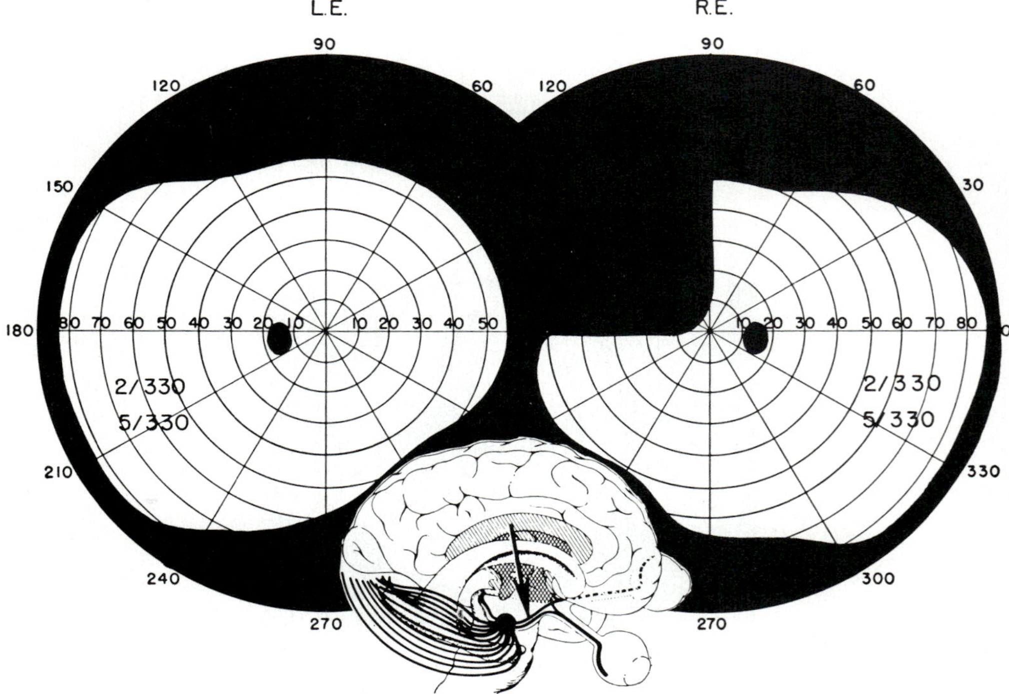

Fig. 15-25. Apparently unilateral quadrantanopsia in case of multiple sclerosis involving right optic tract. Homonymous nature of defect was elicited only with small test objects. This is, in effect, extreme degree of incongruity in homonymous hemianopsia.

hilar and paratracheal adenopathy, typical of pulmonary sarcoidosis. There was a past history of recurrent uveitis, and a mediastinal biopsy of the lymph nodes was positive for sarcoid. The CAT scan indicated a large lesion in the suprasellar cistern with extension into the left temporal lobe along the optic tract.

Intensive corticosteroid therapy resulted in restoration of vision, marked improvement of the visual field defect, decrease in the pulmonary hilar adenopathy, and almost complete resolution of the temporal lobe lesion.

Posterior tract lesions have symptomatology associated with the basal ganglia and are generally indistinguishable from disease affecting the external geniculate ganglion (Figs. 15-26 and 15-27).

When pressure is exerted lateral to the tract, the field is most affected on the side of the lesion, whereas the contralateral field is most severely affected by lesions between or mesial to the tracts (see Plate 7). In all cases of pressure on the optic tract, optic atrophy eventually ensues, although it may require months for development.

Hoyt and Kommerell found objective evidence of homonymous hemiretinal atrophy, documented by red-free fundus photography, in patients with homonymous hemianopsia resulting from lesions of the optic tract. Injury to an optic tract

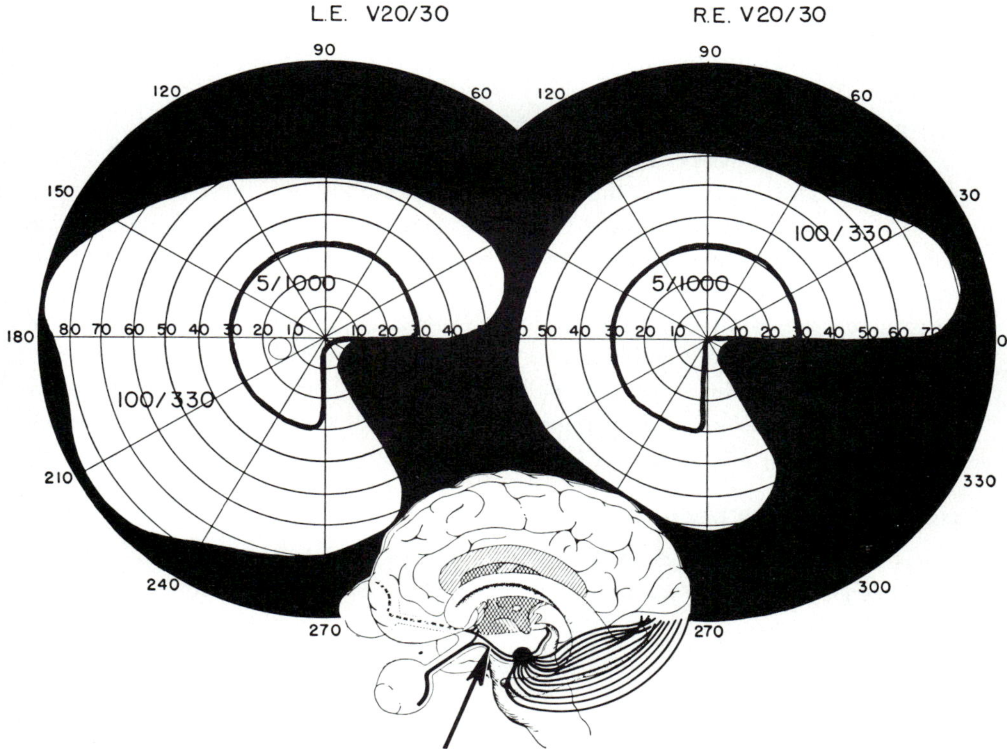

Fig. 15-26. Right homonymous inferior quadrantanopsia of sudden onset in patient with advanced and long-standing multiple sclerosis with episodes of transient partial paralysis, anesthesia, diplopia and nystagmus, and optic atrophy.

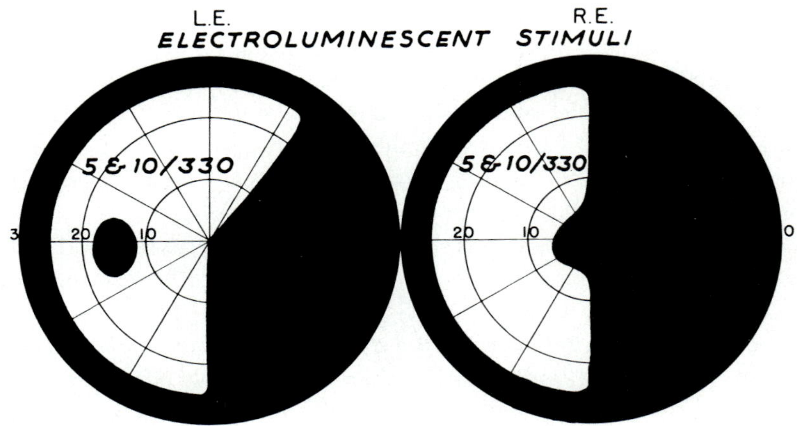

Fig. 15-27. Demyelinating lesion of midbrain with involvement of external geniculate body, third nerve nucleus, superior colliculus, and supranuclear crossed pyramidal tracts. This resulted in (1) incongruous homonymous hemianopsia, (2) Weber's syndrome of ipsilateral third nerve palsy and contralateral hemiplegia, and (3) Perinaud's syndrome of paralysis of upward gaze, ipsilateral oculomotor palsy, and contralateral facial and glossopharyngeal palsy.

leads to retrograde degeneration of the involved nerve fibers as far as the retinal ganglion cells.

Two of their patients had sustained a laceration of the right optic tract, whereas two other patients had presumed early injury of the right occipital lobe with transsynaptic degeneration through the lateral geniculate body into the retina.

In the eye with the blind nasal hemiretina (temporal hemianopsia), an atrophic band was found running diagonally over the papilla. In the eye with the blind temporal hemiretina (nasal heminopsia), an oval papillary excavation was seen, similar to a glaucomatous alteration. These optic disc changes correspond to the areas of retinal nerve fiber bundle and ganglion cell atrophy.

The homonymous hemiretinal atrophy may appear as early as 2 to 3 months after optic tract injury, whereas many years are required for the development of retinal nerve fiber atrophy after injury to the visual cortex.

External geniculate body

It is rarely possible to diagnose lesions of the external geniculate body during life. The characteristic visual field defect would be a markedly incongruous homonymous hemianopsia identical to that produced by a lesion of the posterior part of the tract or the anterior portion of the optic radiation.

In theory a lesion of the medial aspect of the geniculate body would produce a homonymous lower quadrantanopsia of the opposite side, whereas a lesion affecting the lateral aspect of the ganglion would give rise to a homonymous upper quadrantanopsia of the opposite side.

Gunderson and Hoyt have reported quantitative perimetric studies in two patients with involvement of the lateral geniculate nucleus with strikingly incongruous defects in the contralateral homonymous visual fields. One patient had an astrocytoma proven at autopsy and the other had a small arteriovenous malformation demonstrated in vertebral arteriograms. The patterns of these hemianopsias were correlated anatomically with the patterns of retinal projections within the six cellular lamina of the geniculate body (see Fig. 4-8).

Their studies confirm the findings of Minkowski that crossed retinal projections terminate in geniculate laminae, 1, 4, and 6, while uncrossed projections terminate in laminae 2, 3, and 5.

Corresponding points in the two retinae are represented in the external geniculate body in vertical columns of cells from all six laminae. In this way the monocular organization of rods and cones is transformed into a binocular arrangement of lateral geniculate body neurons, most of which is devoted to macular vision. Thus, it is apparent that irregular or partial involvement of several laminae will produce different effects in the corresponding homonymous fields of vision.

Frisen and co-workers have reported on two patients with sectorial optic atrophy and homonymous, horizontal, wedge-shaped sectoranopia. Neuroradiologic investigations localized the visual pathway lesion to the lateral geniculate body. The peculiar nature of the field defect and the optic atrophy could be explained by ischemia in the territory of the lateral choroidal artery.

The close association of the external geniculate body with the thalamus may cause hemianesthesia on the side of the hemianopsia. Involvement of the nearby pyramidal tract may cause motor weakness or hemiplegia on the side opposite the lesion.

All of these symptom complexes may also be found in patients with lesions affecting the internal capsule and the beginning of the optic radiation, in association with homonymous hemianopsia.

Optic radiations or geniculocalcarine pathway

The optic radiations constitute the third and final neuron in the visual pathway. They are the longest, most widespread, and, except for the chiasmal decussation, most vulnerable portion of the visual pathway. Because of the tortuous course of the geniculocalcarine pathway and the wide area that it occupies in the cerebral hemisphere, it is subject to interruptions at many points and from lesions of many types. For this reason, the morphology of its visual field defects is extremely variable, and the interpretation of these variations is diagnostically important.

A brief review of the anatomy of the optic radiation shows it leaving the external geniculate body to run laterally through the retrolenticular segment of the internal capsule behind the sensory fibers in a compact mass, the optic peduncle. The fibers then fan out rapidly in the medullary optic lamella, so that the fibers from the upper and lower retinal quadrants are separated by the macular fibers between them.

The fibers from the medial aspect of the external geniculate body that have come from the upper retinal quadrant run dorsally in the optic lamella in a straight course through the white matter of the parieto-occipital lobe and then descend in a horizontal fan over the caudal end of the calcarine fissure to enter the cortex in the dorsal portion of the striate area.

The fibers from the lateral aspect of the external geniculate body that have come from the lower retinal quadrant run in the ventral portion of the lamella that runs forward in the temporal lobe to form Meyer's temporal loop. This may reach far forward to envelop the temporal horn of the lateral ventricle and then pass along its body and around its posterior horn to end in the ventral portion of the calcarine cortex.

The macular fibers run from the dorsal part of the external geniculate ganglion as a flat bundle between the dorsal and ventral fibers, to end in the posterior pole or operculum of the occipital cortex (see Fig. 4-12).

For convenience the optic radiations may be divided into three parts:

1. The anterior radiation and, in particular, that portion within the internal capsule.
2. The midportion of the radiation, which includes the wide band of fibers traversing the temporal and temporoparietal lobes in the external sagittal stratum.
3. The posterior radiation, made up of that portion of the fibers in the external sagittal stratum of the parietal and parieto-occipital lobes.

Lesions of the forward portion of the internal capsule may not affect the optic radiations, producing only motor and sensory changes. Lesions in the posterior limb of the internal capsule almost invariably affect the optic peduncle and give rise to homonymous hemianopsia of the opposite side and are usually associated with hemianesthesia or hemiplegia, or both.

If the area of fiber interruption in the internal capsule is posterior and small, the hemianopsia may be accompanied by hemianesthesia alone.

Because of the compact area occupied by the optic peduncle, small lesions usually produce total homonymous hemianopsia, and the congruity or incongruity of the field defects cannot be determined.

The lesion most commonly affecting the internal capsule is a vascular one. Obstruction of or hemorrhage from the lenticulostriate and lenticulo-optic branches of the middle cerebral artery (the arteries of cerebral "stroke") account for most of these cases. The visual field defects produced by such damage are usually permanent, although a small area of field recovery may occur in some patients.

As in most vascular lesions, whether caused by hemorrhage, thrombosis, embolism, or angiospasm, the onset of symptoms is sudden. Thrombosis may occur gradually over a period of 1 or 2 days. Angiospasm is usually transient but if sufficiently prolonged may produce permanent infarct. Tumors and injuries of the internal capsule are rare.

Intracranial space-consuming lesions with unilateral cerebral edema occasionally give rise to herniation of the hippocampal gyrus over the edge of the tentorium into the tentorial hiatus (Fig. 15-28). This gives rise to rapidly developing third nerve palsy associated with signs and symptoms of acute rise in intracranial pressure, hom-

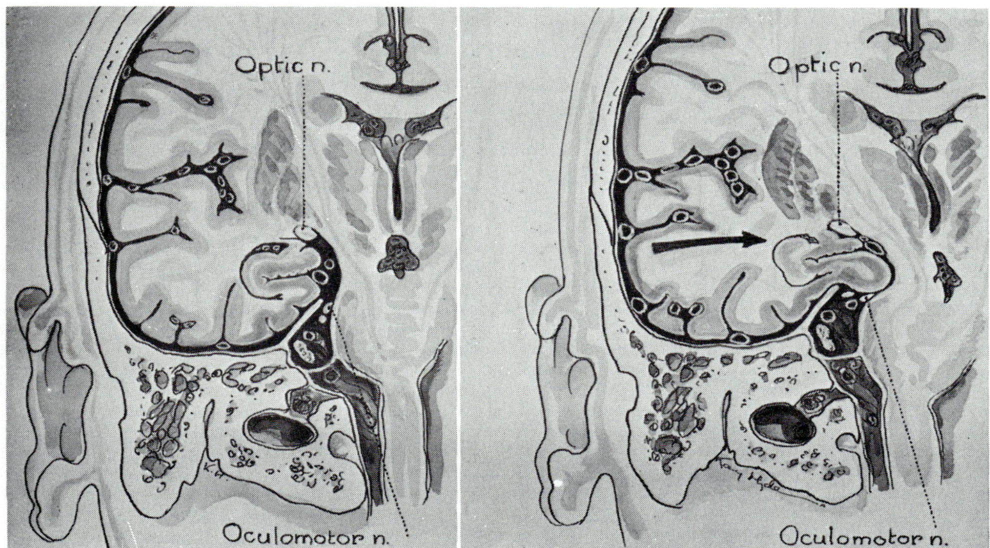

Fig. 15-28. Left, Normal position of hippocampal gyrus of temporal lobe in relation to edge of tentorium and third nerve. **Right,** Medial displacement of temporal lobe produced by tumor, resulting in herniation of hippocampal gyrus over tentorial edge and production of ipsilateral third nerve palsy and contralateral homonymous hemianopsia.

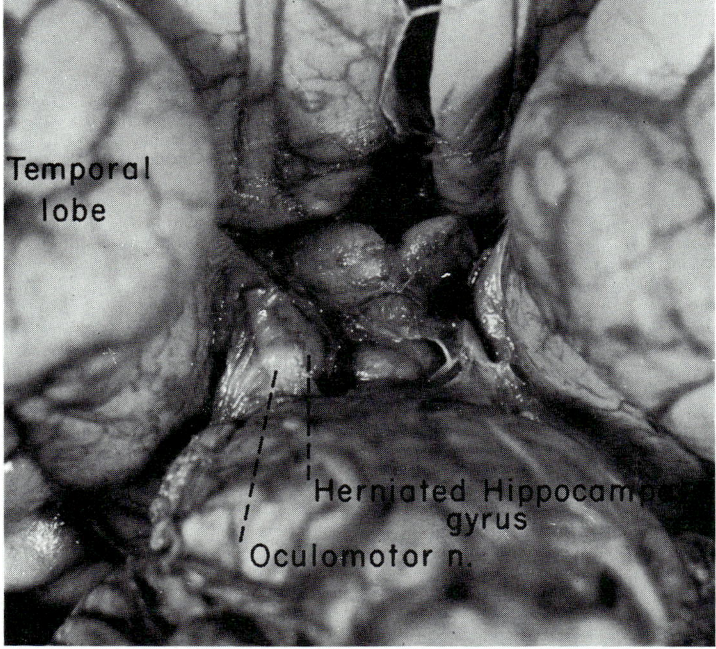

Fig. 15-29, Hippocampal gyrus hernia resulting from tumor of frontal lobe, producing ipsilateral third nerve compression and palsy. There was also compression of posterior cerebral artery with calcarine cortex infarction and contralateral homonymous hemianopsia.

onymous hemianopsia, and development of brain stem compression, hemorrhage, coma, and death. The visual field defect may result from interruption of the fiber bundles in the temporal lobe or from calcarine cortex ischemia and infarction caused by compression of the posterior cerebral artery (Fig. 15-29). The lesion producing the temporal lobe herniation may be far removed from the site of the hernia.

The exact course of the fibers of the optic radiation immediately after they leave the optic peduncle has been the subject of much debate. From both the anatomic and the clinical points of view, the majority of observers appear to favor the concept that the fibers fan out widely in the external sagittal stratum. The dorsal fibers run laterally for a short distance to the outside of the lateral ventricle and thence straight back into the parietal and occipital lobe. The ventral fibers run forward for a considerable distance in the temporal lobe, passing around and over the temporal horn of the lateral ventricle in the temporal loop of Meyer before turning backward in the lower part of the temporal lobe, where they are closely applied to the lateral wall of the body and posterior horn of the lateral ventricle, until they reach the occipital lobe. The macular fibers run between these two bundles.

The chief controversy seems to center around the degree of forward looping of the fibers in the temporal lobe. In my own dissections I have found some variation

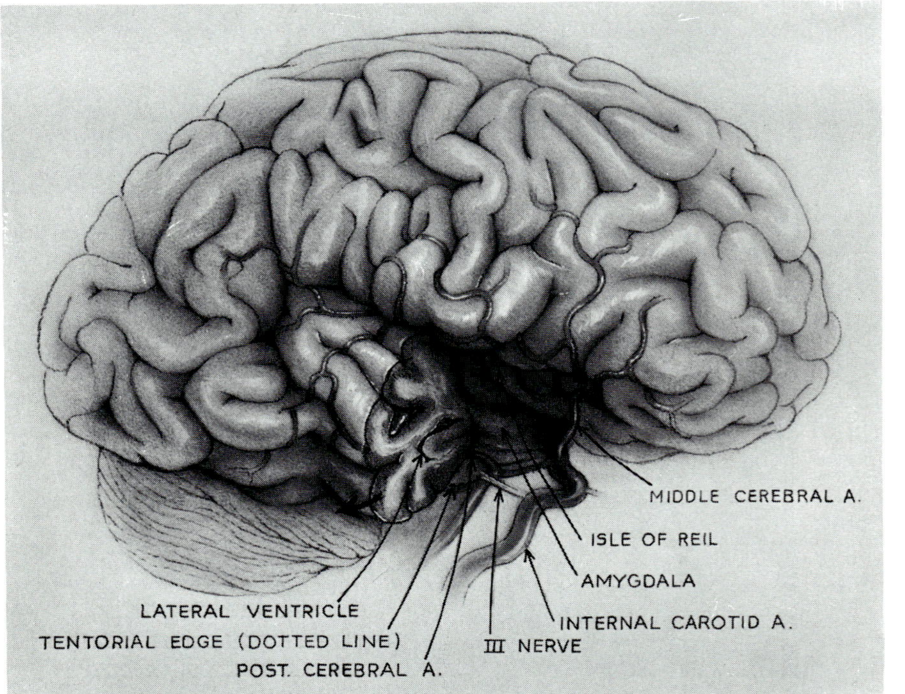

Fig. 15-30. A, Anatomic sketch showing ablation of tip of right temporal lobe for intractable epilepsy. Anterior 5 cm of lobe was resected and tip of temporal horn of lateral ventricle was entered.

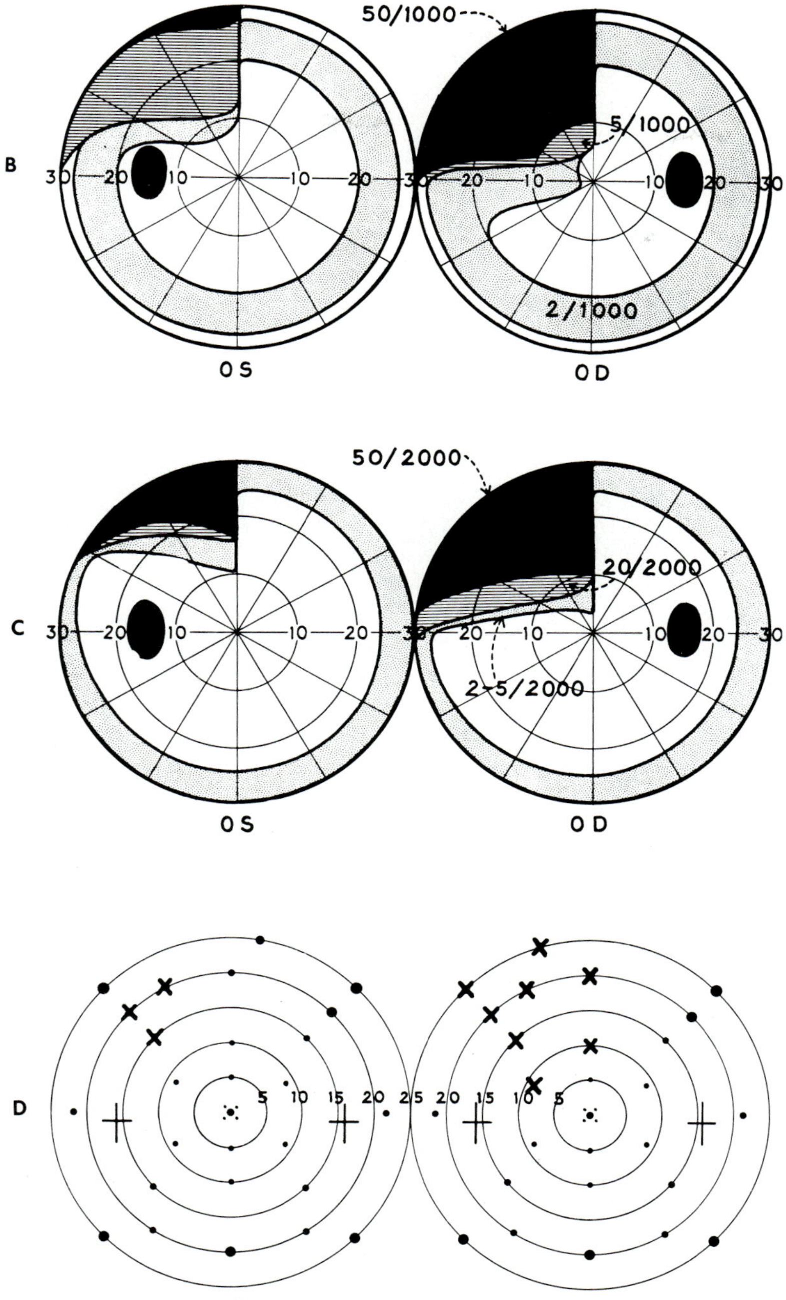

Fig. 15-30, cont'd. B, One month after temporal lobe resection. Tangent screen examination shows left homonymous incongruous quadrantanopsia. Incongruity is most clearly demonstrated in isopters for large stimuli (50/1000). **C,** Ten months after right temporal lobectomy. Tangent screen examination shows slight regression of quadrantanopsia, which is still markedly asymmetric. **D,** Harrington-Flocks multiple pattern visual field examination of defect. Incongruity of homonymous hemianopsia is demonstrated.

Continued.

E

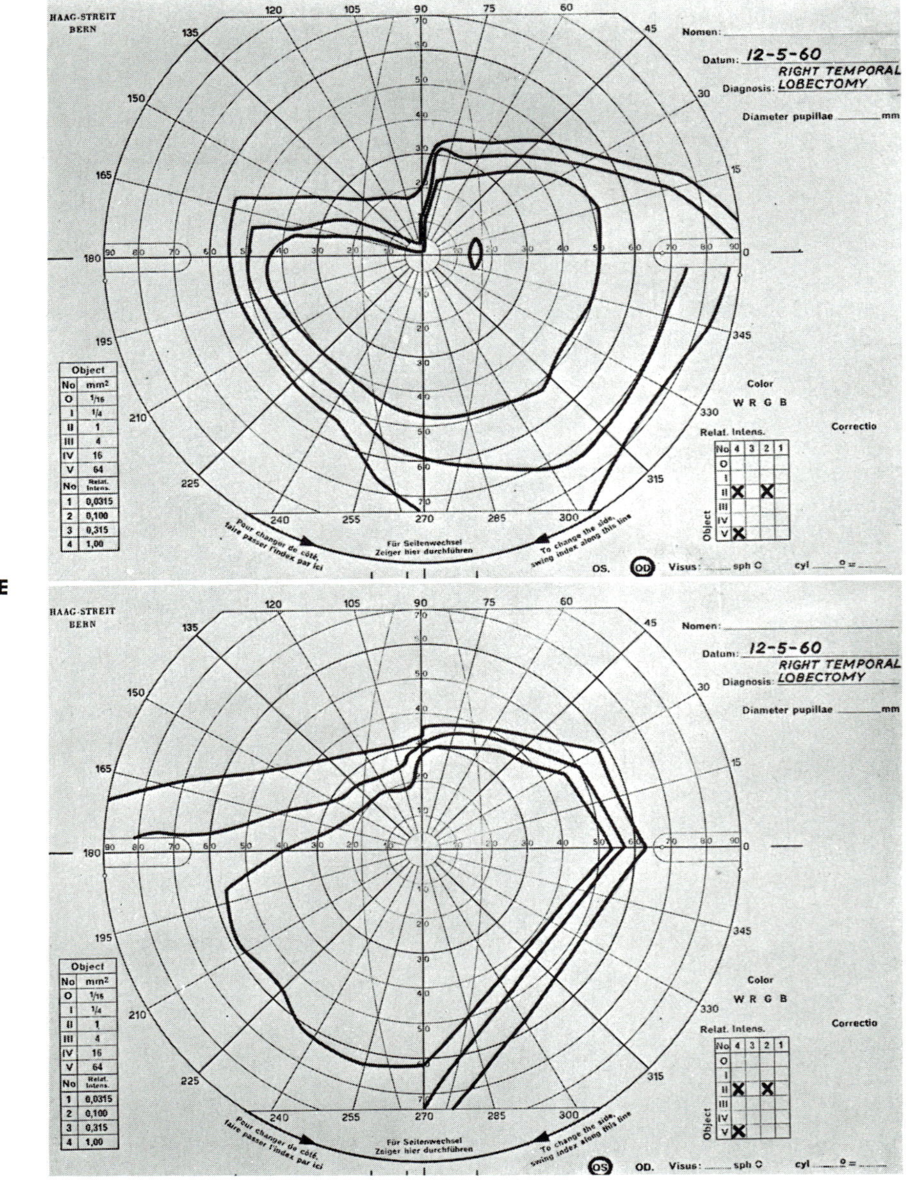

Fig. 15-30, cont'd. E, Above, Right eye field. **Below,** Left eye field. Goldmann perimeter examination showed incongruity best in larger isopters.

among individual brains. In most brains, however, the temporal loop was fairly easy to demonstrate and, in fact, was probably even more extensive than could be readily shown in the average gross dissection.

Because of this widespread disposition of the visual fibers in the temporal lobe, tumors of various portions of the lobe may obstruct the fibers, giving rise to homonymous hemianoptic visual field defects of widely varying morphology.

Lesions of the extreme anterior tip of the temporal lobe may not encroach on the visual pathway and thus do not cause a visual field defect. If only a few of the ventral fibers are involved, however, the result is a homonymous hemianopsia. Tumors of the temporal lobe have a great tendency to produce a depressional-type field loss in which the typical characteristics are an incongruous upper homonymous quadrantanopsia with sloping margins. Such typical visual field defects have been repeatedly demonstrated by many observers in proved lesions of the temporal lobe. One of the outstanding features of the homonymous hemianopsias in these cases is their incongruity (Fig. 15-30).

With regard to the anatomic explanation of this incongruity, there is great diversity of opinion. Cushing predicated his explanation of the existence of asymmetric quadrantanopsias in patients with temporal lobe tumor on his belief in the existence of Meyer's temporal loop.

Traquair expressed doubt as to the existence of the temporal loop and explained the incongruity on the basis of pressure on the optic tract from the closely overlying temporal lobe.

Peter suggested that one explanation for asymmetry could be found in the "dissociation of nerve fibers from corresponding retinal points from chiasm to cortical centers."

Putnam and Putnam believed that different bundles of fibers must keep their relative positions accurately in the optic radiation but adjacent fibers in the radiation do not necessarily supply closely adjacent points in the cortex. They stated that projection fibers proceeding from homologous points in the two retinas are farthest apart at the geniculate body and gradually approach one another as they draw near the visual cortex.

Clinical data from a large number of cases reported in the literature by various observers generally confirm the incongruous character of the temporal lobe visual field defects and the exquisite symmetry of those defects produced by occipital lobe lesions. But there are some authors who take exception, and these should be noted. Cushing's paper on the temporal lobe illustrated ten of a series of thirty-three tumors with homonymous hemianoptic defects, all of which were incongruous. The precise quantitative perimetric examinations were conducted by Dr. Clifford Walker (see Fig. 15-4). No mention was made of the significance or diagnostic value of the asymmetry of the two half-fields, but it is clearly present if one studies the illustrations. Holmes and Lister, on the other hand, illustrated case after case of occipital area injury with precisely symmetric homonymous defects in the visual fields (see Figs. 15-18 and 15-19). Dubois-Poulson illustrated an incongruous homonymous hemianopsia following partial temporal lobectomy. The largest and most intense stimuli on the Goldmann perimeter show the asymmetry to best advantage.

Spalding's study of wounds of the visual radiation and striate cortex beautifully illustrated the anatomic distribution of the geniculocalcarine fibers in the radiation and the visual field representation in the occipital cortex. He did not comment on the matter of congruity of defects following injury to the radiation, but all six of his field studies showed some degree of incongruity, and in some the asymmetry was considerable. In his study of the striate cortex, the congruity of the homonymous scotomas was striking.

Falconer and Wilson, Brodie Hughes, and Wendland and Nerenberg, on the other hand, stated that all homonymous hemianoptic field defects produced by lesions of the radiation are congruous, whereas Teuber, Battersby, and Bender concluded from their study of penetrating missile wounds of the brain that all the resulting visual field defects are incongruous regardless of the portion of the visual pathway involved. None of their cases was studied by quantitative perimetric methods, and, even with the rather gross stimuli used, several of their illustrations contradict their statement.

J. Lawton Smith concluded from a study of his own cases that lesions of the temporal lobe produce basically incongruous homonymous hemianopsias whereas occipital lobe damage causes basically congruous visual field defects.

Walsh and Hoyt stated that most of the partial homonymous upper quadrantanopsias resulting from lesions of the temporal lobe are incongruous; and they agreed with me that the field defects from occipital lobe lesions are congruous.

Van Buren and Baldwin studied the visual fields of forty-one patients after temporal lobectomy for relief of epilepsy. Thirty-three patients showed major defects in the fields, and, of these, ten demonstrated homonymous congruous defects whereas twenty-three developed incongruous deficits. The incongruities were most obvious in the larger isopters. These authors believe that "all fibers derived from a given retinal point do not lie close together in the optic radiation." They believe that lesions affecting the occipital area give rise to entirely symmetric field defects in the two eyes and that "in the posterior portion of the optic system, fibers from homologous areas of the two retinas must lie side by side."

From my own clinical data (Figs. 15-31 and 15-32), I believe that the incongruity so often seen in homonymous hemianopsia in lesions of the temporal lobe is best explained by the dissociation in the temporal lobe of fibers from corresponding retinal points and that this separation of homologous fibers persists in lessening degree throughout the optic radiation as far posterior as the postparietal area almost to the neuron ending in the striate cortex.

Regardless of its cause, asymmetry or incongruity of incomplete homonymous hemianopsia is a clinical entity quite regularly present in visual field defects resulting from lesions of the temporal lobe (Fig. 15-33).

Vascular and traumatic lesions are less common in this area than tumors (Fig. 15-34). Brain abscess of otogenic origin may involve the temporal lobe and give rise to typical visual field defects through visual fiber compression.

Text continued on p. 366.

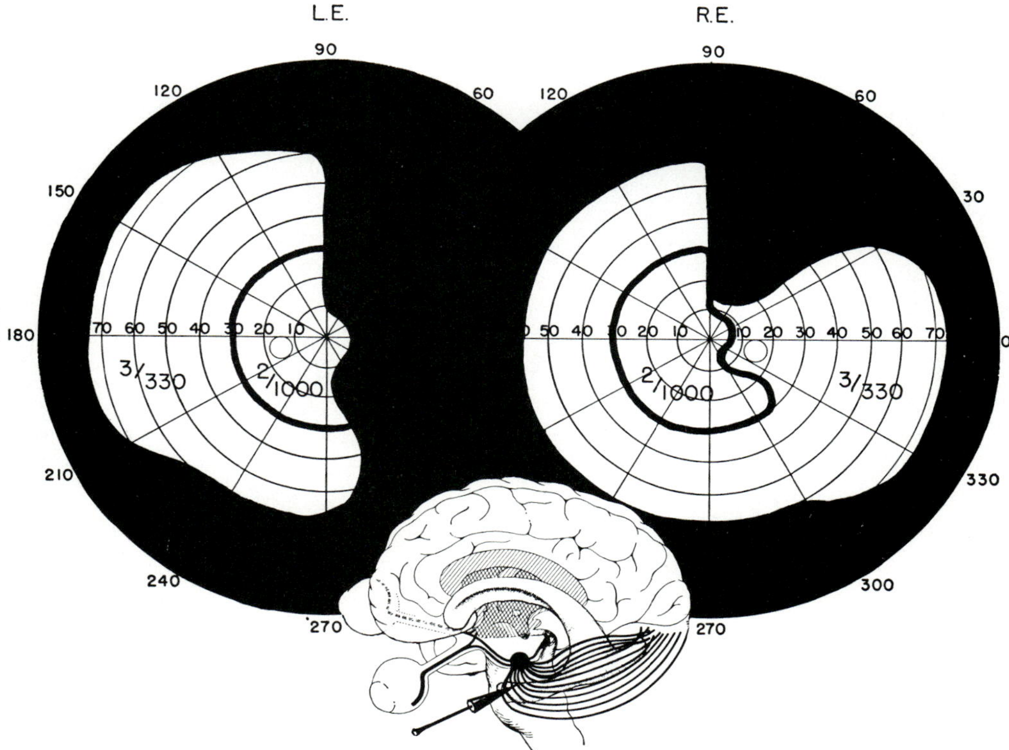

Fig. 15-31. Typical incongruous right homonymous hemianopsia in case of glioma of left temporal lobe. Tumor was large, and patient had had jacksonian epilepsy, headache, increased reflexes in right arm and leg, and severe papilledema.

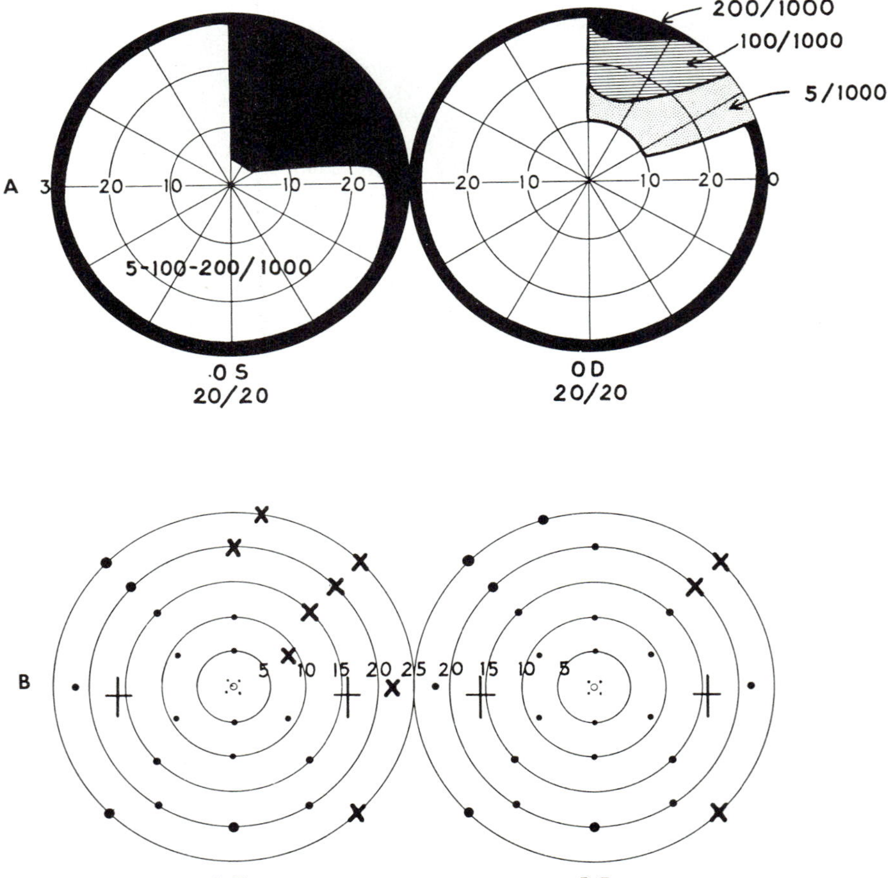

Fig. 15-32. A, Tangent screen 4 years after left temporal lobectomy for relief of epilepsy. Resection did not enter ventricle. Gross incongruity is most evident in larger isopters. **B,** Multiple pattern visual field. Asymmetry is marked. **C, Above,** Field for right eye. **Below,** Field for left eye. Goldmann perimeter examination of patient shows incongruity best with largest and brightest stimuli.

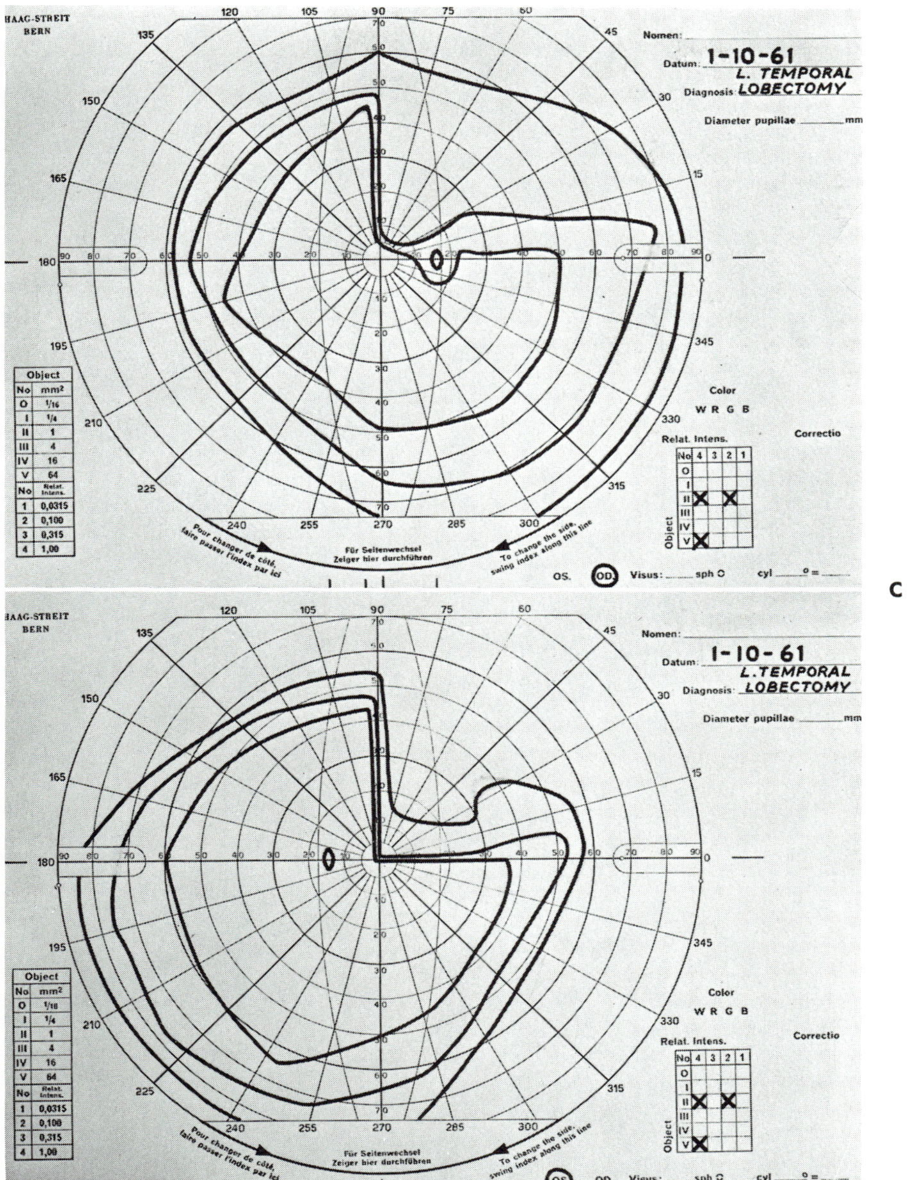

Fig. 15-32, cont'd. For legend see opposite page.

A

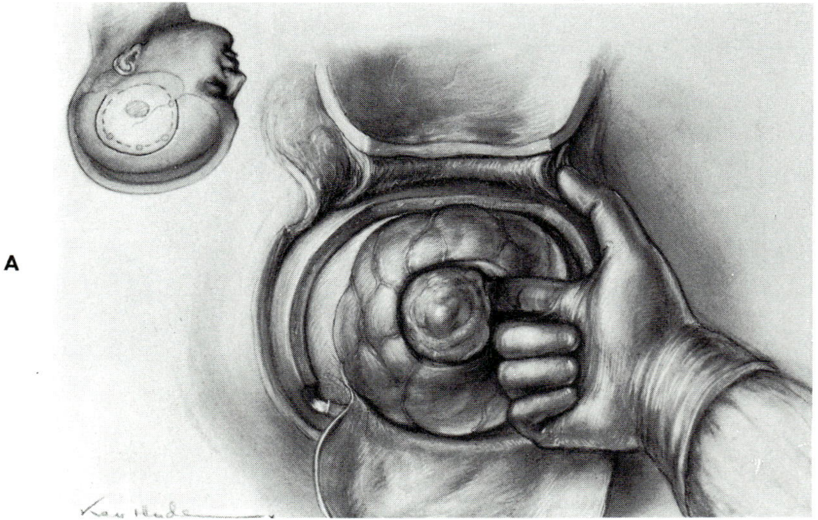

B

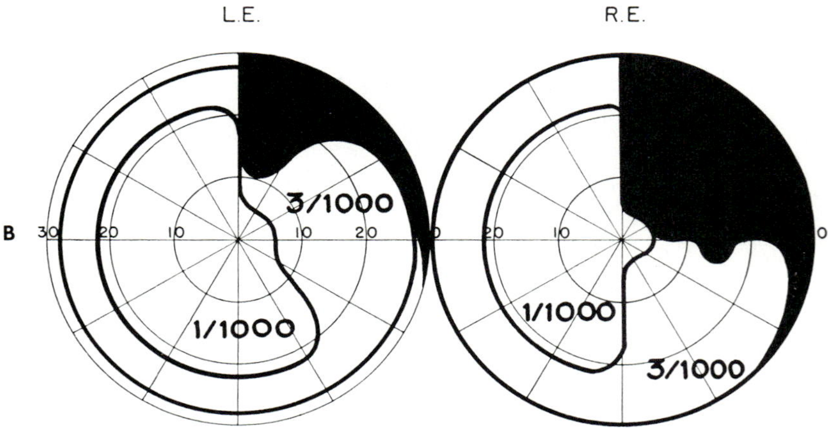

Fig. 15-33. A, Large cystic tumor mass in lower portion of left temporal lobe. Incongruous right homonymous quadrantanopsia produced by this tumor is illustrated in **B.** Tumor was encapsulated and was removed with partial resolution of visual field defect.

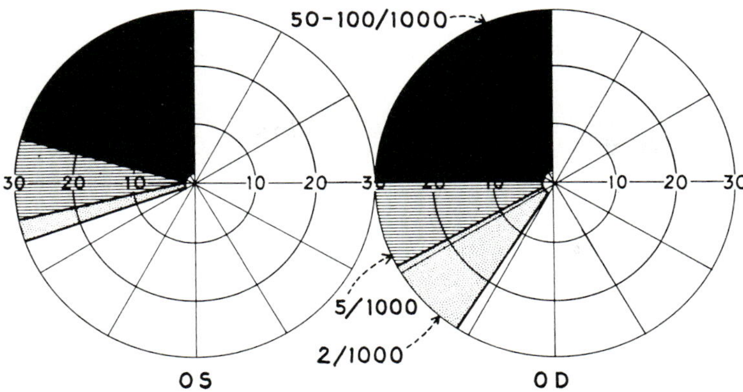

Fig. 15-34. Incongruous homonymous quadrantanopsia resulting from intracerebral hematoma in right temporal lobe. Margins of defect were unusually straight and exact for each isopter studied.

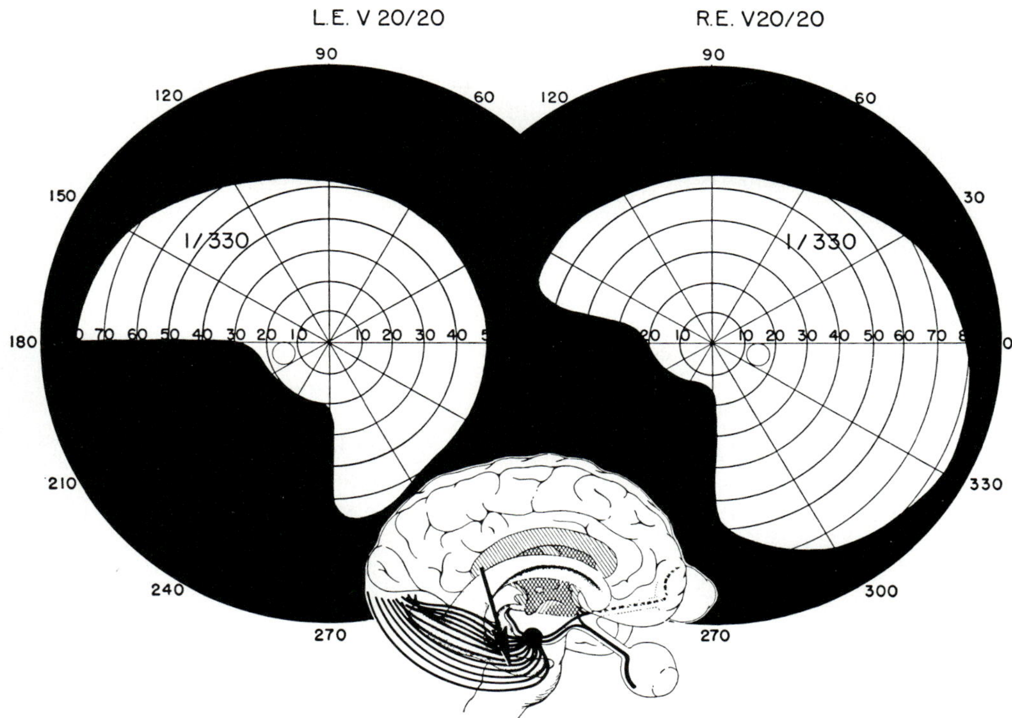

Fig. 15-35. Left inferior homonymous quadrantanopsia produced by degenerative lesion of right temporoparietal area. Patient had grand mal epilepsy of jacksonian type, preceded by aura of formed visual hallucinations of bright, multicolored geometric figures in left visual field.

Certain other neurologic signs and symptoms of localizing value may accompany the characteristic homonymous hemianopsia described above. Some of these are as follows:

1. Uncinate attacks or fits, in which the patient complains of abnormal smells or taste and occasionally of complex or formed visual hallucinations of persons, animals, or known objects.

   This aura is often followed by localized epileptiform attacks involving the arm and the leg on the side opposite the lesion. These uncinate fits are caused by involvement of the uncinate gyrus beneath the temporal lobe (Fig. 15-35).
2. Aphasia occurring in right-handed persons with tumors of the left temporal lobe.
3. Papilledema caused by general increase in intracranial pressure.
4. Neighborhood signs, such as weakness of the facial muscle, conjugate deviation of the eyes, and partial third nerve palsy caused by involvement of nearby structures.

The parietal lobe is large, and the optic radiation occupies a wide flat band close to the lateral wall of the body of the lateral ventricle. It is bounded anteriorly by the central sulcus, laterally by the sylvian fissure, posteriorly by the parieto-occipital fissure, and medially by the cingulum. Its vascular supply is principally through the ascending and posterior parietal branches of the middle cerebral artery laterally and branches of the anterior cerebral artery medially.

The clinical manifestations of parietal lobe disease are among the most interesting in neurology and are often associated with characteristic visual difficulties and field deficits (Figs. 15-36 to 15-40). The precise function of the various areas of the lobe is poorly understood, but in a general way lesions of the anterior and lateral portions of the lobe give rise to somatic disorders whereas those located posteriorly and superiorly cause visual imperception.

The syndromes related to parietal lesions display a disorder of awareness of the disturbance no matter where the lesion. The patient is neglectful of and fails to perceive the nature of his disability. This behavioral defect applies equally to somatic and visual perception (Anton's syndrome).

It is in lesions of the parietal lobe that the extinction phenomenon becomes most manifest. The patient may easily detect a moving finger or even a small test object held consecutively in each quadrant of the visual field, thus demonstrating that simple sensation is preserved. When stimuli are exposed simultaneously in both sides of the visual field, the patient fails to recognize the one in the field contralateral to the lesion even though it may be a gross one easily detected when presented alone. Often these patients are unable to maintain a central fixation and involuntarily shift their gaze to the finger or other target in the normal field.

When asked to bisect a horizontal line, the patient crosses the line well to the side of the unaffected field (i.e., away from the lesion). Writing and drawing will often deviate from the horizontal, and constructional apraxia may be manifested by inability to copy a cube or draw a clock face.

A

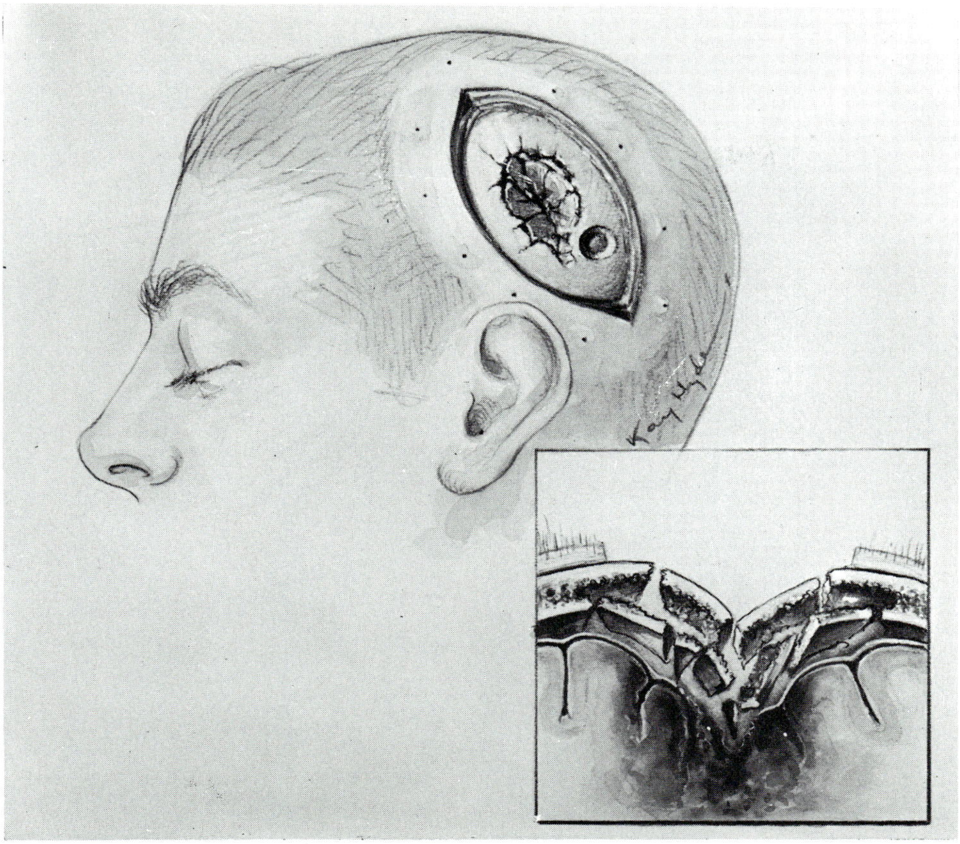

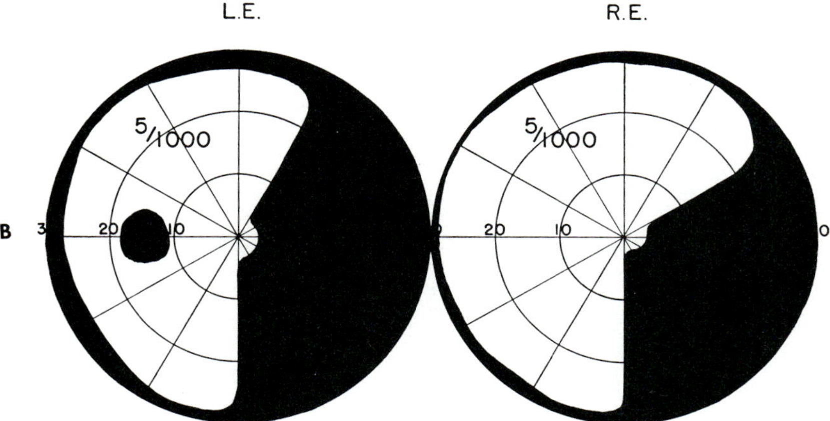

Fig. 15-36. A, Fracture of parietal area of skull with spicules of bone from inner table of skull penetrating dura and brain. **B,** Slightly incongruous right homonymous hemianopsia resulting from this injury. There was moderate aphasia.

A

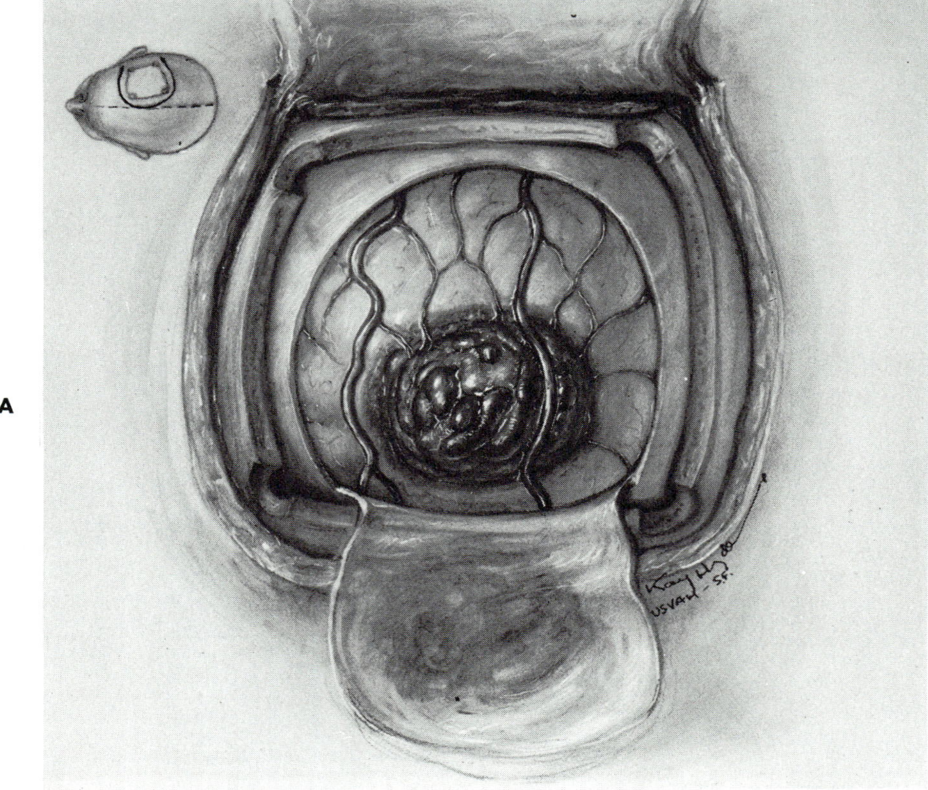

B

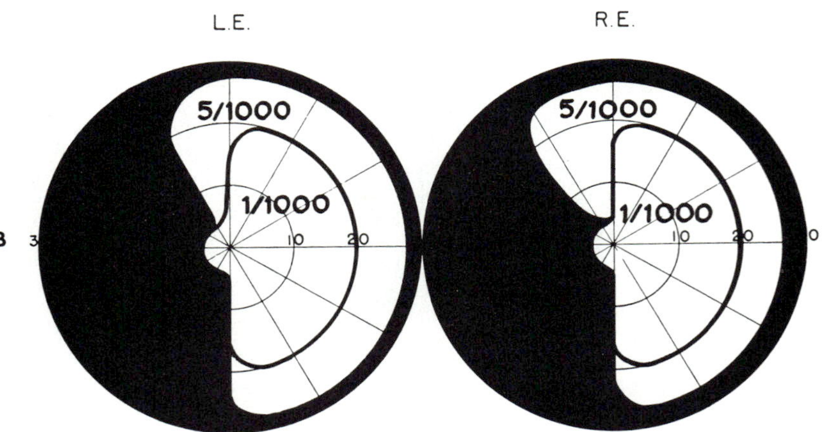

Fig. 15-37. A, Large tumor of upper portion of right parietal lobe showing surgical approach for its removal. (See also Fig. 15-1.) **B,** Left homonymous hemianopsia resulting from this tumor.

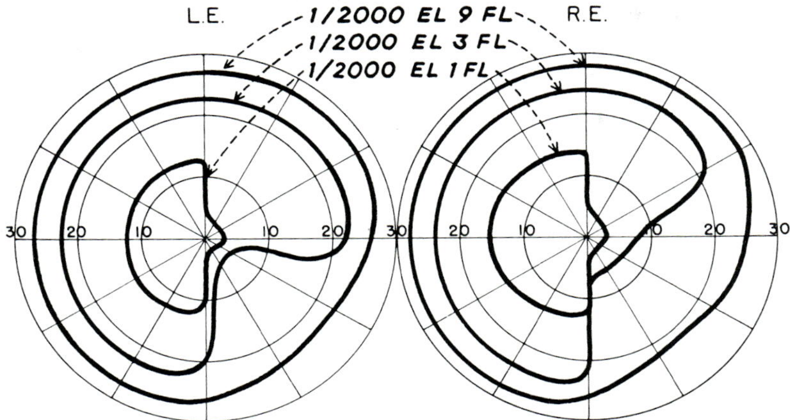

Fig. 15-38. Varying degrees of right homonymous hemianopsia produced by left parietal lobe tumor as demonstrated with electroluminescent stimuli of varying luminance from 9 footlamberts to 3 footlamberts to 1 footlambert.

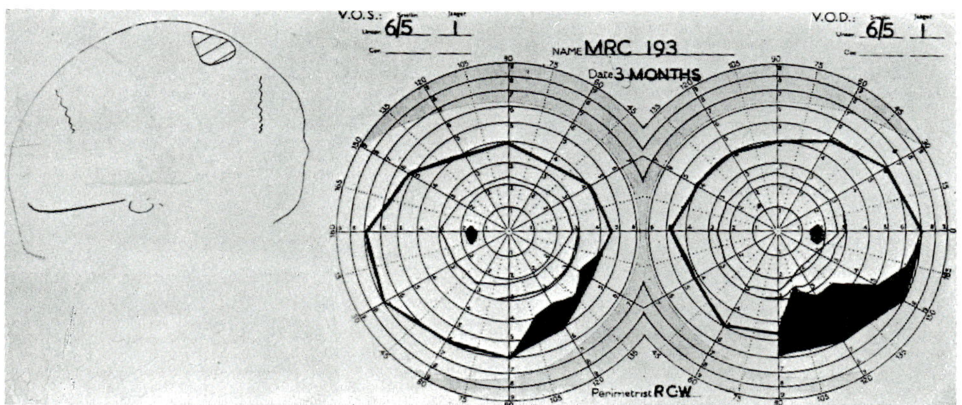

Fig. 15-39. Spalding's case 4. Minimal incongruous inferior homonymous quadrantanopsia resulted from injury to extreme upper margin of anterior radiation. (From Spalding, J. M. K.: J. Neurol. Neurosurg. Psychiatry **15:**99, 1952.)

A

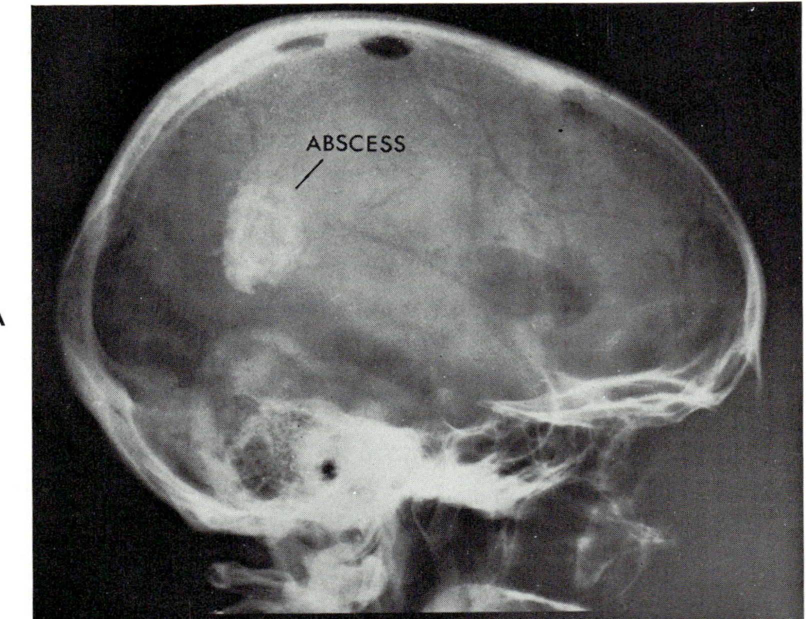

Fig. 15-40. A, Roentgenogram of Lipiodol-injected right parietal lobe abscess. **B,** Multiple pattern visual field examination in case of parietal lobe abscess. Total homonymous hemianopsia is due to simultaneous double stimulation used in this test as compared with single stimulation. **C,** Tangent screen and perimeter field defects, using single stimuli, due to parietal lobe abscess shown in **A** and **B.** Note that defects involve inferior quadrant and are incongruous.

All these visual manifestations may be associated with somatic perceptual disorders such as extinction of tactile stimuli on one side when the other side of the body is tested simultaneously, astereognosis, and even unawareness by the patient of his own limb.

Many left cerebral lesions with visual perceptual disturbance are complicated by aphasia, which interferes with examination of the patient. Reading and writing disability is common, and visual acuity may appear to be grossly depressed due to failure to recognize letters on the Snellen chart. When the patient is tested with numbers or the illiterate E chart, vision may be normal.

Visual loss is usually more severely affected in the lower quadrants, and the most common visual field defect is an inferior homonymous quadrantanopsia, with perhaps a slight degree of incongruity, and is most clearly demonstrated on the tangent screen by the method of simultaneous double stimulation. Superior quadrant loss in association with parietal lobe disease is so rare as to be suspect and is more likely to result from temporal lobe involvement.

The association of homonymous hemianopsia with pain in the eye and orbit has been reported by Knox and Cogan as a symptom of vascular accident in the parieto-occipital area. The pain, which occurs on the side of the lesion, is presumed to be mediated through the dural branches of the first division of the fifth nerve. In two

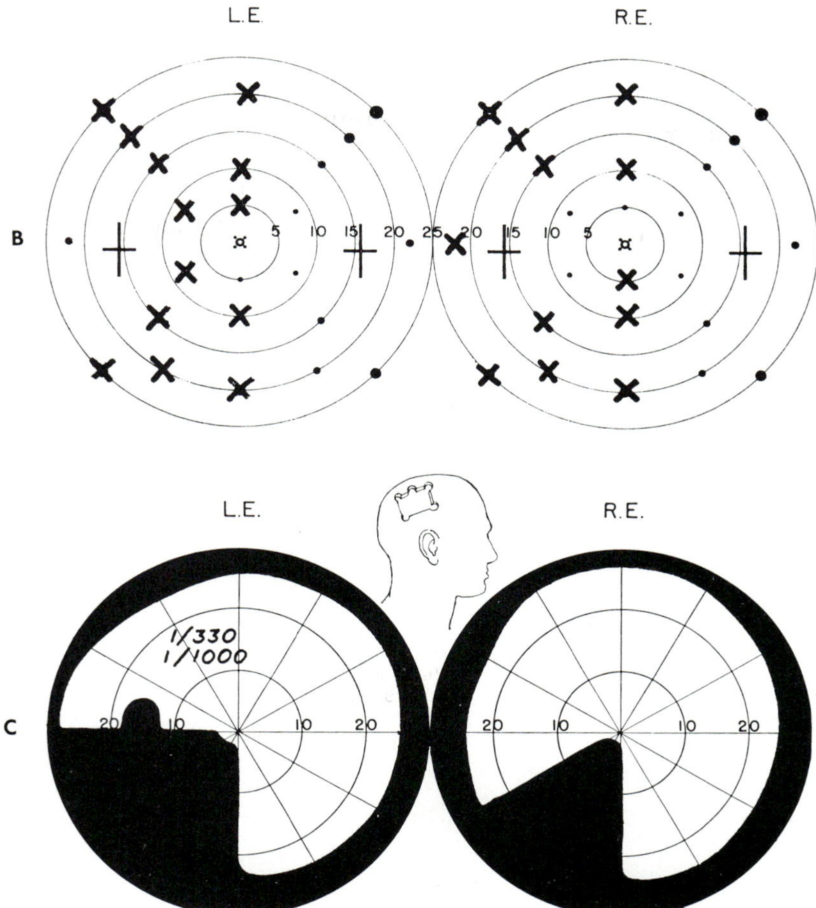

Fig. 15-40, cont'd. For legend see opposite page.

cases observed by me, the pain was severe and was the presenting symptom, leading to detection of the contralateral homonymous field loss of which the patient had been unaware.

Bilateral parietal disease is not uncommon as a complication of diffuse cerebrovascular disease. It results in devastating visual disability. Patients become lost in familiar places, fail to recognize friends, and finally lose all evidence of visual function. The facial expression becomes vacuous and the patient appears to be blind. Pupillary reactions to light and accommodation are retained, however.

Parieto-occipital lesions may produce visual hallucinations, usually in the area of the affected visual field.

Mooney has reported a series of most unusual and vivid visual hallucinations in a patient with a parieto-occipital meningioma. The patient was an artist and was able to reproduce his various hallucinations in brilliant color. Some of them were abstract in nature and some were distortions of human figures. All were in the nonseeing right field of vision, and quantitative perimetry revealed an irregular but congruous homonymous hemianopsia.

A positive or asymmetric optokinetic nystagmus response is always present in association with homonymous hemianopsia due to lesions of the parietal lobe.

Occipital striate cortex

The characteristic visual field defect associated with lesions of the striate cortex is a congruous homonymous hemianopsia, complete or incomplete, with macular sparing, steep margins, and uniform density.

Both tumors and vascular lesions of the occipital lobe frequently involve adjacent cerebral areas so that pure area striate involvement is probably rare. Injuries, on the other hand, may involve relatively small and isolated areas of the occipital cortex and give rise to discrete and isolated central and peripheral homonymous field defects that precisely localize the site of the damage.

The most common vascular lesion involving the occipital lobe is thrombosis of one posterior cerebral or calcarine artery (Fig. 15-42). This lesion usually causes extensive damage in the cortex with complete homonymous hemianopsia. The macula is frequently spared, sometimes in a wide area.

Thrombosis or embolism of small branches of the posterior cerebral artery may produce homonymous hemianoptic sector defects, quadrantanopsias or scotomas (Fig. 15-43). The macular portion of the occipital cortex, supplied in part by the middle cerebral artery, may escape damage and thus account for the widespread area of macular sparing seen in these patients. Bilateral or double homonymous hemianopsia is not uncommon.

The appearance of bright orange-yellow cholesterol crystals in the retinal arte-

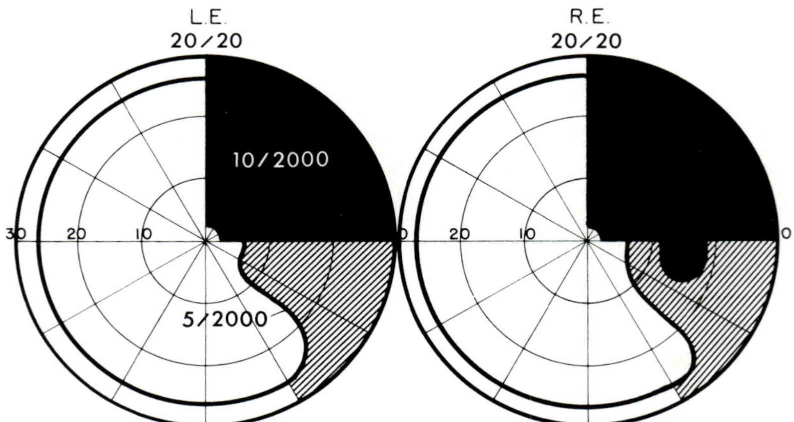

Fig. 15-41. Occipital lobe glioblastoma. Initial symptom reading difficulty and periodic transient visual loss. Congruous right homonymous quadrantanopsia was found on routine visual field examination. Field loss gradually extended into the lower quadrants. There was associated alexia and lack of comprehension. Neurologic examination was otherwise normal.

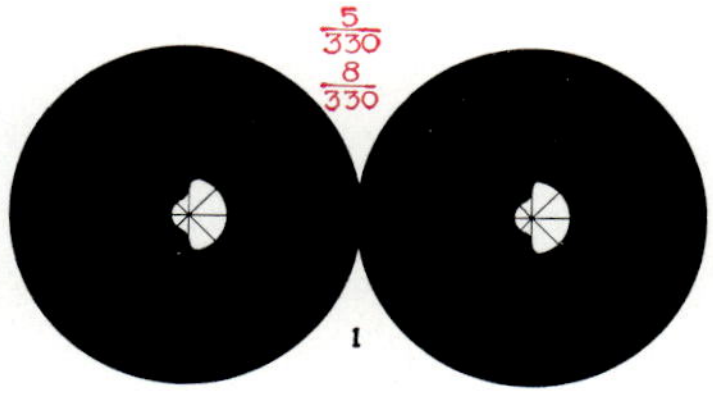

Bilateral Occipital Lobe injury. Double Homonymous Hemianopsia. Destruction of both Occipital Lobes.

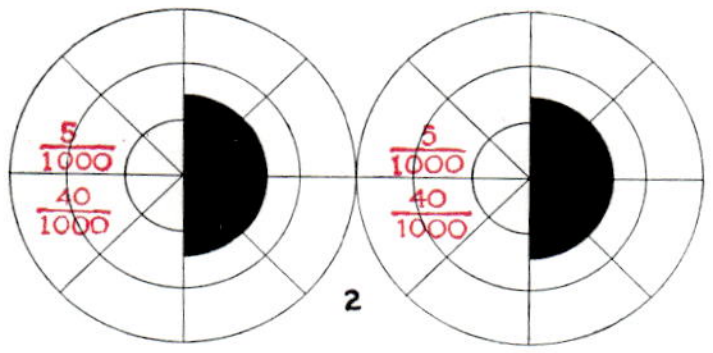

Lesion of the left Operculum or external surface of the Occipital Pole.

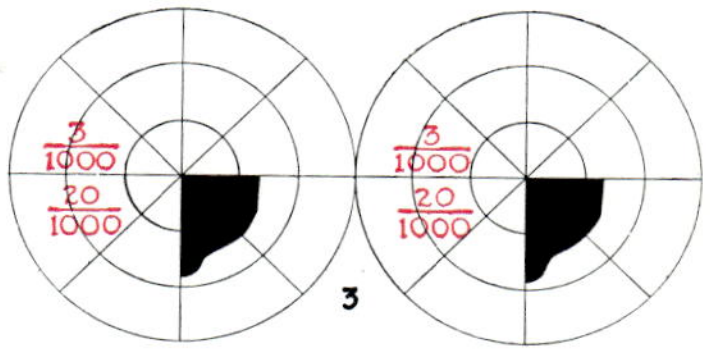

Occipital Pole. Posterior tip of the Upper Lip of the left Calcarine Fissure.

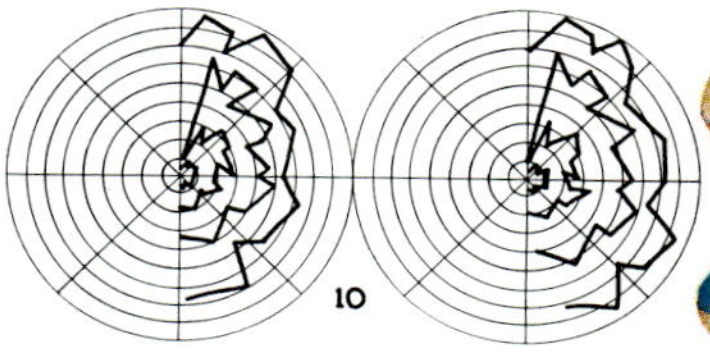

Successive phases in the Homonymous Scintillating Scotoma (Fortification Specter) of Migraine.

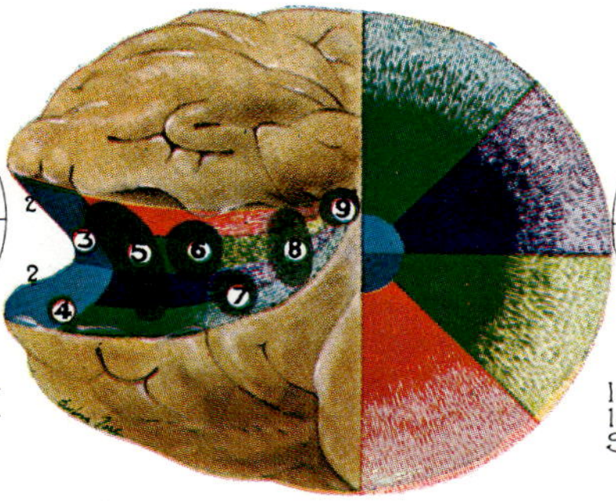

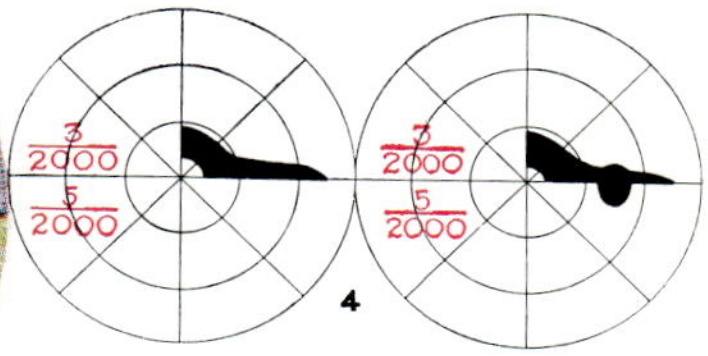

Inferior, Anterior portion of the Macular Projection in the left Area Striata. Ice pick wound.

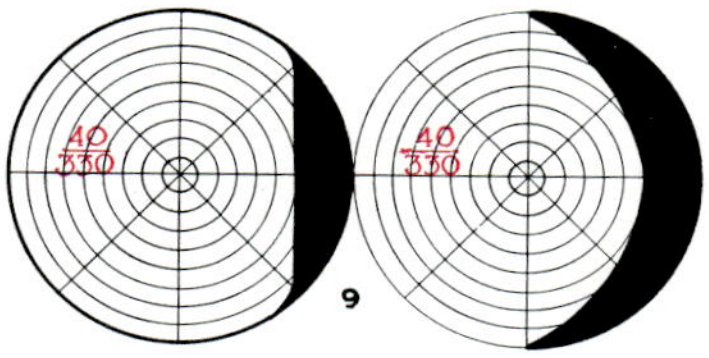

Mesial surface of the left occipital lobe showing the Area Striata (Brodmann's area 17) with the lips of the Calcarine Fissure held apart and the projection of the area on the visual field. The extension of area 17 on to the external surface of the hemisphere, (the Operculum) is not shown.

The visual defects are characterized by complete symmetry (congruity), sharp outline with steep edges and great density. The macula is usually spared.

Anterior Tip of the Calcarine Fissure. The Temporal Crescent

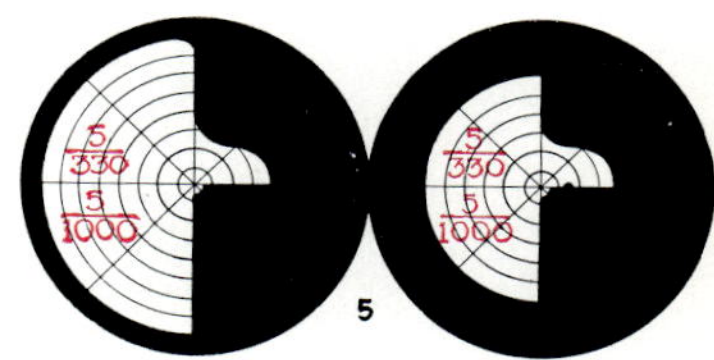

Inferior Quadrant Anopsia combined with partial Superior Quadrant-defect.

Very large area of Macular sparing. Anterior portion of both Lips of the Calcarine Fissure.

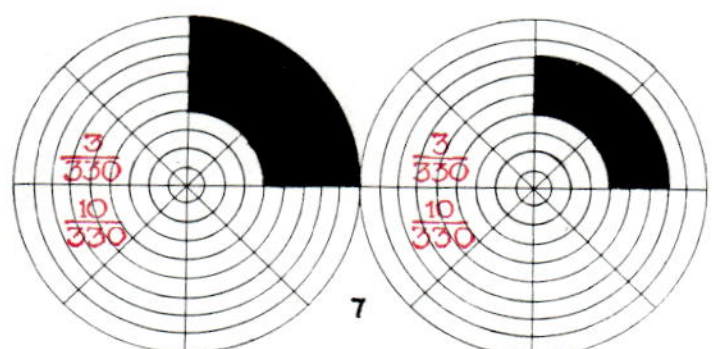

Anterior, Inferior Lip of the Calcarine Fissure.

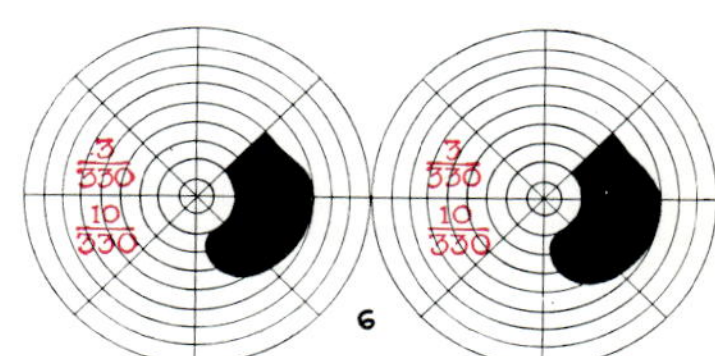

Middle Superior portion of the Calcarine Fissure.

Plate 9. Visual field defects produced by lesions of visual cortex.

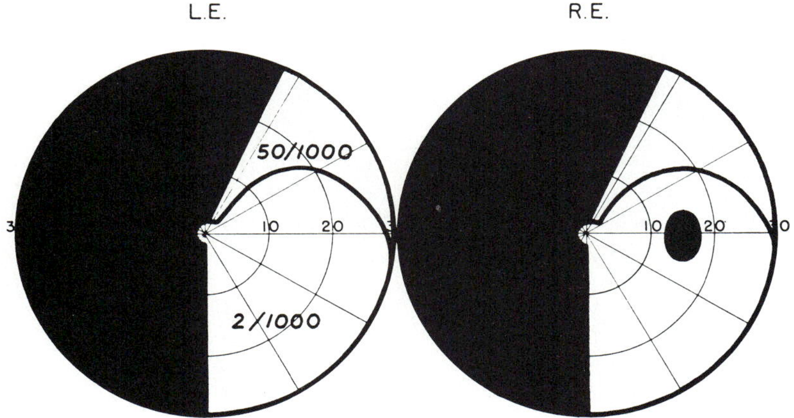

Fig. 15-42. Right calcarine cortical cerebrovascular accident with completely congruous left homonymous hemianopsia and evidence of partial involvement of left striate cortex. Field loss was sudden in onset. There are other evidences of cerebrospinal and vascular syphilis, including Argyll Robertson pupils.

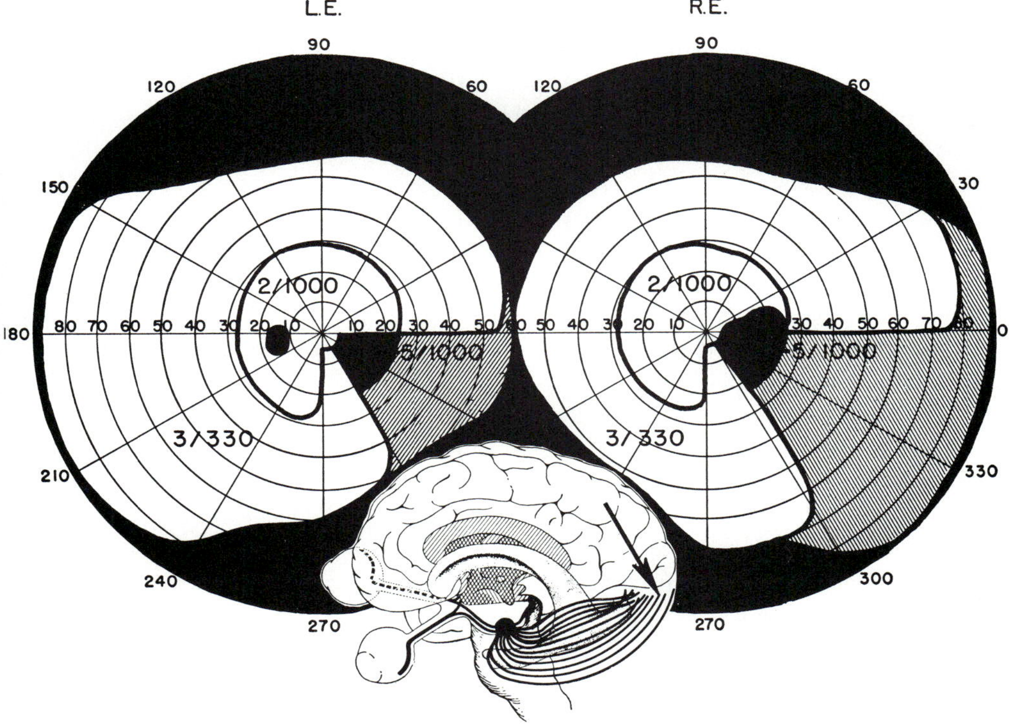

Fig. 15-43. Congruous right homonymous quadrantanopsia with homonymous quadrantanoptic scotoma resulting from thrombosis of a branch of left posterior cerebral artery. Apparent incongruity in the scotomas is due to inclusion of blind spot in right field defect.

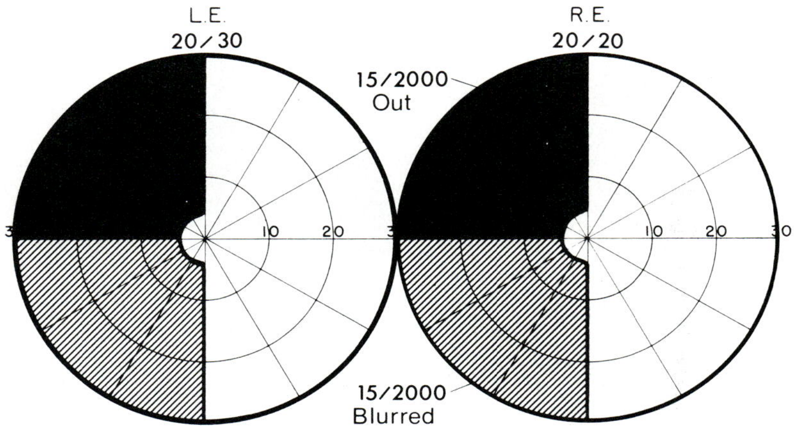

Fig. 15-44. Right cerebellar astrocytoma with pressure occlusion of right posterior cerebral artery and occipital lobe infarction. Unusual picture of cerebellar ataxia and nystagmus associated with congruous homonymous heminopsia. CAT scan revealed large cerebellar mass that was subsequently removed.

rioles (Hollenhorst plaques) in association with transient visual loss (amaurosis fugax) or transient or permanent homonymous hemianoptic visual field defects is a warning of impending disaster in the cardiovascular system (see Chapter 10). These atheromatous emboli give rise to frequent strokes, transient ischemic attacks, ischemic heart disease, and peripheral atherosclerosis obliterans in addition to the visual disturbances resulting from retinal and cerebral infarction. When seen, they call for an urgent evaluation of the entire cardiovascular system.

The large and small arteries to the striate area of the occipital lobe can now be identified in clinical angiographic studies when magnification and subtraction techniques are employed. Neuroradiologic studies of occlusive vascular disease in these vessels reveal sites of occlusion and areas of cortical avascularity. Sources of collateral circulation and delayed flow in involved arteries are also seen. Angiographic signs usually, but with some exceptions, correlate well with visual field deficits.

McAuley and Ross Russell studied thirty-nine patients with various types of isolated homonymous hemianopsias resulting from ischemic lesions in the posterior parts of the cerebral hemispheres. All were examined by CAT scanning. Most had localized low-density lesions within the distribution of the posterior cerebral artery. The location of these lesions (deduced from a separate anatomic study of postmortem brains cut in the plane of the CAT scanner) was correlated with visual field defects. Lesions giving rise to quadrantic defects were smaller than those with total hemianopsias. Lower quadrantic defects tended to occur in superior cuts and vice versa. Macular sparing was associated with survival of the occipital pole in some instances. Bilateral cases had more associated neurologic deficits.

The same type of congruous homonymous hemianopsia may occur as a complication of cardiopulmonary bypass surgery with occipital cortical infarction.

Tumors of the occipital lobe may occur as the various types of infiltrative or

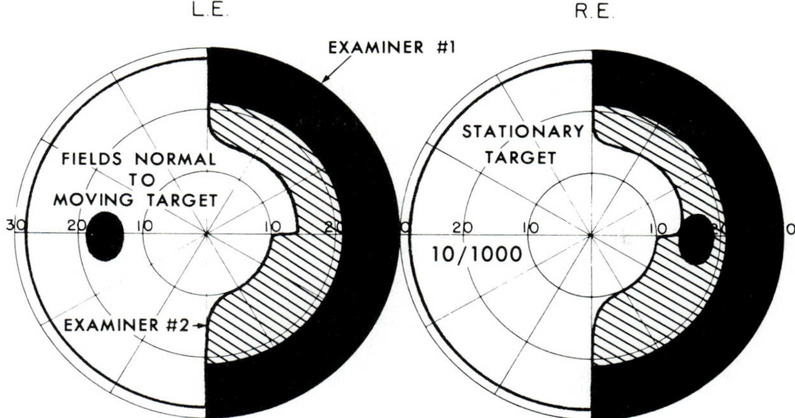

Fig. 15-45. Homonymous hemianopsia from lesion of striate cortex of occipital lobe demonstrating Riddoch phenomenon. Note that field defect varies in size with rate of movement of test object. Stationary stimuli (as used in static perimetry) show complete homonymous hemianoptic deficit. Field defects differ between examiner No. 1 and examiner No. 2 because of difference in speed of stimulus movement in kinetic examination. Anoptic portion of visual field is responsive to motion but not to form.

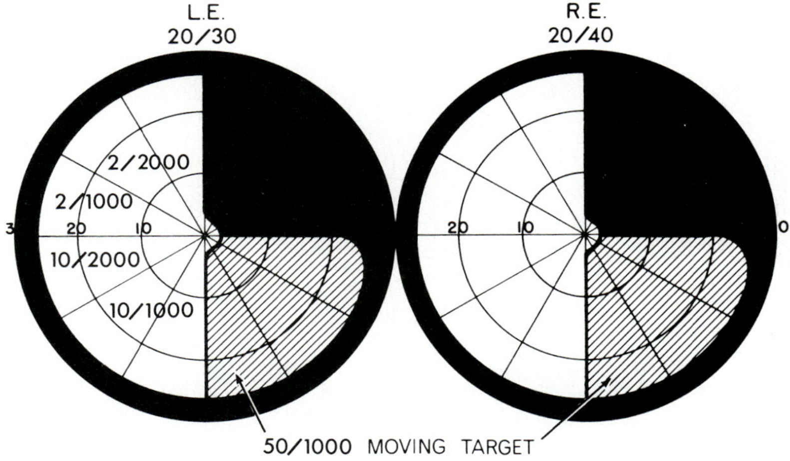

Fig. 15-46. Homonymous hemianoptic hypoplasia. Left cerebral hypoplasia with optic disc hypoplasia and hemianoptic retinal nerve fiber atrophy detectable with red-free ophthalmoscopy. Visual field defect first noted during routine perimetry 6 years earlier. The patient was unaware of the deficit. Nystagmus, alternating esotropia, and psychomotor epilepsy have been present since childhood. The left side of each optic disc shows segmental atrophy.

cystic gliomas, often arising in the parietal lobe and extending backward into the occipital area (see Fig. 15-41). These lesions frequently involve the optic radiations before they reach the striate cortex. Most of them arise lateral to the radiation; and in their medial growth, to involve the visual cortex, they interrupt the optic radiations. The field defects are therefore more or less identical with those found in the postparietal area.

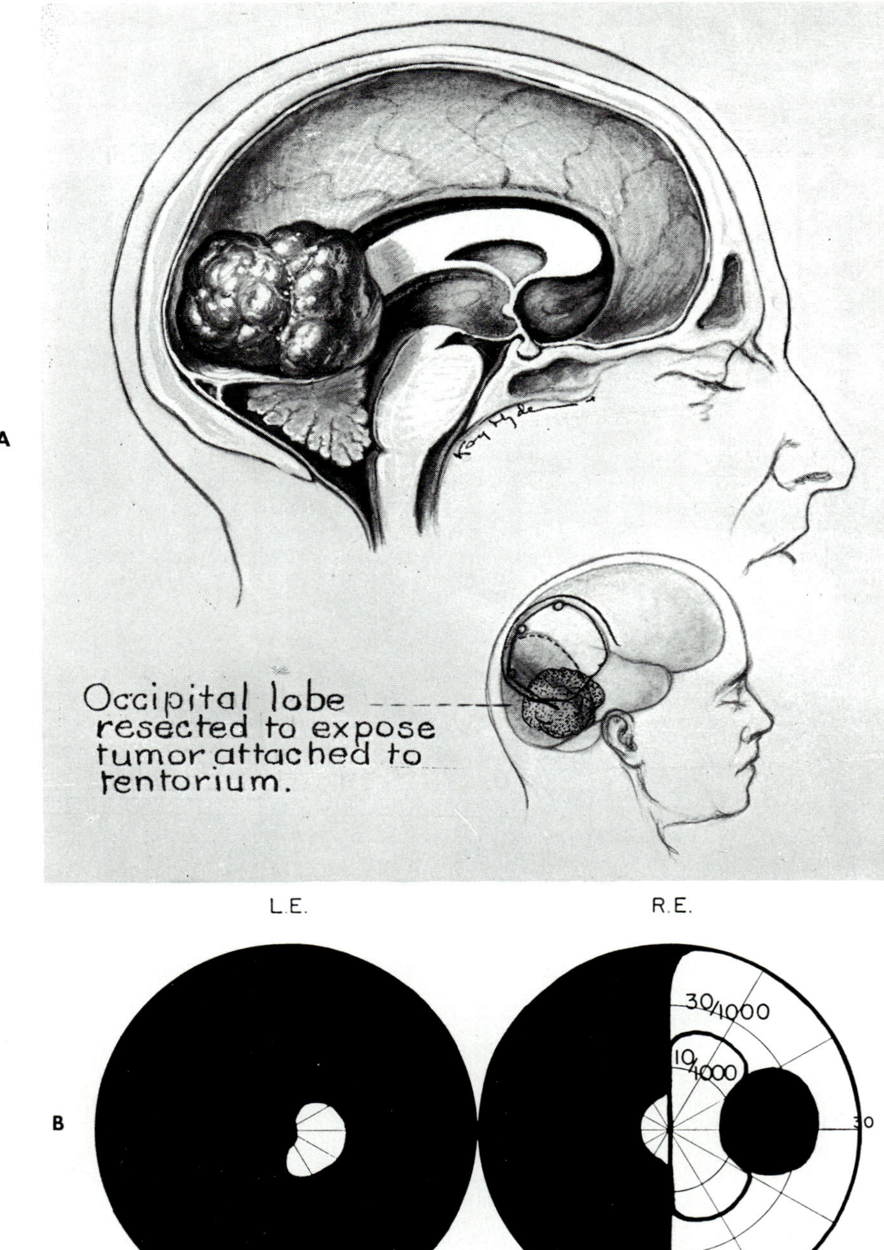

Fig. 15-47. A, Very large meningioma occupying most of right occipital lobe. There was chronic papilledema with secondary optic atrophy. Angiography showed asymmetry of occipital vessels on right, and ventriculograms showed displacement of posterior ventricles to left. Tumor was lying on tentorium and attached to falx and required almost total occipital lobectomy for its removal. Both tumor and area of resection are shown. **B,** Preoperative left homonymous hemianopsia in same patient.

A tumor frequently affecting the occipital cortex and therefore giving early perimetric evidence of its presence is the meningioma (see Fig. 15-47). This tumor may involve any part of the occipital lobe and occasionally attain enormous size before it produces neurologic signs other than vague visual defects. When such meningiomas begin their growth at the posterior pole or operculum, they produce depression-like homonymous hemianopsias that are best analyzed in the central isopters. The peripheral isopters are usually normal in such cases until a late stage of progression. On occasion such lesions cause homonymous hemianoptic scotomas.

When the tumors are farther forward, they usually compress the radiations before they reach the cortex, except for the rather uncommon meningioma arising from the falx (see Fig. 15-48). These tumors of the falx may give unique opportunities for diagnosis and localization and are one of the few examples of pure striate cortex involvement. They are midline in position and may compress the calcarine fissure on either or both sides. They usually grow to one side and indent the calcarine cortex, causing ischemia and cellular destruction. When they are located posteriorly, the associated visual field defects may be hemianoptic scotomas in sharp contrast to radiation lesions. Quadrants are involved only if the tumor compresses the upper or lower lip of the calcarine fissure unequally. Inferior quadrantanopsia is much more common than superior quadrantanopsia. Wide areas of macular vision may be preserved, because either the tumor is anterior in position or it does not involve the depths of the fissure into which are projected the fibers for the horizontal meridian of the field.

An interesting diagnostic finding in visual field examination of some patients with occipital lobe lesions is known as the Riddoch phenomenon (see Fig. 15-45). In

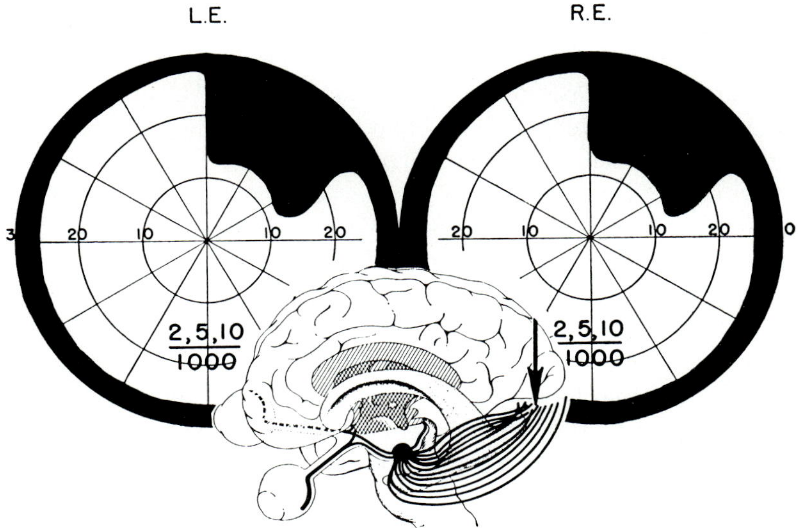

Fig. 15-48. Congruous right homonymous hemianopsia with wide macular sparing in patient with meningioma of falx involving lower lip of left calcarine fissure. There was partial restoration of visual field after removal of tumor.

certain of these lesions, routine testing of the field with moving stimuli (kinetic perimetry) fails to reveal a homonymous hemianopsia, whereas stationary targets demonstrate it readily. This must be kept in mind whenever a suspected lesion of the striate cortex is under investigation, and it calls for some ingenuity and variation from routine testing technique. It may account for marked differences in the visual field deficits found in the same patient by two different perimetrists. The discrepancy is due to variation in the speed of movement of the stimulus in the hemianoptic visual field. The ideal method for detecting such defects is the light threshold sensitivity test or static perimetry as measured with the Goldmann or Tübinger perimeter.

Recent studies by Safran and Glaser have also documented the Riddoch phenomenon, or statokinetic dissociation, in defective visual fields in lesions of the anterior visual pathway. They determined that the most sensitive technique of elaborating field defects is the static presentation of white or red stimuli and chromatic recognition of static or kinetic red objects. They suggest the addition of chromatic recognition of kinetic red stimuli to the application of standard kinetic white stimuli.

Generally, some recovery may be expected in those patients who exhibit the ability to detect motion in the affected fields. Recovery develops first in the peripheral field, leaving residual homonymous paracentral scotomas.

When tumors involve the area striata, the visual field defect is usually dense and has steep margins and the hemianoptic borders are completely congruous.

Traumatic lesions of the occipital cortex are relatively common.

Depressed fracture of the occiput with bone spicule penetration of the dura is a common injury in crimes of violence and to some extent in automobile accidents. Gunshot and shrapnel wounds of the head have afforded military surgeons unequaled opportunity to study the effects of sharply localized lesions of the occipital cortex.

When brain damage is extensive, as in large depressed fracture or extensive war wounds, the visual field changes are in keeping with the damage (i.e., a total homonymous hemianopsia). This type of brain injury sometimes causes the very disabling double homonymous hemianopsia previously mentioned. On the other hand, small areas of brain damage may occasionally occur, giving rise to minute, irregular, complex but completely congruous homonymous hemianoptic or quadrantanoptic scotomas (Figs. 15-50 and 15-51; Plate 9, *4*).

The upper portions of the radiation and occipital cortex appear to be more vulnerable to injury, hence the higher incidence of inferior homonymous quadrantanopsia and scotomas in traumatic lesions. When both sides of the upper lips of the calcarine fissure or the occipital pole are injured, the resulting visual field defect is likely to be a superior altitudinal hemianopsia or scotoma that is symmetric in each half-field (Fig. 15-52). Severe injury to the lower occipital lobes is usually fatal because of intracranial bleeding from laceration of the dural sinuses (Holmes).

The field defects in injury of the occipital area may be depressional in type, with sloping margins and a tendency to recovery; but they are more often total for all stimuli, with steep margins and permanent loss. The depression-type field defect

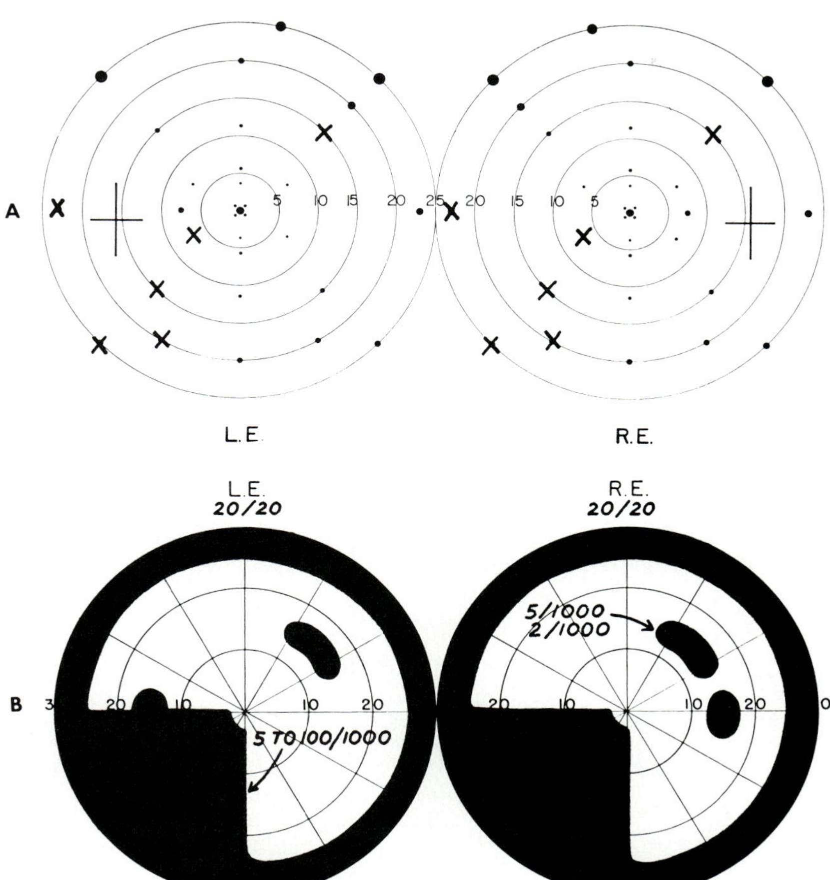

Fig. 15-49. A, Routine multiple pattern visual field examination showing left inferior homonymous quadrantanopsia with small homonymous defect in opposite field. Patient was unaware of any visual disturbance. **B,** Tangent screen examination of visual field defect, same patient. This double homonymous nature, density, and complete congruity of defects is readily apparent with large and small stimuli.

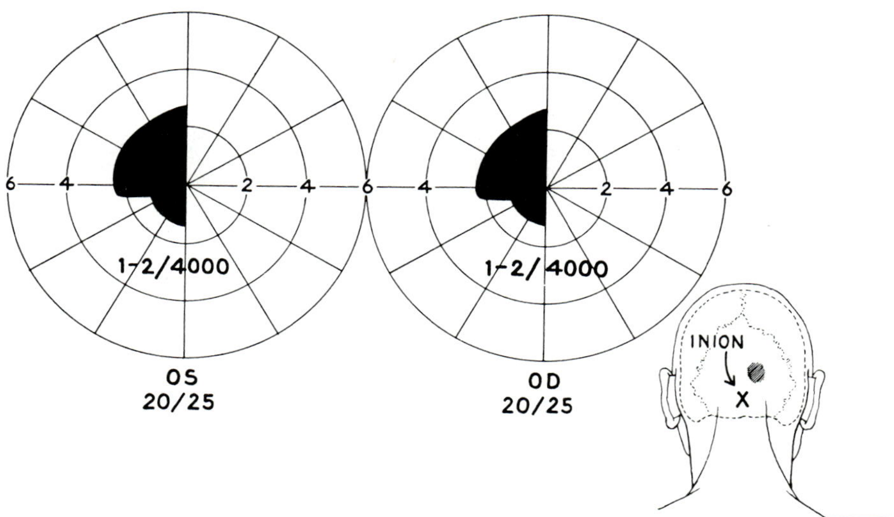

Fig. 15-50. Completely symmetric left homonymous hemianoptic scotomas resulting from hammer blows to occiput. Area of depressed fracture in relation to inion (external occipital protuberance) was drawn from x-ray tracings and operative notes. Note that tangent screen examination was conducted at 4 meters with 1-mm and 2-mm test objects and that scotoma is only 2 degrees in diameter. Defect was not detected on 1-meter screen. Patient was aware of her left-sided visual deficit. Fixation area was truly split, and visual acuity was 20/25 in each eye.

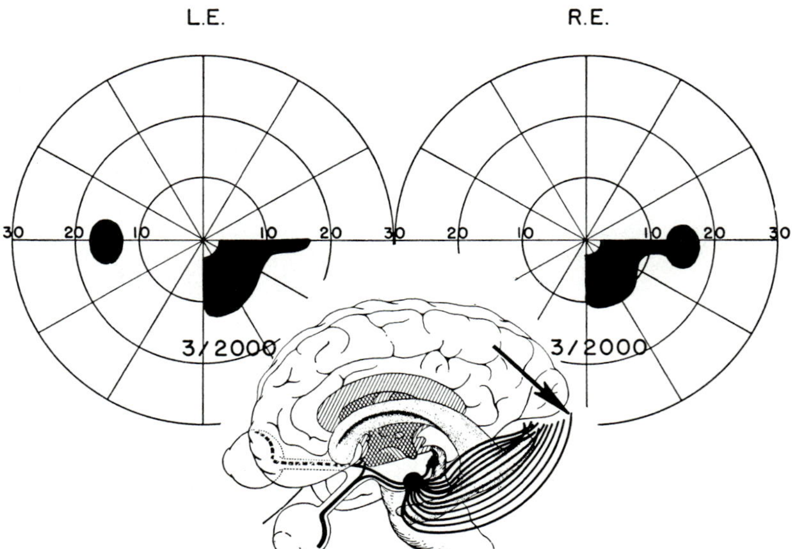

Fig. 15-51. Completely congruous right homonymous quadrantanoptic scotoma due to injury of left upper occipital pole. Apparent asymmetry of right field defect is due to connection of scotoma with normal blind spot. Site of lesion is indicated by arrow in anatomic sketch and was due to ice-pick stab wound through skull.

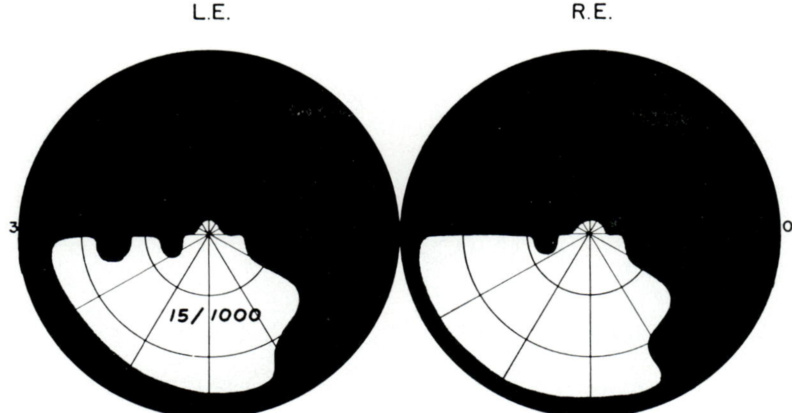

Fig. 15-52. Double homonymous superior quadrantanopsia resulting from inferior calcarine fissure infarction secondary to basilar artery thrombosis with bilateral posterior cerebral artery involvement. Note complete symmetry of defects carried into smallest irregularity. Patient had transient right hemiplegia, aphasia, and facial weakness with repeated attacks of amaurosis fugax. Diastolic pressure in ophthalmic artery was lower on right side.

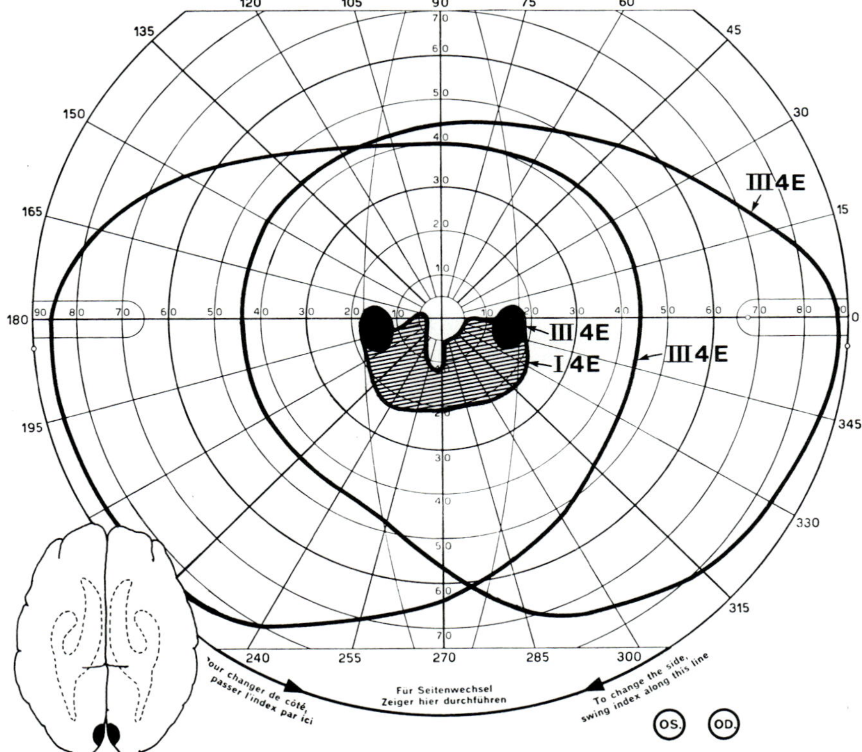

Fig. 15-53. Double (bilateral) homonymous hemianoptic scotomas (two superimposed Goldmann perimeter fields) from small meningiomas of falx involving medial lips of both calcarine fissures at occipital pole.

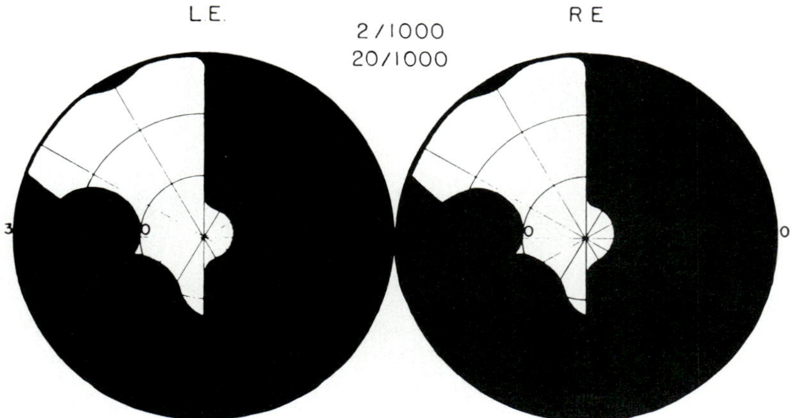

Fig. 15-54. Completely congruous, irregular, double homonymous hemianopsia due to thrombosis of both posterior cerebral arteries with ischemia and degeneration of entire left occipital lobe and upper lip of right occipital lobe.

may be caused by contusion or concussion with immediate severe functional loss followed by varying degrees of edema and vascular damage. The degree of recovery of the field is dependent on the amount of actual cell damage secondary to these vascular changes. When the primary site of injury is in the cortex, with cell destruction in the visual end organ, the hemianopsia is steep-margined and permanent.

Macular sparing usually occurs to some degree in injury to the occipital cortex but is less striking than with tumor and vascular lesions of this area.

Injury to both occipital lobes with production of double or bilateral homonymous hemianopsia is not uncommon in war wounds. It is usually the result of a gunshot wound traversing the two occipital areas, and the character of the defect is determined by the course of the bullet in the brain. In most instances the visual field loss is inferior and the defect is a double inferior homonymous quadrantanopsia with or without macular sparing (Fig. 15-54). Occasionally both upper and lower fields of both sides are involved, giving rise to an apparent concentric contraction with only a small area of double macular sparing remaining (Plate 9, *1*). Injury of the posterior tip of both occipital lobes would produce a double homonymous hemianoptic scotoma, which would appear in the fields as a bilateral, circular, central scotoma with or without minute areas of macular sparing (see Fig. 15-53).

Crossed quadrant hemianopsia is a form of bilateral or double homonymous hemianopsia due to injuries to the upper lip of the calcarine fissure on one side and the lower lip of the opposite cortex (see Fig. 15-49).

Visual phenomena associated with lesions of cortex

In considering disturbances of the visual cortex, mention should be made of four visual phenomena associated with physiologic or pathologic lesions of this area: (1) visual hallucinations, (2) cortical blindness, (3) paroxysmal scintillating scotomas

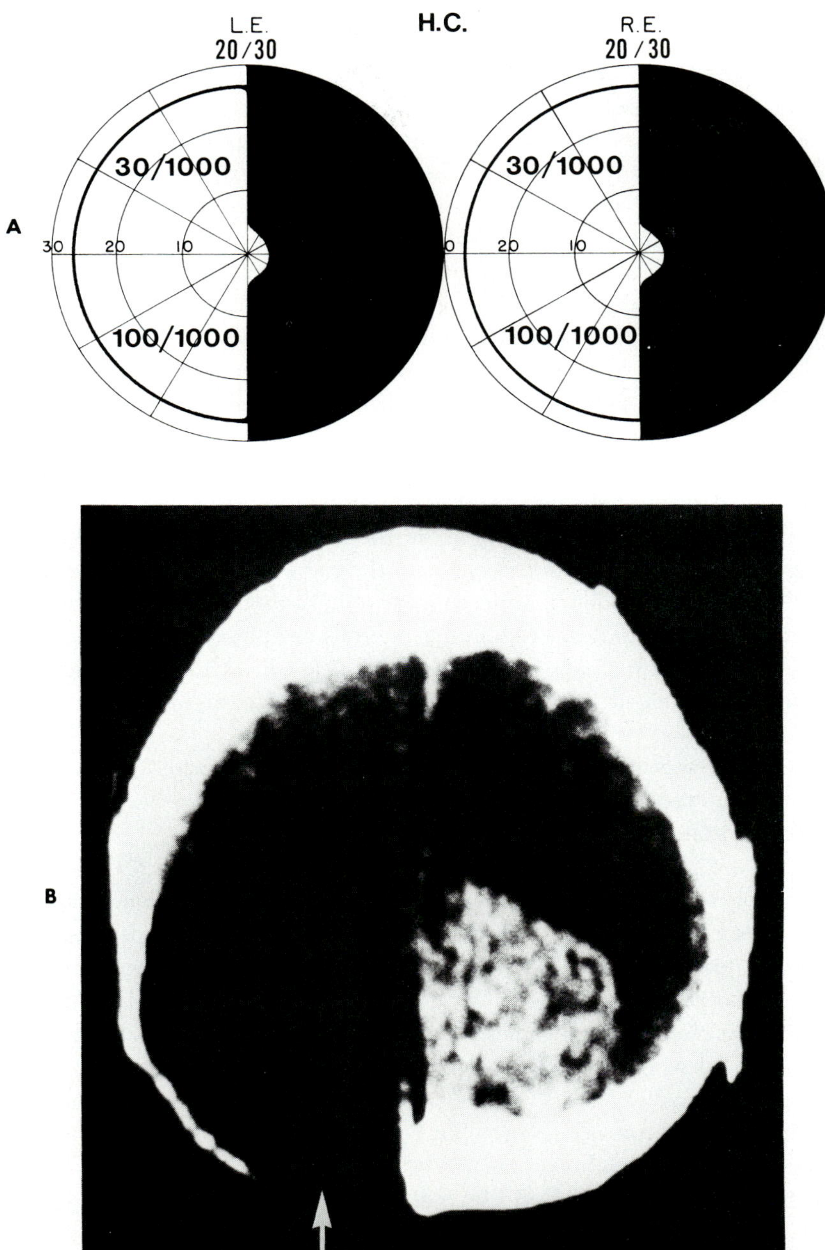

Fig. 15-55. A, Total right homonymous hemianopsia, with macular sparing, resulting from extirpation of a large meningioma of left occipital lobe. Defect same for all stimuli. Later removal of large meningioma of right occipital lobe produced a total left homonymous hemianopsia with macular sparing so that a few degrees of central vision were retained. **B,** CAT scan of case illustrated in **A** shows extirpation of tumor of left occipital lobe *(arrow)* and residual tumor in right occipital lobe.

and hemianopsia of migraine, and (4) light flashes and homonymous visual field dimming or loss associated with occipital lobe arteriovenous malformations.

Visual hallucination. A visual hallucination is the apparent perception of an object or visual stimulus not actually present. As previously noted, such hallucinations may occur in association with lesions of the temporal and parietal areas of the brain. They also accompany disturbance in the visual cortex of the occipital lobe.

Visual hallucinations are generally described as "formed or complex" or "unformed or simple." Formed hallucinations usually appear as specific objects or persons, although they may occur as elaborate abstract patterns, grotesque animals or humans, or well-inown panoramas. Complex hallucinations may merge into simpler forms and simple forms may be interpreted by the patient as complex familiar objects, much as Rorschach blots are given form and substance.

In general, the simple hallucination results from abnormal stimuli to the neurons of the visual pathway and particularly the receptor of the retina and the end organ of the calcarine cortex. The complex hallucination is generally initiated by irritation of the associational areas of the cortex.

Usually the visual hallucination appears in the blind portion of a visual field defect, although it has been reported to occur in the seeing portion of the field.

Practically, the simple hallucination consists of lightning streaks, pinwheels, exploding stars or Roman candles, or shimmering veils of light occupying the anoptic half of a homonymous hemianopsia produced by a lesion of the calcarine cortex. When unilateral, hallucinations are usually the result of irritation of the rod and cone layer of the retina.

Care must be exercised in questioning the patient to be certain that what may appear to him as a monocular scintillation in the left eye is not, in fact, a left homonymous hemianoptic hallucination.

In contrast, the formed hallucination appears as a familiar object, face, person, animal, or complex scene in the blind portion of the homonymous hemianopsia resulting from a lesion of the temporal or parietal lobe affecting the optic radiations.

Although the foregoing generalizations apply to most cases and are of some diagnostic value, it should be remembered that the very nature of a visual hallucination is so complex that there must be many exceptions to the general rule. Thus, the hallucination of light when the optic nerve is cut is a well-known exception to these rules, whereas extremely complex visions are common in psychosis, delirium, and drug addiction and are not necessarily the result of organic irritation of the optic radiations or associational pathways.

Cortical blindness. Cortical blindness, unlike double homonymous hemianopsia, is a total loss of vision caused by bilateral destruction, either transient or permanent, organic or functional, of the occipital visual area. There is no other visual end organ and its removal, usually due to vascular or traumatic accident, results in a striking and unusual visual loss in which the patient is unaware of his blindness. This is in contrast to the strong sense of blindness exhibited by patients after loss of both eyes.

Denial of visual loss (Anton's syndrome), so characteristic of cortical blindness, also occurs in persons with homonymous hemianopsia from cortical lesions so that, although only half the vision is gone, the patient suffers from partial cortical blindness and is not conscious of his one-sided visual loss until he repeatedly bumps into objects on that side. Also, because of the phenomenon of completion, patients with this type of homonymous hemianopsia often will accurately complete images only half of which are actually seen.

The clinical features of complete cortical blindness are (1) complete loss of vision, including light perception often without awareness of such loss, (2) loss of reflex closure of the lid on sudden exposure to light or danger, (3) normal pupillary reaction to light and convergence, (4) normal ophthalmoscopic appearance of the ocular fundi, and (5) normal ocular rotations.

Frequently associated with these signs and symptoms are various forms of aphasia, visual memory loss, spacial disorientation, amnesia, and mental deterioration, and, in fact, the entire symptom complex may be considered as a form of visual agnosia.

Recovery from complete cortical blindness may occur when cell destruction has not been too great. Such a recovery is most likely to take place in cases of traumatic

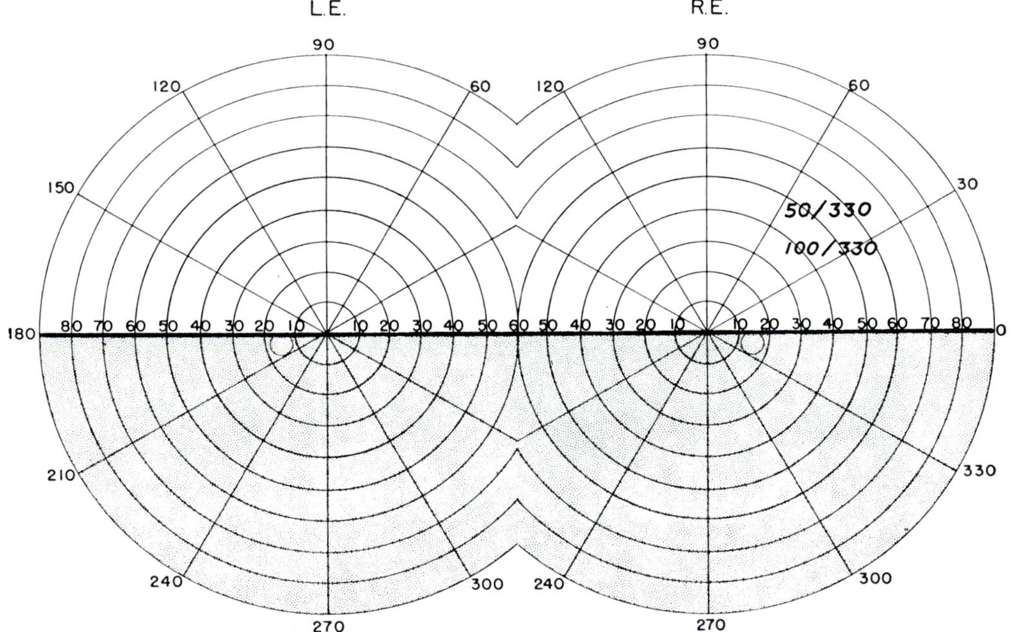

Fig. 15-56. Partially recovered complete cortical blindness with residual bilateral homonymous inferior quadrantanopsia. Vision eventually returned to normal. On recovering from severe asphyxia with prolonged anoxemia, patient was totally blind for several days but refused to recognize that he could not see. Pupillary reactions were normal. Recovery was gradual with restoration of upper field as shown here and finally development of normal fields and vision.

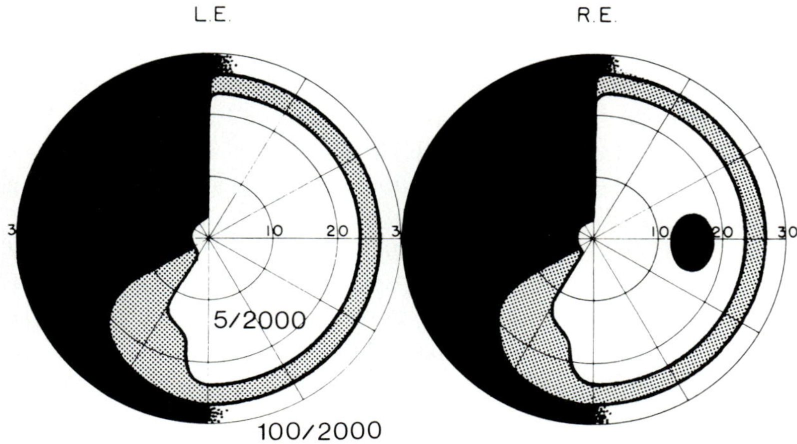

Fig. 15-57. Congruous left homonymous hemianopsia resulting from infarct of right calcarine cortex secondary to transient traumatic vertebral-basilar cerebral artery occlusion. Patient was struck in back of neck near occiput during chiropractic "adjustment" and suffered immediate total visual loss followed by abstract hallucinations "as though looking into a bowl of cracked ice with a bright light behind it." This cortical blindness cleared, but completely symmetric homonymous hemianopsia persisted.

or concussional damage to the visual cortex, and it may be complete or incomplete (Figs. 15-56 and 15-57). Return of vision is gradual with a vague sense of brightness followed by an ill-defined light perception and finally by a return of the form and color sense. Vision may return slowly while varying degrees of amnesia, spacial disorientation, anxiety, and nervous fatigue persist.

Cortical blindness may be caused by cerebral softening due to vascular occlusion, by hypoxia or anoxia, by tumor, and by trauma. It may be difficult to differentiate from hysterical amaurosis.

Migraine. Migraine is a paroxysmal disorder in which transient, scintillating scotomas and homonymous hemianopsia are prominent features of the symptom complex (Figs. 15-58 and 15-59).

Migraine is very common and because of its visual disturbances is frequently first seen by the ophthalmologist. It is a physiologic disturbance of unknown etiology, occurring primarily in young persons of superior intellect with perfectionist personality patterns.

Migraine attacks assume many and varied forms, and it would not be suitable to discuss them here. Nor can we discuss the theories of pathogenesis and the details of diagnosis and treatment.

The typical migraine attack is made up of several parts:

1. The patient experiences an aura of vague uneasiness or increased activity or depression so that the chronic migraine sufferer recognizes the signs of an impending attack.
2. A scintillating scotoma may start at the fixation point of each visual field and expand into the homonymous hemianoptic fields of both eyes to finally dis-

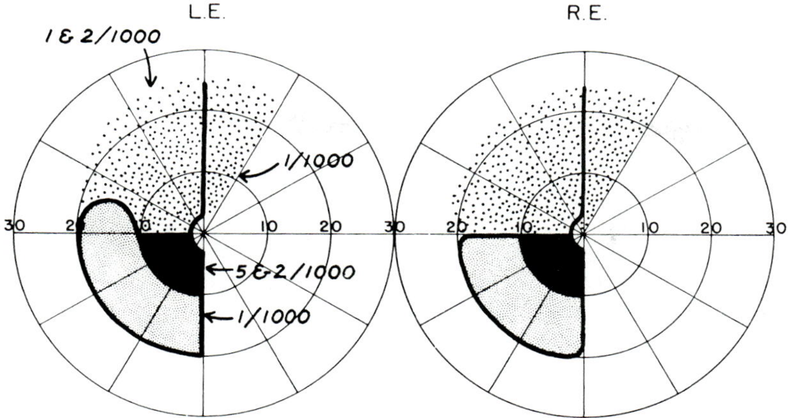

Fig. 15-58. Left homonymous hemianoptic scotomas mapped during initial stages of migraine attack immediately following scintillating scotoma. Scotomatous areas were clear cut, congruous, and steep margined, and they lasted about ½ hour. Remainder of left field was vaguely involved, and there was slight extension of this deficit into upper right quadrant beyond midline.

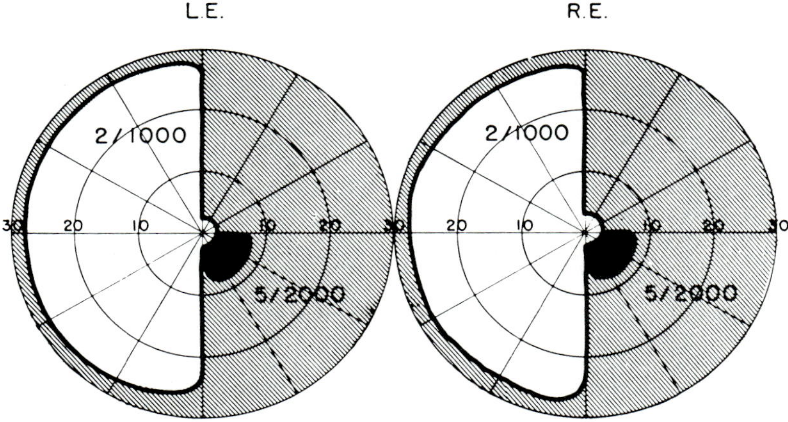

Fig. 15-59. Right homonymous hemianopsia with denser area of right homonymous quadrantanoptic scotoma charted immediately following subsidence of right homonymous hemianoptic scintillating scotoma, and just preceding severe left hemicrania of attack of migraine.

appear from the peripheral field. Some patients describe these scotomas as occurring in only one eye. Scintillating scotomas assume many forms and are, in essence, a type of simple or unformed visual hallucination. Usually they occur as jagged light streaks that begin as a pinpoint of flickering light adjacent to fixation and gradually widen out into the right or left halves of the visual fields as a series of irregular connecting streaks of light, sometimes white and sometimes colored. They form a crooked half-circle and have been called the fortification specter because of their resemblance to maps of old fortification systems. Other patients describe these scotomas as ill-defined circles of whirling light analogous to star nebulas. Still others see them as exploding balls of light that fill the homonymous half-fields with brilliant color. Often the scintillating scotoma is barely perceptible, as though objects were seen through a heat haze rising from an asphalt pavement. Some patients described the visual disturbance as ripples of light on a pond into which a stone has been cast, and others relate it to the snow (horizontal or vertical) on an ill-tuned television screen. All these disturbances of visual perception occur in the half-field of vision that subsequently develops the characteristic homonymous hemianopsia. Other disturbances noted and reported are macropsia, micropsia, distortion of straight lines, diplopia, polyopia, pulsation phenomenon, and loss of stereopsis. In almost every case the scotoma lasts but a few minutes and its place is occupied by an area of visual loss, either relative or complete.

3. Homonymous hemianopsia associated with migraine is a transient loss of visual field that may vary in duration from a minute to several hours. A few cases have been reported in which, after many transient attacks, a permanent hemianopsia developed. The usual duration of the field defect is 15 to 20 minutes. The homonymous hemianopsia may be total or partial. It may involve the macula or spare it. Most patients describe their visual field defects as involving the entire half-field including fixation, the visual loss being relative or partial. Objects, movement, and color may be dimly seen in the blind portion of the field, but details are obscured. This common description is borne out by tangent screen examination on those relatively rare occasions when it is possible to examine the field before disappearance of the defect. In my own personal experience with migraine attacks, the homonymous hemianopsia has spared a minute area around fixation and has obscured test objects under 3 mm in size but was relative for larger stimuli. In five other patients on whom I have been able to perform adequate tangent screen examinations during migraine attacks, the anoptic portion of the fields has varied from total visual loss to a vague depression of vision through which the 1/2000 stimulus was dimly seen. One patient clearly demonstrated a dense homonymous hemianoptic scotoma close to fixation within a more peripheral field loss that was less dense for the same stimulus. The homonymous hemianopsia of migraine appears to be a positive visual loss. The patient is quite aware of the defect and can describe it accurately. Some persons are insistent that only one eye is involved, whereas others readily recognize the homonymous nature of the bilateral defect in the fields.
4. The headache that follows the homonymous hemianopsia, and from which migraine takes its name, is characteristically a hemicrania involving the side of the head opposite the visual field loss. Its variety is almost infinite. It may be so mild as to be overlooked unless specifically questioned for, or it may be prostrating in its severity. It may be located in any area and described as deep or superficial, and it may start in one area and spread to involve the en-

tire head. It may last from a few minutes to several days. Symptoms and signs frequently associated with migrainous headache are nausea and vomiting and marked vasomotor changes that are sometimes unilateral.

The scintillating scotoma and the homonymous hemianopsia are occasionally accompanied by other sensory disturbances such as transitory aphasia, hemianesthesia, and paresthesia. There may even be motor involvement manifested as diplopia or partial hemiplegia.

The cause of migraine is unknown. It is of interest to the perimetrist chiefly because of the frequent presence of homonymous hemianopsia and hemianoptic scintillating scotoma. There is good clinical and experimental evidence that these visual field defects are caused by intense vasomotor disturbance in the arterial supply of the occipital cortex.

It is well known and of interest that, in young women, episodic migraine attacks are often premenstrual in onset and closely follow the menstrual cycle. It is also significant that migraine attacks of considerable severity may be precipitated by the use of various contraceptive pills and that aggravation of migraine by the use of these contraceptives may be so severe as to force their discontinuance.

Occipital lobe arteriovenous malformations. The differentiation of migraine headache preceded by scintillating scotoma and transient homonymous hemianopsia from the occipital epilepsy produced by occipital lobe arteriovenous malformations may be difficult unless certain criteria for each condition are kept in mind.

Troost and Newton have reported the clinical and radiologic features of 26 cases of occipital epilepsy and occipital apoplexy resulting from occipital lobe arteriovenous malformations.

In occipital epilepsy, focal seizures are fairly common with visual auras indicating the focus in the occipital lobe. These consist of poorly formed, episodic, brief visual sensations unlike the scintillating figures of a migraine attack. Epileptic photopsias last only seconds or rarely for a few minutes before the onset of a generalized seizure. Typical seizure activity may not be present. Transient homonymous hemianopsia may or may not occur. Headache usually precedes the attack, unlike the hemicrania that follows a migraine attack.

The syndrome of occipital apoplexy is characterized by the sudden onset of severe headache and homonymous hemianopsia produced by hemorrhage and hematoma formation within the occipital lobe. Some of the effects of compression can be reversed by prompt surgical evacuation of the hematoma. The size of the arteriovenous malformation bears no relation to the presence of the homonymous visual field deficit.

BEHAVIOR PATTERNS IN SPLIT-BRAIN ANIMALS

In any consideration of the interpretation of homonymous hemianoptic visual field defects, the split-brain experiments, which cast much light on the connections between visual cortex and prefrontal cortex and between right and left side of the brain, should be mentioned.

If the optic chiasm is sectioned midsagittally so that all crossing fibers are cut, then the afferent connections from each eye go only to the hemisphere on the same side. When such an animal is trained to choose consistently between a circle and a square with one eye open, the animal retains the habit when the open eye is closed and the closed eye is opened. If however, both optic chiasm and corpus callosum are sectioned, the transfer of monocularly learned visual discrimination habits does not occur. Such sectioning isolates the two cerebral hemispheres from each other. With the left eye open and the right eye closed, all behavior dependent on visual stimuli will be determined by the left cerebral hemisphere, and vice versa. In such a situation, a unilateral cerebral lesion can be produced, and its effect determined by comparing the response of the animal to visual stimuli with either one or the other eye open.

In one experiment on such a split-brain monkey, a right prefrontal lobe resection was performed. The right eye was left open and the left eyelids were sutured together. Immediately there appeared many of the behavioral patterns described in animals with bilateral prefrontal lobe resections. Whereas before the resection the animal would bare its teeth and attempt to attack any person approaching it, following removal of the prefrontal lobe the monkey responded placidly and peacefully to the approach of the person and accepted raisins from his hand. When the left eye was opened and the right eye was closed, the visual stimulus was projected to the undamaged side of the brain and there was an abrupt change in the animal's behavior back to the preoperative level with aggressive response at the appearance of the person.

Other experiments have been performed in which the optic tract and corpus callosum have been sectioned, followed by prefrontal lobectomy on one or the other side. If, in a split-brain monkey, the right optic tract is sectioned and the right prefrontal lobe resected, the animal can see with both eyes and the remaining or left visual and prefrontal cortex are sufficient for learning to discriminate between a circle and a square. If, on the other hand, the right optic tract is cut, the corpus callosum is split, and the left prefrontal lobe is resected, the animal can still see with both eyes through the left visual cortex but neither visual cortex can communicate with either prefrontal lobe and the monkey can no longer learn to solve new problems. In other words, at least one visual cortex must have connections with at least one prefrontal cortex.

CHAPTER 16

Disturbances of psychogenic origin

When we speak of psychogenesis, we refer to physiologic processes consisting of excitations in the central nervous system that can be studied by psychologic methods because they are perceived subjectively in the form of emotions, ideas, or wishes.

Ocular disturbances of psychogenic origin may be divided into (1) conversion symptoms, (2) vegetative neuroses, and (3) psychoses with ocular symptoms. A conversion symptom is a symbolic expression of a well-defined emotional content as an attempt at relief. A vegetative neurosis is not an attempt to express an emotion but is the physiologic accompaniment of constant or periodically recurring emotional states. Psychotic persons, such as schizophrenics and manic-depressive psychotics, not uncommonly appear to suffer from visual disturbances that are nonorganic in origin. These may take the form of delusions regarding loss of the eyes or loss of vision, inability to look directly at an object or person, inability to open the eyes, etc. Rarely are the visual fields abnormal in the psychoses. The perimetrist is interested in these psychogenic disorders as they affect the visual fields. The most typical examples of field loss occur in conversion hysteria.

Loss of vision, either total or partial, in a person with hysteria is a psychogenic reaction of which the patient is unaware, an attempt to escape from an intolerable situation. If the patient is conscious of this reaction, he is malingering. The diagnosis of hysteria must be made by exclusion of organic disease, differentiation from malingering, and, finally and most important, psychologic evaluation of the patient as a whole and his personality pattern. Examination of the visual fields may play an important part in the differential diagnosis of organic from psychogenic disease.

The fundamental characteristic of visual field defects in the person with hysteria is that they do not ordinarily simulate the defects of organic disease of the visual pathway. Thus rarely do hemianoptic field defects occur in association with hysteria; and if a visual field defect has a hemianoptic character, it should be viewed with suspicion and considered as organic in origin until proved otherwise. I followed one patient for over 6 years who consistently demonstrated a dense bitemporal hemianopsia. Complete physical, radiologic, and neurologic examinations were normal, and exploration of the chiasmal area through a frontal craniotomy yeilded negative

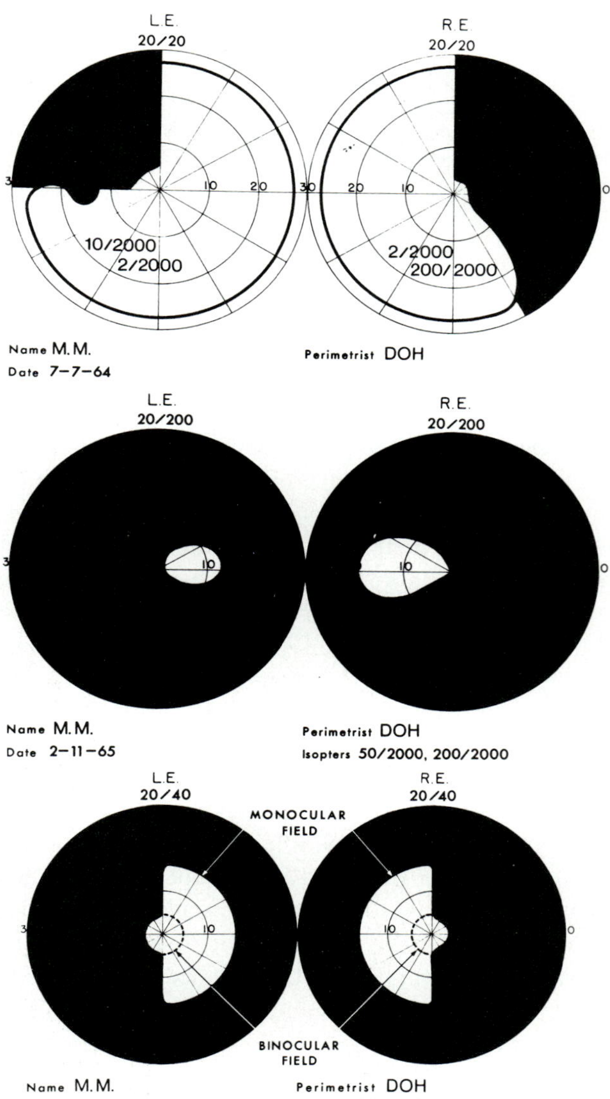

Fig. 16-1. Bitemporal hemianopsia with hysterical amblyopia. Each field, tested separately, showed total temporal loss but, when tested binocularly, there was a typical functional tubular defect the same size at both 1 and 2 meters on the tangent screen. Patient showed marked variation in visual acuity and field deficits over a 5-year period. Surgical exploration of chiasmal area revealed no pathological lesion. Diagnosis later confirmed by psychiatric evaluation. (From Harrington, D. O.: Some unusual and difficult visual field defects. Trans. Ophthalmol. Soc. U.K. **92:**15, 1972, London, Churchill Livingstone Ltd.)

findings. Visual fields varied through the years with periodic concentric contraction of the nasal fields but always with complete bitemporal loss. When both eyes were tested simultaneously, the binocular field was grossly contracted and was the same size in centimeters at both 1 and 2 meters distance on the tangent screen. Visual acuity was 20/40 in each eye, and there was no optic atrophy. Careful questioning finally elicited the story that a close female friend had suffered marked visual loss from a pituitary adenoma. The patient had been relatively undisturbed by her visual field loss, and no amount of suggestion or psychotherapy has affected it through the years (Fig. 16-1).

Another type of functional or hysterical hemianopsia is the "missing half" field defect reported by Keane. The deficit is best appreciated on confrontation testing and, in fact, a hemianoptic pattern is encouraged by this method of testing. The usual pattern consists of decreased vision in one eye, an ipsilateral hemianopsia on testing the "affected" eye, full fields in the other eye, and a complete hemianopsia toward the affected side with both eyes open. The incompatibility of the monocular and binocular fields quickly demonstrates the functional nature of this alleged visual loss.

Central, paracentral, nerve fiber bundle defects, and other types of scotoma are rarely, if ever, found in association with hysteria; when present, they should be considered as the result of organic disease. On the other hand, the variation in morphology in the visual field defects of hysteria is almost infinite, and in some cases nearly any type of field defect may be demonstrated, depending on the examiner's use of suggestion.

The visual field defect may change from one type to another on successive examinations or even during the same examination, if the patient is given sufficient leeway to exercise his imagination. Suggestion by the examiner, if strong enough, may cause the patient to demonstrate a scotoma, particularly of the ring type, and I have even been able to elicit an irregular hemianoptic defect by telling the patient that it should be present. A fairly common example of this type of defect is found when the normal blind spot is demonstrated to the patient in the temporal field and it is then suggested that the same type of scotoma should be present in the same location in the nasal field of the same eye.

Before charting the visual fields of the person suspected of having hysterical amblyopia or visual field loss, the examiner may obtain certain information from watching the person's reaction to and avoidance of external obstacles. The hysterical person views his disability with a certain nonchalance not in keeping with his tested visual acuity or field loss. He carefully avoids obstacles placed in his path, never falling over them or hurting himself as does the organically blind individual with grossly restricted visual fields. The malingerer exaggerates his disability and either dashes into obstacles or stands, like a catatonic, refusing to move at all.

When the visual fields are tested in a patient with hysterical amblyopia, the various methods of examination will usually elicit different types of field defects. This vagary in the fields is in itself a useful diagnostic sign.

When the perimeter is used, a common result is the spiral or fatigue field. If the test object is moved from the periphery toward fixation along successive meridians on the perimeter arc, the stimulus will at first be seen in the normal position; but as each meridian is examined, the test object will appear closer and closer to fixation. Thus the chart of the field will assume the appearance of a contracting spiral until finally the stimulus will be seen only at fixation. The opposite of this defect, in the form of an expanding spiral, may be elicited by starting the test object close to fixation and moving it outward into the peripheral field along successive meridians (Fig. 16-2).

When opposite ends of a meridian are successively tested on the perimeter arc, as the two ends of the 180-degree meridian or the 45- and 135-degree meridians, the resultant visual field chart is very likely to appear star-shaped (Fig. 16-2).

Both the spiral field and the star-shaped field are, in essence, the result of rapid fatigability, itself psychogenic in origin. As such they are found in persons with neurasthenia and the anxiety neuroses as well as hysteria. I have, for example, seen several patients with typical spiral fields in association with neurocirculatory asthenia. Such cases, as would be expected, are much more common in military than in civilian practice.

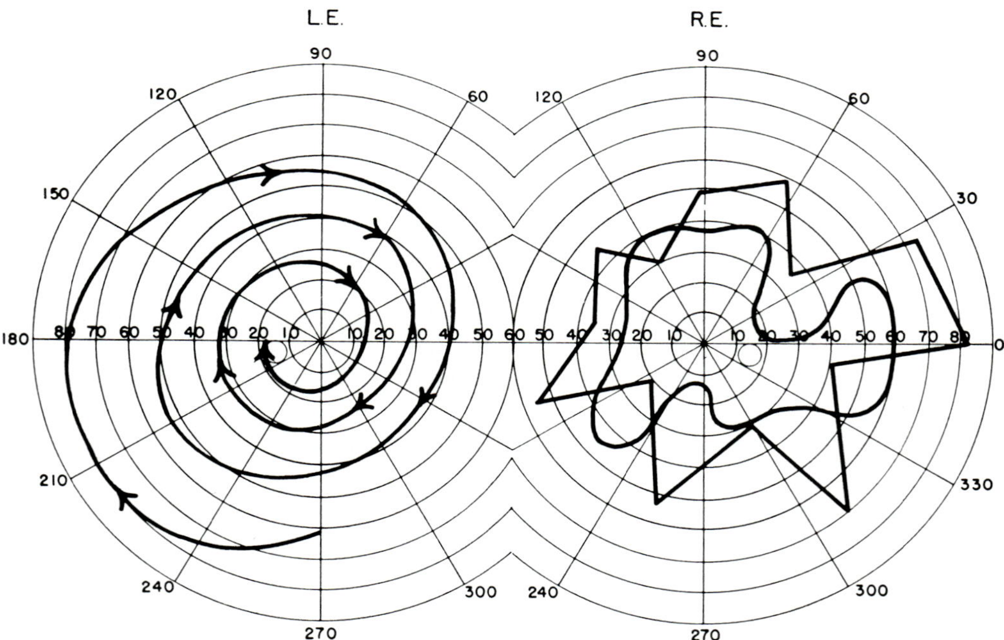

Fig. 16-2. Two examples of visual field defects seen in association with hysterical amblyopia. Right eye shows star-shaped interlacing field resulting from alternately testing the opposite ends of various meridians. This was a form of fatigue field. Left eye shows typical spiral fatigue field often found in hysterical amblyopia and resulting from testing each meridian separately while rotating perimeter arc repeatedly around fixation.

Inversion of the fields is another characteristic psychogenic disturbance. In normal persons, if a test object is carried in toward fixation from the periphery, the field will be somewhat smaller than if the test object is moved outward from fixation and the patient asked to note its disappearance. In the same manner, the normal blind spot will often appear to be slightly smaller if the stimulus is moved from seeing to blind area than if it is moved from blind to seeing. In a person with hysteria, this tendency may be reversed, and the field to an outwardly moving test object is smaller than when the object is brought in from the periphery.

The visual field defects that are most typical of hysteria are the various forms of concentric contraction or tubular field (Fig. 16-3). This type of field loss is so common in hysteria as to be almost pathognomonic of the condition. Its character is such that it can only be functional or psychogenic in origin.

Needless to say, there is considerable variation in tubular fields. Some are extremely small, whereas others may show only slight reduction in size from the normal isopters. Some have sloping margins, whereas most show extremely steep borders. In all instances of true tubular field in association with hysteria, there is one common factor of utmost diagnostic importance: The visual field is cylindric instead of cone-shaped. This can result only from disturbances of psychogenic origin and cannot be an organic visual field defect.

The result of this cylindric-type field loss is that the visual field measures the same size in millimeters regardless of the distance of the test object from the patient's eye, assuming that visual stimuli subtending the same visual angle are used

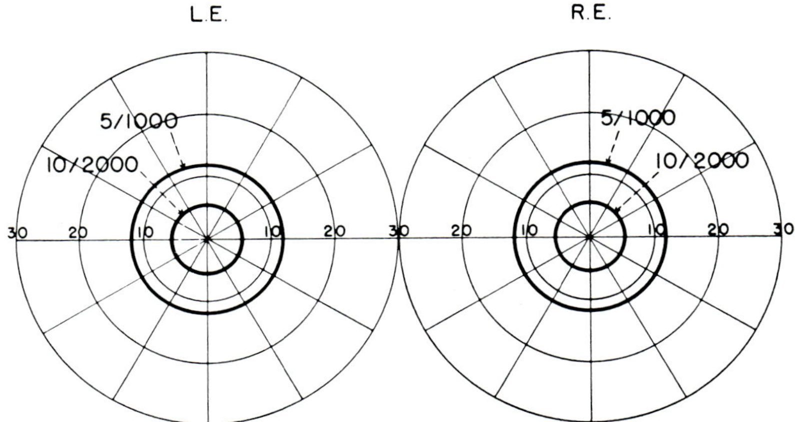

Fig. 16-3. Tubular or cylindric type of concentric contraction of visual field seen in hysteria. Patient was 16-year-old girl whose sister had died shortly before of brain tumor. Vision with Snellen chart was 20/200, although patient could see 1-mm fixation target at 2 meters. Field in each eye was same size in centimeters at both 1 and 2 meters and was charted as though taken directly from tangent screen, with 2000 isopter charted 6 degrees from fixation and 1000 isopter charted 12 degrees from fixation. On tangent screen both fields fell on same circle. To avoid confusion in charting such fields, notation should always be made that radius of field is same in centimeters (not degrees) regardless of distance at which test is performed.

at the varying distances. In instances of hysterical tubular fields with sloping margins, this calculation of the visual angle of the test objects may be important. Most tubular fields, however, have steep margins so that the size of the test object may be of no consequence. In examining such a visual field the tangent screen must be used so that the distance may be varied; an unmarked screen is preferred.

The patient is seated before the screen at a distance of 1 meter and a suitably large fixation target is attached to the center of the screen. One or two meridians may be rapidly tested with 5-, 20-, and 50-mm test objects. If, in these meridians, the border of the field is approximately the same for all three stimuli (i.e., the margin is steep), the larger of the test objects would be chosen to complete the test.

Eight to twelve meridians are tested on the tangent screen at 1 meter, and the points of appearance of the test object are marked on the screen. It is advisable to be ostentatious about this demarcation of the field so that the patient is made aware of the limits of his field. The field is usually circular in shape and may be contracted to a radius of 20, 15, or 10 cm from fixation. The patient is now moved up to a distance of 500 mm from the screen or back to 2 meters (i.e., the distance is halved or doubled).

If the field margins are not steep, the size of the test object should be halved for the 500-mm distance or doubled for the 2-meter distance. If the margins are steep, it matters little what test object is used.

With the patient in the new position, the examination is repeated using the same meridians and the same speed of movement of the test object. Care should be taken to approach the previous markings slowly in order to give the patient time to respond to the appearance of the object.

In hysterical contraction of the visual field, the patient will see the test object at exactly the same spot on the tangent screen at 500 mm or 2 meters as he did at 1 meter. The field will measure the same diameter in millimeters for both distances, whereas if recorded in degrees it would appear to be twice as large for the 500-mm distance and one half as large for the 2-meter distance.

In charting such a field, notation should be made that the test was performed at varying distances and that the field measured the same size in millimeters, not degrees, for the different distances.

In general, the tubular field of hysteria is remarkably constant in size, shape, and steepness of margins, It may vary slightly from one examination to the next, but rarely significantly. In this it differs from the contracted field of malingerers.

Within the area of the tubular field, visual acuity may be good. Outside the circle is almost total blindness.

An interesting variant of the tubular field may occasionally be demonstrated. If the test object is held well outside the alleged area of the visual field and the patient is directed sharply to look at it, he will often involuntarily shift fixation accurately from the central target to the peripheral test object. If he is now asked how many objects he sees he will often respond "two," even when the central fixation target is smaller than the test object.

When the Goldmann perimeter is used to test the field of a hysterical or malingering patient, use of the mechanism that enables the perimetrist to flash the target on and off while moving it from one part of the field to another will be of benefit. If a large target is used in the ordinary manner of kinetic perimetry, the patient may deny seeing it until it approaches fixation, thus demonstrating a grossly constricted field. If, however, the same target is rapidly moved from one area of the field to another, extinguishing the stimulus each time before it is moved, the patient will often involuntarily shift his gaze to the new area of appearance of the target. Even slight shifts of fixation are easily detected through the telescopic sight of the instrument.

If a bright simulus is suddenly exposed in an area of the field that has previously been demonstrated as blind and the patient is sharply commanded to "look at the light," he will usually involuntarily look in the direction of the stimulus, thus indicating that it is, in fact, within his field of vision.

The same methods may be used on the tangent screen with the electroluminescent stimuli of the Lumiwand.

In a number of instances, the multiple pattern method of visual field examination has proved useful in exposing the spurious nature of the hysterical tubular field. Although the field, as tested on the cover of the instrument in the usual manner of a tangent screen field, was found to be contracted to a few centimeters from fixation, the patient's response to the multiple patterns was quite normal.

Keltner found the Fieldmaster automated perimeter especially useful in the detection of visual field loss due to hysteria and malingering.

Unilateral tubular visual fields in patients with hysteria are uncommon. Even though central visual acuity may differ in the two eyes, the contracted visual fields are usually remarkably symmetirc.

Although hysterical amblyopia and visual field loss are commonly seen in military personnel, they are far from rare in civilian life and, when suspected and searched for, are frequently found in children. In soldiers it is usually a manifestation of a desire to escape from duty, whereas in children it may be an unconscious escape mechanism to avoid domination by a parent or as an excuse for deficiencies in schoolwork or social adjustment.

The possibility of visual loss, either peripheral or central, of psychogenic origin superimposed on organic defects must always be borne in mind. I have seen a number of such cases where organic disease with legitimate visual loss was probably the reason why the hysterical conversion reaction elected the eye as the site or organ to demonstrate functional loss. It is obvious that such cases present a difficult differential diagnostic problem in which one must evaluate what degree of visual loss is organic and what is functional. An example of such a case is a patient who had severely contracted visual fields, typical of hysteria, associated with bilateral central scotomas resulting from bilateral macular choroiditis. It was quite certain that the patient's inability to read and his markedly defective central vision were organic in nature, but his completely normal locomotion in the face of extreme contraction of the peripheral fields made him immediately suspect. The tubular nature of the peripheral fields confirmed the suspicion of hysteria, and the subsequent "cure" of this aspect of his visual field loss was easily accomplished.

Many students of hysteria believe that the visual field defects noted in hysteria are entirely the result of suggestion. Some authors believe that the nature of the field defect will be determined by the instrumentation and technique of perimetry in any given case, and that almost any desired type of visual field loss may be produced according to the method employed by the examiner.

Although it is true that skillful perimetry may strongly suggest a certain type of visual field loss and the complicated instruments for visual field examination imply the presence of disease to the patient who faces them, there are many patients for whom the simplest and briefest of tests will demonstrate a functional type of visual field loss.

The basic elements of hysteria must be present before an individual will demonstrate hysterical amblyopia. Treatment must be directed toward these underlying psychogenic elements rather than toward the symptoms by which they manifest themselves.

The vegetative neuroses give rise to physiologic disturbances that, if severe or prolonged, may produce secondary vasomotor changes, edema, and organic cell pathology resulting in loss of function. Thus a constant or periodically recurring emotional state may give rise to secondary organic changes in the eye resulting in visual loss. Examples of this type of disturbance of psychogenic origin may be seen in the homonymous hemianopsia of migraine, some instances of which have been reported as permanent field defects.

Another example is the macular edema associated with retinal angiospasm in susceptible individuals with vasoneurotic diathesis. These persons with labile vasomotor systems, when exposed to emotional trauma, may exhibit various signs and symptoms of peripheral circulatory disturbance of greater or lesser degree. They finally develop an ophthalmoscopically visible edema of the foveal area, often bilateral and variously known as central angiospastic retinopathy or central serous detachment of the retina. The visual field defect is a central scotoma. With relief from emotional tension, the edema may subside, leaving little or no residual visual loss, depending on the duration of the edema.

A third example of this psychosomatic type of disturbance may be demonstrated by angioscotometry in the widening of the normal angioscotoma pattern that accompanies fright or psychic shock.

Although such phenomena are still somewhat controversial, they are, in my opinion, sufficiently common to deserve serious consideration and further study.

Malingering or conscious simulation of visual loss and visual field defects is usually for purposes of gain of a material or monetary nature. Many instances of malingering occur in an attempt to collect compensation for alleged industrial injury. Malingering or simulation of disease and loss of function is not uncommon in accident liability cases in the law courts. Large sums of money are often involved in these lawsuits, and payment hinges on the differentiation of organic disease from simulation.

Simulated blindness of both eyes, and even simulation of severe bilateral visual field defects, is relatively rare. The pretense of marked visual loss is too difficult to sustain for more than a short period of time. Close observation of such a person or moving pictures of his activities extending over a few days or even hours will reveal some inconsistency in behavior that labels his visual defect as fradulent.

Unilateral visual loss either central or peripheral is more easily simulated and can be sustained indefinitely. Because it is unilateral, however, it is readily subject to detection by means of the many different confusion tests, which lead the patient to believe that his good eye is being examined when in fact the eye in which he is simulating visual loss is undergoing scrutiny. Such tests may be simple or elaborate. They are myriad in number, and great ingenuity has been used in devising them.

The most common visual field defect in ocular malingering is concentric contraction. This may take the form of the tubular or cylindric field seen in hysteria, or it may be a simple depression of all isopters. In the latter type of contraction, the outline of the visual field may be very irregular and obviously unrelated to any anatomic or pathologic condition.

In simple, tubular fields the outline is usually circular and the margins extremely sharp and steep, but unlike the field in hysteria the defect is likely to vary, especially if plotted on an unmarked tangent screen or on the perimeter.

When the field is examined on the tangent screen, its outline should be clearly shown with pins or chalk. The patient is then taken to another room for another examination, such as a test for color perception. While he is absent, the markings on the screen are shifted in position, usually closer to fixation. The patient is then returned to face the screen and the visual field is reexamined. In the majority of instances, the new field will conform to the new markings on the screen. Shift of the fixation target between two examinations of the visual field may deceive the malingerer into locating the second field eccentrically around fixation.

Use of a prism over one eye while testing the binocular field may confuse the patient so that significant alteration in the size of the field is obtained.

Rapid shifting of test objects on the carrier wand, with the patient unaware of these changes, may uncover a visual acuity inconsistent with that obtained by the test with the Snellen letters.

It must be remembered that one form of malingering is exaggeration of an organic defect. Evaluation of the actual field loss as opposed to that simulated may be quite difficult.

The general statements that apply to the simulator of disease or malfunction of any organ also apply to the simulator of visual field defects. Malingerers vary in their shrewdness and native wit and also in their intent to deceive. Many malingerers are stupid; others are ashamed of themselves and therefore clumsy in their deceit. Some are psychopathic and their condition is extremely difficult to differentiate from hysteria; in fact, they themselves may become convinced of their illness and so merge into hysteria.

The hysterical patient believes in his illness. He is cooperative in undergoing the most rigorous examination. The malingerer is afraid to be examined. He resorts to any trickery to avoid it, and all through the examination he makes excuses for not continuing with it. The ophthalmoscopic light produces intense photophobia. Refraction causes excessive watering, headache, blurring of vision, and dizziness. If all else fails, he will resort to abuse of the examiner. The malingerer grossly exaggerates his symptoms during questioning and examination and is belligerent about his suffering. When he is alone and unconscious of observation, however, his entire attitude changes.

When hysterical amblyopia is cured, the patient is pleased and full of praise for his doctor. The malingerer is stubborn and, when detected in his falsehood, is either surly and defiant or confused and ashamed. Occasionally, when confronted with his proved simulation, the malingerer becomes dangerous.

The detection of visual loss, either foveal or extrafoveal, of psychogenic origin or from simulation presents one of the most interesting challenges in perimetry and frequently requires ingenuity, shrewdness, wit, and a keen understanding of people and psychology.

BIBLIOGRAPHY

The literature on the subject of the visual fields is so voluminous that a complete bibliography would occupy as many pages as this entire book.

The following list of references has been selected to include (1) those textbooks and review articles that, in themselves, contain extensive bibliographic material and (2) those articles that are particularly pertinent to certain phases of the subject, many of which have become classics in the literature of perimetry and most of which contain their own large bibliography. No textbooks, monographs, or articles are listed that I have not read personally, mostly in their entirety, but a few in abstract form or in earlier editions.

This bibliography has been compiled over a period of many years in full knowledge that numerous excellent and important contributions to the literature will be omitted. This I regret, and for these omissions I apologize. I believe, however, that for the student of perimetry the combined bibliographies of the following list of references will be as complete as is practicable, short of an encyclopedic listing in a separate volume. The list of references has been considerably enlarged for this fifth edition.

PART ONE

Textbooks, monographs, and review articles that contain extensive bibliographic material:

Acta XVIII Concilium Ophthalmologicum, 1958, Belgica, pp. 873-964, articles on functional loss in the glaucomatous eye (various authors), Brussels, 1959, Imprimerie Medicale et Scientifique, S. A.

Annual reviews: Glaucoma (various authors), Arch. Ophthalmol. 1950 to present.

Annual reviews: Neuro-ophthalmology (various authors), Arch. Ophthalmol., November issues, 1950 to present.

Becker, B., and Shaffer, R. N.: Diagnosis and therapy of the glaucomas, St. Louis, 1962, The C. V. Mosby Co.

Bender, M. E.: Disorders in perception, Springfield, Ill., 1952, Charles C. Thomas, Publisher.

Bregeat, P.: Les syndromes opto-chiasmatique, Paris, 1979, Masson et Cie.

Brockhurst, R. J., Boruchoff, S. A., Hutchinson, B. T., and Lassell, S., editors: Controversy in ophthalmology, Philadelphia, 1977, W. B. Saunders Co.

Cant, J. S., editor: The optic nerve, St. Louis, 1972, The C. V. Mosby Co.

Cogan, D. G.: Neurology of the visual system, Springfield, Ill., 1966, Charles C Thomas, Publisher.

Critchley, M.: The parietal lobes, London, 1953, Edward Arnold & Co.

Cushing, J., and Eisenhardt, L.: Meningiomas, their classification, regional behavior, life history and surgical end results, Springfield, Ill., 1938, Charles C Thomas, Publisher.

Dubois-Poulsen, A.: Le champ visuel, Société Française d'Ophthalmologie, Paris, 1952, Masson et Cie.

Duke-Elder, W. S.: System of ophthalmology, St. Louis, The C. V. Mosby Co.

Ellenberger, C., Jr.: Perimetry: principles, technique and interpretation, New York, 1980, Raven Press.

Frankhauser, F.: Octopus visual field atlas, ed. 2, Zurich, Switzerland, 1979, Interzeag Ag Schlieven, Publisher.

Fankhauser, F., and others: Proceedings First International Meeting on Automated Perimetry System Octopus, Zurich, Switzerland, 1979, Interzeag Ag Schlieven Publisher.

Glaser, J. S., editor: Neuro-ophthalmology, St. Louis, 1975, The C. V. Mosby Co.

Grant, M. W.: Toxicology of the eye, Springfield, Ill., 1962, Charles C Thomas, Publisher.

Greve, E. L.: Single and multiple stimulus static perimetry in glaucoma: the two phases of perimetry, The Hague, Holland, 1973, Dr. W. Junk B. V. Publishers.

Hayreh, S. S.: Anterior ischemic optic neuropathy, New York, 1975, Springer-Verlag.

Henderson, W. R.: The pituitary adenomata, Br. J. Surg. **26**:811, 1939.

Huber, A.: Eye symptoms in brain tumors, St. Louis, 1961, The C. V. Mosby Co.

Hughes, B.: The visual fields, Springfield, Ill., 1954, Charles C Thomas, Publisher.

Kooi, K. A., and Marshall, R. E.: Visual evoked potentials in central disorders of the visual system, New York, 1979, Harper & Row, Publishers.

Ourgaud, A-G., and Etienne, R.: L'exploration functionelle de l'oeil glaucomateux, Société Française d'Ophthalmologie, Paris, 1961, Masson et Cie.

Polyak, S. L.: The retina, Chicago, 1941, University of Chicago Press.

Polyak, S. L.: The vertebrate visual system, Chicago, 1957, University of Chicago Press.

Reed, H., and Drance, S. M.: The essentials of perimetry, ed. 2, London, 1972, Oxford University Press.

Scott, G. I.: Traquair's clinical perimetry, ed. 7, St. Louis, 1957, The C. V. Mosby Co.

Smith, J. L.: Optokinetic nystagmus, Springfield, Ill., 1963, Charles C Thomas, Publisher.

Straatsma, B. R., Hall, M. O., Allen, R. A., and Crescitelli, F.: The retina. U.C.L.A. Forum in Medical Sciences, no. 8, Berkeley, 1969, University of California Press.

Tate, G. W., and Lynn, J. R.: Principles of quantitative perimetry, New York, 1977, Grune & Stratton, Inc.

Teuber, H. L., Battersby, W. S., and Bender, M. D.: Visual field defects after penetrating missile wounds of the brain, Cambridge, Mass., 1960, Harvard University Press.

Walsh, F. B., and Hoyt, W. F.: Clinical neuro-ophthalmology, ed. 3, Baltimore, 1969, The Williams & Wilkins Co.

Whitnall, S. E.: Anatomy of the human orbit and accessory organs of vision, ed. 2, London, 1932, Oxford University Press.

Wolff, H. G.: Headache and other head pain, ed. 2, New York, 1963, Oxford University Press.

Year book of ophthalmology, Chicago, published annually, Year Book Medical Publishers, Inc.

PART TWO

List of articles most of which contain bibliographies pertinent to their specific subject matter:

Abbie, A. A.: Blood supply of the visual pathways, Med. J. Aust. **2**:199, 1938.

Amsler, M.: Earliest symptoms of disease of the macula, Br. J. Ophthalmol. **37**:521, 1953.

Anderson, D. R., and Hendrickson, A.: Effect of intraocular pressure on rapid axoplasmic transport in monkey optic nerve, Invest. Ophthalmol. **13**:771, Oct. 1974.

Archer, D. B., Ernest, J. T., and Krill, A.: Retinal, choroidal, and papillary circulations under conditions of induced ocular hypertension, Am. J. Ophthalmol. **73**:834, 1972.

Armaly, M. F.: Ocular pressure and visual fields, Arch. Ophthalmol. **81**:25, 1969.

Armaly, M. F.: Visual field defects in early open angle glaucoma, Trans. Am. Ophthalmol. Soc. **69**:147, 1971.

Armaly, M. F.: Selective perimetry for glaucomatous defects in ocular hypertension, Arch. Ophthalmol. **87**:518, 1972.

Armaly, M. F., Araki, M.: Optic nerve circulation and ocular pressure, Invest. Ophthalmol. **14**: 724, 1975.

Asselman, P., Chadwick, D. W., and Marsden, C. D.: Visual evoked responses in the diagnosis and management of patients suspected of multiple sclerosis, Brain **98**:261, 1975.

Aulhorn, E., and Harms, H.: Early visual field defects in glaucoma. In Glaucoma Tutzing Symposium, proceedings of the Twentieth International Congress of Ophthalmology, Basel, 1967, S. Karger, pp. 151-186.

Austin, G. M., Lewey, F. H., and Grant, F. C.: Studies on the occipital lobe. I. Significance of small areas of preserved central vision, Arch. Neurol. Psychiatr. **62**:204, 1949.

Baker, H. L., Jr., Kearns, T. P., Campbell, J. K., and Henderson, J. W.: Computerized transaxial tomography in neuro-ophthalmology, Trans. Am. Ophthalmol. Soc. **72**:49, 1974.

Ballantyne, A. J.: The nerve fiber pattern of the human retina, Trans. Ophthalmol. Soc. U.K. **66**:179, 1946.

Barber, A. N., Ronstrom, G. N., and Muelling, R. J., Jr.: Development of the visual pathway: optic chiasm, Arch. Ophthalmol. **52**:447, 1954.

Beasley, H.: The visual fields in aphakia, Trans. Am. Ophthalmol. Soc. **63**:364, 1965.

Begg, I. S., Drance, S. M., and Sweeney, V. P.: Ischemic optic neuropathy in chronic simple glaucoma, Br. J. Ophthalmol. **55**:73, Feb. 1971.

Bender, M. B., and Furlow, L. T.: Phenomenon of visual extinction in homonymous fields and the psychologic principles involved, Arch. Neurol. Psychiatr. **53**:29, 1945.

Bender, M. B., and Kanzer, M. G.: Dynamics of homonymous hemianopsias and preservation of central vision, Brain **62**:404, 1939.

Bender, M. B., and Strauss, I.: Defects in visual field in one eye only in patients with a lesion of one optic radiation, Arch. Ophthalmol. **17**: 765, 1937.

Bender, M. B., and Teuber, H. L.: Phenomenon of fluctuation, extinction, and completion in visual perception, Arch. Neurol. Psychiatr. **55**: 627, 1946.

Benton, C. D., Jr., and Calhoun, F. P., Jr.: Ocular effects of methyl alcohol poisoning: report of a catastrophe involving 230 persons, Trans. Am. Acad. Ophthalmol. Otolaryngol. **56**:875, 1952.

Benton, S., Levy, I., Swash, M.: Vision in the temporal crescent in occipital infarction, Brain **103**:83, March 1980.

Bergland, R., and Ray, B. S.: Arterial supply of human optic chiasm, J. Neurosurg. **31**:327, Sept. 1969.

Björk, A., Laurell, C. G., and Laurell, U.: Bilateral optic nerve hypoplasia with normal visual acuity, Am. J. Ophthalmol. **86**:524, 1978.

Blum, F. G., Gates, L. K., and James, N. R.: How important are peripheral fields? Arch. Ophthalmol. **61**:1, 1959.

Blumenthal, M., Gitter, K. A., Best, M., and Galin, M. A.: Fluorescein angiography during induced ocular hypertension in man, Am. J. Ophthalmol. **69**:39, 1970.

Boldt, H. A., Armin, F. H., Tourtellette, W. W., and DeJong, R. N.: Retrochiasmal visual field defects from multiple sclerosis, Arch. Neurol. **8**:565, 1963.

Brais, P., and Drance, S. M.: The temporal field in chronic simple glaucoma. Arch. Ophthalmol. **88**:518, 1972.

Brouwer, B.: Projection of the retina on the cortex in man, localization of function in the cerebral cortex, Ass. Res. Nerv. Ment. Dis. Proc. **13**:529, 1934.

Brouwer, B., and Zeeman, W. P. C.: Experimental anatomical investigations concerning the projection of the retina on the primary optic centers in apes, J. Neurol. Psychopathol. **6**:1, 1925.

Brouwer, B., and Zeeman, W. P. C.: The projection of the retina in the primary optic neurone in monkeys, Brain **49**:1, 1926.

Brown, G. C., Shields, J. A., and Goldberg, R. E.: Congenital pits of the optic nerve head, Ophthalmology **87**:51, Jan. 1980.

Buchanan, W. S., and Gloster, J.: Automatic device for rapid assessment of the central visual field, Br. J. Ophthalmol. **49**:57, 1965.

Campbell, C. J., and Rittler, M. C.: The diagostic value of flicker perimetry in chronic simple glaucoma, Trans. Am. Acad. Ophthalmol. Otolaryngol. **63**:89, 1959.

Cappin, J. M., and Nissim, S.: Visual evoked responses in the assessment of field defects in glaucoma, Arch. Ophthalmol. **93**:9, 1975.

Carroll, F. D.: "Alcohol" amblyopia, pellagra polyneuritis, report of ten cases, Arch. Ophthalmol. **16**:919, 1936.

Carroll, F. D.: The etiology and treatment of tobacco-alcohol amblyopia, Trans. Am. Ophthalmol. Otolaryngol. Soc. **41**:385, 1943.

Chacko, L. W.: Laminar pattern of the lateral geniculate body in the primates, J. Neurol. Neurosurg. Psychiatry **11**:211, 1948.

Chamlin, M.: Minimal defects in visual field studies, Arch. Ophthalmol. **42**:126, 1949.

Chamlin, M., and Davidoff, L. M.: The 1/2000 field in chiasmal interference, Arch. Ophthalmol. **44**:53, 1950.

Chamlin, M., Davidoff, L. M., and Feiring, E. H.: Ophthalmologic changes produced by pituitary tumors, Am. J. Ophthalmol. **40**:353, 1955.

Clark, W. E. L.: A morphological study of the lateral geniculate body, Br. J. Ophthalmol. **16**:264, 1932.

Clark, W. E. L.: The visual centers of the brain and their connections, Physiol. Rev. **22**:205, 1942.

Clark, W. E. L., and Penman, G. G.: The projection of the retina in the lateral geniculate body, Proc. Roy. Soc. London **114**:291, 1934.

Cogan, D. G.: Hemianopsia and associated symptoms due to parieto-temporal lobe lesions, Am. J. Ophthalmol. **50**:1056, 1960.

Cohn, T. E., and Perolman, J.: The Diodewand: a device for tangent screen perimetry, Am. J. Optom. Physiol. Opt. **51**:993, Dec. 1974.

Copenhaver, R. M., and Beinhocker, G. D.: Evoked occipital potentials recorded from scalp electrodes in response to focal visual illumination, Invest. Ophthalmol. **2**:393, 1963.

Cordes, F. C.: Hereditary optic atrophy (Leber's disease), Trans. Am. Ophthalmol. Soc. **31**:289, 1933.

Cordes, F. C., and Harrington, D. O.: Toxic amblyopia due to tobacco and alcohol: treatment with vasodilators; a report of eight cases, Arch. Ophthalmol. **13**:435, 1935.

Council on Industrial Health of American Medical Association: Estimation of loss of visual efficiency, Arch. Ophthalmol. **12**:439, 1955.

Cushing, H.: Distortions of the visual fields in cases of brain tumor; the field defects produced by temporal lobe lesions, Brain **44**:341, 1922.

Cushing, H.: The chiasmal syndrome of primary optic atrophy and bitemporal field defects with a normal sella turcica, Arch. Ophthalmol. **3**: 505, 704, 1930.

Cushing, H., and Walker, C. B.: Distortion of the visual fields in cases of brain tumor, binasal hemianopsia, Arch. Ophthalmol. **41**:559, 1912.

Cushing, H., and Walker, C. B.: Distortions of the visual fields in cases of brain tumor (chiasma lesions with especial reference to bitemporal hemianopsia), Brain **37**:341, 1914-1915.

Daniel, P. M., and Whitteridge, D.: The representation of the visual field on the cerebral cortex in monkeys, J. Physiol. **159**:203, 1961.

Dawson, B. H.: Blood vessels of human optic chiasm and their relation to those of hypophysis and hypothalamus, Brain **81**(2):207, 1958.

Dobelle, W. H., Turkel, J., Henderson, D. C., and Evans, J. R.: Mapping the representation of the visual field by electrical stimulation of human visual cortex, Am. J. Ophthalmol. **88**: 727, 1979.

Dollery, C. T., Henkind, P., Kohner, E. M., and Paterson, J. W.: Effect of raised intraocular pressure on the retinal and choroidal circulation, Invest. Ophthalmol. **7**:191, 1968.

Donahue, H. C.: Migraine and its ocular manifestations, Trans. Am. Ophthalmol. Soc. **47**:554, 1949; Arch. Ophthalmol. **43**:96, 1950.

Douglas, G. R., Drance, S. M., and Schulzer, M.: The visual field and nerve head in angle-closure glaucoma, Arch. Ophthalmol. **93**:409, June 1975.

Drance, S. M.: Susceptibility of the eye to raised intraocular pressure, Arch. Ophthalmol. **68**:478, 1962.

Drance, S. M.: The glaucomatous visual field, Br. J. Ophthalmol. **56**:186, 1972.

Drance, S. M., Lynn, J. R., Pinkerton, R. M. H., Harrington, D. O., and Armaly, M. F.: Symposium on the effect of glaucoma on visual function, Invest. Ophthalmol. **8**:75-124, Feb. 1969.

Drance, S. M., Wheeler, C., and Pattullo, M.: The use of static perimetry in the early detection of glaucoma, Can. J. Ophthalmol. **2**:249, 1967.

Drance, S. M., Wheeler, C., and Pattullo, M.: Uniocular open-angle glaucoma, Am. J. Ophthalmol. **65**:891, 1968.

Drance, S. M., and Begg, I. S.: Sector hemorrhage—a probably acute ischemic disc change in chronic simple glaucoma, Can. J. Ophthalmol. **5**:137, 1970.

Drance, S. M.: Is ischemia the villain in glaucomatous cupping and atrophy? In Brockhurst, R. J., Boruchoff, S. A., Hutchinson, B. I., and Lessell, S., editors: Controversy in ophthalmology, Philadelphia, 1977, W. B. Saunders Co., pp. 292-300.

Ellenberger, C., and Ziegler, S. B.: Visually evoked potentials and quantitative perimetry in multiple sclerosis, Ann. Neurol. **1**:561, 1977.

Elwyn, H.: Calcified carotid artery with atrophy of the optic nerve, cupping and low tension, Arch. Ophthalmol. **24**:476, 1940.

Ernest, J. T.: Pathogenesis of glaucomatous optic nerve disease, Trans. Am. Ophthalmol. Soc. **73**: 366, 1975.

Esterman, B.: Grid for scoring visual fields. I. Tangent screen, Arch. Ophthalmol. **77**:780, 1967.

Esterman, B.: Grid for scoring visual fields. II. Perimeter, Arch. Ophthalmol. **79**:400, 1968.

Fankhauser, F., and Schmidt, T.: Die Untersuchung der räumlichen Summation mit stehender und bewegter Reizmarke nach der Methode der quantitativen Lichtsinnperimetrie, Ophthalmologica **135**:660, 1958.

Fankhauser, F., Spahr, J., and Bebie, J.: Three years' experience with the Octopus Automatic Perimeter, Doc. Ophthalmol. Proc. Ser. 2nd Int. Visual Field Symp. **14**:7, 1977.

Flindall, R. J., and Drance, S. M.: Visual field studies of benign choroidal melanomata, Arch. Ophthalmol. **81**:41, 1969.

Flocks, M., Rosenthal, A. R., and Hopkins, J. L.: Mass visual screening via television, Trans. Am. Acad. Ophthalmol. **85**:114, Nov. 1978.

Forstot, S. L., Weinstein, G. W., and Feicock, K. P.: Studies with the Tübinger perimeter of Harms and Aulhorn, Ann. Ophthalmol. **2**:834, 1970.

Foulds, W. S., Chisholm, I. A., Bronte-Stewart, J., and Reid, H. C. R.: Investigation and therapy of the toxic amblyopias, Trans. Ophthalmol. Soc. U.K. **90**:739, 1970.

Fox, J. C., Jr., and German, W. J.: Macular vision following cerebral resection, Arch. Neurol. Psychiatry **35**:808, 1936.

François, J., and Neetens, A.: Vascularization of optic pathway. I. Lamina cribrosa and optic nerve, Br. J. Ophthalmol. **38**:472, 1954.

François, J., and Neetens, A.: Central retinal artery and central optic nerve artery, Br. J. Ophthalmol. **47**:21, 1963.

François, J., Neetens, A., and Collette, J. M.: Vascular supply of the optic pathway. II. Further studies by micro-arteriography of the optic nerve, Br. J. Ophthalmol. **39**:220, 1955.

François, J., Neetens, A., and Collette, J. M.: Vascularization of the optic pathway. IV. Optic tract and geniculate body, Br. J. Ophthalmol. **40**:341, 1956.

François, J., Neetens, A., and Collette, J. M.: Vascularization of primary optic pathways, Br. J. Ophthalmol. **42**:62, 1958.

Friedman, A. I.: Serial analysis of changes in visual fields, Ophthalmologica **152**:1, 1966.

Frisen, L.: A versatile color confrontation test for the central visual field, Arch. Ophthalmol. **89**:3, Jan. 1973.

Frisen, L., Holmgaard, L., and Rosencrantz, M.: Sectorial optic atrophy and homonymous horizontal sectoranopia: a lateral choroidal artery syndrome? J. Neurol. Neurosurg. Psychiatry **41**: 374, 1978.

Galvin, R. J., Regan, D., and Heron, J. R.: Impaired temporal resolution of vision after acute retrobulbar neuritis, Brain **99**:255, 1976.

Glaser, J. S., Hoyt, W. F., and Corbett, J.: Visual morbidity with chiasmal glioma, Arch. Ophthalmol. **85**:3, Jan. 1971.

Globus, J. H., and Silverstone, S. M.: Diagnostic value of defects in the fields and other ocular disturbances associated with supratentorial tumors of the brain, Arch. Ophthalmol. **14**:325, 1935.

Goldmann, H.: Demonstration unseres neuen Projektionskugelperimeters samt theoretischen und klinischen Bemerkungen über Perimetric, Ophthalmologica **111**:187, 1946.

Gregorius, F. K., Hepler, R. S., and Stern, W. E.: Loss and recovery of vision with suprasellar meningioma, J. Neurosurg. **42**:69, 1975.

Guidetti, B., and LaTorre, E.: Management of carotid-ophthalmic aneurysms, J. Neurosurg. **42**:438, 1975.

Gunderson, C. H., and Hoyt, W. F.: Geniculate hemianopia: incongruous homonymous field defects in two patients with partial lesions of the lateral geniculate nucleus, J. Neurol. Neurosurg. Psychiatry **34**:1, 1971.

Halstead, W. C., Walker, E. A., and Bucy, P. C.: Sparing and nonsparing of macular vision associated with occipital lobectomy in man, Arch. Ophthalmol. **24**:948, 1940.

Harms, H.: Neue Methoden der Perimetric. In Zeitfragen der Augenheilkunde, Stuttgart, 1957, Georg Thieme Verlag.

Harrington, D. O.: The optic radiations in the temporal lobe, Trans. West. Ophthalmol. Soc. **2**:131, 1936-1937.

Harrington, D. O.: Localizing value of incongruity in defects in the visual fields, Arch. Ophthalmol. **21**:453, 1939.

Harrington, D. O.: Autonomic nervous system in ocular disease, Am. J. Ophthalmol. **29**:1405, 1946.

Harrington, D. O.: Ocular manifestations of psychosomatic disorders, J.A.M.A. **133**:669, 1947.

Harrington, D. O.: Perimetry with ultraviolet (black) radiation and luminescent test objects, a preliminary report, Arch. Ophthalmol. **49**:637, 1953.

Harrington, D. O.: The pathogenesis of the glaucoma field, Am. J. Ophthalmol. **47**:177, 1959.

Harrington, D. O.: Pathogenesis of the glaucomatous visual field defect, Transactions of the Fifth Conference on Glaucoma, New York, 1960, Josiah Macy Jr. Foundation.

Harrington, D. O.: Character of the visual field in lesions of the temporal and occipital lobe, Arch. Ophthalmol. **66**:778, 1961.

Harrington, D. O.: Visual field character in temporal and occipital lobe lesions, Trans. Am. Ophthalmol. Soc. **59**:333, 1961.

Harrington, D. O.: Amblyopia due to tobacco, alcohol and nutritional deficiency, Am. J. Ophthalmol. **53**:967, 1962.

Harrington, D. O.: Self-illuminated stimulus for tangent screen perimetry, Am. J. Ophthalmol. **54**:301, 1962.

Harrington, D. O.: The Bjerrum scotoma, Trans. Am. Ophthalmol. Soc. **62**:324, 1964.

Harrington, D. O.: Tangent screen stimuli of variable luminance, Arch. Ophthalmol. **72**:23, 1964.

Harrington, D. O.: Differential diagnosis of the arcuate scotoma, Invest. Ophthalmol. **8**:96, 1969.

Harrington, D. O.: Analysis of some unusual and difficult visual field defects, Trans. Ophthalmol. Soc. U.K. **92**:15, 1973.

Harrington, D. O.: The art of perimetry, Part I, Am. J. Ophthalmol. **80**:414, 1975.

Harrington, D. O., and Flocks, M.: Visual field examination by a new tachystoscopic multiple pattern method, Am. J. Ophthalmol. **37**:719, 1954.

Harrington, D. O., and Flocks, M.: Multiple

pattern method of visual field examination, J.A.M.A. **157**:645, 1955.

Harrington, D. O., and Flocks, M.: The multiple pattern method of visual field examination, a five-year evaluation, Arch. Ophthalmol. **61**:755, 1959.

Harrington, D. O., and Hoyt, W. F.: Ultraviolet radiation perimetry with monochromatic blue stimuli, Arch. Ophthalmol. **53**:870, 1955.

Harrington, D. O., Leinfelder, P. J., and Lyle, D. J.: Symposium: The value of perimetry as a diagnostic aid, Trans. Am. Acad. Ophthalmol. Otolaryngol. **66**:744, 1962.

Hart, W. M., Burde, R. M., Klingele, T. G., and Purlmutter, J. C.: Bilateral optic nerve sheath meningioma, Arch. Ophthalmol. **98**:149, Jan. 1980.

Hayreh, S. S.: The central artery of the retina, Br. J. Ophthalmol. **47**:651, 1963.

Hayreh, S. S.: Blood supply of optic nerve head and its role in optic atrophy, glaucoma, and edema of optic disk, Br. J. Ophthalmol. **53**:721, 1969.

Hayreh, S. S.: Pathogenesis of occlusion of central retinal vessels, Am. J. Ophthalmol. **72**:998, 1971.

Hayreh, S. S.: Anatomy and physiology of the optic nerve head, In Symposium: Glaucoma, Trans. Am. Acad. Ophthalmol. Otolaryngol. **78**:240, March 1974.

Hayreh, S. S., Revie, I. H. S., and Edwards, J.: Vasogenic origin of visual field defects and optic nerve changes in glaucoma, Br. J. Ophthalmol. **54**:461, July 1970.

Hayreh, S. S., and Walker, W. M.: Flourescent fundus photography in glaucoma, Am. J. Ophthalmol. **63**:982, 1967.

Henkind, P., and Levitsky, M.: Angioarchitecture of the optic nerve. I. The papilla, II. Lamina cribrosa, Am. J. Ophthalmol. **68**:979, 1969.

Hetherington, J., Jr.: Symposium glaucoma, Trans. Am. Acad. Ophthalmol. Otolaryngol. **78**:239, March 1974.

Hines, M.: Recent contributions to localization of vision in the central nervous system (review), Arch. Ophthalmol. **28**:913, 1942.

Hobbs, H. E., Sorsby, A., and Freedman, A.: Retinopathy following chloroquine therapy, Lancet **2**:478, 1959.

Hochheimer, B. F., D'Anna, S. A., and Calkins, J. L.: Retinal damage from light, Am. J. Ophthalmol. **88**:1039, Dec. 1979.

Hollenhorst, R. W.: Carotid and vertebralbasilar arterial stenosis and occlusion, neuro-ophthalmologic considerations, Trans. Am. Acad. Ophthalmol. Otolaryngol. **66**:166, 1962.

Holmes, G.: The cortical localization of vision, Br. Med. J. **2**:193, 1919.

Holmes, G., and Lister, W. T.: Disturbances of vision from cerebral lesions with special reference to the cortical representation of the macula, Brain **39**:34, 1916.

Holmes, G. A.: Contribution to the cortical representation of vision, Brain **54**:470, 1931.

Horrax, G.: Visual hallucinations as a cerebral localizing phenomenon, with special reference to their occurrence in tumors of the temporal lobe, Arch. Neurol. Psychiatry **10**:532, 1923.

Horrax, G., and Putnam, T. J.: Distortions of visual fields in cases of brain tumors: the field defects and hallucinations produced by tumors of the occipital lobe, Brain **55**:499, 1932.

Horton, J. C., Greenwood, M. M., and Hubel, D. H.: Non-retinotopic arrangement of fibers in the cat optic nerve, Nature **282**:720, Dec. 1979.

Hoyt, C. S.: Autosomal dominant optic atrophy: a spectrum of disability, Ophthalmology **87**:245, March 1980.

Hoyt, W. F.: Anatomic considerations of arcuate scotomas associated with lesions of the optic nerve and chiasm, a nauta axon degeneration study in the monkey, Bull. Hopkins Hosp. **3**(2): 57, 1962.

Hoyt, W. F.: Correlative functional anatomy of the optic chiasm, Clin. Neurosurg. **17**:189, 1969.

Hoyt, W. F., Frisén, L., and Newman, N. M.: Funduscopy of nerve fiber layer defects in glaucoma, Invest. Ophthalmol. **12**:814, Nov. 1973.

Hoyt, W. F., and Kommerall, G.: Ocular fundus in homonymous hemianopsia, Klin. Monatsbl. Augenheilkd. **162**:456, 1973.

Hoyt, W. F., and Luis, O.: Visual fiber anatomy in the infrageniculate pathways of the primate: uncrossed and crossed retinal quadrant fiber projections studied with nauta silver stain, Arch. Ophthalmol. **68**:94, 1962.

Hoyt, W. F., and Luis, O.: The primate chiasm: details of visual fiber organization studied by silver impregnation techniques, Arch. Ophthalmol. **70**:69, 1963.

Hoyt, W. F., Rios-Montenegro, E. N., Behrens, M. M., and Eckelhoff, R. J.: Homonymous hemianoptic hypoplasia: funduscopic features in standard and red-free illumination in three patients with congenital hemiplegia, Br. J. Ophthalmol. **6**:537, 1972.

Hoyt, W. F., Schlicke, B., Eckelhoff, R. J.: Funduscopic appearance of a nerve fiber bundle defect, Br. J. Ophthalmol. **56**:577, 1972.

Hoyt, W. F., and Tudor, R. C.: The course of the parapapillary temporal retinal axons through the anterior optic nerve, Arch. Ophthalmol. **69**:503, 1963.

Hubel, D. H., and Wiesel, T. N.: Receptive fields of single neurons in the cat's striate cortex, J. Physiol. (London) **148**:574, 1959.

Hubel, D. H., and Wiesel, T. N.: Receptive fields, binocular interaction and functional architecture in the cat's cortex, J. Physiol. (London) **26**:106, 1962.

Hubel, D. H., and Wiesel, T. N.: Binocular interaction in straite cortex of kittens reared with artificial squint, J. Neurophysiol. **28**:1041, 1965.

Huber, A.: Homonymous hemianopsia following occipital lobectomy, Schweiz. Med. Wochenechr. **80**:1227, 1950.

Huber, A.: Ocular symptoms of cerebral aneurysms, Ophthalmologica **167**:165, 1973.

Hughes, B.: Blood supply of optic nerve and chiasm and its clinical significance, Br. J. Ophthalmol. **42**:106, 1958.

Irvine, S. R.: Measuring scotomas with the prism displacement test, Am. J. Ophthalmol. **61**:(II) 117, 1966.

Jaffe, N. S., and Durkin, L. S.: Geniculocalcarine injuries in war casualties, Arch. Ophthalmol. **49**:591, 1953.

Jayle, G.: Study of a standard mesoptic and scotopic isopter, Ann. Oculist **194**:881, 1961.

Jefferson, G.: Compression of chiasm, optic nerves and optic tracts by intracranial aneurysms, Brain **60**:444, 1937.

Johnson, C. A., Keltner, J. L., and Balestrery, F. G.: Suprathreshold static perimetry in glaucoma and other optic nerve disease, Ophthalmology **86**:1278, July 1979.

Jonkers, G. H.: Static perimetry, Ophthalmologica **141**:494, 1961.

Kass, M. A., Kolker, A. E., and Becker, B.: Prognostic factors in glaucomatous visual field loss, Arch. Ophthalmol. **94**:1274, Aug. 1976.

Keane, J. R.: Hysterical hemianopia: the "missing half" field defect, Arch. Ophthalmol. **97**:865, 1977.

Kearns, T. P., and Rucker, C. W.: Arcuate defects in the visual fields, Am. J. Ophthalmol. **45**:505, 1958.

Kearns, T. P., Wagener, H. P., and Millikan, C. H.: Bilateral homonymous hemianopia, Arch. Ophthalmol. **53**:560, 1955.

Keltner, J. L., Johnson, C. A., and Balestrery, F. G.: Suprathreshold static perimetry: initial clinical trials with the Fieldmaster Automated Perimeter, Arch. Ophthalmol. **97**:260, Feb. 1979.

Kjer, P.: Infantile optic atrophy with dominant inheritance. In Handbook of clinical neurology, vol. 13, Amsterdam, 1973, North-Holland Publishing Co., p. 111.

Kline, L. B., and Glaser, J. S.: Dominant optic atrophy: the clinical profile, Arch. Ophthalmol. **97**:1680, 1979.

Knapp, A.: On the association of sclerosis of the cerebral basal vessels with optic atrophy and cupping: report of ten cases, Trans. Am. Ophthalmol. Soc. **30**:343, 1932.

Knight, C. L., Hoyt, W. F., and Wilson, C. B.: Syndrome of incipient prechiasmal optic nerve compression, Arch. Ophthalmol. **87**:1, Jan. 1972.

Knox, D. L., and Cogan, D. G.: Eye pain and hemianopia, Am. J. Ophthalmol. **54**:1091, 1962.

Koerner, F., and Teuber, H. L.: Visual field defects after missile injuries to the geniculo-striate pathway in man, Exp. Brain Res. **18**:88, 1973.

Kolker, A. B., Becker, B., and Mills, D. W.: Intraocular pressure and visual fields: effects of corticosteroids, Arch. Ophthalmol. **72**:772, 1964.

Kronfeld, P. C.: The temporal half moon, Trans. Am. Ophthalmol. Soc. **30**:431, 1932.

Lansche, R. K., and Rucker, C. W.: Progression of defects in visual fields produced by hyaline bodies in the optic disks, Arch. Ophthalmol. **58**: 115, 1957.

Lee, P.-F.: Importance of status of visual field and optic disk in management of open-angle glaucoma, Am. J. Ophthalmol. **53**:435, 1962.

Levene, R. Z.: Low tension glaucoma: a critical review and new material, Surv. Ophthalmol. **24**: 621, May 1980.

Levy, N. S.: Effects of elevated intraocular pressure on slow axonal protein flow, Invest. Ophthalmol. **13**:691, Sept. 1974.

Lippman, O.: Eye screening, Arch. Ophthalmol. **68**:692, 1962.

Liversedge, A., and Smith, V.: The place of ophthalmodynamometry in the investigation of cerebrovascular disease, Brain **84**:274, 1961.

Locket, S.: Blindness associated with hemorrhage, Br. J. Ophthalmol. **33**:543, 1949.

Long, A. E.: Amaurosis following nasal hemorrhage, Am. J. Ophthalmol. **26**:1179, 1943.

Lorente de Nó, R.: Studies on the structure of the cerebral cortex, Jehrb. Psychol. Neurol. **45**:381, 1934; **46**:113, 1934.

Lorentzen, S. E.: Drusen of the optic disc: a clinical and genetic study, Acta Ophthalmol. (Suppl. 90), 1966.

McAuley, D. L., and Ross Russell, R. W.: Correlation of C.A.T. scan and visual field defects in vascular lesions of the posterior visual pathways, J. Neurol. Neurosurg. Psychiatry **42**:298, April 1979.

McLaurin, E. B., and Harrington, D. O.: Intracranial sarcoidosis with optic tract and temporal lobe involvement, Am. J. Ophthalmol. **86**:656, 1978.

Marlow, S. B.: Fields of vision in chronic glaucoma; a comparison of fields with full and reduced illumination, Arch. Ophthalmol. **38**:43, 1947.

Martin, P., and Cushing, H.: Primary gliomas of the chiasm and optic nerves in their intracranial portions, Arch. Ophthalmol. **52**:209, 1923.

Mayer, L. L.: The evolution of flash perimetry, Am. J. Ophthalmol. **20**:828, 1937.

Meyer, A.: The connections of the occipital lobes and the present status of the cerebral visual affections, Trans. Assoc. Am. Physicians **22**:7, 1907.

Miles, P.: Flicker fusion fields, technique and interpretation, Am. J. Ophthalmol. **33**:1069, 1950.

Miles, P.: Testing visual fields by flicker fusion, Arch. Neurol. Psychiatry **65**:39, 1951.

Miller, B. A.: A review of practical tests for ocular malingering and hysteria, Survey Ophthalmol. **17**:241, 1973.

Mooney, A. J.: Perimetry and angiography in the diagnosis of lesions in the pituitary region, Trans. Ophthalmol. Soc. U.K. **72**:49, 1952.

Mooney, A. J.: On the color of the optic disc and its relation to various field defects, Trans. Ophthalmol. Soc. U.K. **84**:227, 1964.

Moore, J. E., and Woods, A. C.: Pathology and pathogenesis of syphilitic primary optic atrophy; critical review, Am. J. Ophthalmol. **23**:1, 1940.

Morin, J. D.: Changes in visual fields in glaucoma: static and kinetic perimetry in 2000 patients, Trans. Am. Ophthalmol. Soc. **77**:622, 1979.

Nettelship, E.: Lebers' disease (Bowman lecture), Trans. Ophthalmol. Soc. U.K. **29** (Appendix VI), 1909.

Nikoskelainen, E.: Clinical, prognostic, and etiological studies on optic neuritis, Departments of Ophthalmology, Neurology, and Clinical Chemistry, Turku University Central Hospital, Turku, Finland, Acta Ophthalmologica **53**:254, 1975.

O'Connell, J. E. A., and DuBoulay, E. P. G. H.: Binasal hemianopia, J. Neurol. Neurosurg. Psychiatry **36**:697, 1973.

Okun, E., Gouras, P., Bernstein, H., and Von Sallman, L.: Chloroquine retinopathy, Arch. Ophthalmol. **69**:59, 1962.

O'Rourke, J. R., and Schlezinger, N. S.: Evaluation of ocular signs and symptoms in verified brain tumors, J.A.M.A. **157**:659, 1955.

Patterson, V. H., and Heron, J. R.: Visual field abnormalities in multiple sclerosis, J. Neurol. Neurosurg. Psychiatry **43**:205, March 1980.

Pederson, J. E., and Anderson, D. R.: The mode of progressive disc cupping in ocular hypertension and glaucoma, Arch. Ophthalmol. **98**:490, March 1980.

Penfield, W., Evans, J. P., and Macmillan, J. A.: Visual pathways in man: with particular reference to macular representation, Arch. Neurol. Psychiatry **33**:816, 1935.

Pevehouse, B. C., Bloom, W. H., and McKissock, W.: Ophthalmologic aspects of diagnosis and localization of subdural hematoma, Neurology **10**:1037, 1960.

Phelps, G. K., and Phelps, C. D.: Blood pressure and pressure amaurosis, Invest. Ophthalmol. **14**:237, March 1975.

Phillips, G.: Perception of flicker in lesions of the visual pathways, Brain **56**:464, 1933.

Polyak, S.: A contribution to the cerebral representation of the retina, J. Comp. Neurol. **57**:541, 1933.

Polyak, S.: Projection of the retina upon the cerebral cortex, based upon experiments with monkeys, Assoc. Res. Nerv. Ment. Dis. Proc. **13**: 535, 1934.

Portney, G. L., and Hanible, J. E.: A comparison of four projection perimeters, Am. J. Ophthalmol. **81**:678, 1976.

Posner, A., and Schlossman, A.: Development of changes in the visual fields associated with glaucoma, Arch. Ophthalmol. **39**:623, 1948.

Posner, A., and Schlossman, A.: The value of changes in the visual fields in the prognosis in glaucoma, Am. J. Ophthalmol. **33**:1391, 1950.

Potts, A., Hodges, D., Shelman, C., Fritz, K., Levy, N., and Mangnall, Y.: Morphology of the primate optic nerve III: Fiber characteristics of the foveal outflow, Invest. Ophthalmol. **11**: 1004, Dec. 1972.

Pruett, R. C., and Wepsic, J. G.: Chiasmal compression, Am. J. Ophthalmol. **76**:229, Aug. 1973.

Putnam, T. J.: II. A comparative study of the form of the geniculo-striate visual system of mammals, Arch. Neurol. Psychiatry **16**:285, 1926.

Putnam, T. J.: III. The general relationships between the extra-geniculate body, optic radiations and visual cortex in man, Arch. Neurol. Psychiatry **16**:566, 1926.

Putnam, T. J.: IV. The details of the organization of the geniculo-striate system in man, Arch. Neurol. Psychiatry **16**:683, 1926.

Putnam, T. J., and Putnam, I. K.: Studies on the central visual system. I. The anatomic projection of the retinal quadrants on the striate cortex of the rabbit, Arch. Neurol. Psychiatry **16**:1, 1926.

Richardson, J. H., Alderfer, H. H., and Reid,

J. D.: Response of eye and brain to micro-emboli, Ann. Intern. Med. **57:**1013, 1962.

Riddoch, G.: Dissociation of visual perception due to occipital injuries with especial reference to appreciation of movement, Brain **40:**15, 1917.

Roberts, W.: The multiple pattern tachistoscopic visual field screener in glaucoma, Arch. Ophthalmol. **58:**244, 1957.

Robertson, L.: Use of the Harrington multiple pattern field screener in industry, Trans. Am. Acad. Ophthalmol. **60:**806, 1956.

Rock, W. J., Drance, S. M., and Morgan, R. W.: Modification of Armaly visual field screening technique for glaucoma, Can. J. Ophthalmol. **6:**283, 1971.

Rönne, H.: The different types of defects of the field of vision, J.A.M.A. **89:**1860, 1927.

Rönne, H.: Ueber die Form der nasalen Gesichtsfeldesdefekte bei Glaucom, Arch. Ophthalmol. **71:**52, 1909.

Rönne, H.: Ueber die Inkongruenz und Asymmetrie im Homonym hemianopischen Gesichtsfeld, Klin. Mbl. Augenheilk. **54:**309, 1915.

Rönne, H.: Zur Theorie und Technik der Bjerrumchen Gesichtsfelduntersuchung, Arch. Augenheilk. **78:**284, 1915.

Rosen, E. S., and Boyd, T. A. S.: New method of assessing choroidal ischemia in open angle glaucoma and ocular hypertension, Am. J. Ophthalmol. **70:**912, Dec. 1970.

Rovit, R. L., and Duane, T. D.: Eye signs in patients with Cushing's syndrome and pituitary tumors, Arch. Ophthalmol. **79:**512, 1968.

Rucker, C. W., and Kernohan, J. W.: Notching of optic chiasm by overlying arteries in pituitary tumors, Arch. Ophthalmol. **51:**161, 1954.

Safran, A., and Glaser, S.: Statokinetic dissociation in lesions of anterior visual pathways, Arch. Ophthalmol. **98:**291, Feb. 1980.

Sanders, T. E., Gay, A. S., and Newman, M.: Drusen of optic disk: hemorrhagic complications, Trans. Am. Ophthalmol. Soc. **68:**186, 1970.

Saper, J. R.: Migraine I. Classification and pathogenesis, J.A.M.A. **239:**2480, 1978.

Saper, J. R.: Migraine II. Treatment, J.A.M.A. **239:**2480, 1978.

Sears, M. L.: Visual field loss in glaucoma, Am. J. Ophthalmol. **88:**493, 1979.

Seeley, R., and Smith, J. L.: Visual field defects in optic nerve hypoplasia, Am. J. Ophthalmol. **73:**882, 1972.

Shaffer, R. N., and Hetherington, J.: The case for conservatism in open angle glaucoma management, Can. J. Ophthalmol. **3:**11, 1968.

Shellshear, J. L.: A contribution to our knowledge of the arterial supply of the cerebral cortex in man, Brain **50:**236, 1927.

Shenkin, H. A., and Leopold, I. H.: Localizing value of temporal crescent defects in the visual fields, Arch. Neurol. Psychiatry **54:**97, 1945.

Sloan, L. L.: Area and luminance of test objects as variables in examination of the visual field by projection perimetry, Vision Res. **1:**121, 1961.

Sloan, L. L., and Brown, D. J.: Area and luminance of test objects as variables in projection perimetry, clinical studies, Vision Res. **2:**527, 1962.

Smith, C. G., and Richardson, W. F. G.: The course and distribution of the arteries supplying the visual (striate) cortex, Am. J. Ophthalmol. **61:**1391, 1966.

Smith, J. L.: Homonymous hemianopia: a review of one hundred cases, Am. J. Ophthalmol. **54:** 616, 1962.

Smith, J. L.: Color perimetry, Am. J. Ophthalmol. **54:**1085, 1962.

Smith, J. L., Hoyt, W. F., and Susac, J. O.: Ocular fundus in acute Leber optic neuropathy, Arch. Ophthalmol. **90:**349, Nov. 1946.

Spalding, J. M. K.: Wounds of the visual pathway, J. Neurol. Neurosurg. Psychiatry **15:**99, 169, 1952.

Stansburg, F. C.: Neuromyelitis optica (Devic's disease); presentation of five cases with pathologic study and review of the literature, Arch. Ophthalmol. **42:**292, 465, 1946.

Susanna, R., Drance, S. M., Douglas, G. R.: Disk hemorrhages in patients with elevated intraocular pressure, Arch. Ophthalmol. **97:**284, 1979.

Taub, R. G., and Rucker, C. W.: Relationship of retrobulbar neuritis to multiple sclerosis, Am. J. Ophthalmol. **37:**494, 1954.

Toland, J., and Mooney, A.: On the enlarged sella, Trans. Ophthalmol. Soc. U.K. **93:**717, 1973.

Traquair, H.: The nerve fiber bundle defect, Trans. Ophthalmol. Soc. U.K. **64:**122, 1944.

Traquair, H. M., Dott, N. J., and Russell, W. R.: Traumatic lesions of the chiasm, Brain **58:**398, 1935.

Trobe, J. D., and Glaser, J. S.: Quantitative perimetry in compressive optic neuropathy, Arch. Ophthalmol. **96:**1210, 1978.

Troost, B. T., and Newton, T. H.: Occipital lobe arteriovenous malformations, Arch. Ophthalmol. **93:**250, April 1975.

Tsamparlakis, J. C.: Effects of transient induced elevation of the intraocular pressure on the visual field, Br. J. Ophthalmol. **48:**237, 1964.

Vail, D.: Syphilitic opto-chiasmatic arachnoiditis, Am. J. Ophthalmol. **22**:505, 1939.

Van Buren, J. M., and Baldwin, M.: The architecture of the optic radiation in the temporal lobe of man, Brain **81**:15, 1958.

Wagener, H. P., and Cusick, P. L.: Chiasmal syndromes produced by lesions in the posterior fossa, Arch. Ophthalmol. **18**:887, 1937.

Wagener, H. P., and Love, J. G.: Fields of vision in cases of tumor of Rathke's pouch, Arch. Ophthalmol. **29**:873, 1943.

Walls, G. L.: The lateral geniculate nucleus and visual histophysiology, Berkeley and Los Angeles, Calif., 1953, University of California Publications in Physiology, University of California Press, vol. 9, no. 1.

Walsh, F. B.: Pathological-clinical correlations. I. Indirect trauma to optic nerves and chiasm. II. Certain cerebral involvements associated with defective blood supply, Invest. Ophthalmol. **5**:433, 1966.

Weekers, R.: L'exploration des fonctions visuelles en clinique par la mesure de la frequence critique de fusion, Bull. Soc. Franc. Ophthalmol. **60**:331, 1947.

Weekers, R., and La Vergne, G.: Applications cliniques de la périmétrie statique, Bull. Soc. Belg. Ophthalmol. **119**:418, 1958.

Weinstein, G. W.: Clinical aspects of visually evoked potentials, Trans. Am. Ophthalmol. Soc. **75**:627, 1977.

Werner, E., and Drance, S. M.: Early visual field disturbances in glaucoma, Arch. Ophthalmol. **95**:1173, 1978.

Wilbrand, H., and Saenger, A.: Die Neurologie des Auges, Wiesbaden, 1917, J. F. Bergmann, vol. 7.

Wilson, W. B., and Keyser, R. B.: Comparison of the pattern and diffuse-light visual evoked responses in definite multiple sclerosis, Arch. Neurol. **37**:30, Jan. 1980.

Wolff, E.: The causation of amblyopia following gastric and other hemorrhages, Trans. Ophthalmol. Soc. U.K. **55**:342, 1935.

Wollschlaeger, P. B., Wollschlaeger, G., Ide, C. H., and Hart, W. M.: Arterial blood supply of the human optic chiasm and surrounding structures, Ann. Ophthalmol. **3**:862, Aug. 1971.

Wolter, J. R.: Human optic papilla, demonstration of new anatomic and pathologic findings, Am. J. Ophthalmol. **44**:48, 1957.

Wood, E. H.: Normal optic nerve, Arch. Ophthalmol. **39**:305, 1948.

Wortis, S. B., Bender, M. B., and Teuber, H. L.: The significance of the phenomenon of extinction, J. Nerv. Ment. Dis. **107**:382, 1948.

Yasuna, E. R.: Hysterical amblyopia; its differentiation from malingering, Am. J. Ophthalmol. **29**:570, 1946.

Yasuna, E. R.: Hysterical amblyopia in children and young adults, Arch. Ophthalmol. **45**:70, 1951.

Index

A

Page numbers in *italics* indicate illustrations.
Page numbers followed by *t* indicate tables.

N

S

T

X

Z